WRITING

A Guide for College and Beyond

FOURTH EDITION

LESTER FAIGLEY
University of Texas at Austin

New!
2016
MLA
Updates

PEARSON

Boston   Columbus   Hoboken   Indianapolis   New York   San Francisco   Amsterdam
Cape Town   Dubai   London   Madrid   Milan   Munich   Paris   Montréal   Toronto   Delhi   Mexico City
São Paulo   Sydney   Hong Kong   Seoul   Singapore   Taipei   Tokyo

Vice President and Editor in Chief: Joseph Opiela
Program Manager: Katharine Glynn
Product Marketing Manager: Allison Arnold
Field Marketing Manager: Mark Robinson
Executive Digital Producer: Stefanie A. Snajder
Digital Editor: Stefanie A. Snajder
Content Specialist: Erin Jenkins
Project Manager: Ellen MacElree
Project Coordination and Electronic Page Makeup:
Lumina Datamatics, Inc.
Program Design Lead and Cover Design: Beth Paquin
Cover image: Lester Faigley
Senior Manufacturing Buyer: Roy L. Pickering, Jr.
Printer/Binder: R. R. Donnelley/Crawfordsville
Cover Printer: Lehigh-Phoenix Color/Hagerstown

Dorling Kindersley Education
Text design by Stuart Jackman and
Anthony Limerick
Design Director: Stuart Jackman
Publisher: Sophie Mitchell

Image Credits

p. 5: Library of Congress; **p. 6–7:** Julian Baum/Dorling Kindersley Ltd.; **p. 20:** Library of Congress; **p. 33:** Library of Congress; **p. 33:** Library of Congress; **p. 71:** Trekandphoto/Fotolia; **p.114:** Mike Goldwater/Alamy; **p. 123:** Natta Ang/Shutterstock; **p. 125–128:** Library of Congress; **p. 154:** NASA EOS Earth Observing System; **p. 156:** NASA EOS Earth Observing System; **p. 156:** NASA EOS Earth Observing System; **p. 188:** NASA EOS Earth Observing System; **p. 208:** NASA EOS Earth Observing System; **p. 210:** NASA EOS Earth Observing System; **p. 211:** NASA EOS Earth Observing System; **p. 326:** Christie's Images/Bridgeman Art Library; **p. 426:** NASA EOS Earth Observing System; **p. 459:** Marshall Ikonography/Alamy; **p. 518:** Courtesy of Denver Water, 9/19/2014; **p. 543:** Library of Congress.

All Write Now images: Oonal/iStock/360/Getty Images

All Staying on Track images: Tobias Machhaus/Getty Images

Unless otherwise credited, all photos © Lester Faigley.

Acknowledgments of third-party content appears on page 662, which constitute an extension of this copyright page.

Library of Congress Control Number: 2014040446

3 2019

www.pearsonhighered.com

Student Edition ISBN-10: 0-13-458635-2
Student Edition ISBN-13: 978-0-13-458635-9
A la Carte ISBN-10: 0-13-458252-7
A la Carte ISBN-13: 978-0-13-458252-8

PART 1
The Academic Writer

PART 2
The Persuasive Writer

Writing to Reflect

Writing to Inform

Writing to Analyze

Writing Arguments

PART 3
The Multimedia Writer

PART 4
The Writer as Researcher

PART 5
The Writer as Editor

Preface

The title of this book, *Writing: A Guide for College and Beyond*, emphasizes the often-overlooked fact that writing courses make students better writers not just for other college courses, but for writing situations throughout their lives. Students who learn to write well become far more successful in their professional and public lives.

I am pleased and grateful for the enthusiastic response of many instructors and students to the previous editions of *Writing: A Guide for College and Beyond*. When writing the first edition of this book, I started with the question: How do students learn best? That question continues to guide my work on this fourth edition, and I have developed this edition with the following principles in mind.

Students learn best when a guide to writing is student oriented	It should start from the student's point of view, not the teacher's.
Students learn best when a guide to writing is easy to use	No matter where you open the book, the content on a particular page and the place of that content in the overall organization should be evident.
Students learn best when a guide to writing shows what readers and writers actually do	Students learn best from *showing* how writers compose, not from lengthy discussions.
Students learn best when they can see examples of what works and what doesn't work	Putting effective and ineffective examples side by side shows students strategies to employ and pitfalls to avoid.
Students learn faster and remember longer when a book is well designed	Textbooks don't have to be dull; visual elements in a book can help students recall important information.

The fourth edition also maintains that the broad goals for a first-year college writing course are those identified in the 2014 Outcomes Statement from the Council of Writing Program Administrators.

1. Rhetorical knowledge	Students should respond to different situations and the needs of different audiences, understand how genres shape reading and writing, and write in several genres.
2. Critical thinking, reading, and composing	Students should find, evaluate, and analyze material from printed books and articles, scholarly databases, Web sources, and informal Internet sources. They should use strategies such as interpretation, synthesis, and critique to compose texts that integrate their ideas with those of others.
3. Processes	Students should develop flexible strategies for generating, revising, and editing across a variety of media and in different contexts. They also should understand how to collaborate effectively with others.
4. Knowledge of conventions	Students should learn the common formats for different kinds of texts, practice appropriate documentation, and master the conventions of grammar, mechanics, and spelling.

What's New in This Edition

More attention to academic writing	Part 1, "The Academic Writer," includes new content on academic reading and writing. Chapter 1, "Thinking as an Academic Writer," invites students to think about their medium and genre at the outset along with their topic, purpose, and audience. Chapter 2, "Reading as an Academic Writer," instructs students in annotating, making notes, keeping a reading journal, mapping, and outlining. Students are guided on how to write summaries and paraphrases, how to start an annotated bibliography, and how to synthesize readings and visuals. The remaining chapters prepare students for planning, drafting, and revising academic writing.
More examples of academic writing	Each chapter in Part 2, "The Persuasive Writer," includes an extended example of a student writing an academic project, starting with doing the research for that project. All chapters provide examples of either MLA or APA documentation.
Expanded instruction in multimedia composing	Smartphones, tablets, and laptops provide students with enormous capabilities in creating multimedia texts. In order to take advantage of the power they carry in their pockets, purses, and backpacks, students need to understand how to compose in multimedia. *Writing: A Guide for College and Beyond* explains how careful planning must be done before a multimedia project is initiated and how resources must be gathered and organized before composing begins. This coverage is spread throughout the book, but it is especially concentrated in Part 3, "The Multimedia Writer."
More multimedia assignments and examples	All eight chapters in Part 2 have a new "Writing in Multimedia" assignment option at the end of each chapter. Chapter 9 has a new sample series of a "Writer at Work," showing how a student developed an analysis of Russell Lee's Pie Town, New Mexico, photographs. The new Chapter 14, "Composing in Multimedia," has new instruction on the process of multimedia composing and creating audio and video texts along with a new example of a photo essay. Chapter 15, "Designing for Print and Digital Readers," offers practical advice on designing and evaluating print and digital texts.
More help on doing research	The emphasis on academic writing in Part 1 now includes new sections on writing a summary, writing a paraphrase, starting an annotated bibliography, and synthesizing readings and visuals. Coverage of research in Part 4, "The Writer as Researcher," has been updated to include the latest MLA and APA guidelines for citing e-books and postings on *Facebook*, *Twitter*, and other social media.

New engaging readings	This edition includes provocative new readings on topics such as pickup soccer in the slums of Rio de Janeiro, the pluses and minuses of dual credit courses in high school, why police departments ignore bicycle theft, why walkable cities attract the brightest young people, why free parking is one of the biggest boondoggles and environmental disasters in the United States, why traffic congestion is made worse by what we think is common sense, and why doodling leads to creative thinking.

Key Features

The quintessential attributes, which have made *Writing* a best-selling rhetoric, continue to be mainstays of the fourth edition.

Unique "process maps"	Show students at a glance what is expected of them for each of the major writing assignments (Chapters 6–13). These process maps give students an overview of the whole writing process and help them to stay oriented as they discover ideas, draft, and revise their own papers.
"Writer at Work" sections	Give examples of student writers working through the writing process, from invention through revision to a final paper (Chapters 6–13). Instead of just showing a finished paper, these sections let students see another student working through the whole messy, creative process of writing.
Writing "Projects"	The projects that conclude Chapters 6–13 offer a range of assignments, including personal narratives, descriptive and informative essays, rhetorical analyses, several kinds of arguments, and various multimedia genre.
Most reading selections are designed to look like original publications	Students are exposed to a diversity of genres that they will encounter in college and beyond.
"Staying on Track"	The boxes which are included throughout the book focus on common writing problems and give students concrete advice for how to avoid such problems, including both "off track" and "on track" examples.
Instruction in and strategies for the research process	Part 4 includes strong coverage of avoiding plagiarism, evaluating sources, and using library databases and the Internet as research tools.
Abundant student papers	Twelve student papers, all with sources and citations, give students realistic, accurate models.
Richly illustrated	More than 300 visuals, many of them photographs taken by the author, serve to support the main points made in each chapter.
Style, grammar, punctuation, and ESL issues	Guidance on these topics is covered in Part 5.

Resources for Teachers and Students

Instructor's Resource Manual

The Instructor's Resource Manual, prepared by Rick Iadonisi of Grand Valley State University, offers detailed chapter-by-chapter suggestions to help both new and experienced instructors. For every chapter in the student text, this manual includes chapter goals and chapter challenges, suggestions for different ways to use the assignments and boxed tips in the chapter, additional activities and resources, and more. It also features an overall discussion of teaching a writing class, including discussion of the Writing Program Administrators Outcomes for first-year composition. Finally, the manual offers suggested syllabi and ideas for teaching students with different learning styles.

MyWritingLab™

MyWritingLab is an online homework, tutorial, and assessment program that provides engaging experiences for teaching and learning. Flexible and easily customizable, MyWritingLab helps improve students' writing through context-based learning. Whether through self-study or instructor-led learning, MyWritingLab supports and complements course work. Particularly noteworthy are these three features: ***Writing at the Center***–With the new composing space and Review Plan, MyWritingLab unites instructor comments and feedback on student writing with targeted remediation via rich multimedia activities, allowing students to learn from and through their own writing. ***Writing Help for Varying Skill Levels***–For students who enter the course under-prepared, MyWritingLab identifies those who lack prerequisite skills for composition-level topics, and provides personalized remediation. ***Proven Results***–No matter how MyWritingLab is used, instructors have access to powerful gradebook reports, which provide visual analytics that give insight to course performance at the student, section, or even program level.

An Interactive Pearson eText in MyWritingLab™

Pearson eText gives students access to *Writing: A Guide for College and Beyond* whenever and wherever they can access the Internet. The eText pages look exactly like the printed text, and include powerful interactive and customization functions. Users can create notes, highlight text in different colors, create bookmarks, zoom, click hyperlinked words and phrases to view definitions, and view as a single page or as two pages. Pearson eText also links students to associated media files, enabling them to view videos as they read the text, and offers a full-text search and the ability to save and export notes. The Pearson eText also includes embedded URLs in the chapter text with active links to the Internet.

The Pearson eText app is a great companion to Pearson's eText browser-based book reader. It allows existing subscribers who view their Pearson eText titles on a Mac or PC to additionally access their titles in a bookshelf on the iPad or an Android tablet either online or via download.

Acknowledgments

I am quite fortunate to work with several of the same team who have been with the book from the beginning. Editor in Chief Joseph Opiela has been involved in all the books and editions I've written for Pearson, and it was a pleasure to work with him again. Katharine Glynn, Program Manager, has collaborated with me on every edition of *Writing*, and I am grateful to her both for the success the book has enjoyed and for her support and perspective through the long process of development. Project Manager Ellen Macelree skillfully coordinated the production. Wayne Butler, Michael Greer, and Lynn Huddon gave me valuable assistance in planning the book and preparing the manuscript. At Lumina Datamatics, Inc., Senior Project Manager Katy Gabel guided the book into print with patience and close attention to details. My splendid copy editor Elsa van Bergen was once again a delight along with her extraordinary competence. Across the Atlantic the DK design team, Anthony Limerick and Stuart Jackman, again worked their magic.

I have learned from the students I teach each semester at the University of Texas at Austin. They continually impress me with their creativity. Some of their splendid work is represented in this book. The wise advice of reviewers has benefitted me greatly in this and previous editions. They include Susan Achziger, *Community College of Aurora*; Devon Adams, *Mesa Community College*; Diana Agy, *Jackson College*; Matthew Allen, *Wright College*; Jade Bittle, *Rowan-Cabarrus Community College*; Rea Crane Bizzaro, *Indiana University of Pennsylvania*; Joel R. Brouwer, *Montcalm Community College*; Gina Burkart, *University of Northern Iowa*; Dan Butcher, *University of Alabama at Birmingham*; M. L. Byrd, *Virginia State University*; Mechel Camp, *Jackson State Community College*; Chandra Speight Cerutti, *East Carolina University*; Ron Christiansen, *Salt Lake Community College*; Ruth L. Copp, *Saginaw Valley State University*; Virginia Crank, *University of Wisconsin-LaCrosse*; Linsey Cuti, *Kankakee Community College*; Cherie Dargan, *Hawkeye Community College*; Cathy Decker, *Chaffey College*; Navdeep Singh Dhillon, *Hudson County Community College*; Rocco Ditello, *Broward College*; Gary Dop, *North Central University*; Stacey Donohue, *Central Oregon Community College*; Stephanie L. Dowdle, *Salt Lake Community College*; Sarah Duerden, *Arizona State University*; H. M. (Mickey) Gentry, *College of the Mainland*; Annette M. Formella, *Baker College of Clinton Township*; Mary Val Gerstle, *University of Cincinnati*; Angelina Gonzales, *California State University, Northridge*; David M. Grant, *University of Northern Iowa*; Maya Greene, *Columbia Greene Community College*; Susan Grimland, *Collin County*; Curtis Harrell, *Northwest Arkansas Community College*; Jacqueline Harris, *Utah State University*; Brigitte Harvey, *Broome Community College*; Judy Hauser, *Des Moines Area Community College*; Mark Heimermann, *Saint Cloud State University*; Richard Iadonisi, *Grand Valley State University*; Kristen Isabelle, *Columbia-Greene Community College*; Michael Jackman, *Indiana University Southeast*; Linda S. Jacobs, *Jackson Community College*; MaryAnn Jacobs, *Northern Kentucky University*; John Jones, *West Virginia University*; Kent Kaiser, *University of Minnesota*; Nadene Keene, *Indiana University Kokomo*; Catherine Keohane, *Bergen Community College*; Janet Knepper, *Clarion University*; Julie Kratt, *Cowley College*; Sally Lahmon, *Sinclair Community College*; Fran L. Lassiter, *University of the District of Columbia*; Sara Lewis, *Pine Manor College*; Seeta Mangra, *Des Moines Area Community College*; Gae Heather McAlpin, *Lansing Community College*; Julia McGregor, *Inver Hills Community College*; Janice McIntire-Strasburg, *Saint Louis University*; Rexann A. McKinley, *Kankakee Community College*; Paul A. McNaney, *Corning Community College*; Tim Miank, *Lansing Community College*; Rhonda Morris, *Santa Fe College*; Missy Nieveen Phegley, *Southeast Missouri State University*; David Norman, *Savannah*

Technical College; Lynanne Page, *Eastern Illinois University*; Martha J. Payne, *Ball State University*; Eden F. Pearson, *Des Moines Area Community College*; Mack Perry, *Jackson State Community College*; Ruben Quesada, *Eastern Illinois University*; Timothy Ray, *West Chester University of Pennsylvania*; Charlotte Teresa Reynolds, *Indiana University Southeast*; Tammy Robinson, *Los Angeles City College*; Nina Sabolik, *Arizona State University*; Jack Shear, *Binghamton University*; Deborah A. Shoop, *East Carolina University*; Greta Skogseth, *Montcalm Community College*; Betty H. Stack, *Rowan Cabarrus Community College*; Karla Farmer Stouse, *Indiana University Kokomo*; Theresa Stowell, *Jackson Community College*; Jane Stubbs, *University of New Orleans*; Diane Tetreault, *Bentley College*; Michelle Trim, *Elon University*; Donna Thompson, *Chandler-Gilbert Community College*; Sherri L. Van den Akker, *Springfield College*; Suzanne Van Wert, *Northern Essex Community College*; Nancy Wallin, *St. Cloud State University*; Sara Webb-Sunderhaus, *Indiana University-Purdue University Fort Wayne*; Leslie Kreiner Wilson, *Pepperdine University*; and Carole Yee, *Los Angeles Valley College*.

As always, my greatest debt of gratitude is to my wife, Linda, who makes it all possible.

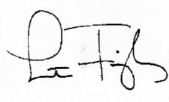

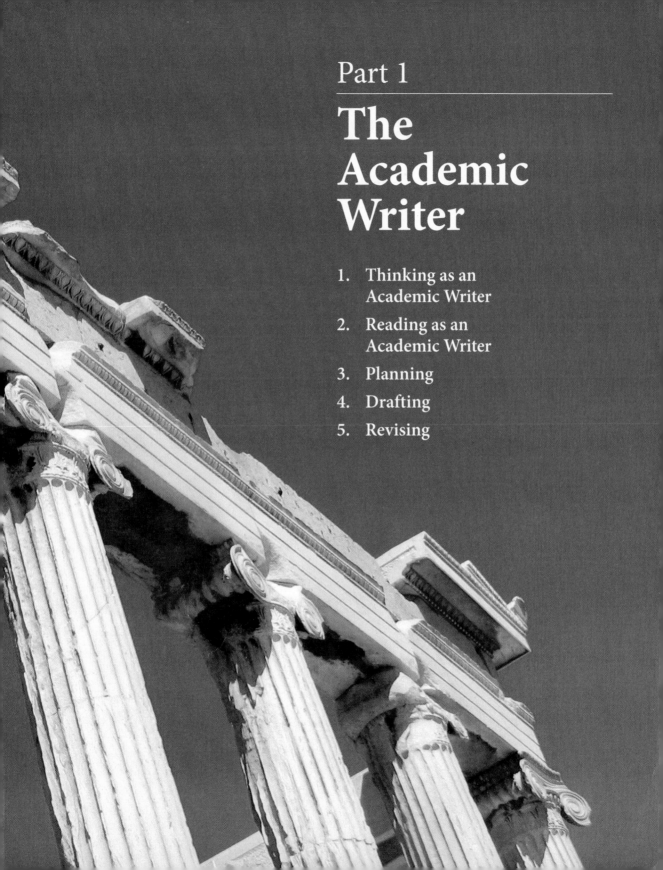

Part 1

The Academic Writer

1 Thinking as an Academic Writer

Learning to write is the most valuable part of your college education.

In this chapter, you will learn to

① Understand the process of writing *(see p. 6)*

② Understand the rhetorical situation *(see p. 7)*

③ Analyze your assignment *(see pp. 8–9)*

④ Think about your genre *(see p. 10)*

⑤ Think about your medium *(see p. 11)*

⑥ Think about your topic *(see pp. 12–13)*

⑦ Think about what your readers expect *(see pp. 14–15)*

⑧ Think about your credibility *(see pp. 16–17)*

Explore Through Writing

From the earliest times in human history to the present, people have always wanted to know more, from finding out what was on the other side of the hill to finding out if life exists beyond our solar system. The effort to find new knowledge is an act of discovery. One of the best ways to discover is by writing.

PREPARING

Exploration begins with an impulse. Sometimes it's curiosity about a place. Sometime it's a hunch. The curiosity or the hunch takes the form of a question. To answer that question, we set out to explore.

As a writer in college you prepare by being open to the possibility of learning new things and revising your ideas as your writing develops.

EXPLORING

Ancient explorers were highly skilled navigators, but in order to find new lands and new peoples, they had to enter unknown regions.

College writers seldom create anything worth reading if everything is common knowledge at the outset. If you can connect what's new to what you know, however, entering the unknown can be a creative time for a writer.

RETURNING

Explorers are successful only if they return or send word back about what they discovered. They must make a difference in the minds of the people they left behind.

Through your writing, you can make a difference to others and enlarge the worlds of your readers.

Understand the Process of Writing

People today write constantly in text messages, e-mail, social networking sites, chat rooms, and message boards, just to name a few. Most of this writing is composed quickly, read quickly, and discarded quickly.

In college, in the workplace, and in public life, however, you will often engage in writing that is composed slowly, read carefully, and stored for future reference. This more engaged kind of writing is similar to exploring in many ways. Indeed, Ralph Waldo Emerson observed that "the writer is an explorer. Every step is an advance into a new land."

Like explorers, writers prepare by assembling materials and establishing goals, they plan and organize, they explore by reading and writing, and they offer what they have learned to others.

But unlike explorers who travel to distant lands and have distinct stages in the process, writers intermingle different activities during writing. The process of writing may seem linear when described, but in practice, a diagram of how a writer actually works would look more like a plate of spaghetti. This messiness, however, often generates new ideas.

PREPARE

Analyze the assignment and take stock.

See the rest of this chapter.

EXPLORE BY READING

Read to broaden your knowledge of your topic and to help you identify different views.

See Chapter 2.

PLAN AND ORGANIZE

Narrow your topic, draft a working thesis, and create a working outline.

See Chapter 3.

DRAFT

Use your working outline to draft paragraphs and to explore your topic further through writing.

See Chapter 4.

Be prepared to go back and forth

Revising will often take you back to exploring and organizing.

REVIEW AND REVISE

Switch from writer to reader to review your draft and identify goals for revising.

See Chapter 5.

Understand the Rhetorical Situation

Successful writers understand that all acts of writing and speaking include three essential elements that interact with each other: the **writer** or speaker, the **subject**, and the **audience**. Every piece of writing is a negotiation among these three elements, even if we are jotting down a grocery list for our own use.

Every instance of writing, which we will define as **text**, is also of a particular category, called a **genre**, or a mixture of genres. Each text is delivered using a particular **medium**, or a combination of media. For example, Twitter messages (tweets) are a well-defined genre. They have to be text only and are limited to no more than 140 characters. The medium is digital.

The rhetorical triangle

These elements—writer, audience, subject, and text—are often represented as a triangle

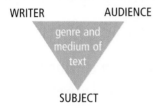

The rhetorical triangle can be used to determine a writer's **purpose** or **aim**. Writers who focus on their own personal experience have a primarily **reflective** aim. Those who are most concerned with explaining a subject have an **informative** aim. Writers who want their audiences to hold certain beliefs or take certain actions have a **persuasive** aim.

The larger context

Communication does not take place in a vacuum. Writers and readers both have knowledge, beliefs, and attitudes about particular subjects. What is happening in the larger world has a great deal to do with how we understand a text.

Take, for example, the first two paragraphs of a press release from the World Bank issued in February 2011.

> **WASHINGTON, February 15, 2011** – Rising food prices have driven an estimated 44 million people into poverty in developing countries since last June as food costs continue to rise to near 2008 levels, according to new World Bank Group numbers released ahead of the G20 Meeting of Finance Ministers and Central Bank Governors in Paris.
>
> "Global food prices are rising to dangerous levels and threaten tens of millions of poor people around the world," said World Bank Group President Robert B. Zoellick. "The price hike is already pushing millions of people into poverty, and putting stress on the most vulnerable, who spend more than half of their income on food."

This press release came from the public relations department of the World Bank and was published on the Bank's Web site.

The World Bank is an international financial institution that was established by wealthy countries to assist developing countries and to reduce poverty. It's not surprising that the World Bank is concerned with rising food prices in developing countries because, according to the Bank's statistics, over 20% of the world's population lives on less than $1.25 a day. The press release is informative in giving statistics, but it is also making a persuasive case that the Bank's mission of reducing poverty will become more difficult if food prices continue to rise.

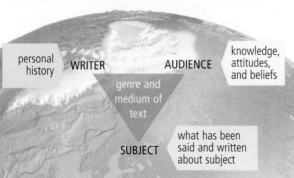

Analyze Your Assignment

When your instructor gives you a writing assignment, look closely at what you are being asked to do. Circle the information about the required length, the due dates, the format, and other requirements. You can attend to these details later.

Make notes on the assignment sheet. You can find examples of eight different kinds of assignments listed on the facing page.

WHAT'S YOUR PURPOSE?

Does your assignment contain words like *reflect, describe, explain, analyze, evaluate, argue,* and *propose* that signal your purpose?

See next page.

WHAT'S YOUR TOPIC?

Do you have some freedom in choosing a topic? What interests you? What can you explore in depth in the length assigned?

See page 12.

WHAT'S YOUR GENRE?

Are you being asked to write an essay, a report, an abstract, an annotated bibliography, a proposal, or something else?

See page 11.

WHAT'S YOUR MEDIUM?

Are you being asked to compose an online text such as a Web site, blog, wiki, an audio, or video text?

See page 10.

WHO IS YOUR AUDIENCE?

Does your assignment specify an audience? If so, what will they likely expect?

See page 14.

HOW DO YOU GAIN CREDIBILITY?

What can you do to make your readers trust you and believe that you know what you're talking about?

See page 16.

AIM	FOCUS	EXAMPLE GENRES
WRITING TO REFLECT	**Reflections:** Narrating personal experience and personal insights for a public audience *(Example assignment on page 90)*	Journals, personal letters, blogs, memoirs, essays
WRITING TO INFORM	**Observations:** Describing accurately and vividly *(Example assignment on page 136)*	Ethnographies, travel accounts, case studies, photo essays
	Informative essays: Communicating information clearly *(Example assignment on page 192)*	Newspaper and magazine articles, academic articles, reports, profiles, essays
WRITING TO ANALYZE	**Rhetorical and literary analysis:** Analyzing what makes a text successful and why the author made particular choices *(Example assignment on page 250)*	Rhetorical analysis, short story analysis, visual analysis, essays
WRITING TO PERSUADE	**Causal arguments:** Exploring why an event, phenomenon, or trend happened *(Example assignment on page 308)*	History, accident analysis, financial analysis, essays
	Evaluation arguments: Assessing whether something is good or bad according to particular criteria *(Example assignment on page 350)*	Reviews, essays, performance evaluations, product evaluations
	Position arguments: Convincing others through reasoned argument to accept or reject a position *(Example assignment on page 408)*	Speeches, letters to the editor, op-ed columns, editorials, essays
	Proposal arguments: Convincing others through reasoned argument to take action *(Example assignment on page 468)*	Speeches, business proposals, grant proposals, essays, advocacy Web sites

Think About Your Genre

The word *genre* may be unfamiliar, but the idea isn't. Netflix and other online movie services classify movies as action and adventure, children and family, classics, comedy, documentary, drama, horror, musical, sci-fi and fantasy, thriller, and so on.

Similarly, academic writing is classified into different types: books, scholarly articles, essays, reviews, research reports, blogs, and so on. These are all genres. Of course, there are many sub-genres within these broad genres.

Research report

A new study by researchers at NASA and the University of California, Irvine, finds a rapidly melting section of the West Antarctic Ice Sheet appears to be in an irreversible state of decline, with nothing to stop the glaciers in this area from melting into the sea.

The study presents multiple lines of evidence, incorporating 40 years of observations that indicate the glaciers in the Amundsen Sea sector of West Antarctica "have passed the point of no return," according to glaciologist and lead author Eric Rignot, of UC Irvine and NASA's Jet Propulsion Laboratory (JPL) in Pasadena, California. The new study has been accepted for publication in the journal *Geophysical Research Letters*.

These glaciers already contribute significantly to sea level rise, releasing almost as much ice into the ocean annually as the entire Greenland Ice Sheet. They contain enough ice to raise global sea level by 4 feet (1.2 meters) and are melting faster than most scientists had expected.

Rasmussen, Carol. "NASA-UCI Study Indicates Loss of West Antarctic Glaciers Appears Unstoppable." *National Aeronautics and Space Administration*, 12 May 2014, www.nasa.gov/press/2014/may/nasa-uci-study-indicates-loss-of-west-antarctic-glaciers-appears-unstoppable/#.VwAk-kfVvf0.

Blog

Why are the East Coast and Gulf of Mexico hotspots of sea level rise?

Global average sea level has increased 8 inches since 1880. Several locations along the East Coast and Gulf of Mexico have experienced more than 8 inches of local sea level rise in only the past 50 years.

The rate of local sea level rise is affected by global, regional, and local factors.

Along the East Coast and Gulf of Mexico, changes in the path and strength of ocean currents are contributing to faster-than-average sea level rise.

In parts of the East Coast and Gulf regions, land is subsiding, which allows the ocean to penetrate farther inland.

"Infographic: Sea Level Rise and Global Warming." *Union of Concerned Scientists*, 30 Apr. 2014, www.ucsusa.org/global_warming/science_and_impacts/impacts/infographic-sea-level-rise-global-warming.html#.VwAtAEfVvf0.

Think About Your Medium

A medium is a channel of communication. All humans communicate by talking (oral or sign language) and through body language. Across centuries analog media were gradually added to the human repertoire—handwriting, print, telephone, radio, and film. Analog media have increasingly been supplanted by new digital media. Today we are never far from the Web, social media, e-mail, texting, photo services, online mapping services, and audio and video sites. We're accustomed to using an app for whatever we want to read, see, or hear.

The challenge now is when to use what media.

- Would a chart, graph, or diagram help to explain your message?
- Would one or more photographs allow your readers to see what you are discussing?
- Would a video support your presentation?
- Would an audio recording add to your presentation?

You'll find more about multimedia composing in Part 3.

The Union of Concerned Scientists created this infographic on the rise of sea levels along the coasts of the United States. This infographic accompanied the blog on the facing page.

WRITE NOW MyWritingLab™

Compare styles across genres and media

Find a newspaper article on a current social, economic, political, or scientific issue. Then find a scholarly article on the same subject using *Google Scholar* or one of the databases on your library's Web site. Next, search blogs for the same subject using *Google Blog Search*.

Compare the styles of the scholarly article, the newspaper article, and the blog using the following criteria: overall length, paragraph length, sentence length, word choice, relationship with the reader, and use of graphics and images. Write a summary of your analysis.

Think About Your Topic

Writers begin by exploring. When they start writing, exploration doesn't stop. Once they start, writers find things they could not have imagined. Where writers end up is often far away from where they thought they were going.

Most writing in college concerns exploration because academic disciplines seek to create new knowledge and to rethink what is known. Colleges and universities bring together people who ask interesting questions: How does recent archaeological evidence change our understanding of Homer's *Iliad* and *Odyssey*? Why does eyesight deteriorate with age? How do volcanoes affect the world climate? How do chameleons regenerate lost body parts? How do Rousseau's ideas about nature continue to shape notions about wilderness? How do electric eels generate voltage and not get shocked in the process? How can a poll of a thousand people represent over 300 million Americans with only a 3% margin of error?

Writers in colleges and universities respond to these questions and many others. They challenge old answers and contribute new answers. Readers of college writing expect to learn something when they read—new knowledge, a fresh interpretation, another point of view that they had not considered.

At first glance the expectations of college writing seem impossible. How can you as an undergraduate student expect to contribute new knowledge? But just as there is a great deal that maps do not show, you can find many uncertainties, controversies, and unresolved problems in any field of study. You just have to ask the right questions.

Local questions are often more interesting than broad, general questions. For example, should historic neighborhoods be preserved, or should they give way to urban renewal and gentrification, as has happened to Chinatown in Washington, DC?

Ask interesting questions

Good questions can take you to places that will interest you and your readers alike.

- Focus on an area you don't know and want to know more about.

- Find out where experts disagree. What exactly is the source of the disagreement? Why do they come to different conclusions using the same evidence?

- Analyze explanations of current trends and events. What possible causes might be left out?

- Examine proposals to solve problems. Does the solution fix the problem? Will people support the solution if it costs them effort or money?

- Compare what people claim and the reality. Often people (especially politicians) represent things and their role in making things much better than they actually are.

Use strategies for finding a topic

Sometimes your instructor will assign a topic, but more often you will have to come up with your own topic. Look first at material from your course. You might find a topic to explore in the readings or from class discussion.

Start with what interests you. It's hard to write about topics that you care little about. If your assignment gives you a range of options, make more than one list.

PERSONAL	1. History of Anime in Japan
	2. Cave exploration and conservation
	3. Learning to windsurf
CAMPUS	1. Pros and cons of technology fees
	2. Excessive litter on campus
	3. Fellowships for study-abroad programs
COMMUNITY	1. Safe bicycle commuting
	2. Bilingual education programs
	3. Better public transportation
NATION/WORLD	1. Advertising aimed at preschool children
	2. Censorship of the Internet
	3. Genetically altered crops

WRITE NOW   MyWritingLab™

Mapping your campus

Your campus likely has an information desk for students and visitors. Information centers typically will have several brochures with maps. Visit the information desk and collect everything that includes a map. Then compare the maps. Make a checklist for what the maps show and don't show (building names, streets, shuttle bus routes, bicycle routes, parking, landmarks, hotels, and more).

Create a map for new students on your campus that contains insider knowledge that would not appear on the maps your school produces. For example, where can you find the best burger on or close to campus? The best cup of coffee or cookies? A quiet place to study? A great place to meet friends?

Make a list of places that need to be included on your map. Then draw the map. Google Maps is an excellent tool for making maps of campuses and neighborhoods.

Think About What Your Readers Expect

When you talk with someone face-to-face, you receive constant feedback from that person, even when you're doing all the talking. Your listener may nod in agreement, frown, act bored, and give you a variety of other signals.

Imagine your readers

When you write, you rarely receive immediate response from readers. Most of the time you don't know exactly how readers will react to what you write. You have to think consciously about your readers and anticipate how they might respond.

Readers of college writing

Readers of college writing expect more than what they can find out from a *Google* search or an online encyclopedia. Facts are easy to obtain from databases and print sources. Readers want to know how these facts are connected.

Good college writing involves an element of surprise. If readers can predict exactly where a writer is going, even if they fully agree, they will either skim to the end or stop reading. Readers expect you to tell them something that they don't already know.

Writing in college …	Writers are expected to …
States explicit claims	Make a claim that isn't obvious. The claim is often called a thesis statement.
Develops an argument	Support their claims with facts, evidence, reasons, and testimony from experts.
Analyzes with insight	Analyze in depth what they read and view.
Investigates complexity	Explore the complexity of a subject, challenging their readers by asking "Have you thought about this?" or "What if you discard the usual way of thinking about a subject and take the opposite point of view?"
Organizes with a hierarchical structure	Make the major parts evident to readers and indicate which parts are subordinate to others.
Signals with transitions	Indicate logical relationships clearly so readers can follow a pathway without getting lost.
Documents sources carefully	Provide the sources of information so readers can consult the same sources the writer used.

Know what college readers expect

Readers expect to be challenged.
Simple answers that can be easily looked up are not adequate.

OFF TRACK
The United States entered World War II when the Japanese attacked Pearl Harbor on December 7, 1941. *(This fact is well known and not informative for college readers.)*

ON TRACK
The war with Japan actually began on July 25, 1941, when President Franklin Roosevelt froze Japanese assets and declared an oil embargo, leaving the Japanese with the choices of abandoning the war with China or neutralizing the United States Navy in order to secure oil resources in Indonesia.

Readers expect claims to be backed up with reasons and evidence.
Simple explanations without support are not adequate.

OFF TRACK
New York City is an exciting place to live, but I wouldn't want to move there because of the crime. *(Is crime really that much higher in New York City?)*

ON TRACK
Many people don't know that New York City is the safest large city in the United States according to FBI crime statistics. It even ranks in the top 20 safest cities among the 210 cities with populations over 100,000.

Readers expect complex answers for complex problems.
Simple solutions for complex problems are not adequate.

OFF TRACK
We need posters urging students not to litter so much on campus. *(Are posters alone likely to solve the problem?)*

ON TRACK
Most of the litter on our campus is paper, bottles, and cans—all recyclable—yet there are almost no recycle containers on campus. Putting recycle containers in high-litter locations along with a "don't litter" campaign could go a long way toward making our campus cleaner.

Readers expect writers to be engaged.
Readers expect writers to be curious and genuinely concerned about their subjects.

OFF TRACK
Older people have to deal with too much bureaucracy to obtain health care. *(The statement rings true but doesn't motivate readers.)*

ON TRACK
After spending a day with my 78-year-old aunt sorting through stacks of booklets and forms and waiting on a help line that never answered, I became convinced that the Medicare prescription drug program is an aging American's worst nightmare.

Think About Your Credibility

Some writers begin with credibility because of who they are. If you wonder what foods compose a balanced meal for your dog, you probably would listen carefully to the advice of a veterinarian. Most writers, however, have to convince their readers to keep reading by demonstrating knowledge of their subject and concern with their readers' needs.

Think about how you want your readers to see you

To get your readers to take you seriously, you must convince them that they can trust you. You need to get them to see you as

Concerned

Readers want you to be committed to what you are writing about. They also expect you to be concerned with them as readers. After all, if you don't care about them, why should they read what you write?

Well informed

Many people ramble on about any subject without knowing anything about it. If they are family members, you have to suffer their opinions, but it is not enjoyable. College writing requires that you do your homework on a subject.

Fair

Many writers look at only one side of an issue. Readers respect objectivity and an unbiased approach.

Ethical

Many writers use only the facts that support their positions and often distort facts and sources. Critical readers often notice what is being left out. Don't try to conceal what doesn't support your position.

Considerate

Writers who don't bother to create new paragraphs when they move to new idea or fail to signal that they are making a transition to a new topic force readers to make extra effort. Readers can become annoyed in a hurry.

Aware of writing in a discipline

Different disciplines use different vocabularies, formats, and evidence to make and support claims.

Careful

No one likes to read sloppy, error-filled writing. Readers appreciate writers who take extra time to get the little things right.

Visually fluent

Digital technologies have made it easy to insert images and graphics in your writing and to publish on the Web. But these technologies don't tell you if, when, and how images and graphics should be used.

STAYING ON TRACK

Build your credibility

Know what's at stake

What you are writing about should matter to your readers. If its importance is not evident, it's your job to explain why your readers should consider it important.

OFF TRACK

We should be concerned about two-thirds of Central and South America's 110 brightly colored harlequin frog species becoming extinct in the last twenty years. *(The loss of any species is unfortunate, but the writer gives us no other reason for concern.)*

ON TRACK

The rapid decline of amphibians worldwide due to global warming may be the advance warning of the loss of cold-weather species such as polar bears, penguins, and reindeer.

Have your readers in mind

If you are writing about a specialized subject that your readers don't know much about, take the time to explain key concepts.

OFF TRACK

Reduction in the value of a debt security, especially a bond, results from a rise in interest rates. Conversely, a decline in interest rates results in an increase in the value of a debt security, especially bonds. *(The basic idea is here, but it is not expressed clearly, especially if the reader is not familiar with investing.)*

ON TRACK

Bond prices move inversely to interest rates. When interest rates go up, bond prices go down, and when interest rates go down, bond prices go up.

Think about alternative solutions and points of view

Readers appreciate a writer's ability to see a subject from multiple perspectives.

OFF TRACK

We will reduce greenhouse gas and global warming only if we greatly increase wind-generated electricity. *(Wind power is an alternative energy source, but it is expensive and many people don't want windmills in scenic areas. The writer also doesn't mention using energy more efficiently.)*

ON TRACK

If the world is serious about limiting carbon emissions to reduce global warming, then along with increasing efficient energy use, all non-carbon-emitting energy sources must be considered, including nuclear power. Nuclear power now produces about 20% of U.S. electricity with no emissions—the equivalent of taking 58 million passenger cars off the road.

MyWritingLab™   Visit Ch. 1 in MyWritingLab to complete the chapter exercises and to test your understanding of the chapter objectives.

2 Reading as an Academic Writer

Along with learning to write well, learning to think critically is essential in a college education.

In this chapter, you will learn to

1. Become a critical reader *(see p. 19)*
2. Become a critical viewer *(see p. 20)*
3. Annotate academic readings *(see p. 21)*
4. Recognize fallacies *(see pp. 24–25)*
5. Write a summary *(see p. 26)*
6. Write a paraphrase *(see p. 27)*
7. Move from reading to invention *(see pp. 28–30)*
8. Start an annotated bibliography *(see p. 31)*
9. Synthesize readings and visuals *(see pp. 32–33)*

Become a Critical Reader

Critical thinking begins with critical reading. For most of what you read, one time through is enough. When you start asking questions about what you are reading, you are engaging in critical reading. Critical reading is a four-part process. First, begin by asking where a piece of writing came from and why it was written. Second, read the text carefully to find the author's central claim or thesis and the major points. Third, decide if you can trust the author. Fourth, read the text again to understand how it works.

---

1. Where did it come from?

- Who wrote this material?
- Where did it first appear? In a book, newspaper, magazine, or online?
- What else has been written about the topic or issue?
- What do you expect after reading the title?

2. What does it say?

- What is the topic or issue?
- What is the writer's thesis or central idea?
- What reasons or evidence does the writer offer?
- Who are the intended readers? What does the writer assume the readers know and believe?

3. Can you trust the writer?

- Does the writer have the necessary knowledge and experience to write on this subject?
- Do you detect a bias in the writer's position?
- Are the facts relevant to the writer's claims?
- Can you trust the writer's facts? Where did the facts come from?
- Does the writer acknowledge opposing views and unfavorable evidence? Does the writer deal fairly with opposing views?

4. How does it work?

- How is the piece of writing organized? How are the major points arranged?
- How does the writer conclude? Does the conclusion follow from the evidence the writer offers?
- How would you characterize the style? Describe the language that the writer uses.
- How does the writer represent herself or himself?

WRITE NOW   MyWritingLab™

Analyze information for students on your campus

No doubt your school sent you a great deal of information when you were admitted. Schools continue to distribute information to students when they get to campus. You can find informative brochures and flyers at your school's student services building and informative pages on your school's Web site. Pick one of the brochures or Web pages to analyze. Remember that you are the intended audience.

Write a one-page evaluation about why the brochure or Web page is effective or ineffective for an audience of college students. If it is ineffective, what changes need to be made to make it effective? If it works, what does it do well?

Become a Critical Viewer

Critical viewing, like critical reading, requires thinking about where the image or visual came from. Begin by asking the following.

- What kind of an image or visual is it?
- Who created this image (movie, advertisement, television program, and so on)?
- What is it about? What is portrayed in the image?
- Where did it first appear? Where do you usually find images like this one?
- When did it appear?

The following questions are primarily for still images. For animations, movies, and television, you also have to ask questions about how the story is being told.

- What attracts your eye first? If there is an attention-grabbing element, how does it connect with the rest of the image?
- What impression of the subject does the image create?
- How does the image appeal to the values of the audience? (For example, politicians love to be photographed with children.)
- How does the image relate to what surrounds it?
- Was it intended to serve purposes besides art and entertainment?

Arthur Rothstein made this photograph of black clouds of dust rising over the Texas Panhandle in March 1936. Look closely at the photo. What attracts your eye first? Snapshots usually put the horizon line in the center. Why did Rothstein put the horizon at the bottom? What impression does this photo convey to you?

Annotate Academic Readings

If you own what you are reading (or are able to make yourself a photocopy of borrowed materials), read with a pencil in hand. Pens and highlighters don't erase, and often you don't remember why you highlighted a particular sentence.

Using annotating strategies will make your effort more rewarding.

Mark major points and key concepts	Sometimes major points are indicated by headings, but often you will need to locate them.
Connect passages	Notice how ideas connect to each other. Draw lines and arrows. If an idea connects to something a few pages before, write a note in the margin with the page number.
Ask questions	Note anything that is unfamiliar, including words and concepts to look up.
Note sources	Pay attention to the outside sources the writer uses.

Below is an annotated passage from Jeff Speck's "The Walkability Dividend" (see the full text of this reading in Chapter 12), in which Speck discusses Portland, Oregon, and the benefits it enjoys as a "walkable" city.

"[W]hat really makes Portland unusual is how it has chosen to grow. While most American cities were building more highways, Portland invested in transit and biking. While most cities were reaming out their roadways to speed traffic, Portland implemented a Skinny Streets program. While most American cities were amassing a spare tire of undifferentiated sprawl, Portland instituted an urban growth boundary. These efforts and others like them, over several decades—a blink of the eye in planner time—have changed the way that Portlanders live.

This para talks about how Portland became walkable.

What is this program?

This change is not dramatic—were it not for the roving hordes of bicyclists, it might be invisible—but it is significant. While almost every other American city has seen its residents drive farther and farther every year and spend more and more of their time stuck in traffic, Portland's vehicle miles traveled per person peaked in 1996. Now, compared to other major metropolitan areas, Portlanders on average drive 20 percent less. Cortright 1

Speck uses a lot of info from this source.

Small change? Not really: according to Cortright, this 20 percent (four miles per citizen per day) adds up to $1.1 billion of savings each year, which equals fully 1.5 percent of all personal income earned in the region. And that number ignores time not wasted in traffic: peak travel times have actually fallen from 54 minutes per day to 43 minutes per day (1-2). Cortright calculates this improvement at another $1.5 billion. Add those two dollar amounts together and you're talking real money."

What are the savings mentioned here? Gas money? What else? Check Cortright.

Read Actively

Engage in a dialogue with what you read. Talk back to the author. If you are having trouble understanding a difficult section, read it aloud and listen to the author's voice. Hearing something read will sometimes help you to imagine being in a conversation with the author.

Make notes

As you read, write down your thoughts.

- Imagine that the author is with you. What points does the writer make that you would respond to in person?
- What questions would you have of the author? These indicate what you might need to look up.
- What ideas do you find that you might develop or interpret differently?

Keep a reading journal

One place to keep track of your notes on readings is in a reading journal. Record your first impressions, note any ideas you find stimulating or useful, explore relationships, and write down questions. Often you can connect ideas from different readings. A reading journal is a great place to test ideas that you can later develop for a writing assignment.

Map what you read

Drawing a map of a text can help you to identify key points and understand the relationships among ideas in a reading. Below is one idea for mapping the opening paragraphs from Jeff Speck's "The Walkability Dividend" (included in Chapter 12).

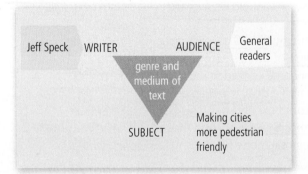

Thesis: There are real benefits to living in a walkable city

Example: Portland

Portland's urban growth strategies

Today, Portlanders drive 20% less than people in other cities

Money saved from driving less

Map the rhetorical situation

Remember that it's always helpful to understand the rhetorical situation when you are working with a reading. Use search tools to explore the larger conversation about the issue your author identifies.

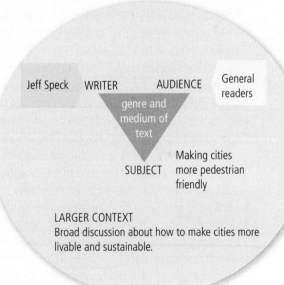

Outline a reading

Another strategy that you can use to better understand a text that you're reading is to outline it. Creating a working (or informal) outline that describes what a reading says, paragraph by paragraph, will help you see how a reading is organized and how the different ideas in the reading relate to each other and to the main thesis. When outlining a reading, you'll want to include the main thesis of the reading as well as a sentence or phrase that recaps each paragraph of the reading.

Below is a working outline for the opening paragraphs from "The Walkability Dividend" by Jeff Speck.

Thesis: There are real benefits to living in a walkable city

1. How is Portland different from other cities [Background info]

2. How are Portland's urban growth strategies different from those in other cities [Background info]

3. Today, Portlanders drive 20% less than people in other cities [Why Portland is used as the example in this reading]

4. Billions of dollars saved from driving less in Portland [Evidence to support main thesis]

5. Where does saved money go? Above-average spending on recreation in Portland.

WRITE NOW

Outline or map a reading

Create an outline or a map for one of the readings in Part 2. The key for either a map or an outline of a reading is to determine the subject of each paragraph and how they are connected. An example outline for Jeff Speck's "The Walkability Dividend" is above.

A map represents the structure visually and verbally. A map can help you to understand the relationship of key concepts.

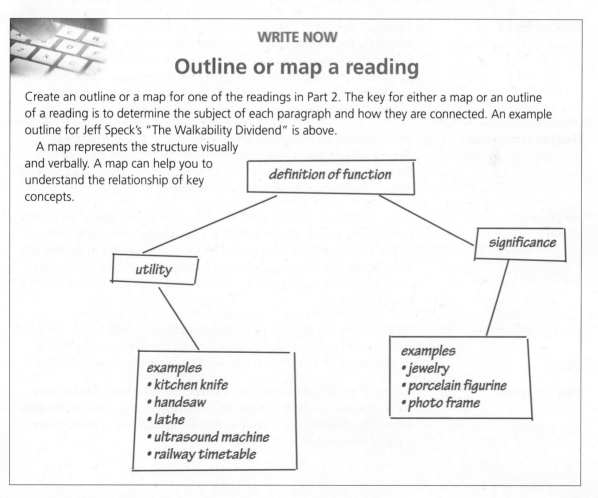

definition of function

significance

utility

examples
• kitchen knife
• handsaw
• lathe
• ultrasound machine
• railway timetable

examples
• jewelry
• porcelain figurine
• photo frame

Recognize Fallacies

Writers of arguments make claims based on reasons and evidence (see Chapters 10–13). When you read critically, you stay alert for flaws in reasoning and evidence. The kinds of faulty reasoning called logical fallacies reflect a failure to provide sufficient evidence for a claim that is being made.

Fallacies of logic

Begging the question	*Politicians are inherently dishonest because no honest person would run for public office.* The fallacy of begging the question occurs when the claim is restated and passed off as evidence.
Either-or	*Either we eliminate the regulation of businesses or else profits will suffer.* The either-or fallacy suggests that there are only two choices in a complex situation. Rarely, if ever, is this the case. (In this example, the writer ignores the fact that Enron was unregulated and went bankrupt.)
False analogies	*Japan quit fighting in 1945 when we dropped nuclear bombs on them. We should use nuclear weapons against other countries.* Analogies always depend on the degree of resemblance of one situation to another. In this case, the analogy fails to recognize that circumstances today are very different from those in 1945; many countries now possess nuclear weapons, and we know their use could harm the entire world.
Hasty generalization	*We have been in a drought for three years; that's a sure sign of climate change.* A hasty generalization is a broad claim made on the basis of a few occurrences. Climate cycles occur regularly over spans of a few years; climate trends must be observed over centuries.
Non sequitur	*A university that can raise a billion dollars from alumni should not have to raise tuition.* A *non sequitur* (which is a Latin term meaning "it does not follow") ties together two unrelated ideas. In this case, the argument fails to recognize that the money for capital campaigns is often donated for special purposes such as athletic facilities and is not part of a university's general revenue.
Oversimplification	*No one would run stop signs if we had a mandatory death penalty for doing it.* This claim may be true, but the argument would be unacceptable to most citizens. More complex, if less definitive, solutions are called for.
Post hoc fallacy	*The stock market goes down when the AFC wins the Super Bowl in even years.* The *post hoc* fallacy (from the Latin *post hoc ergo hoc,* which means "after this, therefore this") assumes that things that follow in time have a causal relationship.

Rationalization	*I could have finished my paper on time if my printer was working.* People frequently come up with excuses and weak explanations for their own and others' behavior that often avoid actual causes.
Slippery slope	*We shouldn't grant citizenship to illegal immigrants now living in the United States because no one will want to obey our laws.* The slippery slope fallacy maintains that one thing inevitably will cause something else to happen.

Fallacies of emotion and language

Bandwagon appeals	*It doesn't matter if I copy a paper off the Web because everyone else does.* This argument suggests that everyone is doing it, so why shouldn't you? But on close examination, it may be that everyone really isn't doing it— and in any case, it may not be the right thing to do.
Name calling	Name calling is frequent in politics and among competing groups (*radical, tax-and-spend liberal, racist, fascist, right-wing ideologue*). Unless these terms are carefully defined, they are meaningless.
Polarization	*Feminists are all man-haters.* Polarization, like name-calling, exaggerates positions and groups by representing them as extreme and divisive.
Straw man	*Environmentalists won't be satisfied until not a single human being is allowed to enter a national park.* A straw man argument is a diversionary tactic that sets up another's position in a way that can be easily rejected. In fact, only a small percentage of environmentalists would make an argument even close to this one.

WRITE NOW MyWritingLab™

Analyze opinion writing

Examine writing that expresses opinions: blogs, discussion boards, editorials, advocacy Web sites, the letters to the editor on the editorial pages of your campus or local newspaper. Read with a pencil in hand, and mark where you think there may be fallacies.

Select the example that has the clearest fallacy. Explain in a paragraph the cause of the fallacy.

Write a Summary

When you summarize, you state the major ideas of an entire source or part of a source in your own words. A summary can be as short as a sentence or a few sentences, and it can also be longer especially if you are trying to summarize a long academic argument. Short summaries can be an important strategy in critical reading. Longer, formal summaries are sometimes assigned as stand-alone writing. Because summaries focus on the key ideas of a reading, they often will not include any of the specific language or words from the reading. But if you do use exact words from a reading in your summary, then you have to put those words within quotation marks and cite them correctly. Below is a sample summary of Jeff Speck's "The Walkability Dividend."

"The Walkability Dividend" appears early in Jeff Speck's 2012 book, Walkable City: How Downtown Can Save America, One Step at a Time. *It gives a strong justification for the steps Speck recommends for making cities more accessible for pedestrians and bicycle riders. Speck poses the question: What kind of city encourages economic productivity and attracts college-educated 25- to 34-year-olds, the most prized demographic? Which kind of city does the talented millennial generation prefer—sprawling cities like Atlanta, Phoenix, and Riverside, California, or compact cities like Washington, DC and San Francisco? Speck uses the example of Portland, Oregon, where the rate of well-educated young people moving to the city is five times higher than the national average. Portland's economy is booming with over twelve hundred technology companies. Speck stands the conventional argument that a strong economy attracts people and jobs on its head. Instead Speck argues that people will flock to cities with a higher quality of life and that the jobs will follow.*

Write a Paraphrase

When you paraphrase, you represent the ideas articulated in a source in your own words at about the same length as the original. If you use the exact words from the source, then you will need to put them within quotation marks and cite the page number. Also cite the page number for the source of any facts you include.

In "The Walkability Dividend," Jeff Speck examines the economic benefits that Portland enjoys from reducing the vehicle miles driven per person by 20% since 1996 (29). Drawing on statistics from Joe Cortright, Speck concludes that the people of Portland save over $2.6 billion by driving less. Furthermore, Speck argues that the money saved on cars and gasoline—which almost all leaves the city—gets invested in housing, which Speck says is "about as local as it gets" (29).

Decide when to summarize and when to paraphrase

When you want to discuss a text that you've read, you'll need to decide if you should summarize or paraphrase or even quote from the reading. In general, if you want to discuss the details of a reading or some particular part of an argument, then it works best to paraphrase or quote from the reading. However, if you want to mention a only the basic argument or main point of a reading, or if you want to broadly compare one reading to another, then it works best to use a short summary.

WRITE NOW
MyWritingLab™

Respond to what you read

Select a reading in one of the chapters in Part 2 that interests you. Write a one-paragraph summary of either the entire reading or of a part that contains a stimulating idea.

Write a second paragraph that develops one or more of the ideas in the reading. Think of some way of expanding or extending one of the author's ideas, either by relating it to your own experience or to something else you have read.

Move from Reading to Invention

When you read broadly about a topic, you'll find that many writers respond to the ideas and opinions of other writers. Any important topic in our culture is the site of an ongoing conversation. By considering what you write as just one move in a larger conversation might end up helping you think about what you want to say. In the process of researching what has been said and written on a particular issue, often your own view is expanded and you find an opportunity to add your voice to the ongoing conversation.

Writer at work

Patrice Conley was given an assignment that called for taking a position on a current controversial issue. Patrice enjoys playing and watching sports, so she started by making a list of current controversial issues in college sports.

COLLEGE SPORTS CONTROVERSIES

1. Equal opportunities for women athletes

2. Big-time sports overshadow education

3. Financing college sports

4. Paying student-athletes in big-time college sports

5. Ethics: win-at-all-costs philosophy

6. The BCS championship system in big-time college football

She decided she was most interested in the issue of paying college athletes who participate in big-time college sports. She had wondered why student-athletes could be paid nothing when their coaches in big-time college football and basketball often have seven-figure salaries. She made her initial search using the search terms "student athlete salaries" on *Google*, which turned up many relevant articles.

Patrice began reading about the issue and making notes. She found an article by a sports attorney that explained how colleges through the National Collegiate Athletic Association (NCAA) justify defining big-time athletes as amateurs.

NCAA's justification for not paying salaries to athletes in big-time sports or allowing them to endorse products

McCann, Michael. "NCAA Faces Unspecified Damages, Changes in Latest Anti-Trust Case." *Sports Illustrated*, 21 July 2009, www.si.com/more-sports/2009/07/21/ncaa.

"Indeed, if student-athletes were paid salaries or received income through endorsement or licensing deals, they may begin to resemble professional athletes more than college students. The professionalization of student-athletes would frustrate the NCAA's focus on amateurism, possibly making it more difficult for schools to comply with Title IX, a federal law that commands gender equity in sports. Professionalization could also create economic divisions among student-athletes on the basis of their commercial appeal. Student-athletes' exposure to professional opportunities might also lead to exploitation by unsavory businesspersons, whom colleges and universities do not want on their campuses or near their student bodies."

After reading several articles and a book, Patrice began to identify specific issues in the debate over paying college athletes. She imagined the writers being in a conversation about these issues.

"The NCAA draws a clear line between professionalism and amateur sports."

"But that line seems to be for the players alone in big-time college sports. The coaches, networks, and schools make millions."

"Too few college athletes graduate or go on to lucrative professional careers."

"Colleges argue that scholarships are adequate payment for big-time college athletes."

"The NCAA should return to an older definition of amateur, which comes from Latin meaning "lover of." If students are lucky enough to be paid for doing what they love, so be it."

Imagining different positions as turns in a conversation helped her to think about what she might contribute.

WRITE NOW

MyWritingLab™

Imagine a conversation about a controversial issue

Think of a controversial issue that you know something about. It could be a local issue such as the overpopulation of deer in a neighborhood or the creation of bicycle lanes on busy streets. Or it could be a national or global issue such as Internet privacy or nuclear energy.

Think about the positions as turns in a conversation. What can you add to what's been said? Use the template below.

Some people claim that ....

Other people respond that ....

Still others claim that..

I agree with X's and Y's points, but I maintain that ....

because ....

Start an Annotated Bibliography

A working bibliography is an alphabetized list of sources with complete publication information that you collect while researching your topic. An annotated bibliography builds on the basic citations of a working bibliography by adding a brief summary or evaluation of each source. Annotated bibliography must include

- a complete citation in the documentation style you are using (MLA or APA), and
- a concise summary of the content and scope.

In addition, your instructor may ask you to comment on the relevance of the source or the qualifications of the author.

Conley 1

Patrice Conley

Professor Douglas

English 101

14 April 2014

Annotated Bibliography

"Money and March Madness." *Frontline*, WGBH/Boston, 29 Mar. 2011, www.pbs.org/
wgbh/pages/frontline/money-and-march-madness/. This video reports on a
lawsuit, O'Bannon v. NCAA, filed by former UCLA basketball star Ed O'Bannon
on behalf of other college athletes. The suit tackles the issue of using likenesses
of athletes in DVDs and video games without compensation to the athletes.
Attorneys for student athletes claim that the NCAA has violated federal antitrust
law by refusing to allow athletes to license their images and likenesses as other
entertainers are allowed to do. In 2014, the case is still in court.

Zaiger, Alan Scher. "Study: NCAA Graduation Rate Comparisons Flawed." *ABC News*,
20 Apr. 2010, abcnews.go.com/topics/sports/ncaa-football.htm. The University
of North Carolina's College Sport Research Institute accuses the NCAA of fudging
the numbers of athletes who graduate. The NCAA claims that athletes graduate
at a higher percentage than that of the total student body, but the research
institute shows that the NCAA's percentage is fraudulent because it includes
part-time students. When athletes are compared with other full-time students,
their graduation rate is 20% lower than other students.

Synthesize Readings and Visuals

Synthesize readings

When you read more than one text on the same topic, you will naturally start to compare ideas and argument among the different texts. What does each have to say on the topic? Which source do you find the most persuasive and why? Which offers surprising ideas or counterarguments? In short, how do these different texts talk to one another? When you bring together information and ideas from several sources into a coherent discussion of a topic, you are synthesizing readings.

Often your own questions will guide you to what you need to synthesize. For example, Patrice Conley recognized that the NCAA's defense of not paying college athletes depends on its definition of amateurism. She wanted to know where this definition came from, and she did historical research. (You can read Conley's completed essay on pages 416–421.)

> The definition of amateur arose in the nineteenth century in Great Britain, when team sports became popular. Middle-class and upper-class students in college had ample time to play their sports while working-class athletes had only a half-day off (no sports were played on Sundays in that era). Teams began to pay top working-class sportsmen for the time they had to take off from work. Middle-class and upper-class sportsmen didn't want to play against the working-class teams, so they made the distinction between amateurs and professionals. The definition of amateur crossed the Atlantic to the United States, where college sports became popular in the 1880s. But it was not long until the hypocrisy of amateurism undermined the ideal. Top football programs like Yale had slush funds to pay athletes, and others used ringers—players who weren't students—and even players from other schools (Zimbalist 7).

Compare your sources using this list of questions.

- What subjects, problems, or issues do your sources examine?
- What are their strongest arguments about these subjects, problems, or issues?
- How much do they agree?
- On what points do they disagree?
- Do you find the same facts cited or do the facts differ?

Synthesize visuals

Often examining a single visual doesn't tell you why the photographer or artist created it. For example, Dorothea Lange took a series of photographs of rich people on the streets of Manhattan in 1939. Lange is known today for her photographs of desperately poor people during the Great Depression. So what was Lange's intent for taking a set of photographs of the rich? Was she portraying the end of the Great Depression? Probably she was not because the United States did not emerge from the Great Depression until World War II began late in 1941.

A key clue to why Lange took these set of photos is one titled *"Social Justice," Founded by Father Coughlin, Sold on Important Street Corners and Intersections, New York City*. Father Coughlin was leader of the National Union for Social Justice, which was a rabidly anti-Semitic movement. In his radio broadcasts and in his newspaper, Couglin spewed his hatred of Jews and his support for the policies of Adolf Hitler. Only after Germany declared war on the United States did the government force the cancellation of the radio broadcasts and the newspaper. The popularity of *Social Justice* among wealthy of New York City suggests that they shared Father Coughlin's pro-Nazi sympathies.

Dorothea Lange, *Fifth Avenue Approaching 57th Street. New York City. Some New Yorkers Use Personally Owned Limousines Driven by Private Uniformed Drivers.* 1939.

Dorothea Lange, *"Social Justice," Founded by Father Coughlin, Sold on Important Street Corners and Intersections, New York City.* 1939.

MyWritingLab™ Visit Ch. 2 in MyWritingLab to complete the chapter exercises and to test your understanding of the chapter objectives.

3 Planning

Developing a plan for writing is the key to success.

In this chapter, you will learn to

1. Move from a general topic to a writing plan *(see p. 35)*
2. Narrow your topic *(see pp. 36–37)*
3. Write and evaluate a thesis *(see pp. 38–39)*
4. Make a plan *(see pp. 40–41)*

Move from a General Topic to a Writing Plan

After you have found a topic (see Chapter 1) and likely have read about the topic (see Chapter 2), you need to formulate a plan for writing. Planning in advance will make your time more productive and lead to better results.

IDENTIFY YOUR PURPOSE	Often your assignment will direct your purpose. Look for words like these.
	Reflect: Think about an event or a concept in terms of your own experience. → **See Chapter 6**
	Describe: Observe carefully, make notes, and report what you saw, heard, and experienced. → **See Chapter 7**
	Inform: Report information or explain a concept or idea. → **See Chapter 8**
	Analyze: Interpret a text or event to find connections and reach conclusions. → **See Chapter 9**
	Analyze causes: Identify probable causes of a trend, event, or phenomenon. → **See Chapter 10**
	Evaluate: Determine whether something is good or bad according to criteria that you identify. → **See Chapter 11**
	Argue: Take a position on an issue or propose a course of action. → **See Chapters 12 and 13**
NARROW YOUR TOPIC	If your topic is too broad, you will find too much information and will not be able to cover the topic adequately. → **See page 36**
WRITE A WORKING THESIS	Avoid sentences that begin "I'm going to write about computer games and children," or "My topic is computer games and children." Write a complete sentence that states your main idea and makes an assertion about that main idea. (For example, "Computer games are valuable because they improve children's visual attention skills and literacy skills.") → **See page 38**
EVALUATE YOUR THESIS	Your working thesis should progress to a statement that is of increasing interest to your readers → **See page 39**
MAKE A VISUAL PLAN OR A WORKING OUTLINE	A visual plan or a working outline will list the major sections and sketch the overall development. → **See page 40**

Narrow Your Topic

Until you can focus a broad topic, you will not be able to organize your project and treat your subject in enough depth.

Take, for example, the broad topic of whether genetically modified foods (GM foods) are safe for consumers. The topic is much too large to cover adequately in a course project. Ask questions and brainstorm (see page 12).

- Who is involved in the issue? Governments? corporations? farmers? consumers?
- Which crops are genetically modified?
- What time period is involved?
- What countries are involved?
- Why are GM foods controversial?

You may need to do research to find out more about your topic in order to narrow it (see Chapter 20). Your readers will stay better focused if you have a specific topic, and you will be better equipped to cover your topic thoroughly.

Broad topic
Are GM foods safe for consumers?

Narrower topic
What is the European Union's policy on selling and labeling GM foods?

Specific topic
Why did France and other European countries ban Monsanto's MON0810 corn and similar genetically modified crops in 2007?

Map your topic

Mapping is another method of narrowing your topic. Mapping can also help you to create a working outline if you connect the ideas you set out. See the facing page for how Patrice Conley used mapping to narrow her topic.

To create a map you can use either pen and paper or mapping software available on the Internet. Google Docs has a free drawing program that can make diagrams.

Writer at work

Patrice Conley decided to make a map in order to find a center for her broad topic of whether student athletes in big-time college sports should be paid.

She started with her general topic, stating it in a few words and drawing a box around it.

Next Patrice asked additional questions:
- What is the current situation?
- Who is involved?
- How long has it been going on?
- What else is like it?
- What exactly is the problem?
- What possible solutions are there for the problem?

She thought of some general categories for her topic in response to those questions and drew boxes for each.

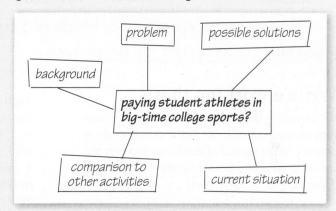

She then looked at her notes from what she had read. She began to generate ideas for each of the subcategories and put them on her map.

When she finished she took stock of her map. She picked up a marker and drew a box around a possible central idea for her project.

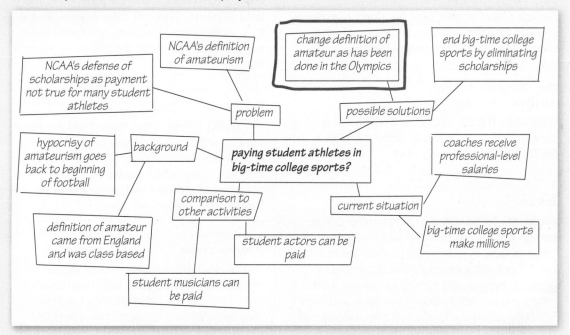

She succeeded in narrowing her general topic to the more specific topic of changing the definition of amateur as it applies to student athletes.

Write a Thesis

The thesis announces your topic and states what point or points you want to make about that topic. A thesis is a statement, not a question. A thesis has a subject and an assertion.

Subject | **Assertion** |

Advertisers use *Facebook's* list of friends to determine where you live and what you buy in order to send you targeted ads.

Write a working thesis

Your working thesis should follow the direction your assignment calls for. These examples show how the broad subject of databases and privacy can be approached from different directions, depending on your purpose.

Describe

WORKING THESIS: My Amazon.com account has a list of every book I have purchased from them dating back ten years, plus Amazon records every item I browse but don't buy. No wonder Amazon's recommendations of what I might like are so uncannily accurate!

Analyze

WORKING THESIS: Understanding how the concept of privacy is legally defined is critical for strengthening privacy laws.

Inform

WORKING THESIS: Imagine a government that compels its citizens to reveal vast amounts of personal data, including your physical description, your phone number, your political party, your parents' and spouse's names, where you work, where you live, what property you own, and every legal transaction in your life, and then making that data available to anyone on the Web—which is exactly what federal, state, and local governments are doing today in the United States.

Argue

WORKING THESIS: Unlike the government, companies have almost no restrictions on what information they collect or what they do with it. Laws should be passed that make companies responsible for the misuse of personal information and allow people to have greater participation in how that information is used.

Evaluate

WORKING THESIS: Using personal consumer data to refuse service or offer inferior service to customers who likely will not spend much money is an example of the misuse of personal information.

Reflect

WORKING THESIS: I had never thought about the consequences of data profiling until I read about Netflix's policy of "throttling" frequent users, which explained why deliveries of movies I had requested from Netflix grew slower and slower.

Analyze causes

WORKING THESIS: Many laws to protect privacy are on the books, but these laws are ineffective for the digital era because they were written to protect people from government spying and intrusion rather than from the collection and selling of personal information by companies.

Evaluate your working thesis

Ask yourself these questions about your working thesis.

1. Is it specific?
2. Is it manageable in terms of the assigned length and the amount of time you have?
3. Is it interesting to your intended readers?

Example 1

WORKING THESIS: Steroids are a problem in Major League Baseball.

- Specific? The thesis is too broad. What exactly is the problem? Is the problem the same now as it was a few years ago?

- Manageable? Because the thesis is not limited, it cannot be discussed adequately.

- Interesting? The topic is potentially interesting, but many people are aware that baseball players used steroids. How can you lead readers to think about the topic in a new way?

Example 1 revised

THESIS: Home run records from 1993 through 2004 should be placed in a special category because of the high use of steroids in Major League Baseball before testing began in 2004.

Example 2

WORKING THESIS: "Nanotechnology" refers to any technology that deals with particles measured in units of a nanometer, which is one billionth (10^{-9}) of a meter.

- **Specific?** The thesis is specific, but it is too narrow. It offers only a definition of nanotechnology.

- **Manageable?** The thesis states a fact.

- **Interesting?** Nanotechnology could be interesting if some of its potential effects are included.

Example 2 revised

THESIS: Nanotechnology may soon change concepts of social identity by making it possible for individuals to alter their physical appearances either through cosmetic surgery performed by nanorobots or changes in genetic sequences on chromosomes.

WRITE NOW   MyWritingLab™

Write a bold thesis

Too much of what we read says what we've all heard before. Instead of serving up what readers likely know, try challenging readers. For example, in *Everything Bad Is Good for You*, Steven Johnson argues that video games are not a total waste of time but teach children valuable problem-solving skills.

Think of something that many people accept as common sense or general wisdom—that junk food is bad for you, reality television is garbage, or graffiti is vandalism—and argue the opposite. Or that something thought of as boring might be really interesting: bird watching, classical Indian music, or ancient Greek drama. Write a thesis that stands common wisdom on its head.

Then write a paragraph about how you might argue for your controversial thesis. What evidence might you supply?

Make a Plan

Get out your notes and all the information you have collected. You may find it helpful to write major points on sticky notes so you can move them around. If your topic is the effects of nanotechnology on the body, you might produce an organization plan similar to this one.

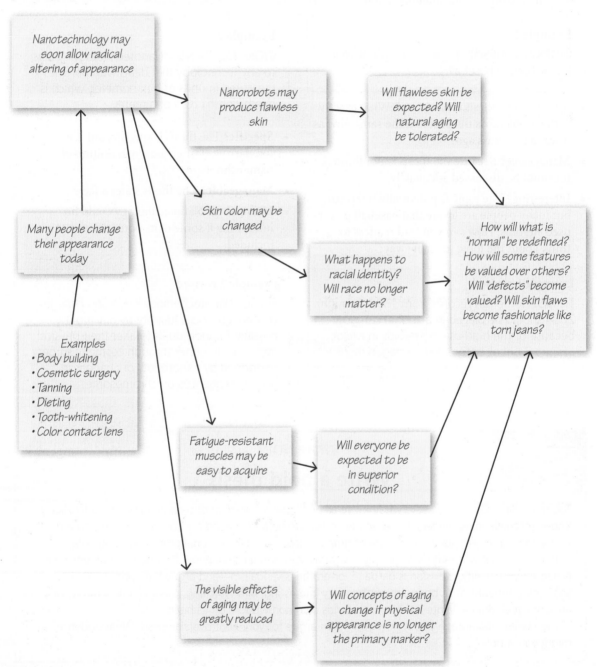

Writing plans often take the form of outlines, either formal outlines or working outlines.

A **formal outline** typically begins with the working thesis, which anchors the entire outline.

A **working outline** is a sketch of how you will arrange the major sections.

WORKING THESIS: Nanotechnology may soon allow radical altering of the human body, which will have major social consequences.

I. Altering the appearance of the body has become common.
   A. Cosmetic surgery is now routine.
   B. Body building is popular.
   C. Most people are aware of diet and many attempt to control their weight.
   D. Tanning, changing eye color, and tooth-whitening are frequent.

II. Nanotechnology may soon radically accelerate these trends.
   A. Nanorobots may produce flawless skin.
   B. Skin color may be changed.
   C. Wrinkles and other signs of aging may be eliminated or reduced.
   D. Muscle tissue may be enhanced.

Effects of nanotechnology on the body

SECTION 1: *Begin with how people change the appearance of their bodies today.*

SECTION 2: *Discuss how nanotechnology will accelerate these trends, giving people the potential for perfect skin, changing their skin color, and reducing aging.*

SECTION 3: *Move to the questions these technologies raise, such as how aging will be perceived and how race will be understood.*

SECTION 4: *Raise the issue of how "normal" will be defined if people can choose how they look.*

SECTION 5: *Expand the idea of "normal" to who will control what is desirable and how social hierarchies might be changed or reinforced.*

SECTION 6: *End by connecting body issues to larger issues such as who gets to live for how long.*

WRITE NOW   MyWritingLab™

Compare planning methods

First, write a working thesis. Ask the questions on page 39.

• Is the thesis specific?   • Is it manageable?   • Is it interesting?

Revise your thesis if necessary.

   Then use two of the three methods—a visual organization plan, a formal outline, or a working outline—to develop a plan for writing a paper based on the thesis. When you finish, compare the plans. Which will be easier to use for writing your paper?

MyWritingLab™ Visit Ch. 3 in MyWritingLab to complete the chapter exercises and to test your understanding of the chapter objectives.

4 Drafting

Drafting is easier when you think ahead with strategies in mind for writing.

In this chapter, you will learn to

❶ Draft with strategies in mind *(see p. 43)*

❷ Write a zero draft *(see p. 44)*

❸ Draft from a working outline *(see p. 46)*

❹ Start fast with an engaging title and opening paragraph *(see p. 48)*

❺ Develop paragraphs *(see p. 49)*

❻ Conclude with strength *(see p. 50)*

❼ Link within and across paragraphs *(see p. 51)*

❽ Write an essay exam *(see p. 52)*

Draft with Strategies in Mind

People who write frequently on the job or who make their living as writers have many different strategies for producing a successful piece of writing. Some plan extensively in advance, specifying what will go in each section.

Other writers find that putting ideas into words often changes the ideas and generates new ones. These writers start with what is sometimes called a zero draft or discovery draft, which resembles a sculptor's untouched clay to be molded later into the finished project.

FIND A DRAFTING STRATEGY THAT WORKS FOR YOU	Think about how you will write your project. **Write a zero draft:** If you do not have a plan, you may want to write a zero draft, then determine your plan. **→ See page 44** **Write from an outline:** If you have a formal or working outline, you can use the outline to write individual paragraphs. **→ See page 46**
WRITE AN ENGAGING TITLE AND INTRODUCTION	Get off to a fast start. Make your readers interested in your topic. **→ See page 48**
DEVELOP YOUR BODY PARAGRAPHS	Paragraphs, like essays, have a beginning, middle, and end organized around a central idea. **→ See page 49**
WRITE A STRONG CONCLUSION	Conclusions that offer only a summary bore readers. Effective conclusions are interesting and provocative, leaving readers with something to think about. **→ See page 50**
CHECK YOUR LINKS WITHIN AND BETWEEN PARAGRAPHS	Writing that flows is coherent, which means that readers understand how sentences and paragraphs fit together. Repeating key words and phrases and signaling transitions builds coherence. **→ See page 51**

Write a Zero Draft

One method of drafting is to start writing before you know where you are headed. A zero draft or discovery draft is similar to freewriting, where you write quickly for a set time, often five to ten minutes.

The idea of a zero draft is to get as much down as you can and not worry about producing a finished product. Don't worry about grammar, spelling, or gaps in logic. If you start writing about side issues, don't worry about that either; it might eventually turn into the focus of your project.

Writer at work

For assigned writing in her classes, Patrice Conley prefers writing first and then determining her organization. She knows in advance that nearly all of what she writes will not make it into the final draft she submits to her instructor. Nevertheless, she finds writing as fast as she can frees up her thinking and gives her words to start with rather than a blank page.

Patrice later goes back to her zero draft to identify key ideas, which she underlines.

PATRICE'S ZERO DRAFT

I can't believe how much colleges and universities that play big-time football and basketball are making off the student athletes. It's ridiculous. The schools are making a fortune, the networks that televise the games are making a fortune, and the coaches are making a fortune. Everybody is getting filthy rich except the stars of the show, the players, who get nothing out of it. They can't even be paid after they graduate if their school uses their names and images to make money. I know the NCAA—that's the organization that runs college sports—claims that student athletes are paid with scholarships. But that assumes that they will graduate, and a lot of them will drop out. They spend so much time on athletics that once their eligibility is gone, they are way behind and don't have the athletics' tutors to help them. I know this has been going on for years, but it just isn't right. Why don't the players sue? Other students can get paid for working as professionals. Our music school has a service for helping talented musicians to find jobs. I know other students who have had bit parts in movies. How can students who aren't athletes work professionally in their specialty and get paid when athletes can't. The reason colleges get by with treating athletes unfairly is because they define them as amateurs. The Olympics used to do this too, but they have dropped this distinction. Professional athletes compete in the Olympics in every sport except boxing. The definition needs to be changed.

When Patrice finished her zero draft, she let it sit for a day and then took stock of the key points that she had underlined. She rearranged these key points into a working outline.

PATRICE CREATES A WORKING OUTLINE FROM HER ZERO DRAFT

WORKING TITLE: *Should Student Athletes in Big-Time College Sports Be Paid?*

SECTION 1: *Student athletes in college sign away their rights for payment.*

SECTION 2: *College athletics are big business, and top coaches receive multimillion-dollar salaries.*

SECTION 3: *NCAA defends classifying student athletes as amateurs to protect them from exploitation.*

SECTION 4: *The history of amateurism arose in 19th c. Britain when middle- and upper-class sportsmen didn't want to play against working-class teams. The Olympics abandoned the distinction in 1988.*

SECTION 5: *Student musicians and student actors get paid when they perform professionally.*

SECTION 6: *Student athletes cannot be paid for use of their names and images even after they graduate.*

SECTION 7: *Defenders of the current system claim that student athletes are paid with scholarships, but in big-time sports many do not graduate.*

SECTION 8: *NCAA should adopt a different definition of amateur that allows those lucky enough to be paid for what they earn for their schools.*

WRITE NOW   MyWritingLab™

Your drafting strategies

Think about two or three pieces of writing you have done for school or work recently. What method did you use? Did you make an outline or a visual plan or did you start writing?

Write a paragraph for each piece of writing about your writing process. What was easy for you? What was most difficult?

Draft from a Working Outline

Writers who like to lay out sections in advance of writing use formal or working outlines. These advance planners want to know where they are headed when they start typing sentences.

One issue to consider is where to place the thesis for the project. You may have been told at some point that your thesis should be the last sentence in the first paragraph. In some kinds of writing, especially arguments, the organization builds toward a thesis, which may come as late as the conclusion. Nonetheless, the opening paragraph should clearly indicate your topic and where you are headed.

This working outline on the risks of nanotechnology describes potential risks before presenting the thesis in the final paragraph.

TITLE:	Managing the Risks of Nanotechnology While Reaping the Rewards
SECTION 1:	Begin by defining nanotechnology—manipulating particles between 1 and 100 nanometers (nanometer is a billionth of a meter). Describe the rapid spread of nanotechnology in consumer products including clothing, food, sports equipment, medicines, electronics, and cars. State projection of 15% of global manufactured goods containing nanotechnology in 2014: But is it safe?
SECTION 2:	Most Americans know nothing about nanotechnology. Companies have stopped advertising that their produces contain nanotechnology because of fear of potential lawsuits. Asbestos, once thought safe, now is known to be toxic and has cost companies $250 billion in lawsuits in the United States alone.
SECTION 3:	Relatively little research has been done on the safety of nanotechnology. No testing is required for new products because the materials are common, but materials behave differently at nano-scale (example—aluminum normally inert but combustible at nano-scale).
SECTION 4:	Nanoparticles are highly mobile and can cross the blood-brain barrier and through the placenta. They are toxic in brains of fish and may collect in lungs.
SECTION 5:	Urge that the federal government develop a master plan for identifying and reducing potential risks of nanotechnology and provide sufficient funding to carry out the plan. The federal government needs to create a master plan for risk research and to increase spending at least tenfold to ensure sufficient funding to carry out the plan.

The working thesis is stated as the conclusion.

Use your working outline to write paragraphs

Using a working outline to guide a writing project requires you to decide how you convert sections into paragraphs. Some sections might translate into a single paragraph; other sections might require two or more paragraphs.

For example, the first section of the working outline on the opposite page might be the first paragraph.

Construct effective paragraphs

For each paragraph you will need either to identify the main idea or write a topic sentence. Paragraphs are organized much like essays with an introduction, a body, and a conclusion. The topic sentence often is the first sentence and serves as the introduction. The body expands the main idea of the paragraph. The conclusion either reinforces the main point or it provides a bridge to what follows in the next paragraph and beyond.

Opening paragraphs need to do more than provide information about the topic. They need either to include the thesis statement or else they need to cue the reader to where the project is headed. In this case, the writer poses a question. This opening paragraph develops section 1 of the working outline.

Managing the Risks of Nanotechnology While Reaping the Rewards

Topic sentence →

The revolutionary potential of nanotechnology for medicine, energy production, and communication is now at the research and development stage, but the future has arrived in consumer products. Nanotechnology has given us products we hardly could have imagined just a few years ago: socks that never smell; pants that repel water yet keep you cool; eyeglasses that won't scratch; "smart" foods that add nutrition and reduce cholesterol; DVDs that are incredibly lifelike; bandages that

Details build the paragraph →

speed healing; tennis balls that last longer; golf balls that fly straighter; pharmaceuticals that selectively deliver drugs; various digital devices like palm pilots, digital cameras, and cell phones that have longer battery lives and more vivid displays; and cars that are lighter, stronger, and more fuel efficient. These miracle products are now possible because scientists have learned how to manipulate nano-scale particles from 1–100 nanometers (a nanometer is a billionth of a meter; a human hair is about 100,000 nanometers in width). Experts estimate that 15% of all consumer

A question indicates the direction for the rest of the paper →

products will contain nanotechnology by 2014. In the rush to create new consumer products, however, one question has not been asked: Is nanotechnology safe for those who use the products and the workers who are exposed to nanoparticles daily?

Start Fast with an Engaging Title and Opening Paragraph

Often you have but a few seconds to convince a reader to keep reading what you've written. Make those few seconds count.

Titles

Vague titles give no motivation to read on.

VAGUE

Good and Bad Fats

Specific titles are like a tasty appetizer; if you like the appetizer, you'll probably like the main course.

SPECIFIC

The Secret Killer: Hydrogenated Fats

Cut out empty phrases and sentences

Writers often start a draft with empty phrases and sentences, much as speakers clear their throats before starting.

~~Americans have seen many new digital technologies in just a few years. These technologies are capable of delivering massive amounts of information almost instantly.~~ Unlike the past two centuries, when many celebrated each new communication technology as the means to a glorious future, few now claim that more information will lead to better lives. The glut of information that is readily accessible has not led to broader global understanding but instead in the view of many observers has led to increased fragmentation, confusion, and exhaustion.

Don't apologize

Readers dismiss writers who begin by making excuses. Do your homework as a writer and you can offer an informed perspective.

WEAK

I'm not an economics major, and 1 don't know much about financial issues, but it costs a lot to fill up my car each week.

STRONGER

Could small changes in behavior lead to big economic changes in the lives of Americans? I tested that question for a week by walking, biking, and taking public transportation to avoid driving and by eating healthy foods bought in bulk or from the farmers market rather than more expensive packaged foods.

Develop Paragraphs

Readers expect paragraphs in essays to be developed.

This paragraph gives the main ideas but with no examples. The writing is abstract and limp.

THIN

We now live in a global economy where all countries are connected. When something happens to the economy in one country, it affects others. Many factories have moved to developing nations, and the economic activity in advanced nations focuses more on concept development and marketing.

Developed paragraphs often include examples that illustrate main points. Key ideas are emphasized in vivid sentences.

DEVELOPED

We now live in a global economy, where more than a trillion dollars is exchanged in currency markets daily and where a burp in Malaysia can tumble stock exchanges in the West. The creation of wealth has moved from production in fortress-like factories to global networks of management and distribution, so that, when you buy a product at your local Walmart or Costco, the purchase data are sent not only to a corporation but also to the manufacturer of that product. Tomorrow's production in distant developing nations is determined by what is purchased today in the United States and other affluent nations. In the fast and light capitalism of the new economy, how and where goods are produced has become relatively unimportant compared to creating new concepts and marketing those concepts.

Pay attention to paragraphs when you revise

In revising, focus on each paragraph—one at a time. For each one, ask yourself what your reader will notice and remember.

- Is the main point fully developed?
- Does the paragraph include examples?
- Are key ideas emphasized in vivid sentences?

Conclude with Strength

The challenge in ending paragraphs is to leave the reader with something provocative, something beyond pure summary of the previous paragraphs.

Issue a call to action	Although ecological problems in Russia seem distant, students like you and me can help protect the snow leopard by joining the World Wildlife Fund campaign.
Make a recommendation	Russia's creditors would be wise to sign on to the World Wildlife Fund's proposal to relieve some of the country's debt in order to protect snow leopard habitat. After all, if Russia is going to be economically viable, it needs to be ecologically healthy.
Give an example that illustrates a key point	Poachers are so uncowed by authorities that they even tried to sell a leopard skin to a reporter researching a story on endangered species.
Speculate about the future	Unless Nepali and Chinese officials devote more resources to snow leopard preservation, these beautiful animals will be gone in a few years.
Ask rhetorical questions	In general the larger and more majestic (or better yet, cute) an endangered animal is, the better its chances of being saved. Bumper stickers don't implore us to save blind cave insects; they ask us to save the whales, elephants, and tigers. But snow leopards aren't cave bugs; they are beautiful, impressive animals that should be the easiest of all to protect. If we can't save them, do any endangered species stand a chance?

Link Within and Across Paragraphs

Transitions at the beginnings and ends of paragraphs guide readers. They explain why a paragraph follows from the previous one. They offer writers the opportunity to highlight the turns in their thinking.

Build coherence

The first paragraph introduces the metaphor of the "Information Superhighway" and connects the metaphor to the American myth of the frontier. The words in bold are repeated verbatim or with synonyms in the next paragraph.

The second paragraph begins with the frontier and examines how roads are also tied to ideas of a free-market economy.

The metaphor of the "Information Superhighway," popularized by Al Gore in the 1990s, sprang from a long-standing American myth about the freedom of **the open road**. Throughout the twentieth century the automobile represented freedom of action—not just the pleasures of driving around aimlessly for recreation but the possibility of exploring new territories and reaching **the frontier**. When talking about the Internet, both Republicans and Democrats in the 1990s invoked the idealized highway in the American imagination—**the highway** that leads to **the frontier.**

Exploration of the **frontier** is linked to democracy in this rhetoric. From Thomas Jefferson onward, American leaders have maintained that **good roads** are a prerequisite to democracy. With **good roads** farmers could transport their crops directly to local markets and competitive railheads.

WRITE NOW MyWritingLab™

What makes a paragraph good or bad?

Find examples of well-written paragraphs and poorly written paragraphs in print or on the Web using the criteria covered in this chapter. Look for examples of opening and concluding paragraphs as well as body paragraphs. What exactly makes the good examples well written? Likewise, what makes the bad examples poorly written?

Revise one of the bad examples to improve it.

Write an Essay Exam

Like any writing task, writing essay exams is a learned skill. Practice and careful preparation are your keys to success.

Preparing for the examination

Use common sense before an essay exam. Get a good night's sleep. Don't wait until the last minute to study. Be prepared.

1. Learn what to expect. Ask the instructor about the exam format. How much time will you have? How many points will each question be worth?

2. Study early and often. Review your notes and assigned readings to determine the major concepts and terms being tested. Practice explaining, applying, and analyzing them. Think about how the texts or concepts relate to one another.

3. Anticipate possible questions. Generate essay questions you think might appear on the exam, and outline possible responses.

4. Make a plan. Have a plan for budgeting your time and approaching the questions. You may want to tackle questions worth the most points first. Allow time to plan, revise, and proofread in addition to actually writing the essay.

Writing a successful exam

After "Be Prepared," the best piece of advice for writing essay examinations is "Don't Panic." It's easy to feel pressure as you hear the clock ticking away during an exam. Although time is limited, don't forsake the writing process during an essay exam.

Understand the question	Take the time to read the question carefully. Underline important words or phrases. If the question asks you to address more than one issue, number them. Be on the lookout for prompting words, which tell you what kind of essay the instructor wants.
Analyze	*Analyze the good and bad effects of requiring students to take mandatory standardized tests to graduate from high school.* Make an original argument that seeks to illuminate some aspect of the issue at hand for the reader. Will students be better educated if they must pass a test at the end of high school? Or will they be less well educated because teachers will be forced to teach what's on the test and neglect other essential knowledge?
Assess or evaluate	*The president's long-standing rationale for recommending most-favored nation (MFN) status for trade relations with China is that our openness encourages human rights reforms in China. Assess whether China's MFN status since 2001 has been a success on those grounds.* Make a judgment based on well-supported reasons. For example, has China's human rights record improved with increased trade with the United States?

Compare/contrast	*Compare Jamaica Kincaid's relationship with her mother in* Annie John *with Amy Tan's relationship with her mother in* The Joy Luck Club. Make an argument about similarities or differences between texts or issues. A compare and contrast essay should not simply describe similarities or differences; it should argue for what can be learned by comparing the two books.
Describe	*Describe how aphasia can affect sufferers' language skills.* "Describe" questions usually ask you to present relevant material from the course readings and lectures.
Discuss	*Discuss Giotto's reputation as a transitional figure between medieval and renaissance painting.* Make a specific and manageable argument with plenty of detail. Since *discuss* can be a vague prompting word, ask your instructor if you need clarification.
Explain	*Explain why we would die of thirst if we only drank salt water.* Take on the role of teacher. Your goal is to make the reader understand a concept. Begin by breaking the subject down into categories or steps. Carefully detail and illustrate those categories or steps. Use the terms covered in the course where appropriate.
Explore	*Explore the environmental risks of offshore drilling.* Like "discuss" questions, "explore" questions tend to be vague. Develop a focused argument. Avoid the temptation to respond with an equally vague thesis: Offshore drilling has minimal environmental risks if done correctly.

Plan your essay

After you read the essay question, take a few minutes to sketch an outline of your answer. Decide what argument you want to make. Break the argument into manageable chunks, logical steps, or categories. Note the examples you want to analyze in order to illustrate each chunk of the argument.

Write the essay

An essay exam is not the place to be subtle. Your instructor probably won't have time to hunt for your argument. Highlight your argument clearly toward the beginning of the essay and map out the upcoming paragraphs. Use strong transitions between paragraphs. Relate the point of each paragraph clearly to the larger argument. Offer examples to prove your point. And remember, examples aren't self-explanatory. Analyze your examples to support your argument. Then write a conclusion that once again emphasizes the argument and the steps you took to prove it.

Revise and proofread

While your instructor won't expect essay exam answers to be as polished as other types of writing, your prose still affects your credibility. Reserve time at the end of the exam period to revise your essay, expanding on explanations, adding any examples that strengthen your argument, and clarifying muddled sentences. Then read the essay for errors in spelling, punctuation, and grammar.

MyWritingLab™ Visit Ch. 4 in MyWritingLab to complete the chapter exercises and to test your understanding of the chapter objectives.

5 Revising

To revise effectively, you must "re-see" what you have written, which, after all, is what revision means.

In this chapter, you will learn to

1 Evaluate your draft *(see p. 56)*

2 Learn strategies for rewriting *(see p. 57)*

3 Respond to the writing of others *(see p. 58)*

4 Edit and proofread carefully *(see p. 59)*

5 Revise using your instructor's comments *(see pp. 60–61)*

Revising and Editing

Revision is a two-step process that involves both revising and editing. The revising step can involve a major overhaul of your paper or media project. You may have to rewrite entire sections. The editing step deals with local concerns: making sentences read better, inserting transitions between sentences and paragraphs, checking for correct format, and eliminating errors in grammar, punctuation, and spelling.

Experienced writers know that both steps are critical for success. Even the best writers have to revise several times to get the result they want. Inexperienced writers too often skip the revising step and go straight to the issues of copyediting and proofreading. They are unwilling to make major changes.

To be able to revise effectively, you have to plan your time. You cannot revise a paper or a media project effectively if you wait until the last minute to begin working. Allow at least a day between the time you finish your draft and when you begin revising to let what you write cool off.

A good method to begin your revision is to read your paper out loud to someone else. Ask that person to give you a quick response. Is the organization clear? Is anything confusing? Is there anything that the listener wants to know more about? You'll likely also notice rough spots in your writing because these places will be difficult to read. What you are after is an overall sense of how well you have accomplished what you set out to do.

EVALUATE AND REVISE YOUR DRAFT	Start with the big picture. Does your project meet the assignment? Does it have a clear focus? Are the main points adequately developed? Is the organization effective? ➔ **See page 56**
RESPOND TO OTHERS	Responding to the writing of others is one of the most practical skills you learn in a writing class. College-educated people write frequently in their jobs and professions—often as a team—and they are regularly asked to review what coworkers have written. ➔ **See page 58**
PAY ATTENTION TO DETAILS LAST	Your sentences should be clearly written and free of errors in grammar and punctuation. ➔ **See page 59**
REVISE USING YOUR INSTRUCTOR'S COMMENTS	Your instructor's comments give you the benefit of advice from an expert reader. ➔ **See page 60**

Evaluate Your Draft

Use these questions to evaluate your draft. Note any places where you might make improvements.

Does your paper or project meet the assignment?	• Look again at your assignment and especially at the key words such as *analyze, define, evaluate,* and *propose.* Does your paper or project do what the assignment asks for? If not, how can you change it?
	• Look again at the assignment for specific guidelines including length, format, and amount of research. Does your work meet these guidelines? If not, how can you change it?
Do you have a clear focus?	• Underline your thesis. Think how you might make your thesis more precise.
	• Underline the main idea of each paragraph. Check how each paragraph connects to your thesis. Think about how you can strengthen the connections.
Are your main points adequately developed?	• Put brackets around the reasons and evidence that support your main points.
	• Can you find places to add more examples and details that would help to explain your main points?
Is your organization effective?	• Make a quick outline of your draft if you have not done so already.
	• Mark the places where you find abrupt shifts or gaps.
	• Think about how you might rearrange sections or paragraphs to make your draft more effective.
Do you consider your potential readers' knowledge and points of view?	• Where do you give background if your readers are unfamiliar with your subject?
	• Where do you acknowledge any opposing views your readers might have?
Do you represent yourself effectively?	• To the extent you can, forget for a moment that you wrote what you are reading. What impression do you have of you, the writer?
	• Does the writer have an appropriate tone?
	• Is the writer visually effective? Is the type easy to read? Does the writer use headings and illustrations where they are helpful?

When you finish, make a list of your goals in the revision. You may have to scrap the draft and start over, but you will have a better sense of your subject and your goals.

Strategies for rewriting

Now it's time to go through your draft in detail. You should work on the goals you identify in your review. Also, look for other opportunities using this checklist.

1.

KEEP YOUR AUDIENCE IN MIND

Reread each of your paragraphs' opening sentences and ask yourself whether they are engaging enough to keep your readers interested.

2.

SHARPEN YOUR FOCUS WHEREVER POSSIBLE

You may have started out with a large topic but most of what you wrote concerns only one aspect. You may need to revise your thesis and supporting paragraphs.

3.

CHECK IF KEY TERMS ARE ADEQUATELY DEFINED

What are your key terms? Are they defined precisely enough to be meaningful?

4.

DEVELOP YOUR IDEAS WHERE NECESSARY

Key points and claims may need more explanation and supporting evidence. Look for opportunities to add support without becoming redundant.

5.

CHECK LINKS BETWEEN PARAGRAPHS

Look for any places where you make abrupt shifts and make the transitions better. Check if you signal the relationship from one paragraph to the next.

6.

CONSIDER YOUR TITLE

Many writers don't think much about titles, but they are very important. A good title makes the reader want to see what you have to say. Be as specific as you can in your title, and if possible, suggest your stance.

7.

CONSIDER YOUR INTRODUCTION

In the introduction you want to get off to a fast start and convince your reader to keep reading. Cut to the chase.

8.

CONSIDER YOUR CONCLUSION

Restating your thesis usually isn't the best way to finish; conclusions that offer only summary bore readers. The worst endings say something like "in my paper I've said this." Effective conclusions are interesting and provocative, leaving readers with something to think about.

9.

IMPROVE THE VISUAL ASPECTS OF YOUR TEXT

Does the font you selected look attractive using your printer? Would headings and subheadings help to identify key sections? If you include statistical data, would charts be effective? Would illustrations help to establish key points?

Respond to Others

Your instructor may ask you to respond to the drafts of your classmates. Responding to other people's writing requires the same careful attention you give to your own draft.

First reading:
Read at your normal rate the first time through without stopping. When you finish you should have a clear sense of what the writer is trying to accomplish.

- **Main idea:** Write a sentence that summarizes what you think is the writer's main idea in the draft.
- **Purpose:** Write a sentence that summarizes what you think the writer was trying to accomplish in the draft.

Second reading:
In your second reading, you should be most concerned with the content, organization, and completeness of the draft. Make notes as you read.

- **Introduction:** Does the writer's first paragraph effectively introduce the topic and engage your interest?
- **Thesis:** Where exactly is the writer's thesis? Note in the margin where you think the thesis is located.
- **Focus:** Does the writer maintain focus on the thesis? Note any places where the writer seems to wander off to another topic.
- **Organization:** Are the ideas presented in effective order? Can you suggest a better order for the paragraphs?
- **Completeness:** Are there sections and paragraphs that lack adequate development? Where do you want to know more?
- **Sources:** If the draft uses outside sources, are they cited accurately? If there are quotations, are they used correctly and worked into the fabric of the draft?

Third reading:
In your third reading, turn your attention to matters of audience, style, and tone.

- **Audience:** Who is the writer's intended audience? What does the writer assume the audience knows and believes?
- **Style:** Is the writer's style engaging? How would you describe the writer's voice?
- **Tone:** Is the tone appropriate for the writer's purpose and audience? Is the tone consistent throughout the draft? Are there places where another word or phrase might work better?

When you have finished the third reading, write a short paragraph on each bulleted item above—audience, style, and tone—referring to specific paragraphs in the draft by number. Then end by answering these two questions:

1. **What does the writer do especially well in the draft?**

2. **What one or two things would most improve the draft in a revision?**

Pay Attention to Details Last

When you finish revising, you are ready for one final careful reading, keeping the goals of improving your style and eliminating errors in mind.

Edit different elements in turn

1. Check the connections between sentences.	Notice how your sentences are connected. If you need to signal the relationship from one sentence to the next, use a transition word or phrase.
2. Check your sentences.	If you notice that a sentence doesn't sound right, think about how you might rephrase it. Often you will pick up problems by reading aloud. If a sentence seems too long, then you might break it into two or more sentences. If you notice a string of short sentences that sound choppy, then you might combine them.
3. Eliminate wordiness.	Writers tend to introduce wordiness in drafts. Look for long expressions that can easily be shortened ("at this point in time" –> "now") and for unnecessary repetition. Remove unnecessary words like *very, really,* and *totally.* See how many words you can take out without losing the meaning.
4. Use active verbs.	Anytime you can use a verb besides a form of *be* (*is, are, was, were*) or a verb ending in *–ing,* take advantage of the opportunity to make your style more lively. Sentences that begin with "There is (are)" and "It is" often have better alternatives.

Proofread carefully

In your final pass through your text, eliminate as many errors as you can. To become an effective proofreader, you have to learn to slow down. Some writers find that moving from word to word with a pencil slows them down enough to find errors. Others read backward to force concentration on each word.

1. Know what your spelling checker can and can't do.	Spelling checkers are the greatest invention since peanut butter. They turn up many typos and misspellings that are hard to catch. But spelling checkers do not catch wrong words (e.g., "to much" should be "too much"), where you leave off endings ("three dog"), and other similar errors.
2. Check for grammar and punctuation.	Nothing hurts your credibility more than leaving many errors in what you write. Many job application letters get tossed in the reject pile because an applicant made a single, glaring error. Readers probably shouldn't make such harsh judgments when they find errors, but in real life they do.

Revise Using Your Instructor's Comments

After you have put in a great deal of work writing a paper, sometimes you may find it discouraging to get your paper back with numerous comments from your instructor. Revising with your instructor's comments, however, is the best way to learn how to become a better writer.

Here are a few points to keep in mind.

- **Think of your instructor as a coach whose goal is to make you the best writer you can be.**
  When your coach tells you that your writing can improve, it's not the same thing as telling you that you are a bad writer. Don't take your instructor's advice personally.

- **Read the comments carefully.**
  Often what your instructor is asking you to do is not difficult.

- **Talk with your instructor if you do not understand a comment.**
  Your instructor can explain the comment, and both you and your instructor will benefit from the conversation.

- **Go to your writing center.**
  The consultants at your writing center will help you to interpret your instructor's comments and to plan strategies for using the comments.

Identify your instructor's local and global comments

Your instructor likely will make local and global comments, and it's important to distinguish them. Start with the global comments. These may be comments in the margins like "I can't follow your logic here" and "This section appears out of place." Or they may be in a final comment like "Your organization would be more effective if you presented other proposed solutions first and held your solution until the end." Address these big issues first.

Local comments may be circled or underlined words and punctuation and short comments. Understand that your instructor is not editing the paper for you and will not mark every error. Your instructor wants you to recognize categories of errors; for example, if you have one problem with using commas, you likely have others.

Don't limit your revisions to addressing your instructor's comments. Many times revising a paper will bring new ideas. Realize too that it's your responsibility to make sure that your paper is error-free when you submit the final draft.

WRITE NOW   MyWritingLab™

Make a reverse outline

Find a paper that you wrote for another course. Number the paragraphs in the paper. On a separate sheet of paper, write the main point of the first paragraph. Then, write the main point of the second paragraph. Go through the entire paper this way. When you have gone through the whole paper, you will have a reverse outline, an outline done after writing the paper.

Look at your reverse outline. Does the outline fulfill what you promise in the introduction? Can any ideas be deleted without losing content? Can any ideas be moved? Can you revise the outline to better organize your paper?

Writer at work

Patrice Conley received both global and local comments from her instructor. Patrice first dealt with her instructor's global comments.

RETURNED DRAFT WITH COMMENTS

College athletics are big business. The most visible college sports—big-time men's football and basketball—generate staggering sums of money. Even more money comes in from video games, clothing, and similar licenses.

Your major claims need to be supported with evidence. Give specific examples.

Patrice did additional research to find examples to support her claim.

PATRICE'S REVISION

Make no mistake: college athletics are big business. The most visible college sports—big-time men's football and basketball—generate staggering sums of money. For example, the fourteen universities in the Southeastern Conference receive $205 million each year from CBS and ESPN for the right to broadcast its football games (Smith and Ourand). Even more money comes in from video games, clothing, and similar licenses. In 2010, *The New York Times* reported, "the NCAA's licensing deals are estimated at more than $4 billion" per year (Thamel). While the staggering executive pay at big corporations has brought public outrage, coaches' salaries are even more outlandish. Kentucky basketball coach John Calipari is paid over $4 million a year for a basketball program that makes about $35–40 million a year, more than 10% of the entire revenue.

Then she moved on to her instructor's local comments. Her instructor noted a transition is needed between two paragraphs, and Patrice added a sentence, highlighted in yellow below.

PATRICE'S REVISION

The college sports empire in the United States run by the NCAA is the last bastion of amateurism for sports that draw audiences large enough to be televised. Colleges might be able to defend the policy of amateurism if they extended this definition to all students. A fair policy is one that treats all students the same. A fair policy doesn't result in some students getting paid for professional work, while other students do not.

You can read Patrice's completed paper on pages 416–421.

MyWritingLab™ Visit Ch. 5 in MyWritingLab to complete the chapter exercises and to test your understanding of the chapter objectives.

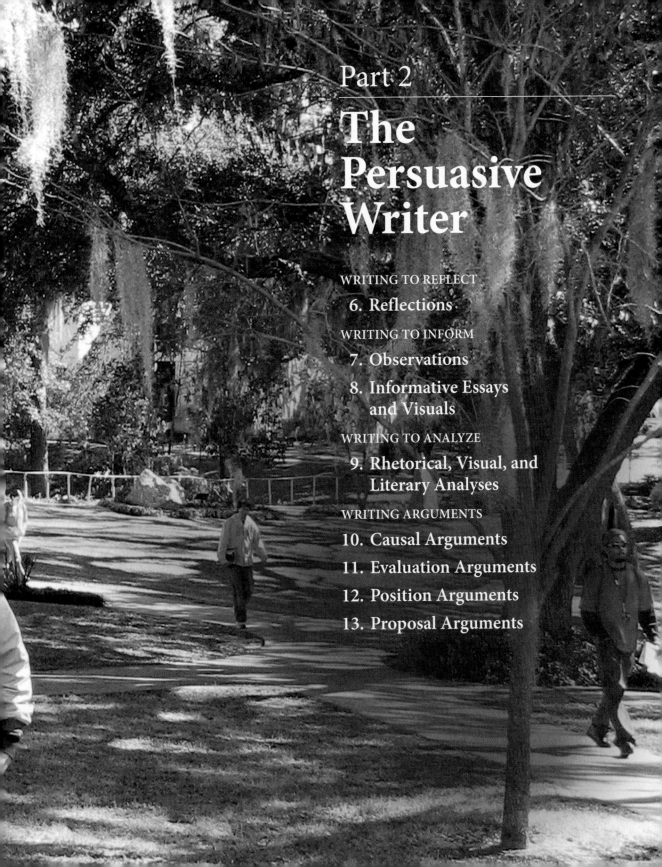

Part 2
The Persuasive Writer

6 Reflections

A successful reflection challenges readers to learn something about themselves.

In this chapter, you will learn to

1. Describe the elements of a good reflection *(see p. 65)*
2. Write a short reflection on a photograph or visual text *(see p. 66)*
3. Read and analyze reflections to understand their organization and language *(see pp. 67–85)*
4. Describe the steps involved in the process of writing a reflection *(see pp. 86–87)*
5. Apply flexible strategies to write and revise a reflection *(see pp. 88–101)*

Writing a Reflection

When we reflect, we consider an idea or experience in order to come to a greater understanding of its significance. Reflecting is a way of understanding ourselves. By connecting memories of the past with our knowledge of the present, we learn about who we were and who we have become.

The goal of a reflection should not be simply to vent pent-up emotions or to expose secrets (although when done well, these techniques can be effective). Instead, a reflection should allow readers to share with the writer a discovery of significance.

Genres of reflective writing

- **Memoirs** reflect on personal memories and life experiences.
- **Narratives** tell stories about other people as well as the writer's life and offer unique perspectives.
- **Personal statements** are often required for admission to graduate and professional schools.
- **Blogs** reflect on events of the day, books, films, music, and popular culture.

What Makes a Good Reflection?

1

Find an interesting topic

Think about how interesting your topic will be to your potential readers. Your greatest moment in sports or the time you met your current partner may be peak experiences for you, but how engrossing with they be for your readers?

2

Engage readers at the beginning

Get your readers' attention with your title and first sentences.

3

Write with a personal voice

Reflections should not sound like they were written by a committee. Your reflection should convey your personality.

4

Introduce a complication

A conflict or a tension usually motivates a reflection. While the complication is often between people, it can involve objects and ideas.

5

Provide concrete details

Details make reflections come alive. Don't limit details to what you can see. Include sounds, smells, textures, physical actions, and tastes where possible.

6

Use dialogue when possible

People come to life when you let them talk.

7

Identify a central theme

Sometimes a central theme is at the heart of a reflection such as David Sedaris's reflection on his family. In other cases the theme is implied but still provides a center for the reflection.

8

Come to a new understanding

Effective conclusions invite readers to reflect further. Ending by inviting readers to think about what they have just read is usually better than trying to sum up with a moral lesson.

Reflections About Visuals

The Kodak Brownie, introduced in 1900, popularized snapshot photography and allowed families to construct their own histories in the family album. Kodak urged consumers to "celebrate moments of your life." Photographs indeed freeze moments in the past, documenting that the camera was present at a precisely datable time.

But photographs also take on lives of their own much like our memories of the past, where seemingly insignificant conversations and events from years ago keep popping into our heads. Photographs show us people we have known as adults when they were children and remind us that they too were once young. By reflecting on photographs, we imagine people, including ourselves, at times in the past.

Two girls in a park near Union Station, Washington, D.C. (1943).

WRITE NOW MyWritingLab™

Reflecting on photographs

1. Look at personal photographs on *Flickr, Instagram, Photobucket, Picasa, Shutterfly*, or another Web-hosting service and find a set of images that stick with you.

2. Select three or four photographs of people by one photographer that appear to be taken within an hour or a few hours. Make a list of people in each photograph. What can you infer about them by the way they are dressed and what they are doing? Where were the photographs taken? What do you associate with the place?

3. Write a narrative about what you think was going on when the pictures were taken. What was the relationship between the people in the photographs and the photographer? What might they have been thinking at the time? Why were they in this particular place? Why were the photographs taken?

Some Lines for a Younger Brother . . .
Sue Kunitonomi Embrey

Sue Kunitonomi Embrey (1923–2006) was born in Los Angeles. Instead of starting college in 1942, she was forced to move to the Manzanar Relocation Center in Inyo County, California, with other Japanese Americans. She spent the years during World War II in the concentration camp. After the war most of the people who were interned did not want to talk about the experience, but Embrey became an activist and made a pilgrimage in 1969 to remember what happened at Manzanar. She eventually was successful in getting Manzanar declared a national historic site. "Some Lines for a Younger Brother . . ." was published in *Gidra* in 1970.

HOW IS THIS READING ORGANIZED?

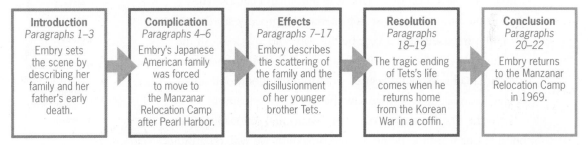

| **Introduction** *Paragraphs 1–3* Embry sets the scene by describing her family and her father's early death. | **Complication** *Paragraphs 4–6* Embry's Japanese American family was forced to move to the Manzanar Relocation Camp after Pearl Harbor. | **Effects** *Paragraphs 7–17* Embry describes the scattering of the family and the disillusionment of her younger brother Tets. | **Resolution** *Paragraphs 18–19* The tragic ending of Tets's life comes when he returns home from the Korean War in a coffin. | **Conclusion** *Paragraphs 20–22* Embry returns to the Manzanar Relocation Camp in 1969. |

Some Lines for a Younger Brother . . .

1   I still remember the day he was born. It was early April and Papa came into the kitchen with a smile on his face. He said we had a baby brother. In the months to follow, we were busy carrying and cuddling the brother who was many years younger than the rest of us. When he cried from hunger and Mama was busy, one of us would run into the bedroom and rock the bed or pick him up and quiet him.

2   We were a family of five sons and three daughters. Money was scarce. My father ran a moving and transfer business in L'il Tokyo, the Japanese community in the shadow of City Hall in Los Angeles, but people had little money to pay him. He came home with boxes of books bartered for his services, and we spent many hours curled up in a corner reading some popular fiction story.

Introduction: Embrey begins with her earliest memory of her brother, making it clear that he will be the focus of her reflection.

3   Tets, as we called him, was eight years old when Papa was killed in an automobile accident a week before Christmas. Tets cried because he could not give his dad the present he had made at school. The bullies would beat him up now that he had no father, he said.

4   Pearl Harbor was attacked by the Japanese when Tets was in elementary school. Rumors of sabotage couldn't be separated from the facts. Soon there was a clamor on the West Coast for wholesale evacuation of all Japanese into inland camps. The democratic process was lost in hysteria. The grocery store which we had purchased only a year before was sold at a loss. All the furniture we couldn't sell, the plants my mother had tenderly cared for, our small personal treasures went to a neighborhood junk dealer. Tears came when we saw the truck being loaded.

5   On the first Sunday in May, 1942, Manzanar Relocation Center became our war-time home. Before breakfast, we walked around the dry, dusty land, to get acquainted with the landscape. The sun sparkled against the Sierra Nevada mountains to the west. The brown Inyo hills were high-rising barriers, more formidable than the barbed wire which was soon to enclose us. As we wondered how the pioneers had crossed over the Sierras, someone asked, "How long do we have to stay here?" and someone quoted from the military instructions, "For the duration of the war, and six months thereafter." Six months are forever, and forever is a long, long time.

6   Some order became evident within a few months after the fear, confusion and shock of transplantation from the big city to the arid land of Manzanar. Catholic nuns, who had joined the evacuees, found empty barracks and started a school. The War Relocation Authority recruited teachers from the "outside." Many of them were Quakers with a real desire to serve their fellow man.

7   When I asked Tets what he was studying, he shrugged his shoulders. There were no chairs, no desks, no supplies, he said.

Complication:
Outside events are fitted into the family's personal chronology. Embrey shows vividly the impact of the decision to intern Japanese Americans.

Details:
Details about the relocation camp reinforce the sense of isolation and hopelessness it evokes.

Dialogue:
Embrey uses dialogue to recount a significant conversation she had with her brother, one that she has remembered for many years.

"What's the use of studying American history when we're behind barbed wires?" he asked. I tried to tell him that it would matter some day, but I was not sure any more. "Someday," I said, "the government would realize it had made a mistake and would try to correct it." His eyes were narrow against the noon sun, his whole body positioned badly to the right as he looked at me and said, "You 'da kind'? I lose fight." The colloquial speech was everywhere among the second generation. "Da kind" categorically placed me among those who argued for and defended American democracy. The second expression was used constantly, but it meant different things to different people.

8   "Try walking out that gate," he added. "See if they don't shoot you in the back." With that, he walked away.

9   The rest of us managed to get out of confinement—to Chicago, to Madison, Wisconsin. Three brothers entered the United States Army. Tets was left with his aging mother and he was to spend almost three years behind barbed wires.

10   By 1948 when the family was partially reunited and settled in Los Angeles, Tets was in high school, or we thought he was. One day a school counselor came to the door. He reported that Tets had not been in school for several weeks and that he had been missing school sporadically for several months. He saw the shock on our faces. We had been too busy working to be suspicious.

11   "I'm looking for a job," Tets said, when confronted.

12   "But you can't find a job without a high school diploma," I protested.

13   "So I found out," he answered. "Learning to say 'isn't' instead of 'ain't' doesn't get you a job. They want us to have experience to land a job, but how can we get experience if we can't get a job?"

14   I asked him what he was going to do.

15   "I'm going to join the Army," was his reply.

Effects:
Again, Embrey uses dialogue to show viewers a turning point in her brother's life. As in the internment camp, this argument centers on whether he should go to school, but it is clear there are deeper issues at play for Embrey and for Tets.

16   Day in and day out, this was his argument. "I'm going to join the Army when I'm eighteen. You won't have me around to bother you and I'll be doing some traveling. I'm tired of holding up the buildings in L'il Tokyo. There's nothing to do and no place to go where I can be with my friends."

17   He was sure that wars were over for a while and there would be no danger. He signed up one day and was gone the next. He came home on furlough, husky and tanned, a lot taller and more confident than when he had left. He had been in training camp in Louisiana and had seen much of the country. Before he left, he broke the news to us that he had signed up for another three years so he wouldn't have to serve in the reserves. He was transferred to the West Coast and we saw him often when he hitch-hiked home on weekends. One day he phoned collect from San Jose. He was being shipped out to Japan and it would probably be a year before he would be back.

18   His hitch was almost over when the Korean War broke out. Soon after his 22nd birthday, he wrote that he hoped to be home for Christmas. He explained that he had not been sleeping well lately since some veterans had been brought into his barracks. They had nightmares and they screamed in the night. The stories of war they told could not be shut out of his mind. There was a rumor going around that his company might be going over to replace the first groups. He hoped his timetable for discharge would not change. He was worried and that was why he had not written.

19   Tets came home before Christmas. He came home in a flag-draped coffin, with one of his buddies as a military escort. The funeral at the Koyasan Buddhist Church was impressive. There was a change of guards every few minutes. Their soft-spoken order mixed with the solemn chants. The curling incense smoke made hazy halos of the young faces who came mourning a dead friend.

Resolution: Embrey uses vivid detail to re-create her dead brother's funeral.

20   On December 27, 1969, I joined several hundred young people who made a day-long pilgrimage to the Manzanar cemetery. While I helped clean out the sagebrush and manzanilla, pulled tumbleweeds out of my boots, I was interrupted many times to recall facts and figures for the NBC and CBS television crews who were there to record the event.

21   Mt. Williamson's peak crested somewhere in the gray clouds that drew menacingly closer as the hours passed. Soon there was no sun. No seven-mile shadow lay across Owens Valley.

22   Dedication services ended that freezing, windswept and emotional day. I looked beyond the crowd and the monument. Out of the painful memories my mind dusted out of the past, I saw again the blurred impressions of the barbed-wire fence, the sentry towers and the tar-papered barracks. For a moment I saw again the 12-year-old boy with his head cocked, his shoulders sagging, his eyes fighting to keep open in the sun, while the long and lonely desert stretched out behind him.

Conclusion: Embrey ends with an almost wistful recollection of her brother.

Mt. Williamson

Let It Snow
David Sedaris

David Sedaris is a writer, playwright, and radio commentator whose work often has an autobiographical focus. He became famous for *The Santaland Diaries*, a play about his job as a Christmas elf in Macy's department store. In this essay, from his collection *Dress Your Family in Corduroy and Denim*, he recalls a single day from his childhood in North Carolina.

Return to these questions after you have finished reading.

Analyzing the Reading

1. On the surface, this story centers around a snowstorm and children playing in it. Underlying these events are the much darker issues of the narrator's mother, her drinking, and her treatment of her children. How exactly does the snowstorm focus Sedaris's investigation of his family's past?

2. The narrator, as a fifth-grader, thinks that having his sister get hit by a car would be "the perfect solution" to their problem. What do you believe the adult narrator thinks of this "solution"? Are there any other clues that the narrator feels differently now?

3. The humor turns a potentially sad story into a ridiculous one. Think about how this essay might have been written without the humor. Could it be as effective?

4. Although this story deals with intensely personal issues, the tone is quite ironic and detached. Given the tone, what do you make of the story's ending, with the children surrounding their mother "tightly on all sides," finally going back to their house?

Exploring Ideas and Issues

In the essay, Sedaris shows how his mother's alcoholism affected his family. However, episodes in the life of a family can also be positive. Whether they are negative or positive, vivid memories can present a snapshot, a moment in time that can be representative of larger patterns in a family and its relationships.

1. In the essay, the author comes up with a plan to teach his parents a lesson. Most children probably have the wish, at one time or another, to punish their parents. Recall a time you thought your parents treated you unjustly. Did you feel angry, sad, confused, or ashamed? Describe the incident and your response at the time. Then reflect on whether or not your feelings have remained the same. Explain why.

2. Think of a snapshot moment in your life that could reflect a larger pattern or situation. The experience could concern your family life, work, school, or friendships. Describe the incident and explain how it represents a larger reality. For example, you might show how the cutting remark made by a coworker was typical of the atmosphere at your first job.

3. Think of a relationship—for example, with a sibling, teacher, or grandparent—that you particularly treasure. In a two-page essay, describe two or three experiences you've had that demonstrate why you value this relationship. Be sure to express how you felt about these incidents or what you learned from them.

Let It Snow

In Binghamton, New York, winter meant snow, and though I was young when we left, I was able to recall great heaps of it, and use that memory as evidence that North Carolina was, at best, a third-rate institution. What little snow there was would usually melt an hour or two after hitting the ground, and there you'd be in your windbreaker and unconvincing mittens, forming a lumpy figure made mostly of mud. Snow Negroes, we called them.

The winter I was in the fifth grade we got lucky. Snow fell, and for the first time in years, it accumulated. School was canceled and two days later we got lucky again. There were eight inches on the ground, and rather than melting, it froze. On the fifth day of our vacation my mother had a little breakdown. Our presence had disrupted the secret life she led while we were at school, and when she could no longer take it she threw us out. It wasn't a gentle request, but something closer to an eviction. "Get the hell out of my house," she said.

We reminded her that it was our house, too, and she opened the front door and shoved us into the carport. "And stay out!" she shouted.

My sisters and I went down the hill and sledded with other children from the neighborhood. A few hours later we returned home, surprised to find that the door was still locked. "Oh, come on," we said. I rang the bell and when no one answered we went to the window and saw our mother in the kitchen, watching television. Normally she waited until five o'clock to have a drink, but for the past few days she'd been making an exception. Drinking didn't count if you followed a glass of wine with a cup of coffee, and so she had both a goblet and a mug positioned before her on the countertop.

"Hey!" we yelled. "Open the door. It's us." We knocked on the pane, and without looking in our direction, she refilled her goblet and left the room.

"That bitch," my sister Lisa said. We pounded again and again, and when our mother failed to answer we went around back and threw snowballs at her bedroom window. "You are going to be in so much trouble when Dad gets home!" we shouted, and in response my mother pulled the drapes. Dusk approached, and as it grew colder it occurred to us that we could possibly die. It happened, surely. Selfish mothers wanted the house to themselves, and their children were discovered years later, frozen like mastodons in blocks of ice.

My sister Gretchen suggested that we call our father, but none of us knew his number, and he probably wouldn't have done anything anyway. He'd gone to work specifically to escape our mother, and between the weather and her mood, it could be hours or even days before he returned home.

"One of us should get hit by a car," I said. "That would teach the both of them." I pictured Gretchen, her life hanging by a thread as my parents paced the halls of Rex Hospital, wishing they had been more attentive. It was really the perfect solution. With her out of the way, the rest of us would be more valuable and have a bit more room to spread out. "Gretchen, go lie in the street."

"Make Amy do it," she said.

Amy, in turn, pushed it off onto Tiffany, who was the youngest and had no concept of death. "It's like sleeping," we told her. "Only you get a canopy bed."

Poor Tiffany. She'd do just about anything in return for a little affection. All you had to do was call her Tiff and whatever you wanted was yours: her allowance money, her dinner, the contents of her Easter basket. Her eagerness to please was absolute and naked. When we asked her to lie in the middle of the street, her only question was "Where?"

We chose a quiet dip between two hills, a spot where drivers were almost required to skid out of control. She took her place, this six-year-old in a butter-colored coat, and we gathered on the curb to watch. The first car to happen by belonged to a neighbor, a fellow Yankee who had outfitted his tires with chains and stopped a few feet from our sister's body. "Is that a person?" he asked.

"Well, sort of," Lisa said. She explained that we'd been locked out of our house and though the man appeared to accept it as a reasonable explanation, I'm pretty sure it was him who told on us. Another car passed and then we saw our mother, this puffy figure awkwardly negotiating the crest of the hill. She did not own a pair of pants, and her legs were buried to the calves in snow. We wanted to send her home, to kick her out of nature just as she had kicked us out of the house, but it was hard to stay angry at someone that pitiful-looking.

"Are you wearing your loafers?" Lisa asked, and in response our mother raised her bare foot. "I was wearing loafers," she said. "I mean, really, it was there a second ago."

This was how things went. One moment she was locking us out of our own house and the next we were rooting around in the snow, looking for her left shoe. "Oh, forget about it," she said. "It'll turn up in a few days." Gretchen fitted her cap over my mother's foot. Lisa secured it with her scarf, and surrounding her tightly on all sides, we made our way back home.

My Hips, My Caderas
Alisa Valdes-Rodriguez

MyWritingLab™

Alisa Valdes-Rodriguez is the author of several books, including *The Dirty Girls Social Club* (2003), *Playing With Boys* (2004), and *The Three Kings* (2010). Valdes-Rodriguez is the daughter of Nelson Valdes, a retired sociology professor who emigrated from Cuba, and Maxine Conant, a poet and novelist of Irish descent. This essay appeared on MSN's *Underwire*, in April 2000.

Return to these questions after you have finished reading.

Analyzing the Reading

1. Valdes-Rodriguez observes that in cultures where more "traditional" roles for women are observed, such as on her Cuban side of the family, big hips and rounded curves are considered beautiful. What accounts for this preference? What beauty traits are valued in cultures where women have less traditional roles?

2. How does the author feel about her hips and her body? About the different opinions people have of her shape? Identify areas in her essay where she clearly reveals her view.

3. How does Valdes-Rodriguez describe her mother's side of the family? Her father's? Which does she prefer?

4. The author describes different phases in her life when she tried to change her body to please others or meet a cultural ideal. Can you think of a time in your own life in which you tried to change something about yourself to please others or to fit in? Explain.

Exploring Ideas and Issues

In April 2010, Gad Saad blogged in *Psychology Today* that while social constructivists argue that there are no universal metrics of beauty, studies indicate that our appreciation of beauty is hard-wired universally into our brains and that we innately prefer the symmetry of phi—also called the "golden ratio." He observes, "You can visit Bedouins in the Middle East, the Yanomamo in the Amazon, and Inuits in the Canadian north, and they will all agree as to who is or is not beautiful. . . . Rotund Rubanesque women, heavier women preferred in Central Africa, and catwalk thin models, while varying greatly in terms of their weight, all tend to have hourglass figures that correspond roughly to a waist-to-hip ratio of 0.70."

1. Images of female bodies are everywhere, selling everything from food to cars. Models and women actors have become younger, taller, and thinner. Articles in women's magazines proclaim that if women can just lose those last twenty pounds, they'll have a happy life at home and at work. Media critics argue that unnatural and often altered images of thin female bodies cause women and girls to lose self-esteem, become depressed, and develop unhealthy eating habits. Write an essay in which you argue either that the media have a powerful influence on our notion of female beauty or you argue that, in reality, the media have little influence.

2. Write a personal narrative in which you recount a moment when your self-esteem was influenced by what others thought about your physical appearance.

3. Research the "golden ratio," phi. Then view popular celebrities from several cultures, such as India, Mexico, Germany, and Japan. Contrast the differences, if any, you see in physical attributes, including faces, hair, and body types. What do your observations reveal about the social and innate influences of beauty?

MY HIPS, MY CADERAS

MY FATHER IS CUBAN, with dark hair, a cleft in his chin, and feet that can dance the Guaguanco.

My mother is white and American, as blue-eyed as they come.

My voluptuous/big hips are both Cuban and American. And neither. Just like me. As I shift different halves of my soul daily to match whichever cultural backdrop I happen to face, I also carefully prepare myself for how differently my womanly/fat hips will be treated in my two realities.

It all started 15 years ago, when my hips bloomed in Albuquerque, New Mexico, where I was born. I went from being a track club twig—mistaken more than once for a boy—to being a splendidly curving thing that Chicano men with their bandanas down low whistled at as they drove by in their low-riders. White boys in my middle school thought I suddenly had a fat ass, and had no problem saying so.

But the cholos loved me. San Mateo Boulevard . . . remember it well. Jack in the Box on one corner, me on a splintered wooden bench with a Three Musketeers bar, tight shorts, a hot summer sun, and those catcalls and woof-woofs like slaps. I was 12.

My best friend Stacy and I set out dieting right away that summer, to lose our new hips so boys from the heights, like the nearly albino Tom Fairfield with the orange soccer socks, would like us. In those days, I was too naïve to know that dismissing the Chicano guys from the valley and taking French instead of Spanish in middle school were leftovers of colonialism. Taking Spanish still had the stigma of shame, like it would make you a dirty wetback. So Stacy and I pushed through hundreds of leg lifts on her bedroom floor, an open *Seventeen* magazine as a tiny table for our lemon water, and the sound of cicadas grinding away in the tree outside.

In Spanish, the word for hip is *caderas*—a broad term used to denote everything a real woman carries from her waist to her thighs, all the way around. Belly, butt, it's all part of your caderas. And caderas are a magical sphere of womanhood. In the lyrics of Merengue and Salsa, caderas are to be shaken, caressed, admired and exalted. The bigger, the better. In Spanish, you eat your rice and beans and sometimes your *chicharrones* because you fear your caderas will disappear.

In my work as a Latin music critic for a Boston newspaper, I frequent nightclubs with wood-paneled walls and Christmas lights flashing all year long. I wear short rubber skirts and tall shoes. There, I swing my round hips like a metronome. I become fierce. I strut. In the red disco lights, my hips absolutely torture men. I can see it on their faces.

"Mujeron!" they exclaim as I shimmy past. Much woman. They click their tongues, buy me drinks. They ask me to dance, and I often say "no," because I can. And these men suffer. Ironically, this makes the feminist in me very happy. In these places, my mujeron's hips get more nods than they might at a pony farm.

In English, your hips are those pesky things on the sides of your hipbones. They don't *"menear,"* as they do in Spanish; they "jiggle." In English, hips are something women try to be rid of. Hips are why women bruise themselves in the name of lipsuction.

My mother's people hate my hips. They diet. My aunt smokes so she won't eat. And in the gym where I teach step aerobics—a habit I took up in the days when I identified more with my mother's than my father's people—I sometimes hear the suburban anorexics whisper in the front row: "My God, would you look at those hips." Sometimes they walk out of the room even before I have begun teaching, as if hips were contagious. In these situations, I am sad. I drive home and examine my hips in the mirror, hit them for being so imprudent, and like great big ears on the side of my body. Sometimes I fast for days. Sometimes I make myself puke up rice and beans. Usually I get over it, but it always comes back.

Sociologists will tell you that in cultures where women are valued for traditional roles of mother and caregiver, hips are in, and that in cultures where those roles have been broken down and women try to be like men were in traditional societies—i.e., have jobs—hips are out.

So when I want to be loved for my body, I am a Latina. But most Latino men will not love my mind as they do my body, because I am an Americanized professional. Indeed, they will feel threatened, and will soon lose interest in hips that want to "andar por la calle come un hombre" (carry themselves like a man).

When I want to be loved for my mind, I flock to liberal intellectuals, usually whites. They listen to my writings and nod . . . and then suggest I use skim milk instead of cream. These men love my fire and passion—words they always use to describe a Latina—but they are embarrassed by my hips. They want me to wear looser pants.

In some ways I am lucky to be able to move between two worlds. At least my hips get acknowledged as beautiful. I can't say the same for a lot of my bulimic friends, who don't have a second set of standards to turn to. But still, I dream of the day when bicultural Latinas will set the standards for beauty and success, when our voluptuous caderas won't bar us from getting through those narrow American doors.

Mother Tongue
Amy Tan

MyWritingLab™

Amy Tan is well known for novels that concern the bonds between Chinese American mothers and daughters. She has introduced a rich world of Chinese myth and history to a global audience, but her themes of love and forgiveness are universal. Tan began writing fiction along with playing the piano to curb her workaholic tendencies, but with the publication of *The Joy Luck Club* in 1989, her talent as a writer became widely celebrated. She reflects on her career in this essay.

Return to these questions after you have finished reading.

Analyzing the Reading

1. How did Tan's attitude toward her mother's use of language change over the years? Use evidence from the text to support your statements.

2. Tan writes about value judgments based on language. How does Tan account for these judgments?

3. Why was Tan's awareness of different Englishes important to her development as a writer?

4. Tan says that an insight she had as a beginning writer was to imagine a reader. Why was imagining a reader so important?

Exploring Ideas and Issues

Linguists describe going back and forth between different languages, or between varieties of one language, as *code switching*. Tan tells how she goes back and forth between standard English and her home dialect in her own speaking and writing. Code switching used to be considered nonstandard usage, but more recently linguists consider code switching a natural product of language use. Just as we dress differently for more formal and less formal occasions, so too we adjust our language depending on the situation.

Indeed, we all code switch constantly. New digital technologies have led to new forms of code switching, especially in media such as *Twitter*, that force extreme brevity. Without giving it much conscious thought, we adjust our language to the medium we're using as well as to who will be reading our message and what we are trying to accomplish.

1. Tan says, "Recently I was made aware of all of the different Englishes I do use." What different Englishes, or other languages, do you use? List each and explain the different contexts and relationships in which you use them. Write an essay in which you compare two different "languages" (either styles of English or English and another language) that you use. Give examples of when, where, and how you use them.

2. You may have grown up in an ethnically diverse neighborhood or a neighborhood with little diversity. Either way, you were aware of prevailing attitudes and beliefs about race and ethnicity as you grew older. Write an essay describing one positive and one negative belief you encountered and the reasons people had for holding these beliefs. Include examples from the experiences of people you know.

3. Do you think being a "good" American depends on speaking English? Can people have an American identity without being able to speak English? Write a short essay in which you answer yes or no to these questions. Include examples of specific people you have known to support your view.

MOTHER TONGUE

I am not a scholar of English or literature. I cannot give you much more than personal opinions on the English language and its variations in this country or others. I am a writer. And by that definition, I am someone who has always loved language. I am fascinated by language in daily life. I spend a great deal of my time thinking about the power of language—the way it can evoke an emotion, a visual image, a complex idea, or a simple truth. Language is the tool of my trade. And I use them all—all the Englishes I grew up with.

Recently, I was made keenly aware of the different Englishes I do use. I was giving a talk to a large group of people, the same talk I had already given to half a dozen other groups. The nature of the talk was about my writing, my life, and my book, *The Joy Luck Club*. The talk was going along well enough, until I remembered one major difference that made the whole talk sound wrong. My mother was in the room. And it was perhaps the first time she had heard me give a lengthy speech, using the kind of English I have never used with her. I was saying things like, "The intersection of memory upon imagination" and "There is an aspect of my fiction that relates to thus-and-thus"—a speech filled with carefully wrought grammatical phrases, burdened, it suddenly seemed to me, with nominalized forms, past perfect tenses, conditional phrases, all the forms of standard English that I had learned in school and through books, the forms of English I did not use at home with my mother.

Just last week, I was walking down the street with my mother, and I again found myself conscious of the English I was using, the English I do use with her. We were talking about the price of new and used furniture and I heard myself saying this: "Not waste money that way."

My husband was with us as well, and he didn't notice any switch in my English. And then I realized why. It's because over the twenty years we've been together I've often used that same kind of English with him, and sometimes he even uses it with me. It has become our language of intimacy, a different sort of English that relates to family talk, the language I grew up with.

So you'll have some idea of what this family talk I heard sounds like, I'll quote what my mother said during a recent conversation which I videotaped and then transcribed. During this conversation, my mother was talking about a political gangster in Shanghai who had the same last name as her family's, Du, and how the gangster in his early years wanted to be adopted by her family, which was rich by comparison. Later, the gangster became more powerful, far richer than my mother's family, and one day showed up at my mother's wedding to pay his respects. Here's what she said in part:

Du-Yusong having business like fruit stand. Like off the street kind. He is Du like Du Zong—but not Tsung-ming Island people. The local people call putong, the river east side, he belong to that side local people. That man want to ask Du Zong father take him in like become own family. Du Zong father wasn't look down on him, but didn't take seriously, until that man big like become a mafia. Now important person, very hard to inviting him. Chinese way, came only to show respect, don't stay for dinner. Respect for making big celebration, he shows up. Mean gives lots of respect. Chinese custom. Chinese social life that way. If too important won't have to stay too long. He come to my wedding. I didn't see, I heard it. I gone to boy's side, they have YMCA dinner. Chinese age I was nineteen.

You should know that my mother's expressive command of English belies how much she actually understands. She reads the *Forbes* report, listens to *Wall Street Week*, converses daily with her stockbroker, reads all of Shirley MacLaine's books with ease—all kinds of things

I can't begin to understand. Yet some of my friends tell me they understand 50 percent of what my mother says. Some say they understand 80 to 90 percent. Some say they understand none of it, as if she were speaking pure Chinese. But to me, my mother's English is perfectly clear, perfectly natural. It's my mother tongue. Her language, as I hear it, is vivid, direct, full of observation and imagery. That was the language that helped shape the way I saw things, expressed things, made sense of the world.

Lately, I've been giving more thought to the kind of English my mother speaks. Like others, I have described it to people as "broken" or "fractured" English. But I wince when I say that. It has always bothered me that I can think of no way to describe it other than "broken," as if it were damaged and needed to be fixed, as if it lacked a certain wholeness and soundness. I've heard other terms used, "limited English," for example. But they seem just as bad, as if everything is limited, including people's perceptions of the limited English speaker.

I know this for a fact, because when I was growing up, my mother's "limited" English limited my perception of her. I was ashamed of her English. I believed that her English reflected the quality of what she had to say. That is, because she expressed them imperfectly her thoughts were imperfect. And I had plenty of empirical evidence to support me: the fact that people in department stores, at banks, and at restaurants did not take her seriously, did not give her good service, pretended not to understand her, or even acted as if they did not hear her.

My mother had long realized the limitations of her English as well. When I was fifteen, she used to have me call people on the phone to pretend I was she. In this guise, I was forced to ask for information or even to complain and yell at people who had been rude to her. One time it was a call to her stockbroker in New York. She had cashed out her small portfolio and it just so happened we were going to go to New York the next week, our very first trip outside California. I had to get on the phone and say in an adolescent voice that was not very convincing, "This is Mrs. Tan."

And my mother was standing in the back whispering loudly, "Why he don't send me check, already two weeks late. So mad he lie to me, losing me money."

And then I said in perfect English, "Yes, I'm getting rather concerned. You had agreed to send the check two weeks ago, but it hasn't arrived."

Then she began to talk more loudly. "What he want, I come to New York tell him front of his boss, you cheating me?" And I was trying to calm her down, make her be quiet, while telling the stockbroker, "I can't tolerate any more excuses. If I don't receive the check immediately, I am going to have to speak to your manager when I'm in New York next week." And sure enough, the following week there we were in front of this astonished stockbroker, and I was sitting there red-faced and quiet, and my mother, the real Mrs. Tan, was shouting at his boss in her impeccable broken English.

We used a similar routine just five days ago, for a situation that was far less humorous. My mother had gone to the hospital for an appointment, to find out about a benign brain tumor a CAT scan had revealed a month ago. She said she had spoken very good English, her best English, no mistakes. Still, she said, the hospital did not apologize when they said they had lost the CAT scan and she had come for nothing. She said they did not seem to have any sympathy when she told them she was anxious to know the exact diagnosis, since her husband and son had both died of brain tumors. She said they would not give her any more information until the next time and she would have to make another appointment for that. So she said she would not leave until the doctor called her daughter. She wouldn't budge. And when the doctor finally called her daughter, me, who spoke in perfect English—lo and behold—we had assurances the CAT scan would be found, promises that a conference call on Monday would be held, and apologies for any suffering my mother had gone through for a most regrettable mistake.

I think my mother's English almost had an effect on limiting my possibilities in life as well. Sociologists and linguists probably will tell you that a person's developing language skills are more influenced by peers. But I do think that the language spoken in the family, especially in immigrant families which are more insular, plays a large role in shaping the language of the child. And I believe that it affected my results on achievement tests, IQ tests, and the SAT. While my English skills were never judged as poor, compared to math, English could not be considered my strong suit. In grade school I did moderately well, getting perhaps B's, sometimes B-pluses, in English and scoring perhaps in the sixtieth or seventieth percentile on achievement tests. But those scores were not good enough to override the opinion that my true abilities lay in math and science, because in those areas I achieved A's and scored in the ninetieth percentile or higher.

This was understandable. Math is precise; there is only one correct answer. Whereas, for me at least, the answers on English tests were always a judgment call, a matter of opinion and personal experience. Those tests were constructed around items like fill-in-the-blank sentence completion, such as, "Even though Tom was _____, Mary thought he was _____." And the correct answer always seemed to be the most bland combinations of thoughts, for example, "Even though Tom was shy, Mary thought he was charming," with the grammatical structure "even though" limiting the correct answer to some sort of semantic opposites, so you wouldn't get answers like, "Even though Tom was foolish, Mary thought he was ridiculous." Well, according to my mother, there were very few limitations as to what Tom could have been and what Mary might have thought of him. So I never did well on tests like that.

The same was true with word analogies, pairs of words in which you were supposed to find some sort of logical, semantic relationship—for example, "*Sunset is to nightfall* as _____ is to _____." And here you would be presented with a list of four possible pairs, one of which showed the same kind of relationship: *red* is to *stoplight*, *bus* is to *arrival*, *chills is to fever*, *yawn* is to *boring*. Well, I could never think that way. I knew what the tests were asking, but I could not block out of my mind the images already created by the first pair, "*sunset* is to *nightfall*"—and I would see a burst of colors against a darkening sky, the moon rising, the lowering of a curtain of stars. And all the other pairs of words—red, bus, stoplight, boring—just threw up a mass of confusing images, making it impossible for me to sort out something as logical as saying: "A sunset precedes nightfall" is the same as "a chill precedes a fever." The only way I would have gotten that answer right would have been to imagine an associative situation, for example, my being disobedient and staying out past sunset, catching a chill at night, which turns into feverish pneumonia as punishment, which indeed did happen to me.

I have been thinking about all this lately, about my mother's English, about achievement tests. Because lately I've been asked, as a writer, why there are not more Asian Americans represented in American literature. Why are there few Asian Americans enrolled in creative writing programs? Why do so many Chinese students go into engineering? Well, these are broad sociological questions I can't begin to answer. But I have noticed in surveys—in fact, just last week—that Asian students, as a whole, always do significantly better on math achievement tests than in English. And this makes me think that there are other Asian-American students whose English spoken in the home might also be described as "broken" or "limited." And perhaps they also have teachers who are steering them away from writing and into math and science, which is what happened to me.

Fortunately, I happen to be rebellious in nature and enjoy the challenge of disproving assumptions made about me. I became an English major my first year in college, after being enrolled as pre-med. I started writing nonfiction as a freelancer the week after I was told by my former boss that writing was my worst skill and I should hone my talents toward account management.

But it wasn't until 1985 that I finally began to write fiction. And at first I wrote using what I thought to be wittily crafted sentences, sentences that would finally prove I had mastery over the English language. Here's an example from the first draft of a story that later made its way into *The Joy Luck Club*, but without this line: "That was my mental quandary in its nascent state." A terrible line, which I can barely pronounce.

Fortunately, for reasons I won't get into today, I later decided I should envision a reader for the stories I would write. And the reader I decided upon was my mother, because these were stories about mothers. So with this reader in mind—and in fact she did read my early drafts—I began to write stories using all the Englishes I grew up with: the English I spoke to my mother, which for lack of a better term might be described as "simple"; the English she used with me, which for lack of a better term might be described as "broken"; my translation of her Chinese, which could certainly be described as "watered down"; and what I imagined to be her translation of her Chinese if she could speak in perfect English, her internal language, and for that I sought to preserve the essence, but neither an English nor a Chinese structure. I wanted to capture what language ability tests can never reveal: her intent, her passion, her imagery, the rhythms of her speech and the nature of her thoughts.

Apart from what any critic had to say about my writing, I knew I had succeeded where it counted when my mother finished reading my book and gave me her verdict: "So easy to read."

How to Write a Reflection

These steps for the process of writing a reflection may not progress as neatly as this chart might suggest. Writing is not an assembly-line process. Writing about a remembered event, place, or person is, in itself, a powerful way to reflect. Be open to uncovering insights and understanding more broadly the significance.

1 CHOOSE A SUBJECT

- Analyze the assignment.

- Explore possible topics. Make lists of memories connected with your family, work, school, friends, and travels.

- Examine your lists for what might interest readers.

- Consider why this person, place, event, or object is significant to you.

2 IDEAS AND TEXT

- Describe the scene in as much detail as you can remember with visual details, sounds, smells, tastes, and tactile feelings.

- Tell the story of what happened, capturing actions with active verbs.

- Make people come alive. Recreate conversations that reveal character. Record gestures and other details that make people unique.

- Think about the context. What was happening at the time for you and the larger community?

- Relate your experience to the experiences of others.

3
WRITE A DRAFT

- Plan your organization, either chronologically or conceptually.

- Write an engaging title that suggest the direction or the significance of your reflection.

- Draft a strong beginning that establishes a focus and makes your readers want to continue.

- Introduce a tension between people or a problem early on that motivates your reflection.

- Select vivid details and dialogue that let readers experience what you experienced.

- Describe how the tension or problem was resolved.

- Leave your readers with something to think about. Your conclusion should invite readers to reflect on what you've written.

4
REVISE, REVISE, REVISE

- Check that your paper or project fulfills the assignment.

- Make sure that the subject is focused.

- Add details, description, or dialogue.

- Make sure your voice and tone will engage readers.

- Examine your organization and think of possible better ways to organize.

- Review the visual presentation.

- Proofread carefully.

5
SUBMITTED VERSION

- Make sure your finished writing meets all formatting requirements.

1: Choose a Subject

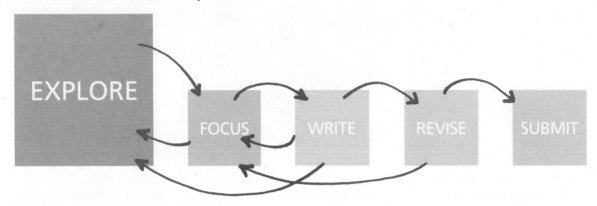

Analyze the assignment

Read your assignment slowly and carefully. Look for key words like *reflection, memoir,* or *personal narrative,* which signal a reflective essay. Identify any information about the length specified, date due, formatting, and other requirements. You can attend to this information later. At this point you want to give your attention to your topic and the focus of your reflection.

Explore possible topics

The challenge is to find a topic that will be interesting to your readers, presents a complication that must be resolved, and offers you the opportunity to reflect on the person, event, or experience.

Start by making lists.

- Your childhood: What do you remember most vividly from your childhood? What scared you as a child? When were the happiest times you can remember?

- Your family: What memories stand out about your parents? your brothers and sisters? your grandparents and other relatives? family vacations and other family experiences? How has your perspective on your family changed over time?

- Your work experience: What was your first job? Did you ever have a great boss or a horrible boss? What important learning experiences did you have while working?

- Your school experience: What school memories stand out? Did a particular teacher have a strong influence on you?

- Your friends and social relationships: What stands out among memories of your friends? about people you have dated? about your experiences on social networks?

Remember places and objects

Is a particular place important to you? Why is it critical? For example how did you gain an understanding of your mother's attitudes when you visited the place where she grew up? Is a particular object important to you, such as something that belonged to your great-grandmother and was passed down to you?

Consider the importance in your life

Ask yourself: Why is this person, event, place, or object significant to me? Think about why the person, place, event, or object seems more important today than it did in your initial experience. Think about how the person, place, event, or object changed you as a person.

Analyze your potential readers

What do your readers likely know about your subject? What might your readers gain from reading your reflection? What might you need to tell your readers about the background? For example, Amy Tan (see page 78) provides more background about her Chinese American mother than David Sedaris (see page 72) does about his mother. Tan examines how her mother's use of language became important to Tan as a writer whereas Sedaris' focus is on how he and his sisters resolved the problem of their mother locking them out of the house.

WRITE NOW   MyWritingLab™

Explore memories

- Select one of the items that you have checked on your lists.

- Write nonstop for five minutes to explore the event, situation, place, or object. What was your initial reaction? Who else was there? Did you share your reaction at the time?

- Write nonstop for five minutes to explore your current perspective. How did an experience change you? Why do you remember this person, event, place, or object so well? Looking back, what do you see now that you didn't recognize at the time?

- Stop and read what you have written. Do you see possibilities for writing at length about this person, event, or situation? If you do, then begin generating more content. If the idea seems limited, try writing nonstop about another person, event, place, or object.

Writer at work

Janine Carter received the following assignment in her Introduction to Archeology class. She made notes on her assignment sheet as the class discussed the assignment.

Archeology 201
Reflection on an Artifact

We have read about and discussed artifacts at great length in this unit — how and where they are found, what they indicate about human cultures, and what they mean to archeologists. But not all artifacts are found in museums. Almost any human-made object can be considered an artifact, because it contains information about its makers. Archeologists study artifacts because they teach us about people we do not know, and because they teach us things about ourselves.

For your first paper, I would like you to find an artifact in your daily life. This might be a family heirloom with a great deal of personal meaning, or it might be something you have no emotional attachment to at all, like a soda can or a discarded newspaper. Write a 4–6 page essay reflecting upon your artifact. Describe it in as much detail as you can. Consider what its construction tells you about its maker. Why was it made? When? By whom? What clues does the artifact contain about its own history? *"Think like a detective"*

Use lots of detail

Spend some time considering what the artifact means to you. What is your relationship to the person who created the artifact? What can you construct about the culture and conditions in which it was created? What sorts of things can you not figure out about it?

Writing Process
Bring in a good draft of your essay on October 3rd. We will discuss them in class so you can revise carefully before you turn your essay in on October 10. *Two weeks for first draft*
One week for revision

Grading
I will look for the following qualities in your essay: detailed description, logical deduction, and an interesting account of the artifact's significance or meaning.

Then Janine made a list of possible objects to write about.

<u>HEIRLOOMS/EMOTIONAL CONNECTION</u>
- *Aunt Marie's tulip quilt—shows my connection to a long line of quilters*
- ~~Sea shells from Girl Scout camp~~—NOT MAN-MADE
- *Bracelet from graduation*
- *Terry's photo*
- *Stuffed elephant–shows how much I have grown up. Where was it made?*
 - *Garage sale quilt—don't know much about this; could guess a lot though.*
- *Diploma*

<u>LESS IMPORTANT OBJECTS</u>
- *Cereal box—ingredients show lack of nutrition. Pictures show how kids are bombarded with cartoons and colorful images. Expiration date and other clues to where it was made.*
- *Desk in dorm room— Must have been used by dozens of people like me (?)*
- *Old calendar*
- *Old cookbook*
- *Old cell phone—Could talk about how fast technology is changing. Do I have one?*

2: Develop Ideas and Text

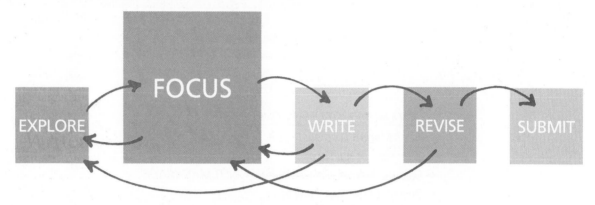

Writing a draft will be much easier if you generate ideas and text in advance. Having some material to work from will help you to plan your organization.

Set the scene

Describe the setting of your reflection in as much detail as you can remember. Write down all the sights, sounds, smells, tastes, and tactile feelings you associate with your topic. If the subject of your reflection is a photograph or an object, write a detailed description of it.

Describe what happened

Tell the story of what happened in as much detail as you can remember. Capture the action with active verbs (*giggled, whistled, devoured, sauntered, witnessed*).

Make people come alive

Use dialogue to let readers hear people talk, which reveals much about character. Recreate a conversation between key people in your reflection. Also, record the little mannerisms, gestures, clothing, and personal habits that distinguish people. Don't forget to make yourself come alive. If you are reflecting on an incident from your childhood, how old were you? What do you remember about yourself at that age?

Consider the larger context

Write about what else was going on at the time, both with the immediate people involved and in the larger culture. How does your memory compare with similar experiences you have read or heard about from others? Does your memory connect to larger trends going on at the time?

Think about the significance

Write about the meaning the person, place, event, or object has for you today. The fact that you find the topic memorable means there is something you can share with others. What do you notice, as you reflect, that other people might not notice? This is the "added value" that will make your reflection more than a mere description or memory.

Writer at work

Janine Carter sat down with her garage-sale quilt and a pen and paper. She observed it carefully and made a list of detailed observations about its physical appearance. Then, she added her conclusions and guesses about the quilt, its history, and its maker, based on these clues.

Janine thought about her relationship to the quilt. She jotted down, in no particular order, what she remembered about buying the quilt, conversations she had had with her grandmother about quilting, and ideas that occurred to her.

- Unbleached muslin, pink calico, coral calico
- Most stitching is white thread and quilting is pink thread
  - All these materials are very cheap

- Nine-patch plus a 5-patch alternating throughout; binding is plain muslin
  - I do not know the name of this pattern. Looks a little like Churn Dash.

- Batting is coming through in many areas
- Lots of stains, even some paint
  - Has been used a lot and has been used for unintended purposes—discarded?

- Large muslin patches are cut on bias
  - Means the person knew what she was doing and planned ahead

- Quilting is in nested L-blocks. Is there a name for that?
- 1,372 patches (approx.) Small squares are 1-1/2 inches
- Quilting is about 5 stitches/inch on average, 1" apart. Over 100 yards total.

- The two colors clash and are not mixed together; one runs out and the other starts. Why?
  - New quilter? Poor planning? To make it bigger? Unforeseen accident?
  - Grandma would have had a fit if I ever made a quilt this ugly. So why did I buy it?

3: Write a Draft

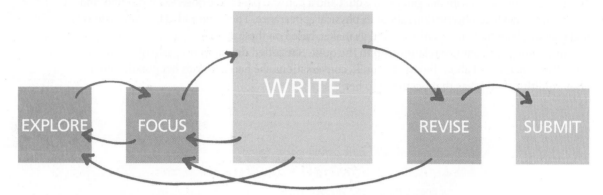

Plan your organization

Consider how to tell your story. Embrey (see page 67), Sedaris (see page 72), and Valdes-Rodriguez (see page 75) narrate events in chronological order. Tan (see page 78) focuses on a central idea and organizes according to different aspects of that idea.

Write an engaging title

Your title should suggest the direction or the significance of your reflection.

Draft a strong beginning

You might start by describing the setting of your reflection. You might narrate the central event, which you will expand and reflect on later. Or you might give critical background.

Introduce a complication early on

The complication is a tension or problem that motivates the reflection. Embrey's family is relocated to a concentration camp. Sedaris and his sisters are locked out of their house by their drunken mother. Both writers describe the immediate reactions of the people involved.

Select vivid details and dialogue

Let your readers experience what you experienced. Small details can say a great deal. Likewise, dialogue reveals the character of people in your reflection.

Describe how the complication was resolved

How did the people involved resolve the complication? Sometimes the resolution is the solution to a practical problem like getting locked out, and in other cases the resolution is coming to terms with an idea.

Leave your readers with something to think about

Your conclusion should invite readers to reflect on what you've written. Sedaris concludes with a recollection of how his dysfunctional family somehow muddled through. Tan ends with her mother's appreciation of her writing. Valdes-Rodriguez expands her reflection to challenge prevailing ideals of female beauty.

Writer at work

Janine Carter tried several organizational patterns for her essay. Because she knew so little about the quilt's history, she did not feel chronological organization would be a good strategy. However, as she worked through her draft she realized that readers would appreciate a firsthand account of her purchase of the quilt. She decided to include this story near the beginning of her essay, after describing the quilt. She organized the rest of her essay around the questions that occurred to her as she considered the quilt's appearance. As she worked, she referred back to her assignment frequently to make sure she was fulfilling all its terms. She decided to cut one section, about the names of various quilt patterns, because it was too general and distracted from the main focus of her essay. Here is the original outline Janine began working from, along with revisions she made.

I.   Intro—describe quilt with detail
       < tell story of "Miracle" salesman

II. Cheap material and clashing colors–poor person, or some other reason?

III. Bias-cut material indicates experienced quilter

IV. ~~Names and meanings of quilt patterns.~~

V.   Number of patches, stitching: this information means more to quilters than to average people. Explain.

VI. Quilting's meaning for women (cultural use). Tell Grandma's story about the work on the farm.

VII. My relationship with the quilt
       < contrast w/how much I know about quilts in our family
       < add more detail here, and talk about quilt's probable history

4: Revise, Revise, Revise

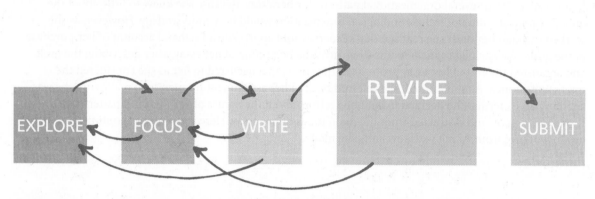

Skilled writers know that the secret to writing well is rewriting. Even the best writers often have to revise several times to get the result they want. You also must have effective strategies for revising if you're going to be successful. The biggest trap you can fall into is starting off with correcting errors. Leave the small stuff for last.

Does your paper or project meet the assignment?	• Look again at the assignment for specific guidelines, including length, format, and amount of research. Does your work meet these guidelines?
Is the subject focused?	• Will readers find your subject early on? • Is the significance evident?
Can you add dialogue, description, and other details?	• Can you make events and memories from the past more concrete?
Is your tone engaging?	• Will readers sympathize and identify with you, or will they find your tone too negative, angry, or intensely personal? • Does your tone fit your topic? Some intensely personal topics may not be suited to humorous treatment.
Is your organization effective?	• Are links between concepts and ideas clear? • Are there any places where you find abrupt shifts or gaps? • Are there sections or paragraphs that could be rearranged to make your draft more effective?
Is the writing project visually effective?	• Is the font attractive and readable? • Are the headings and visuals effective? • If you have included an image associated with your reflection, where should it be placed for maximum impact?
Save the editing for last.	• When you have finished revising, edit and proofread carefully.

A peer review guide is on page 58.

Writer at work

Janine Carter was not satisfied with her opening paragraph, or her title. After talking to a consultant at her campus writing center, she worked on ending her opening paragraph with a surprising twist that would engage readers. She also realized that she could draw out the concept of "miracles" from within her essay to tie together the beginning and end. Here are the first drafts of Janine's opening and concluding paragraphs, with her notes.

<u>My Mystery Quilt</u>   *This is so boring!*

[introduction]   *Too obvious. That's sort of the point of the assignment, looking for clues.*

The quilt folded at the foot of my bed <u>is a mystery</u>. It is made of cotton: plain muslin and two patterns of calico, with a cotton batt inside, sewn by hand with careful stitches. Some of its thread is white and some is pink. It is frayed around the edges, so someone has obviously used it. But unlike quilts in my own family, this quilt was not handed down as a cherished heirloom. I rescued it from a garage sale and have tried to <u>"piece together"</u> its history.

Consultant says puns are usually a bad idea—especially in opening.

[conclusion]

When I am cold at night I pull the quilt up over my knees and think about the stranger who made it, wondering who she was, who her loved ones were, whether she was happy. Her quilt gives me warmth, and I give her thanks. There is a bond <u>between us because of this quilt.</u>

This is boring/obvious. Can I make it more special?

97

5: Submitted Version (MLA Style)

MyWritingLab™

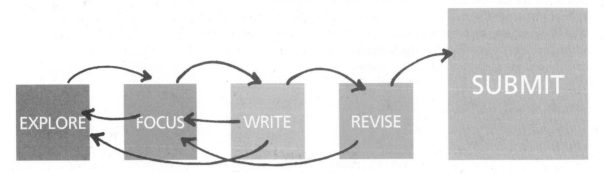

Carter 1

Janine Carter

Dr. Shapiro

Archeology 201

10 October 2014

The Miracle Quilt

The quilt folded at the foot of my bed has a long history. It is made of cotton: plain muslin and two patterns of calico, with a cotton batt inside, sewn by hand with careful stitches. Some of its thread is white and some is pink. It is frayed around the edges and has obviously lived a long, useful life. It is steeped in memories. Unfortunately, I don't know what any of them are.

I found the quilt at a city-wide garage sale. At the end of the auditorium, taking up half of the bleachers, was a vendor's booth called "Miracles by the Pound." The gentleman who ran the booth went around buying up vintage fabrics in bad condition. He would dump huge piles of them on the bleachers for people to pick through. When you had found what you wanted, he would weigh it on a scale and tell you how much it cost. Everything was five dollars per pound. As he weighed your purchase, he would call out the price so everyone at the garage sale could hear what a good deal you were getting. My quilt weighed three pounds. "Fifteen dollar miracle!" the vendor sang out as I opened my purse.

My quilt had already been dug out of the pile and discarded by another woman at the garage sale, who had two or three other vintage quilts in her arms. She told me

Fig. 1.   Detail of the miracle quilt.

she bought old, damaged quilts and cut them up to make sofa pillows. My quilt didn't interest her because it wasn't in very good shape, and the blocks were the wrong size for the pillow forms she used. I come from a family of quilters, so when I saw the quilt I felt it needed a good home. I didn't like the idea of someone using it to wrap around furniture in a moving van, or even cutting it up for pillows. I took it home and washed it, and put it on my bed, and took a good look at it.

The quilt was probably made by someone poor, or at least very frugal, I decided. The muslin, which provides the background, is the cheapest unbleached kind. Even the binding around the edges, which in most quilts is a bright, contrasting color, is plain muslin. Whoever pieced the quilt—and it was almost certainly a woman, because quilting has always been women's work—started out using a coral-toned calico. But before she finished, she ran out and had to switch to a rose-colored calico. The effect is jarring, as the colors do not complement each other. The coral marches two-thirds of the way across the quilt, and then stumbles into rose. I do not know why the quiltmaker did not work the two colors evenly throughout the quilt; this is what my own grandmother taught me to do when I didn't have enough of one color. Perhaps she was inexperienced; perhaps this was her first quilt, or perhaps she hadn't intended to make the quilt as large as it is. The coral would have been sufficient to cover a single bed; maybe, I think to myself, someone proposed to her while she was making it, and she ended up enlarging it to fit a double bed after she got married.

But there are other clues that suggest experience and planning. The octagon-shaped patches of muslin that center the five-patch blocks are cut so that the lines of quilting cross them on the bias—that is, diagonally across the up-and-down and side-to-side warp and woof threads of the fabric. Fabric is more flexible on the bias (this, my grandmother once explained to me, is why clothing cut on the bias fits and looks better, and is more expensive). A needle slips in and out between the threads more easily, so a quilter is wise to arrange pieces so as to maximize bias quilting. The quilting itself (that is the stitching through all the layers of the quilt) is respectable enough, about five stitches per inch. No fancy 12-stitch-per-inch quilting like you would see in a showpiece quilt, but quite firm and straight, in neat pink rows spaced an inch apart. The quilting pattern is in L-shaped blocks, which I have never seen before. There must be over one hundred yards of quilting all together; the length of a football field, taken one stitch at a time.

The quilt's pattern looks like a variation of wagon tracks, but it uses an octagonal block like a "churn-dash" pattern that sets it apart from a more straightforward Irish chain. Nine-patch and five-patch blocks alternate across it. By my count it contains 1,372 separate pieces, all cut, sewn, and quilted by hand. The nine-patch blocks use 1-1/2-inch patches. These may seem like insignificant details to most people, but to quilters they are important. They tell you how much work went into the quilt. The first nine-patch quilt I made with my grandmother contained a grand total of 675 patches, and I thought it would take forever to sew it (even using a sewing machine!). I remember asking my grandmother how she ever made her more complicated quilts: the flower garden with its thousands of tiny hexagons; the Dutchman's puzzle that was so mesmerizing you could hardly stop your eyes from running over it, trying to pick out the "real" pattern. "Doesn't quilting drive you crazy sometimes?" I asked her. She thought that was pretty funny. "Quilting was how we used to keep from going crazy," she told me.

When she first married my grandfather and moved to a farm in the Brazos River bottom over sixty years ago, there was no television and no neighbors for miles. In the spring, rain would turn the roads to thick clay mud and no one could get off their property for days at a time. Quilting was the way women dealt with the isolation. "That is what the pioneer women did too," she told me. Stuck out alone on the prairies and in the mountains, they kept their sanity by cutting and arranging hundreds of pieces of cloth in different patterns, methodically assembling quilts to bring some order into their own bleak lives.

"It looks like hard work to you now," my grandmother explained, "but for us it was like a vacation. So much of women's work was never done, but you could sit down after dinner in the evening and finish a quilt block and feel like you had done something that would last. You might have spent the whole day dirtying and washing the same set of dishes three times, feeding the same chickens and milking the same cows twice, and you knew you'd have to get up in the morning and do the same things all over again, from top to bottom. But quilt blocks added up to something. Nobody was going to take your finished quilt block and sit down at the breakfast table and pick it apart, and expect you to sew it back together again before lunch. It was done, and it stayed done. There wasn't much else you could say that about, on a farm."

In my family, quilts are heirlooms and are handed down with stories about who made them, who owned them, what they were used for, and what events they had been part of. Some were wedding presents, others were made for relatives when they were first born. I don't know the stories that go with my miracle quilt. It has had a hard life; that is easy to see. Most of the binding has frayed off and there are some spots where the quilt has holes worn straight through it—top, batting, and backing. There are stains that suggest coffee or tea or perhaps medicines from a sickbed spilled on it. There are some spots of dried paint. Evidently at some point it was used as a drop-cloth. But at least, I tell myself, it has found a home with someone who appreciates the work that went into it, and can guess at some of its history.

When I am cold at night I pull the quilt up over my knees and think about the stranger who made it, wondering who she was, who her loved ones were, whether she was happy. Her quilt gives me warmth, and I give her thanks. Though we will never meet, or even know each other's identity, there is a bond between us because of this quilt. And so it seems that the man who sold me this quilt was right: it is a sort of miracle.

Projects

Reflections focus on people, places, events, and things—past and present—that have significance in the writer's life.

Reflection on the past

List people, events, or places that have been significant in your life or in some way changed you. Many reflections focus on a conflict of some kind and how it was resolved. Look back over your list and check the items that seem especially vivid to you.

Take a few minutes to write first about the person, event, or place as you remember it, and then write about how you regard it today. What was your initial reaction? Did your initial reaction change over time? Why do you feel differently now?

Think about the significance of the person, event, or place in your life. What details best convey that significance? If conversations were involved, remember what was said and create dialogue.

Organize your essay around the focus. Start fast to engage your readers. If there is a conflict in your reflection, get it up front.

Show the significance through describing, vivid details, and dialogue. Make the characters and the places come to life.

Literacy narrative

Think about a childhood memory of reading or writing that remains especially vivid. The memory may be of a particular book you read, of something you wrote, or a teacher who was important in teaching you to read or write. Or think of a more recent experience of reading and writing. What have you written lately that was especially difficult? Or especially rewarding? List as many possibilities as you can think of.

Look over the items on the list and pick one that remains significant to you. Begin writing by describing the experience in as much detail as you can remember. Describe who was involved and recall what was said. Describe the setting of the experience: where exactly were you and what difference did it make? Remember key passages from what you either read or wrote. How did you understand the experience at the time? How do you understand it now? What makes it special?

Review what you have written and consider how to shape your raw material into an engaging essay. You may want to narrate the experience in the order it happened; you may want to start in the middle of the experience and give the background later; or you may want to start in the present as you look back. Above all, start fast. Somewhere along the way, you will need to convey why the experience was significant for you, but avoid the temptation to end with a moral. Don't forget to include a title that makes your readers want to read your literacy narrative.

Personal blog

Read blogs on sites such as blogger.com (click on the BLOGS OF NOTE link). You'll find that personal blogs take on a wide range of subject matter from thoughts about life in general to reflections on specific subjects like art, films, fashion, education, music, and family. Many blogs are multimedia including vlogs (video blogs), sketchblogs (portfolios of sketches), and photoblogs (photographic records of daily life).

Decide on a general subject matter for your blog. The most interesting blogs come from writers who spend much time thinking about that subject, perhaps to the point of obsession. Write about what you love. If you have strong dedication to a particular subject, likely you can get others interested.

Write your blog with your readers in mind. Write with a personal voice that engages your readers. Make your blog fun to read. Use paragraphs and pay attention to the little things. Error-filled writing is not enjoyable to read, no matter how fresh the content.

Encourage your readers to respond. Web hosting sites allow you to have a comment section so that readers can interact with you.

Publish your blog on a Web hosting site or a site at your school. Commit to a schedule of posting blog entries with regular frequency such as once a week..

Family photograph

Family photographs and cherished objects can be subjects for reflection. Try carefully observing (or picturing in your mind) an object or photograph that has special meaning for you. Write down all the details you can. What memories does each observation evoke? Do you find that different aspects of the photograph make you feel different ways?

Choose as a topic something that is significant to you, and which you can recall with a reasonable amount of detail. But also consider how interesting this topic will be to others. Will an audience want to share in your experience?

Write a reflective essay about that photograph. What does the photograph convey that other similar snapshots do not? What does it hide or not show? What does it say about your family?

 Visit Ch. 6 in MyWritingLab to complete the chapter exercises, explore an interactive version of the Writer at Work paper, and test your understanding of the chapter objectives.

7 Observations

Effective observations capture readers' attention through details that may be unfamiliar or surprising but always fresh and vivid.

In this chapter, you will learn to

1. Describe the elements of a good observation (*see p. 105*)

2. Write or photograph a visual observation (*see p. 106*)

3. Read and analyze observations to understand their organization and language (*see pp. 107–131*)

4. Describe the steps involved in the process of writing an observation (*see pp. 132–133*)

5. Apply flexible strategies to write and revise an observation (*see pp. 134–151*)

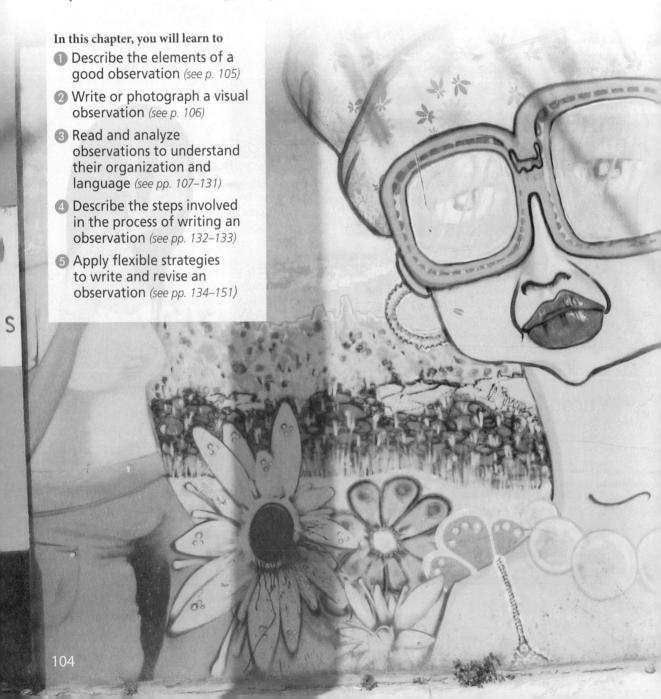

Writing an Observation

Observing is often the first step to understanding. In fields such as anthropology, sociology, and psychology, scientists observe people and processes and use their observations to answer questions like these: How is death regarded in Navajo societies? What groups of people are most likely to visit an urban parkland? How do primates interact?

Observations begin with thorough research. Your firsthand impressions must be carefully recorded in as much detail as possible. These observations, often called field notes, provide your raw material. When you write as an observer, you place yourself in the background, and give readers the clearest, most detailed view you can of your subject.

Genres of observations

- **Descriptive essays** use details to give a vivid experience of a place, event, or object.

- **Documentaries** are a broad category of films and photographic essays, sometimes combined with written text.

- **Ethnographies** collect data from observations, interviews, and daily participation to describe human cultures in rich detail.

- **Case studies** are used in a wide range of fields such as nursing, psychology, business, and anthropology to create in-depth portraits.

What Makes a Good Observation?

1

Identify your subject
Be specific about who or what you are observing. If it is a certain group of people, what sets them apart as a group? Do they share a common interest? If it is a place, what makes it special?

2

Assemble your observations
You may approach your observations chronologically, leading readers through your day-to-day or hour-by-hour experience as an observer. Or you may find other ways to organize that work better for your purposes: perhaps starting with the most surprising discovery you made while observing.

3

Provide vivid sensory details
Build your observation with concrete details. For example, think about the sounds of food as well as how it looks and tastes.

4

Place your observations in a larger context
What questions are left unanswered by your observations? How might your observations be atypical? Give your readers a framework within which to understand your observations.

5

Know when you are expected to be objective
Field observations in the sciences and social sciences keep the writer in the background, focusing instead on the subject. Ask your instructor what is expected.

6

Provide visuals if needed
Photographs and other images can work in combination with words to enhance observations. Close attention to details is critical for both descriptive writing and descriptive visuals.

Visual Observations

Photographs and other images can work in combination with words to enhance observations.

Photographs are valuable for providing concrete examples. For instance, Frank Lloyd Wright's attention to detail is evident in his 1905 design for the lobby of the Rookery Building in Chicago.

WRITE NOW   MyWritingLab™

Visit a place or event

In small groups of three or four students, visit the same place or event, such as a museum, a parade or festival, or a political rally. Each group member should make notes about what he or she observes and write a short synopsis of the visit (one to two pages). Then, as a group, read each other's synopses. How different was each person's experience? What, if anything, did they have in common?

Working together, draft a short introduction that summarizes the different perspectives your observations provide. What can an audience learn by reading multiple accounts of the same experience?

The Old Man Isn't There Anymore
Kellie Schmitt

During the two years she spent in China, the journalist Kellie Schmitt was a frequent contributor to CNNgo, a travel and lifestyle Web site. Her articles have also appeared in the *Wall Street Journal, Marie Claire, Afar Magazine,* and *The Economist's Business China*.

HOW IS THIS READING ORGANIZED?

Introduction *Paragraphs 1–6*	Setting *Paragraph 7*	Complication *Paragraphs 8–13*	Details *Paragraphs 14–34*	Conclusion *Paragraphs 35–38*
Schmitt begins with a dialogue with her cleaning lady.	The setting is an apartment in Shanghai.	Schmitt attempts to befriend her neighbors only to be rebuffed.	The old man, the delivery of sympathy, and the funeral come alive through details.	Schmitt uses humor to describe her surprise that she didn't know whose funeral she attended.

The Old Man Isn't There Anymore

1 I found myself in a Chinese funeral parlor because of a phone call I made to my cleaning lady.

2 The previous evening, my husband Gregg had seen our neighbors crying in the hallway. We'd wondered if the old grandpa, the one with the buzz-cut hair, had died. Gregg had suggested we shouldn't interfere, but curiosity had gotten the best of me. I'd called the all-knowing cleaning lady.

3 "Do you know why the neighbors," I paused. I knew the word in Mandarin for "crying" but not hallway.

4 "Do you know why the neighbors are very sad?" I asked.

5 "The old man isn't there anymore," she replied, which I guessed was her baby Chinese way of telling me he died.

6 "Ah, the old man who lives on the second floor?" I asked.

7 Even though we had lived in this old three-story house in Shanghai for more than a year, I couldn't map out the neighbors and where they resided. While we lived in a spacious apartment

Introduction:
Schmitt gets off to a fast start by beginning with a dialogue with her cleaning lady.

Setting:
She describes the scene of where she lived in Shanghai and the others who lived there.

on the renovated top floor, the other two floors remained as they had been during the height of Communism: cheap, basic and subdivided. As a result, we shared the house with many neighbors. They'd pop out of doorways, hallways, and hidden bathrooms, often wearing just slippers and underwear. There were at least a dozen, all local Shanghainese.

8   When we had first seen the apartment, I had created stories in my head of the relationships we'd establish with our cohabitants. I'd wander into their kitchens in the late afternoon and we'd sit around sipping green tea and chatting in Chinese about our lives. That fairy-tale ended when we moved in: Nobody would even say hello to us.

9   I grilled our Chinese teacher for an explanation. Am I saying *ni hao* wrong? Was there some moving-in etiquette that I'd forgotten? In China, do people not speak to those who walk around in their underwear under the same roof? My teacher said she wasn't sure.

10   Still, I was persistent. I would repeatedly try to engage them, saying hello at every encounter. Sometimes, I'd offer a comment on the weather, or tell the grandpa with the buzz cut: "We're off to America for two weeks! See you when we get back!"

11   Around month three, I got a disgruntled nod from one of the underwear men. One day, the second-floor dad, who was always cooking in the communal kitchen, told me his family's white cat liked me. And, miraculously, when I returned from Christmas vacation with two heavy suitcases, the burly second-floor mom helped me lug them up the steep wooden stairs. We had turned a corner.

12   I was so grateful that I wanted to show my appreciation. I dashed down the stairs and offered the mom and grandpa a plate of fresh brownies. Grandpa didn't say anything, just looked at me with a bemused smile. I shoved one onto his plate, blushing as it occurred to me that Chinese traditionally don't like excessively sweet Western desserts.

Complication: Schmitt's expectation of being able to talk with her neighbors was frustrated when they wouldn't speak to her.

13   From there, I progressed to exchanging pleasantries, mostly commenting on the lazy white cat who liked to sleep all day in the nook beneath the banister.

14   When I hung up the phone with the cleaning lady, I made the bold decision to buy sympathy flowers. After all, grandpa and I had often exchanged hellos. He would stand in his undershirt in the doorway, a stout man with full cheeks and an easy smile. His face had few wrinkles though it was patterned with age spots, and I had imagined he was in his 70s. He always looked perplexed by our presence and I'd sometimes wonder what the China of his youth was like, when the country was closed to the West. What a contrast to be spending his final days living a floor away from two Americans.

Details:
Schmitt paints a vivid portrait of her memory of the old man, her culturally unaware delivery of sympathy flowers, and later the experience of the funeral.

15   With my basket of roses in hand, I knocked on the family's door. The dad, dressed in loose white fabric, opened it with a surprised smile. In Chinese, he said, over and over, that I was too polite. For the first time, he beckoned me into their one-room space, now covered in white floral arrangements. The sweet scent of lilies perfumed the air.

16   My local florist didn't do funeral-specific arrangements so I'd asked her to create an appropriate alternative. Apparently something got lost in the translation. Nobody had mentioned I should have requested white, the color associated with death in China.

17   The mom wrote my Chinese name, 可莉, on a long paper scroll and hung it across my scarlet-colored flowers like a beauty pageant sash. Great, I thought. Now everyone will know who got the wrong color.

18   Their rarely-seen, 25-year-old daughter, Lili, spoke up in English. She explained that her grandfather had died from cancer, and while they were very sad, it was considered a good omen for the family that he had a long life.

19   "We would be very honored if you'd attend the funeral on Saturday," she said. "Since he died at 91, it's a joyous occasion and we want you to be there."

20   I deflected the offer, using the words I had learned for "don't want to bother you." I was aware that the Chinese often extended invites just to be polite. It was my job to refuse. Still, they insisted and insisted, which made me wonder if they were seriously asking me to attend grandpa's funeral. When they mentioned that it would mean a lot to the deceased, I wavered. And when they told me that everyone who attends will also live a long life, I finally agreed.

21   As soon as our coach arrived at the funeral home that Saturday, Lili began translating the remarks of the passersby: Wow a foreigner is here! What is a foreigner doing here? We've never seen a foreigner here.

22   As we silently filed into the room, trumpets and saxophones sounded, a little off-key, punctuated with a clash of cymbals. We all wore black fabric swatches pinned to our arms to acknowledge we were part of the grieving party. Inside, there were about 30 people, mostly family and some old friends. I urged Lili to join her family in the front while I shuffled to the back of the room.

23   The emcee orchestrated the order of events with short commentaries. Soon, the microphone was given to the mom's older sister. I was able to follow her speech for about two sentences, up to the point where she said she'd be representing her siblings. She quickly lost me, but I still understood the parts where she cried, "Baba," or daddy, then sobbed. She wailed, her voice broke, and then she repeated it, "Baba, Baba." In the front row, her three sisters joined the chorus.

24   There was something about the sister's impassioned cry to her daddy that stirred my own emotions. Suddenly the grandpa was my own father, or my mother's father, who'd died young, years before I was born. Tears filled my eyes, and before long, I was turning my face toward the lilies to hide my sobs. Now I wasn't just the foreigner, I was the foreigner drawing attention to herself by crying at her old neighbor's funeral, a neighbor with whom she had only exchanged ni haos.

25   I watched Lili in the front row, leaning slightly against her father, and I was filled with longing for my own family. They were thousands of miles away in Baltimore, and I hadn't seen them in months.

26   After the speeches, we filed around the coffin in a circle. I could see my red flowers positioned on the mantle directly in front of the casket. I snuck a glimpse at the grandfather. He was mostly obscured under mounds of flowers, but his bruised face looked much older than I remembered, his hair grayer. I focused on the actions of the people going before me—a ritual sequence of pauses and bows. I sighed with relief when I passed the casket and entered the receiving line of grieving family members.

27   The ceremony ended at the crematorium. We walked down a hallway past orange plastic chairs and crammed, elbow to elbow, into a small room. The casket, now closed, sat in an elevator shaft of sorts with a row of buttons. This was the last chance to say goodbye before plunging grandpa into the depths.

28   Lili whispered: "We paid extra so he'd go to the fire alone." Apparently, there had been some problems with getting the wrong ashes if you went economy style, and had your loved one cremated alongside other people.

29   Perhaps Chinese are more comfortable with the inner workings of cremation since, in crowded cities like Shanghai, the rate of cremation approaches 100 percent. I felt uneasy though as I watched the staff send grandpa into the fire.

30   Afterward, we did a final walk around the place, this time tossing the black fabric patches we had worn on our arms into an outdoor fireplace. Then we each took one leaping step forward—away from the fire—to help the deceased transcend the gap between life and death. Before boarding the bus, we all sipped sugar water, a symbol of heavenly bliss that came in the form of iced tea juice boxes.

31   As we headed back on the bus, I tried to justify my presence at grandpa's funeral.

32   "Once, I brought him a freshly-made extra chocolate brownie," I told Lily, brightly. "I am not sure if he ate it, but he was sitting there smiling in the kitchen."

33   "Really?" she said, looking at me a bit strangely. I figured she didn't know the English for brownie so she wasn't quite sure what I had offered him. We didn't have much more to chat about, so we sat in silence and watched the skyscrapers emerge again.

34   Back downtown, at the post-ceremony lunch, I struggled to eat a helping of chicken feet as the entire table watched. Apart from that, though, it seemed as if I had made it through my first Chinese funeral with minimal social missteps. Maybe I was finally getting into the swing of life in China.

35   Then one day I breezed down the stairs and saw a familiar silhouette in the second-floor kitchen. I grasped the banister and stared. If I believed in ghosts, I might have fainted in fear. It was the old grandfather, the same buzz-cut hair, the thin white undershirt, even that same bemused look he always gave me.

36   This elderly man, I realized, must have been just another of the numerous neighbors, without any familial relation to mom, dad and Lili. But, if it wasn't the buzz-cut man in the coffin, who was it? And had I ever even met him?

37   I realized that I had unknowingly committed the most egregious of cultural misunderstandings. Forget the glaring red bouquet, my self-conscious sobs, or my battle with the chicken feet; I have absolutely no idea whose funeral I attended.

38   I kept that information to myself, though, and focused on getting to know the family downstairs. Since the funeral, our relationship achieved a new level of familiarity.

39   The dad offered to teach me how to cook Kung Pao chicken. Lili invited me for tea, and asked for advice on her latest love interest. The mom insisted on carrying my luggage down the stairs, even if it was only a duffel bag. And, without fail, every single time we passed in the hallway, they gave me a friendly ni hao.

Style:
Schmitt uses humor to describe her revelation that she had no clue whose funeral she attended.

Conclusion:
In spite of Schmitt's confusion about the funeral, the family accepts her as a friend.

Pelada
Gwendolyn Oxenham

MyWritingLab™

Gwendolyn Oxenham played varsity soccer at Duke and later professionally in Brazil. After her soccer career ended, Oxenham, her boyfriend, and two friends received a grant to make a documentary film about "pickup" soccer around the world, which in Brazil is called *pelada* (literally "naked"). The four visited twenty-five countries from 2007 to 2009 to complete the award-winning film *Pelada*, (2010), and Oxenham published a book, *Finding the Game* (2012), which includes this selection.

Return to these questions after you have finished reading.

Analyzing the Reading

1. Oxenham builds a strong sense of place with images such as, "Homes web up the steep hillside." Analyze the text for similar examples of vivid details evoking place.

2. The author observes the *favela* and then plays in the *pelada*. What is the effect of the juxtaposition of places, events, and tones on the main idea of the essay?

3. The author employs sounds to show her experience: "the sound of a *cuica*, ... made to imitate a monkey's screech." In what other ways do sounds show rather than tell? With what effect?

4. Oxenham alludes to movies, books, art, and pop-culture. What might be her purpose in doing so? What is the effect of these allusions?

Exploring Ideas and Issues

Favela is Portuguese for urban slum. Soldiers seeking a place to live built the earliest ones in the nineteenth century. Over the years, freed slaves and rural Brazilians settled in mostly outlying sections of cities lacking urban planning and services. According to the Brazilian Institute of Geography and Statistics, in 2010 11.4 million of Brazil's 190 million residents lived in such "subnormal agglomerations." While *favelas* experience high poverty and crime rates, with drug lords competing with police to create social order, they are also fertile sites of vibrant social life and musical subgenres such as *funk carioca*. *Favela* culture has been explored in films, celebrated by theme clubs worldwide, and sought out by tourists.

1. Reflect on pick-up games and activities (i.e., basketball, chess, musical jams) you've participated in, and write an observation on the nature and importance of "pick-up" in personal development, society, and culture.

2. Oxenham employs sound to evoke memories, to build a sense of place, and to create tones. Undoubtedly, you've heard a song or sound that sparks a memory. Write a personal observation exploring how a sound or song evoked some memory in you, and reflect on the possible mechanisms by which sound creates such strong memory sensations.

3. Oxenham assumes the center mid-fielder position, "the person who's everywhere, all the time. On the wing, you can . . . fall into a trance, to watch. There's no risk of that in the center: all points connect through you." Such reflections often signal a metaphor, one that might underscore a larger essay theme or worldview. Write an analysis of how the passage above might work as a metaphor, and how it contributes to a theme in the essay or life generally.

Pelada

Rio de Janeiro has a murder rate comparable to war zones; most of those deaths happen in the favelas facing the city. During Luke's summer in Rio, he played in a Friday *pelada* between two warring favelas that neighbored his apartment. (They stuck the blond guy in goal until he proved his way out of it.) On the court, there were no problems.

According to legend, the Rio favelas may be where *futebol arte* was born. "After the British brought what is now the most popular sport on the planet to South America about 115 years ago, it was initially adopted by the elite," writes Brazilian architect Fernando Luiz Lara. "Around the same time, the occupation of a hill in downtown Rio created its first favela. Once the game reached the Brazilian peripheries, it broke away with the European formalism and transformed itself into the exuberant game now well known." Many of the one-name Brazilian stars—Adriano, Ronaldo, Ronaldinho—grew up in the favelas. On Thursday, a friend of Luke's friend will take us into Rocinha to see *peladas* in the largest favela in South America.

A cab drops us off at the base of Rocinha at 6:45 the next morning. This favela's not quiet like the one we went to with Nike. The Internet told us it's home to somewhere in the narrow range of fifty thousand to five hundred thousand people.

Pelada, *"pickup" soccer in Brazil*

We didn't want to be late so now we are early. This is the city where you don't stop at red lights at night unless you want to get robbed, the city where people get sandals stolen while napping on the beach, the city where Luke got held up at gunpoint. And we are four tourists hanging out in front of a favela run by drug lords.

I've got *Tropa de elite* on my mind, the Brazilian movie about heavily armed police squads trained in urban warfare who come into the favelas to clear out drug traffickers. Even though the film hasn't been released yet, most of Brazil has already seen it; bootleg copies of a leaked cut were sold all over the street.

City of God, the other famous favela movie, put all of the action—the shoot-outs, the drug wars—to the sound of a *cuica*, a samba instrument made to imitate a monkey's screech, a sound that makes it feel like something is going to happen. That's the sound I'm hearing in my head as we stand and wait.

The drug lords is the part that scares me, even though Luke explained that, weirdly, the drug dealers make the favela safe: everybody follows their law. Even to enter the favela, we need approval from the gunmen. We're waiting on Washington and Emerson, Brazilians with names that sound more American than our own. They run an after-school program in Rocinha and are willing to get us the drug lords' permission.

In front of us, commuter vans empty out and then fill up again, women off to work, boys on their way to sell soft drinks or sunglasses on the beach in Ipanema.

"Lucas?" we hear as two guys approach. We shake hands, and then Emerson says, "Shall we go?"

We weave between men selling acai, tank tops, and cell phones. Washington walks with his hands behind his back and whistles something eerie, something that sounds startlingly familiar.

To the soundtrack of the *Kill Bill* whistle, we enter Rocinha. Guys on both sides of the road carry guns so big they look like toys. Right in front of us, a teenager props himself up on an AK-47 the way someone in an old-fashioned photo might lean against an umbrella. He's smiling and it seems like he's smiling at us, but I'm also trying not to look directly in his face, so I'm not really sure until he says in perfect English, "Hello, my friends. Welcome to Rocinha, the most beautiful place on earth."

I keep my hands on the straps of the camera backpack and stare ahead of me as we head into the favela. It's like walking into a cross between *Alice in Wonderland* and an M. C. Escher. Homes web up the steep hillside and into the horizon—homes made out of exposed terra-cotta, concrete oozing out from between the blocks; homes made out of cement, blotches of mildew staining their sides; homes coated in brightly painted stucco. Most are three or four stories, stacked topsy-turvy on top of one another, the floors on the bottom often smaller than the ones on the top.

The base of Rocinha bustles with business: Internet cafés, local bars, and stands with blue-tarp roofs selling candy, jewelry, and electronics. I stare at a telephone pole with hundreds of cables shooting out from it, crosshatched like an Etch A Sketch drawing. A dozen motorcycles wait at the bottom, ready to taxi people up to the top.

All the sound is morphing together. Cars with giant speakers bungee-corded to their roofs blare advertisements. A man hawks pirated movies, chanting, "DVD, DVD, DVD." A chicken roasts on a spit on the sidewalk. A television blares a rerun of the Flamengo match, an announcer shouting, "Bellllllleza." Washington's whistling, the *cuica* noise is playing in my head, and I can still hear the gunman saying *The most beautiful place on earth.*

The road, while wide at the bottom of the hill, contracts as we climb higher, too narrow for cars. We walk along winding mazes that shrink smaller and smaller before opening up again. Sound softens as we turn down side streets; noises are delicate—the echo of kids laughing, the voices of a *telenovela* escaping through an open window, the distant rumble of a scooter funneling down the alley. A boy on a tricycle streaks by us, heading straight down the hill. We walk through a doorway, down a teal blue hallway, and up a winding staircase that leads to the roof.

Up top, we look down at the favela. Washington's next to me. He seems like a guy we'll never know. No telling what his mind's doing while he's whistling, hands in his pockets. I lean over the side and look out at his neighborhood, the Jenga-like towers of homes, rooftops dotted with blue water bins, and mothers pinning T-shirts onto clotheslines.

"Do you play?" I ask Washington, my foot nudging the ball toward him.

"No …" he says. His pause stretches out. "But later, I'll take you to people who do."

Around 8 P.M., Emerson drops us off at the big field on the outer lip of the favela. Men linger in pockets around the dusty sidelines. The sun has just gone down. The lights around the field are not bright. Each gives off a six-inch glow, making it feel like we'll be playing in candlelight. It's too dark to film.

One guy wears a shirt with green and white stripes that make his belly look even bigger than it is. A gold chain and a bright pink stopwatch hang around his neck. Everyone comes up to him, giving him a hand-over-fist shake. I get the sense that he's the center, the one who runs it.

The guys put Luke on one team and me on another. My team is off first, so we sit on a bench off to the side and watch. I don't try to talk to anyone. I wouldn't even if I spoke Portuguese. You don't talk if no one's seen you play.

Watching the game, I realize there's a good chance I'm not going to be good enough. The *futebol* in front of me is everything Brazilian soccer is supposed to be. Players invent in the dust. I'm jealous Luke gets to play right away, while I sit here and psych myself out. I've never been good at watching, I get sucked in, transfixed by everyone else, less sure of myself.

I don't understand what makes the game end, but it does, and my team starts walking out onto the field. Someone tosses me a red bib that says FAMÍLIA VALÃO in a font made to imitate dripping blood. *Valão,* Luke tells me, is the name of the street they all live on in Rocinha. The word means both "sewer" and "open grave." A big sewer runs under their street; the blood-dripping font presumably takes advantage of the word's other, more-intimidating meaning.

"Que posição você joga?" one guy calls out to me.

"Meio-campo," I say, hoping I'm saying "midfield." He points to the center of the field. By midfield. I'd meant outside, on the wing, where you can turn it into a one-on-one battle. I had not meant to ask for the all-the-best-players-play-here center.

I jog to the middle, my heartbeat scattered and out of control. The whistle blows, the game begins. A center mid has to check to the ball, which means you've got to think you deserve it. I know if I can win a tackle, my confidence will shoot up enough for me to go ask for the ball.

A player on the other team is close to me, and his touch, while not sloppy, isn't perfect either. I lunge hard for the ball and knick it, slipping in the dust but catching my balance enough to break for it, getting my body between the guy and the ball, I take one touch and send it to the forward. I overlap up the field, and the guy lays it back to me. I one-time it, taking a left-footed shot that has decent pace. The keeper catches it easily enough, and I start jogging back the other direction, keeping my face blank, even though what I feel is unbelievably lucky.

Now I have to maintain it. My mom always told me. "Fake it 'til you make it," and I never liked the expression—I thought, it was too cutesy—but that's often what I end up doing. I pretend like I belong until I believe it.

Center midfielder—the person who's everywhere, all the time. On the wing, you can go long stretches without seeing the ball. It's easy to fall into a trance, to watch. There's no risk of that in the center: all points connect through you.

I get megged once—the ball whooshing between my legs before I know what's happening. The move's so fantastic I don't even feel bad about it.

And otherwise, I'm playing well. I check to my forwards and my defenders and then I lay it off, my passes clean. I'm not stupid enough to try to dribble. It's cluttered and cramped in the center; taking more than two touches is asking for it. Someone will appear out of nowhere, materializing right in front of you, usurping the ball. On the field, there's very little worse than that.

Of course, I want to dribble, I want it badly. Dribbling is what I'm good at, even though it feels stupid to say that in Brazil. I'm good but they're better. Still, I want to impress them. But I've got to wait. You have to fan the field with passes so consistently that no one will expect you to dribble—and that's when you go for it.

The big guy wearing the bright pink stopwatch blows a whistle, Our game is up. No one scored. I head back to the bench, Luke touching my hand as he walks by me.

Now that I've played, it doesn't feel bad to watch; I can sit back and appreciate. I see the meg again, the one that got me. A man charging forward suddenly changes directions, turning right into the person chasing him. Using the sole of his foot, he pulls the ball through the outspread legs, going through the defender so completely it's as if the guy was never there.

When I go on again, it no longer feels like there's an earthquake in my heart. This time my team puts me on the wing, space I know how to navigate. I hit in passes, one and then two and then three—and then I try something. I don't know what, I'm just moving, sprinting down the line, feigning a cut right but continuing left, my legs making a bow around the ball until I've stolen a couple inches of space. I shoot the hell out of it, as quickly as I can, scared I've taken one touch too many and that I'm about to get caught. I hit it cleanly. I hear the bang of the crossbar and the ripple of surprise.

For the rest of the game, the guy running the wing with me lays down move after move. I grab his shorts and try not to lose him. He beats me a lot. Bur I feel sort of proud about it, like I've proved I'm good enough to be worth beating. I'm playing as hard as I can, the kind of hard playing you don't even feel.

At midnight, Anderson, the man in the green and white stripes with the pink stopwatch, whose name we know from hearing everyone call it on the field, blows the whistle again, and this time it means the end.

Everyone stands clustered together, pushing down socks and taking off bibs, running fingers through sweaty hair. One guy brushes my shoulder and says, "Joga bem." *You play well.* He's the one who kept beating me up the line. My hands are on my waist, and my breathing hasn't quite evened out. For as long as I can remember, *futebol* has been how I come all the way alive.

Interview with the Bear

John Muir

MyWritingLab™

Born in Dunbar, Scotland, John Muir (1838–1914) grew up in Wisconsin and attended the University of Wisconsin. Muir became an explorer and environmental activist, and he was cofounder of the Sierra Club. "Interview with the Bear" is taken from *My First Summer in the Sierra*, Muir's account of a season working as a shepherd in Yosemite in 1868. Carlo was his sheep dog.

Return to these questions after you have finished reading.

Analyzing the Reading

1. Muir employs figurative language (i.e., personification and similes) to ascribe human characteristics to nature and animals. For example, " . . . Carlo . . . seemed to be saying . . . like a hunting cat. . . ." Identify other examples of figurative language and discuss the effects on what you believe to be the main idea.

2. Sentence style can show as well as tell. Find and read the sentence starting "How long our . . ." ending with ". . . very much nor trusting me." Note how this sentence captures a number of discrete actions by bear and narrator in one continuous sequence, mimicking the "slow fullness of time." Examine other passages and discuss how the sentence style promotes the author's desired effects.

3. As all authors know, no conflict, no story. Muir describes "Muir vs. Bear." Explore the story for other conflicts driving the action, and discuss what these conflicts or tensions reveal about Muir's worldview.

4. What do you believe to be Muir's main point? What might the piece tell us about Muir's worldview? Pay close attention to Muir's use of personification and similes such as "a place for angels" to shape your hypothesis about Muir.

Exploring Ideas and Issues

In Muir's various roles as an environmentalist and activist, he engaged in public debates and protests. A famous debate, one that continues to this day, involved the Hetch Hetchy Dam controversy. The 1906 San Francisco earthquake and fires taught San Francisco's leaders the city's water supply was inadequate. Leadership endeavored to dam the Tuolumne River and fill the Hetch Hetchy Valley to provide water and hydroelectric power. Muir's Sierra Club fought the plan for twelve years, but in 1923, the dam was completed. Today a debate continues over the dam's future: should it be updated or demolished to restore the Hetch Hetchy Valley.

1. Conduct research about the Hetch Hetchy Valley, and write an analysis of the positions and roles Muir and the Sierra Club took, as well as the current state of the controversy.

2. Observe an animal closely over a defined period. What human attributes might you assign to it? Write an observation mimicking Muir's style employing vivid details, personification, and similes.

3. Choose a landscape and observe the features, listen for sounds, and smell for aromas. Write a description employing vivid details to "show" readers the setting.

4. Muir was a great walker. Before he spent the summer in Yosemite, he walked a thousand miles from Indiana to Florida. How does walking change how you see a landscape, whether it's a city street, an urban park, or a wild area? Take a walk in your neighborhood, and consider how that activity differs from the experience of driving or even riding a bicycle.

INTERVIEW WITH THE BEAR

July 21. —Sketching on the Dome, —no rain; clouds at noon about quarter filled the sky, casting shadows with fine effect on the white mountains at the heads of the streams, and a soothing cover over the gardens during the warm hours.

Saw a common house fly and a grasshopper and a brown bear. The fly and grasshopper paid me a merry visit on the top of the Dome, and I paid a visit to the bear in the middle of a small garden meadow between the Dome and the camp where he was standing alert among the flowers as if willing to be seen to advantage. I had not gone more than half a mile from camp this morning, when Carlo, who was trotting on a few yards ahead of me, came to a sudden, cautious standstill. Down went tail and ears, and forward went his knowing nose, while he seemed to be saying "Ha, what's this? A bear, I guess." Then a cautious advance of a few steps, setting his feet down softly like a hunting cat, and

Half Dome, Yosemite National Park

questioning the air as to the scent he had caught until all doubt vanished. Then he came back to me, looked me in the face, and with his speaking eyes reported a bear near by; then led on softly, careful, like an experienced hunter, not to make the slightest noise, and frequently looking back as if whispering "Yes, it's a bear, come and I'll show you." Presently we came to where the sunbeams were streaming through between the purple shafts of the firs, which showed that we were nearing an open spot, and here Carlo came behind me, evidently sure that the bear was very near. So I crept to a low ridge of moraine boulders on the edge of a narrow garden meadow, and in this meadow I felt pretty sure the bear must be.

Grizzly bears were common in Yosemite when Muir was there in 1868 but they largely disappeared by 1900

I was anxious to get a good look at the sturdy mountaineer without alarming him; so drawing myself up noiselessly back of one of the largest of the trees I peered past its bulging buttresses, exposing only a part of my head, and there stood neighbor Bruin within a stone's throw, his hips covered by tall grass and flowers, and his front feet on the trunk of a fir that had fallen out into the meadow, which raised his head so high that he seemed to be standing erect. He had not yet seen me, but was looking and listening attentively, showing that in some way he was aware of our approach. I watched his gestures and tried to make the most of my opportunity to learn what I could about him, fearing he would catch sight of me and run away. For I had been told that this sort of bear, the cinnamon, always ran from his bad brother man, never showing fight unless wounded or in defense of young. He made a telling picture standing alert in the sunny forest garden. How well he played his part, harmonizing in bulk and color and shaggy hair with the trunks of the trees and lush vegetation, as natural a feature as any other in the landscape. After examining at leisure, noting the sharp muzzle thrust inquiringly forward, the long shaggy hair on his broad chest, the stiff erect ears nearly buried in hair, and the slow heavy way he moved his head, I thought I should like to see his gait in running, so I made a sudden rush at him, shouting and swinging my hat to frighten him, expecting to see him make haste to get away. But to my dismay he did not run or show any sign of running. On the contrary, he stood his ground ready to fight and defend himself, lowered his head, thrust it forward, and looked sharply and fiercely at me. Then I suddenly began to fear that upon me would fall the work of running; but I was afraid to run, and therefore, like the bear, held my ground. We stood staring at each other in solemn silence within a dozen yards or thereabouts, while I fervently hoped that the power of the human eye over wild beasts would prove as great as it is said to be. How long our awfully strenuous interview lasted, I don't know; but at length in the slow fullness of time he pulled his huge paws down off the log, and with magnificent deliberation turned and walked leisurely up the meadow, stopping frequently to look back over his shoulder to see whether I was pursuing him, then moving on again, evidently neither fearing me very much nor trusting me. He was probably about five hundred pounds in weight, a broad rusty bundle of ungovernable wildness, a happy fellow whose lines have fallen in pleasant places. The flowery glade in which I saw him so well, framed like a picture, is one of the best of all I have yet discovered, a conservatory of Nature's precious plant people. Tall lilies were swinging their bells over that bear's back, with geraniums, larkspurs, columbines, and daisies brushing against his sides. A place for angels, one would say, instead of bears.

Yosemite meadow

In the great cañons Bruin reigns supreme. Happy fellow, whom no famine can reach while one of his thousand kinds of food is spared him. His bread is sure at all seasons, ranged on the mountain shelves like stores in a pantry. From one to the other, up or down he climbs, tasting and enjoying each in turn in different climates, as if he had journeyed thousands of miles to other countries north or south to enjoy their varied productions. I should like to know my hairy brothers better, —though after this particular Yosemite bear, my very neighbor, had sauntered out of sight this morning, I reluctantly went back to camp for the Don's rifle to shoot him, if necessary, in defense of the flock. Fortunately I couldn't find him, and after tracking him a mile or two towards Mt. Hoffman I bade him Godspeed and gladly returned to my work on the Yosemite dome.

Photographs of Japanese Americans at Manzanar MyWritingLab™
Ansel Adams

Ansel Adams (1902–1984) was an American photographer known for his black-and-white photographs capturing the splendor of the American West. His photographs are acclaimed for their clarity and depth, and are featured in many museums, including the Museum of Modern Art. During World War II, Adams requested permission to photograph the Manzanar War Relocation Center, a Japanese internment camp, in Owens Valley in California. His resulting photo-essay first appeared in a Museum of Modern Art exhibit and was later published in *Born Free and Equal: The Story of Loyal Japanese-Americans*.

Return to these questions after you have finished reading.

Analyzing the Reading

1. Read Kunitomi Embrey's account of life in Manzanar on pages 67–71. What do we learn about Manzanar from Embrey's account that we do not learn from Adams's photographs? Conversely, what do the photographs tell us that her narrative does not?

2. Adams was known for his skill in photographing landscapes and the natural environment. Look at the landscape in these images. How does Adams capture the relationship of the people at Manzarar with their environment?

3. What details caught Adams's eye? Why do you think these details were important?

4. The people in these photographs were posed. What directions do you think Adams gave his subjects, and why?

Exploring Ideas and Issues

Ansel Adams's Manzanar photographic collection is a departure from the landscape photography for which he is best known. Although a majority of the photographs are portraits, his images also include carefully composed scene of daily life at the camp. When he gave the collection to the Library of Congress in 1965, Adams wrote, "The purpose of my work was to show how these people, suffering under a great injustice, and loss of property, businesses and professions, had overcome the sense of defeat and despair by building for themselves a vital community in an arid (but magnificent) environment . . . All in all, I think this Manzanar Collection is an important historical document, and I trust it can be put to good use."

1. View the Adams exhibit at the Library of Congress at http://international.loc.gov/ammem/collections/anseladams. How is the Library using the photographs? Do you think that Adams would agree that the collection has indeed been "put to good use"?

2. When viewed as a collection, what "story" does Adams's photography tell? Write an essay exploring the message(s) conveyed by this collection, as a group or as individual works of art.

3. Adams chose to use his camera to record and expose a great injustice. Write an essay exploring the ways photography can raise awareness of social and political injustice. Connect your points to a current issue locally or globally.

Manzanar from guard tower, view west

Dressmaking class: Mrs. Ryie Yoshizawa, instructor

Catholic church

Yonehisa Yamagami, electrician

Joyce Yuki Nakamura, eldest daughter

Farm workers, Mt. Williamson in background

Richard Kobayashi, farmer with cabbages

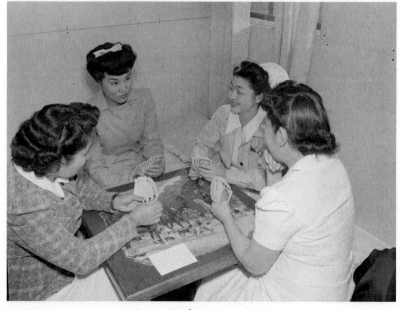

Bridge game

Yellowstone's Geothermal Resources
National Park Service

MyWritingLab™

Yellowstone National Park, which is located primarily in Wyoming but also includes parts of Idaho and Montana, is home to almost half of the Earth's geothermal resources. Geothermal features include hot springs, geysers, mudpots (pools of hot bubbling mud), and fumaroles (openings in the Earth's crust that emit steam and gases). In fact, its more than 300 geysers make up two thirds of all those found on Earth. Yellowstone's vast collection of thermal features attest to the park's volcanic past. Geothermal resources invite us to consider ways to use the Earth's interior as an energy source.

Return to these questions after you have finished reading.

Analyzing the Reading

1. Yellowstone National Park is the largest ecosystem in the northern temperate zone that is still largely intact. Why is its preservation important?

2. The Yellowstone Caldera, where Yellowstone Lake is located today, is the largest volcanic system in North America. It has been called a "super volcano" because the caldera was formed by a series of massive explosive eruptions. Each year there are many minor earthquakes, and the possibility of major future seismic activity is high. Should the National Park Service give greater emphasis to the dangers of visiting Yellowstone?

3. Acts of vandalism have harmed Yellowstone's geothermal resources. Why do you think people vandalize these features?

Exploring Ideas and Issues

In a 2009 article on the human impact on geyser basins, Alethea Steingisser and W. Andrew Marcus noted that "many of the world's geysers have already been altered or completely extinguished by geothermal energy development and tourism. Yellowstone National Park was set aside as the world's first national park due primarily to its multiple geyser basins, an act that set the stage for protecting lands deemed unique in the world. The park has lost a relatively small number of geysers to tourism-related activities, but there is potential for greater damage if geothermal development occurs outside the park."

1. Write about the geologic processes at work in one of Yellowstone's natural wonders—a geyser, hot spring, mudhole, or fumerole.

2. Alethea Steingisser and W. Andrew Marcus are concerned about geothermal development. Write an essay describing what geothermal development is. What are the pros and cons of this type of development?

3. In your opinion, if harnessing the energy Old Faithful (or other geothermal resources) could help power a city but destroy the landmarks in the process, would it be worth it? Why or why not?

YELLOWSTONE'S GEOTHERMAL RESOURCES

Nowhere else in the world can we find the array or number of geysers, hot springs, mudpots, and fumaroles found in Yellowstone. More than 75% of the world's geysers, including the world's largest, are here in 7 major basins. Steamboat, the world's tallest active geyser, is in the Norris Geyser Basin. Old Faithful, Grand, Castle, Giantess, Beehive, and Lion geysers may be frequently observed in the Upper Geyser Basin. Old Faithful Geyser has never been either the largest or most regular of geysers, yet it has been the most regular and frequent geyser that erupts to a height of more than 100 feet; the average time between eruptions ranges between about 60 and 110 minutes, although occasionally visitors must wait two hours between eruptions of Old Faithful. For other major geysers in the Old Faithful and Norris geyser basins, eruption frequencies, durations, and heights change fairly often, especially in response to seismic activity.

The park's thermal features lie in the only essentially undisturbed geyser basins left worldwide. In Iceland and New Zealand, geothermal drill holes and wells have reduced geyser activity and hot spring discharge. Despite the proximity of roads and trails in the largest basins, few park features have ever been diverted for human use (such as bathing pools or energy). YNP offers visitors and scientists an opportunity to appreciate thermal features in their natural, changing state. For example, research on thermophilic bacteria, algae mats, predators, and their environments is applied elsewhere to energy fuel production and extraction, bio-mining, control and removal of toxic wastes, development of new surfactants and fermentation processes, and other fields.

Park features have always been subject to some influence from human vandalism. In the park's early years it was common for visitors to use thermal features as "wishing wells," and this practice continues to some degree today. Coins, rocks, trash, logs or stumps, and other paraphernalia are found in the narrow vents of geysers and hot springs. Features have been plugged up, and little can be done to repair the damage. Radical attempts to siphon surface water and induce eruptions have occasionally been tried on famous features such as Morning Glory Pool, with varying degrees of success. Damage also occurs when people leave walkways and climb on features, or occasionally break pieces of sinter or travertine off for souvenirs.

Features can also be affected by nearby ground-disturbing activities. The presence of water, sewer, and other utility systems adjacent to thermal areas has likely affected features in the past. Since many major features are located near roads and developed areas, major maintenance and construction activities must be carefully designed and monitored so as not to alter thermal features.

Volcanic and seismic processes are very active in the park. A network of seismic monitoring stations in the park provides data to help understand overall seismicity in the region and gauge the magnitude of earth tremors. Thermal features and basins respond violently to volcanic and seismic activity, which creates both a serious hazard to humans and an opportunity to study and possibly predict major geologic hazards. Thus, maintenance of a long-term geothermal database also helps us manage visitor use to increase public safety in a naturally hazardous environment.

How to Write an Observation

These steps for the process of writing an observation may not progress as neatly as this chart might suggest. Writing is not an assembly-line process. As you write, you are constantly reading what you have written and rethinking.

Writing may help you to remember details about what you have observed.

1 CHOOSE A SUBJECT

- Analyze the assignment.
- Identify your goals.
- Choose a person or people.
- Choose a place.
- Plan your observations.
- Analyze your genre. Observations in the sciences and social sciences aim for objectivity and minimize personal reactions.

2 OBSERVE & ANALYZE

- Make observations. Carefully record details of what you see, hear, smell, touch, and taste.
- Record the exact names of people, places, and things.
- Observe more than one time and note what changes.
- Analyze the observations by organizing them into categories.
- Analyze patterns and draw implications.
- Be a "participant observer." You often can learn a great deal by talking to people.

3
WRITE A DRAFT

- Determine your point of view. If you are writing an "objective" description, your point of view is the fly on the wall, describing everything you observe.

- If you are writing a more personal description, think about the ideas and impressions you want to convey.

- Determine an organizational strategy.

- Select details. Give the names of places, people, and things. Give sensory details of sight, sound, smell, touch, and taste.

- "Objective" descriptions in the social sciences and sciences conclude with summarizing your observations in light of your goals.

- Personal descriptions do not have to summarize, but you do want to leave readers with something to think about.

4
REVISE, REVISE, REVISE

- Check that your paper or project fulfills the assignment.

- Make sure that you have a focused thesis or a clear overall impression.

- Revise your introduction, if needed, to draw readers in.

- Examine the organization.

- Add details to make the description more concrete.

- Check that the conclusion gives a sense of the significance of the observations.

- Review the visual presentation.

- Proofread carefully.

5
SUBMITTED VERSION

- Make sure your finished writing meets all formatting requirements.

1: Choose a Subject

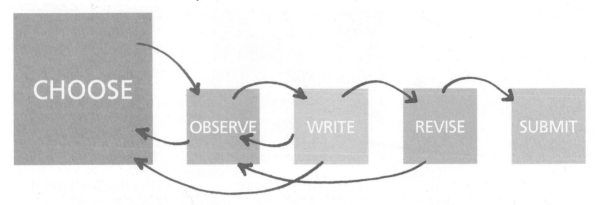

Analyze the assignment

Read your assignment slowly and carefully. Look for words like *observe, field research,* or *field observation,* which tell you that you are writing about your firsthand observations. Identify any information about the length specified, date due, formatting, and other requirements. You can attend to this information later. At this point you want to give your attention to your subject and your goals.

Identify your genre and goals

Different kinds of observing have different goals. What exactly would make an observation effective for your assignment? If your assignment to observe is in the sciences, social sciences, and education, your readers will expect you to be objective and not to emphasize your personal reactions.

Choose a person or people

If your assignment asks you to observe a person or people, think about whom you might observe—a front-desk person, an athlete on and off the field, players of video games and other games, people building something, people exercising, and so on. Consider how each person interacts with others or how a group maintains its identity.

Choose a place

If your assignment asks you to observe a place or object, think about where or what you might observe—a park, a downtown street, a market, a factory, a bowling alley, and so on. Consider what recurring activities you can observe at this place.

Choose an event

If your assignment asks you to observe an event, look at the event calendars on your school's Web site and in your local newspaper. You'll find many possibilities. Observe what goes on besides the main event. For example, if you attend a sports event, observe the concession stands, the first-aid station, the ticket staff, and other people besides the players.

Be aware of ethical considerations

Be open and honest about what you are doing. Observing should not involve becoming a spy. If you need permission to visit a site, obtain it in advance.

Plan your observations

Determine what times you will need to visit and what will be going on. Plan to spend a long time observing. The longer you observe, the more likely you will encounter something out of the ordinary that will give your description a special insight.

WRITE NOW   MyWritingLab™

Find a place

Think about possible places that might work for your assignment. Divide a sheet of paper into four columns and label them place, people, activities, and times. List your places in the first column. Then list the people who go there, their behavior, and the times they are present.

PLACE	PEOPLE	ACTIVITIES	TIMES
Television room in student union	Some of the same people every day	They view particular programs but also talk	Most busy around lunch time

When you have at least five possible places, select the one you feel will work best.

Writer at work

Sarah Cuellar was asked to conduct observations for her Early Childhood Development class and write a report about them. She made notes on and highlighted important parts of her assignment sheet.

Early Childhood Development 324
Observation Assignment

For this assignment you will (observe) preschool children during normal school activities. You will (analyze) the behavior you observe within the context of a behavioral theory we have studied in class. To start this project, you will need to

- Choose the age of student and type of behavior you want to observe.
- Review the readings and your class notes covering theories about that behavior.
- Schedule at least three observation periods of thirty to sixty minutes each, about three to five days apart. Our class will observe students at the Babiya Montessori school at 1700 Crown Ave.
- Fill out the informed consent form for your observation and have it signed by one of the instructors at Babiya Montessori.

Make sure you do the following in your paper:

EXPLAIN the theory

(1) Introduce the behavior you are studying, summarize the thoery or theories you are working with, and explain why you want to study it.
(2) Provide substantial detailed observations from your field journal, with context and explanations.

DESCRIBE what you saw

(3) Relate the behaviors you observe to the theories about behavior we are studying.
(4) Conclude by noting how your observations did or did not align with a given theory, OR suggesting how your observations may indicate a need for further research to clarify or test the theory, OR explaining how the behaviors you observed may support a new theory.

Did observing help you understand the theory any better?

(5) Use APA-style documentation. You do not need to include a title page or abstract.

Due dates:
March 17: Informed consent forms and observation schedules due
April 14: Draft due
April 28: Final version due

After she felt she understood the assignment, Sarah listed several theories discussed in class that interested her. For each theory, she wrote down questions that occurred to her about the behavior. Then she considered which of these questions she might be able to learn more about by observing preschool children.

POSSIBLE BEHAVIORS TO OBSERVE:

Make-believe/imaginative play—*How much variation in ages when it begins?*

Oppositional behavior—*Do students "talk back" more to some teachers than others?*

Solitary/parallel/group play—*What is the progression and how do children learn group play skills?*

Object play—*Are there differences between boys and girls (frequency, purpose, and so on)?*

Because she planned to teach preschool, Sarah decided to observe children's solitary, parallel, and group play patterns. She felt that learning more about how children's play skills progressed might help her discover whether teachers could help students develop their social play skills.

Sarah then reviewed her notes from class and from her readings. She summarized the readings that addressed types of play.

Parten, M. (1932). Social participation among preschool children. *Journal of Abnormal and Social Psychology, 27,* 242–269.

> Classic study of preschool behavior. Parten's scale of solitary and group play assumes each "step up" requires better social skills.
>
> (1) unoccupied play   (2) solitary play
> (3) onlooker play   (4) parallel play
> (5) associative play   (6) cooperative play

Smith, P. K. (1978). A longitudinal study of social participation in preschool children: solitary and parallel play reexamined. *Developmental Psychology, 14,* 517–523.

> Data did not prove that children progress "through" parallel play as a stage, so posited that it is "optional," and that some kids do while others don't.

Bakeman, R., & Brownlee, J. R. (1980). The strategic use of parallel play: A sequential analysis. *Child Development, 51,* 873–878.

> Parallel play does not ever become the dominant play style. Children use it a lot but they do not go through a stage where they use primarily parallel play. "Parallel play often functions in the stream of activities as a bridge to group play."

2: Make Observations and Analyze Them

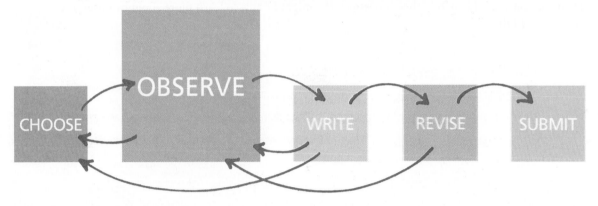

Make observations

Take notes that record what you use in detail, using either pen and paper notebook or a tablet computer or mobile device. If you use pen and paper, leave space for comments after your observations are complete. Pay attention to all your senses—smell, taste, touch, and hearing as well as sight. Take photos if possible.

Be a "participant observer"

Talk to the people you observe. Ask them questions about their activities, opinions, and feelings. If you are polite and unobtrusive, you will learn a great deal more than if you keep silent. Keep your own language distinct, in your notes, from the language of your subjects.

Record times, places, and names of people

Always note exactly where you were, when you were there, and the people you talked with.

Assemble your observations

Gather your notes and read them carefully. You may want to do an initial sorting by putting them in chronological order or else categorizing them by major theme.

Analyze the observations

How many different activities were going on during your observations? Which activities were particular to this place? Were there significant differences among the subjects you observed? Were these differences behavioral or of some other type? Did anything unusual happen? Why were the subjects there?

Analyze patterns and draw implications

What patterns can you identify? What implications can you draw from these patterns?

Writer at work

After observing, Sarah went back over her notes and made comments on them in order to analyze what she had observed.

3/24/14

10:15 a.m.

Sadie is playing with blocks. Lilly is putting away some books nearby. The teacher shows Lilly another bin of blocks and asks if she would like to build something, "like Sadie." Lilly looks at Sadie and Sadie's blocks and then says "yes." Both girls play separately for about two minutes. They watch each other work but do not speak. Then Lilly knocks down her blocks and laughs. She looks at Sadie who also laughs. Sadie pushes over her own blocks and then they both laugh again.

Encouragement from teacher

Laughing is the first real communication between the two girls. Lilly is looking at Sadie when she laughs. Sadie copies Lilly's action and response. She seems to be saying, "I like to do what you like to do.

Lilly: "Now we have to clean up."

Both girls put some blocks back in their bins.

Sadie: "I made a tower all of orange bricks."

Cooperative activity

Lilly: "One time I made a big, big house, so big."

Sadie: "You can have green blocks."

The girls begin to sort the blocks into colors, sharing blocks. The teacher comes by and says "Are you making a house together?"

The teachers have been talking about sharing a lot. The girls do not use the word "share" but they are mimicking the behavior the teachers have modeled.

Lilly: "Yes, and I made the green blocks."

Sadie: "I like orange because orange is my best color."

Teacher: "It's a pretty house. You are both working very hard! I like to see you sharing."

Verbal reinforcement

3: Write a Draft

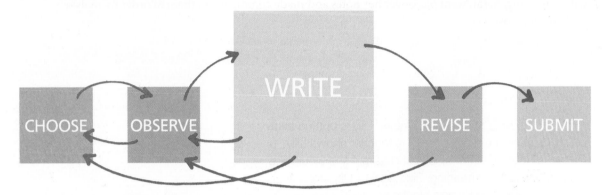

Determine your thesis or the overall impression you want to convey

If your assignment asks you to observe for a particular purpose, likely you will need to provide a clear, significant thesis early on. If you are writing a travel account or describing a place, you may not have an explicit thesis, but you will want to convey an overall impression through the details you select.

Determine your point of view

If you are observing for a science or social science class, focus on when and what you observed. If you are writing a travel account or describing a place, you may want to foreground yourself as a participant—why you went there and how you responded to the place and people.

Determine an organization

You might organize by chronology or by special location. You may need to classify your observations into subtopics and organize accordingly.

Select details

Give accurate, specific information about the place and, if present, the people. Include short quotations if you record conversations and attribute them accurately.

Grab readers at the beginning and leave them with something to think about

Choose an appropriate title that will immediately get readers' attention. Conclude by leaving your readers with a sense of why your observations matter. Press beyond the superficial.

Work for precise description

Show, not tell

OFF TRACK

It is very difficult to hike cross-country in the Arctic National Wildlife Refuge.

ON TRACK

Every inch of ground challenges human walking: meadows of waist-high muskeg brush, quicksand beside the streams and slick rocks in them, loose shale on the hillsides, and uneven tundra hillocks on flat sections that offer no good way to negotiate—plant your foot on them and they collapse sideways, step between them and you sink to your calf.

Provide exact details

OFF TRACK

Grizzly bears and black bears look different.

ON TRACK

Rely on body shape rather than size and color to distinguish grizzly bears from black bears. Grizzlies have a hump above their front shoulders; black bears lack this hump. In profile, grizzlies have a depression between their eyes and nose, while black bears have a "Roman" profile with a straight line between the forehead and nose.

Give names where possible

OFF TRACK

The courthouse stands in the center of the town square, bordered by streets named for Civil War generals.

ON TRACK

The courthouse stands in the center of the town square, bordered by streets named for Confederate heroes: Lee, Jackson, Stuart, and Davis.

Writer at work

Sarah needed to synthesize her observations with the behavioral theories discussed in her class. She went back to her notes on parallel play and looked for specific concepts that helped explain the behaviors she had observed. She made an outline of the points she thought she should cover in her paper. This outline also helped her make certain she was fulfilling all the requirements of her assignment.

From Bakeman & Brownlee:

"Those who play beside others may indeed desire their company and use parallel play as a strategy (albeit not necessarily in a conscious sense) that often brings them into group play" (877).

Sometimes the kids send pretty obvious signals that they would like to be playing with the child next to them. Ellen pretty clearly wanted to play with Lilly and set up her own doll so she could suggest a shared activity. Keyshawn often will put down a toy he is playing with and change to the type of toy another child has. Does this imitation send a "cue" to the other child that he would like to play?

"Parallel play among preschoolers may be important then, not as a type of play which dominates or characterizes a given developmental stage but as a type of play which frequently initiates or leads into group play" (877).

I didn't see any child who used primarily parallel play. Generally the kids represented a pretty wide range of developmental levels, so if parallel play was associated with one stage it should have been evident in certain kids. However, it was really common for group play to come about after a period of parallel play.

"It may be that parallel play often serves as a brief interlude during which preschoolers have both an increased opportunity to socialize as well as a chance to 'size up' those to whom they are proximal. In fact, such a pause for evaluation and initial coordination of one's actions to those of another might be one of the more important functions of parallel play" (877).

There were many times kids did not move into group play from parallel play. Was this because they decided it would be a "bad fit"?

Playing in Traffic: How Parallel Play Helps Preschool Children "Merge" into Group Play

I. Theories of parallel play
A. Parten theorized developmental play stages in 1932.
B. Smith proposed that parallel play is an "optional stage" in 1978.
C. Bakeman and Brownlee viewed parallel play as a transition.

II. My observations
A. I observed a class of 11 children, 32 to 50 months of age, at Babiya Montessori preschool.
B. My observations were not a formal study.

III. Thesis
A. I did not observe parallel play as a stage.
B. I did not observe parallel play as social adaptation.
C. "Merge lane" might be a better metaphor than "bridge."

IV. Detailed observations
A. Lilly and Sadie play with blocks.
　1. Lilly and Sadie use parallel play to "size up," as Bakeman and Brownlee describe.
　2. Sharing has been modeled by teachers.
B. Ellen and Lilly play with dolls.
　1. Ellen uses parallel play to "size up" Lilly.
　2. She uses parallel play again with Sadie later.

V. Teachers' involvement shifts to group play
A. The playroom was set up to encourage parallel play.
B. Teachers sometimes facilitate group play, but they allow the children to decide.

VI. Different rates of parallel play related to social comfort
A. Keyshawn uses more parallel play than other children.
B. He is developmentally equal with other kids his age.

VII. Conclusion
A. Even the most mature children frequently played alone.
B. Children use different kinds of play at different times for different purposes.

4: Revise, Revise, Revise

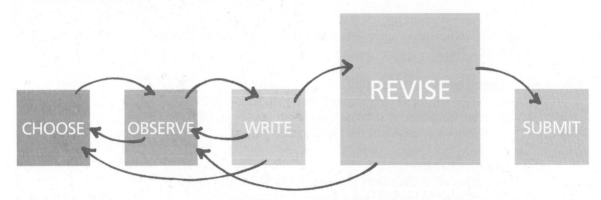

Skilled writers know that the secret to writing well is rewriting. Even the best writers often have to revise several times to get the result they want. You also must have effective strategies for revising if you're going to be successful. The biggest trap you can fall into is starting off with the little stuff first. Leave the small stuff for last.

Does your paper or project meet the assignment?	• Look again at the assignment for specific guidelines, including length, format, and amount of research. Does your work meet these guidelines?
Do you have a focused thesis or a clear overall impression?	• Is it clear to readers what is most important about your observations?
Is your introduction effective?	• Will your title grab people's attention? • Does your introduction draw readers in?
Is your organization effective?	• Is the order the best for your purpose? Possibly you may need to shift the order of some of your paragraphs.
Do you provide vivid, well-chosen details?	• Can you add details to increase interest and paint a clearer picture?
Is your conclusion effective?	• Do you place your observations in a larger overall context? • Do you leave readers with the feeling that they have learned something valuable?
Is the writing project visually effective?	• Is the font attractive and readable? • Are the headings and visuals effective?
Save the editing for last.	• When you have finished revising, edit and proofread carefully.

A peer review guide is on page 58.

Writer at work

Sarah took a draft of her paper to her instructor's office hours and discussed it with him. She made notes during their conversation and used his comments to guide her revisions. Her completed revision of the entire paper begins on the next page.

Add date after Brownlee

Bakeman and Brownlee theorized that parallel play, instead of being a developmental stage children go through, is actually a social adaptation that allows them to move from solitary play into group play in specific situations. In their study, parallel play often preceded group play, indicating that children used it to transition into group play. "[T]hose who play beside others may indeed desire their company and use parallel play as a strategy (albeit not necessarily in a conscious sense) that often brings them into group play" (p. 877).

Incorporate this quote more smoothly

Focus should not be on what I believe, but on what the evidence shows. Also nothing has been "proven"; B&B say more research is called for

After observing a group of eight preschool children, ages 38–50 months, at Babiya Montessori preschool, I believe that Bakeman and Brownlee were right. Parallel play is a social adaptation rather than a developmental stage. I observed many instances in which children used parallel play to move into group play, or to try to do so. But while Bakeman and Brownlee conclude that parallel play is a "bridge to group play" (p. 873), I think a better analogy is that parallel play works like the merge lane on a highway. It allows kids to get "up to speed" and find the right way to work themselves into a specific group play situation. For example, if one kid did not want to participate in group play, his preference was often made evident during parallel play. He might move away from the other child near him, or provide a verbal or physical clue that he wanted to remain solitary.

Change "kids" to "children"– more formal tone is needed for this paper

5: Submitted Version (APA Style)

MyWritingLab™

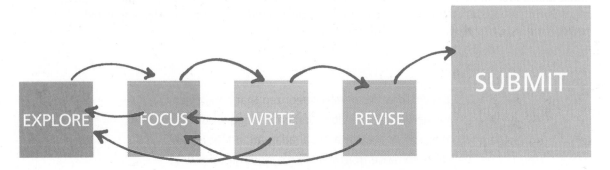

EXPLORE FOCUS WRITE REVISE SUBMIT

PLAYING IN TRAFFIC   1

Sarah Cuellar

Professor Barone

Early Childhood Development 324

28 April 2014

Playing in Traffic: How Parallel Play Helps Preschool Children

"Merge" into Group Play

The term "parallel play" was invented by Mildred Parten (1932) to describe the way preschool age children will play next to each other, doing the same things, but without interacting. Parten thought that parallel play was a developmental stage between solitary play and group play. However, later research showed that most children do not develop along a simple track from solitary play to parallel play and then to group play. Parallel play is very common in almost all children, but children do not go through a stage where it dominates their play. It is more mixed along their developmental path.

Smith (1978) proposed that parallel play may be an "optional" stage that only some children go through, which could explain why it doesn't show up as a definite developmental phase in large studies. However, other researchers make the case that parallel play isn't a developmental stage at all. Bakeman and Brownlee (1980) theorized that parallel play, instead of being a developmental stage children go through, is actually a social adaptation that allows them to move from solitary play into group play in specific situations. In their study, parallel play often preceded group play, meaning that children used it to transition into group play. Bakeman and Brownlee posit that "those who play beside others may indeed desire their company and use parallel play as a strategy (albeit not necessarily in a conscious sense) that often brings them into group play" (p. 877). Group play requires complex social skills that children develop gradually, like sharing, patience, and communication. It also requires multiple focuses of attention. Children playing in a group have to focus on toys and on playmates. Parallel play may be a way for children to coordinate all these skills and get them all working at the same time so that they can play successfully with others.

My reading about types of play has left me with many questions. How accurately does play activity reflect a child's developmental level? How can I as a teacher encourage play that promotes development? How much conflict during play is normal and healthy? How can a teacher identify and minimize play behavior that impedes development? I had all these questions in mind when I began my observations.

I observed a class of 11 children, 32 to 50 months of age, at Babiya Montessori preschool over a two-week period. Six were girls and five were boys. They came from a variety of backgrounds but none of them could really be described as disadvantaged, according to the teachers at the school. I did not conduct a formal study like Parten, Smith, or Bakeman and Brownlee; thus my observations cannot be directly compared to their findings. Those researchers recorded children's play and divided time up into small increments for analysis. I simply observed and made notes. But what I observed did seem to align more closely with Bakeman and Brownlee's theories than with those of Parten or Smith.

My observations tend to support Bakeman and Brownlee's theory that parallel play is a social adaptation rather than a developmental stage. In my observations, age was not a good predictor of which children used parallel play most. If parallel play were a developmental stage, I would expect to see more use of it in younger children, and less use by older children who had matured and moved away from the solitary play stage, into the group play stage. However, I did observe many instances in which children of all ages used parallel play to move into group play, or to try to do so.

While Bakeman and Brownlee describe parallel play as a "bridge to group play" (p. 873), I think a better analogy is that parallel play works like the merge lane on a highway. Parallel play allows children to get "up to speed" and find the right way to move into a specific group play situation. For example, I observed that if a child wanted to play with another child near him, he could signal his intentions by talking, touching, or some other means of expressing his interest in group play. If a child did not want to participate in group play, his preference was often made evident during parallel play. He might move away from the other child near him, or provide a verbal or physical clue that he wanted to remain solitary.

Here is a typical shift from parallel to group play as I observed it:

3/24/08

10:15 a.m.

Sadie is playing with blocks. Lilly is putting away some books nearby. The teacher shows Lilly another bin of blocks and asks if she would like to build something, "like Sadie." Lilly looks at Sadie and Sadie's blocks and then says "yes." Both girls play separately for about two minutes. They watch each other work but do not speak. Then Lilly knocks down her blocks and laughs. She looks at Sadie who also laughs. Sadie pushes over her own blocks and then they both laugh again.

Lilly: "Now we have to clean up."

Both girls put some blocks back in their bins.

Sadie: "I made a tower all of orange bricks."

Lilly: "One time I made a big, big house, so big."

Sadie: "You can have green blocks."

The girls begin to sort the blocks into colors, sharing blocks. The teacher comes by and says "Are you making a house together?"

Lilly: "Yes, and I made the green blocks."

Sadie: "I like orange because orange is my best color."

Teacher: "It's a pretty house. You are both working very hard! I like to see you sharing."

Here we see Lilly and Sadie using parallel play the way Bakeman and Brownlee describe it, as "a chance to 'size up' those to whom they are proximal" (p. 877). Lilly knocks down her blocks in part to see if she can get a reaction from Sadie. When Sadie notices her, Lilly laughs. She looks at Sadie while she is laughing, which encourages Sadie to laugh too. When Sadie laughs with her, and then knocks over her own blocks, imitating Lilly, Lilly knows that Sadie has accepted her "invitation" to play. At that point they are willing to work together. When Lilly orders "We have to clean up," Sadie goes along with her and puts the blocks away. They verbally share information with each other about things they like or that they have done. They also make a joint decision to share the blocks by dividing them into the colors each girl likes best. This decision making is a complicated process and requires some cooperation by each girl, who must be willing to "give up" some blocks to her friend.

I noticed that the teachers had been talking often about sharing during the time I was there, and I concluded that Lilly and Sadie were actually mimicking some behaviors the teachers had modeled for them already. Doing so helped them play together successfully. This observation leads me to believe that there are many strategies that children use to learn social interaction, and that some of them, like the concept of sharing, can be taught. Others, like parallel play, may be more developmental in character.

Many times I observed parallel play that did not lead to group play. Often neither child really made an effort to join the other perhaps because children use parallel play when they see someone doing something interesting and want to try it themselves, not because they have the explicit goal of wanting to play with another child. This type of parallel play can lead into group play, but the children often seemed just as happy staying in parallel play. In fact, it seemed to me that parallel play is in some ways easier for the teacher, because then the children don't fight with each other.

Sometimes one child tried to move from parallel to group play and was rejected. Here is the way one attempted shift ended.

3/26/08

1:30 p.m.

Lilly is dressing a doll. Ellen comes in from the playground and finds another doll. She dresses her doll and then puts it on the floor and covers it with a towel.

Ellen (pointing at her doll): "Nap!"

Ellen tugs on Lilly's dress and points to her doll. Lilly looks at Ellen and makes a face.

Ellen: "Lilly! Naptime!"

Lilly: "No!"

Lilly turns her back.

By demonstrating a play activity and indicating that Lilly should share or imitate it, Ellen has used her "turn signal" to let Lilly know she would like to merge into Lilly's "lane" on the "play highway." By shouting "No!" and making a face, Lilly is honking her horn to tell Ellen she is not interested in sharing her lane. Instead of playing with Lilly, Ellen took her doll to another area of the classroom and played alone. After a few minutes she and Sadie took the doll "on a ride" in the toy shopping cart Sadie was pushing. So Ellen managed to transition successfully into group play, but only after finding a child who (unlike Lilly) was interested in playing with her. Parallel play allowed her to determine who would welcome her as a playmate.

After my observations were concluded, I talked to the teachers about the shift from parallel to group play. I wanted to see if they ever intervened to move children from one state to another, or if such shifts were entirely up to the children. They said the classroom was set up in part to encourage parallel play, with similar toys grouped in certain areas (the doll corner, the block wall, and so on). They also said they will sometimes facilitate parallel play by providing similar toys for children. If the children do start playing together, the teachers will encourage them by praising them and by intervening if there are arguments, reminding them to share. But they let the children figure out if they are ready to play together.

As noted earlier, I did not observe children using parallel play more at one age than at another. However, I did notice that children who were newer to the group did use parallel pay more than those who already had friends in the school. This observation supports Bakeman and Brownlee's claim that parallel play is a tool that the children use to help them function socially. For example, Keyshawn, the newest child at the school, used parallel play the most, and often stayed in parallel play for long periods. This behavior may have been because he was trying to get to know the other children better and to figure out who was likely to play well with him. Keyshawn was almost four years old, and all of his other behaviors that I observed (like vocabulary, drawing skills, motor coordination) were equal to those of the older children. Keyshawn's greater use of parallel play does not seem to be tied to his developmental level. I predict that as Keyshawn becomes more comfortable at the school, he will spend less time in parallel play and more time in group play.

My observations suggest that Parten's concept of "development" of play skills distorts what really happens when children play. Even the most mature children in the group played alone frequently. The teachers said this time alone is necessary because social play is hard work for children, and they need "down time." Just like adults, children need some time without the stimulus of others. Thinking of group play as a goal, with solitary play as a basic skill that should be left behind during normal development, is a mistake. Instead, it is better to see types of play as different tools children use to develop their mental, physical, and social skills. Different children will use different tools in different situations, and it is the teacher's job to make sure students have all the tools they need and to suggest using certain ones when the time seems right. Tools like parallel play and sharing skills let children merge onto the highway of social play successfully, with as few fender benders as possible.

References

Bakeman, R., & Brownlee, J. R. (1980). The strategic use of parallel play: A sequential analysis. *Child Development, 51,* 873-878.

Parten, M. (1932). Social participation among preschool children. *Journal of Abnormal and Social Psychology, 27,* 242-269.

Smith, P. K. (1978). A longitudinal study of social participation in preschool children: Solitary and parallel play reexamined. *Developmental Psychology, 14,* 517-523.

Projects

Observations span a wide range of writing, from objective scientific reports to highly personal descriptions of places. Accurate, detailed description is valued in all kinds of observations.

Description of a place

Write an essay describing a place. Select one of these options:

Visit an urban neighborhood that is not familiar to you. Pay close attention to what distinguishes this neighborhood from other neighborhoods in the city.

or

Visit a small town near you, preferably one that is not on a major highway. Likely you will find that many of the businesses that once thrived on Main Street or on the courthouse square are gone. Pay close attention to signs and other things that give indications to what goes on in the town.

Visit some stores, a local coffee shop, and other places where you can talk to people. Ask them about their neighborhood or their town. Then reconstruct conversations in your notebook.

Natural observation

Find a setting in which you can observe animals or natural phenomena such as tides, weather patterns, or erosion. In a large city, you might watch pigeons interacting with people in a park, observe feeding time at a zoo, or watch how insects behave during a rainstorm.

Use your observations to generate a list of questions that would help you fill in any gaps in what you observed. Can you explain the behavior of any animals you observed? If not, how could you determine the causes of their behavior? Can your localized observation of a spring-fed pool uncover the causes of the heavy algae growth there, or do you need to look further to find an explanation?

Analyze your observations by placing them in categories. Note any patterns. Think about what generalizations you can make from the patterns.

Write a brief description about what you observed, including the questions your observation raised, and any answers you found.

Field observation

Observe people in a public setting you
frequent, such as your student union, a library, a coffee shop, a dormitory lounge, a gym, a basketball court, or bus route. Think of one or more questions that field observation might answer. For example, students who use your campus library go there for multiple reasons: to study, to find books, to find journal articles, to use a computer, to watch movies on DVD, to meet their friends, and others.

Collect field notes by observing. Take a
tablet computer or a paper notebook and write only on the right-hand pages. Use the left-hand pages later to analyze your data. Plan to spend at least three hours a week at your site for two weeks. You should gather at least ten pages of notes per week. Listen carefully to conversations and record direct quotations. After you leave the site, make comments on your notes on the left-hand page.

Analyze your notes after two weeks of
observations. What constitutes abnormal behavior? How do people learn the normal behavior for that setting? What happens when the norm is violated by someone?

Write a detailed field observation that
includes concrete details and quotations from people at your site. Make your paper interesting to readers by showing them something about the setting they didn't already know or had never noticed.

COMPOSE IN MULTIMEDIA

Photo essay of a place

Select a place that potentially is an interesting
subject for a photo essay. Places that have people and activities are often more interesting than places without people. Check if it is possible to take photographs. Many malls, stores, and other private spaces do not allow to you take photos. Public spaces are unrestricted.

Think about the focus and purpose of
your photo essay. If, for example, you decide to photograph an animal shelter, will your focus be on the work volunteers do or on the animals?

Visit the place several times. Don't take
photographs at the outset but instead get a sense of the place first at different times of the day. Record the dates of your visits and what was going on. Note the lighting conditions

Take photographs that give an overall sense of
the place and take others that show key details.

Select and edit photographs with a photo
editor. Arrange them so they tell a story and add captions. You can show your photo essay with presentation software like PowerPoint or upload your photos to a Web site like *Flickr*.

MyWritingLab™
Visit Ch. 7 in MyWritingLab to complete the chapter exercises, explore an interactive version of the Writer at Work paper, and test your understanding of the chapter objectives.

8 Informative Essays and Visuals

Successful informative writing begins with what the reader needs to know.

In this chapter, you will learn to

1. Describe the elements of good informative writing *(see p. 155)*

2. Read and use informative visuals *(see p. 156)*

3. Read and analyze an example of informative writing *(see pp. 157–187)*

4. Describe the steps involved in the process of writing an informative essay *(see pp. 188–189)*

5. Apply flexible strategies to write and revise an informative essay *(see pp. 190–213)*

Reporting Information

Whether reading the news, following a recipe, hooking up a new computer, deciding which course to take, or engaging in a multitude of other events in our daily lives, we depend on reliable and clear information.

In one sense, most kinds of writing, including writing to reflect and writing to persuade, also report information. The main difference is that the focus of a report and other informative kinds of writing is on the subject, not on the writer's reflections or on changing readers' minds or on getting them to take action.

Genres of informative writing

- **Reports** often require analysis of data, which readers use to make decisions.
- **News articles** inform us about events around the world.
- **Scholarly articles** report original research.
- **Instructions** help readers to accomplish a task efficiently.

What Makes Good Informative Writing?

1
Focus on a central idea
The key to success is limiting your topic to one you can cover adequately.

2
Stay objective
Writers whose purpose is to inform usually stay in the background, taking the stance of an impartial, objective observer. Absence from bias helps readers to believe that you are trustworthy.

3
Do the necessary research and document your sources
If you use sources in a college assignment, you will be expected to document those sources.

4
Start fast
Your title and introduction should entice readers to want to read the rest. Readers become bored quickly if they have heard it all before. Once you have made your readers curious to know more, don't disappoint them.

5
Define key terms
Define any key terms and concepts that might be unfamiliar.

6
Present information clearly with relevant examples
Organize for the benefit of readers, establishing your major points early on. Define any key terms and concepts that might be unfamiliar. The examples and details make or break informative writing, whether it is a news article, a profile, or even a cookbook.

7
Conclude with strength
Leave your readers something to think about—a memorable example, a key point, an anecdote, implications of the information you have provided, or a projection into the future.

8
Use visuals where appropriate
Charts and graphs show facts and relationships that are often difficult to communicate with words alone. Maps, drawings, and photographs can provide concrete evidence for what is being described in words.

Informative Visuals

Effective informative visuals can communicate complex ideas and phenomena at a glance. NASA frequently uses computer-enhanced imagery for examining objects and events in space and on earth.

A 9.0-magnitude earthquake off the coast of Japan on March 11, 2011, triggered tsunami waves up to 33 feet that devastated coastal areas. The city of Ishinomaki was one of the hardest hit. On March 14, 2011, three days after the tsunami, the Advanced Spaceborne Thermal Emission and Reflection Radiometer (ASTER) on NASA's Terra satellite acquired the right-hand image with water

still inundating the city. The left-hand image, from August 8, 2008, shows water levels under normal circumstances.

NASA uses false color to interpret these images. Water is dark blue, plant-covered land is red, exposed earth is tan, and the city is silver. Water is standing in the flat, open places that were once fields.

WRITE NOW   MyWritingLab™

Examine informative media

1. Popular articles versus scholarly articles: Find an article in a newspaper or an online popular magazine like *Time* or *Newsweek* that reports a scientific discovery or experiment. Select key words from the article that you can use to find a scholarly article in a database. Use a database like *Google Scholar* or *Academic Search Complete*, which allows you to limit the search to scholarly journals. Read both articles and make a list of the differences between them. Notice differences in the language used, the overall length, the format, and the listing of sources.

2. Profiles: On your school's Web site or in the school newspaper, find several written profiles of

people at your school. Likely you can find profiles of the president, deans, coaches, athletes, some professors, and award-winning students. Read the profiles and note what kinds of information are included about each person and what information is left out. Are the profiles written for different audiences? If so, how does the information included depend on the audience?

3. Instructional videos: *YouTube*, *MyVideo*, *Vimeo*, and other video hosts have thousands of instructional videos. Think of something you would like to learn how to do, and combine the name of this activity with "instruction" in a search on *YouTube* or another video host. Watch the two videos. Which one is more effective? Why?

Is Faster Always Better?
Katherine Mangan

After graduating from Williams College in 1981, Katherine Mangan served as a reporter and editor for *The Fort Lauderdale News*, *Sun-Sentinel*, and the *Associated Press*. As a reporter for *The Chronicle of Higher Education* since 1986, she has written about community colleges, professional schools, and workforce issues. Currently, she focuses on student issues ranging from access and preparedness to remediation and completion.

HOW IS THE READING ORGANIZED?

Introduction	Description of the issue	Background information	Complications	Conclusion
Paragraphs 1–5	*Paragraphs 6–15*	*Paragraphs 16–41*	*Paragraphs 42–49*	*Paragraphs 50–55*
Mangan begins with a case study of James Hinkston, a student who began college with advanced courses because of dual credit.	The article gives the larger context of dual credit and continues the case study in paragraphs 12–15.	This section examines why dual-credit programs are booming.	Many high school students are not prepared for the accelerated pace of dual-credit courses.	Mangan returns to the case study of James Hinkston, who realizes he lacked the necessary skills to succeed immediately in college.

Is Faster Always Better?

1   James I. Hinkson graduated from Orem High School in 2011 with two years of college under his belt. His senior year here outside Provo, Utah, was a blur of 13 college courses, most of them beamed onto a TV screen in a multimedia room at Orem High, where a stuffed tiger, its mascot, dangles from a light fixture, and a Utah Valley University banner hangs on the wall.

2   Like thousands of students straddling high school and college in dual-credit classes that start as early as ninth grade, Mr. Hinkson wanted to save money and move faster toward a degree.

3   Algebra, art, astronomy, ethics, history, psychology. He sat watching instructors at Utah Valley lecture to their university classes, as well as to students at several high schools across the region. At Orem High, a facilitator monitored attendance from a

Introduction:
Mangan begins with an individual student who earned college credits in high school and started college in advanced courses, giving a concrete example of a larger issue.

control room. To ask a question, students would press a button, then speak into a microphone.

4   Sometimes it was a challenge to stay motivated, says Mr. Hinkson, the 11th of 12 children in a blended family. "When you're trying to be a college student in high school, you're surrounded by students who don't really understand what college is all about," he says. "A lot of my classmates figured this is the easiest and cheapest way to get through college. If you do your work at the last minute, that's fine, as long as you get a C and get your credit."

5   Two weeks after his high-school graduation, with an associate degree from Utah Valley in hand, Mr. Hinkson moved into a dorm at Brigham Young University. He was already a junior. Three days later, he found himself immersed in upper-level courses, including honors government and economics and the New Testament.

6   Dual enrollment in high school and college—common since the late 1980s—is proliferating as the nation's completion agenda takes hold. Earning tuition-free college credit in high school, the thinking goes, saves students time and money and gives them the confidence and momentum to continue on with higher education. But such acceleration, skeptics say, compromises rigor and doesn't do students any favors.

Description of dual credit:
The focus goes from an individual student to a national perspective on the trend toward earning college credit while in high school.

7   In theory, dual-credit courses use the same syllabi and adhere to the same standards as those on campus. Advocates of the model point to at-risk students who go on to thrive in college and cite studies showing that students with early college credits are more likely to progress and to graduate with at least a two-year degree. It's hardly surprising that at least some students with a head start get to the finish line faster. But is it a race?

8   As lawmakers, educators, and parents worry about soaring college costs and high dropout rates, the pressure on 15- to 17-year-olds to earn college credits early has intensified. The message: Get core courses "out of the way."

9   For years, programs like Advanced Placement have given that chance mainly to high-achieving students at affluent schools. Dual enrollment, in contrast, is now growing fastest at schools with predominantly minority populations.

10   Never mind that many districts struggle to produce graduates who have mastered high-school material. Some educators worry that many of the students hurried through are being set up to fail.

11   "We're steering students toward a course on the assumption that cheaper, earlier, faster is better," says Kristine Hansen, a professor of English at Brigham Young and co-editor of a collection of essays about earning college credit in high school. "I'm afraid we're going to see the fallout later."

12   Mr. Hinkson kept his stride at Brigham Young until he decided he'd earned the right to slack off a bit. "I'm so far ahead," he remembers thinking, "it doesn't matter." He went hiking when he should have been studying, stayed out all night with friends, and then crammed to catch up.

Continuation of case study: Hinkston questions why he was in such a hurry to complete college.

13   His grades suffered, and he got discouraged. Within three months, he had put college on hold and moved back home, an experience he called humbling. "It shot all the confidence I'd built based on having done so much more than everyone else," he says. "I realized I wasn't so great."

14   In retrospect, he wishes he hadn't been in such a hurry.

15   "One of the things they always told us is, 'We want you to get ahead,'" says Mr. Hinkson, pausing with a smile and shaking his head. "What am I trying to get ahead of? Myself?"

16   Dual enrollment spread in part to keep high-schoolers from slacking off. Individual courses existed as early as the 1950s, and in the '70s Syracuse University pitched them to local schools as a cure for "senioritis." A decade later, the first statewide programs rolled out.

Background: Magnan looks at the history and kinds of dual-credit programs along with offering current statistics on the number of students enrolled in dual-credit courses.

17   While most high schools now offer dual-credit courses à la carte, special early-college high schools provide a prix fixe selection. Variations on both models abound: Much instruction is at the high

schools, by teachers the credit-granting colleges approve. Elsewhere, video technology links professors with high-school classrooms. Sometimes high-school students commute to the college campus.

18   When high-school teachers are at the helm, colleges typically insist on the same qualifications as for adjunct instructors, often a master's degree in the subject being taught. The National Alliance of Concurrent Enrollment Partnerships, which accredits 89 partnerships, requires colleges to provide teachers with training and professional development. But for the vast majority of partnerships, which are not accredited by the alliance, regulation and oversight are spotty.

19   Meanwhile, demand for dual enrollment is booming. The number of dual-enrollment courses taken increased by 67 percent from 2002–3 to 2010–11, according to federal data. At schools with higher shares of minority students, the expansion has been explosive. In that eight-year span, the number of dual-credit courses taken at predominantly minority schools rose by 145 percent.

Minority Enrollment Is Key to Rapid Rise In Dual-Enrollment Classes

Classes that award both high-school and college credit are gaining popularity across the country, most notably at high schools with large numbers of minority students.

Numbers of dual-enrollment students by minority-enrollment level of high school

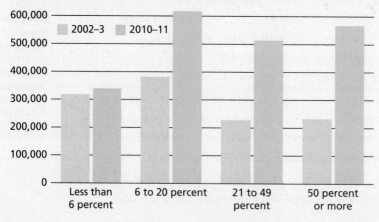

Source: National Center for Education Statistics

20   About 1.4 million high-school students nationally were enrolled in dual-credit courses in 2010–11, the most recent year for which data are available. More than eight in 10 high schools offered the courses.

21   Extending opportunities to low-income and minority students— to take academic as well as career or technical courses—has become a key goal in many education-reform campaigns. Advanced Placement and International Baccalaureate courses aren't necessarily available to everyone, one argument goes. Others, too, could benefit from an early college start.

22   The fast-track approach is popular among advocates of the national college-completion agenda. Groups like the Bill & Melinda Gates Foundation have promoted dual enrollment as a way to improve graduation rates, particularly among minority students, and to produce more educated workers. Early-college high schools took off in 2002 as part of a Gates project. Today more than 280 such schools serve around 80,000 students in 32 states.

Extending educational opportunity: Another argument for dull-credit courses is to improve college graduation rates, especially for low-income students.

23   The nonprofit group Jobs for the Future helps carry the banner. "The populations we're targeting need a clear pathway," says Joel Vargas, a vice president there. "The systems are disjointed, and these students have a particularly hard time navigating them."

24   An early-college experience, if well designed, helps students build successful habits, Mr. Vargas says. "A blended high school-college environment gives them support before they're ready to leave the nest."

25   Early-college opportunities in all their forms continue to grow. Up to two years of free college credit, along with a high-school diploma, sounds like a good offer, and about a dozen states have policies requiring schools or school districts to make dual credit available. The courses are a crucial ingredient in efforts in Texas and Florida to piece together a four-year degree costing $10,000 or less.

26   Numerous studies, including one by ACT, have found that students who earn college credits in high school are more likely to continue in college and to graduate on time; some reports have

shown a correlation with better grades. Anecdotally, however, professors complain that students come in ill-prepared for upper-level coursework.

27   While AP or IB classes require students to take a standardized national exam, and a college might grant credit only for the highest scores, in dual enrollment all a student must do is pass the class to chalk up credits.

28   Many dual-credit courses taught at high schools rely on memorization, contends Harrison Keller, vice provost for higher-education policy and research at the University of Texas at Austin. "They're really a high-school course on steroids," he says. "If you simply credential a teacher with a master's degree and say, 'Here's your syllabus, and sixth period is now college,' it doesn't translate into an authentic college-level learning experience."

29   Questions about rigor have prompted some colleges, especially more-selective private ones, to deny credit for dual-enrollment courses that students try to transfer in. But on many campuses, that credit is the new normal.

30   Ken W. Smith, a professor of mathematics and statistics at Sam Houston State University, wrote with Diana Nixon in a recent column in *The Chronicle* about an 18-year-old student who landed in his precalculus class as a junior, with 65 credits she'd earned in high school. She struggled with his tests, she told him, because her learning style was suited to multiple-choice questions.

31   Across Texas, enrollment in dual-credit courses has quadrupled in the past decade. The state approved 30 early-college high schools in January, bringing the total to 95. More are expected this month.

32   Many of the schools that have been converted to the early-college model have a pattern of low test scores and high dropout rates. The state is changing them over on the theory that academic rigor and the chance to save time and money will motivate students.

33   Lyndon B. Johnson High School, in Austin, was deemed "academically unacceptable" by the state of Texas in 2010–11. So

LBJ, which serves predominantly minority students whose parents did not go to college, teamed up with Austin Community College to offer an early-college curriculum.

34   Students have to pass a test proving they're ready to take college courses. About 130 of 831 students are enrolled in at least one such course, says the principal, Sheila Henry. The rest are in what she calls "pre-college prep."

35   The school has recently extended its offerings to let students pursue certifications in firefighting, for example, and media technology. "If they're not on a track to college," Ms. Henry says, "we want them on a pathway to a great career."

36   The school aims to lift all students' ambitions. Inside a glass case across from the principal's office is an honor roll that ranks students, based on their latest report cards, as professors, department chairs, provosts, or chancellors. Halls are lined with reminders of admissions deadlines and photos of smiling seniors displaying the pennants of the colleges that have accepted them.

37   Ms. Henry wants to see more students qualify for dual credit. But she's not willing to compromise rigor. "Don't water down the work for our kids," she tells instructors.

38   The straight-talking principal encourages students in college-level courses to take as many as they can handle. "It's money that doesn't come out of their pockets," she says. "Loans they don't have to take out."

39   Maya Pierce, 17, is enrolled in five dual-credit courses this year. "Before, I didn't think I'd be able to get the work done," says Ms. Pierce, a petite, serious student. Now she's hoping to get into Texas A&M University to study petroleum engineering. Her college-level courses, she says, have boosted her confidence.

40   Her classmate Casey Brady says he now knows what to expect in college. The lanky 18-year-old with a mop of sandy hair was "never a fan of hard work," he says. But after an auto-mechanics class he'd signed up for was canceled, he landed in a college-level engineering course.

41   "I was bummed out," says Mr. Brady. "I'd always wanted to be one of those guys working in a garage who could bring an old car back to life." Beyond a brief period of procrastinating and "freaking out" when the workload piled up, he says, he did pretty well. A senior, he has applied to the state's two flagship campuses, with dreams now not of repairing cars but of designing them.

42   Things don't always go so smoothly. On a recent rainy morning in one of a cluster of portable buildings at LBJ, about a dozen students are in "British Literature," an ambitious blend of Chaucer, Milton, and Shakespeare taught by Richard Price, an instructor at Austin Community College.

Complications: Many high school students are not prepared for the accelerated pace of dual-credit courses.

43   The class starts with a recap of works from Chaucer and Milton. Then students break into groups of four or five, dragging their chairs together, to act out scenes from Chaucer's poem *Troilus and Criseyde*. Mr. Price encourages the students to sit "eyeball to eyeball and knee to knee" and assign roles to each group member.

44   Amid much conversation, two students excitedly plan their costumes as Eve and the serpent. The problem is that they're picturing a scene from Milton's *Paradise Lost*. They're supposed to be in Chaucer's Troy.

45   Mr. Price senses the confusion. "You're in the wrong garden," he tells them, smiling sympathetically. "It's OK. We're moving quickly."

46   Colleges seeing surges of students with early credit will have to adapt, if they're not already. Some institutions may find that enrollment is falling in entry-level courses and rising in upper-level ones, says Adam I. Lowe, executive director of the national dual-enrollment alliance. "Departments need to rethink how the sequence of courses are delivered," he says.

47   The University of Texas at Austin has responded with an attempt at quality control: a blended-learning program called OnRamps. Its goal is to ensure that dual-enrollment and community-college courses align with expectations at the university. Faculty members there, guided by learning specialists, design the courses and train high-school instructors to teach them.

48   At Sam Houston State, the Student Advising and Mentoring Center offers extensive support to students who find themselves in over their heads. About a third of the incoming class last fall came in with dual credit, an average of 17 credit hours. Some students start with 30 or more hours, allowing them to skip freshman year altogether.

49   Missing out on first-year courses designed in part to introduce students to college work puts them at a disadvantage—and puts institutions in a bind, says Ms. Hansen, of Brigham Young. "We have to do remedial work," she says, "because they haven't mastered the basics."

50   James Hinkson landed in classes at Brigham Young with juniors, he says, who knew how to be college students. They had learned to write two or three drafts before turning in a 10-page English paper. To turn down the music and pass on parties when they need to study. Some of those skills, he says, he hadn't developed yet.

Conclusion: Magnan returns to the case study of James Hinkson. Looking back, Hinkson realizes that he lacked the necessary skills to succeed immediately in advanced college courses.

51   After Mr. Hinkson put his studies on hold, he tried his hand at sales. He enrolled in BYU courses here and there. He went to work at a call center. But then, tired of dead-end jobs, he felt that he needed to immerse himself in college to figure out what would come next. This past fall, he returned to Brigham Young full time.

52   With several accounting classes this term, Mr. Hinkson is thinking of becoming a consultant. As long as he works hard and stays focused, he has five or six semesters left, he calculates. But he hopes to set out on a Mormon mission this summer before coming back to finish.

53   Earnest and reflective, he is grateful for the money he saved through dual enrollment. Not so much for the years he tried to shave off college.

54   "I have a healthy understanding of who I am now," says Mr. Hinkson. "I'm still motivated and driven, but I'm operating on a more realistic time frame."

55   Now, at 21, he is right where he might have been if he hadn't started college in high school.

Understanding China's Middle Class

MyWritingLab™

Kheehong Song and Allison Cui

Kheehong Song is a partner of Monitor Group, a marketing consultation firm. He is also the head of M2C (Monitor's marketing practice) Asia and managing director of Monitor's Shanghai office. Allison Cui, who is based in Shanghai, is a senior consultant for Monitor Group. Monitor consultants Angela Wang, Moon Heo Koo, Min Tian, James Bian, and Wendy Yu also contributed to this article, which was published in the March 2008 issue of *China Entrepreneur.*

Return to these questions after you have finished reading.

Analyzing the Reading

1. Who do you think is the audience for this reading? What is the reading's purpose?

2. Much of the selection is focused on defining the Chinese middle class and its purchasing habits. What criteria, in addition to income, do the authors say are important to understanding the consumer habits of middle-class Chinese?

3. What kinds of evidence do the authors use to support their points? Give at least two examples. How persuasive is their choice of evidence?

4. The authors divide the Chinese middle class into subsegments. How many subsegments do they identify? Do the descriptions of these groups seem useful? In what ways? What is the purpose of giving names to these subsegments?

Exploring Ideas and Issues

Identifying consumers' needs is a vital step in successful marketing. Companies like the Monitor Group specialize in systematically and objectively gathering and analyzing marketing information for producers. Though marketing research uses many of the tools of statistical analysis, it also depends to a great extent on the expertise of knowledgeable people in the field for interpretation of results.

1. The authors looked at the buying habits of middle-class Chinese. Think of three specific people you know in terms of their buying habits. Maybe one is an impulse buyer and another buys only high-status items, for example. How typical are these habits? Write an essay in which you generalize from your observations about these people to create three consumer "types."

2. Think of a widely known company—for example, Coca-Cola or Jeep. How does the company reach different U.S. population segments? Do some research, including observing TV commercials, print ads, and Internet marketing, on the company's products. What information do the ads convey? Which consumers do you think the company is trying to reach? Why? Write an essay in which you describe your research and give your conclusions.

3. With its rapidly growing middle class—340 million by 2016, according to Song and Cui—China has become a very desirable market for many companies worldwide. Do some research on marketing to China or another country with a growing economy, such as Brazil or India. Identify a marketing trend. Then write a short report to an imaginary U.S. company suggesting how the company can take advantage of that trend. You may use "Understanding China's Middle Class" as an information source for your essay.

Understanding China's Middle Class

Targeting key segments of China's diverse and rapidly emerging middle class will be crucial as household incomes rise

Gone are the days when companies looked at China as a monolithic land of 1 billion potential customers. Companies are now focusing on how to capture small segments of China's giant market, and none of these segments is as attractive or as full of potential as the country's rapidly growing—and multifaceted—middle class. As China's economy continues to grow, more people will migrate to China's booming metropolises to find better-paying jobs. These working consumers, once among the country's poorest, will steadily climb the income ladder and join the new middle class. Companies that can effectively understand the composition and needs of this diverse group will be positioned to reap massive rewards.

WHY THE MIDDLE CLASS?

Though many foreign companies have remarked on the importance of China's middle class as a consumer segment, few realize just how dramatic its ascendance is. From 1995 to 2005, the population of China's middle class—defined here as households with annual incomes ranging from $6,000 to $25,000—grew from close to zero in 1995 to an estimated 87 million in 2005, according to MasterCard Worldwide, Asia Pacific. China's middle class will jump to 340 million by 2016. The purchasing power—disposable income minus savings—of China's middle class is also growing. In 2006, around 39 percent of urban households were middle class. By 2016, that percentage will likely rise to 60 percent. At present, the middle class accounts for 27 percent of China's total urban disposable income. By 2015, that percentage is expected to rise to more than 40 percent (see Figure 1). Considering its swelling numbers,

purchasing power, and trajectory, China's middle class presents marketing opportunities that companies cannot afford to miss.

WHAT DOES IT MEAN TO BE MIDDLE CLASS?

Different types of companies have different concepts of exactly what it means to be middle class in China. For example, HSBC Holdings plc and Deutsche Bank AG have used income to differentiate the middle class from the affluent and laboring classes in China. From an investment bank's perspective, using income level as the defining criterion makes sense. But simply judging a group by income is far from sufficient for marketers of consumer goods. Such marketers trying to reach the middle class have to know more than their salaries: They must know what makes middle class consumers tick.

Income plays a powerful role in most purchasing decisions for any consumer segment, but other elements play a role that is sometimes greater than income. When products are relatively inexpensive, income has little influence on a consumer's decisionmaking process. Deciding to buy chocolate, for example, depends significantly more on consumers' emotion and shopping experience—a store's ambience, for example—than it does on how much money they make. Using income as the only indicator of spending habits allows much information to slip through the cracks. In addition, income is a difficult variable to act upon, in part because the data on income in China tends to be either unavailable or unreliable. Thus, companies must find meaningful alternatives to predict what consumers can afford and what they are willing to pay for certain goods and services. Studies by the Monitor Group indicate that scores of non-income-related hooks—including age, the stage in a consumer's career, and location of purchase—influence purchase decisions.

The Chinese badminton industry is a good example. Most Chinese school kids who play badminton do so in an outdoor playground with a group of friends, wear non-professional badminton sportswear, and purchase a relatively inexpensive racket in a sports stadium or shop near school. Professionals and businesspeople, however, usually play badminton in indoor badminton clubs, gyms, or stadiums. One of the major reasons they play badminton is to make friends or develop business relationships. They are aware of racket brands and wear professional sportswear to display social status.

The differences between school kids and professionals are mainly due to their disparate life stages and buying power. If a sports equipment and apparel company understands the differences between these two segments, it will use varying products and prices to target them through different channels. Nonetheless, even within the professional segments, consumers exhibit distinct buying behavior based on their occupation and level of career development. For example, engineers usually exhibit different buying behavior from marketing professionals, and senior managers may not care as much about brands as junior managers, who tend to buy famous brands to show their emerging social status.

PURCHASING POWER AND HOW THE MIDDLE CLASS BUYS

Of all the challenges that the middle class presents to marketers, understanding the specific needs and purchasing power of the group is of

Quick Glance

■ China's middle class, defined here as those earning $6,000 to $25,000, will increase from 87 million in 2005 to 340 million in 2016.

■ Several non–income-related hooks, such as age, the stage in a consumer's career, and location of purchase, influence purchase decisions for China's middle-class consumers.

■ Monitor identified six subsegments within China's middle class, each with its own unique needs and consumption patterns.

utmost importance. Though middle-class consumers have rising purchasing power and are increasingly willing to pay more for higher quality, brand names, and differentiated features, they are still price sensitive. Recognizing differences in behavior within middle-class segments is essential to success in the Chinese marketplace.

When Inter IKEA Systems B.V. first entered China in 1998, its strategy was to offer stylish furniture at premium prices. The strategy was a flop. Middle-class customers filled IKEA's stores to look around but bought less than expected.

In the last few years, however, IKEA has repositioned itself as a brand targeting segments with annual household incomes above ¥40,000 ($5,857). Thanks to achievements in localization, the company has been able to cut prices by an average of 54 percent in more than 1,000 categories since 2005. IKEA broke the bottleneck and succeeded in China because it recognized that middle-class consumers wanted and would pay for high-quality products, but not at the same premiums as the affluent class.

MEET THE MIDDLE CLASS

China's relatively new middle class consists of a rapidly shifting, diverse population. At present, China's lower middle class accounts for 44 percent of the total middle class. As the middle class matures, however, the number of people in the upper middle class—households that earn $12,000 to $25,000—will spike dramatically. Companies must prepare for the different shopping behaviors of each sub-segment within the middle class. Lower-middle-class shoppers, for example, tend to buy top-tier products that can display their wealth and status. These middle-class consumers sometimes spend a large portion of their income on expensive goods. By contrast, upper-middle-class shoppers, who are more experienced with different types of brands, will seek out relatively high-quality products without paying as much attention to brands or will pick out products that merely reflect personal tastes.

To differentiate customer segments, Monitor Group has used "action segmentation," a market analysis strategy that draws on statistical data from a customer survey with several thousand samples and wide coverage. This methodology identifies multiple consumer segments to help companies address core organizational issues, achieve a well-designed marketing mix, reach growth targets, and more effectively engage their market. In the case of China's middle class, Monitor focused on purchasing behavior and demographic features, rather than income, as the key measures for understanding the middle class.

In one case, Monitor examined the correlation between consumer occupation and purchasing decisions within the tourism industry, the results of which allowed companies to customize their tourist packages more effectively. Monitor found three distinct segments of Chinese tourists: business, leisure, and backpacking travelers. Business travelers have fairly stable travel schedules throughout the year. They are reimbursed for some expenses and tend to spend more than leisure travelers. Leisure travelers enjoy sightseeing and recreational activities and tend to be more cost-conscious and self-organized. Chinese backpackers are willing to spend more and care most about uniqueness and experience. They want more personalized services, such as global positioning systems and specially trained tour guides. Unlike US backpackers, they have money and time and backpack mainly to be fashionable and gain new experiences.

In another case, an examination of the different levels of daily exercise among men and women revealed that although men tend to exercise at a more or less constant rate throughout their lives, women exercise less after marriage and still less after having children. This information helped sportswear companies

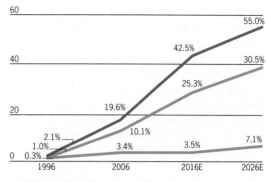

% of total China households **% of total urban households**
% of total rural households

Note: E = estimate
Sources: Global Demographics, DRC, and Monitor

Figure 1: Middle-class Consumer Households as a Percentage of Total Households, 1996–2026

identify which demographic segments were most profitable to target.

Applying the action segmentation methodology to the Chinese middle class, Monitor identified six sub-segments within the group, each with its own unique needs and consumption patterns. These include Early Heavy Buyers, the Smarts, the Quality-Oriented, Trend Followers, Driven Businesspeople, and Value Seekers.

To serve the specific needs of China's diverse middle class, companies must understand the desires of these six sub-segments and learn how to reach them. Early Heavy Buyers are energetic consumers, consisting primarily of professionals in tertiary industries and junior managers at multinational corporations. They tend to be young and well-educated, with an interest in and exposure to the world outside China. As consumers, they are early adopters of the latest products and aggressively seek out fashion that can help them stand out from their peers. Because they serve as trendsetters, members of this group actively search for information online and share that information with peers. They predominantly make purchases online or by mail order and have a high willingness to spend, especially on discretionary goods such as fashion items and lifestyle products and services. This group of trendsetters stands out from Trend Followers, who attempt to emulate Early Heavy Buyers in certain ways but approach purchasing decisions differently. Trend Followers tend to be junior white-collar workers and civil servants who have some leisure time and a stable salary but are new to the middle class and have less room for discretionary spending. They are less well-informed than Early Heavy Buyers and consequently place more emphasis on the shopping experience. They are also more price sensitive. Though Early Heavy Buyers may be more concerned with being the first to get a new product, Trend Followers will wait for discounts and tend to take advantage of promotions.

Like Trend Followers, Value Seekers are usually junior white collar office workers or government employees. As their incomes rise, they increasingly demand better quality and service, but remain sensitive to price. Though they purchase some goods from relatively inexpensive luxury brands to help show their status, they remain more concerned about value than other middle-class segments. Trend Followers may choose products that are in fashion, while Value Seekers tend to look for the best quality-to-price ratio regardless of how popular the item may be at the time.

The final three—the Smarts, the Quality-Oriented, and Driven Businesspeople—tend to be older and to have been in the middle class longer. The Smarts are usually more sophisticated shoppers who prefer to buy from specialty stores and boutiques instead of major outlets. They regularly order business and fashion magazines to stay on top of trends but also rely on word of mouth.

Like the Smarts, Driven Businesspeople are willing to pay premiums for convenience. Driven Businesspeople are relatively wealthy and lead extremely busy lives. They do not have much time to gather information and compare different brands or clothes, but they have higher purchasing power. They usually trust friends'

recommendations, develop brand preferences before they buy, and are not price sensitive. They are experienced consumers with high degrees of brand loyalty, especially in fashion. For this group, product and service quality are much more important than price. The Quality-Oriented share much in common with the Smarts and Driven Businesspeople but tend to have more leisure time. More than either of those groups, family is a priority for the Quality-Oriented and has a strong influence on their purchasing decisions. For example, large markets and department stores that carry a range of products important to a family are the major purchasing channels for the Quality-Oriented, and television is their dominant information resource for new products.

Monitor helped a sportswear client target two of the six middle class segments—Driven Businesspeople and Value Seekers—by understanding different buying habits. To better target Driven Businesspeople, Monitor recommended that its client market products in mid-range to high-end gyms and fitness clubs, where many businesspeople usually go, to develop brand awareness and attract customers. Monitor also recommended that its client place mid-to-high-end products in department stores and flagship shops, where Driven Businesspeople usually go to buy sportswear. By contrast, to target Value Seekers, Monitor recommended that the client become more aware of Value Seekers' tendency to spend time comparing products, shopping at hypermarkets, and buying less expensive products.

WHAT IT MEANS FOR YOUR BUSINESS

There is no denying the enormous benefit that companies can gain from a better understanding of China's emerging middle class. Marketing effectively to any group of middle-class consumers requires an understanding of the needs of specific segments and the recognition of which segments provide the greatest potential profitability for a particular product.

Bicycle Theft

MyWritingLab™

Shane D. Johnson, Aiden Sidebottom, and Adam Thorpe

The Office of Community Oriented Policing Services (COPS) in the US Department of Justice is dedicated to advancing the practice of community police in the United States. It works principally distributing information and making grants to police departments. COPS makes available a series of reports on common policing problems, helping police analyze and address problems. This excerpt is taken from *Bicycle Theft*, Problem-Oriented Guides for Police, No. 52. Its authors Shane D. Johnson and Aiden Sidebottom are researchers in Crime Science at the University of London, and Adam Thorpe is a researcher involved in the Design Against Crime initiative.

Return to these questions after you have finished reading.

Analyzing the Reading

1. According to the authors, why is bicycle theft a low-priority crime for police?

2. Have you or a friend had your bicycle stolen? Did you or your friend report the crime to police? If no, why didn't you make a report? If yes, what was the response of the police?

3. Interview a campus police officer at your school to learn what is being done to prevent bike theft.

4. What do the authors suggest police might do to lower the number of stolen bicycles?

Exploring Ideas and Issues

Many college students are well aware that bike theft is a major problem. Transportation Alternatives estimates that over a million bicycles are stolen annually, and most thefts are not reported. The FBI reports that the value of stolen bicycles and parts each year is over $350 million. A major cause of the problem is that nearly all bike thieves get a free pass. Police have little incentive to pursue bike thieves. Identifying suspects is difficult because usually the thief is unknown to the victim. Victims also often lack proof of ownership, which means that even if the police recover the bike and identify the thief, the suspect will be released if the victim didn't register the bike or keep the receipt. Furthermore, if thieves want to steal parts, locks secure only the locked parts of the bike.

1. Bicycling has many advantages for the health of individuals and the quality of the air we breathe. Many cities have expanded dedicated bike lanes and built new bike paths separated from traffic. Nevertheless, bike theft works against promoting bicycling. Many people cannot afford to replace a stolen bicycle and many others don't. Write an essay about what your city or campus might do to prevent bicycle thefts such as installing more bike racks, providing more surveillance, educating students on secure methods of locking, and offering electronic bike tags.

2. The country with the highest rate of bicycle ownership is the Netherlands, with one bicycle for every person. The Dutch make 27% of all trips by bicycle. Amsterdam is one of the most bicycle-friendly large cities in the world. Yet bike theft remains a big problem. Research what the Dutch are doing to prevent bike theft in comparison to the United States.

3. Japan is another nation with a high percentage of people owning bicycles (about 57%). Japanese people frequently ride bicycles to train stations for health reasons and to avoid traffic jams. Often they do not lock their bicycles, yet the rate of theft is low. Write about why bicycle theft is much rarer in Japan than in the United States and affluent European countries like Norway and Sweden.

BICYCLE THEFT

General Description of the Problem

Bicycle theft is typically seen as a low police priority, its impact and magnitude often overlooked because police often consider incidents on a case-by-case basis. This picture is often misleading, however, and when viewed at the aggregate level, bicycle theft represents a much larger problem, one with harmful economic and societal effects that warrant greater police attention.

The Rise of the Bicycle

The bicycle has become increasingly popular as a healthier and environmentally friendlier mode of transport. In London, for example, cycle use has increased by 83 percent between 2000 and 2007. In the United States, between 1992 and 2006, bicycle sales have increased from 15.3 million to 18.2 million per year (an increase of roughly 20 percent), illustrating an increase in cycle use there. While cycles enjoy the greatest share of transit options within campus towns, several major towns and cities such as Portland, Oregon, are continually improving cycling infrastructure to encourage cycling. Moreover, anticipating consumer demand, General Motors has developed the Flex-Fix® system, a retractable bicycle rack that is hidden in a car's bumper. These changes in bicycle usage and provision have been influenced in recent years by the following:

- Increased awareness of the detrimental effect of automobile carbon dioxide emissions, and pursuit of air quality and emission reduction targets
- Concerns over growing traffic congestion and accompanying noise pollution
- Rising levels (and fear) of obesity and heart disease
- Recognition that most trips are relatively short, or "bike-sized"
- Savings in road maintenance and improvement of street infrastructure
- Responses to policies such as charging fees to alleviate traffic congestion.

Several studies suggest that fear of cycle theft may discourage bicycle use, and that many bicycle theft victims do not buy a replacement. Combating bicycle theft, therefore, is a necessary step toward increasing the use of this sustainable form of transport, an increase that unexpectedly may also improve cyclist safety. To elaborate, a recent international review of programs to encourage walking and cycling found strong evidence indicating that as the number of cyclists and walkers increased, the frequency of collisions between those groups and motorists actually decreased. The authors concluded that an effective means of improving the safety of cyclists and walkers is therefore to *increase* the numbers of people cycling and walking. Despite this, little attention has been paid to the prevention of bicycle theft. Car theft has received much more attention, for example, yet according to data collected as part of the International Crime Victim Survey, for all countries for which data were available (including the United States), bicycle owners are far more likely to have their bikes stolen (4.7 percent) than car owners their cars (1.2 percent) and motorcyclists their motorcycles (1.9 percent).

Bicycle Theft Data

Understanding the problem of bicycle theft is hampered because police data typically underrepresent the problem. This is illustrated by data from the International Crime Victim Survey (2000), which show that across the 17 countries surveyed (including the United States), on average only 56 percent of bicycle thefts were reported to the police.

U.S. crime statistics are collated using both National Crime Victim Survey (NCVS) data from a yearly national survey, and data recorded by the police. Comparing the two data sources highlights the problem of underreporting. For example, in 2004, bicycle theft accounted for 3.6 percent of all incidents of larceny (Federal Bureau of Investigation, 2005), which equates to more than 250,000 bicycles stolen each year. According to an estimate from the NCVS, in 2006 the number of incidents of theft-of or theft-from bicycles was more like 1.3 million (just under 2.5 incidents per minute). This suggests that for every crime reported, another four (or more) may have occurred.

Interviews with bicycle theft victims indicate that underreporting is largely due to victims' belief that the police are not interested in bicycle theft and cannot do anything about catching the offender and returning the stolen bicycle. A further reason for an underrepresentation of the problem is that police departments record bicycle theft in different ways that, however inadvertently, may serve to conceal the full scope of the problem. For example, police may record a bicycle theft as a burglary from a residential property.

Clearance Rates

Clearance rates for bicycle theft remain consistently low. In the United States, 18.3 percent of incidents of larceny-theft were cleared by arrest, but this figure (which includes all categories of larceny) is likely to be a gross overestimate of the arrest rate for bicycle theft. For example, in Sweden, only 1 percent of bicycle thefts are cleared by arrest. One reason for this is that there typically exists little relationship between the victim and the offender, and hence it is difficult to identify suspects. Bicycle theft is also largely a crime of stealth, or one that goes unnoticed or unchallenged. A further problem is proof of ownership. As will be discussed below, even when crimes are reported to (and recorded by) the police, the majority of bicycle owners cannot supply sufficient details to assist in an investigation. As a consequence, even when an offender is detained for cycle theft, if the owner cannot provide proof of ownership for the retrieved cycle, then the suspect may be released without charge and may be given the stolen bike on release. Addressing the proof-of-ownership problem is important to alleviate storage costs for recovered bikes and improve the process of bicycle identification, recovery, and reunification with legitimate owners.

Offenders

Not all bicycles are stolen for financial gain. Some offenders may take a bicycle simply to get from one place to another, and then abandon it. Research suggests that the motivations of bicycle thieves can be categorized in the following way:

- **To joyride**—those who steal any type of bicycle for transportation and/or enjoyment. These offenders generally abandon the stolen bicycle after use. Younger offenders (16 and under) typically fit this group.
- **To trade for cash**—those who exploit easy opportunities to steal any type of bicycle and trade it for cash or goods (such as drugs).
- **To fill a request**—those who steal specific types of bicycles to order.

Understanding what types of offenders steal bicycles in your area can inform your approach to crime prevention. Unfortunately, low clearance rates for this type of crime make it difficult to gather detailed information on active bicycle thieves. Available evidence does indicate, however, that the majority of offenders are male and below the age of 20. Moreover, an examination of the frequency with which bicycles are abandoned can provide useful insights into offenders' motivations. For example, in a bicycle theft study in Ellensberg, Washington, police recovered 25 percent of stolen bicycles, suggesting that around 25 percent of bicycles were probably stolen by "joyrider" offenders. In a Dayton, Ohio, police initiative, the problem was reversed, with approximately 80 percent of stolen bicycles being recovered, suggesting that many more offenses were committed for the purposes of transportation or enjoyment than for financial gain.

It is important to be aware that victims and offenders may not always represent distinct groups. For example, studies suggest that victims of bicycle theft sometimes either steal bicycles themselves to compensate for their loss, or knowingly buy bicycles that are themselves stolen. This type of pattern illustrates a concept referred to as a *crime multiplier*, whereby one offense leads to the commission of several others. These offenses may include the fencing or receiving of stolen goods. Thus, a single bicycle theft does not necessarily equate to one offense, but may lead to a series of related crimes.

Recovery Rates

As noted above, not all stolen bicycles are sold for financial gain. The police recover many of them. Nonetheless, few recovered bicycles are returned to their rightful owners, often because of the proof-of-ownership problem. Surveys indicate that most cyclists do not know their bicycle serial number, nor can they provide legal evidence of bicycle ownership, such as a purchase receipt. As a result, the police cannot return many recovered bikes to their owners and, instead, store them until they can be checked as roadworthy and donated to charity or sold at auction.

Bicycle theft is largely ignored by police.

The Current and Future Consequences of Climate Change

MyWritingLab™

National Aeronautics and Space Administration

The National Aeronautics and Space Administration (NASA) is the government agency responsible for the space program but its mission involves better understanding Earth. NASA's Earth science mission studies changes in the oceans, the land, and Earth's atmosphere. The scientists at NASA investigate how climate change is affecting people worldwide. For example, NASA's Soil Moisture Active Passive (SMAP) satellite collects data that farmers and water managers need. Farmers who know how much moisture is in the ground can make informed decisions about when to plant crops for the best yields. NASA's summary article below gives a long-term picture on the effects of climate change.

Return to these questions after you have finished reading.

Analyzing the Reading

1. Who is the audience for this report? How much does the audience have to know about climate change to understanding the forecasts contained in the report?

2. NASA reports the findings of the Intergovernmental Panel on Climate Change (IPCC), a scientific intergovernmental body established under the auspices of the United Nations. The IPCC does not carry out its own research but provides summaries of peer-reviewed scientific literature. While the IPCC concludes that some regions will benefit from climate change and some will be harmed, the IPCC's ultimate objective is to stabilize the increase of greenhouse gasses in the atmosphere. In contrast, the NASA Web page describes projected effects of climate change, but NASA does not propose solutions. Why do you think NASA gives the projected risks but doesn't argue for changes in human behavior?

3. Does NASA's Web page succeed in conveying the importance of the information? Why or why not?

Exploring Ideas and Issues

The description of climate change as "global warming" has been misleading. While the temperatures in the Arctic and Antarctic have indeed risen rapidly, the effects elsewhere have not followed a consistent pattern. In general, weather has moved toward the extremes. Places that have high levels of precipitation have experienced more rain and snow; places that suffer from drought have become dryer.

1. One of the arguments against taking steps to mitigate climate change in the United States is that the US is a small player on the global stage. At a time when China is adding a new coal-fired electric plant every week, some argue that it hardly matters what policy the US adopts. Others argue that the US should be setting a good example for the rest of the world to follow. Do research to find out what you can about how much the United States, Europe, India, and China are causing climate change.

2. Climate change has been ongoing in the recent history of Earth. Around 12,000 years ago sea levels were 140 meters below what they are today. Humans walked from Europe to England as late as 8,500 years ago. The end of the last ice age brought a rapid sea rise, and many of the places where people lived then are now under water. Given that humans survived an enormous rise in sea levels, are rising oceans a threat to humans today? Or does the fact that the global population has risen from a few million 12,000 years ago to over 7 billion today mean that the threat is much more serious?

3. Several scientists including E. O. Wilson and Elizabeth Kolbert argue that climate change is leading to a mass extinction on the scale of the asteroid impact that wiped out the dinosaurs. Do you agree or disagree with Wilson that animals have at minimum a basic right to exist? If you agree, would you include insects and tiny forms of life?

The Current and Future Consequences of Climate Change

Global climate change has already had observable effects on the environment. Glaciers have shrunk, ice on rivers and lakes is breaking up earlier, plant and animal ranges have shifted and trees are flowering sooner.

Effects that scientists had predicted in the past would result from global climate change are now occurring: loss of sea ice, accelerated sea level rise and longer, more intense heat waves.

"Taken as a whole, the range of published evidence indicates that the net damage costs of climate change are likely to be significant and to increase over time."

—Intergovernmental Panel on Climate Change

Scientists have high confidence that global temperatures will continue to rise for decades to come, largely due to greenhouse gasses produced by human activities. The Intergovernmental Panel on Climate Change (IPCC), which includes more than 1,300 scientists from the United States and other countries, forecasts a temperature rise of 2.5 to 10 degrees Fahrenheit over the next century.

According to the IPCC, the extent of climate change effects on individual regions will vary over time and with the ability of different societal and environmental systems to mitigate or adapt to change.

The IPCC predicts that increases in global mean temperature of less than 1.8 to 5.4 degrees Fahrenheit (1 to 3 degrees Celsius) above 1990 levels will produce beneficial impacts in some regions and harmful ones in others. Net annual costs will increase over time as global temperatures increase.

"Taken as a whole," the IPCC states, "the range of published evidence indicates that the net damage costs of climate change are likely to be significant and to increase over time."[1]

Below are some of the regional impacts of global change forecast by the IPCC:

- ❑ **North America:** Decreasing snowpack in the western mountains; 5-20 percent increase in yields of rain-fed agriculture in some regions; increased frequency, intensity and duration of heat waves in cities that currently experience them.[2]

- ❑ **Latin America:** Gradual replacement of tropical forest by savannah in eastern Amazonia; risk of significant biodiversity loss through species extinction in many tropical areas; significant changes in water availability for human consumption, agriculture and energy generation.[3]

- ❑ **Europe:** Increased risk of inland flash floods; more frequent coastal flooding and increased erosion from storms and sea level rise; glacial retreat in mountainous areas; reduced snow cover and winter tourism; extensive species losses; reductions of crop productivity in southern Europe.[4]

- ❑ **Africa:** By 2020, between 75 and 250 million people are projected to be exposed to increased water stress; yields from rain-fed agriculture could be reduced by up to 50 percent in some regions by 2020; agricultural production, including access to food, may be severely compromised.[5]

- ❑ **Asia:** Freshwater availability projected to decrease in Central, South, East and Southeast Asia by the 2050s; coastal areas will be at risk due to increased flooding; death rate from disease associated with floods and droughts expected to rise in some regions.[6]

Global Climate Change: Recent Impacts[7]

Phenomena	Likelihood that trend occurred in late 20th century
Cold days, cold nights and frost less frequent over land areas	Very likely
More frequent hot days and nights	Very likely
Heat waves more frequent over most land areas	Likely
Increased incidence of extreme high sea level*	Likely
Global area affected by drought has increased (since 1970s)	Likely in some regions
Increase in intense tropical cyclone activity in North Atlantic (since 1970)	Likely in some regions

* Excluding tsunamis, which are not due to climate change.

Global Climate Change: Future Trends[8]

Phenomena	Likelihood of trend
Contraction of snow cover areas, increased thaw in permafrost regions, decrease in sea ice extent	Virtually certain
Increased frequency of hot extremes, heat waves and heavy precipitation	Very likely to occur
Increase in tropical cyclone intensity	Likely to occur
Precipitation increases in high latitudes	Very likely to occur
Precipitation decreases in subtropical land regions	Very likely to occur
Decreased water resources in many semi-arid areas, including western U.S. and Mediterranean basin	High confidence

Definitions of likelihood ranges used to express the assessed probability of occurrence: *virtually certain >99%, very likely >90%, likely >66%.*

Source: *Summary for Policymakers, IPCC Synthesis report, November 2007* http://www.ipcc.ch/

[1]IPCC 2007, Summary for Policymakers, in *Climate Change 2007: Impacts, Adaptation and Vulnerability. Contribution of Working Group II to the Fourth Assessment Report of the Intergovernmental Panel on Climate Change,* Cambridge University Press, Cambridge, UK, p. 17.

[2]IPCC 2007, Summary for Policymakers, in *Climate Change 2007: Synthesis Report,* p. 11.

[3]Ibid.

[4]Ibid.

[5]Ibid.

[6]Ibid.

[7]Adapted from IPCC 2007, Summary for Policymakers, *Synthesis Report,* p. 13.

[8]Adapted from Ibid, p. 8.

A Degree of Difference

So, the Earth's average temperature has increased about 1 degree Fahrenheit during the 20th century. What's the big deal?

One degree may sound like a small amount, but it's an unusual event in our planet's recent history. Earth's climate record, preserved in tree rings, ice cores, and coral reefs, shows that the global average temperature is stable over long periods of time. Furthermore, small changes in temperature correspond to enormous changes in the environment.

For example, at the end of the last ice age, when the Northeast United States was covered by more than 3,000 feet of ice, average temperatures were only 5 to 9 degrees cooler than today.

The main source for water in Las Vegas, Lake Mead, is in danger of emptying by 2025. The reduced flow of the Colorado River also threatens thirty million people in Arizona and California and much of the nation's agricultural production.

MyPlate Brochure
US Department of Agriculture

Today's US Department of Agriculture (USDA) grew out of the Department of Agriculture founded during the Lincoln administration. Grover Cleveland elevated its commissioner to Cabinet status in 1889. The USDA develops and executes federal policies on farming, agriculture, forestry, and food. MyPlate is the eighth nutrition guideline since 1916. The guide has been updated every decade or so to reflect advances in nutritional science, consumer behavior, and media.

Return to these questions after you have finished reading.

Analyzing the Reading

1. Examine MyPlate's photos, graphics, and language, and infer the audience. To whom is the brochure "speaking"? To whom is it not speaking?

2. The brochure is informational, but what other purposes might the author had had in mind? Discuss the brochure's features, including text and graphics, to support your ideas about alternative purposes.

3. The information and advice in this brochure also might have been presented as an essay, a research report, or other forms of informational writing. Discuss the effect of the brochure format on the audience, purpose, and thesis.

4. "Read" the MyPlate logo (dinner setting with food groups). How do you interpret the nutritional information embedded in the logo?

Exploring Ideas and Issues

In 1920, public health expert and Yale professor Charles-Edward Amory Winslow declared that public health is "the science and art of preventing disease, prolonging life and promoting health through the organized efforts and informed choices of society, organizations, public and private, communities and individuals." The USDA's efforts to educate citizens about healthy lifestyle choices are part of a larger effort to improve public health. Poor public health not only reduces the quality and length of individual lives; it has significant economic impact, too. According to the Center for Disease Control, for example, America spends over $130 billion annually on medical care of adult smokers. The news, however, is not all bleak. Partly due to public information campaigns by government and public health organizations, the number of both adult and youth smokers has been cut in half since the Surgeon General's initial 1964 report on the dangers of smoking. Public attitudes have changed too, as evidenced by a Gallup poll in 2011, which found a majority of Americans supported smoking bans in all public places.

1. Nutrition, exercise, and healthy living discussions, advertisements, and advice have become central to the American national conversation. Write an informative narrative essay in the first (about yourself) or third person (about somebody else) about the challenges and effects of healthy lifestyle choices.

2. "Diets" are a multimillion-dollar industry, but much debate exists regarding the effectiveness of dieting. Write an informational research report exploring the history and effectiveness of various diets in US history.

3. Create a graphical presentation (brochure, Web site, collage, or other multimedia) for a specific audience explaining a controversial, contemporary lifestyle or public health issue. Issues might include smoking (tobacco, vapor, hookahs), legalizing marijuana, bariatric surgery, and so on.

Let's eat
for the health of it

ChooseMyPlate.gov

Start by choosing one or more tips to help you ...

**Build a
healthy plate**

**Cut back on
foods high in solid
fats, added sugars,
and salt**

**Eat the right
amount of
calories for you**

**Be physically
active your way**

▶ Build a healthy plate

Before you eat, think about what goes on your plate or in your cup or bowl. Foods like vegetables, fruits, whole grains, low-fat dairy products, and lean protein foods contain the nutrients you need without too many calories. Try some of these options.

Make half your plate fruits and vegetables.

- Eat red, orange, and dark-green vegetables, such as tomatoes, sweet potatoes, and broccoli, in main and side dishes.
- Eat fruit, vegetables, or unsalted nuts as snacks—they are nature's original fast foods.

Switch to skim or 1% milk.

- They have the same amount of calcium and other essential nutrients as whole milk, but less fat and calories.
- Try calcium-fortified soy products as an alternative to dairy foods.

Make at least half your grains whole.

- Choose 100% whole-grain cereals, breads, crackers, rice, and pasta.
- Check the ingredients list on food packages to find whole-grain foods.

Vary your protein food choices.

- Twice a week, make seafood the protein on your plate.
- Eat beans, which are a *natural* source of fiber and protein.
- Keep meat and poultry portions small and lean.

Keep your food safe to eat—learn more at www.FoodSafety.gov.

▶ Cut back on foods high in solid fats, added sugars, and salt

Many people eat foods with too much solid fats, added sugars, and salt (sodium). Added sugars and fats load foods with extra calories you don't need. Too much sodium may increase your blood pressure.

Choose foods and drinks with little or no added sugars.

- Drink water instead of sugary drinks. There are about 10 packets of sugar in a 12-ounce can of soda.
- Select fruit for dessert. Eat sugary desserts less often.
- Choose 100% fruit juice instead of fruit-flavored drinks.

Look out for salt (sodium) in foods you buy— it all adds up.

- Compare sodium in foods like soup, bread, and frozen meals—and choose the foods with lower numbers.
- Add spices or herbs to season food without adding salt.

Eat fewer foods that are high in solid fats.

- Make major sources of saturated fats—such as cakes, cookies, ice cream, pizza, cheese, sausages, and hot dogs—occasional choices, not everyday foods.
- Select lean cuts of meats or poultry and fat-free or low-fat milk, yogurt, and cheese.
- Switch from solid fats to oils when preparing food.*

*Examples of solid fats and oils	
Solid Fats	**Oils**
Beef, pork, and chicken fat	Canola oil
Butter, cream, and milk fat	Corn oil
Coconut, palm, and palm kernel oils	Cottonseed oil
Hydrogenated oil	Olive oil
Partially hydrogenated oil	Peanut oil
Shortening	Safflower oil
Stick margarine	Sunflower oil
	Tub (soft) margarine
	Vegetable oil

▶ Eat the right amount of calories for you

Everyone has a personal calorie limit. Staying within yours can help you get to or maintain a healthy weight. People who are successful at managing their weight have found ways to keep track of how much they eat in a day, even if they don't count every calorie.

Enjoy your food, but eat less.

- Get your personal daily calorie limit at www.Choose**MyPlate**.gov and keep that number in mind when deciding what to eat.
- Think before you eat ... is it worth the calories?
- Avoid oversized portions.
- Use a smaller plate, bowl, and glass.
- Stop eating when you are satisfied, not full.

Cook more often at home, where *you* are in control of what's in your food.

When eating out, choose lower calorie menu options.

- Check posted calorie amounts.
- Choose dishes that include vegetables, fruits, and/or whole grains.
- Order a smaller portion or share when eating out.

Write down what you eat to keep track of how much you eat.

If you drink alcoholic beverages, do so sensibly—limit to 1 drink a day for women or to 2 drinks a day for men.

▶ Be physically active your way

Pick activities that you like and start by doing what you can, at least 10 minutes at a time. Every bit adds up, and the health benefits increase as you spend more time being active.

Note to parents

What you eat and drink and your level of physical activity are important for your own health, and also for your children's health.

You are your children's most important role model. Your children pay attention to what you ***do*** more than what you ***say***.

You can do a lot to help your children develop healthy habits for life by providing and eating healthy meals and snacks. For example, don't just ***tell*** your children to eat their vegetables—***show*** them that you eat and enjoy vegetables every day.

Use food labels to help you make better choices

Most packaged foods have a Nutrition Facts label and an ingredients list. For a healthier you, use this tool to make smart food choices quickly and easily.

Check for calories. Be sure to look at the serving size and how many servings you are actually consuming. If you double the servings you eat, you double the calories.

Choose foods with lower calories, saturated fat, *trans* fat, and sodium.

Check for added sugars using the ingredients list. When a sugar is close to first on the ingredients list, the food is high in added sugars. Some names for added sugars include sucrose, glucose, high fructose corn syrup, corn syrup, maple syrup, and fructose.

Dietary Guidelines for Americans

The *Dietary Guidelines for Americans, 2010* are the best science-based advice on how to eat for health. The Guidelines encourage all Americans to eat a healthy diet and be physically active.

Improving what you eat and being active will help to reduce your risk of chronic diseases such as diabetes, heart disease, some cancers, and obesity. Taking the steps in this brochure will help you follow the Guidelines.

For more information, go to:

- www.DietaryGuidelines.gov
- www.Choose**MyPlate**.gov
- www.Health.gov/paguidelines
- www.HealthFinder.gov

USDA Publication number: Home and Garden Bulletin No. 232-CP
HHS Publication number: HHS-ODPHP-2010-01-DGA-B

June 2011

The U.S. Departments of Agriculture and Health and Human Services are equal opportunity providers and employers.

A Map of the British and French Dominions in North America, 1755

MyWritingLab™

John Mitchell

John Mitchell (1711–1768) was neither a mapmaker nor a geographer but a practicing physician and botanist in coastal Virginia. He received his medical training at Edinburgh University in Scotland, and after returning to Virginia, he became ill and left for London in 1746. In London he became upset at the lack of interest in the American colonies, especially the threat from the French. Mitchell created his first map of North America in 1750, and it so impressed Lord Halifax that he wanted Mitchell to make a larger and better map. The map printed in 1755 was an impressive 4 feet 6 inches by 6 feet 5 inches. The map shows a strong pro-British bias in extending the colonies across the continent into established Spanish territory west of the Mississippi and claiming the land of the Iroquois, allies of Britain, as British territory. When the American Revolutionary War ended in 1783, the Mitchell Map was the most accurate available, and it was used to draw the boundaries of the new United States.

Return to these questions after you have finished reading.

Analyzing the Reading

1. What do you notice that is different about the Mitchell Map from a map today?

2. Names on maps are as important as the boundaries drawn. Above New France on the Mitchell Map there is the pink color, indicating British territory even though much of this territory had not been explored. A notation above New France says: "The long and barbarous names lately given to some of the northern parts of Canada and the lakes we have not inserted, as they are of no use, and uncertain authority." Why were these names omitted?

3. The Mitchell Map identifies the locations of Indian villages, including those that no longer exist such as the Tuscaroras. (See the detail below.) What does the map imply about the future for Indians east of the Mississippi in British eyes?

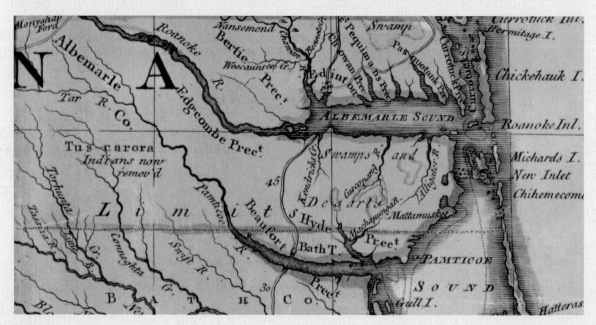

Exploring Ideas and Issues

In 1992 Denis Wood published *The Power of Maps*, which has led to what has been called the "new cartographies." The key idea is that maps do not so much represent the world as they make arguments through careful choice of content. In their 2008 book, *The Natures of Maps*, Wood and Fels insist that "The map is not a picture." Instead "everything about a map, from top to bottom, is an argument."

1. Do a search for "tourist map" and a place (e.g., Cancun). Explain in a short analysis what argument the map is making.

2. What we consider a "normal" map of Earth puts the Northern Hemisphere on top, but the reason for doing so is nothing more than habit and prejudice. Citizens of Australia and New Zealand are fond of maps that put Antarctica on top. Things seem upside down to us, but it is just another point of view. Our word "orientation" comes from the Latin *oriens*, the Latin word for "rising" or "east," because that's where the sun rises. Change the orientation of a map of your town or state or of a country. Write about the difference that a change in orientation makes.

3. Compare the street and satellite maps of major mapping services such as *Bing Maps*, *Google Maps*, and *OpenStreetMap*. At first glance these services provide similar maps, but if you look more closely, you will find subtle differences in how they use labels and colors, differences in what they choose to represent (for example, subway stops, bus stops, restaurants, and so on), and differences in how they give directions. Write a short essay that compares how two or three of the map services represent a particular place. Include screen captures that illustrate the differences that you find.

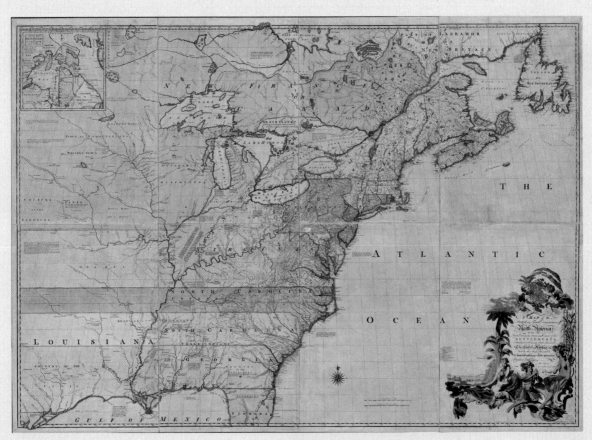

How to Write to Inform

These steps for the process of informative writing may not progress as neatly as this chart might suggest. Writing is not an assembly-line process. As you write, you are constantly reading what you have written and rethinking.

Keep your readers in mind while you are writing, and if you don't know who your readers might be, imagine someone. What questions might that person have? Where would they appreciate a more detailed explanation?

1 EXPLORE THE WRITING TASK

- Read the assignment, carefully noting key words.

- Determine what kind of writing is required. Who are the potential readers?

- Find the limits of your topic. What do you not need to cover? How far do you need to go in breaking down your explanations?

- Review class notes and textbooks; talk to instructor and peers.

- Search for topic ideas in Web subject directories and your library's online catalog.

2 FOCUS YOUR TOPIC AND WRITE A THESIS

- Within the scope of the assignment, explore what interests you.

- Ask yourself, "Who else will be interested in this topic?"

- Make a list of issues, questions, or problems associated with the topic area.

- Make idea maps about possible topics.

- Discuss possible choices with your peers, coworkers, or instructor.

- Ask questions:
  What happened? What do people need to know?

  Who is my audience?

  How can I connect with them on this topic?

- Narrow your topic. When you learn more about your topic, you should be able to identify one aspect or concept that you can cover thoroughly.

- Write a working thesis that describes what you plan to report or explain.

- If you are unsure if you can follow through with your thesis, do additional research and revise your thesis.

3
WRITE A DRAFT

- Write your revised thesis and main points.

- Think about how you will organize your main points.

- Make a working outline that lists the sections of your essay.

- Draft an introduction that will make readers interested in your subject.

- Build the organization by identifying the topic of each paragraph.

- Draft a conclusion that does more than summarize.

- Write an engaging title.

- If you have statistical information to present, consider using charts or graphs.

4
REVISE, REVISE, REVISE

- Reorganize your ideas for clarity.

- Add detail or further explanation where needed.

- Cut material that distracts from your thesis.

- Check that all key terms are defined.

- Frame your report with an introduction that interests readers and a conclusion that makes a point or raises an interesting question.

- Check that any sources are appropriately quoted or summarized and that they are documented correctly.

- Revise the title to be more accurate and to make readers more interested.

- Review the visual presentation of your report for readability and maximum impact.

5
SUBMITTED VERSION

- Make sure your finished writing meets all formatting requirements.

1: Explore the Writing Task

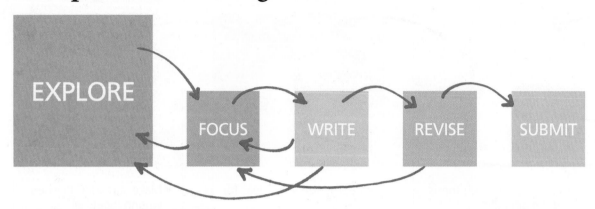

Analyze the assignment

Read your assignment slowly and carefully. Mark off any information about the length specified, date due, formatting, and other requirements. You can attend to this information later. At this point you want to zero in on the subject you will write about and how you will approach that subject.

What kind of informative writing is required?

Look for key words such as *analyze, compare and contrast*, or *explain*. Often these key words will help you in determining what direction to take.

- **Analyze:** Find connections among a set of facts, events, or things, and make them meaningful.

- **Compare and contrast:** Examine how two or more things are alike and how they differ.

- **Explain:** Go into detail about how something works or make an unfamiliar subject comprehensible.

Is the audience specified?

If the audience is mentioned in the assignment, how much will they know about your subject? How much background will you need to provide? What terms will you need to define?

Is the topic assigned?

If the topic is assigned, how much do you know about it? Think about which aspects might interest you. What angle or perspective might you take to make the topic interesting?

Are you able to choose a topic?

Think first about what is most interesting to you. Do you have any special knowledge about a hobby, job, or sport that you want to share with others? A good first step is to make an inventory of what you know. Make a list of possible ideas. After you write down as many ideas as you can, go back through the list and place a star beside the ideas that seem most promising.

- **What ideas can you find in your course notes, class discussions, and your textbooks?** Think about subjects raised in lectures, in class discussions, or in your textbooks for potential ideas.

- **What can you find in a database or online library catalog?**

- Subject directories on databases and your library's online catalog can be valuable sources of potential topics. See Chapter 20.

- **What might you find on the Web?** *Google* searches and other search engines often turn up promising ideas to pursue. *Yahoo* has a subject directory that breaks down large topics into subtopics. See Chapter 20.

- **What might you find doing field research?** Sometimes the information you need cannot be found in libraries or on the Web, and you have to collect the information firsthand through interviews, surveys, or observations. See Chapter 22.

WRITE NOW   MyWritingLab™

Make a mind map

A good way to explore a topic is to make a mind map. You can create a mind map by using pen and paper or presentation software including Google Docs, which is a free service that allows you to collaborate with others.

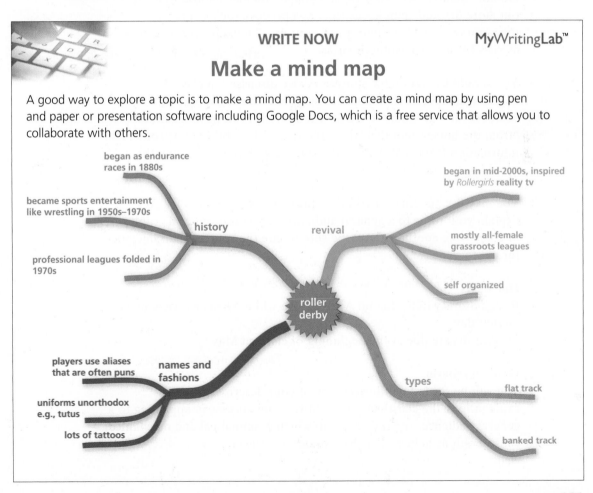

Writer at work

Astronomy 101
Writing Assignment #2

*Use examples
(Show, don't just tell)
Galaxy 999 shows
this process at work*

Explain an astronomical process, and the current theory that accounts for it, to a general audience. Use examples of specific phenomena to illustrate the process. Be sure to discuss observations or data that aren't well understood or don't fit the theory. Your paper should seek to make an astronomical process accessible and interesting to an average adult.

Do not "dumb down" your topic. Though you may choose to leave out more dry and complex aspects of a process, such as precise temperature ranges or time spans, your essay must be as accurate as possible given existing theories.

Keep it simple but be accurate. Interest

You should use reputable sources. As we discussed in class, newsmagazines and newspaper articles are fine as supporting sources, but you should make an attempt to get your information "from the horse's mouth." Given the ready availability of astronomical information from NASA and other publicly funded programs, this should not be difficult.

Check NASA

You may use any kind of visual features that you think helps you explain your topic to a general audience. If you reproduce a graph or chart from another source, be sure to cite the source. The same goes for photographs.

Due dates *Have two weeks for research and writing rough draft*
Rough drafts will be due on April 22. We will have peer review in class on that day.
Final drafts are due at the beginning of class on May 6.

Two more weeks to revise

Grading criteria
You will be graded on the accuracy of your descriptions and explanations, the clarity of your writing, your success in appealing to a general audience, and the extent to which grammatical and mechanical considerations help, rather than hinder, your essay.

Assess the assignment

Lakshmi Kotra wrote a report in response to this assignment in her Introduction to Astronomy course. She made the following notes and observations to help determine what her essay needed to accomplish, and to explore how she might find a good topic.

Highlight key words

Lakshmi began by highlighting the words in the assignment that gave her specific information about the writing tasks she was to perform.

Identify goals

Then, she made notes on the assignment sheet to specify what she needed to do.

Note time frame

She also made notes about the time frame she has to work in.

Plan strategy

Lakshmi made notes about possible sources for her paper. Then she sketched out a brief time line to follow.

<u>SOURCES</u>

- Go back over lecture notes—Unit 3 was easiest for me to understand so may be best for a general audience?

- Review theories—what makes an idea a theory; who decides what is the accepted theory?

- See book also, esp. Table of contents, for topic ideas.

- Library subject index

- Online subject index

- Check NASA archives online for good pictures. Maybe categories there would help too.

- Ask Dr. Jenson if we can do something we haven't covered in class yet.

***Get to the library by <u>Friday</u> so topic is ready over the weekend. See if Karen wants to go too. Check reference librarian hours first, just in case.

- Outline over the weekend so I have next week to ask Dr. Jenson for help with the rough draft, if I need it.

- Visuals will help make the essay interesting and appealing to a general audience, and also can help explain. So maybe pick two or three topics and then look at NASA images and other visuals to see what is available. This should help narrow down my choices.

2: Focus Your Topic and Write a Thesis

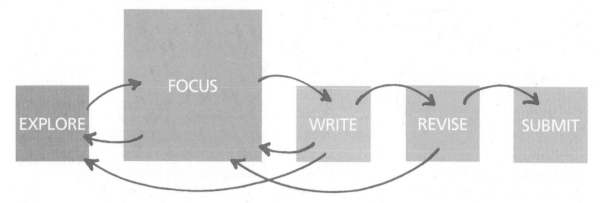

Choose a topic you will enjoy writing about

After you have done preliminary research and collected ideas, it's time to list possible topics and begin making connections. Circle the most interesting possibilities. Writing is fun when you discover new things along the way. If your topic isn't interesting for you, it likely won't be for your readers either.

Choose a topic that your readers will enjoy reading about

Readers may ask, "Why are you telling me this?" Your subject should be interesting to your readers. If the subject isn't one that is immediately interesting, think about ways you can make it so.

Choose a topic that either you know something about or for which you can find the information you need

A central difficulty with writing to inform is determining where to stop. The key to success is to limit the topic. Choose a topic for which you can find the information you need and which you can cover thoroughly in the space you have. If you choose an unfamiliar topic, you must be strongly committed to learning much about it in a short time.

Focus your topic and write a thesis

Look for ways of dividing large topics into smaller categories, and select one that is promising.

1. What is your topic exactly? (Try to state your answer in specific terms.)

   The grassroots revival and rapid spread of roller derby in the 2000s.

2. What points do you want to make about your topic?

   The revival of roller derby changed the character of roller derby from the staged sports entertainment of the 1950s–1970s period to a grassroots, women-organized, participatory sport that emphasizes athleticism.

3. What exactly is your purpose in this project? To analyze? compare? explain?

   Most people don't know about the revival of roller derby, so I will have to introduce the sport and explain who is involved, how it spread, and why it happened.

4. Develop a working thesis that draws on your answers to questions 1 and 2 and that reflects the purpose you described in your answer to question 3.

   The grassroots, women-organized revival and spread of roller derby in the 2000s reflects a new image of women as athletic and empowered.

STAYING ON TRACK
Evaluate your thesis

Your thesis should fulfill the assignment

If your assignment is informative, your purpose is not to argue something is good or bad (see Chapter 11), not to argue for a position (see Chapter 12), and not to argue for change (see Chapter 13).

OFF TRACK

The electoral college is an antiquated system that results in unfair election results.
(evaluates rather than informs)

ON TRACK

Considering the huge impact the electoral college system has on American presidential elections, it is surprising that few people understand how it actually works.

Your thesis should be interesting

If your readers already know everything that you have to say, you will bore them. Likewise, your thesis should be significant. Readers will care little about what you have to say if they find your subject trivial.

OFF TRACK

There are many steps involved before a bill becomes a law.
(vague, bland)

ON TRACK

Only a tiny fraction of the bills proposed in Congress will ever become laws, and of those, most will accrue so many bizarre amendments and riders that they will barely resemble the original document.

Your thesis should be focused

You cannot tell the story of the Cold War in five pages. Narrow your thesis to a topic you can treat in depth.

OFF TRACK

Many new products were developed in the 1950s to support the boom in housing construction.
(possibly interesting if particular products are described)

ON TRACK

The rush to create new housing for returning WWII veterans in the 1950s resulted in many houses that are now extremely hazardous to live in.

Writer at work

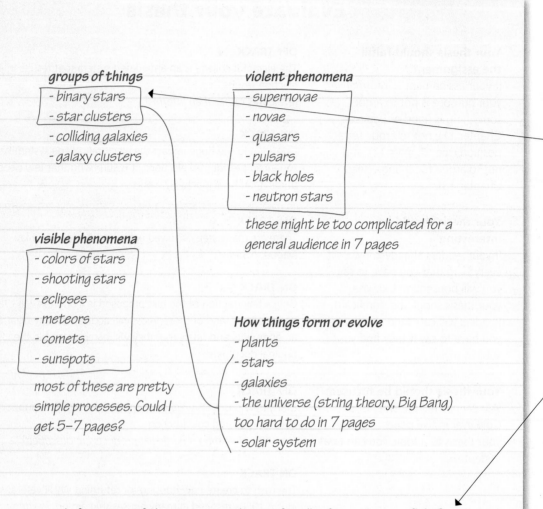

groups of things
- binary stars
- star clusters
- colliding galaxies
- galaxy clusters

violent phenomena
- supernovae
- novae
- quasars
- pulsars
- black holes
- neutron stars

these might be too complicated for a
general audience in 7 pages

visible phenomena
- colors of stars
- shooting stars
- eclipses
- meteors
- comets
- sunspots

most of these are pretty
simple processes. Could I
get 5–7 pages?

How things form or evolve
- plants
- stars
- galaxies
- the universe (string theory, Big Bang)
too hard to do in 7 pages
- solar system

Is formation of planets a normal part of stellar formation or a fluke?
Can binary star systems have planets?
How common are supernovae? Or black holes?
What will happen to the Sun when it runs out of hydrogen?
How do sunspots fit in with atomic processes in stars?
Why do stars start forming in the first place?

Map possible topics

Lakshmi Kotra began by reviewing her class notes and her textbooks. She also looked in the library's online catalog subject index and an online subject index. She listed all the possible topics she came across in these sources. Then she made an idea map of the topics that appealed to her, clustering types of theories, and adding new ones as they occurred to her. She made a few notes on some of her topic areas, describing how well they would meet the needs of her assignment. And she jotted down questions she had about some topics as well.

Narrow the search

Lakshmi narrowed her search by considering how complicated a topic she wanted to take on. Since she had to explain the theory to a general audience, she ruled out topics like black holes and string theory. She noticed that stellar processes showed up several times in her lists of interesting topics.

Identify the topic

Lakshmi settled on stellar formation as a theory that interested her and which she felt confident she could explain in layman's terms. Her preliminary research also indicated there was a wealth of observational data and photos that she could use in her report.

Find images and get source information

Lakshmi wanted to include photographs of star formation, and on NASA's Web site she located images that she could use legally. She carefully recorded all the information she would need to find the images again and to document the images in her paper.

AUTHOR: United States National Aeronautics and Space Administration

DATE: April 1, 1995

PAGE TITLE: The Eagle nebula.

SITE TITLE: Great Images in NASA

URL: grin.hq.nasa.gov/ABSTRACTS/GPN-2000-000987.html

197

3: Write a Draft

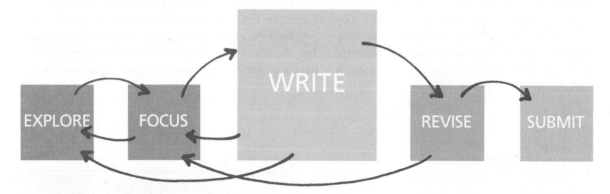

Organize your information

Gather your notes and other materials. Think about how you want to convey the information to your readers.

- If your subject matter occurs over time, you might want to use a chronological order.

- If you need to discuss several aspects, identify key concepts and think about how they relate to each other.

- If you are comparing two or more things, think about how these things are similar and how they are different.

Make a working outline

A working outline is a tool that you can use as you write your first draft. The more detailed it is, the better. List the sections in the order that you expect them to appear.

Working thesis: The grassroots, women-organized revival and spread of roller derby in the 2000s reflects a new image of women as athletic and empowered.

1. *Introduction: Give description of bout—loud rock music, noisy crowd, teams of five armored women*

2. *Brief history: began as endurance racing 1880s–1930s. Theatrical sports entertainment like wrestling in 1950s–1970s*

3. *Contemporary revival: Began in 2002 in Austin, Texas—grassroots, strictly amateur, open to women only with emphasis on athleticism*

4. *New image of women: aggressive attitudes, derby names often sexual puns, punk and "bad girl" costumes, lots of tattoos*

5. *Sudden growth in 2006: Reality TV show Rollergirls gave the sport exposure. Many new leagues and spread outside the U.S.*

6. *Move toward mainstream sports: In 2009 players in some leagues start using their real names.*

7. *Conclusion: Will roller derby remain popular or die like it did in the 1970s?*

Think of an effective title

An effective title motivates your readers to want to read what you have written.

DULL:
The Revival of Roller Derby in the 2000s

BETTER:
Tatts, Tutus, and Fishnets: The Grassroots Roller Derby Revival

Stay objective

You may have a strong opinion about your subject, but if your purpose is to inform rather than convince readers of your opinion, stay in the background. Readers appreciate a balanced, objective presentation.

Use quality sources

Unless you are writing about a subject well known to you, likely you will need to do library and online research. A well-written report is useless if the information is suspect. See Chapters 20 and 21 for how to find and evaluate sources.

Think about design

Headings are frequent in informative writing, especially in long essays and reports. A list of items usually reads better in numbered or bulleted points. Charts and graphs help readers to understand data, maps help them to understand locations, and photographs let them see what you are talking about.

STAYING ON TRACK
Write an effective introduction and conclusion

Write an effective introduction
Get off to a fast start. Cut to the chase: no empty sentences or big generalizations at the beginning.

OFF TRACK
Because we all live such busy, hectic lives in these modern times, everyone wants to know why we must wait for hours and hours at the airport before boarding a flight.
(boring, predictable beginning—a signal that the paper will be dull)

ON TRACK
It's a traveler's worst nightmare: the long line of people at the security gate, snaking back and forth across the waiting area. What exactly goes on in an airport screening area, and how does it help to keep us safe?

Write an effective conclusion
Remember that a summary of what you have just written is the weakest way to conclude. Think of something interesting for your reader to take away such as an unexpected implication or a provocative example.

OFF TRACK
In conclusion, we have seen how peer-to-peer file sharing works.
(ineffective; says only that the paper is finished)

ON TRACK
The peer-to-peer file-sharing process is relatively simple. Unfortunately, in many cases it is also illegal. It is ironic that a technology intended to help people has resulted in turning many of them into *de facto* criminals.
(ends with a significant point, which helps readers remember the paper)

Writer at work

Lakshmi Kotra began with the following rough outline of the process she planned to write about.

Introduction—connect with audience and make them interested
(explain what the clouds are first—composed of what elements?)

I. molecular clouds—collapse begins

will need to explain HOW that happens. No one seems sure so this is a good place to "discuss things that don't fit the theory." Maybe start with one possibility and then describe an alternate explanation in the next paragraph, then go back to process.

II. protostar stage

describe cocoon nebulae—good image

III. fusion begins

will need to explain fusion process

IV. equilibrium

Before getting to equilibrium stage, describe how nebula is blown away and planetary disk forms (for some stars). Mention Earth's origin to interest readers again.

V. death
- white dwarfs
- supernova

End with supernova to connect back up with interstellar matter/cycle of star formation.

Conclusion can highlight "cycle," and that can be built in at beginning too.

Think about organization

Lakshmi recognized that the process she was describing naturally lent itself to chronological, or time-order, organization, because one thing has to happen after another for a star to form. However, she found that she had to "break out" from the simple time line of stellar formation at some points, to explain in more detail or to trace multiple possibilities.

Stars have a complex and fascinating life cycle. Saying it's fascinating doesn't make it fascinating to readers.

Make notes on how to develop the subject

She made notes on her outline indicating where she would step away from the chronological pattern to do this explaining. As she considered how she wanted to end her essay, she realized the idea of a "life cycle" for stars could point back toward the essay's beginning. This strategy helped her focus her thesis.

Have you ever looked up at the stars at night and wondered why they are there? Vague. Kind of sounds like I'm going to talk about religious or spiritual issues.

Astronomers have spent many years studying the life cycle of stars. So? Anyway, I just want to talk about what they've found, not how long it took them.

If "sunshine on your shoulders" makes you happy, you will be even happier to know that the sun will keep shining for at least another 8 billion years. Too corny. Does anyone even remember that song? Anyway, "happy" isn't the way I want readers to feel. But using a familiar phrase might be good.

Connect with readers

Lakshmi realized that stellar formation would probably seem like a distant and forbidding topic to a general audience, so she thought carefully about making a connection with her readers. She began by trying out some different ways to introduce her essay. Here are some of her initial attempts and the comments she made on them. Lakshmi decided to work with the last of these openings and see how well she could integrate it with the rest of her essay.

"Twinkle, twinkle little star. How I wonder what you are." Good—more personal than "Have you ever looked up at the stars and wondered . . ." Astronomers wonder too. That could be the connection between them and scientists' work. More familiar song, also.

4: Revise, Revise, Revise

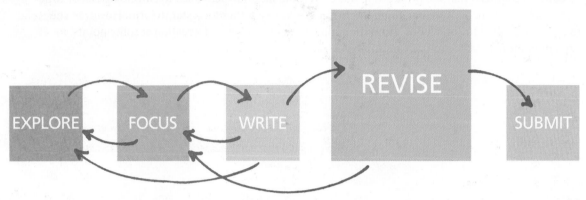

Skilled writers know that the secret to writing well is rewriting. Even the best writers often have to revise several times to get the result they want. You also must have effective strategies for revising if you're going to be successful. The biggest trap you can fall into is starting off with the little stuff first. Leave the small stuff for last.

Does your paper or project meet the assignment?	• Look again at your assignment. Does your paper or project do what the assignment asks? • Look again at the assignment for specific guidelines, including length, format, and amount of research. Does your work meet these guidelines?
Is your title specific?	• Vague titles suggest dull treatment of the topic. Can you make your title more accurate?
Does your writing have a clear focus?	• Does your project have an explicitly stated thesis? If not, is your thesis clearly implied? • Is each paragraph related to your thesis? • Do you get off the track at any point by introducing other topics? • Have you defined all terms that might be unfamiliar to your readers? • Can you add more examples and details that would help to explain your main points?
Is your organization effective?	• Is the order of your main points clear to your reader? • Are there any places where you find abrupt shifts or gaps? • Are there sections or paragraphs that could be rearranged to make your draft more effective?

Is your introduction effective?	• Do you have any general statements that you might cut to get off to a faster start?
	• Can you think of a vivid example that might draw in readers?
	• Can you use a striking fact to get readers interested?
	• Does your introduction make clear where you are headed?
Is your conclusion effective?	• Conclusions that only summarize tend to bore readers. Does your conclusion add anything new to what you've said already?
	• Can you use the conclusion to discuss further implications?
	• Have you left your audience with a final provocative idea that might invite further discussion?
Do you represent yourself effectively?	• To the extent you can, forget for a moment that you wrote what you are reading. What impression do you have of you, the writer?
	• Does "the writer" create an appropriate tone?
	• Has "the writer" done his or her homework?
Is the writing project visually effective?	• Is the font attractive and readable?
	• Are the headings and visuals effective?
Save the editing for last	• When you have finished revising, edit and proofread carefully.

STAYING ON TRACK

Reviewing your draft

Give yourself plenty of time for reviewing your draft. For detailed information on how to participate in a peer review; how to review it yourself; and how to respond to comments from your classmates, your instructor, or a campus writing consultant, see pages 58–61.

Some good questions to ask yourself when reviewing informative writing

• Are the explanations in the essay easy to follow?

• Are there gaps or places where you feel you need more information?

• Are any unusual or discipline-specific words defined for readers?

• Can the reader construct a clear picture of what the essay describes?

• Is the essay interesting enough to catch readers' attention and keep them reading?

Writer at work

Lakshmi Kotra gave a copy of her first draft to her instructor for feedback. She used his comments to guide her revision of the essay.

Once a section of a dust cloud starts to collapse, gravity relentlessly pulls the material together into a much smaller area. Gradually, the cloud becomes denser and less cloudlike. At this stage, astronomers refer to the object as a "protostar." For a star the size of our sun, the journey from cloud to protostar may take about 100,000 years (Chaisson and McMillan 429). Bigger clouds of gas will develop faster—but they will also have shorter lives. The larger the star, the faster it uses up its "fuel." But first the fuel must start burning. As the atoms of gas crowd into a smaller and smaller space, they bounce off one another faster and faster, and the protostar heats up. However, it is not a true star yet. That comes later, when nuclear fusion begins. If a cloud segment is less than .08 solar masses, it won't get hot enough, and it will never become a star.

When the protostar is dense enough, its nuclear heart finally starts to beat. This happens when hydrogen atoms are pushed close enough together to fuse into helium. This requires a total of six hydrogen atoms, which must combine in a specific sequence: hydrogen—deuterium—helium 3—helium + hydrogen. Every time fusion takes place, a small amount of energy is released.

You bring up a number of concepts here that don"t quite fit with the main idea of the paragraph. It might make sense to move the information about mass and lifespan to later in the paper

The "sequence" isn't clear. Can you break this down into simpler steps?

Determine a plan for revision in light of your instructor's comments

Based on her instructor's comments, Lakshmi decided to shift some information on the rates at which stars burn nuclear fuel from an earlier section of the paper to her later discussion of the fates of stars with different masses. This strategy also allowed her to flesh out the description of "brown dwarfs"—starlike objects that do not develop into stars.

Act on specific comments

She also took her instructor's advice about simplifying her explanation of hydrogen fusion.

Read your paper aloud to catch mistakes and awkward phrasing

Lakshmi also read her essay aloud to help identify spelling errors and missing or poorly chosen words.

Visit your writing center

Finally, Lakshmi visited her school's writing center. She asked for specific help in making the paper accessible for an audience without a scientific background. Working with a consultant, she recognized the need to define scientific terms, like *nebulae*, *protostar*, and *equilibrium*, that might not be familiar to a general audience.

5: Submitted Version (MLA Style)

MyWritingLab™

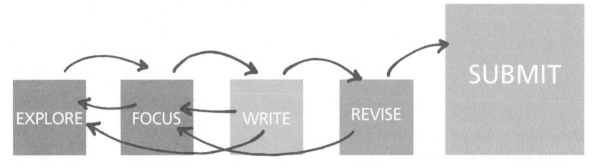

EXPLORE   FOCUS   WRITE   REVISE   SUBMIT

Kotra 1

Lakshmi Kotra

Professor Jenson

Astronomy 101

6 May 2014

The Life Cycle of Stars

"Twinkle, twinkle, little star; how I wonder what you are." This old nursery rhyme may not seem profound, but it echoes some of the biggest questions astronomers puzzle over: What are stars made of? How do they form? How are they born and how do they die? Current theories of star formation answer some of these questions, but not all of them. We do know that, even though stars are separated from one another by vast amounts of space, their life cycles are intertwined.

Twinkling stars are born in dark, cold clouds of dust and gas called nebulae. These clouds consist mainly of hydrogen, and may be as cold as 10 degrees Kelvin (Chaisson and McMillan 427). Nebulae are very dense compared to the near-vacuum of interstellar space. But something must concentrate this dust and gas even more if a star is to form. This first part of the star-forming process is not fully understood. Some force has to cause a portion of the nebula to begin collapsing. Magnetism and rotation are two forces already at work in most clouds, but astronomers have long thought that these forces are more likely to counteract the collapsing force of gravity (Chaisson and McMillan 427). However, new research may have found a solution to this problem. In some clouds, magnetic fields may cancel out some or all of the rotational force. This reorganization would allow gravity to begin collapsing the star (Farivar).

Another theory is that a shock wave from some outside event or object might trigger the collapse of a cloud. The Eagle Nebula provides a good illustration of this theory. Ultraviolet radiation from super-hot stars in the nebula has been observed bombarding the surrounding dust and gas. The radiation has stripped away a lot of dust but left dense columns of cloud where stars are believed to be forming. The impact of this "stellar wind" may have also triggered the star formation. Smaller clumps of denser gas are contracting within the columns, taking their first step on the journey to stardom (see fig. 1).

Once a section of a dust cloud starts to collapse, gravity relentlessly pulls the material together into a much smaller area. Gradually, the center of the cloud becomes denser and less cloudlike. At this stage, astronomers refer to the object as a "protostar." For a star the size of our sun, the journey from cloud to protostar may take about 100,000 years (Chaisson and McMillan 429). As the atoms of gas crowd into a smaller and smaller space, they bounce off one another faster and faster, and the protostar heats up. However, it is not a true star yet. That comes later, when nuclear fusion begins. For now, the developing protostar is still surrounded by a shroud of dust

Fig. 1. Eagle Nebula
The columns of interstellar gas in the
Eagle Nebula are incubators for new stars
(United States, NASA, "Eagle").

that hides it from view. This dust mantle is called a cocoon nebula. Some protostars can be detected by the infrared glow of their cocoon nebulae (Chaisson and McMillan 435-36).

Over millions of years, the protostar continues to grow and change, like a butterfly in its cocoon. Gravity keeps compacting it, making it smaller in size and denser. When the protostar is dense enough, its nuclear heart finally starts to beat. This happens when hydrogen atoms are pushed close enough together to fuse into helium. The fusion process involves several steps. First, two hydrogen atoms will fuse to form an atom of deuterium, or heavy hydrogen. When a third hydrogen atom joins the deuterium atom, an isotope called helium 3 results.

Finally, when two helium 3 atoms fuse together, an atom of regular helium plus two of hydrogen are created. But the crucial part of this process is that, every time fusion takes place, a small amount of energy is released. The radiation emitted from the fusion of hydrogen into helium is what makes the majority of stars shine. Fusion radiation from the Sun lights our planet in the daytime, makes the moon shine at night—and gives you sunburn.

Hydrogen atoms must be moving at extremely high speeds in order to fuse. Another way to say this is that the temperature in the core of a protostar must be very high for fusion to take place: at least 10 million degrees Kelvin (Chaisson and McMillan 431). Now nuclear forces, not just gravity's grip, are controlling the star's development. In fact, these two forces will compete throughout the star's life. Gravity tries to collapse the star, while the pressure of its fast-moving, superheated atoms pushes it outward. As long as the two forces balance each other, the star will remain stable. Astronomers call this state "equilibrium."

During the intense heating at the end of the protostar stage, and when hydrogen fusion is beginning, intense radiation streams off the young star. The dust and gas that have surrounded the protostar are swept away by this energy bombardment, and the star emerges from its cocoon. This phenomenon can be observed visually in NGC 4214. Young stars in this nebula are pouring out radiation that has created "bubbles" in the surrounding gas. Brighter and older stars have pushed away more of the dust and gas. The bubbles around these stars are bigger than those around younger or cooler stars in the nebula (see fig. 2).

Sometimes, not all of a protostar's dust cocoon blows away. According to one theory, you can look around our own solar system and see the remnants of the dust that once surrounded our Sun. In fact, you are standing on some of it. The Earth and the rest of the planets in our solar system are believed to have formed from a disk of dust and gas left over after the sun formed. The reasons this happens are not entirely clear, but astronomers now think that many stellar systems have planetary disks around them. The Orion Nebula provides some confirmation of this theory. There, astronomers have observed many glowing disks of dust, called "proplyds." They think these disks are actually young stars surrounded by material that will eventually form a system of orbiting planets (see fig. 3).

Fig. 2. Star Formation
Clusters of new stars form from interstellar gas and
dust in galaxy NGC 4214 (United States, NASA, "Star").

The size of the original dust cloud a star is born from will also determine how it dies. Some protostars don't quite have what it takes to become a star. Clumps of dust and gas that are smaller than .08 solar masses never get hot enough to begin fusing hydrogen (Chaisson and McMillan 433). These "brown dwarfs" produce infrared radiation, but they never shine visibly.

True stars burn through their nuclear fuel at different rates. The larger the star, the faster its fuel is fused. Smaller stars, like our Sun, are called "dwarf stars." If they began life with less than eight times the mass of our Sun, they will quietly burn hydrogen for perhaps ten billion years. Toward the end of their lives, as they begin to run out of

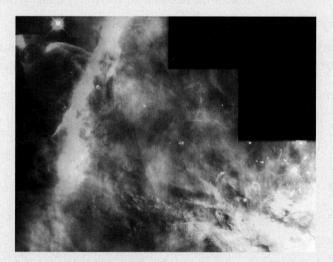

Fig. 3. Orion Nebula
This composite photo of the Orion nebula assembled from images taken by the Hubble Space Telescope shows the beginnings of new solar systems surrounding young stars (United States, NASA, "Orion").

fuel, they will swell briefly into red giant stars, fusing their helium into carbon, and cooling substantially. Finally, they will subside into "white dwarf" stars, about the size of the planet Earth. Provided they do not have nearby neighboring stars that might interact with them, white dwarfs gradually dim and cool, until they go dark altogether (Chaisson and McMillan 459). This cooling process is what astronomers predict will some day happen to our Sun.

A star of more than about eight solar masses has a shorter but much more spectacular life. It will fuse all its available fuel in well under one billion years—perhaps in as little as one million years. When a giant star has run through all its available nuclear fuel, it develops a core of iron atoms, which cannot be fused into anything else. When this core has grown to about 1.4 solar masses, the star will explode in a supernova. All that will be left of the original star is a dark neutron star or black hole (Chaisson and McMillan 475). But the shock wave from the supernova may go on to trigger new star formation in dust clouds nearby. In this way, dying stars contribute to the birth of new ones, and the life cycle of stars continues.

Works Cited

Chaisson, Eric, and Steve McMillan. *Astronomy Today*. 6th ed.,
Prentice Hall, 2008.

Farivar, Cyrus. "Galactic Map Aids Stellar Formation Theory." *The Daily Californian*, 23 Jan. 2002, archive.dailycal.org/article.php?id=7441.

United States, National Aeronautics and Space Administration. "The Eagle Nebula." *Great Images in NASA*, 1 Apr. 1995, grin.hq.nasa. gov/ABSTRACTS/GPN-2000-000987.html.

---, ---. "Fireworks of Star Formation Light Up a Galaxy." *Great Images in NASA*, 6 Jan. 2000, grin.hq.nasa.gov/ABSTRACTS/GPN-2000-000877.html.

---, ---. "The Orion Nebula." *Great Images in NASA*, 20 Nov. 1995, grin. hq.nasa.gov/ABSTRACTS/GPN-2000-000983.html.

Projects

No matter how diverse its forms, successful informative writing begins with the basics.

- What do readers already know about a subject?
- What do readers need to know about a subject?
- What kind of writing is best suited for particular readers?

Instructions

Be aware that instructions are much harder to write than most people expect. They usually require a lot of detail, yet if they are too complex, people will be confused or intimidated.

Think of a fairly simple device you have learned to use, like an smart phone or an app.

Write a one- or two-page set of instructions explaining how to perform a simple task, such as creating a play list on your smart phone, using your school's Web-based e-mail service, or changing the toner cartridge in your printer. When you are finished, have a friend volunteer to try out your instructions. How easy is it to follow them? Do they work?

Profile of an individual

Choose a person to profile. The more interesting the person, the more interesting your profile will be. Make a list of possible people. Think about people who are known in your community such as politicians, business leaders, athletes, musicians, and other entertainers. Also think of people who have unusual occupations or unusual hobbies, complex life histories, or who have overcome challenges.

Arrange to interview the person at a time and place comfortable for the person. Ask if you can bring a digital recorder and a camera.

Find out as much as you can about the person before the interview. See if the person shows up on a *Google* search. If the person is in the public eye, use the *LexisNexis* database or other databases for newspapers (see pages 538–539) to learn what has been written about the person.

Prepare questions in advance. Take brief notes during the interview. If you record the interview, transcribe the parts that you find important.

Decide what is most interesting about the person and make that the focus of your profile. Choose the details and quotations that are the most vivid. Then think about how you will organize your profile. Will you give the person's background first or will you start with your interview and work in the background later?

Report

Think of a subject you know a great deal about but most other people, especially those who are your intended readers, do not.

Your subject might come from your life experience

- What's it like to grow up on a family farm?
- What's it like to be an immigrant to the United States?

Your hobbies

- What's the best way to train for a marathon?
- How can you avoid injuries in sports by stretching?

Your personal interests

- Why everyone over age 20 should pay attention to cholesterol

A place that you have found fascinating, or a subject you have studied in college

- The misunderstood nature of conceptual art
- Breakthroughs in nanotechnology in the near future.

Consider what will likely be most interesting about your subject to your readers.

Engage your readers with a provocative title and a thesis that will challenge them to think about your subject in new ways.

Aim for a report of 700–1000 words or about 3–4 double-spaced pages.

COMPOSE IN MULTIMEDIA

Informative audio podcast

Listen to a few informative audio podcasts such as *This American Life* on Public Radio International. Pay attention to how they are organized and how narrators use their voices to signal key points, transitions, and conclusions.

Make a list of possible topics for your podcast. Think about possibilities on your campus, such as the history of a building or the research of a professor whom you could interview. Think about possibilities in your community such as an interesting nonprofit organization or hobby. Then think about the rhetorical situation. Who would be the likely audience?

Conduct research on the topic of your podcast. You may need to interview people in addition to library and online research. Make a working outline for the major segments of your podcast (see page 41).

Learn to use an audio editor. You may have one such as *GarageBand* installed already on your computer or you may download an open-source editor.

Write and record your podcast. If you have clips from interviews, insert them into your audio file. Next, listen to your podcast and revise.

MyWritingLab™ Visit Ch. 8 in MyWritingLab to complete the chapter exercises, explore an interactive version of the Writer at Work paper, and test your understanding of the chapter objectives.

9 Rhetorical, Visual, and Literary Analyses

Every piece of writing, every painting, every building, every movie, every new product, every advertisement is a response to what came before it.

In this chapter, you will learn to

1. Understand the different kinds of analyses *(see p. 217)*
2. Be aware of the elements of a rhetorical analysis *(see p. 218)*
3. Be aware of the elements of a visual analysis *(see p. 219)*
4. Be aware of the elements of a literary analysis *(see p. 220)*
5. Describe the steps involved in the process of writing a rhetorical analysis *(see pp. 256–257)*
6. Apply flexible strategies to write and revise a rhetorical analysis *(see pp. 258–265)*

Writing an Analysis

Critical reading and viewing are essential skills for all kinds of writing. Analysis is a more specific aim where those critical reading and viewing skills are applied to particular subjects. Analysis involves dividing a whole into parts that can be studied both as individual entities and as parts of the whole.

Rhetorical analysis is a kind of analysis that divides a whole into parts to understand how an act of speaking or writing conveys meaning. *Visual analysis* is closely related to rhetorical analysis. The tools of rhetorical analysis have been applied to understanding how other human creations make meaning. The goal of *literary analysis* is to interpret a literary text and support that interpretation with evidence or, more simply, to make a discovery about a text that you share with your readers.

A rhetorical, visual, or literary analysis may be concerned with either text or context, but often it examines both. Textual analysis focuses on the features of a text. Contextual analysis reconstructs the cultural environment, or context.

Keys to analyses

ANALYZE THE TEXT	• What is the subject? • What are the main ideas? • What is the genre? a newspaper article? a short story? a documentary film? • What appeals are used? What facts or evidence does the author present? • How is the text organized? • What style does the author use?
ANALYZE THE CONTEXT	• Who is the author? What else has the author written or said on this subject? What motivated the author to address this issue? • Who is the audience? What is the occasion and forum? • What is the larger conversation? When did the text appear? Why did it appear at that particular moment? Who or what might this text be responding to?

Analyses in the world

Analyses are basic tools for all academic disciplines, which seek to break down complex subjects into smaller parts in order to gain a better understanding. Methods of analysis vary widely across disciplines.

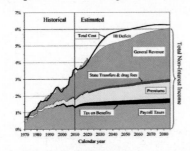

Other genres of analyses
• **Intelligence analyses** are used by business, law enforcement, and the military to inform planners.
• **Engineering analyses** employ scientific principles to understand how components interact in a system.
• **Business analyses** identify problems and opportunities.

Writing a Rhetorical Analysis

People often use the term *rhetoric* to describe empty language. "The governor's speech was just a bunch of rhetoric," you might say, meaning that the governor offered noble-sounding words but no real ideas. But rhetoric originated with a much more positive meaning. According to Aristotle, rhetoric is "the art of finding in any given case the available means of persuasion." Rhetoric is concerned with producing effective pieces of communication.

What makes a good rhetorical analysis?

1
Find an interesting text
Select a text that will be interesting both to you (perhaps because of the subject) and to your readers (perhaps because the text does something unusual with words and images).

2
Analyze the immediate context

- Who is the author? Learn all you can about the author. What was the author's purpose?
- Who is the audience? Learn all you can about the original publication or the occasion for your text.
- What are the medium and genre? What expectations would the audience have about this genre?

3
Analyze the larger context
Find out what else was being said about the subject of your text. What other pieces of "cultural conversation" does your text respond to?

4
Analyze the appeals used

- Analyze the ethos. How does the writer represent herself or himself?
- Analyze the logos. Where do you find facts and evidence in the argument?
- Analyze the pathos. Where do you find appeals to shared values?

5
Analyze the language and style
Is the style formal, informal, satirical, or something else? Are any metaphors used?

WRITE NOW   MyWritingLab™

Analyze a public speech

You can locate public speeches on several Web sites, including American Rhetoric. After answering the questions below, formulate a thesis for a rhetorical analysis.

1. What is the rhetorical purpose?
2. Who is the audience?
3. How does the speaker gain (or not gain) credibility?
4. What is the background of the speech?
5. What appeals does the speaker use?
6. How formal or informal is the style?
7. What metaphors does the speaker use?

Writing a Visual Analysis

We are bombarded by images on a daily basis. They compete for our attention, urge us to buy things, and guide us on our way home from work. These visual texts frequently attempt to persuade us, to make us think, feel, or act a certain way. Yet we rarely stop to consider how they do their work.

Visual texts leave room for the audience to interpret to a greater degree than many verbal texts, which make them particularly rich subjects for analysis.

What makes a good visual analysis?

1
Describe what you see
Is it a single image, part of a series, a sign, a building, or something else? What are the conventions for this kind of visual?

2
Analyze the composition
What elements are most prominent? Which are repeated? Which are balanced or in contrast to each other? Which details are important?

3
Examine the context
Who created the image? When and where did it first appear? Can you determine why it was created?

4
Look for connections
What is the genre? What kind of visual is it? What elements have you seen before? Which remind you of other visuals?

WRITE NOW   MyWritingLab™

Analyze a print or web ad

Find a visually striking advertisement that combines words and images. Analyze how the words and images work together to persuade. To succeed with this assignment, you will need to find an ad that supports an extended analysis.

1. What is the ad really trying to sell? Often it is not a specific product but a brand.

2. Analyze the text of the ad. Is it a single image or part of a series? What does the image depict? Does it employ a visual metaphor (such as the overused images of a fried egg as your brain on drugs)? What is the primary appeal used in the ad: appeals to emotions and values (pathos), appeals to the brand a celebrity featured in the ad (ethos), or appeals to good reasons such as the gas mileage of a hybrid car (logos)?

3. Analyze the context of the ad. Where was it published? What else appears on the Web site or magazine where you found the ad?

4. How ultimately persuasive is the ad?

Writing a Literary Analysis

A literary analysis takes different forms. One form is to analyze patterns, such as how the repetition of particular images and even words contributes to the meaning. Another form is to pose a problem, such as why a particular character behaves in an odd way or why the narrator leaves out key information. Another approach is to use comparison and contrast to analyze two characters, two works of literature, or any pairs that help readers gain insight into a work.

What makes a good literary analysis?

1

Start with a close reading
Examine carefully the plot of your short story or novel, the characters, the setting, patterns of language, imagery, and metaphors. If you are analyzing a poem, study how the individual words and images connect to shape your interpretation.

2

Evaluate and revise your thesis
Make sure your thesis is specific and significant. If you identify a pattern but say nothing about why it is important, your reader will ask "So what?"

3

Select your evidence and examples with an eye on your thesis
Make sure your evidence and examples are relevant to your thesis, and quotations are integrated into your text.

4

Use the present tense
In writing about literature, refer to events in the present tense.

5

Document carefully
Document your sources using the MLA format.

WRITE NOW   MyWritingLab™

Analyze characters in a literary work

A character analysis is assigned frequently in courses that examine literature. To begin a character analysis, make notes on the following.

1. Identify the main characters. Key characters are the protagonist—the main character—and the antagonist—the character who struggles against the main character.

2. Describe elements of the characters.
   Appearance: How does the character look?
   Personality: How does the character act?
   Motives: What does the character seek?
   Background: What in the character's past might explain current motives?
   Conflicts: What conflicts does the character have? internal conflicts? conflicts with other people?
   Choices: Does the character make good or bad choices?
   Change: How does the character change or does the character remain static?

Straight from the Heart
Tim Collins

On July 11, 2005, Marie Fatayi-Williams made an immensely moving speech in London at the site where her son Anthony had been killed in a terrorist bombing four days earlier. Her speech was reported in numerous media outlets. The *Guardian*, a British newspaper, printed Fatayi-Williams's speech on July 13, with an analysis and commentary by Tim Collins. Collins considers the factors that make Fatayi-Williams's speech so powerful, and places it in a larger context of responses to terrorism.

HOW IS THIS READING ORGANIZED?

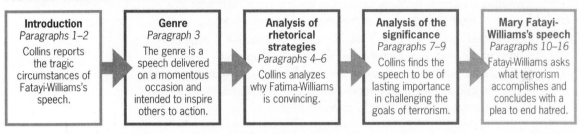

| **Introduction** *Paragraphs 1–2* Collins reports the tragic circumstances of Fatayi-Williams's speech. | **Genre** *Paragraph 3* The genre is a speech delivered on a momentous occasion and intended to inspire others to action. | **Analysis of rhetorical strategies** *Paragraphs 4–6* Collins analyzes why Fatima-Williams is convincing. | **Analysis of the significance** *Paragraphs 7–9* Collins finds the speech to be of lasting importance in challenging the goals of terrorism. | **Mary Fatayi-Williams's speech** *Paragraphs 10–16* Fatayi-Williams asks what terrorism accomplishes and concludes with a plea to end hatred. |

Straight from the Heart

1 Caught in the spotlight of history, set on the stage of a very public event, Marie Fatayi-Williams, the mother of Anthony Fatayi-Williams, 26 and missing since Thursday, appeals for news of her son. Her words are a mixture of stirring rhetoric, heartfelt appeal and a stateswoman-like vision, and so speak on many levels to the nation and the world. Her appeal is a simple one—where is my son? If he has been killed, then why? Who has gained?

Introduction: The subject is announced in the first sentence.

2 Marie has found herself, as I did on the eve of the invasion of Iraq, an unwitting voice, speaking amid momentous events. Her appeal, delivered on Monday not far from Tavistock Square, where she fears her son died in the bomb attack on the number 30 bus, gives a verbal form to the whirlpool of emotions that have engulfed society as the result of last week's bombings. I suspect Marie, like myself, had no idea that her words would find such wide recognition, have fed such an acute hunger for explanation, have slaked such a thirst for expression of the sheer horror of Thursday's events.

Analysis of rhetorical appeals: Collins points out the appeal to pathos—the beliefs and values of the audience—that lies at the heart of Fatayi-Williams's speech.

3 This kind of speech is normally the preserve of the great orators, statesmen and playwrights, of Shakespeare, Churchill or Lincoln. It is

221

often a single speech, a soliloquy or address from the steps of the gallows, that explains, inspires, exhorts and challenges. But always such addresses are crafted for effect and consciously intended to sway and influence, and often, as in the case of Shakespeare's Henry V, they are set in the mouth of a long dead hero or delivered by wordsmiths who are masters of their craft. It is rare in history that such oratory is the genuine article, springing from the heart and bursting forth to an unwitting audience. In Marie's case, her speech gains its power as a vehicle of grief and loss, and of the angst of a mother who yearns for her beloved son. In my case it was the opposite emotion from which I drew inspiration—an appeal to understand, to empathize, to give courage and purpose. I was motivated by a need to warn and teach as well as to encourage. Marie's motivation is a reflection on loss and that most powerful of all emotions, a mother's love.

Genre:
Collins identifies the genre of the speech, which is usually crafted for a specific occasion. Marie's speech is remarkable because it is spontaneous.

4   The form the address takes is as poignant as the language used. There is an initial explanation of the extraordinary circumstances of the loss, a cri de coeur for the innocent blood lost, a rejection of the act by its comparison to the great liberators, and the assertion that her loss is all our loss in the family of humanity. It ends with her personal grief for her flesh and blood, her hopes and pride. The language echoes verses of the Bible as well as from the Koran. It has raw passion as well as heart-rending pathos.

Style:
Several rhetorical techniques used in the speech connect it to a larger historical tradition.

5   With only a photograph of her son and a sheet of paper as a prompt, Marie's words burst out with as much emotion as anger. Her speech stands in stark contrast to the pronouncements of politicians, prepared by aides and delivered from copious notes. It is indeed the raw originality and authentic angst that give the delivery such impact, the plea such effect. No knighted veteran of the Royal Shakespeare Company could deliver such an address without hours or even days of rehearsal. I know from my own experience that only momentous events can provoke such a moment, only raw emotion can inspire such a spontaneous plea. I am often asked how long it took me to write my speech, delivered to my regiment, the Royal Irish, on the eve of the invasion of Iraq on March 19, 2003, at Fort Blair Mayne camp in the Kuwaiti desert. My answer is simple—not one moment. There was no plan; I spoke without notes. For me there was only the looming specter of actual warfare and the

Personal connection:
Collins's own experience informs his understanding of what Fatayi-Williams might have been feeling. This helps assure his audience that he is qualified to comment on the meaning of her speech.

certainty of loss and killing, and I was speaking to myself as well as to my men. I suspect for Marie there was only the yawning black void of loss, the cavern left behind in her life caused by the loss of a son who can never be replaced.

6 What, then, can we take from this? Marie's appeal is as important as it is momentous. Her words are as free from hatred as they are free from self-interest; it is clear that no man can give her her heart's desire—her son. I was also struck by the quiet dignity of her words, the clarity of her view and the weight of her convictions. She does not condemn, she appeals; her words act as an indictment of all war and violence, not just acts of terror but also the unnecessary aggression of nation states. Her message is simple: here is a human who only wanted to give, to succeed and to make his mother proud. Where is the victory in his death? Where is the progress in his destruction? In her own words: "What inspiration can senseless slaughter provide?"

Analysis of rhetorical appeals: Collins examines how Marie creates her ethos, which convinces her audience of her sincerity and lack of malice.

7 I am certain that Marie's appeal will go down as one of the great speeches of our new century. It will give comfort to the families and friends of the dead and injured, both of this act and no doubt, regrettably, of events still to come. It should act as a caution to statesmen and leaders, a focus for public grief and, ultimately, as a challenge to, as well as a condemnation of, the perpetrators.

Style: Collins sees Fatayi-Williams's directness as perhaps the most important aspect of her speech. She responds to historic events in a way that personalizes them and shows their human cost.

8 Marie is already an icon of the loss of Thursday July 7. Having travelled from Africa to find a better life, Anthony Fatayi-Williams carried the hopes and pride of his family. Now, as his mother has traveled to London, arguably one of the most cosmopolitan and integrated cities in the world, and standing nearby a wrecked icon of that city, a red double-decker bus, she has made an appeal which is as haunting as it is relevant, as poignant as it is appealing. It is a fact that such oratory as both Marie and I produced is born of momentous events, and inspired by hope and fears in equal measure.

9 But Marie's appeal is also important on another level. I have long urged soldiers in conflict zones to keep communicating with the population in order to be seen as people—it is easier to kill uniforms than it is to kill people. On July 7 the suicide bombers attacked icons of a society that they hated more than they loved life,

the red London bus and the tube. Marie's speech has stressed the real victims' identities. They are all of us.

Marie's speech

10   This is Anthony, Anthony Fatayi-Williams, 26 years old, he's missing and we fear that he was in the bus explosion ... on Thursday. We don't know. We do know from the witnesses that he left the Northern line in Euston. We know he made a call to his office at Amec at 9.41 from the NW1 area to say he could not make [it] by the tube but he would find alternative means to work.

> **Marie Fatayi-Williams's speech:** She begins with the fact that her son is missing. She asks poignantly what terrorism accomplishes, and she concludes with a plea to end hatred.

11   Since then he has not made any contact with any single person. Not New York, not Madrid, not London. There has been widespread slaughter of innocent people. There have been streams of tears, innocent tears. There have been rivers of blood, innocent blood. Death in the morning, people going to find their livelihood, death in the noontime on the highways and streets.

12   They are not warriors. Which cause has been served? Certainly not the cause of God, not the cause of Allah because God Almighty only gives life and is full of mercy. Anyone who has been misled, or is being misled to believe that by killing innocent people he or she is serving God should think again because it's not true. Terrorism is not the way, terrorism is not the way. It doesn't beget peace. We can't deliver peace by terrorism, never can we deliver peace by killing people. Throughout history, those people who have changed the world have done so without violence, they have won people to their cause through peaceful protest. Nelson Mandela, Martin Luther King, Mahatma Gandhi, their discipline, their self-sacrifice, their conviction made people turn towards them, to follow them. What inspiration can senseless slaughter provide? Death and destruction of young people in their prime as well as old and helpless can never be the foundations for building society.

13   My son Anthony is my first son, my only son, the head of my family. In African society, we hold on to sons. He has dreams and hopes and I, his mother, must fight to protect them. This is now the fifth day, five days on, and we are waiting to know what happened

to him and I, his mother, I need to know what happened to
Anthony. His young sisters need to know what happened, his
uncles and aunties need to know what happened to Anthony,
his father needs to know what happened to Anthony. Millions of
my friends back home in Nigeria need to know what happened
to Anthony. His friends surrounding me here, who have put this
together, need to know what has happened to Anthony. I need to
know, I want to protect him. I'm his mother, I will fight till I die to
protect him. To protect his values and to protect his memory.

14 Innocent blood will always cry to God Almighty for reparation. How
much blood must be spilled? How many tears shall we cry? How
many mothers' hearts must be maimed? My heart is maimed. I pray
I will see my son, Anthony. Why? I need to know, Anthony needs to
know, Anthony needs to know, so do many other unaccounted for
innocent victims, they need to know.

15 It's time to stop and think. We cannot live in fear because we are
surrounded by hatred. Look around us today. Anthony is a Nigerian,
born in London, worked in London, he is a world citizen. Here today
we have Christians, Muslims, Jews, Sikhs, Hindus, all of us united in
love for Anthony. Hatred begets only hatred. It is time to stop this
vicious cycle of killing. We must all stand together, for our common
humanity. I need to know what happened to my Anthony. He's the
love of my life. My first son, my first son, 26. He tells me one day,
"Mummy, I don't want to die, I don't want to die. I want to live, I want
to take care of you, I will do great things for you, I will look after you,
you will see what I will achieve for you. I will make you happy." And
he was making me happy. I am proud of him, I am still very proud of
him but I need to now where he is, I need to know what happened to
him. I grieve, I am sad, I am distraught, I am destroyed.

16 He didn't do anything to anybody, he loved everybody so much.
If what I hear is true, even when he came out of the underground
he was directing people to take buses, to be sure that they were
OK. Then he called his office at the same time to tell them he was
running late. He was a multi-purpose person, trying to save people,
trying to call his office, trying to meet his appointments. What did he
then do to deserve this? Where is he, someone tell me, where is he?

The Collapse of Big Media: The Young and the Restless

David T. Z. Mindich

MyWritingLab™

David T. Z. Mindich, a former assignment editor at CNN, holds a PhD in American studies from New York University. He is a professor of media studies, journalism, and digital arts at St. Michael's College in Colchester, Vermont, and the author of *Tuned Out: Why Americans under 40 Don't Follow the News* (2005). "The Collapse of Big Media: The Young and the Restless" was published in the *Wilson Quarterly* in spring 2005.

Return to these questions after you have finished reading.

Analyzing the Reading

1. What is Mindich's thesis? What kind of evidence does he provide to support the points he makes? Is his evidence persuasive?

2. What does the author say are the causes of the situation he writes about? What evidence does he give to support his analysis of causes? Is the evidence persuasive?

3. At the end of the essay, the author makes some recommendations? What are these? Do these recommendations seem valuable?

4. What are the author's credentials? Do the author and the publication seem to be reliable sources of information and analysis?

Exploring Ideas and Issues

The Founding Fathers of the United States thought so highly of the role of a free press in a democracy that they enshrined that right in the First Amendment to the Constitution. Over the centuries, the press has changed in a number of ways—not the least of which is technologically—but its role as a "watchdog" has remained throughout.

Possibilities for Writing

1. Make a log for one entire day on all the news you read, watch, or listen to: newspapers, radio, television news broadcasts, comedy reporting of news like *The Daily Show*, comic monologues commenting on events, news flashes at the bottom of other television programs, news on the Web, blogs, and personal news sources such as e-mail. Make notes about what the news contained and keep track of the time you spent reading, viewing, or listening. On the next day total the time for each category. Write a short analysis of your data. Bring your analysis to class to compare with other students' totals.

Do the results for the entire class surprise you in any way?

2. Do you agree with Mindich that young people display a "detachment" from political issues? Why or why not? Write a short essay explaining your reasons. Include examples from your own and your friends' personal experience of recent political events.

3. Mindich, writing in 2007, says that "the theory that younger people are more reliant on the Internet for news than their elders doesn't hold up." However, the 2014 *State of the Media* study conducted by the Pew Research Journalism Project reports that three in ten adults in America get some news from *Facebook*. Do some additional research on the state of Internet news. Do you agree with Mindich's assessment, or do you think he has not sufficiently credited the online delivery of news for young adults? Write an essay in which you analyze your research and reach a conclusion.

The Collapse of Big Media:
The Young and the Restless

When news executives look at the decline over the past few decades in the number of people who read or watch the news, they're scared silly. But then they reassure themselves that the kids will come around. Conventional wisdom runs that as young men and women gain the trappings of adulthood—a job, a spouse, children, and a house—they tend to pick up the news habit, too. As CBS News president Andrew Heyward declared in 2002, "Time is on our side in that as you get older, you tend to get more interested in the world around you." Unfortunately for Heyward and other news executives, the evidence suggests that young people are not picking up the news habit—not in their teens, not in their twenties, not even in their thirties.

When they aren't reassuring themselves, editors and publishers are lying awake at night thinking about the dismaying trends of recent decades. In 1972, nearly half of 18-to-22-year-olds read a newspaper every day, according to research conducted by Wolfram Peiser, a scholar who studies newspaper readership. Today, less than a quarter do. That younger people are less likely to read than their elders is of grave concern, but perhaps not surprising. In fact, the baby boomers who came of age in the 1970s are less avid news consumers than their parents were. More ominous for the future of the news media, however, is Peiser's research showing that a particular age cohort's reading habits do not change much with time; in other words, as people age, they continue the news habits of their younger days. Thus, the real danger, Peiser says, is that cohort replacement builds in a general decline in newspaper reading. The deleterious effects of this phenomenon are clearly evident: In 1972, nearly three-quarters of the 34-to-37 age group read a paper daily. Those thirtysomethings have been replaced by successive crops of thirtysomethings, each reading less than its predecessor. Today, only about a third of this group reads a newspaper every day. This means that fewer parents are bringing home a newspaper or discussing current events over dinner. And fewer kids are growing up in households in which newspapers matter.

A similar decline is evident in television news viewership. In the past decade, the median age of network television news viewers has crept up from about 50 to about 60. Tune in to any network news show or CNN, and note the products hawked in the commercials: The pitches for Viagra, Metamucil, Depends, and Fixodent are not aimed at teenyboppers. Compounding the problem of a graying news audience is the proliferation of televisions within the typical household, which diminishes adult influence over what's watched. In 1970, six percent of all sixth graders had TVs in their bedrooms; today that number is an astonishing

77 percent. If you are in sixth grade and sitting alone in your room, you're probably not watching Peter Jennings.

One of the clearest signs of the sea change in news viewing habits was the uproar following the appearance last fall by Jon Stewart, host of *The Daily Show*, a parody of a news program, on CNN's *Crossfire*, a real one. With a median age of 34, *The Daily Show*'s audience is the envy of CNN, so when Stewart told *Crossfire*'s hosts that their show's predictable left/right approach to debates of current issues was "hurting America," one could have guessed that CNN bigwigs would pay attention. But who could have foreseen that CNN president Jonathan Klein would cancel *Crossfire*? "I agree wholeheartedly with Jon Stewart's overall premise," he told the *New York Times*. News executives are so desperate to get to consumers before the AARP does that they're willing to heed the advice of a comedian.

If the young (and not so young) are not reading newspapers or watching network television news, many assume that they are getting news online. Not so. Only 18 percent of Americans listed the Internet as a "primary news source" in a survey released earlier this year by the Pew Internet and American Life Project and the Pew Research Center for the People and the Press. And the theory that younger people are more reliant on the Internet for news than their elders doesn't hold up. Certainly an engaged minority of young people use the Net to get a lot of news, but studies show that most use it primarily for e-mailing,

instant messaging, games, and other diversions. You only need to wander into a computer lab at your local college or high school and see what the students have on their screens for the dismal confirmation of these choices.

If the youth audience is tuned out of newspaper, television, and Internet news, what, exactly, is it tuning in to? To answer this question, I traveled the country in 2002 speaking with groups of young people about their news habits. My research confirmed what many people already suspect: that most young people tune in to situation comedies and "reality" TV to the exclusion of news. I was surprised, though, by the scope of the trend: Most of the young people I interviewed had almost no measurable interest in political news. At Brandeis University in Massachusetts, one student explained that watching the situation comedy *Friends* creates a "sense of emotional investment" and "instant gratification." This engagement contrasts with the "detachment" young people feel from public issues such as campaign finance reform and news sources such as CNN and Peter Jennings. And when the news and its purveyors are seen simply as alternative forms of entertainment, they can't compete with the likes of *CSI, Las Vegas, American Idol*, and *Fear Factor*.

The entertainment options competing with the news for the attention of the youth audience have multiplied exponentially. In the 1960s, there were only a handful of television stations in any given market. When Walter Cronkite shook the nation by declaring in a February 1968 report on the Vietnam War that the United States was "mired in stalemate," he spoke to a captive audience. New York City, for example, had only seven broadcast stations. At 10:30 p.m. on the night of Cronkite's remarks, channels 4 and 11 ran movies, channels 5 and 9 had discussion shows, and channel 7 was showing *NYPD Blue*, a cop show. In this media universe of limited competition, nearly 80 percent of all television viewers watched the nightly news, and from the late 1960s on, Cronkite won the lion's share of the total news audience. Today, young people can choose from hundreds of stations, less than a tenth of which are devoted to news. And that's not to mention the many competing diversions that weren't available in 1968, from video games to iPods. Amid this entertainment cornucopia, the combined network news viewership has shrunk significantly—from some 50 million nightly in the 1960s to about 25 million today. (In comparison, CNN's audience is minuscule, typically no more than a million or so viewers, while public television's *NewsHour with Jim Lehrer* generally reaches fewer than three million viewers.)

The effects of this diet are evident in how little Americans know about current events. True, Americans have been extremely uninformed for a long time. Most follow public affairs only in a vague way, and many don't bother to engage at all. In the 1950s and 1960s, at the height of the Cold War, a poll revealed that only 55 percent of Americans knew that East Germany was a communist country, and less than half knew that the Soviet Union was not part of NATO, report political scientists Michael X. Delli Carpini and Scott Keeter in *What Americans Know about Politics and Why It Matters* (1996). In short, there was never a golden age of informed citizenry. But in recent decades, Americans' ignorance has reached truly stupefying levels, particularly among young adults. A series of reports published over the past two decades by the Pew Research Center for the People and the Press (and its predecessor, the Times Mirror Center) suggest that young adults were once nearly as informed as their elders on a range of political issues. From 1944 to 1968, the interest of younger people in the news as reported in opinion surveys was less than five percent below that of the population at large. Political debates and elections in the 1940s, the Army-McCarthy hearings of the 1950s, and the Vietnam War in the 1960s generated as much interest among the young as among older people. But Watergate in the 1970s was the last in this series of defining events to draw general public attention. (Decades later, in 2001, the bombing of the World Trade Center towers revived general public engagement, at least for a few weeks.) Soon after Watergate, surveys began to show flagging interest in current affairs among younger people.

There is no single explanation for this sudden break. Many of the young people I spoke with in doing my research were disaffected with the political process and believed that it was completely insulated from public pressure. Why, in that case, keep up with public affairs? The blurring line between entertainment and journalism, along with corporate consolidation of big media companies, has also bred in some minds a deep skepticism about the news media's offerings. At bottom, however, the sense of community has declined as Americans are able to live increasingly isolated lives, spending long hours commuting to work and holing up in suburban homes cocooned from the rest of the world.

The extent of this withdrawal from civic involvement is evident in a poll conducted during the height of the 2004 Democratic presidential primaries. In response to the question, "Do you happen to know which of the presidential candidates served as an army general?" about 42 percent of the over-50 crowd could name Wesley Clark. Only 13 percent of those under 30 could. While these results reveal a general lack of political knowledge across ages, they also underscore the growing gap between ages.

The shrinking audience for news is undermining the health of many major news media outlets. The most recent symptom was the revelation last year that a number of major newspapers, notably the *Chicago Sun-Times* and New York's *Newsday*, had cooked their books, inflating circulation figures in order to mask declines and keep advertising revenues from falling. More insidious—and less widely decried—is the industry-wide practice of bolstering profits by reducing news content. In newspapers, this is done by cutting back on the number of reporters covering state government, Washington, and foreign affairs, and by shrinking the space in the paper devoted to news. The news media are, in a very real sense, making our world smaller. On the broadcast networks, this shrinkage is easily measurable: In 1981, a 30-minute nightly newscast on CBS, minus commercials, was 23 minutes and 20 seconds, according to Leonard Downie, Jr., and Robert G. Kaiser's *The News about the News: American Journalism in Peril* (2002). In 2000, the same newscast was down to 18 minutes and 20 seconds. That's a lot of missing news.

The failing health of the nation's news media is not only a symptom of Americans' low levels of engagement in political life. It is a threat to political life itself. "The role of the press," writes news media critic James W. Carey, "is simply to make sure that in the short run we don't get screwed." Independent, fair, and accurate reporting is what gives "We the People" our check on power. Reporters dig up corruption and confront power; they focus the public's attention on government policies and actions that are unwise, unjust, or simply ineffective. It was the news media that exposed the Watergate burglary and cover-up engineered by Richard Nixon, sparked the investigation of the Iran-contra affair during the watch of Ronald Reagan and George H. W. Bush, ferreted out Bill Clinton's Whitewater dealings, and turned a searchlight on George W. Bush's extrajudicial arrests of American citizens suspected of terrorism.

A shrinking audience impairs the news media's ability to carry out their watchdog role. It also permits the powers that be to undermine journalism's legitimate functions. Where was the public outrage when it was revealed that the current Bush administration had secretly paid journalists to carry its water, or when the White House denied a press pass to a real journalist, Maureen Dowd of the *New York Times*, and gave one to a political hack who wrote for purely partisan outlets using a fake identity? The whole notion of the news media as the public's watchdog, once an unquestioned article of the American civic faith, is now in jeopardy. A recent study commissioned by the John S. and James L. Knight Foundation showed that more than a third of high school students feel that newspaper articles should be vetted by the federal government before publication.

If we are entering a post-journalism age—in which the majority of Americans, young and old, have little interaction with mainstream news media—the most valuable thing we are losing is the marketplace of ideas that newspapers and news broadcasts uniquely provide, that place where views clash and the full range of democratic choices is debated. You usually don't get that on a blog. You don't get that in the left-leaning *Nation* or on right-wing talk shows. But any newspaper worth its salt, and there are plenty, presents a variety of views, including ones antithetical to its editorial page positions. These papers are hardly immune from criticism—they sometimes err, get sloppy, or succumb to partisan or ideological bias—but they do strive to be accurate and independent sources of fact and opinion, and more often than not they fulfill that indispensable public function.

America's newspapers and television news divisions aren't going to save themselves by competing with reality shows and soap operas. The appetite for news, and for engagement with civic life itself, must be nurtured and promoted, and it's very much in the public interest to undertake the task. It's not the impossible assignment it may seem. During the course of my research, I met a group of boys in New Orleans who were very unlikely consumers of news: They were saturated with television programs and video games, they were poor, and they were in eighth grade. Yet they were all reading the *New York Times* online. Why? Because one of their teachers had assigned the newspaper to them to read when they were in sixth grade, and the habit stuck. There's no reason why print and broadcast news shouldn't be a bigger part of the school curriculum, or why there shouldn't be a short civics/current affairs section on the SAT for college-bound students, or why all high school seniors shouldn't have to take a nonbinding version of the civics test given to immigrants who want to become U.S. citizens. And why shouldn't broadcasters be required to produce a certain amount of children's news programming in return for their access to the public airwaves? These are only the most obvious possibilities.

Reporters, editors, producers, and media business executives will all need to make their own adjustments to meet the demands of new times and new audiences, but only by reaching a collective judgment about the value and necessity of vigorous news media in American democracy can we hope to keep our public watchdogs on guard and in good health.

The Ray and Maria Stata Center, Massachusetts Institute of Technology

MyWritingLab™

Frank Gehry

Frank Gehry, born in Toronto in 1929, has become one of most famous architects in the world for his sculptural approach to building design. His buildings feature shiny, curved surfaces, bizarre color combinations, and warped forms. One of his most famous and most controversial buildings is The Ray and Maria Stata Center on the Massachusetts Institute of Technology campus, which opened in March 2004. Housed in the Stata Center are the Computer Science and Artificial Intelligence Laboratory, the Laboratory for Information and Decision Systems, and the Department of Linguistics and Philosophy.

The Stata Center has been controversial from the start. *The Kaplan College* Guide describes MIT has having the "hottest" architecture of any campus. *Boston Globe* architecture columnist Robert Campbell wrote that "the Stata's appearance is a metaphor for the freedom, daring, and creativity of the research that's supposed to occur inside it." But others have criticized the Stata Center as poorly designed for day-to-day use, extremely overpriced (the official cost is $283.5 million), and garishly ugly.

Return to these questions after you have finished reading.

Analyzing the Reading

1. A campus joke goes "No worry at Stata about earthquakes—it already had one." Why do you think MIT wanted a building so different and whimsical on its campus?

2. Some of the world's best-loved structures including the Statue of Liberty and the Eiffel Tower were hated by many when they were erected. Why do people have such strong feelings about buildings and statues when they first appear, only to accept them soon afterwards?

3. The Stata Center was built on the site of Building 20, which was hastily constructed during World War II for research on radar. Building 20 was plain and ugly, yet it has been claimed that it was the most productive building for research in the history of the United States. Does the architecture of a building influence what happens inside? Think of examples that you have experienced.

4. Does your campus or city have a "signature" building? What does that building say about your school or your city?

Exploring Ideas and Issues

1. Frank Gehry said his goal was to create spaces for MIT scientists and faculty to meet one another, make connections, and spawn new ideas. How much can a building contribute to encouraging connections and creativity? Think about the buildings on your campus.

2. Think about your daily experience in the buildings of your campus. In some buildings, you feel comfortable and at ease right away. But in others you always feel disoriented, even after you memorize the route to your classroom. How does the layout of a building affect how you experience it? Discuss one campus building.

GEHRY: THE RAY AND MARIA STATA CENTER

The Story of an Hour
Kate Chopin

MyWritingLab™

Kate Chopin (1850–1894) began writing as a source of therapy and to earn income after she was widowed with six children. She wrote "The Story of an Hour" in the spring of 1894; *Vogue* magazine published the story in December 1894 under the title "The Dream of an Hour." In her day, Chopin's work was evocative, at times controversial, and often dismissed. While Chopin herself did not participate in the women's suffrage movement, 1960s feminists embraced her as among the first feminist authors.

Return to these questions after you have finished reading.

Analyzing the Reading

1. How has Chopin employed imagery to create a tone for the story? Upon your second reading, reflect upon the imagery within the context of your knowledge of the plot and ending.

2. In the first sentence, Chopin refers to the main character as Mrs. Mallard. Later in the story, we learn her first name. What might be the significance of the different ways Chopin names and describes Louise Mallard?

3. Conflict, and how characters respond to it, drives plot. Authors employ plot twists to move the story forward by exploiting readers' preconceived expectations. Identify several plot twists and describe what expectations the author exploits and with what effect.

4. Discuss the story's last sentence. It can be read from a literal perspective offering one meaning, but think about it in symbolic terms. What does a symbolic reading of the last line add to the story?

Exploring Ideas and Issues

Artists create within the context of their experiences; readers and viewers interpret through the lens of their experiences. Chopin's work may not seem radical or controversial in our contemporary context, but in the late nineteenth century, women had not yet won the right to vote or enjoyed the wide range of opportunities we take for granted today. Chopin was a married (then widowed) middle-class woman lacking a college education and living in the post-Reconstruction American South during her adulthood and child-rearing days. While her depictions and critique of the society, its values, and the mores of her time often startled early-twentieth-century readers, contemporary readers without understanding Chopin's context might wonder what the fuss was all about.

1. Feminism, a nineteenth-century movement launched to fight for women's equal rights, serves as a lens to examine the female experience in history, politics, and art. Research feminist literary theory and write an essay arguing why Chopin should or should not be considered a feminist author.

2. Examine the passage that begins, "She could see in the open square . . ." up to ". . . sparrows were twittering in the eaves." Write an analysis of how this image contributes to what you consider the larger theme of the story.

3. Place yourself in the role of a writer in the Mallard's community. Write a sequel to the story from Brently Mallard's perspective as a nineteenth-century male in which he interprets what happened to his wife. How did he perceive her and her relationship? How would he tell the story of their life together?

4. Write a critical literary analysis in which you connect figurative language, metaphors, or symbols of your choosing to your interpretation of the theme. Be sure to cite specific passages from the text to support your analysis and claims.

The Story of an Hour

Knowing that Mrs. Mallard was afflicted with a heart trouble, great care was taken to break to her as gently as possible the news of her husband's death.

It was her sister Josephine who told her, in broken sentences; veiled hints that revealed in half concealing. Her husband's friend Richards was there, too, near her. It was he who had been in the newspaper office when intelligence of the railroad disaster was received, with Brently Mallard's name leading the list of "killed." He had only taken the time to assure himself of its truth by a second telegram, and had hastened to forestall any less careful, less tender friend in bearing the sad message.

She did not hear the story as many women have heard the same, with a paralyzed inability to accept its significance. She wept at once, with sudden, wild abandonment, in her sister's arms. When the storm of grief had spent itself she went away to her room alone. She would have no one follow her.

There stood, facing the open window, a comfortable, roomy armchair. Into this she sank, pressed down by a physical exhaustion that haunted her body and seemed to reach into her soul.

She could see in the open square before her house the tops of trees that were all aquiver with the new spring life. The delicious breath of rain was in the air. In the street below a peddler was crying his wares. The notes of a distant song which some one was singing reached her faintly, and countless sparrows were twittering in the eaves.

There were patches of blue sky showing here and there through the clouds that had met and piled one above the other in the west facing her window.

She sat with her head thrown back upon the cushion of the chair, quite motionless, except when a sob came up into her throat and shook her, as a child who has cried itself to sleep continues to sob in its dreams.

She was young, with a fair, calm face, whose lines bespoke repression and even a certain strength. But now there was a dull stare in her eyes, whose gaze was fixed away off yonder on one of those patches of blue sky. It was not a glance of reflection, but rather indicated a suspension of intelligent thought.

There was something coming to her and she was waiting for it, fearfully. What was it? She did not know; it was too subtle and elusive to name. But she felt it, creeping out of the sky, reaching toward her through the sounds, the scents, the color that filled the air.

Now her bosom rose and fell tumultuously. She was beginning to recognize this thing that was approaching to possess her, and she was striving to beat it back with her will—as powerless as her two white slender hands would have been.

When she abandoned herself a little whispered word escaped her slightly parted lips. She said it over and over under her breath: "free, free, free!" The vacant stare and the look of terror that had followed it went from her eyes. They stayed keen and bright. Her pulses beat fast, and the coursing blood warmed and relaxed every inch of her body.

She did not stop to ask if it were or were not a monstrous joy that held her. A clear and exalted perception enabled her to dismiss the suggestion as trivial.

She knew that she would weep again when she saw the kind, tender hands folded in death; the face that had never looked save with love upon her, fixed and gray and dead. But she saw beyond that bitter moment a long procession of years to come that would belong to her absolutely. And she opened and spread her arms out to them in welcome.

There would be no one to live for during those coming years; she would live for herself. There would be no powerful will bending hers in that blind persistence with which men and women believe they have a right to impose a private will upon a fellow-creature. A kind intention or a cruel intention made the act seem no less a crime as she looked upon it in that brief moment of illumination.

And yet she had loved him—sometimes. Often she had not. What did it matter! What could love, the unsolved mystery, count for in face of this possession of self-assertion which she suddenly recognized as the strongest impulse of her being!

"Free! Body and soul free!" she kept whispering.

Josephine was kneeling before the closed door with her lips to the keyhole, imploring for admission. "Louise, open the door! I beg; open the door—you will make yourself ill. What are you doing, Louise? For heaven's sake open the door."

"Go away. I am not making myself ill." No; she was drinking in a very elixir of life through that open window.

Her fancy was running riot along those days ahead of her. Spring days, and summer days, and all sorts of days that would be her own. She breathed a quick prayer that life might be long. It was only yesterday she had thought with a shudder that life might be long.

She arose at length and opened the door to her sister's importunities. There was a feverish triumph in her eyes, and she carried herself unwittingly like a goddess of Victory. She clasped her sister's waist, and together they descended the stairs. Richards stood waiting for them at the bottom.

Some one was opening the front door with a latchkey. It was Brently Mallard who entered, a little travel-stained, composedly carrying his grip-sack and umbrella. He had been far from the scene of accident, and did not even know there had been one. He stood amazed at Josephine's piercing cry; at Richards' quick motion to screen him from the view of his wife.

But Richards was too late.

When the doctors came they said she had died of heart disease—of joy that kills.

EXAMPLE FOR ANALYSIS

Love in L.A.
Dagoberto Gilb

Dagoberto Gilb's mother was an illegal immigrant from Mexico. She settled in Los Angeles, where she and his father, an ex-Marine sergeant of German ancestry, started a relationship that ended quickly. Born in 1950, Gilb grew up in Los Angeles, attended college, and worked for many years as a carpenter, which gave him time to write. He is now the Director of Centro Victoria at the University of Houston-Victoria and has published novels and collections of short stories and essays.

A student's analysis of "Love in L.A." follows the story.

Return to these questions after you have finished reading.

Analyzing the Reading

1. From whose point of view is the story told? Do you think the narrator is a neutral observer?

2. Does Jake act responsibly after the accident? What other choices did he consider? What does his response tell you about his character?

3. What do we learn about Mariana from her response, her car, and her mention of her parents? Do you find her behavior credible and realistic? Support your response with evidence from the text.

4. How does the setting on a freeway shape how we understand the two characters? Imagine the story told in a rural setting. Do you think the main characters would behave differently?

5. Put forth an argument about whether the title is appropriate for the story. Use details from the story to support your position.

6. Gilb often writes about lives of working-class Latinos. Do you think Gilb is sympathetic to Jake's behavior? Explain.

Exploring Ideas and Issues

Gilb's story narrates the accidental meeting of two young people in a large, sprawling metropolis. The author keeps the action straightforward and confines it to one location and a limited time period. Yet, though the story seems simple, it raises many issues of character, societal interaction, and even fate.

1. Mariana and Jake seem to come from different worlds. What might we assume about their backgrounds and positions in society? What assumptions do they seem to make about each other? Is it likely that the two characters would have met under any other circumstances? Are they attracted to one another? Write a short essay in which you answer these questions. Give quotations from the story to support your answers.

2. Think of Jake's conversation with the girl as a rhetorical act, and write a short analysis. Make sure you address the following questions: What is his purpose? What strategies does he use? How does he adjust his presentation to his audience? Is his presentation effective? Why or why not? Give examples from the story to illustrate your answers.

3. The story starts and ends with Jake sitting in "this '58 Buick he drove," fantasizing about a better life. What effect does the car accident have on his sense of himself and of his future? Does Jake have the capacity to "change his whole style"? Why or why not? Write an essay examining what you think the story says about people's ability to change in general. Remember to include quotations from the story to support your views.

Love in L.A.

Jake slouched in a clot of near motionless traffic, in the peculiar gray of concrete, smog, and early morning beneath the overpass of the Hollywood Freeway on Alvarado Street. He didn't really mind because he knew how much worse it could be trying to make a left onto the onramp. He certainly didn't do that everyday of his life, and he'd assure anyone who'd ask that he never would either. A steady occupation had its advantages and he couldn't deny thinking about that too. He needed an FM radio in something better than this '58 Buick he drove. It would have crushed velvet interior with electric controls for the LA summer, a nice warm heater and defroster for the winter drives at the beach, a cruise control for those longer trips, mellow speakers front and rear of course, windows that hum closed, snuffing out that nasty exterior noise of freeways. The fact was that he'd probably have to change his whole style. Exotic colognes, plush, dark nightclubs, maitais and daquiris, necklaced ladies in satin gowns, misty and sexy like in a tequila ad. Jake could imagine lots of possibilities when he let himself, but none that ended up with him pressed onto a stalled freeway.

Jake was thinking about this freedom of his so much that when he glimpsed its green light he just went ahead and stared bye bye to the steadily employed. When he turned his head the same direction his windshield faced, it was maybe one second too late. He pounced the brake pedal and steered the front wheels away from the tiny brakelights but the smack was unavoidable. Just one second sooner and it would only have been close. One second more and he'd be crawling up the Toyota's trunk. As it was, it seemed like only a harmless smack, much less solid than the one against his back bumper.

Jake considered driving past the Toyota but was afraid the traffic ahead would make it too difficult. As he pulled up against the curb a few carlengths ahead, it occurred to him that the traffic might have helped him get away too. He slammed the car door twice to make sure it was closed fully and to give himself another second more, then toured front and rear of his Buick for damage on or near the bumpers. Not an impressionable scratch even in the chrome. He perked up. Though the car's beauty was secondary to its ability to start and move, the body and paint were clean except for a few minor dings. This stood out as one of his few clearcut accomplishments over the years.

Before he spoke to the driver of the Toyota, whose looks he could see might present him with an added complication, he signaled to the driver of the car that hit him, still in his car and stopped behind the Toyota, and waved his hands and shook his head to let the man know there was no problem as far as he was concerned. The driver waved back and started his engine.

"It didn't even scratch my paint," Jake told her in that way of his. "So how you doin? Any damage to the car? I'm kinda hoping so, just so it takes a little more time and we can talk some. Or else you can give me your phone number now and I won't have to lay my regular b.s. on you to get it later."

He took her smile as a good sign and relaxed. He inhaled her scent like it was clean air and straightened out his less than new but not unhip clothes.

"You've got Florida plates. You look like you must be Cuban."

"My parents are from Venezuela."

"My name's Jake." He held out his hand.

"Mariana."

They shook hands like she'd never done it before in her life.

"I really am sorry about hitting you like that." He sounded genuine. He fondled the wide dimple near the cracked taillight. "It's amazing how easy it is to put a dent in these new cars. They're so soft they might replace waterbeds soon." Jake was confused about how to proceed with this. So much seemed so unlikely, but there was always a possibility. "So maybe we should go out to breakfast somewhere and talk it over."

"I don't eat breakfast."

"Some coffee then."

"Thanks, but I really can't."

"You're not married, are you? Not that that would matter that much to me, I'm an openminded kinda guy."

She was smiling. "I have to get to work."

"That sounds boring."

"I better get your driver's license," she said.

Jake nodded, disappointed. "One little problem," he said. "I didn't bring it. I just forgot it this morning. I'm a musician," he exaggerated greatly, "and, well, I dunno, I left my wallet in the pants I was wearing last night. If you have some paper and a pen I'll give you my address and all that."

He followed her to the glove compartment side of her car.

"What if we don't report it to the insurance companies? I'll just get it fixed for you."

"I don't think my dad would let me do that."

"Your dad? It's not your car?"

"He bought it for me. And I live at home."

"Right." She was slipping away from him. He went back around to the back of her new Toyota and looked over the damage again. There was the trunk lid, the bumper, a rear panel, a taillight.

"You do have insurance?" she asked, suspicious, as she came around the back of the car.

"Oh yeah," he lied.

"I guess you better write the name of that down too."

He made up a last name and address and wrote down the name of an insurance company an old girlfriend once belonged to. He considered giving a real phone number but went against that idea and made one up.

"I act too," he lied to enhance the effect more. "Been in a couple of movies."

She smiled like a fan.

"So how about your phone number?" He was rebounding maturely.

She gave it to him.

"Mariana, you are beautiful," he said in his most sincere voice.

"Call me," she said timidly.

Jake beamed. "We'll see you, Mariana," he said holding out his hand. Her hand felt so warm and soft he felt like he'd been kissed.

Back in his car he took a moment or two to feel both proud and sad about his performance. Then he watched the rear view mirror as Mariana pulled up behind him. She was writing down the license plate numbers on his Buick, ones that he'd taken off a junk because the ones that belonged to his had expired so long ago. He turned the ignition key and revved the big engine and clicked into drive. His sense of freedom swelled as he drove into the now moving street traffic, though he couldn't stop the thought about that FM stereo radio and crushed velvet interior and the new car smell that would even make it better.

Quandre Brown

Professor Okafor

English 102

6 October 2014

Fender-bender Romance in Dagoberto Gilb's "Love in L.A."

The title of the story "Love in L.A." serves as metaphor for the nature of love and relationships in Los Angeles, and Hollywood in particular, has a reputation for being superficial. The setting in L.A. means everything; it is an L.A. story, not a New York City story, and certainly not a small town story. Everything is artifice and acting. The story "Love in L.A." describes a brief encounter following a fender-bender between a young man, Jake, and a young woman, Mariana. Jake and Mariana seem to be interested in each other, but we as the audience watching the scene unfold know that they are unlikely to ever see each other again. In fact, most of entire exchange between them was a lie—a big act. The two meet, flirt, lie, and then leave. Is this what love in L.A. is like?

The uninvolved narrator reveals that Jake is, at his core, a liar. In fact, he even lies to himself. Before the accident, the unemployed Jake is stuck in a traffic jam, daydreaming about owning a nicer car than his '58 Buick and living a finer lifestyle. As he watches the cars go up the onramp (on to steady jobs presumably in L.A.), Jake muses how much better it is not to have to do that, "He certainly didn't do that everyday of his life, and he'd assure anyone who'd ask that he never would either" (240). But while Jake may *tell* anyone who asked that he prefers his freedom, that doesn't necessarily mean he feels that way himself. Jake is really trying to convince himself that he has it better than the alternative. The fact that much of his daydream involves things that a steady job could provide—a nicer car, nightclubs, well-dressed women—reveals that he really wishes his life were different. The onramp represents an impediment to Jake's freedom (he is pleased that he doesn't have to cut across traffic to reach it) but it also represents the lifestyle a steady job can provide.

After the accident, we learn more about how far Jake's lying will go. In an honest moment, Jake sees the driver of the car he hit and admits to himself that her "looks might present him with an added complication" (241). The driver of the car is pretty, and *perhaps* this makes him more genuinely sorry he is about to lie through his teeth to her. The audience can't really tell, because the narrator leaves us wondering. " 'I really am sorry about hitting you like that.' He sounded genuine" (241). *Sounding* genuine is not necessarily *being* genuine, and it is interesting that the narrator uses this word to describe Jake's comment. Later in the story, when Jake tells Mariana that she is beautiful, the narrator relates that he says this "in his most sincere voice" (242). Another interesting word choice that leaves the audience to make up its own mind about the honesty of Jake's feelings. The fact that the accident happens just past the underpass of the Hollywood Freeway is significant. The setting is vital to the message the story is trying to convey. Love in L.A., it seems, is more about sounding the part, acting it out and delivering your lines the right way. Typical Hollywood.

Jake lies about not having his license with him, and makes up a false address with false auto insurance information, all the while trying to still pick Mariana up. Mariana flirts back with him, and does give him her phone number asking him to give her a call. But of course, we cannot be certain that the number she gave him was a real one. The narrator doesn't let us know what Mariana is thinking. For example, Mariana says she lives at home, but her car, however, has Florida license plates. While she may be a student home for summer break, she also may be lying to Jake about where she is from. Because the narrator does not tell us what Mariana is thinking, we have no way of knowing how truthful she is being. Before leaving, Mariana takes down Jake's license plate numbers, a clear indication that she really doesn't believe him.

Accidental meetings, superficial exchanges, a whole lot of acting, and two people going their separate ways sums up the nature of romance in a place like L.A. As he drives off, pleased with his performance, Jake resumes his daydream where he left off. Mariana will resume her trek to work. Cue the next act.

Work Cited

Gilb, Dagoberto. "Love in L.A." *Writing: A Guide for College and Beyond*, edited by Lester
    Faigley, 4th ed., Pearson, 2016, pp. 240-42.

How to Write an Analysis

These steps for the process of writing a rhetorical analysis may not progress as neatly as this chart might suggest. Writing is not an assembly-line process.

As you write, be open to new insights about the subject you are analyzing. Writing often generates new ideas that you can use to strengthen your analysis.

1 SELECT A TEXT TO ANALYZE

- Examine the assignment.
- Find a text or one or more visuals.
- Read the text carefully.
- Research the context.
- Research the author and audience.

2 ANALYZE CONTEXT AND TEXT

- Consider the medium and genre.
- Analyze the appeals. How does the author establish credibility? How logical are the arguments? What values does the author appeal to?
- Situate the text in its context. Where do you find evidence that the text was responding to other texts and events?
- Consider the style and tone.
- Make an analytical claim.

3
WRITE A DRAFT

- Decide on an organization. Make a working outline before you start writing.

- Write an introduction that describes briefly the text you are analyzing and gives information about the medium, the genre, when and where the text or visuals first appeared, and the author.

- State your thesis. Make sure your thesis is not an over-generalization and can be supported by textual and contextual evidence.

- Analyze the text. Discuss elements that show a pattern or illustrate specific techniques that you want to talk about.

- Analyze the context. Connect the text to events and discussions that were going on at the time it was composed. Explain how the text took part in a larger conversation.

- Build a strong conclusion. Your conclusion is a good place to draw implications about larger issues.

- Write a descriptive title.

4
REVISE, REVISE, REVISE

- Check that your paper or project fulfills the assignment.

- Make sure your analysis has a clear focus and claim.

- Check that each point of your analysis is supported with evidence.

- Make sure your voice and tone will engage readers.

- Examine your organization and think of possible better ways to organize.

5
SUBMITTED VERSION

- Make sure your finished writing meets all formatting requirements.

1: Select a Text or Visuals to Analyze

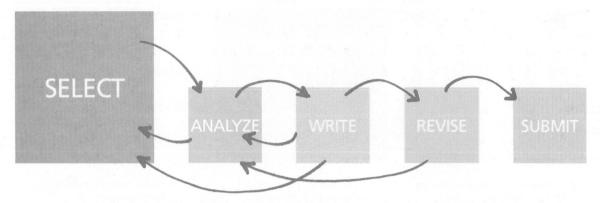

Examine the assignment

Read your assignment slowly and carefully. Look for words like *analyze* or *critique*, which tell that you are writing an analysis. Highlight any information about the length specified, date due, formatting, and other requirements. You can attend to this information later. At this point you want to zero in on the subject of your analysis.

Find a text to analyze

Choose a text that will be engaging for you and your readers. Your assignment may indicate what kind of text to analyze. Newspaper editorials, activist Web sites, speeches, proposals, and visual arguments are all good sources of texts for analysis. Look for a text that does something interesting, such as Tim Collins's comparison of his own battlefield speech with Marie Fatayi-Williams's emotional speech on the loss of her son.

Read the text carefully

In your first and second readings, your goal is to make sure you understand the text fully. Look up any names or events you don't know.

Research the context

What else was being written and said about this subject at the time the text was written? What events were taking place that might have influenced the author?

Research the author and the audience

Who is the author? What else has he or she said on this subject? What motivated him or her to produce this text? Who is the audience? Where did the text first appear (or, why was this image made or created)? Why did it appear at that particular moment?

Find a Verbal Text to Analyze

Find at least three examples of verbal texts that intend to persuade you in some way. They may ask you to do something specific such as buy a product or vote for a candidate, or else they may aim at changing your attitude. Note what makes each text interesting and make a tentative claim.

Text	Deadspin
What makes it interesting	Takes a humorous look at sports, exposing the pretensions and lack of honesty among sports figures.
Claim	Deadspin represents the spirit of many digital news sites in going for the truth underneath layers of hype and having fun along the way.

Find a Visual Text to Analyze

Identify at least three visual texts for possible analysis. Look for a visual text that in some way attempts to influence the viewer—an advertisement, a public building, a statue, a controversial work of art, a dramatic photograph, a television commercial, a corporate logo, and so on. Note what makes it interesting and make a tentative claim.

Text	Logos of competing political candidates
What makes it interesting	Candidate X's logo appears much better than candidate Y's logo among people I have asked, but they cannot explain why.
Claim	Candidate X has a better logo than candidate Y because the typeface and colors of X's logo express strength, energy, and movement while those on Y's logo suggest indecision and weakness.

Writer at Work

Chris Gonzalez's assignment asked him to analyze four photographs of a place taken by one of the Farm Security Administration photographers during the late 1930s and early 1940s. He searched for a place near his grandparents' home in Socorro, New Mexico. He found a few images of Socorro County taken by Russell Lee in 1940, but that search brought him to a far larger collection of Lee's photographs of Pie Town.

Project 2: Documentary photographs of a place

Complete draft due at the beginning of class on October 14

Final version due at the beginning of class on October 28

Length: 1100-1500 words (about 4-6 double-spaced pages not including the space for photos)

Follow MLA style described in Chapter 23, *Brief Penguin Handbook*, 5th Ed.

The foremost collection of documentary photographs from the late 1930s and early 1940s is the *Farm Security Administration-Office of War Information Collection* in the Library of Congress. Use the search engine or browse the geographic location index to find a place. You will also need to conduct additional research.

Select four photos by one photographer to analyze how the photographer chose to represent the place. Ask these questions.

- Who took the photograph?
- Why did the photographer choose this place? Most of the FSA photographs had some freedom in selecting the places they photographed.
- How was the photograph taken? Consider where the photographer was standing or sitting. If people are in the photographs, were they posing or are the shots candid?
- Look at the entire set of images of the place. What overall impression do they give of the place and the people?

Also think about the following.

- The composition of the image (point of view of photographer, lighting, framing, cropping, posing)
- The influence of the caption or title

Download your four photographs to your desktop and insert them in your project. Include the original captions under each photo.

Writer at Work

Chris selected four of Russell Lee's Pie Town photos from the *Farm Security Administration-Office of War Information Collection* in the Library of Congress. (See pages 260–265 to read the full essay.) He began by asking questions based on the instructor's assignment and the Visual Analysis section of this chapter. Here are the questions and his answers.

Where and when were the photos created?
—Pie Town, NM in October 1940; high-mountain desert of western New Mexico of 200+ families on the Great Divide

What was the purpose?
—To document the effects of the Great Depression and Dust Bowl on rural America to highlight the plight of the poor
—Smithsonian.com article suggests project was propaganda effort to promote President Roosevelt's New Deal legislation

Who was the photographer?
—Russell Lee (1903–1986)
—Raised in Illinois and earned degree in Chemical Engineering from Lehigh University, PA
—Became painter, using photos for subjects, then took interest in photography
—Hired by Farm Security Administration in 1936 as part of documentation team
Moved to Austin, Texas in 1947. Became first UT photography instructor in 1965

Who did he work for?
—FDR's Farm Security Administration (FSA) under the direction of Roy Stryker
—Stryker was a Columbia-educated economist and photographer hired by FSA to head up Information Division and manage photo documentary project

For whom were the photographs taken?
—The general public through mainstream publications
—FSA provided 77,000 black-and-white and 644 color images for the press

What can you infer about the intended audience?
—1940 US general public recovering from the decade-long Great Depression characterized by high unemployment and increased poverty and the growth of New Deal social and economic stimulus programs by Franklin Delano Roosevelt, elected in 1932
—Woes compounded by severe droughts leading to Dust Bowl in American Southwest creating additional hardships for Midwestern and Southwestern farmers, many of whom were displaced when they could not endure the hardships

— While many suffered, many were less affected. Photo documentary project set out to spread word across America to highlight the plight of fellow citizens with possible goal to develop support for government and social programs designed to improve the economy and lift the downtrodden

<u>What kind of visuals are they?</u>
—Color photographs; portraits of individuals and couples; groups participating in community events

<u>What was the medium?</u>
—Kodachrome color film; relatively new medium introduced in 1935; known for bright tones favored by amateurs and advertisers; departure from b&w favored by other documentary photographers

<u>How were the photographs composed? (point of view of photographer, lighting, framing, cropping, posing)</u>
—Photo 1: The Caudills
- stark shadows on the Caudills' squinting faces; harsh shadows and Doris's windblown hair; weathered, rugged appearance; Faro's tattered hat and tan skin; hard, long hours in sun?
- Point of view below eye level with the Caudills; looking up to the subjects; literally and figuratively?
- dark, heavy, foreboding clouds in the background contrasting w/ color present in foreground
- Doris is focal point; subtle smile, her red nail polish set her apart; contrast w/ Lange's '36 Migrant Mother?

—Photo 2: Mrs. Bill Stagg
- Holds up quilt w/ 48 states and image of a bird from the state (though not the state bird); proud demeanor?
- Looks (gazes?) directly into the camera; expresses pride and strength?
- Bright late afternoon light illuminates details of dugout cabin pine logs
- Lee portraying as proud, dignified; points to Lee's compassion?

—Photo 3: Barbeque
- Community feast; bbq, pies, cakes; people dressed up in "best" clothes; women in foreground wearing jewelry; bright purple dress; children blowing up balloons, eating ice cream, joyful; boy looks at desserts while grinning; women smiling; men talking; delicious looking pies; crust perfect color
- Photo vivid account of Pie Town life despite poverty; not "poor" people, just people, like other American citizens

—Photo 4: School Choir
- School recital; children dressed in best clothes; four boys in new-looking overalls; girls w/ fresh print dresses (look freshly washed?)
- Half of children without shoes, displaying poverty
- Lined up orderly, all focused on older girl leader

How would you characterize the style?
—Realism reflecting harsh realities of poor rural life offset with pride, dignity, and community

How were the photographs presented?
—Distributed by FSA to popular press to illustrate newspaper and magazine stories about plight of proud Americans challenged by Great Depression, Dust Bowl; victims of circumstances beyond their control

How do the captions or other connected words guide your interpretation?
—All captions include "Pie Town"; slices of life of individuals, couples, children, and community groups facing adversity in specific time and location

What is your claim?
—Pie Town photographs contrast with the stereotypical extreme cases of poverty portrayed by other Great Depression photos.
—Lee's Pie Town collection presents citizens supporting each other a sense of community embracing American values of hard work, family, and faith appealing to another American value of championing the underdog.
—He believed that in order to capture human suffering, a photographer also has to capture human dignity.

2: Analyze Context and Text

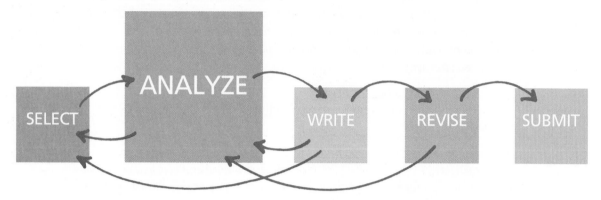

Consider the medium and genre

What is the medium: print, Web, video, or other? What is the genre? Is it an editorial? a proposal? a speech? a documentary film?

Consider the main claim or claims

Summarize the claim or describe the subject.

Consider the evidence

Note all the reasons and evidence given to support the claim.

Analyze the appeals

- **Ethos:** How trustworthy is the author? Does the author give you evidence to think he or she is knowledgeable or fair?
- **Pathos:** What emotions or values does the author appeal to?
- **Logos:** Where does the writer use facts and reasoning to support the claims?

Situate the text in its context

Where do you find evidence that this text was responding to other texts and events? How does the author contribute to the ongoing conversation of which this text is a part?

Consider the style and tone

How would you characterize the style? Is the style formal? informal? academic? How would you characterize the tone? Does the writer or speaker use humor or satire? How is language used to influence the audience? What metaphors are used?

Make an analytical claim

Your claim will be the focus of your analysis. Think about the evidence you will need to support your claim. It may come from the text itself or from your research into the context.

EXAMPLE OF AN ANALYTICAL CLAIM: Sojourner Truth's famous "Ain't I a Woman?" speech, made to an all-white and mostly male audience, uses powerful emotional and logical appeals to connect women's rights with the abolition of slavery.

Writer at Work

Chris Gonzales found a set of color photographs of Pie Town. He carefully reviewed the photos to select the four he would use in his visual analysis.

Interesting contrast to happy community shot. Portrait of couple under foreboding clouds; look more like hardscrabble people in other Dust Bowl photos; harsh features, tattered hat, defiant pose of woman.

Portrait of individual could balance well with community, couple, and children shots. Handmade folk art; states w/ birds; subject looking directly at camera displaying pride, dignity; bright afternoon light reveals details on the quilt and the texture of the log wall of the cabin.

Chris pulled together his thoughts on the photos and created a working thesis for his paper.

Pie Town collection portrays how residents support each other and display a sense of community and American values of hard work, family, and faith, hence appealing to the American value of championing the underdog.

3: Write a Draft

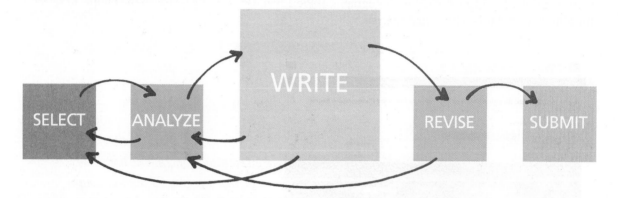

Decide on an organization

Make a working outline before you start writing.

- One method of organization is to introduce the text, state your thesis, and then give your analysis that supports your thesis.
- A second method is to introduce your text, then analyze the text section by section in order. In your conclusion you will need to come to a summary judgment.

Write a descriptive title

Don't settle for "An Analysis of ____." Give your readers a taste of what's to come.

Write an introduction

Describe briefly the text you are analyzing. Identify the medium and genre and when and where the text first appeared. Name the author and give any details about the author that are relevant. At the end of the introductory section, state your thesis. Make sure your thesis is not an overgeneralization and can be supported by textual and contextual evidence.

Analyze the text

Select the most important parts of the text to focus on.

- Choose elements that will show a pattern or illustrate specific techniques that you want to talk about.
- Build a critical mass of evidence with examples and quotations.
- Make the larger patterns or contrasts visible for your readers. For example, an author might appeal to two different audiences in the same editorial.

Analyze the context

Connect the text to events and discussions that were going on at the time it was composed. Explain how the text took part in a larger conversation.

Build a strong conclusion

Don't merely summarize what you have said. Your conclusion is a good place to draw implications about larger issues.

Writer at Work

Chris created a working outline to determine the best structure for his paper. He decided to introduce the photos, analyze them section by section, and conclude with a summary judgment.

I. *Introduction (Context and Background)*
   A. *Russell Lee*
      1. *Russell Lee joined Historical Section of Resettlement Administration in 1937*
      2. *Managed by Roy Stryker*
      3. *Became Farm Security Administration (FSA)*
   B. *FSA*
      1. *Provided relief for poor Southern and Southwestern sharecroppers during Great Depression*
      2. *Historical Section propaganda arm of the FSA to gain support for New Deal legislation*
   C. *Stryker*
      1. *Sought to document the plight of destitute farmers*
      2. *Employed accomplished Great Depression photographers*
   D. *Lee's Work*
      1. *Pie Town June 1940*
      2. *Returned October 1940 with Kodachrome film*

II. *Lee's Pie Town*
   A. *Lee's photographs give a vivid account of life in Pie Town*
      1. *Didn't gloss over the poverty*
      2. *Pie Towners did not let poverty define who they were as people*
   B. *Example 1: Faro and Doris Caudill . . .*
      1. *Composition*
      2. *Analysis: vivid colors, point of view, and composition elevate Lee's portrait to art*
   C. *Example 2: Mrs. Bill Stagg . . .*
      1. *Holds up a quilt*
      2. *Gaze directly into camera expresses pride and strength*
   D. *Example 3: Cutting the Pies, and Cakes . . .*
      1. *Feasting on barbeque, pies, and cakes*
      2. *Dressed in best clothes*
      3. *Color conveys the spirit*
   E. *Example 4: School Children Singing . . .*
      1. *School represents sense of community*
      2. *Children*

III. *Conclusions (Summary Judgment)*
   A. *Lee does not depict the extreme cases of Great Depression poverty*
   B. *Lee's Pie Town citizens*
      1. *support each other and display a sense of community unity*
      2. *embrace American values of hard work, family, and faith,*

4: Revise, Revise, Revise

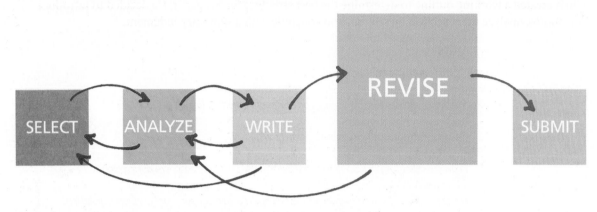

Skilled writers know that the secret to writing well is rewriting. Leave correcting errors for last.

Does your paper or project meet the assignment?	• Look again at your assignment. Does your paper or project do what the assignment asks? • Check the assignment for specific guidelines, including length, format, and amount of research. Does your work meet these guidelines?
Does your analysis have a clear purpose?	• Does it tell readers something they would not have otherwise noticed? • Do you make some kind of claim about the work you are analyzing? Is it a debatable claim?
Do you support your analysis with evidence?	• Do you provide a background about the author, intended audience, and the larger conversation surrounding the text you are analyzing? • Can you provide additional analysis to support your claims?
Is your organization effective?	• Is the order of your main points clear to your reader? • Are there any places where you find abrupt shifts or gaps? • Are there sections or paragraphs that could be rearranged to make your draft more effective?
Is the writing project visually effective?	• Is the font attractive and readable? • Are the headings and visuals effective?
Save the editing for last.	• When you have finished revising, edit and proofread carefully.

A peer review guide is on page 58.

Writer at Work

Chris Gonzalez received comments from his instructor on his draft. He used these comments to revise his draft.

Chris's instructor encouraged him to use precise language and a reliable source so his emerging thesis was not clouded by unintended connotations.

In 1936, Russell Lee joined a talented group of documentary photographers who worked as part of Roy Stryker's Historical Section of the Resettlement Administration, shortly renamed the Farm Security Administration (FSA). The FSA's mission was to provide relief for sharecroppers and very poor landowning farmers who were suffering during the Great Depression, particularly in the South and drought-stricken Southwest. Stryker's Historical Section was effectively the propaganda arm of the FSA, aimed at gaining support for New Deal legislation. Stryker envisioned a massive effort to photograph the plight of destitute farmers, and he employed photographers including Dorothea Lange, Arthur Rothstein, Ben Shahn, Walker Evans, Marion Post Walcott, Carl Mydans, Gordon Parks, and Jack Delano, whose images have come to represent the Great Depression in America.

Chris's emerging thesis was implied but buried as a transition in the first analytical section of the paper. His instructor encouraged Chris to make his thesis more prominent by pulling it up to the end of the introduction section.

Russell Lee sought out Roy Stryker and became the most prolific of the FSA photographers. He was on the road almost constantly documenting urban and rural communities. In June 1940, he arrived in Pie Town, New Mexico, where he took over six hundred black-and-white photographs of homesteaders who had moved there when President Franklin Delano Roosevelt revived the provisions of the Homestead Act under the New Deal. Located on the high-mountain desert of western New Mexico, Pie Town could not support over two hundred families living there at the time, and today the population is estimated to be around seventy, clustered around the Daily Pie Café, which has become a tourist attraction (Hendrickson). Lee returned in October 1940, but this time with Kodachrome film, which had appeared on the market only five years prior (Rosenblum 602).

"Propaganda" carries a strong connotation, usually a negative one associated with totalitarian regimes. Of course, the US has long used persuasive techniques to promote political and economic agendas, so "propaganda" could be appropriate. But, are you making this judgment? If so, why? Will the notion become part of your thesis? Or, has one of your sources offered up this interpretation? Is there a citation for this judgment?

Good background information and context so far, but I'm not sure what your thesis is, yet. Perhaps the first sentence of the paragraph below can serve as one? Maybe moving that sentence below up to this paragraph my make your thesis more clear.

259

5: Submitted Version (MLA Style)

MyWritingLab™

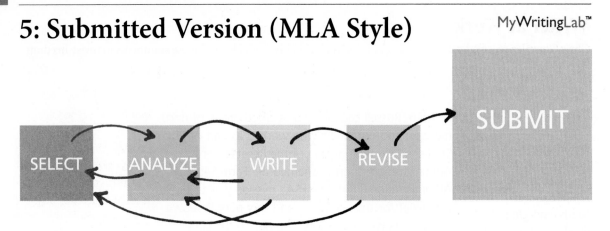

Chris Gonzalez

Professor Harrison

EN 100

28 October 2014

Russell Lee's Pie Town Photographs

    In 1936, Russell Lee joined a talented group of documentary photographers who
worked as part of Roy Stryker's Historical Section of the Resettlement Administration,
shortly renamed the Farm Security Administration (FSA). The FSA's mission was
to provide relief for sharecroppers and very poor landowning farmers who were
suffering during the Great Depression, particularly in the South and drought-stricken
Southwest. According to Jack Hurley, Stryker's Historical Section was effectively
the propaganda arm of the FSA, aimed at gaining support for New Deal legislation.
Stryker envisioned a massive effort to photograph the plight of destitute farmers, and
he employed photographers including Dorothea Lange, Arthur Rothstein, Ben Shahn,
Walker Evans, Marion Post Walcott, Carl Mydans, Gordon Parks, and Jack Delano,
whose images have come to represent the Great Depression in America.

    Russell Lee sought out Roy Stryker and became the most prolific of the FSA
photographers. He was on the road almost constantly documenting urban and rural
communities. In June 1940, he arrived in Pie Town, New Mexico, where he took over
six hundred black-and-white photographs of homesteaders who had moved there when
President Franklin Delano Roosevelt revived the provisions of the Homestead Act under
the New Deal. Located on the high-mountain desert of western New Mexico, Pie Town
could not support the over two hundred families living there at the time, and today

the population is estimated to be around seventy, clustered around the Daily Pie Café, which has become a tourist attraction (Hendrickson). Lee returned in October 1940, but this time with Kodachrome film, which had appeared on the market only five years prior (Rosenblum 602). Other creative and documentary photographers largely ignored color film, leaving its bright tones to amateurs and advertisers. Lee demonstrated the potential of color for documentary photography with his photographs of Pie Town, which captured the resiliency and sense of community of its residents.

In particular, Lee became close to Faro and Doris Caudill, whose lives he followed as he assembled a collection of photographs during his stay in Pie Town (see fig. 1).

The stark light on the Caudills' squinting faces, coupled with the harsh shadows from Faro's hat and Doris's windblown hair, give them a weathered, rugged appearance. Faro's tattered hat and tan skin testify that he labors long hours in the sun. Russell Lee took the picture below the Caudills' eye level so that the viewer looks up to them—literally and figuratively. Also notable in the photograph are the dark,

Fig. 1. Lee, Russell. *Faro and Doris Caudill, Homesteaders, Pie Town, New Mexico.* Library of Congress, Oct. 1940, www.loc.gov/pictures/item/fsa1992000345/PP/.

heavy, foreboding clouds in the background contrasting to the colorful foreground, particularly Doris Caudill's dress. Her confident pose, subtle smile, and red nail polish set her apart from other impoverished women in FSA collection such as Dorothea Lange's famous 1936 photograph of Florence Owens Thompson known as *Migrant Mother*. The vivid colors, point of view, and composition elevate Lee's portrait of the Caudills to art as well as a document.

Several other color portraits from October 1940 show Lee's compassion for Pie Town residents (see fig. 2). Mrs. Bill Stagg proudly holds up a quilt with names of the then forty-eight states and a quilted image of a bird from the state (though not the state bird). With her gaze directly into the camera, she too expresses pride and strength. The bright light of late afternoon shows the detail of the pine logs in her dugout cabin.

In addition to the portraits, Lee's photographs give a vivid account of life in Pie Town. He didn't gloss over the poverty. His 656 black-and-white photographs taken in June 1940 depict how close to the edge the Pie Town residents lived, how they had to dig new dugout cabins to get closer to water, how their crops shriveled in the dry wind. But

Fig. 2. Lee, Russell. *Mrs. Bill Stagg with State Quilt Which She Made, Pie Town, New Mexico*. Library of Congress, Oct. 1940, www.loc.gov/pictures/item/fsa1992000355/PP/.

Lee's photographs also suggest that Pie Towners did not let poverty define who they were as people, even though nearly all of them had to move elsewhere eventually. (The few that stayed met a severe drought in the 1950s that was even worse than the Dust Bowl years.)

They celebrated life as best they could. Clearly, they looked forward all year to the county fair, where they feasted on barbeque, pies, and cakes (see fig. 3). They all are dressed in their best clothes. Children are blowing up balloons and eating ice cream. A boy looks at the desserts with a broad grin. The women are smiling; the men are talking. Again, the color conveys the spirit. The sumptuous flavor of the pies is indicated by the perfect color of the crust. The happiness of the two women in the foreground is expressed not only by the joy on their faces but by what they are wearing—one with a handsome necklace, the other in a lavender dress.

The Pie Town sense of community is embodied in the school, which was held in the Farm Bureau building constructed by the residents. The children singing in this photograph are also dressed in their best clothes. Four of the boys wear new overalls,

Fig. 3. Lee, Russell. *Cutting the Pies and Cakes at the Barbeque Dinner, Pie Town, New Mexico Fair*. Library of Congress, Oct. 1940, www.loc.gov/pictures/item/fsa1992000386/PP/.

and the girls have clean print dresses. The telling detail, however, is that only half have shoes (see fig. 4). Still they all are focused on the older girl who is leading them.

Lee's Pie Town color photographs do not depict the extreme cases of poverty of the California migrant workers or the sharecroppers of the South that we have now come to associate with the Great Depression. What stands out about Pie Town in the larger collection, however, is how its citizens support each other and display a sense of community. Lee portrays the residents of Pie Town as embracing American values of hard work, family, and faith, and hence they appeal to another American value of championing the underdog. Not all the FSA photographers bought in to Roy Stryker's goal of creating empathy for the rural poor; Russell Lee was a natural fit because of his belief in social justice for all.

The head of the photographic archive that houses Lee's collection, Linda Peterson, observes, "His essential compassion for the human condition shines forth in every image" (Griffith). From Lee's work in Pie Town, we can see today why he became one of the most influential teachers of documentary photographers.

Fig. 4. Lee, Russell. *School Children Singing, Pie Town, New Mexico Fair.* Library of Congress, Oct. 1940, www.loc.gov/pictures/item/fsa1992000401/PP/.

Works Cited

Griffith, Vivé. "Compassionate Lens." *University of Texas at Austin,* Apr. 2007, www.
    utexas.edu/features/2007/lee/.

Hendrickson, Paul. "Savoring Pie Town." *Smithsonian.com*, Feb. 2005,
    www.smithsonianmag.com/history/savoring-pie-town-85182017/?no-ist.

Hurley, Jack F. "Lee, Russell Werner." *The Handbook of Texas*, Texas State Historical
    Association, 15 June 2010, tshaonline.org/handbook/online/articles/fle71.

Rosenbaum, Naomi. *A World History of Photography*. 4th ed., Abbeville Press, 2007.

Projects

Analyzing is valuable for clarifying and developing your own thinking as well as for giving your readers a broader understanding.

Rhetorical Analysis

Select a text to analyze—a speech, a sermon, an editorial, a persuasive letter, an essay, a Web site, a pamphlet, a brochure, or another kind of text.

Explain briefly what kind of text it is, when and where it was first published or spoken, and its main argument.

Make a claim about the text, which you support with close analysis.

Analyze the context. Is the text part of a larger debate? What other texts or events does it respond to? Who is the author? What motivated the author to write this text? What can you infer about the intended audience?

Analyze the appeals. What appeals to values and emotions are used? What appeals to logic are used? Do you find any logical fallacies (see pages 24–25)? Do you trust the writer?

Analyze the organization and style. What are the major parts and how are they arranged? Is the style formal, informal, satirical, or something else? Are any metaphors used?

Visual analysis

Find a visual text to analyze. You might analyze a popular consumer product, a public building, advertising, art, or a map.

Make a claim about the visual text. Support your claim with close analysis. Describe key features.

Analyze the context. Where and when was the visual created? What was the purpose? Who created it? What can you infer about the intended audience?

Analyze the visual text. What kind of visual is it? What is the medium? How is it arranged? How would you characterize the style? Are any words connected?

Critical literary analysis

Read carefully a short story or other literary text. Map out the plot. What is the conflict and how is it resolved?

Examine the characterization, including the major and minor characters. Characters are not real people, but instead they are constructed for a purpose. What role does each character perform? The setting, too, is a character. What role does the setting play in the story?

Consider the point of view. Does a character tell the story? Or is the narrator an all-knowing observer? Describe the language, style, and tone of the story. Identify any important images, symbols, and metaphors.

Identify the story's central theme. How does the title of the story relate to the theme?

Write an arguable thesis that connects one or more elements—characters, setting, language, metaphors, and so on—to the overall theme. A paper that begins with an engaging thesis arouses the reader's interest. Support your thesis with evidence from the text. A successful paper shares a discovery with the reader.

COMPOSE IN MULTIMEDIA

Analytical presentation

Choose a subject to analyze. Just as for rhetorical, visual, and literary analyses, an interesting text will help you to produce a presentation that will interest your audience. You will also need to do the same kind of close analysis of the text and research about the context (see page 217).

Plan your presentation. Just as for a written analysis, you will need to write a working thesis to make a working outline. Make a list of key points and think about the best order to present them. Plan your introduction to gain the attention of the audience and to introduce your topic. End by giving the audience something to take away—a compelling example or an idea that gives the gist of your presentation.

Create visuals that will help keep you and your audience oriented. Keep the visuals simple with one point per slide. Don't force your audience to read your presentation on the screen.

Deliver your presentation. Practice in advance so you don't have to fumble with your notes. Avoid the temptation to read to your audience. The best presentations make the audience feel like they have been in a conversation with the speaker. Invite response from your audience during and after your presentation.

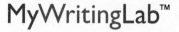 Visit Ch. 9 in MyWritingLab to complete the chapter exercises, explore an interactive version of the Writer at Work paper, and test your understanding of the chapter objectives.

10 Causal Arguments

An effective causal argument moves beyond the obvious to examine complex underlying causes.

In this chapter, you will learn to

1 Recognize the basic forms of causal arguments *(see p. 269)*

2 Understand how to make a visual causal argument *(see p. 270)*

3 Read and analyze a causal argument *(see pp. 271–303)*

4 Describe the steps involved in the process of writing a causal argument *(see pp. 304–305)*

5 Apply flexible strategies to write and revise a causal argument *(see pp. 306–321)*

Writing a Causal Argument

Causal arguments take three basic forms.

1. One cause leads to one or more effects.

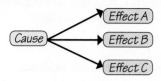

The invention of the telegraph led to the commodities market, the establishment of standard time zones, and news reporting as we know it today.

2. One effect has several causes.

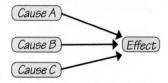

Hurricanes are becoming more financially destructive to the United States because of the greater intensity of recent storms, an increase in the commercial and residential development of coastal areas, and a reluctance to enforce certain construction standards in coastal residential areas.

3. A series of events form a chain, where one event causes another, which then causes a third, and so on.

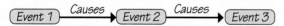

Making the HPV vaccination mandatory for adolescent girls will make unprotected sex seem safer, leading to greater promiscuity, ultimately resulting in more teenage pregnancies.

What Makes a Good Causal Argument?

1

Identify what is at stake

Because a strong causal claim may inspire people to change policies or behaviors or take other action, some readers may reject your claim. For example, although the causal link between cigarette smoke and cancer was widely accepted in scientific circles for many years, tobacco companies argued vociferously that no such link existed.

2

Move beyond the obvious to identify underlying causes

A well-thought-out causal analysis will trace multiple causes and consider their cumulative effect.

269

3

Avoid mistaking correlation for causations

A common pitfall of causal analysis is confusing causation with correlation. Events can be correlated without one being the cause of the other. Deaths by drowning and baseball games are correlated. But does one cause the other? Or is it because both occur most frequently in the summer?

4

Pay attention to effects

It's not enough to simply identify causes. In order for a causal analysis to matter, you must make clear why the effects are important. Otherwise, readers are apt to ask, "So what?"

5

Acknowledge other possible causes and make counterarguments

When causes are uncertain, disagreements often arise when various causes are proposed. Acknowledge possible causes that you think are flawed and explain why they are unlikely.

6

Support your causal claims with evidence

Do research to find evidence to back up your claims.

7

Conclude with strength

Simply repeating your claim often isn't the best way to end. Leave your readers with a memorable image, point, or implication.

Visual Causal Arguments

Causal arguments can be made in charts.

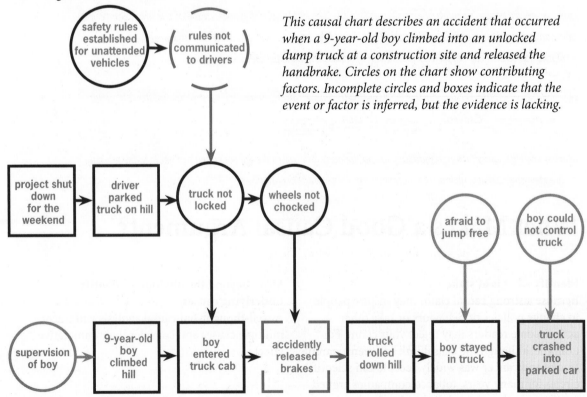

This causal chart describes an accident that occurred when a 9-year-old boy climbed into an unlocked dump truck at a construction site and released the handbrake. Circles on the chart show contributing factors. Incomplete circles and boxes indicate that the event or factor is inferred, but the evidence is lacking.

The French Paradox
Laura Fraser

Laura Fraser started counting calories in kindergarten when she was a slightly plump child. Her parents' obsession with her weight drove her to bulimia, which she describes in her 1997 book *Losing It: America's Obsession with Weight and the Industry That Feeds on It*. She comes to the conclusion that diets don't work. In the "The French Paradox," published in the online magazine *Salon* in 2000, Fraser examines why the French can eat a high-fat, high-calorie diet and be far healthier than Americans.

HOW IS THIS READING ORGANIZED?

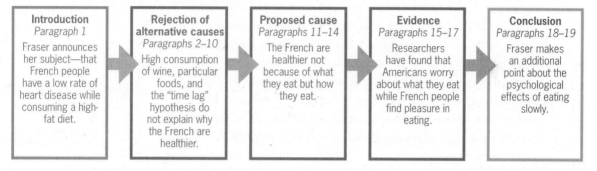

Introduction *Paragraph 1*	Rejection of alternative causes *Paragraphs 2–10*	Proposed cause *Paragraphs 11–14*	Evidence *Paragraphs 15–17*	Conclusion *Paragraphs 18–19*
Fraser announces her subject—that French people have a low rate of heart disease while consuming a high-fat diet.	High consumption of wine, particular foods, and the "time lag" hypothesis do not explain why the French are healthier.	The French are healthier not because of what they eat but how they eat.	Researchers have found that Americans worry about what they eat while French people find pleasure in eating.	Fraser makes an additional point about the psychological effects of eating slowly.

The French Paradox

1 For much of the past decade, American and British scientists have been annoyed by the phenomenon known as the French Paradox. Nutritionally speaking, the French have been getting away with murder: They eat all the butter, cream, foie gras, pastry and cheese that their hearts desire, and yet their rates of obesity and heart disease are much lower than ours. The French eat three times as much saturated animal fat as Americans do, and only a third as many die of heart attacks. It's maddening. ◄

Introduction: Fraser starts fast, setting out the central question: Why are the French healthier than Americans considering their respective diets?

2 Baffled, scientists struggled to come up with a few hypotheses: Maybe it was something in the red wine, they said. But while winemakers worldwide celebrated that news, more sober research has suggested that any alcohol—whether Lafite Rothschild, a banana daiquiri or a cold Bud—pretty much has the same nice, relaxing effect. So while a little wine is apt to do you good, the French aren't so special in having a drink now and then (though

the fact that they drink wine moderately and slowly with meals, instead of downing shots at the bar, could make a difference). ◄

First rejected cause: Wine consumption isn't the answer.

3   After the wine argument, scientists ventured that it must be the olive oil that keeps the French healthy. But this doesn't explain the butter or brie. Then, voilà, French scientist Serge Renaud (made famous on *60 Minutes* as an expert on the French Paradox) said it's the foie gras that melts away cholesterol. This, too, is dicey: While people in Toulouse— the fattened force-fed duck-liver-eating area of France—do indeed have one of the lowest rates of heart disease in the developed world, they actually only eat the delicacy about six times a year. And they're a lot more likely to die of stroke than we are anyway.

4   Other researchers, perhaps sponsored by the garlic and onion industry, suggested that the French Paradox effect is due to garlic and onions. Claude Fischler, a nutritional sociologist at INSERM, the French equivalent of America's National Institutes of Health, says all these single hypotheses are more wishful thinking than science. ◄

Second rejected cause: Particular foods don't explain why the French are healthier.

5   "The government loves the French Paradox because it sells red wine—Bordeaux wine in particular—it sells French lifestyle and a number of other French products," he tells me over dinner at an outdoor Paris bistro. "It's something in the cheese! Something from the fat from ducks! It's butter! Really, we're a long way from science here."

6   More than anything, Fischler thinks the French Paradox is a kind of cultural Rorschach test. "Americans think it's unfair, and Francophiles think it's wonderful."

7   Last May, researchers writing in the *British Medical Journal* came up with the least cheerful hypothesis of all. They argued that it's just a matter of time before the French—who are in fact eating more hamburgers and french fries these days—catch up with Americans, and begin suffering the same high rates of cardiovascular disease.

8   These researchers, Malcolm Law and Nicholas Wald (who must have thought up their hypothesis over dry kidney pie, while dreaming of the kind of duck in red wine and honey sauce I had with Claude Fischler), call this the "time lag explanation" for the French Paradox. As far as they are concerned, the McDonaldization (this is a French catch-all term for the importation of fast food and

other American cultural horrors) of France will continue at a frantic pace, and it is as inevitable that French men will start keeling over of heart attacks as it is that French women will eventually wear jean shorts and marshmallow tennis shoes on the streets of Paris.

9   Nutritionists on this side of the Atlantic are just as dour in their predictions. Marion Nestle, chair of New York University's department of nutrition, says that the wonderful food she found on every street corner in Paris when she lived there in 1983 has changed. "Then you could go into some local bar, and you would be given a little tart, a little salad and a little quiche that would knock your socks off," she says wistfully. But now, she says, the quality of ingredients, the concern about flavor and the freshness of the food has declined. "Last time I was in Paris, everything seemed bigger, softer and more commercially prepared. If you wanted really high quality food, you had to pay for it." When she looked at food data in France, she saw that indeed the amount of fat has risen, and the French are snacking more, eating fewer long meals and visiting McDonald's more often on the sly. She, like Law and Wald, says, "Just wait."

10   The French, however, disagree about this time lag hypothesis. Nor do they believe that Parisian women will start wearing Nikes with skirts to work anytime soon. "It's hilarious!" says Fischler, finishing a fresh ricotta-stuffed tortellini appetizer. "The American attitude is always to look for a silver bullet—it's the wine, the cheese—or else it has to be nothing, we'll get worse, we haven't had time to get the terrible consequences of modern eating." Instead, says Fischler, the deeply rooted French traditions of eating not only explain the French Paradox, but will insure that it continues, even if it decreases somewhat. ◄──────

Third rejected cause: Fraser refutes that the French will become as unhealthy with an American diet.

11   Americans, he says, are always painting the picture in extremes. The French, he continues over a piece of grilled fish, pouring me another glass of that medicinal red wine, have a long-evolved culture of eating that emphasizes pleasure—and order. The French eat *comme il faut*, "the way it should be done." They may eat whatever they want, but they eat by strict rules: no snacking, no seconds,

no skipping meals, no bolting down food, no heading straight for dessert before first filling up on vegetables, salad and meat. They savor their food and eat smaller portions than Americans do. ◄

Actual cause:
The difference between the French and Americans is not what they eat but how they eat.

12   They also eat a greater diversity of food, which could have something to do with their health, too. And while traditions are loosening in France—more women are working, and so people are more apt to grab a sandwich at lunch—a recent survey Fischler took showed that while more people will skip the cheese course or the first course once or twice a week, they still don't skip meals. The French sit down at the table for well-prepared meals, with high-quality foods, and between times they don't eat. Period.

13   "In France, we eat in a socially controlled and regulated way, but it's pleasant," says Fischler. "Structure is something that constrains you but also supports you." Fischler and a food-loving University of Pennsylvania psychologist, Paul Rozin, say the fact that the French have lower rates of coronary artery disease and are skinnier than Americans doesn't have so much to do with what they eat, but how they eat—especially their positive attitudes about food. Talk to a French woman about whether she ever feels guilty about what she eats and she will tell you, as one impossibly young-looking 46-year-old dancer told me, "Absolutely not—I eat exactly what I please."

14   Then try to find a woman in the U.S. who will answer the same way. There's no magic ingredient that keeps French arteries clear, but instead a whole system of eating that allows them to indulge without overdoing it, and without feeling guilty. Fischler and Rozin say that the biggest predictor of health may not be the content of someone's diet, but how stressed out they are about food, and how relaxed they are about eating. In other words, the more pleasurable it is to eat, the healthier it is for you.

15   In a study published in the October issue of the journal *Appetite*, Fischler and Rozin surveyed 1,281 French, American, Japanese and Flemish people about their attitudes toward food. Participants were asked how much they worried about food and the healthiness of their diet, whether they bought low-fat and other diet foods and how much importance they placed on food as a positive force in life.

Americans, it turned out, were much more likely than the French to worry about what they eat, buy diet foods and still think of themselves as unhealthy eaters. The French and Belgians were at the other extreme, thinking about food as mainly a great pleasure, and feeling fine about how healthy their diet was. In word association tests, given "chocolate cake," the French would say "celebration," and Americans, "guilt." Given "heavy cream," the French said "whipped," while the Americans responded "unhealthy." Says Rozin, "The French are more inclined to think of food as something you eat and experience, and the Americans are thinking about some sort of chemicals that are getting into your body." ◄

Evidence for claim:
Fraser summarizes a study that supports the anecdotal evidence she has given.

16   Americans have the worst of both worlds, Rozin says—they have greater concerns about their diets, and they are much more dissatisfied with what they eat. And that sort of stress, he says, can result in a lot of poor eating habits for Americans—extreme dieting, bingeing, overeating and constantly obsessing about food—which are ultimately unhealthy. The real paradox, Rozin says, isn't that the French enjoy food and remain thin and heart disease-free. It's that Americans worry so much about food, do so much more to control their weight and end up so much more dissatisfied with their meals. ◄

Conclusion:
Fraser reverses the paradox: Americans worry more about food than the French yet are fatter and less healthy.

17   American researchers are tentative about Fischler and Rozin's pleasure hypothesis. Eric Rimm, a nutritional epidemiologist at Harvard, says a pleasurable way of eating may be part of the puzzle. "There is something to eating patterns that makes a difference to overall health," he says. "It can't just be the total calories you get at the end of the day."

Eating slowly, he points out, may make a difference. And then there are psychosocial effects. "In France they eat with large families and social networks, which may be important to peace of mind, which has been linked to coronary disease." He hesitates. "Maybe there are psychological effects to the way they eat in France, too." ◄

Conclusion:
Fraser offers an additional point for her readers to think about.

18   As the French would say, with just a hint of derision, "*Mais oui*— but of course." And then, like Claude Fischler and me, they would finish off a long, perfect meal with a couple little spoonfuls of intensely rich chocolate soufflé.

Why Should I Be Nice to You? Coffee Shops and the Politics of Good Service

MyWritingLab™

Emily Raine

> **Emily Raine** recently received a Master's degree in Communication Studies at McGill University in Montreal. She also writes about graffiti and street art. This essay appeared in the online journal *Bad Subjects* in 2005.

Return to these questions after you have finished reading.

Analyzing the Reading

1. What exactly is Raine's causal argument about why work in coffee chains is worse than in other kinds of service jobs?

2. Raine mixes technical terms with informal language. For example, she says, "Café labor is heavily grounded in the rationalism of Fordist manufacturing principles," which uses the technical term for the method of assembly line production developed by Henry Ford. But she also says she "felt like an aproned Coke machine." Look for other examples of technical and informal language. Why does she mix them?

3. Why is it important that coffee shop employees not act like individuals, from the employer's perspective?

4. Have you ever worked in a restaurant, coffee shop, retail store, or another service industry? If so, how was your experience similar to or different from Raine's? If not, think about your experiences as a customer in coffee shops and similar businesses. How did the employees behave?

5. Look at the last paragraph. Raine makes a new claim that rudeness allows workers to retain their individuality. Why does she put this claim in the conclusion? Does it lead to a strong conclusion?

Exploring Ideas and Issues

Raine presents a sophisticated analysis, explaining both employers' requirements and employees' responses. She uses expert opinion, historical facts, and personal experience to support her contention that the very way in which coffee bars are organized works against employers' demand that employees provide "good service."

1. Think about the causal argument that Raine presents and your own experiences as an employee or as a customer at a coffee shop, restaurant, store, or other service-oriented establishment. Do you agree with Raine's explanation of rudeness? Has she overlooked other possible causes of this behavior? Write a short rebuttal to Raine's argument, discussing at least one factor that Raine has overlooked.

2. Raine contends that uniforms obscure workers' individuality. However, people in many occupations—for example, police, military, medical personnel—must wear uniforms or adhere to specific grooming regimens. Write a short essay in which you discuss the effects that various kinds of uniforms can have. Is making practioners themselves seem "uniform" something that all have in common? Draw on examples from your personal experience to support your ideas.

Bad Subjects

Why Should I Be Nice to You?
Coffee Shops and the Politics of Good Service

"There is no more precious commodity than the relationship of trust and confidence a company has with its employees."

–STARBUCKS COFFEE COMPANY CHAIRMAN HOWARD SCHULTZ

I actually like to serve. I'm not sure if this comes from some innate inclination to mother and fuss over strangers, or if it's because the movement and sociability of service work provides a much-needed antidote to the solitude of academic research, but I've always found something about service industry work satisfying. I've done the gamut of service jobs, from fine dining to cocktail waitressing to hip euro-bistro counter work, and the only job where I've ever felt truly whipped was working as a barista at one of the now-ubiquitous specialty coffee chains, those bastions of jazz and public solitude that have spread through urban landscapes over the last ten years or so. The pay was poor, the shifts long and oddly dispersed, the work boring and monotonous, the managers demanding, and the customers regularly displayed that unique spleen that emerges in even the most pleasant people before they've had the morning's first coffee. I often felt like an aproned Coke machine, such was the effect my sparkling personality had on the clientele. And yet, some combination of service professionalism, fear of termination and an imperative to be "nice" allowed me to suck it up, smile and continue to provide that intangible trait that the industry holds above all else, good service.

Bad Subjects

Good service in coffee shops doesn't amount to much. Unlike table service, where interaction with customers spans a minimum of half an hour, the average contact with a café customer lasts less than ten seconds. Consider how specialty cafés are laid out: the customer service counter is arranged in a long line that clients move along to "use" the café. The linear coffee bar resembles an assembly line, and indeed, café labor is heavily grounded in the rationalism of Fordist manufacturing principles, which had already been tested for use in hospitality services by fast food chains. Each of the café workers is assigned a specific stage in the service process to perform exclusively, such as taking orders, using the cash registers, or handing clients cups of brewed coffee.

The specialization of tasks increases the speed of transactions and limits the duration of any one employee's interaction with the clientele. This means that in a given visit a customer might order from one worker, receive food from the next, then brewed coffee or tea from yet another, then pay a cashier before proceeding down the line of the counter, finishing the trip at the espresso machine which is always situated at its end. Ultimately, each of the café's products is processed and served by a different employee, who repeats the same preparation task for hours and attends to each customer only as they receive that one product.

Needless to say, the productive work in cafés is dreary and repetitive. Further, this style of service severely curtails interaction with the clientele, and the very brevity of each transaction precludes much chance for authentic friendliness or conversation—even asking about someone's day would slow the entire operation. The one aspect of service work that can be unpredictable—people—becomes redundant, and interaction with customers is reduced to a fatiguing eight-hour-long smile and the repetition of sentiments that allude to good service, such as injunctions to enjoy their purchases or to have a nice day. Rather than friendly exchanges with customers, barista workers' good service is reduced to a quick rictus in the customer's direction between a great deal of friendly interaction with the espresso machine.

eserver » bad home » bad editorials » 2006 » raza/race: why support immigrants?

Bad Subjects

home   about   articles   authors   books   contact us   **editorials**   links   news   reviews

As the hospitality industry really took off in the sixties, good service became one of the trademarks of its advertising claims, a way for brands to distinguish themselves from the rest of the pack. One needn't think too hard to come up with a litany of service slogans that holler the good graces of their personnel — at Starbucks where the baristas make the magic, at PSA where smiles aren't just painted on, or at McDonald's where smiles are free. Employee friendliness emerged as one of the chief distinguishing brand features of personal services, which means that the workers themselves become an aspect of the product for sale.

Our notions of good service revolve around a series of platitudes about professionalism — we're at your service, with a smile, where the customer's always right — each bragging the centrality of the customer to everything "we" do. Such claims imply an easy and equal exchange between two parties: the "we" that gladly serves and the "you" that happily receives. There is, however, always a third party involved in the service exchange, and that's whoever has hired the server, the body that ultimately decides just what the dimensions of good service will be.

Like most employees, a service worker sells labor to an employer at a set rate, often minimum wage, and the employer sells the product of that labor, the service itself, at market values. In many hospitality services, where gratuities make up the majority of employment revenue, the worker directly benefits from giving good service, which of course translates to good tips. But for the vast majority of service staff, and particularly those employed in venues yielding little or no gratuities — fast food outlets, café chains, cleaning and maintenance operations — this promises many workers little more than a unilateral imperative to be perpetually bright and amenable.

The vast majority of service personnel do not spontaneously produce an unaffected display of cheer and good will continuously for the duration of a shift. When a company markets its products on servers' friendliness, they

Bad Subjects

must then monitor and control employees' friendliness, so good service is defined and enforced from above. Particularly in chains, which are premised upon their consistent reproduction of the same experience in numerous locations, organizations are obliged to impose systems to manage employees' interaction with their customers. In some chains, namely the fast food giants such as McDonald's and Burger King, employee banter is scripted into cash registers, so that as soon as a customer orders, workers are cued to offer, "would you like a dessert with that?" (an offer of dubious benefit to the customer) and to wish them a nice day. Ultimately, this has allowed corporations to be able to assimilate "good service"—or, friendly workers— into their overall brand image.

While cafés genuflect toward the notion of good service, their layouts and management styles preclude much possibility of creating the warmth that this would entail. Good service is, of course, important, but not if it interferes with throughput. What's more, these cafés have been at the forefront of a new wave of organizations that not only market themselves on service quality but also describe employees' job satisfaction as the seed from which this flowers.

Perhaps the most glaring example of this is Starbucks, where cheerful young workers are displayed behind elevated counters as they banter back and forth, calling out fancy Italian drink names and creating theatre out of their productive labor. Starbucks' corporate literature gushes not only about the good service its customers will receive, but about the great joy that its "partners" take in providing it, given the company's unique ability to "provide a great work environment and treat each other with respect and dignity," and where its partners are "emotionally and intellectually committed to Starbucks success." In the epigraph to this essay, Starbucks' chairman even describes the company's relationship with its workers as a commodity. Not only does Starbucks offer good service, but it attempts to guarantee something even better: good service provided by employees that are genuinely happy to give it.

Bad Subjects

home   about   articles   authors   books   contact us   **editorials**   links   news   reviews

Starbucks has branded a new kind of worker, the happy, wholesome, perfume-free barista. The company offers unusual benefits for service workers, including stock options, health insurance, dental plans and other perks such as product discounts and giveaways. Further, they do so very, very publicly, and the company's promotional materials are filled with moving accounts of workers who never dreamed that corporate America could care so much. With the other hand, though, the company has smashed unionization drives in New York, Vancouver and at its Seattle roaster; it schedules workers at oddly timed shifts that never quite add up to full-time hours; the company pays only nominally more than minimum wage, and their staffs are still unable to subsist schlepping lattes alone.

Starbucks is not alone in marketing itself as an enlightened employer. When General Motors introduced its Saturn line, the new brand was promoted almost entirely on the company's good relations with its staff. The company's advertising spots often featured pictures of and quotes from the union contract, describing their unique partnership between manufacturer, workers and union, which allowed blue-collar personnel to have a say in everything from automobile designs to what would be served for lunch. The company rightly guessed that this strategy would go over well with liberal consumers concerned about the ethics of their purchases. Better yet, Saturn could market its cars based on workers' happiness whether personnel were satisfied or not, because very few consumers would ever have the chance to interact with them.

At the specialty coffee chains, however, consumers have to talk to employees, yet nobody ever really asks. The café service counter runs like a smooth piece of machinery, and I found that most people preferred to pretend that they were interacting with an appliance. In such short transactions, it is exceedingly difficult for customers to remember the humanity of each of the four to seven people they might interact with to get their coffees. Even fast food counters have one server who processes each customer's order, yet in cafés the workers just become another gadget in the well-oiled café machine. This is a definite downside for the

Bad Subjects

home   about   articles   authors   books   contact us   **editorials**   links   news   reviews

employees—clients are much ruder to café staff than in any other sector of the industry I ever worked in. I found that people were more likely to be annoyed than touched by any reference to my having a personality, and it took no small amount of thought on my part to realize why.

Barista workers are hired to represent an abstract category of worker, not to act as individuals. Because of the service system marked by short customer interaction periods and a homogenous staff, the services rendered are linked in the consumer imagination to the company and not to any one individual worker. Workers' assimilation into the company image makes employees in chain service as branded as the products they serve. The chain gang, the workers who hold these eminently collegiate after-school jobs, are proscribed sales scripts and drilled on customer service scenarios to standardize interactions with customers. The company issues protocols for hair length, color and maintenance, visible piercings and tattoos as well as personal hygiene and acceptable odorific products. Workers are made more interchangeable by the use of uniforms, which, of course, serve to make the staff just that. The organization is a constant intermediary in every transaction, interjecting its presence in every detail of the service experience, and this standardization amounts to an absorption of individuals' personalities into the corporate image.

Many of the measures that chains take to secure the homogeneity of their employees do not strike us as particularly alarming, likely because similar restrictions have been in place for several hundred years. Good service today has inherited many of the trappings of the good servant of yore, including prohibitions against eating, drinking, sitting or relaxing in front the served, entering and exiting through back doors and wearing uniforms to visually mark workers' status. These measures almost completely efface the social identities of staff during work hours, providing few clues to workers' status in their free time. Contact between service workers and their customers is thus limited to purely functional relations, so that the public only see them as workers, as makers of quality coffee, and never as possible peers.

Bad Subjects

Maintaining such divisions is integral to good service because this display of class distinctions ultimately underlies our notions of service quality. Good service means not only serving well, but also allowing customers to feel justified in issuing orders, to feel okay about being served—which, in turn, requires demonstrations of class difference and the smiles that suggest servers' comfort with having a subordinate role in the service exchange.

Unlike the penguin-suited household servant staffs whose class status was clearly defined, service industry workers today often have much more in common from a class perspective with those that they serve. This not only creates an imperative for them to wear their class otherness on their sleeves, as it were, but also to accept their subordinate role to those they serve by being unshakably tractable and polite.

Faith Popcorn has rather famously referred to the four-dollar latte as a "small indulgence," noting that while this is a lot to pay for a glass of hot milk, it is quite inexpensive for the feeling of luxury that can accompany it. In this service climate, the class status of the server and the served—anyone who can justify spending this much on a coffee—is blurry, indeed. Coffee shops that market themselves on employee satisfaction assert the same happy servant that allows politically conscientious consumers who are in many cases the workers' own age and class peers, to feel justified in receiving good service. Good service—as both an apparent affirmation of subordinate classes' desire to serve and as an enforced one-sided politeness—reproduces the class distinctions that have historically characterized servant-served relationships so that these are perpetuated within the contemporary service market.

The specialty coffee companies are large corporations, and for the twenty-somethings who stock their counters, barista work is too temporary to bother fighting the system. Mostly, people simply quit. Dissatisfied workers are stuck with engaging in tactics that will change nothing but allow them to make the best of

eserver » bad home » bad editorials » 2006 » raza/race: why support immigrants?

Bad Subjects

home   about   articles   authors   books   contact us   **editorials**   links   news   reviews

their lot. These include minor infractions such as taking liberties with the uniforms or grabbing little bits of company time for their own pleasure, what Michel de Certeau calls *la perruque* and the companies themselves call "time theft." As my time in the chain gang wore on, I developed my own tactic, the only one I found that jostled the customers out of their complacency and allowed me to be a barista and a person.

There is no easy way to serve without being a servant, and I have always found that the best way to do so is to show my actual emotions rather than affecting a smooth display of interminable patience and good will. For café customers, bettering baristas' lots can be as simple as asking about their day, addressing them by name—any little gesture to show that you noticed the person behind the service that they can provide. My tactic as a worker is equally simple, but it is simultaneously an assertion of individual identity at work, a refusal of the class distinctions that characterize the service environment and a rebuttal to the companies that would promote my satisfaction with their system: be rude. Not arbitrarily rude, of course—customers are people, too, and nobody gains anything by spreading bad will. But on those occasions when customer or management behavior warranted a zinging comeback, I would give it.

Rudeness, when it is demanded, undermines companies' claims on workers' personal warmth and allows them to retain their individuality by expressing genuine rather than affected feelings in at-work interpersonal exchanges. It is a refusal of the class distinctions that underlie consumers' unilateral prerogative of rudeness and servers' unilateral imperative to be nice. It runs contrary to everything that we have been taught, not only about service but about interrelating with others. But this seems to be the only method of asserting one's person-hood in the service environment, where workers' personalities are all too easily reduced to a space-time, conflated with the drinks they serve. Baristas of the world, if you want to avoid becoming a green-aproned coffee dispensary, you're just going to have to tell people off about it.

The New Girl Order

MyWritingLab™

Kay S. Hymowitz

Kay S. Hymowitz is a contributing editor of *City Journal* and the William E. Simon Fellow at the Manhattan Institute. She writes about childhood and education in the United States as well as the breakdown of marriage and how it threatens the nation's future. She has published four books, including *Marriage and Caste in America: Separate and Unequal Families in a Post-Marital Age* (2006), which is a compilation of some of her previously published *City Journal* essays. Her most recent book is *Manning Up: How the Rise of Women is Turning Men into Boys* (2011).

Return to these questions after you have finished reading.

Analyzing the Reading

1. The title of Hymowitz's essay is a play on the phrase "New World Order." Why do you think that she chose this phrase? What does this phrase mean to you? What is the history of this phrase?

2. The author suggests that the SYF lifestyle is spreading worldwide. What three factors does she say contribute to this growth?

3. What exactly is the SYF lifestyle, and why is it so attractive to women, according to Hymowitz?

4. What does Hymowitz see as the societal costs of the "New Girl Order"?

Exploring Ideas and Issues

Women's status has changed dramatically over the past century. It's as recently as 1920 that women's right to vote was recognized in the United States by the adoption of the Nineteenth Amendment. Some changes, such as the right to vote, have been enshrined in law; others, such as those described in Hymowitz's essay, are the result of personal decisions and societal forces.

1. Hymowitz does not directly discuss the role that changes in sexual mores may have played in the development of the SYF lifestyle. Think about your generation's attitude toward sex before marriage and children born out of wedlock. Compare that attitude with your parents' or your grandparents' view of the same issues. Write a short essay in which you analyze the differences and similarities.

2. The essay says, "It's a man's world. ... But if these trends continue, not so much." We can infer from this statement that the author thinks men will lose out in this "New Girl Order." Write an essay in which you either affirm or refute this idea. Give at least three examples to support your thesis.

3. The author ends her essay with dire predictions about the effects of the "New Girl Order" on society. Research at least two other views of demographic change that have predicted desperate outcomes. How often have these predictions come to pass? Write an essay in which you explore these ideas.

The New Girl Order

AFTER MY LOT AIRLINES FLIGHT from New York touched down at Warsaw's Frédéric Chopin Airport a few months back, I watched a middle-aged passenger rush to embrace a waiting younger woman—clearly her daughter. Like many people on the plane, the older woman wore drab clothing and had the short, square physique of someone familiar with too many potatoes and too much manual labor. Her Poland-based daughter, by contrast, was tall and smartly outfitted in pointy-toed pumps, slim-cut jeans, a cropped jacket revealing a toned midriff (Yoga? Pilates? Or just a low-carb diet?), and a large, brass-studded leather bag, into which she dropped a silver cell phone.

Yes: Carrie Bradshaw is alive and well and living in Warsaw. Well, not just Warsaw. Conceived and raised in the United States, Carrie may still see New York as a spiritual home. But today you can find her in cities across Europe, Asia, and North America. Seek out the trendy shoe stores in Shanghai, Berlin, Singapore, Seoul, and Dublin, and you'll see crowds of single young females (SYFs) in their twenties and thirties, who spend their hours working their abs and their careers, sipping cocktails, dancing at clubs, and (yawn) talking about relationships. *Sex and the City* has gone global; the SYF world is now flat.

Is this just the latest example of American cultural imperialism? Or is it the triumph of planetary feminism? Neither. The globalization of the SYF reflects a series of stunning demographic and economic shifts that are pointing much of the world—with important exceptions, including Africa and most of the Middle East—toward a New Girl Order. It's a man's world, James Brown always reminded us. But if these trends continue, not so much.

Three demographic facts are at the core of the New Girl Order. First, women—especially, but not only, in the developed world—are getting married and having kids considerably later than ever before. According to the UN's *World Fertility Report*, the worldwide median age of marriage for women is up two years, from 21.2 in the 1970s to 23.2 today. In the developed countries, the rise has been considerably steeper—from 22.0 to 26.1.

Demographers get really excited about shifts like these, but in case you don't get what the big deal is, consider: in 1960, 70 percent of American 25-year-old women were married with children; in 2000, only 25 percent of them were. In 1970, just 7.4 percent of all American 30- to 34-year-olds were unmarried; today, the number is 22 percent. That change took about a generation to unfold, but in Asia and Eastern Europe the transformation has been much more abrupt. In today's Hungary, for instance, 30 percent of women in their early thirties are single, compared with 6 percent of their mothers' generation at the same age. In South Korea, 40 percent of 30-year-olds are single, compared with 14 percent only 20 years ago.

Nothing-new-under-the-sun skeptics point out, correctly, that marrying at 27 or 28 was once commonplace for women, at least in the United States and parts of northern Europe. The cultural anomaly was the 1950s and 60s, when the average age of marriage for women dipped to 20— probably because of post-Depression and postwar cocooning. But today's single 27-year-old has gone global—and even in the West, she differs from her late-marrying great-grandma in fundamental ways that bring us to the second piece of the demographic story. Today's aspiring middle-class women are gearing up to be part of the paid labor market for most of their adult lives; unlike their ancestral singles, they're looking for careers, not jobs. And that means they need lots of schooling.

In the newly global economy, good jobs go to those with degrees, and all over the world, young people, particularly women, are enrolling in colleges and universities at unprecedented rates. Between 1960 and 2000, the percentages of 20-, 25-, and 30-year-olds enrolled in school more than doubled in the U.S., and enrollment in higher education doubled throughout Europe. And the fairer sex makes up an increasing part of the total. The majority of college students are female in the U.S., the U.K., France, Germany, Norway, and Australia, to name only a few of many places, and the gender gap is quickly narrowing in more traditional countries like China, Japan, and South Korea. In a number of European countries, including Denmark, Finland, and France, over half of all women between 20 and 24 are in school. The number of countries where women constitute the majority of graduate students is also growing rapidly.

That educated women are staying single is unsurprising; degreed women have always been more likely to marry late, if they marry at all. But what has demographers taking notice is the sheer transnational numbers of women postponing marriage while they get diplomas and start careers. In the U.K., close to a third of 30-year-old college-educated women are unmarried; some demographers predict that 30 percent of women with university degrees there will remain forever childless. In Spain—not so long ago a culturally Catholic country where a girl's family would jealously chaperone her until handing her over to a husband at 21 or so—women now constitute 54 percent of college students, up from 26 percent in 1970, and the average age of first birth has risen to nearly 30, which appears to be a world record.

Adding to the contemporary SYF's novelty is the third demographic shift: urbanization. American and northern European women in the nineteenth and early twentieth centuries might have married at 26, but after a long day in the dairy barn or cotton mill, they didn't hang out at Studio 54 while looking for Mr. Right (or, as the joke has it, Mr. Right for Now). In the past, women who delayed marriage generally lived with their parents; they also remained part of the family economy, laboring in their parents' shops or farms, or at the very least, contributing to the family kitty. A lot of today's bachelorettes, on the other hand, move from their native village or town to Boston or Berlin or Seoul because that's where the jobs, boys, and bars are—and they spend their earnings on themselves.

By the mid-1990s, in countries as diverse as Canada, France, Hungary, Ireland, Portugal, and Russia, women were out-urbanizing men, who still tended to hang around the home village. When they can afford to, these women live alone or with roommates. The Netherlands, for instance, is flush with public housing, some of it reserved for young students and workers, including lots of women. In the United States, the proportion of unmarried twentysomethings living with their parents has declined steadily over the last 100 years, despite sky-high rents and apartment prices. Even in countries where SYFs can't afford to move out of their parents' homes, the anonymity and diversity of city life tend to heighten their autonomy. Belgians, notes University of Maryland professor Jeffrey Jensen Arnett, have coined a term—"hotel families"—to describe the arrangement.

Combine these trends—delayed marriage, expanded higher education and labor-force participation, urbanization—add a global media and some disposable income, and voilà: an international lifestyle is born. One of its defining characteristics is long hours of office work, often in quasi-creative fields like media, fashion, communications, and design—areas in which the number of careers has exploded in the global economy over the past few decades. The lifestyle also means whole new realms of leisure and consumption, often enjoyed with a group of close girlfriends: trendy cafés and bars serving sweetish coffee concoctions and cocktails; fancy boutiques, malls, and emporiums hawking cosmetics, handbags, shoes, and $100-plus buttock-hugging jeans; gyms for toning and male-watching; ski resorts and beach hotels; and, everywhere, the frustrating hunt for a boyfriend and, though it's an ever more vexing subject, a husband.

The SYF lifestyle first appeared in primitive form in the U.S. during the seventies, after young women started moving into higher education, looking for meaningful work, and delaying marriage. Think of your SYF Mary Richards, the pre-Jordache career girl played by Mary Tyler Moore, whose dates dropped her off—that same evening, of course—at her apartment door. By the mid-nineties, such propriety was completely passé. Mary had become the vocationally and sexually assertive Carrie Bradshaw, and cities like New York had magically transformed into the young person's pleasure palace evoked by the hugely popular TV show *Sex and the City*. At around the same time, women in Asia and in post-Communist Europe began to join the SYF demographic, too. Not surprisingly, they also loved watching themselves, or at least Hollywood versions of themselves, on television. *Friends*, *Ally McBeal*, and *Sex and the City* became global favorites. In repressive places like Singapore and China, which banned SATC, women passed around pirated DVDs.

By the late 1990s, the SYF lifestyle was fully globalized. Indeed, you might think of SYFs as a sociological Starbucks: no matter how exotic the location, there they are, looking and behaving just like the American prototype. They shop for shoes in Kyoto, purses in Shanghai, jeans in Prague, and lip gloss in Singapore; they sip lattes in Dublin, drink cocktails in Chicago, and read lifestyle magazines in Kraków; they go to wine tastings in Boston, speed-dating events in Amsterdam, yoga classes in Paris, and ski resorts outside Tokyo. "At the fashionable Da Capo Café on bustling Kolonaki Square in downtown Athens, Greek professionals in their 30s and early 40s luxuriate over their iced cappuccinos," a *Newsweek International* article began last year. "Their favorite topic of conversation is, of course, relationships: men's reluctance to commit, women's independence, and when to have children." Thirty-seven-year-old Eirini Perpovlov, an administrative assistant at Associated Press, "loves her work and gets her social sustenance from her *parea*, or close-knit group of like-minded friends."

Sure sounds similar to this July's *Time* story about Vicky, "a purposeful, 29-year-old actuary who … loves nothing better than a party. She and her friends meet so regularly for dinner and at bars that she says she never eats at home anymore. As the pictures on her blog attest, they also throw regular theme parties to mark holidays like Halloween and Christmas, and last year took a holiday to Egypt." At the restaurant where the reporter interviews them, Vicky's friends gab about snowboarding, iPods, credit-card rates, and a popular resort off the coast of Thailand. Vicky, whose motto is "work hard, play harder," is not from New York, London, or even Athens; she's from the SYF delegation in Beijing, China, a country that appears to be racing from rice paddies to sushi bars in less than a generation—at least for a privileged minority.

With no children or parents to support, and with serious financial hardship a bedtime story told by aging grandparents, SYFs have ignited what *The Economist* calls the "Bridget Jones economy"—named, of course, after the book and movie heroine who is perhaps the most famous SYF of all. Bridget Jonesers, the magazine says, spend their disposable income "on whatever is fashionable, frivolous, and fun," manufactured by a bevy of new companies that cater to young women. In 2000, Marian Salzman—then the president of the London-based Intelligence Factory, an arm of Young & Rubicam—said that by the 1990s, "women living alone had come to comprise the strongest consumer bloc in much the same way that yuppies did in the 1980s."

SYFs drive the growth of apparel stores devoted to stylish career wear like Ann Taylor, which now has more than 800 shops in the United States, and the international Zara, with more than 1,000 in 54 countries. They also spend paychecks at the Paris-based Sephora, Europe's largest retailer of perfumes and cosmetics, which targets younger women in 14 countries, including such formerly sober redoubts as Poland and the Czech Republic. The chain plans to expand to China soon. According to *Forbes*, the Chinese cosmetics market, largely an urban phenomenon, was up 17 percent in 2006, and experts predict a growth rate of between 15 and 20 percent in upcoming years. Zara already has three stores there.

The power of the SYF's designer purse is also at work in the entertainment industry. By the mid-1990s, "chick lit," a contemporary urban version of the Harlequin romance with the SYF as heroine, was topping bestseller lists in England and the United States. Now chick lit has spread all over the world. The books of the Irish writer Marian Keyes, one of the first and most successful chick-litterateurs, appear in 29 languages. *The Devil Wears Prada* was an international hit as both a book (by Lauren Weisberger) and a movie (starring Meryl Streep). Meantime, the television industry is seeking to satisfy the SYF's appetite for single heroines with *Sex and the City* clones like *The Marrying Type* in South Korea and *The Balzac Age* in Russia.

Bridget Jonesers are also remaking the travel industry, especially in Asia. A 2005 report from MasterCard finds that women take four out of every ten trips in the Asia-Pacific region—up from one in ten back in the mid-1970s. While American women think about nature, adventure, or culture when choosing their travel destinations, says MasterCard, Asian women look for shopping, resorts, and, most of all, spas. Female travelers have led to what the report calls the "spa-ification of the Asian hotel industry." That industry is growing at a spectacular rate—200 percent annually.

And now the maturing Bridget Jones economy has begun to feature big-ticket items. In 2003, the Diamond Trading Company introduced the "right-hand ring," a diamond for women with no marital prospects but longing for a rock. ("Your left hand is your heart; your right hand is your voice," one ad explains.) In some SYF capitals, women are moving into the real-estate market. Canadian single women are buying homes at twice the rate of single men. The National Association of Realtors reports that in the U.S. last year, single women made up 22 percent of the real-estate market, compared with a paltry 9 percent for single men. The median age for first-time female buyers: 32. The real-estate firm Coldwell Banker is making eyes at these young buyers with a new motto, "Your perfect partner since 1906," while Lowe's, the home-renovation giant, is offering classes especially for them. SYFs are also looking for wheels, and manufacturers are designing autos and accessories with them in mind. In Japan, Nissan has introduced the Pino, which has seat covers festooned with stars and a red CD player shaped like a pair of lips. It comes in one of two colors: "milk tea beige" and pink.

Japan presents a striking example of the sudden rise of the New Girl Order outside the U.S. and Western Europe. As recently as the nation's boom years in the 1980s, the dominant image of the Japanese woman was of the housewife, or *sengyoshufu*, who doted on her young children, intently prepared older ones for the world economy, and waited on the man of the house after his 16-hour day at the office. She still exists, of course, but about a decade ago she met her nemesis: the Japanese SYF. Between 1994 and 2004, the number of Japanese women between 25 and 29 who were unmarried soared from 40 to 54 percent; even more remarkable was the number of 30- to 34-year-old females who were unmarried, which rocketed from 14 to 27 percent. Because of Tokyo's expensive real-estate market, a good many of these young single women have shacked up with their parents, leading a prominent sociologist to brand them "parasite singles." The derogatory term took off, but the girls weren't disturbed; according to *USA Today*, many proudly printed up business cards bearing their new title.

The New Girl Order may represent a disruptive transformation for a deeply traditional society, but Japanese women sure seem to be enjoying the single life. Older singles who can afford it have even been buying their own apartments. One of them, 37-year-old Junko Sakai, wrote a best-selling plaint called *The Howl of the Loser Dogs*, a title that co-opts the term *makeinu* — "loser" — once commonly used to describe husbandless 30-year-olds. "Society may call us dogs," she writes, "but we are happy and independent." Today's Japanese SYFs are world-class shoppers, and though they must still fight workplace discrimination and have limited career tracks — particularly if they aren't working for Westernized companies — they're somehow managing to earn enough yen to keep the country's many Vuitton, Burberry, and Issey Miyake boutiques buzzing. Not so long ago, Japanese hotels wouldn't serve women traveling alone, in part because they suspected that the guests might be spinsters intent on hurling themselves off balconies to end their desperate solitude. Today, the losers are happily checking in at Japanese mountain lodges, not to mention Australian spas, Vietnamese hotels, and Hawaiian beach resorts.

And unlike their foreign counterparts in the New Girl Order, Japanese singles don't seem to be worrying much about finding Mr. Right. A majority of Japanese single women between 25 and 54 say that they'd be just as happy never to marry. Peggy Orenstein, writing in the *New York Times Magazine* in 2001, noted that Japanese women find American-style sentimentality about marriage puzzling. Yoko Harruka, a television personality and author of a book called *I Won't Get Married* — written after she realized that her then-fiancé expected her to quit her career and serve him tea — says that her countrymen propose with lines like, "I want you to cook miso soup for me for the rest of my life." Japanese SYFs complain that men don't show affection and expect women to cook dinner obediently while they sit on their duffs reading the paper. Is it any wonder that the women prefer Burberry?

Post-Communist Europe is also going through the shock of the New Girl Order. Under Communist rule, women tended to marry and have kids early. In the late eighties, the mean age of first birth in East Germany, for instance, was 24.7, far lower than the West German average of 28.3. According to Tomáš Sobotka of the Vienna Institute of Demography, young people had plenty of reasons to schedule an early wedding day. Tying the knot was the only way to gain independence from parents, since married couples could get an apartment, while singles could not. Furthermore, access to modern contraception, which the state proved either unable or unwilling to produce at affordable prices, was limited. Marriages frequently began as the result of unplanned pregnancies.

And then the Wall came down. The free market launched shiny new job opportunities, making higher education more valuable than under Communist regimes, which had apportioned jobs and degrees. Suddenly, a young Polish or Hungarian woman might imagine having a career, and some fun at the same time. In cities like Warsaw and Budapest, young adults can find pleasures completely unknown to previous generations of singles. In one respect, Eastern European and Russian SYFs were better equipped than Japanese ones for the new order. The strong single woman, an invisible figure in Japan, has long been a prominent character in the social landscape of Eastern Europe and Russia, a legacy, doubtless, of the Communist-era emphasis on egalitarianism (however inconsistently applied) and the massive male casualties of World War II.

Not that the post-Communist SYF is any happier with the husband material than her Japanese counterpart is. Eastern European gals complain about men overindulged by widowed mothers and unable to adapt to the new economy. According to *The Economist*, many towns in what used to be East Germany now face *Frauenmangel*—a lack of women—as SYFs who excelled in school have moved west for jobs, leaving the poorly performing men behind. In some towns, the ratio is just 40 women to 100 men. Women constitute the majority of both high school and college graduates in Poland. Though Russian women haven't joined the new order to the same extent, they're also grumbling about the men. In Russian TV's *The Balzac Age*, which chronicles the adventures of four single thirtysomething women, Alla, a high-achieving yuppie attorney, calls a handyman for help in her apartment. The two—to their mutual horror—recognize each other as former high school sweethearts, now moving in utterly different social universes.

There's much to admire in the New Girl Order—and not just the previously hidden cleavage. Consider the lives most likely led by the mothers, grandmothers, great-grandmothers, and so on of the fashionista at the Warsaw airport or of the hard-partying Beijing actuary. Those women reached adulthood, which usually meant 18 or even younger; married guys from their village, or, if they were particularly daring, from the village across the river; and then had kids—end of story, except for maybe some goat milking, rice planting, or, in urban areas, shop tending. The New Girl Order means good-bye to such limitations. It means the possibility of more varied lives, of more expansively nourished aspirations. It also means a richer world. SYFs bring ambition, energy, and innovation to the economy, both local and global; they simultaneously promote and enjoy what author Brink Lindsey calls "the age of abundance." The SYF, in sum, represents a dramatic advance in personal freedom and wealth.

But as with any momentous social change, the New Girl Order comes with costs—in this case, profound ones. The globalized SYF upends centuries of cultural traditions. However limiting, those traditions shaped how families formed and the next generation grew up. So it makes sense that the SYF is partly to blame for a worldwide drop in fertility rates. To keep a population stable, or at its "replacement level," women must have an average of at least 2.1 children. Under the New Girl Order, though, women delay marriage and childbearing, which itself tends to reduce the number of kids, and sometimes—because the opportunity costs of children are much higher for educated women—they forgo them altogether. Save Albania, no European country stood at or above replacement levels in 2000. Three-quarters of Europeans now live in countries with fertility rates below 1.5, and even that number is inflated by a disproportionately high fertility rate among Muslim immigrants. Oddly, the most Catholic European countries— Italy, Spain, and Poland—have the lowest fertility rates, under 1.3. Much of Asia looks similar. In Japan, fertility rates are about 1.3. Hong Kong, according to the CIA's *World Factbook*, at 0.98 has broken the barrier of one child per woman.

For many, fertility decline seems to be one more reason to celebrate the New Girl Order. Fewer people means fewer carbon footprints, after all, and thus potential environmental relief. But while we're waiting for the temperature to drop a bit, economies will plunge in ways that will be extremely difficult to manage—and that, ironically, will likely spell the SYF lifestyle's demise. As Philip Longman explains in his important book *The Empty Cradle*, dramatic declines in fertility rates equal aging and eventually shriveling populations. Japan now has one of the oldest populations in the world—one-third of its population, demographers predict, will be over 60 within a decade. True, fertility decline often spurs a temporary economic boost, as more women enter the workforce and increase income and spending, as was the case in 1980s Japan. In time, though, those women— and their male peers—will get old and need pensions and more health care.

And who will pay for that? With fewer children, the labor force shrinks, and so do tax receipts. Europe today has 35 pensioners for every

100 workers, Longman points out. By 2050, those 100 will be responsible for 75 pensioners; in Spain and Italy, the ratio of workers to pensioners will be a disastrous *one-to-one*. Adding to the economic threat, seniors with few or no children are more likely to look to the state for support than are elderly people with more children. The final irony is that the ambitious, hardworking SYF will have created a world where her children, should she have them, will need to work even harder in order to support her in her golden years.

Aging populations present other problems. For one thing, innovation and technological breakthroughs tend to be a young person's game—think of the young Turks of the information technology revolution. Fewer young workers and higher tax burdens don't make a good recipe for innovation and growth. Also, having fewer people leads to declining markets, and thus less business investment and formation. Where would you want to expand your cosmetics business: Ireland, where the population continues to renew itself, or Japan, where it is imploding?

And finally, the New Girl Order has given birth to a worrying ambivalence toward domestic life and the men who would help create it. Many analysts argue that today's women of childbearing age would have more kids if only their countries provided generous benefits for working mothers, as they do in Sweden and France. And it's true that those two countries have seen fertility rates inch up toward replacement levels in recent years. But in countries newly entering the New Girl Order, what SYFs complain about isn't so much a gap between work and family life as a chasm between their own aspirations and those of the men who'd be their husbands (remember those Japanese women skeptical of a future cooking miso soup). Adding to the SYF's alienation from domesticity is another glaring fact usually ignored by demographers: the New Girl Order is fun. Why get married when you can party on?

That raises an interesting question: Why are SYFs in the United States—the Rome of the New Girl Order—still so interested in marriage? By large margins, surveys suggest, American women want to marry and have kids. Indeed, our fertility rates, though lower than replacement level among college-educated women, are still healthier than those in most SYF countries (including Sweden and France). The answer may be that the family has always been essential ballast to the individualism, diversity, mobility, and sheer giddiness of American life. It helps that the U.S., like northwestern Europe, has a long tradition of "companionate marriage"—that is, marriage based not on strict roles but on common interests and mutual affection. Companionate marriage always rested on the assumption of female equality. Yet countries like Japan are joining the new order with no history of companionate relations, and when it comes to adapting to the new order, the cultural cupboard is bare. A number of analysts, including demographer Nicholas Eberstadt, have also argued that it is America's religiousness that explains our relatively robust fertility, though the Polish fertility decline raises questions about that explanation.

It's by no means certain that Americans will remain exceptional in this regard. The most recent census data show a "sharp increase," over just the past six years, in the percentage of Americans in their twenties who have never married. Every year sees more books celebrating the SYF life, boasting titles like *Singular Existence* and *Living Alone and Loving It*. And SYFs will increasingly find themselves in a disappointing marriage pool. The *New York Times* excited considerable discussion this summer with a front-page article announcing that young women working full-time in several cities were now outearning their male counterparts. A historically unprecedented trend like this is bound to have a further impact on relations between the sexes and on marriage and childbearing rates.

Still, for now, women don't seem too worried about the New Girl Order's downside. On the contrary. The order marches on, as one domino after another falls to its pleasures and aspirations. Now, the *Singapore Times* tells us, young women in Vietnam are suddenly putting off marriage because they "want to have some fun"—and fertility rates have plummeted from 3.8 children in 1998 to 2.1 in 2006.

And then there's India. "The Gen Now bachelorette brigade is in no hurry to tie the knot," reports the *India Tribune*. "They're single, independent, and happy." Young urbanites are pushing up sales of branded apparel; Indian chick lit, along with *Cosmopolitan* and *Vogue*, flies out of shops in Delhi and Mumbai. Amazingly enough, fertility rates have dropped below replacement level in several of India's major cities, thanks in part to aspirant fashionistas. If in India—*India!*—the New Girl Order can reduce population growth, then perhaps nothing is beyond its powers. At the very least, the Indian experiment gives new meaning to the phrase "shop till you drop."

Why I Became a Late Merger (and Why You Should Too)

MyWritingLab™

Tom Vanderbilt

Tom Vanderbilt is a freelance writer, blogger, and consultant who writes and speaks about culture, design, technology, and science. His work has appeared in *Rolling Stone, Slate*, and *The New York Times Magazine* as well other journals and Web sites. His books include *Survival City: Adventures Among the Ruins of Atomic America* (2002) and *Traffic: Why We Drive the Way We Do (and What It Says About Us)* (2008), from which this reading is excerpted.

Return to these questions after you have finished reading.

Analyzing the Reading

1. In the opening of the piece, Vanderbilt employs the second person "you" to set up the problem. What is the effect of his technique? How might the effect be different if Vanderbilt worked entirely in the first person?

2. How is "Why I Became a Late Merger (and Why You Should Too)" an example of a causal argument? Identify passages and sections in the text where the author states or implies his argument.

3. A basic strategy of causal arguments is to offer possible causes and make counterarguments.

Identify sections and passages in the text where you believe Vanderbilt lays out causes and counterarguments.

4. After a narrative, exposition, and analysis of the issue, Vanderbilt launches into a conclusion with "there seems to be a whole worldview contained in each of the merge strategies." How does the author prepare the reader throughout the piece to anticipate his conclusion that "early mergers" are good people whereas "later mergers" are not as good or only as good as circumstances allow.

Exploring Ideas and Issues

Vanderbilt characterizes the Late Merge strategy as "laissez-faire" for giving people a set of circumstances and vague directions on how to behave and leaves the rest up to them. The literal translation of the French term *laissez-faire* is "let them do," but it also implies "let it be" or "leave it alone." The term identifies an eighteenth-century French economic theory emphasizing that the basic unit of society is the individual who has a natural right to freedom. The physical order of nature is a harmonious, self-regulating system and thus, economic markets should be free and competitive. You might recognize the essence of laissez-faire at the center of many policy and economic debates where those on the "right" criticize "big government" and those on the "left" fight against "unfettered capitalism" that must be regulated to create an equal playing field of opportunity.

1. Write a rhetorical analysis of the structure of "Why I Became a Late Merger (and Why You Should Too)" as a causal argument. Make an

outline of the major sections as illustrated in the headnote of "The French Paradox" (see page 271). Use the map to write your formal analysis of the causal argument.

2. Vanderbilt includes worldviews, ideology, and personality types as possible causes for driver behavior. These causes could explain other behaviors in other contexts. Reflect on experiences in your life in which you have had to make a choice between your desires when in conflict with a larger group. Write a causal argument to examine and defend your decisions.

3. Choose a controversial, contemporary political or economic topic, such as, for example, The Affordable Care Act, the Common Core Curriculum, or public funding for education. Conduct research on the issue to learn its history, proponents, and the range of positions. Where do you stand? Write a causal argument to present your position.

WHY I BECAME A LATE MERGER (AND WHY YOU SHOULD TOO)

Why does the other lane always seem to be moving faster?

It is a question you have no doubt asked yourself while crawling down some choked highway, watching with mounting frustration as the adjacent cars glide ahead. You drum the wheel with your fingers. You change the radio station. You fixate on one car as a benchmark of your own lack of progress. You try to figure out what that weird button next to the rear-window defroster actually does.

I used to think this was just part of the natural randomness of the highway. Sometimes fate would steer me into the faster lane, sometimes it would relinquish me to the slow lane.

That was until recently, when I had an experience that made me rethink my traditionally passive outlook on the road, and upset the careful set of assumptions that had always guided my behavior in traffic.

I made a major lifestyle change. I became a *late merger*.

Chances are, at some point you have found yourself driving along the highway when a sign announces that the left lane, in which you are traveling, will close one mile ahead, and that you must merge right.

You notice an opening in the right lane and quickly move over. You breathe a sigh, happy to be safely ensconced in the Lane That Will Not End. Then, as the lane creeps to a slow halt, you notice with rising indignation that cars in the lane you have vacated are continuing to speed ahead, out of sight. You quietly seethe and contemplate returning to the much faster left lane—if only you could work an opening. You grimly accept your condition.

One day, not long ago, I had an epiphany on a New Jersey highway. I was having a typical white-knuckle drive among the scenic oil-storage depots and chemical-processing plants of northern Jersey when suddenly, on the approach to the Pulaski Skyway, the sign loomed: LANE ENDS ONE MILE. MERGE RIGHT.

Seized by some rash impulse, I avoided the instinctual tickle at the back of my brain telling me to get in the already crowded right lane. *Just do what the sign says*, that voice usually counsels. Instead, I listened to another, more insistent voice: *Don't be a sucker. You can do better.* I plowed purposefully ahead, oblivious to the hostile stares of other drivers. From the corner of my eye I could see my wife cringing. After passing dozens of cars, I made it to the bottleneck point, where, filled with newfound swagger, I took my rightful turn in the small alternating "zipper" merge that had formed. I merged, and it was clear asphalt ahead. My heart was beating faster. My wife covered her face with her hands.

In the days after, a creeping guilt and confusion took hold. Was I wrong to have done this? Or had I been doing it wrong all my life? Looking for an answer, I posted an anonymous inquiry on Ask MetaFilter, a Web site one can visit to ask random questions and tap into the "hive mind" of an anonymous audience of overeducated and overopinionated geeks. Why should one lane move faster than the other, I wanted to know, and why are people rewarded for merging at the last possible moment? And was my new lifestyle, that of the late merger, somehow deviant?

I was startled by the torrent of responses, and how quickly they came. What struck me most was the passion and conviction with which people argued their various cases—and the fact that while many people seemed to think I was wrong, almost as many seemed to think I was right. Rather than easy consensus, I had stumbled into a gaping divide of irreconcilable belief.

The first camp—let us name it after the bumper sticker that says PRACTICE RANDOM ACTS OF KINDNESS—viewed early mergers as virtuous souls doing the right thing and late mergers as arrogant louts. "Unfortunately, people suck," wrote one Random Acts poster. "They'll try whatever they can to pass you, to better enjoy the traffic jam from a few car lengths ahead of you. . . . People who feel that they have more pressing concerns and are generally more important than you will keep going, and some weak-spined schmuck will let them in further down, slowing your progress even more. This sucks; I'm afraid it's the way of the world."

Another camp, the minority camp—let's call them Live Free or Die, after the license-plate motto of the state of New Hampshire—argued that the late mergers were quite rationally utilizing the highway's maximum capacity, thus making life better for everyone. In their view, the other group's attempts toward politeness and fairness were actually detrimental to all.

It got more complicated. Some argued that late merges caused more accidents. Some said the system worked much better in Germany, and hinted that my dilemma perhaps revealed some national failing in the American character. Some said they were afraid of not being "let in" at the last moment; some said they would actively try to block someone from merging, the way truckers often do.

So what was going on here? Are we not all driving the same road, did we not all pass the same driving tests? What was puzzling was not just the variety of responses but the sense of moral righteousness each person attributed to his or her highway behavior, and the vitriol each person reserved for those holding the opposite view. For the most part, people were not citing traffic laws or actual evidence but their own personal sense of what was right.

I even found someone claiming to have had a conversion experience exactly the opposite of mine. "Until very recently, I was a 'late merger,'" wrote the author, an executive with a software company, in a business magazine. Why had he become a born-again early merger? "Because I came to realize that traffic flowed faster the sooner people merged." He used this as a metaphor for successful team building in corporate America, in which "late mergers" were those who consistently put their own opinions and motives above the greater company. "Early mergers," he wrote, could help push companies to their "maximum communal speed."

But did traffic flow faster when people merged sooner? Or did it just seem more noble to think that it did?

• • •

You may suspect that getting people to merge in a timely fashion, and without killing one another, is less of a traffic problem and more of a *human* problem. The road, more than simply a system of regulations and designs, is a place where many millions of us, with only loose parameters for how to behave, are thrown together daily in a kind of massive petri dish in which all kinds of uncharted, little-understood dynamics are at work. There is no other place where so many people from different walks of life—different ages, races, classes, religions, genders, political preferences, lifestyle choices, levels of psychological stability—mingle so freely.

What do we really know about how it all works? Why do we act the way we do on the road, and what might that say about us? Are certain people predisposed to drive certain ways? Do women behave differently than men? And if, as conventional wisdom has it, drivers have become progressively less civil over the past several decades, why is that so? Is the road a microcosm of society, or its own place with its own set of rules? I have a friend, an otherwise timorous Latin teacher, who once told me how, in a modest Toyota Corolla, he had defiantly "stuck it" to the driver of an eighteen-wheeler who he felt was hogging the road. Some mysterious force had turned this gentle suburban scholar into the Travis Bickle of the turnpike. (Are you tailgatin' me?) Was it traffic, or had the beast always been lurking within?

The more you think about it—or, rather, the more time you spend in traffic with time to think about it—the more these sorts of puzzling questions swim to the surface. Why can one sit in traffic jams that seem to have no source? Why does a ten-minute "incident" create one hundred minutes of gridlock? Do people really take longer to vacate a parking spot when someone else is waiting, or does it just seem so? Do the car-pool lanes on highways help fight congestion or cause more of it? Just how dangerous are large trucks? How does what we drive, where we drive, and with whom we drive affect the *way* we drive? Why do so many New Yorkers jaywalk, while hardly anyone in Copenhagen does? Is New Delhi's traffic as chaotic as it seems, or does a beautiful order lurk beneath the frenzied surface?

Like me, you may have wondered: What could traffic tell us, if someone would just stop to listen?

The situation that I encountered on the Jersey highway is known in the traffic-engineering world as a "work-zone merge." Work zones, it turns out, are among the most complex and dangerous areas on the highway. Despite the signs often warning of large penalties for striking a worker (or pleas like SLOW DOWN, MY DADDY WORKS HERE), they are much more dangerous for the drivers passing through them than for the workers—some 85 percent of people killed in work zones are drivers or passengers. The reasons are not difficult to imagine. Drivers moving from an incredibly fast, free-flowing environment are suddenly being asked, sometimes unexpectedly, to come to a crawl or even a full stop, perhaps change lanes, and pass through a narrow, constricted space filled with workers, heavy machinery, and other objects of visual fascination.

And then there's the inevitable point at which two lanes of traffic will be forced to become one (or three to become two, etc.), when the early mergers, the late mergers, and everyone in between are suddenly introduced to one another. This can get sticky. It seems that even though (or maybe because) we're all tossed together on the road, drivers are not all that comfortable with interacting; a survey undertaken by the Texas Transportation Institute found that the single most common cause of stress on the highway was "merging difficulties."

Traffic engineers have spent a lot of time and money studying this problem, but it is not as simple as you might think. The "conventional merge" site, the sort I experienced on the highway in New Jersey, works reasonably well when traffic is light. Drivers are warned in advance to move into the correct lane, and they do so at a comfortable distance and speed, without a "conflict" with a driver in the other lane. But the very nature of a work zone means that traffic is often *not* light. A highway going from two lanes to one, or experiencing a "lane drop," loses at least half of its capacity to process cars—even more if drivers are slowing to see what is going on in the work zone itself. Because the capacity is quickly exceeded by the arriving cars, a "queue" soon forms. The queue, inevitably, is longer in the lane that will remain open, probably because signs have told drivers to move there.

This causes more problems. As the queue grows, it may move far back up the highway—engineers call this "upstream"—perhaps even past the signs warning of the lane closure. This means that newly arriving drivers will be encountering an unexpected queue of cars. Seeing no reason for it, they will be unaware that they're in a lane that is due to close. Once they learn this, they will have to "force" their way into the queued line, whose drivers may view the new arrivals, fairly or not, as "cheaters." As the entering drivers slow or even stop to merge, they create a temporary second queue. Drivers who grow frustrated in the queued line might similarly force their way into the faster open lane. This is all a recipe for rear-end collisions, which, as it happens, are among the leading types of crashes in work zones.

To improve things, North American engineers have responded in two basic ways. First, there is the school of Early Merge. To tackle the "forced merge" problem, Early Merge spreads out the whole merging zone. Drivers are warned by a sign several miles in advance of the "taper" that a lane drop is coming, rather than the twelve hundred feet or so in the conventional merge. "No Passing Zones" signs are often placed in the lane that will close. The earlier notice, in theory, means drivers will merge sooner and with less "friction," as engineers politely say, and will be less surprised by a sudden queue of stopped cars. Indeed, a 1997 study of an Indiana construction site using this system showed very few forced merges, few "traffic conflicts," and few rear-end collisions.

Early Merge suffers from a critical flaw, however. It has not been shown to move vehicles through the work zone more quickly than the conventional merge. One simulation showed that it actually took vehicles *longer* to travel through the work zone, perhaps because faster-moving cars were being put behind slower-moving cars in a single lane sooner than they might naturally have gotten there, thus creating an artificial rolling traffic jam. An Early Merge system would also seem to require some kind of active law enforcement presence to make sure drivers do not violate the concept. As we all know, the presence of a police car on the highway has its own unique effects on traffic.

The second school, Late Merge, was rolled out by traffic engineers in Pennsylvania in the 1990s in response to reports of aggressive driving at merge locations. In this system, engineers posted a succession of signs, beginning a mile and a half from the closure. First came USE BOTH LANES TO MERGE POINT, then a ROAD WORK AHEAD or two, and finally, at the lane drop: MERGE HERE TAKE YOUR TURN.

The beauty of the Late Merge system is that it removes the insecurity or anxiety drivers may feel in choosing lanes, as well as their annoyance with a passing "cheating" driver. The Late Merge compresses what may normally be thousands of feet of potential merging maneuvers to a single point. There is, presumably, no lane jumping or jockeying, as the flow or speed should be no better or worse in one lane than another—hence there are fewer chances for rear-end collisions. Because cars are using both lanes to the end point, the queue is cut in half.

The most surprising thing about the Late Merge concept is that it showed *a 15 percent improvement in traffic flow* over the conventional merge. It turns out that the Live Free crowd was right. Merging late, that purported symbol of individual greed, actually makes things better for everyone. As one of my Live Free responders had succinctly put it: "Isn't it obvious that the best thing to do is for both lanes to be full right up to the last moment, and then merge in turn? That way, the full capacity of the road is being used, and it's fair on everyone, rather than a bunch of people merging early and trying to create an artificial one-lane road earlier than necessary."

Beyond simple engineering, there seems to be a whole worldview contained in each of the merge strategies that have been tried. The Early Merge strategy implies that people are good. They want to do the right thing. They want to merge as soon as possible, and with as little negotiation as possible. They can eschew temptation in favor of cooperation. The line might be a little longer, but it seems a small price for working toward the common good. The Late Merge strategy suggests that people are not as good, or only as good as circumstances allow. Rather than having people choose among themselves where and when and in front of whom to merge, it picks the spot, and the rules, for them. Late Merge also posits that the presence of that seductively traffic-free space will be too tempting for the average mortal, and so simply removes it. And the conventional merge, the one that most of us seem to find ourselves in each day? This is strictly laissez-faire. It gives people a set of circumstances and only a vague directive of what to do and leaves the rest up to them. This tosses the late mergers and the early mergers together in an unholy tempest of conflicting beliefs, expectations, and actions. Perhaps not surprisingly, it performs the worst of all.

I suggest the following: The next time you find yourself on a congested four-lane road and you see that a forced merge is coming, don't panic. Do not stop, do not swerve into the other lane. Simply stay in your lane—if there is a lot of traffic, the distribution between both lanes should be more or less equal—all the way to the merge point. Those in the lane that is remaining open should allow one person from the lane to be closed in ahead of them, and then proceed (those doing the merging must take a similar turn). By working together, by abandoning our individual preferences and our distrust of others' preferences, in favor of a simple set of objective rules, we can make things better for everyone.

How to Write a Causal Argument

These steps for the process of writing a causal argument may not progress as neatly as this chart might suggest. Writing is not an assembly-line process. As you write, you are constantly reading what you have written and rethinking.

Continue thinking about causation as you write and revise. The process of writing may lead you to additional causal relationships.

1 MAKE A CAUSAL CLAIM

- Examine a social trend, law, or policy.

- Analyze problems in your neighborhood or at your school.

- Investigate natural phenomena.

- Investigate the impact of human activity on the environment.

- Think about what is at stake. What could or should change if the cause were known?

- Put your claim in the form "____ causes (or does not cause) ____."

2 THINK ABOUT POSSIBLE CAUSES AND EFFECTS

- What are the obvious causes or effects?

- What are the underlying causes?

- What causes or effects might be hidden?

- What are the causes or effects that most people have not recognized before?

- Who is affected by what you are investigating? Do your readers have a stake in what you are analyzing?

- Look for disagreement among your sources. If they all agree on the cause, probably you won't have much to add.

3
WRITE A DRAFT

- Describe the trend, event, or phenomenon.

- Give the background your readers will need.

- If the trend or event you are analyzing is unfamiliar to your readers, explain the cause or the chain of causation.

- Another way to organize the body of your analysis is to set out the causes that have already been offered and reject them one by one. Then you can present the cause or causes that you think are the right ones.

- A third method is to look at a series of causes one by one, analyzing the importance of each.

- Do more than simply summarize in your conclusion. You might consider additional effects beyond those you have previously noted, or explain to readers any action you think should be taken based on your conclusions.

- Choose a title that will interest readers in your essay.

- Include any necessary images or tables.

4
REVISE, REVISE, REVISE

- Check that your causal analysis fulfills the assignment.

- Make sure that your claim is clear and that you have sufficient evidence to convince readers.

- Look at additional potential causes, if necessary.

- Reconsider how multiple causes might interact.

- Go further back in the causal chain, if necessary, showing how the causes you examine have their roots in other events.

- Examine the organization of your analysis and think of possible better ways to organize.

- Review the visual presentation of your analysis for readability and maximum impact.

- Proofread carefully.

5
SUBMITTED VERSION

- Make sure your finished writing meets all formatting requirements.

1: Make a Causal Claim

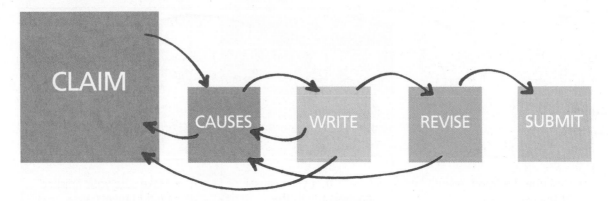

Analyze the assignment

Read your assignment slowly and carefully. Look for words like *causes, effect, result, impact,* and *why,* which signal that you are writing a causal argument. Highlight any information about the length specified, date due, formatting, and other requirements. You can attend to this information later. At this point you want to give your attention to the topic and criteria you will use in your argument.

Explore possible topics

- Make a list of fashion trends including cars, clothing, hairstyles, food, tattoos, and piercing. Look at your list and think about where and why a particular trend originates.

- Make a list of social trends including music, television shows, movies, sports, exercising, childrearing, and leisure. Look at your list and think about where and why a particular trend originates.

- Make a list of important historical events or discoveries that changed the course of civilization. Make notes about what led to these events or discoveries and how people's lives were changed.

- Identify two or three possibilities for a causal argument.

Make an initial causal claim

Select one of your possibilities and make a causal claim. Use the form: "SOMETHING causes (or does not cause) SOMETHING ELSE."

Think about what's at stake

Remember that people often have a stake in the outcome of a causal argument. Ask: Who will agree with me? Who will disagree, and why? If people accept your causal argument, will anything change?

STAYING ON TRACK

Make a claim that matters

MAKE AN ARGUABLE CLAIM

Easy answers generally make bad arguments. If all the sources you consult agree about the cause of the effect you are interested in, there is probably no need for you to make another argument saying the same thing. Look for a phenomenon that hasn't been explained to everyone's satisfaction.

OFF TRACK
Cigarette smoke is a leading cause of lung cancer.

ON TRACK
New research indicates that childhood asthma may be linked to exposure to cockroaches.

EXPLAIN WHY IT MATTERS

Readers need to know why this cause-and-effect relationship is important. If we determine the cause of this phenomenon, what will change? What can we do? What might happen?

OFF TRACK
This paper will investigate the most common causes of foundation failure in US residential housing.

ON TRACK
Foundation failure, especially cracked slabs, can cost anywhere from a few thousand to tens of thousands of dollars to repair. Determining the primary causes of foundation failure can help homeowners and insurers protect themselves against economic loss and inconvenience.

WRITE NOW   MyWritingLab™

Think about causal factors

1. Consider trends or problems you are familiar with—in your daily life, or in the larger world.
2. List these trends and problems on the right side of a piece of paper. On the left side, write down what you think some of the causes of the problems might be. Underline the causes that you are confident about.
3. Look over your two lists. Which topics seem most interesting to you? If an entry has many underlined causes or effects, it may be too obvious to write about.

Writer at work

Armadi Tansal was asked to write a paper analyzing the effects of a current trend in popular culture for his Social Trends and Problems course. He made the following notes on his assignment sheet while his class was discussing the assignment.

Sociology 032
Social Trends and Problems

Macro and micro effects

Identify a trend in American popular culture that interests you, and analyze its impact—postive or negative—on society. Some topics we have discussed in class that might make good papers include the rising number of unwed teenage mothers who keep their babies; the popularity of video games; people ignoring social protocol while talking on cell phones; and the growth of pet ownership over the past fifteen years. Look for large-scale social consequences as well as the effects on individuals for which this trend might be responsible.

Use outside sources to help make your claims, and find authoritative opinions on the topic whenever possible. It usually isn't possible to definitively identify the effects of a social trend, so beware of making a claim that is too sweeping. Social science often relies on probability and plausibility rather than absolute certainty.

Look for causation – not just correlation

Length and deadlines
You should be able to complete this assignment in about four double-spaced, typed pages. Papers are due on October 28, and I will return them to you one week later with a grade. If you then wish to rewrite your paper, you will have one week to do so. I will average the rewrite grade with your first grade to give you your final grade.

I encourage you to share your papers with your discussion groups as you draft them. You should also plan to take your paper to the writing center. This is not required, but it is highly recommended.

Evaluation
Papers will be evaluated according to how well they use logic and evidence to show causation. In addition, I will consider how well you contextualize your analysis for readers. (Why does it matter? Who is affected? And so on.)

Read the assignment closely

Armadi Tansal began by circling the words and phrases that indicated his analytical task. Then he highlighted information about dates and processes for the project.

Choose a topic

Armadi Tansal made a list of trends he might write about. After each item on his list, he made notes about why the topic would matter, and to whom. He also made preliminary observations about where he might find "authoritative opinions" on each topic, wrote down any possible causes that occurred to him at the time, and noted any other observations or questions he had about that topic. Finally, he chose one trend for further research.

POPULARITY OF ANIME

- Is it more popular with certain age groups or other demographic groups?

- Is there any scholarly/authoritative research on it? Maybe in Art History?

- I've seen tons of magazines devoted to it at the bookstore.

- Could interview Sarah about the collection she has.

POPULARITY OF VIDEO GAMES   ** Best research possibilities **

- What types of games are most popular?

- How much time do people spend gaming instead of doing something else? Consequences?

- Effect on friendships/relationships?

- What's the effect of gaming on the brain?

- What about violence in games? Does it affect behavior?

- Is there any scholarly/authoritative research on it?

- Could interview a friend (anonymously).

SUV SALES

- Why do people want to drive "off-roading" cars to work every day?

- What does this do to the environment?

- Are sales declining with rising gas prices?

- Is this even a trend any more? People are buying VWs and Mini Coopers now.

"ILLEGAL" FILE SHARING

- Why do so many people do it if it is "illegal"? (Because you get something for free.)

- Impact on morals—plagiarism?

- What are the arguments saying that it is or isn't illegal?

- Easy answer: people are willing to "steal" in this case because there is still significant disagreement over whether it is really stealing.

2: Think about possible causes and effects

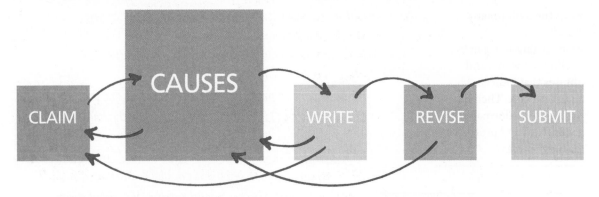

Find the obvious causes and effects, and then dig deeper

- **What factors might be hidden from the general observer, and why?** Use your imagination; hidden causes and subtle effects require new thinking if they are to be uncovered.

- **How do various causal factors interact?** Several causes together might contribute to an effect, rather than any single cause being the determining factor.

- **What "causes the cause" that you have identified?** What prior conditions does each cause arise from? If poor attendance is a factor in dropout rates, what causes some students to have poor attendance in the first place?

Think about common threads

Sometimes causes can be identified because two or more similar events share a common factor. The common factor may be the cause. For example, a mysterious outbreak of deadly *E.coli* bacteria in Germany in 2011 was traced to eating organic bean sprouts.

Think about relevant differences

Relevant difference reasoning attempts to identify causes that produce different effects. For example, studies of identical twins raised apart from each other rule out genetic influences. Differences between the twins in physical characteristics, intelligence, and behavior are determined by environmental factors.

Research your analysis

- **Look for some disagreement among your sources.** If they all agree, your analysis won't matter much.

- **When your sources disagree, ask why.** Does one give more weight to some pieces of evidence than to others? Do they draw different conclusions from the same evidence?

- **Be on the lookout for new potential causes or unexpected effects, or new findings that could help you rule out potential causes and effects.**

Writer at work

Armadi Tansal began his analysis by brainstorming for all the possible effects he could think of. Then, he researched the topic to find information on the effects he had listed and also to learn about other potential effects that had been put forward.

Tansal thought about his own experience with the trend to help define his audience. Finally, Tansal identified what he thought were the most likely effects of playing violent video games.

POSSIBLE EFFECTS OF PLAYING VIOLENT VIDEO GAMES:

- Time spent gaming instead of on other activities: school, sports, friends, family, exercising? Does gaming lead gamers to be unsociable? - Any physical effects? increased heart rate? weight gain?
- Aggressive behavior: Anderson talks about "delinquency, fighting at school and during free play periods, and violent criminal behavior."
- Violent thoughts and feelings: Anderson says there's a link here.
- Players rewarded for being violent: Anderson mentions the active role in video games as opposed to passive experience of violence on TV and in movies. So violent games are a stronger influence than violent shows.

**I've played violent video games. What about "John"? He does a lot of gaming, and he's not a criminal!

**Talk about causation vs. correlation: Is the link between playing violent video games and behaving aggressively just coincidental? See Ferguson and Kilburn on this.

**Also, a main factor vs. a contributing factor: Does playing violent video games lead to criminal behavior in a healthy person?

**Effect on individuals vs. effect on society: Gaming might not have much of an impact on most people, but what about its impact on the small number of people who are already prone to be aggressive?

Most important effects to talk about: link to aggressive or criminal behavior; individuals lose out socially; mass effect on society.

3: Write a Draft

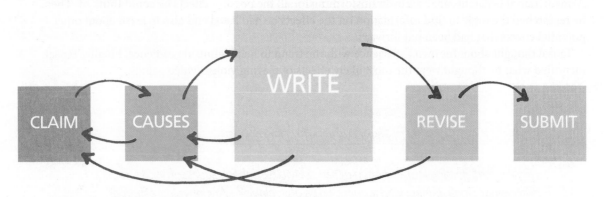

Introduce the subject of your argument

Describe the trend, event, or phenomenon you will be analyzing. Give your readers any background information they will need. Explain why it is important to determine the causes or effects of this phenomenon (you can save this for the conclusion if you wish).

Describe the causal relationship

- Explain how the chain of causation works to produce the effect in question. Break down each step so readers can follow the process.

- Alternatively, set out the causes or effects offered by other people and show how they can be ruled out. Then, introduce your own claim and demonstrate why it is superior to others'.

- A third method is to look at a series of possible causes or effects one at a time. Analyze each cause and make a claim about its relative impact on a phenomenon, or analyze each effect and make a claim about the likelihood that it is a consequence of the phenomenon.

Anticipate and address opposing viewpoints

Acknowledge other stakeholders in the analysis and consider their claims. Demonstrate why your claim is preferable.

Conclude by doing more than summarizing

Spell out the importance of the analysis, if you haven't already done so. Consider additional causes or effects you haven't previously discussed. Explain any action you think needs to be taken on the basis of your conclusion.

Look at the big picture

DON'T CONFUSE CORRELATION WITH CAUSATION

Remember that the relationship of separate events is causal only when all other variables are accounted for.

OFF TRACK

The drop in the number of Americans living in poverty during the Clinton administration was due to a number of factors.

ON TRACK

The lower number of Americans living in poverty during the Clinton administration was due to a number of factors. How much did the Welfare Reform Act contribute to this trend? The general economic prosperity experienced by the entire country during that time probably had a greater impact. Statistics show that the primary effect of the Welfare Reform Act was to simply remove people from welfare rolls, not actually lift them out of poverty.

IDENTIFY THE STAKEHOLDERS IN YOUR ANALYSIS

Be especially alert for opinions about your topic from people who would be adversely affected by a different causal outcome.

OFF TRACK

Can megadoses of vitamin C prevent colds, flu, and other illnesses? Good health is important to everyone, so we should all be interested in the news that vitamin C has many important health benefits.

ON TRACK

Can megadoses of vitamin C prevent colds, flu, and other illnesses? The supplements industry has spent millions of dollars to convince consumers that this is the case. The industry stands to make hundreds of millions more if people believe them. But evidence from independent researchers casts some doubt on the effectiveness of megadoses of vitamin C in preventing illness.

313

Writer at work

Armadi Tansal tested three organizational patterns for his analysis. First he looked at how describing a chain of causation could illuminate his analysis. Next, he considered examining effects one by one and eliminating them before describing the effects he thought most likely and most important. Finally, he structured his analysis as an examination of possible effects, one by one, with accompanying discussion of how likely each effect is to be true. This method seemed to be the best for making his analysis, so he used it to write his draft.

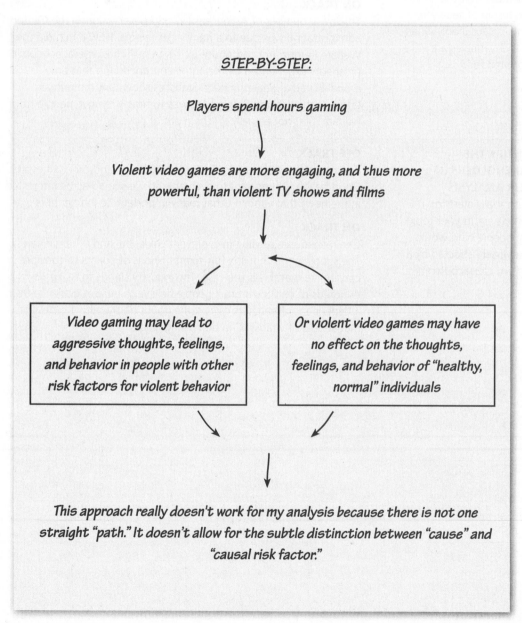

DISPROVING ALTERNATE EFFECTS:

Playing violent video games <u>always</u> leads to violent behavior.
> *- Experts agree there's no definitive proof that this is so.*

Playing violent video games has no impact on the behavior of "healthy, normal" individuals.
> *- Experts seem to concede that this is likely.*

Playing violent video games promotes aggressive behavior in individuals already at risk for violent behavior.
> *- Researchers don't dispute this, but some say the impact of this effect on society is minimal.*

ONE EFFECT AT A TIME:

Anderson thinks video game violence is more influential than TV and movie violence because of the gamer's active role. (Web article)
> *- Gaming is a common activity with little discernible effect anecdotally. (Interview with "John"; my own experience)*

Minimally, violent video games are a "causal risk factor" (Anderson) especially when other risk factors are present (Anderson et al.)
> *- Though the influence on most gamers is probably minor, the impact on society as a whole, even if only a few become more violent, can be great.*

This strategy is the best approach because it lets me look at all the possible effects in detail and finish with a meaningful conclusion.

4: Revise, revise, revise

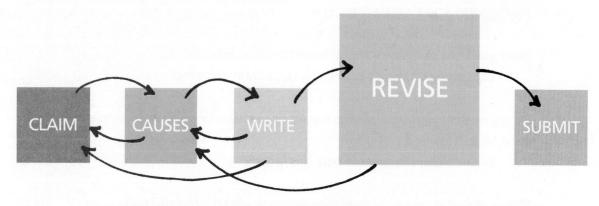

Skilled writers know that the secret to writing well is rewriting. You must have effective strategies for revising if you're going to be successful. The biggest trap you can fall into is starting off with the little stuff first. Leave the small stuff for last.

Does your paper or project meet the assignment?	• Look again at your assignment. Does your paper or project do what the assignment asks?
	• Look again at the assignment for specific guidelines, including length, format, and amount of research. Does your work meet these guidelines?
Is your causal claim arguable?	• Do enough people disagree with you to make the evaluation worthwhile?
	• Who cares about this topic? Do you explain to readers why it is important?
Is your evidence authoritative and convincing?	• Have you found the most accurate available information about your topic?
	• Have you carefully examined the analysis and conclusions of people who have already expressed an opinion on this topic?
Save the editing for last.	When you have finished revising, edit and proofread carefully.

A peer review guide is on page 58.

Writer at work

Armadi Tansal talked with his peer group about his analysis, and he took his draft to the writing center for a consultation. He wrote notes on the draft to help him revise, and then he made some changes to the draft. His peers particularly urged him to cite more research and explain what "violent" means. Here is part of Armadi Tansal's original draft, with notes he made, and the same section as he revised it for his final draft.

Give more details about games so readers can see what "violent" means.

Cite some specific research— not my own opinion. Maybe add a quote?

I've never seen John act violently, and he's never been in trouble with the law. But (new research) on violent video games suggests that John's gaming habit puts him at risk for violent or aggressive behavior. (I agree) that when people play these games a lot, they get used to being rewarded for violent behavior. For example, the multiplayer version of *Modern Warfare 4* and games like *Left 4 Dead*, *Halo*, and *Grand Theft Auto* (are all violent.) To do well in all of these games, you have to commit acts of violence. But does acting violently in games make you more violent in real life?

I've never seen John act violently, and he's never been in trouble with the law. But new research on violent video games suggests that John's gaming habit puts him at risk for violent or aggressive behavior. Dr. Craig Anderson, a psychologist at the University of Iowa, says "the active role required by video games … may make violent video games even more hazardous than violent television or cinema." When people like John play these games, they get used to being rewarded for violent behavior. For example, in the multiplayer version of *Modern Warfare 4*, if the player gets a five-kill streak, he can call in a Predator missile strike. If you kill twenty-five people in a row, you can call in a tactical nuclear strike. Missile strikes help you advance toward the mission goals more quickly, so the more people you kill, the faster you'll win.

Along with *Modern Warfare 4*, John plays games like *Left 4 Dead*, *Halo*, and *Grand Theft Auto*. All these games are rated *M* for "Mature," which according to the Entertainment Software Rating Board means they "may contain intense violence, blood and gore, sexual content and/or strong language." Some M-rated games, like *Grand Theft Auto*, feature random violence, where players can run amok in a city, beat up and kill people, and smash stuff for no reason. In others, like *Modern Warfare 4*, the violence takes place in the context of military action. To do well in all of these games, you have to commit acts of violence. But does acting violently in games make you more violent in real life?

5: Submitted version (MLA Style)

MyWritingLab™

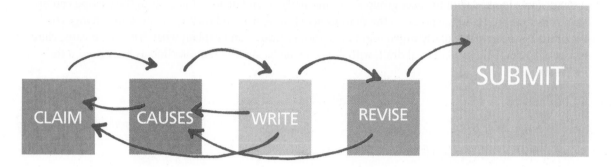

Armadi Tansal

Professor Stewart

English 115

28 October 2014

Modern Warfare: Video Games' Link to Real-World Violence

"John" is a nineteen-year-old college student who gets decent grades. He comes from

a typical upper-middle-class family and plans to get his MBA after he graduates. John is

also my friend, which is why I'm not using his real name.

John has been playing moderately violent video games since he was nine years old.

I started playing video and console games around that age too, and I played a lot in junior

high, but John plays more than anyone I know. John says that over the past year he has

played video games at least four hours every day, and "sometimes all day and night on the

weekends." I have personally witnessed John play *Call of Duty: Modern Warfare 4* for six

hours straight, with breaks only to use the bathroom or eat something.

I've never seen John act violently, and he's never been in trouble with the law. But

new research on violent video games suggests that John's gaming habit puts him at risk

for violent or aggressive behavior. Dr. Craig Anderson, a psychologist at the University

of Iowa, says "the active role required by video games . . . may make violent video games

even more hazardous than violent television or cinema" (Anderson). When people like

John play these games, they get used to being rewarded for violent behavior. For example, in the multiplayer version of *Modern Warfare 4*, if the player gets a five-kill streak, he can call in a Predator missile strike. If you kill twenty-five people in a row, you can call in a tactical nuclear strike. Missile strikes help you advance toward the mission goals more quickly, so the more people you kill, the faster you'll win.

Along with *Modern Warfare 4*, John plays games like *Left 4 Dead, Halo*, and *Grand Theft Auto*. All these games are rated M for Mature, which according to the Entertainment Software Rating Board means they "may contain intense violence, blood and gore, sexual content and/or strong language." Some M-rated games, like *Grand Theft Auto*, feature random violence, where players can run amok in a city, beat up and kill people, and smash stuff for no reason. In others, like *Modern Warfare 4*, the violence takes place in the context of military action. To do well in all of these games, you have to commit acts of violence. But does acting violently in games make you more violent in real life?

Anderson says studies show that "violent video games are significantly associated with: increased aggressive behavior, thoughts, and affect [feelings]; increased physiological arousal; and decreased prosocial (helping) behavior" (Anderson). He also claims that "high levels of violent video game exposure have been linked to delinquency, fighting at school and during free play periods, and violent criminal behavior (e.g., self-reported assault, robbery)."

Being "associated with" and "linked to" violent behavior doesn't necessarily mean video games cause such behavior. Many people have argued that the links Anderson sees are coincidental, or that any effects video games might have on behavior are so slight that we shouldn't worry about them. Christopher Ferguson and John Kilburn, professors of criminal justice at Texas A&M International University, feel that the existing research does not support Anderson's claims. In a report published in the *Journal of Pediatrics*, they point out that in past studies, "the closer aggression measures got to actual violent behavior, the weaker the effects seen."

From what I can tell, John doesn't have any more violent thoughts and feelings than most men his age. When I asked him if he thought the games had made him more violent or aggressive in real life, he said, "I'm actually less violent now. When we were kids we used to play 'war' with fake guns and sticks, chasing each other around the neighborhood and fighting commando-style. We didn't really fight but sometimes kids got banged up. No one ever gets hurt playing a video game."

Anderson admits that "a healthy, normal, nonviolent child or adolescent who has no other risk factors for high aggression or violence is not going to become a school shooter simply because they play five hours or 10 hours a week of these violent video games" (qtd. in St. George). But just because violent video games don't turn all players into mass murderers, that doesn't mean they have no effect on a player's behavior and personality. For example, my friend John doesn't get into fights or rob people, but he doesn't display a lot of prosocial "helping" behaviors either. He spends most of his free time gaming, so he doesn't get out of his apartment much. Also, the friends he does have mostly play video games with him.

Even though the games restrict his interactions with other humans and condition him to behave violently onscreen, John is probably not at high risk of becoming violent in real life. But according to researchers, this low risk of becoming violent is because none of the dozens of other risk factors associated with violent behavior are present in his life (Anderson et al. 160). If John were a high school dropout, came from a broken home, or abused alcohol and other drugs, his game playing might be more likely to contribute to violent behavior.

Anderson contends that violent video games are a "causal risk factor" for violence and aggression—not that they alone cause violent aggression. In other words, the games are a small piece of a much larger problem. People like my friend John are not likely to become violent because of the video games they play. But Anderson's research indicates that some people do. Although there is no simple way to tell who those people are, we should include video games as a possible risk factor when we think about who is likely to become violent. If video games contribute to violent tendencies in only a small fraction of players, they could still have a terrible impact.

Works Cited

Anderson, Craig. "Violent Video Games: Myths, Facts, and Unanswered Questions."
    Psychological Science Agenda, vol. 16, no. 5, Oct. 2003, www.apa.org/science/about/
    psa/2003/10/anderson.aspx.

Anderson, Craig, et al. "Violent Video Game Effects on Aggression, Empathy, and Prosocial
    Behavior in Eastern and Western Countries." *Psychological Bulletin*, vol. 136, no. 2,
    Mar. 2010, pp. 151-73. *APA PsycNET*, doi:10.1037/a0018251.

"ESRB Ratings Guide." *ESRB Ratings*. Entertainment Software Rating Board, www.esrb.org/
    ratings/ratings_guide.aspx. Accessed 2 Oct. 2014.

Ferguson, Christopher J., and John Kilburn. "The Public Health Risks of Media Violence:
    A Meta-Analytic Review." *Journal of Pediatrics*, vol. 154, no. 5, May 2009, pp. 759-63.
    APA PsycNET, doi:10.1037/a0018566.

John. Personal interview. 4 Oct. 2014.

St. George, Donna. "Study Links Violent Video Games, Hostility." *The Washington Post*,
    3 Nov. 2008, www.washingtonpost.com/wp-dyn/content/article/2008/11/02/
    AR2008110202392.html.

Projects

A causal argument answers the question: How did something get that way?

Analyzing claims and stakeholders

Identify a causal relationship that is now generally accepted but was once in doubt, such as Galileo's explanation of the phases of the moon, the link between DDT and the decline of bald eagle populations, or the effects of vitamin B12 on developing fetuses.

Research the arguments that were made for and against these causal relationships. Who initially proposed the cause? What was the reaction? Who argued against them, and why? How did the causal relationship come to be accepted as real? Write a short essay outlining the stakeholders in the issue you have chosen.

Explain the arguments made for and against the now-accepted cause, and the evidence presented. Why were the arguments of the now-accepted cause more effective?

Causal analysis of a trend

Identify a significant change in human behavior over a period of months or years. Why have mega-churches grown rapidly? Why has reality television become popular? Why have the wealthiest one percent of Americans grown significantly richer over the past twenty years? Why have homicide rates dropped to levels not seen since the 1960s? Why are children increasingly obese?

Determine the time span of the trend. When did it start? When did it stop? Is it still going on? You likely will need to do research.

Analyze the possible causes of the trend, arguing for the ones you think are most likely the true causes. Look for underlying and hidden causes.

Remember that providing facts is not the same thing as establishing causes, even though facts can help support your causal analysis.

Causal analysis of a human-influenced natural phenomenon

Find a natural phenomenon or trend that is (or may be) the result of human activity. Is the growing hole in the Earth's ozone layer the result of human-produced chemicals in the atmosphere? Why have populations of American alligators rebounded in the southern United States? Are sinkholes in a Kentucky town the result of new mining activity in the area? Why are more and more bacteria developing resistance to antibiotics? Choose a topic that interests you and that you feel is important. If you think the topic is important, it will be easier to convince your audience that your analysis is important.

Research the possible causes of the phenomenon, focusing on the ones you think are most likely the true causes. Remember to look at underlying and hidden causes.

Think about possible alternative causes. Do you need to incorporate them? If you don't think they are valid causes, then you need to refute them.

Recognize that causal relationships between humans and the natural world are so complex and large in scale that it is often difficult to prove them definitively. Don't oversimplify or make sweeping claims that can't be proven.

COMPOSE IN MULTIMEDIA

Causal argument Web site

Choose a topic for a causal argument (see page 306). You will need to identify your thesis and outline your argument, just as you would for a paper. Decide if you are going to argue for a chain of causes, the effects of a particular cause, or that alternative causes that have been proposed are flawed and the cause you are proposing is the deciding cause.

Divide the elements of your argument into separate Web pages. Give the main argument on the home page and offer evidence and other background on other pages.

Find Web-editing software on your campus if you do not have it on your computer. Campus labs will have programs like Dreamweaver that can produce a handsome site.

Create user-friendly pages with headings and subheadings, a navigation menu with links to move among pages, and visual elements such as graphics and photographs. Avoid large blocks of unbroken text.

Make sure your links work, and proofread carefully before posting your site.

MyWritingLab™ Visit Ch. 10 in MyWritingLab to complete the chapter exercises, explore an interactive version of the Writer at Work paper, and test your understanding of the chapter objectives.

11 Evaluation Arguments

Convincing evaluations rely on selecting criteria and supporting a claim with reasons and evidence.

In this chapter, you will learn to

① Recognize how evaluation arguments use criteria to make judgments (see p. 325)

② Understand how to make a visual evaluation argument (see p. 326)

③ Read and analyze an evaluation argument (see pp. 327–345)

④ Describe the steps involved in the process of writing an evaluation argument (see pp. 346–347)

⑤ Apply flexible strategies to write and revise an evaluation argument (see pp. 348–367)

Writing an Evaluation Argument

You argue for your favorite band, favorite sports team, favorite mobile device, and so on. Evaluation arguments argue for specific criteria and then judge something to be good or bad (or better, or best) according to those criteria.

Evaluative claims argue that SOMETHING is a GOOD (or BAD) — because it meets certain criteria.

Google maps is the best mapping program because it is easy to use, it is accurate, and it provides entertaining and educational features such as Google Earth.

Genres of evaluation arguments

- **Reviews** offer opinions about many products, services, and forms of entertainment like movies and concerts.

- **Policy evaluations** argue what particular policies and laws are good or bad.

- **Evaluations of colleges and universities** use both reputation and statistical criteria such as graduation rates and student selectivity.

- **Evaluations of culture** make judgments about how we eat, work, travel, live in communities, and entertain ourselves.

What Makes a Good Evaluation Argument?

1
Find an interesting topic
A controversial policy, law, or social practice is often a good subject for an evaluation argument.

2
Describe your subject of your evaluation
Because your readers may be unfamiliar with what you are evaluating, describe what you are evaluating.

3
Choose and explain the appropriate criteria

- **Practical criteria** will demand that the thing being evaluated work efficiently or lead to good outcomes (improved conditions, lower costs, and so on).

- **Aesthetic criteria** hinge on the importance and value of beauty, image, or tradition.

- **Ethical criteria** are used to evaluate whether something is morally right, consistent with the law, and upholds fairness.

4
Be fair
Be honest about the strengths and weaknesses of what you are evaluating. Your credibility will increase if you give a balanced view.

5
Support your judgments with evidence
Back up your claims with specific evidence. If you write that a restaurant serves inedible food, describe examples in detail.

Visual Evaluations

Among the first photographs published in newspapers were Jacob Riis's images of slums in New York City in the 1880s, intended to convince readers that living conditions for the poor were intolerable. Beginning in 1908, Lewis Hine worked for a decade photographing child laborers in the United States. Hine's photographs help to mobilize support for state-level child labor laws and later the passage of a federal law to abolish child labor.

Riis's and Hine's photographs were powerful because they provided evidence for larger social movements to improve living conditions in New York City and to end most child labor.

Lewis Hine. *Addie Card, twelve-year-old-spinner (1910)*.

WRITE NOW   MyWritingLab™

What makes an effective review?

1. Look at a several amateur online reviews of a particular film, restaurant, book, or a consumer product such as who makes the best ice cream sundae. You can find movie reviews on IMDB and consumer reviews of thousands of books and products on Amazon, Epionions, and other sites.

2. Select several examples of reviews that you think are persuasive and several that are not (see if you can find some persuasive reviews that you don't necessarily agree with).

3. Analyze the criteria the reviewers use to evaluate. What types of criteria do the persuasive reviewers use? What types do the less persuasive reviews use? Do you see any patterns that make reviews effective?

The Only Way to Have a Cow
Bill McKibben

Bill McKibben is an American environmentalist and author who frequently writes about climate change. He is the author of many books, including *The End of Nature* (1989), *The Age of Missing Information* (1992), and most recently, *Oil and Honey: The Making of an Unlikely Activist* (2013). This essay appeared in the March/April 2010 issue of *Orion* magazine.

HOW IS THIS READING ORGANIZED?

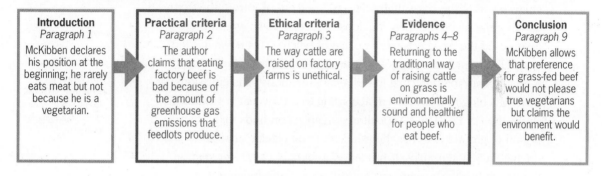

Introduction *Paragraph 1*	**Practical criteria** *Paragraph 2*	**Ethical criteria** *Paragraph 3*	**Evidence** *Paragraphs 4–8*	**Conclusion** *Paragraph 9*
McKibben declares his position at the beginning; he rarely eats meat but not because he is a vegetarian.	The author claims that eating factory beef is bad because of the amount of greenhouse gas emissions that feedlots produce.	The way cattle are raised on factory farms is unethical.	Returning to the traditional way of raising cattle on grass is environmentally sound and healthier for people who eat beef.	McKibben allows that preference for grass-fed beef would not please true vegetarians but claims the environment would benefit.

The Only Way to Have a Cow

1   May I say—somewhat defensively—that I haven't cooked red meat in many years? That I haven't visited a McDonald's since college? That if you asked me how I like my steak, I'd say I don't really remember? I'm not a moral abstainer—I'll eat meat when poor people in distant places offer it to me, especially when they're proud to do so and I'd be an ass to say no. But in everyday life, for a series of reasons that began with the dietary scruples of the woman I chose to marry, hamburgers just don't come into play.

2   I begin this way because I plan to wade into one of the most impassioned fracases now underway on the planet—to meat or not to meat—and I want to establish that I Do Not Have A Cow In This Fight. In recent years vegetarians and vegans have upped their attack on the consumption of animal flesh, pointing out not only that it's disgusting (read Jonathan Safran Foer's new book) but also a major cause of climate change. The numbers range from 18

Beginning paragraph: McKibben starts by announcing his stance on being a vegetarian. He rarely eats meat for several reasons.

percent of the world's greenhouse gas emissions to—in one recent study that was quickly discredited—51 percent. Whatever the exact figure, suffice it to say it's high: there's the carbon that comes from cutting down the forest to start the farm, and from the fertilizer and diesel fuel it takes to grow the corn, there's the truck exhaust from shipping cows hither and yon, and most of all the methane that emanates from the cows themselves (95 percent of it from the front end, not the hind, and these millions of feedlot cows would prefer if you used the word eructate in place of belch). This news has led to an almost endless series of statistical calculations: going vegan is 50 percent more effective in reducing greenhouse gas emissions than switching to a hybrid car, according to a University of Chicago study; the UN Food and Agriculture Organization finds that a half pound of ground beef has the same effect on climate change as driving an SUV ten miles. It has led to a lot of political statements: the British health secretary last fall called on Englishmen to cut their beefeating by dropping at least a sausage a week from their diets, and Paul McCartney has declared that "the biggest change anyone could make in their own lifestyle to help the environment would be to become vegetarian." It has even led to the marketing of a men's flip-flop called the Stop Global Warming Toepeeka that's made along entirely vegan lines.

Introduction of practical criteria: Going vegan reduces greenhouse gas emissions.

3   Industrial livestock production is essentially indefensible—ethically, ecologically, and otherwise. We now use an enormous percentage of our arable land to grow corn that we feed to cows who stand in feedlots and eructate until they are slaughtered in a variety of gross ways and lodge in our ever-larger abdomens. And the fact that the product of this exercise "tastes good" sounds pretty lame as an excuse. There are technofixes—engineering the corn feed so it produces less methane, or giving the cows shots so they eructate less violently. But this type of tailpipe fix only works around the edges, and with the planet warming fast that's not enough. We should simply stop eating factory-farmed meat, and the effects on climate change would be but one of the many benefits.

Introduction of ethical criteria: The way we raise cattle is unethical.

4   Still, even once you've made that commitment, there's a nagging ecological question that's just now being raised. It goes like this: long before humans had figured out the whole cow thing, nature had its own herds of hoofed ungulates. Big herds of big animals—perhaps 60 million bison ranging across North America, and maybe 100 million antelope. That's considerably more than the number of cows now resident in these United States. These were noble creatures, but uncouth—eructate hadn't been coined yet. They really did just belch. So why weren't they filling the atmosphere with methane? Why wasn't their manure giving off great quantities of atmosphere-altering gas?

5   The answer, so far as we can tell, is both interesting and potentially radical in its implications. These old-school ungulates weren't all that different in their plumbing—they were methane factories with legs too. But they used those legs for something. They didn't stand still in feedlots waiting for corn, and they didn't stand still in big western federal allotments overgrazing the same tender grass. They didn't stand still at all. Maybe they would have enjoyed stationary life, but like teenagers in a small town, they were continually moved along by their own version of the police: wolves. And big cats. And eventually Indians. By predators.

6   As they moved, they kept eating grass and dropping manure. Or, as soil scientists would put it, they grazed the same perennials once or twice a year to "convert aboveground biomass to dung and urine." Then dung beetles buried the results in the soil, nurturing the grass to grow back. These grasslands covered places that don't get much rain—the Southwest and the Plains, Australia, Africa, much of Asia. And all that grass-land sequestered stupendous amounts of carbon and methane from out of the atmosphere—recent preliminary research indicates that methane-loving bacteria in healthy soils will sequester more of the gas in a day than cows supported by the same area will emit in a year.

Background information: Cattle and other ungulates in the past contributed to a healthy ecosystem.

7   We're flat out of predators in most parts of the world, and it's hard to imagine, in the short time that we have to deal with climate change, ending the eating of meat and returning the herds

of buffalo and packs of wolves to all the necessary spots. It's marginally easier to imagine mimicking those systems with cows. The key technology here is the single-strand electric fence—you move your herd or your flock once or twice a day from one small pasture to the next, forcing them to eat everything that's growing there but moving them along before they graze all the good stuff down to bare ground. Now their manure isn't a problem that fills a cesspool, but a key part of making the system work. Done right, some studies suggest, this method of raising cattle could put much of the atmosphere's oversupply of greenhouse gases back in the soil inside half a century. That means shifting from feedlot farming to rotational grazing is one of the few changes we could make that's on the same scale as the problem of global warming. It won't do away with the need for radically cutting emissions, but it could help get the car exhaust you emitted back in high school out of the atmosphere.

> **Arguing for criteria:**
> Raising grass-fed beef is a simple system to implement.

8   Oh, and grass-fed beef is apparently much better for you—full of Omega 3s, like sardines that moo. Better yet, it's going to be more expensive, because you can't automate the process the same way you can feedlot agriculture. You need the guy to move the fence every afternoon. (That's why about a billion of our fellow humans currently make their livings as herders of one kind or another—some of them use slingshots, or dogs, or shepherd's crooks, or horses instead of electric fence, but the principle is the same.) More expensive, in this case, as in many others, is good; we'd end up eating meat the way most of the world does—as a condiment, a flavor, an ingredient, not an entrée.

> **More practical criteria:**
> Grass-fed beef is healthier to eat than feedlot beef.

9   I doubt McDonald's will be in favor. I doubt Paul McCartney will be in favor. It doesn't get rid of the essential dilemma of killing something and then putting it in your mouth. But it's possible that the atmosphere would be in favor, and that's worth putting down your fork and thinking about.

> **Conclusion:**
> Strict vegetarians would still disagree with grass-fed beef, but shifting to grass-fed beef would be better for the planet.

In Praise of Fast Food
Rachel Laudan

MyWritingLab™

Rachel Laudan grew up on a farm in England eating fresh food from the family garden. Since earning a PhD in the history and philosophy of science at the University of London, Laudan has taught at universities in Mexico, Argentina, and the United States. She has published in academic and popular presses and authored *Cuisine and Empire: Cooking in World History* (2013) and *The Food of Paradise: Exploring Hawaii's Culinary Heritage* (1996). Laudan also keeps a blog at rachellauden.com.

Return to these questions after you have finished reading.

Analyzing the Reading

1. Reflect upon the title. How does it contribute to the author's argument? What expectations did it create in you? To what degree were your expectations fulfilled?

2. Who is the target audience for this piece? Note this essay appeared in the *Utne Reader*, a self-described "digest of independent ideas and alternative culture. Not right, not left, but forward thinking." Laudan also identifies a category of food critics in the piece. Evaluate the effectiveness of her argument on the intended audience, offering evidence from the text to support your assertions.

3. Which evaluation argument genre best describes this piece? What evaluation criteria does the author employ? Cite examples from the text to support your discussion of genre and evaluation criteria.

4. Describe and evaluate Laudan's evidence supporting her argument. Do you consider the evidence effective? What other kinds of evidence might the author have used to advance the argument?

Exploring Ideas and Issues

Upton Sinclair's novel *The Jungle* (1906) exposed the working conditions of immigrant laborers in a Chicago meat-packing industry. Sinclair's descriptions of dangerous and unsanitary conditions sparked a national conversation on food safety that eventually led to passage of the Pure Food and Drug Act of 1906. More recently, Eric Schlosser published *Fast Food Nation: The Dark Side of the All-American Meal* (2001) in which he examines the rise of fast-food industry since World War II. Schlosser finds that the fast food industry spreads infectious diseases and contributes to the obesity epidemic.

1. Interview several of the oldest people you know, asking them to compare the food culture of their youth to the one we live in today. Ask about their preference and reasons for it. Write an essay in which you explore the changes in food culture as experienced by your interviewee.

2. Write a counterargument to the essay by researching the debates associated with contemporary US diets such as the impact of hormones and additives believed to contribute to obesity, diabetes, and immune deficiencies.

3. In the early nineteenth century "canning" transformed food preservation. In the mid-twentieth century, "TV Dinners" revolutionized food preparation. The microwave oven cooks complete meals in minutes. Write a research report documenting the history of food preservation and preparation technologies and explore the impact, benefits, and drawbacks of how we procure, preserve, and prepare what we eat today.

In Praise of Fast Food

Modern, fast, processed food is a disaster. That, at least, is the message conveyed by newspapers and magazines, on television programs, and in cookbooks. It is a mark of sophistication to bemoan the steel roller mill and supermarket bread while yearning for stone-ground flour and brick ovens; to seek out heirloom apples while despising modern tomatoes; to be hostile to agronomists who develop high-yielding crops and to home economists who invent recipes for General Mills.

My culinary style, like so many people's, was created by those who scorned industrialized food; culinary Luddites, we could call them, after the 19th-century English workers who abhorred the machines that were destroying their way of life. I learned to cook from the books of Elizabeth David, who urged us to sweep our cupboards "clean forever of the cluttering debris of commercial sauce bottles and all synthetic aids to flavoring." I rush to the newsstand to pick up *Saveur* with its promise to teach me to "savor a world of authentic cuisine."

Culinary Luddism has come to involve more than just taste, however; it has also presented itself as a moral and political crusade—and it is here that I begin to back off. The reason is not far to seek: because I am a historian.

As a historian I cannot accept the account of the past implied by this movement: the sunny, rural days of yore contrasted with the gray industrial present. It gains credence not from scholarship but from evocative dichotomies: fresh and natural versus processed and preserved; local versus global; slow versus fast; artisanal and traditional versus urban and industrial; healthful versus contaminated. History shows, I believe, that the Luddites have things back to front.

That food should be fresh and natural has become an article of faith. It comes as something of a shock to realize that this is a latter-day creed.

For our ancestors, natural was something quite nasty. Natural often tasted bad. Fresh meat was rank and tough, fresh fruits inedibly sour, fresh vegetables bitter. Natural was unreliable. Fresh milk soured; eggs went rotten. Everywhere seasons of plenty were followed by seasons of hunger. Natural was also usually indigestible. Grains, which supplied 50 to 90 percent of the calories in most societies, have to be threshed, ground, and cooked to make them edible.

Carl Mydans took this photograph of a twelve-year-old girl of a family of nine, cooking a meal in a lean-to hut in rural Tennessee in 1936.

So to make food tasty, safe, digestible, and healthy, our forebears bred, ground, soaked, leached, curdled, fermented, and cooked naturally occurring plants and animals until they were literally beaten into submission. They created sweet oranges and juicy apples and non-bitter legumes, happily abandoning their more natural but less tasty ancestors. They built granaries, dried their meat and their fruit, salted and smoked their fish, curdled and fermented their dairy products, and cheerfully used additives and preservatives—sugar, salt, oil, vinegar, lye—to make edible foodstuffs.

Eating fresh, natural food was regarded with suspicion verging on horror; only the uncivilized, the poor, and the starving resorted to it. When the ancient Greeks took it as a sign of bad times if people were driven to eat greens and root vegetables, they were rehearsing common wisdom. Happiness was not a verdant Garden of Eden abounding in fresh fruits, but a securely locked storehouse jammed with preserved, processed foods.

As for slow food, it is easy to wax nostalgic about a time when families and friends met to relax over delicious food, and to forget that, far from being an invention of the late 20th century, fast food has been a mainstay of every society. Hunters tracking their prey, shepherds tending their flocks, soldiers on campaign, and farmers rushing to get in the harvest all needed food that could be eaten quickly and away from home. The Greeks roasted barley and ground it into a meal to eat straight or mixed with water, milk, or butter (as Tibetans still do), while the Aztecs ground roasted maize and mixed it with water (as Mexicans still do).

What about the idea that the best food was country food, handmade by artisans? That food came from the country goes without saying. The presumed corollary—that country people ate better than city dwellers—does not. Few who worked the land were independent peasants baking their own bread and salting down their own pig. Most were burdened with heavy taxes and rents paid in kind (that is, food); or worse, they were indentured, serfs, or slaves. They subsisted on what was left over, getting by on thin gruels and gritty flatbreads.

The dishes we call ethnic and assume to be of peasant origin were invented for the urban, or at least urbane, aristocrats who collected the surplus. This is as true of the lasagna of northern Italy as it is of the chicken korma of Mughal Delhi, the moo shu pork of imperial China, and the pilafs, stuffed vegetables, and baklava of the great Ottoman palace in Istanbul. Cities have always enjoyed the best food and have invariably been the focal points of culinary innovation.

Nor are most "traditional foods" very old. For every prized dish that goes back 2,000 years, a dozen have been invented in the last 200. The French baguette? A 20th-century phenomenon, adopted nationwide only after World War II. Greek moussaka? Created in the early 20th century in an attempt to Frenchify Greek food. Tequila? Promoted as the national drink of Mexico during the 1930s by the Mexican film industry. These are indisputable facts of history, though if you point them out you will be met with stares of disbelief.

Were old foods more healthful than ours? Inherent in this vague notion are several different claims, among them that foods were less dangerous, that diets were better balanced. Yet while we fret about pesticides on apples and mercury in tuna, we should remember that ingesting food is and always has been dangerous. Many plants contain both toxins and carcinogens. Grilling and frying add more. Bread was likely to be stretched with chalk, pepper adulterated with the sweepings of warehouse floors, and sausage stuffed with all the horrors famously exposed by Upton Sinclair in *The Jungle*.

By the standard measures of health and nutrition—life expectancy and height— our ancestors were far worse off than we are. Much of the blame was due to diet, exacerbated by living conditions and infections that affect the body's ability to use food. No amount of nostalgia for the pastoral foods of the distant past can wish away the fact that our ancestors lived mean, short lives, constantly afflicted with diseases, many of which can be directly attributed to what they did and did not eat.

Historical myths, though, can mislead as much by what they don't say as by what they do say—and nostalgia for the past typically glosses over the moral problems intrinsic to the labor of producing food. Most men were born to a life of labor in the fields, most women to a life of grinding, chopping, and cooking.

"Servitude," said my mother as she prepared home-cooked breakfast, dinner, and tea for 8 to 10 people 365 days a year. She was right. Churning butter and skinning and cleaning hares, without the option of picking up the phone for a pizza if something goes wrong, is unremitting, unforgiving toil. Perhaps, though, my mother did not realize how much worse her lot might have been. She could at least buy our bread. In Mexico, at the same time, women without servants could expect to spend five hours a day kneeling at the grindstone preparing the dough for the family's tortillas.

In the first half of the 20th century, Italians embraced factory-made pasta and canned tomatoes. In the second half, Japanese women welcomed factory-made bread because they could sleep a little longer instead of getting up to make rice. As supermarkets appeared in Eastern Europe, people rejoiced at the convenience of ready-made goods. For all, culinary modernism had proved what was wanted: food that was processed, preservable, industrial, novel, and fast, the food of the elite at a price everyone could afford. Where modern food became available, people grew taller and stronger and lived longer. Men had choices other than hard agricultural labor; women had choices other than kneeling at the metate five hours a day.

So the sunlit past of the culinary Luddites never existed. So their ethos is based not on history but on a fairy tale. So what? Certainly no one would deny that an industrialized food supply has its own problems. Perhaps we should eat more fresh, natural, local, artisanal, slow food. Does it matter if the history is not quite right?

It matters quite a bit, I believe. If we do not understand that most people had no choice but to devote their lives to growing and cooking food, we are incapable of comprehending that modern food allows us unparalleled choices not just of diet but of what to do with our lives. If we urge the Mexican to stay at her metate, the farmer to stay at his olive press, the housewife to stay at her stove, all so that we may eat handmade tortillas, traditionally pressed olive oil, and home-cooked meals, we are assuming the mantle of the aristocrats of old.

If we fail to understand how scant and monotonous most traditional diets were, we can misunderstand the "ethnic foods" we encounter in cookbooks, at restaurants, or on our travels. We can represent the peoples of the Mediterranean, Southeast Asia, India, or Mexico as pawns at the mercy of multinational corporations bent on selling trashy modern products—failing to appreciate that, like us, they enjoy a choice of goods in the market. A Mexican friend, suffering from one too many foreign visitors who chided her because she offered Italian food, complained, "Why can't we eat spaghetti, too?"

If we assume that good food maps neatly onto old or slow or homemade food, we miss the fact that lots of industrial foods are better. Certainly no one with a grindstone will ever produce chocolate as suave as that produced by conching in a machine for 72 hours. And let us not forget that the current popularity of Italian food owes much to two convenience foods that even purists love, factory pasta and canned tomatoes. Far from fleeing them, we should be clamoring for more high-quality industrial foods.

If we romanticize the past, we may miss the fact that it is the modern, global, industrial economy (not the local resources of the wintry country around New York, Boston, or Chicago) that allows us to savor traditional, fresh, and natural foods. Fresh and natural loom so large because we can take for granted the processed staples—salt, flour, sugar, chocolate, oils, coffee, tea—produced by food corporations.

Culinary Luddites are right, though, about two important things: We need to know how to prepare good food, and we need a culinary ethos. As far as good food goes, they've done us all a service by teaching us how to use the bounty delivered to us by (ironically) the global economy. Their ethos, though, is another matter. Were we able to turn back the clock, as they urge, most of us would be toiling all day in the fields or the kitchen; many of us would be starving.

Nostalgia is not what we need. What we need is an ethos that comes to terms with contemporary, industrialized food, not one that dismisses it; an ethos that opens choices for everyone, not one that closes them for many so that a few may enjoy their labor; and an ethos that does not prejudge, but decides case by case when natural is preferable to processed, fresh to preserved, old to new, slow to fast, artisanal to industrial. Such an ethos, and not a timorous Luddism, is what will impel us to create the matchless modern cuisines appropriate to our time.

We Paved Paradise
Katharine Mieszkowski

MyWritingLab™

Katharine Mieszkowski earned a BA in English from Yale University. Currently she is a health and environment reporter for *The Bay Citizen* and contributes to *Fast Company, The New York Times*, and *Rolling Stone*, among others. "We Paved Paradise" appeared in *Salon.com*.

Return to these questions after you have finished reading.

Analyzing the Reading

1. Describe the core issue of Mieszkowski's argument. Identify specific passages that articulate the issue. Construct a synthesis statement that might serve as a thesis statement.

2. What impact would you expect the essay to have on its intended audience? Consider Mieszkowski's education and other work and affiliations. Note that *Salon.com* considers itself a "progressive" voice publishing "literary luminaries."

3. What evaluation argument genre does the essay best represent, and what kind of evaluation criteria does the author employ? Reference specific passages in the text to support your analysis.

4. Evaluate the kinds and effectiveness of evidence used to support the argument. Is the evidence appropriate for the kind of argument the writer is making? Do you consider the author and her sources credible? Is the evaluation and its evidence fair or biased?

Exploring Ideas and Issues

"We Paved Paradise" alludes to a now famous line in 1960s folk singer Joni Mitchell's song "Big Yellow Taxi." Mitchell echoed the sentiments of environmentalists, social commentators, and citizens concerned by the effects of the suburbanization. While affordable cars and suburban homes signaled a new level of affluence for middle-class Americans, sprawl and urban decline redefined American culture. Pete Seeger's 1963 "Little Boxes" lambasted tract homes and their residents as "ticky tacky" that all look just the same. By the 1980s, New Urbanism advocated a return to traditional neighborhood design and transit-oriented development that encourages people to live, work, and play locally while conserving natural resources.

1. "Having a parking space seems to be one of those amenities that you think is a good thing, but it probably isn't." Brainstorm a list of other "amenities" of modern life that seem like a good thing but may not actually be. Choose one that interests you and write an evaluative argument exploring the issue.

2. Mieszkowski quotes Wiley Norvell, spokesperson for Transportation Alternatives, who argues "the way you manage demand (for parking) is through pricing." In your experience, can the proposed solution work? What might be the impact on mobility? Is the proposal economically equitable? Write an evaluation argument assessing Norvell's solution.

3. Is suburbanization changing your community? Interview elders in your community about their memories of the community. Research the local newspapers to see how your community has changed, for better or for worse, and then write a development history of your community. How did it begin, how did it grow or decline, and how has it changed, for better or for worse, as the result of local, regional, and national transportation policies?

We Paved Paradise

So why can't we find any place to park? Because parking is one of the biggest boondoggles — and environmental disasters — in our country.

In Tippecanoe County, Ind., there are 250,000 more parking spaces than registered cars and trucks. That means that if every driver left home at the same time and parked at the local mini-marts, grocery stores, churches and schools, there would still be a quarter of a million empty spaces. The county's parking lots take up more than 1,000 football fields, covering more than two square miles, and that's not counting the driveways of homes or parking spots on the street. In a community of 155,000, there are 11 parking spaces for every family.

Bryan Pijanowski, a professor of forestry and natural resources at Purdue University, which is located in Tippecanoe, documented the parking bounty in a study released this September. When it made the news, Pijanowski got puzzled reactions from locals. In short, they said: "Are you crazy? I can never find parking where I'm going!"

That's the paradox of parking. No matter how much land we pave for our idle cars, it always seems as if there isn't enough. That's America. We're all about speed and convenience. We don't want to walk more than two blocks, if that. So we remain wedded to our cars, responsible for "high CO_2 emissions, urban sprawl, increased congestion and gas usage, and even hypertension and obesity," says Amelie Davis, a Purdue graduate student who worked on the study.

Despite all the environmental evils blamed on the car and its enablers — General Motors, the Department of Transportation, Porsche, Robert Moses, suburban developers — parking has slipped under the radar. Yet much of America's urban sprawl, its geography of nowhere, stems from the need to provide places for our cars to chill. In the past few years, a host of forward-looking city planners have introduced plans to combat the parking scourge. This year, some are making real progress.

Our story begins in the 1920s with the birth of a piece of esoteric regulation, the "minimum parking requirement." Before parking meters and residential parking permits, cities feared that they were running out of street parking. So municipalities began ordering businesses to provide parking and wrote zoning restrictions to ensure it. Columbus, Ohio, was first, requiring apartment buildings in 1923 to provide parking. In 1939, Fresno, Calif., decreed that hospitals and hotels must do the same. By the '50s, the parking trend exploded. In 1946, only 17 percent of cities had parking requirements. Five years later, 71 percent did.

Today, those regulations could fill a book, and do. The American Planning Association's compendium of regulations, "Parking Standards," numbers 181 pages. It lists the minimum parking requirements for everything from abattoirs to zoos. It is a city planner's bible.

To Donald Shoup, a professor of urban planning at UCLA, parking requirements are a bane of the country. "Parking requirements create great harm: they subsidize cars, distort transportation choices, warp urban form, increase housing costs, burden low income households, debase urban design, damage the economy, and degrade the environment," he writes in his book, *The High Cost of Free Parking*.

Americans don't object, because they aren't aware of the myriad costs of parking, which remain hidden. In large part, it's business owners, including commercial and residential landlords, who pay to provide parking places. They then pass on those costs to us in slightly higher prices for rent and every hamburger sold.

"Parking appears free because its cost is widely dispersed in slightly higher prices for everything else," explains Shoup. "Because we buy and use cars without thinking about the cost of parking, we congest traffic, waste fuel, and pollute the air more than we would if we each paid for our own parking. Everyone parks free at everyone else's expense, and we all enjoy our free parking, but our cars are choking our cities."

It's a self-perpetuating cycle. As parking lots proliferate, they decrease density and increase sprawl. In 1961, when the city of Oakland, Calif., started requiring apartments to have one parking space per apartment, housing costs per apartment increased by 18 percent, and urban density declined by 30 percent. It's a pattern that's spread across the country.

In cities, the parking lots themselves are black holes in the urban fabric, making city streets less walkable. One landscape architect compares them to "cavities" in the cityscape. Downtown Albuquerque, N.M., now devotes more land to parking than all other land uses combined. Half of downtown Buffalo, N.Y., is devoted to parking. And one study of Olympia, Wash., found that parking and driveways occupied twice as much land as the buildings that they served.

Patrick Siegman, a transportation planner, who is a principal with Nelson/ Nygaard Consulting Associates in San Francisco, says Americans are gradually waking up to the downside of parking requirements — at least in one way. "Americans love traditional American small towns, main streets and historic districts," he says. "But largely because of minimum parking requirements, it's completely illegal to build anything like that again in most American cities. It's really hard to build anything where anyone would want to walk from one building to the next."

Parking regulations vary locally, but a typical one in suburban communities requires four parking spaces for every 1,000 square feet of office space. Yet, typically, just over two spaces per 1,000 square feet are used. A classic restaurant parking regulation might require 20 parking spaces per 1,000 square feet of restaurant, which can mean more than five times the space for cars than for diners and chefs.

Wonder why the mall parking lot is half empty most of the time? Developers build parking lots to accommodate shoppers on the busiest shopping day of the year — the day after Thanksgiving — so that shoppers need never, ever park on the street. Similarly, the church parking lot is designed to accommodate

Christmas and Easter services. So a whole lot of land gets paved over that doesn't have to be, transportation planners argue.

The environmental impacts of all this parking go way beyond paving paradise. The impervious surfaces of parking lots accumulate pollutants, according to Bernie Engel, a professor of agricultural engineering at Purdue. Along with dust and dirt, heavy metals in the air like mercury, copper and lead settle onto the lots' surfaces in a process called dry deposition. These particles come from all kinds of diffuse sources, such as industry smokestacks, automobiles and even home gas water heaters.

"If they were naturally settling on a tree or grass, they would wash off those and into the soil, and the soil would hold them in place, so they wouldn't get into the local stream, lake or river," Engel says.

But when the same substances settle on parking lots, rain washes them into streams, lakes and rivers. Engel calculates that the Tippecanoe land used for parking creates 1,000 times the heavy-metal runoff that it would if used for agriculture. Because the surface of the lots doesn't absorb water, it also creates 25 times the water runoff that agricultural land would, which can increase erosion in local waterways.

Parking lots also contribute to the "urban heat island effect." The steel, concrete and blacktops of buildings, roads and parking lots absorb solar heat during the day, making urban areas typically 2 to 5 degrees hotter than the surrounding countryside. "This is most apparent at nighttime, when the surrounding area is cooler, and the urban area starts radiating all this heat from the urban structures," explains Dev Niyogi, an assistant professor at Purdue, who is the Indiana state climatologist.

The urban heat island effect can be so dramatic that it changes the weather. One Indianapolis study found that thunderstorms that reach the city often split in two, going around it, and merging again into one storm after the urban area. "The urban heat island is not simply a temperature issue. It could affect our water availability," says Niyogi.

In Tippecanoe, Pijanowski thinks the county could take steps to keep parking from eating up more land. With changes to zoning laws, a church and a school could share a parking lot, with the worshippers using it on the weekend, and the school kids and teachers parking in it during the week. "These new parking lots that are being built on the urban fringe are huge," says Pijanowski. "They're mega-lots that are servicing mega-buildings for big-box retailers and mega churches. Even our new schools in rural communities have huge parking lots. Having a parking space seems to be one of those amenities that you think is a good thing, but it probably isn't."

Still, there are few frustrations like driving around looking for a parking space, which has its own environmental impacts. Shoup studied a 15-block district in Los Angeles and found that drivers spent an average of 3.3 minutes looking for parking, driving about half a mile each. Over the course of a year, Shoup calculated the cruising in that small area would amount to 950,000 excess miles traveled, equal to 38 trips around the earth, wasting about 47,000 gallons of gas, and producing 730 tons of carbon dioxide that contribute to global warming.

But if simply requiring businesses to build more parking isn't the answer, what is? Today there's a burgeoning movement among urban planners, transportation advocates and city officials to manage parking without blindly building more of it.

Some cities, like Seattle and Petaluma, Calif., are loosening or chucking their minimum parking requirements. Great Britain found that minimum parking requirements bred such bad land-use policies that the nation recently outlawed them entirely. It's a policy that has appeal for both sides of the aisle. "Liberals can love it because it does a huge amount on the affordability of housing, reducing traffic, improving the environment. And conservatives can love it because it's deregulation," says Siegman.

For his part, Shoup wants street parking to be priced at a market rate, so it can compete with lots and garages. Raising rates in the most congested areas will free up space curbside by inspiring thrifty drivers to park farther from their destinations, or — heaven forefend! — take the bus or train. To be politically feasible, he wants to see cities use the money raised by those increased fees to improve the city streets where they're collected, cleaning up graffiti or street cleaning, so shoppers and businesses can see the benefits of where that money is going.

Some cities are putting his theories to the test. In Redwood City, Calif., which boomed during the Gold rush by processing and shipping lumber to San Francisco, city planners are trying to revitalize the historic downtown by luring businesses and shoppers back from the far-flung malls and big-box stores. Yet adding parking spaces would mean adding parking garages, where capital costs can run $20,000 to $30,000 per parking space.

Recently, the city managed to subvert the parking code bible and add a 20-screen movie theater with 4,200 seats without adding more than a thousand parking spaces. Even before the cinema opened, on Friday and Saturday nights, drivers trying to go to restaurants and clubs circled the block searching for the elusive free street spaces, creating gridlock. Meanwhile, parking lots a few blocks away stood half empty. "We had plenty of parking," explains Dan Zack, downtown development coordinator for Redwood City. "What we had was a management problem, not a supply problem."

Transportation planners contend this is true in many urban areas, where street parking is free, and everyone is trying to grab a coveted space right in front of their destination. "You could add another 10,000 parking spaces to a place like downtown Redwood City, and it still wouldn't help you empty out the overfill on street spaces," says Siegman.

To prevent drivers from circling, Redwood City raised the prices of parking on the street from zero in the evening to 75 cents an hour on the main drag, and 50 cents and 25 cents in the surrounding streets until 8 p.m. Even farther from the center of the action, parking is still free on the street. Drivers searching for a good deal quickly caught on and went to the surrounding streets, cheaper parking lots and garages, which can be free with validation. Other cities, such as Ventura and Glendale, both in Southern California, are adopting similar schemes.

In Brooklyn, N.Y., transportation advocates are pushing for the city to consider doing the same. A survey by Transportation Alternatives, an advocacy group for bicyclists, walkers and public-transit users in New York City, found that 45 percent of drivers surveyed in Park Slope were just cruising looking for parking. And street parking was so overcrowded that one in six cars on the main drag, Seventh Avenue, was parked illegally. Only increases in the price of street parking can fix the problem, they contend.

"For the past 100 years, traffic engineers looked at problems like this, and said, 'Oh, the problem is that we don't have enough parking.' That's what got us into the nightmare that we have today," says Wiley Norvell, a spokesperson for Transportation Alternatives. "What we have to start doing is managing the demand for parking, and the way you manage demand is through pricing. The logic with parking for as long as anyone can remember has been supply-oriented. What that does is induce demand: The more roads you have, the more parking you have, the more cars you have." The hope is, of course, to create more incentive to bike, walk or take the bus, instead of driving.

But it's tough to convince drivers to accept that they might have to pay for something that they're used to thinking that they get for nothing, even if they're really paying for it in all kinds of invisible ways. Ever since their first game of Monopoly, Americans have been conditioned to think that parking is free. "I think that we've done things wrong for so long that it takes a while to break all our bad habits of wanting to be freeloaders," says Shoup. "We know that land is fabulously valuable and housing is expensive, but somehow we think we can park for free. We can't."

How to Write an Evaluation Argument

These steps for the process of writing an evaluation may not progress as neatly as this chart might suggest. Writing is not an assembly-line process.

As you write and revise, think about how you might sharpen your criteria and better explain how they apply to what you are evaluating. Your instructor and fellow students may give you comments that help you to rethink your argument from the beginning.

1 CHOOSE A SUBJECT

- Analyze the assignment.

- Explore possible subjects by making lists. Consider which items on your list you might evaluate.

- Analyze a subject by thinking about other things like it.

- Make an evaluative claim that something is good, bad, best, or worst if measured by certain criteria.

- Think about what's at stake. If nearly everyone agrees with you, your claim probably isn't important. Why would some people disagree with you?

2 THINK ABOUT YOUR CRITERIA

- List the criteria that makes something good or bad.

- Which criteria are the most important?

- Which criteria are fairly obvious, and which will you have to argue for?

- How familiar will your readers be with what you are evaluating?

- Which criteria will they accept with little explanation, and which will they possibly disagree with?

- Research your argument by finding evidence and reliable sources.

3
WRITE A DRAFT

- Introduce the issue and give the necesary background.

- Describe each criterion and then analyze how well what you are evaluating meets that criterion.

- If you are making an evaluation according to the effects of something, describe those effects in detail.

- Anticipate where readers might question your criteria and address possible objections.

- Anticipate and address opposing viewpoints by acknowledging how others' evaluations might differ.

- Conclude with either your position, a compelling example, or what is at stake.

- Choose a title that will interest readers in your essay.

4
REVISE, REVISE, REVISE

- Check that your paper or project fulfills the assignment.

- Is your evaluative claim arguable?

- Are your criteria reasonable, and will your audience accept them?

- Is your evidence convincing and sufficient?

- Do you address opposing views?

- Review the visual presentation of your paper or project.

- Proofread carefully.

5
SUBMITTED VERSION

- Make sure your finished writing meets all formatting requirements.

1: Explore the Writing Task

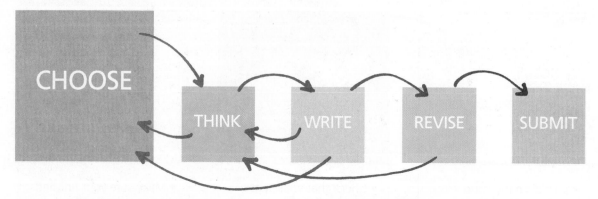

Analyze the assignment

Read your assignment slowly and carefully. Look for key words like *evaluate, rank*, or *review*, which signal an evaluation argument. Identify any information about the length specified, date due, formatting, and other requirements. You can attend to this information later. At this point you want to give your attention to your topic of your evaluation.

Explore possible topics

- **Make a list** of goods and services you consume; sports, entertainment, or hobbies you enjoy; books you have read recently; films you have seen; or policies and laws that affect or concern you.

- **Consider** which items are interesting to you. Which ones also might interest your readers?

- **Choose** something to evaluate that is potentially controversial. You will engage your readers successfully if you can get them to think more about the subject of your evaluation.

Analyze your subject

What does your subject attempt to achieve? What do other similar subjects attempt to achieve? How much do you know about your subject? If it isn't familiar, what research will you need to do?

Analyze your potential readers

What do your readers likely know about your subject? If your readers are knowledgeable, you can introduce technical concepts without much explanation. The more general your audience, the more you will have to define key terms and provide background information. For example, most general readers probably don't know why the practice of breeding dogs for confirmation showing is controversial. If you decide to argue that dog shows that award best in breed are good or bad, you will need to discuss the health issues affecting pedigree dogs.

Think about what is at stake

Why does your evaluation matter? In some cases the stakes are relatively low, such as which food trailer serves the best Thai food. Others, like Bill McKibben's evaluation (see page 327), take on global issues of food production.

Make an arguable claim

A claim that is too obvious or too general will not produce an interesting evaluation. Don't waste your time—or your readers'.

OFF TRACK
Michael Jordan was a great basketball player.

ON TRACK
Bill Russell was the best clutch player in the history of professional basketball.

OFF TRACK
Running is great exercise and a great way to lose weight.

ON TRACK
If you start running to lose weight, be aware of the risks: your body running exerts eight times its weight on your feet, ankles, legs, hips, and lower back, often causing injury to your joints. Swimming, biking, or exercise machines might be the better choice.

Finding a subject to evaluate

1. Make a list of possible subjects to evaluate, and select the one that appears most promising.
2. Write nonstop for five minutes about what you like and dislike about this particular subject.
3. Write nonstop for five minutes about what you like and dislike about things in the same category (Mexican restaurants, world leaders, horror movies, mountain bikes, and so on).
4. Write nonstop for five minutes about what people in general like and dislike about things in this category.
5. Underline the likes and dislikes in all three freewrites. You should gain a sense of how your evaluation stacks up against those of others. You may discover a way you can write against the grain, showing others a good or bad aspect of this subject that they may not have observed.

Writer at work

Jenna Picchi began by underlining the words and phrases that indicated her evaluative task and highlighting information about dates and processes for the project. She then made notes and a list of possible subjects. She selected the policy of producing organic foods on a massive, industrial scale, which she knew about firsthand as a consumer.

English 1302
Evaluating Policy and Law

Write an essay that <u>evaluates</u> a government or corporate policy, or a law. Explain the policy in some detail, <u>and assess</u> it in terms of its impact. Write with the goal of persuading an <u>informed but uncommitted</u> audience to share your opinion. Your paper should be about 4-6 pages long.

Some factors you may want to consider in your assessment are: the people directly affected by the policy; the people indirectly affected; the cost of the policy; the impact of the policy on national security, the environment, international relations, or other sectors of society; and the policy's original purpose. Do not base your assessment solely on practical criteria. Remember that law and policy are intended to effect some good, whether for the public at large, for the benefit of shareholders, or for someone.

Remember to look for __all__ types of criteria.

Think about who will be interested in your topic. <u>Who are you talking to?</u> <u>Who has a stake in this issue?</u> How do you need to tailor your argument to reach your <u>audience</u>?

AUDIENCE

Peer review
You will discuss drafts of your essay in your peer groups during class two weeks from today. Final drafts will be due the following week.

Grading Criteria
I will grade your essay according to how well it does the following:
- Accurately describes the policy or law under consideration.
- Presents persuasive criteria and evidence.
- Appeals to its intended audience.

CLAIMS COULD BE:

1. The prosecution of WikiLeaks founder Julian Assange is not an effective way to address the damage published leaks do to American foreign policy.
2. The campus-wide smoking ban is a policy that protects the health of students, faculty, and staff.
3. <u>The policy of producing organic foods on a massive scale is not as good for the environment or consumers as producing and selling organic foods on a smaller scale.</u>
4. The university's policy of diverting food waste to the composting program is one of the best of its kind.
5. The current policy regarding blood doping and other drug use in professional cycling does not effectively deter drug use.

FREEWRITE:

Many people buy organic foods in the belief that these foods and products are free of pesticides, additives, and other harmful chemicals. A visit to a Whole Foods or even the organic section in an average supermarket is like a trip to a food museum that sets idyllic goods on display. The labels seem to certify that the foods are more wholesome and more humanely raised and harvested than the other choices in the supermarket. Although the marketing message of organic foods seems to be one of purity and natural, simple goodness, the big business that is involved in bringing these foods to consumers is anything but simple. When we imagine organic foods being healthier and grown with traditional methods that are better for the environment, we picture exactly what these marketing messages would prefer. In fact, the companies and farms bringing these foods to us are the same ones producing the cheaper, mass-produced goods from industrial farms.

People have to assert the right to know where their food comes from. The marketing and sales of organic foods tap into consumer desire to have natural, honest food choices. But when giant manufacturers and chains increasingly sell organic products in supermarkets, it is more likely that without scrutiny these organic standards are not being met. Private label organic brands—those sold at a particular chain of stores—allow consumers to get organic goods at lower prices. But when Aurora Dairy, the supplier for many in-house brands of organic milk, was discovered to have broken fourteen of the organic standards in 2007, it took a federal investigation to bring that information to light. Even then Aurora continued to operate without penalty. We can't trust that factory-farming operations are going to follow organic farming principles; they must be required to follow organic certification. If consumers can't trust that organic certification is valid, then the organic label will cease to be meaningful, hurting small family farmers even further. Many who operate smaller, organic family farms are concerned that if the image of organic foods erodes from scandals and exploitation by industrial farms, they will be the ones who suffer the most, even being put out of business.

Even though the goal of "eat local" may not be attainable everywhere for practical reasons, buying local and sensibly traded foods that are sustainably produced is important for the environment and our planet's quickly expanding population.

2: Focus Your Topic and Write a Thesis

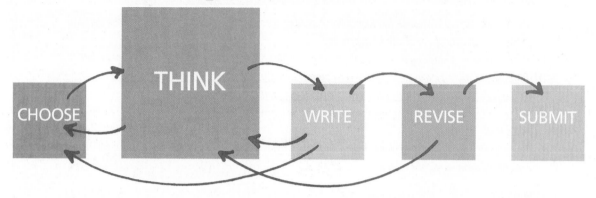

Find the obvious criteria and then dig deeper

Write down the criteria you know you will use in your evaluation. Then think about other criteria that might apply to your evaluation. Think about whether these criteria are practical, aesthetic, or ethical. You may risk losing your readers if you use only one type of criteria, such as aesthetics, and neglect others, like practicality. A beautiful chair that hurts your back isn't a good chair.

Make comparisons based on criteria

Evaluation arguments can look at just one case in isolation, but often they make comparisons. You could construct an argument to preserve the oldest commercial building in your city and turn it into a museum rather than tearing it down as part of a downtown revitalization plan. You might argue that the museum will have economic benefits (a practical criterion), that the carved stone facade is an important example of architecture (an aesthetic criterion), and that the oldest houses have historic preservation status (an ethical criterion of fairness).

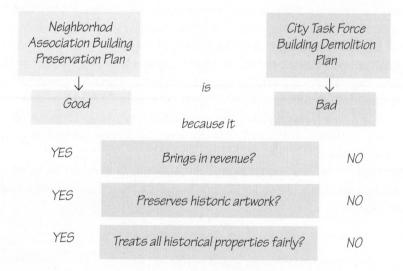

Specify and argue for your criteria

Specify your criteria

Show exactly how your criteria apply to what you are evaluating.

OFF TRACK

Border collies make the best pets because they are smart, friendly, and easy to train. *[Vague; many pets are smart, friendly, and easy to train]*

ON TRACK

Border collies are ideal family pets because their intelligence and trainability enable them to fit into almost any household, no matter how crowded.

Support your criteria

Give evidence to demonstrate why your criteria are valid.

OFF TRACK

Swimming is better exercise than running because you get a better workout. *[How so?]*

ON TRACK

Health professionals maintain that for those who have access to pools or lakes, swimming is the best workout because it exercises all major muscle groups and it's not prone to causing injuries.

Don't assume your audience shares your criteria

It's easy to forget that other people have different concerns and priorities. Your challenge as a writer is finding common ground with people who think differently.

OFF TRACK

Coach X is a bad coach who should be fired because he has lost to our rival school three years in a row. *[For some fans beating the big rival is the only criterion, but not all fans.]*

ON TRACK

While coach X hasn't beaten our big rival in three years, he has succeeded in increasing attendance by 50%, adding a new sports complex built by donations, and raising the players' graduation rate to 80%.

Writer at work

Jenna Picchi made the following notes about her evaluative claim.

TOPIC

The policy of producing and selling organic foods on a massive, industrial scale is not as good for the environment or consumers as producing and selling organic foods on a smaller scale. Although organic foods produced on an industrial scale are less expensive and more convenient, all industrial foods require massive use of fossil fuels to bring them to consumers and may be less sustainably produced.

WHAT ARE INDUSTRIALLY PRODUCED ORGANIC FOODS?

Organic foods are increasingly grown on a mass scale by centralized businesses that run industrial farm operations. These companies replicate many of the practices of mainstream factory farms to keep prices low and maximize profits.

WHO IS AFFECTED?

- Consumers who are looking to organic foods for health and aesthetic reasons
- Those interested in responsible agriculture as a way to protect the environment
- Local organic farmers

MY EXPERIENCE

- Organic options at campus markets are limited to national brands.
- Farmers markets that offer locally grown produce in our community are not easily accessible to students and have limited hours.

CRITERIA

Practical

- Big organic food producers bring organic options at lower cost to more people.
- Organics cost more and bring in high profits. But big corporate producers of organic goods drive down prices for local farmers, making it harder for traditional, local organic farmers to compete.

Ethical

- Big industrial organic companies produce things that are not consistent with organic principles that encourage eating more whole foods (rather than processed ones) that are sustainably grown.
- Large corporations have cut corners. Industrial scale food producers have been caught stretching or breaking organic guidelines and were cited by the federal government.

<u>Aesthetic</u>
- Marketing for organic foods uses images of traditional, idyllic farms, equating organic with naturalness and purity. But the reality of factory-scaled farms is quite different and these images are inaccurate.

AUDIENCE

Who has a stake in this issue? What do they know about it? How should I appeal to them?

<u>Consumers of organic foods</u>
- Consumers want to purchase the healthiest, most environmentally sustainable choices and are often fairly well informed about the issue.
- Organic shoppers often have a strong sense of the ethical importance of sustainable, safely produced foods. They are likely to feel upset if they find that the organic industry is misrepresenting itself.

<u>Local farmers</u>
- Farmers feel direct effect in prices and regulations.

<u>All citizens</u>
- Citizens feel a sense of empathy for the farmers who produce our food.
- All taxpayers benefit when citizens eat whole and organic foods that keep them healthier and reduce disease.

BACKGROUND

Many people know about the benefits of organic foods but may not know how the spread of low-cost, industrially produced organic options involves compromises to organic ideals.

TO RESEARCH

- Need to get info on how organic industry evolved and grew, and what impact this growth had.
- Find anecdotes on the threat to standards posed by the industrial organic industry.
- Find evidence of the effects of eating locally.

3: Write a Draft

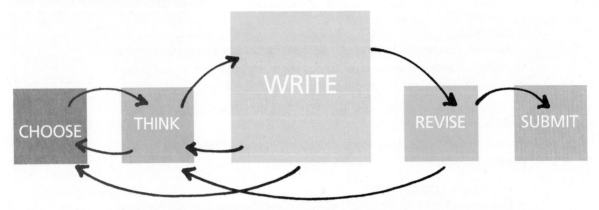

Introduce the issue

Give your readers any background information they will need. State your stance up front, if you wish. Some evaluations work better if the writer's judgment is issued at the beginning; sometimes, it is more effective to build up a mass of evidence and then issue your verdict at the end.

Describe your criteria and offer evidence

Organize the criteria to be as effective as possible. Identify your strongest criterion, and think about if you want to lead with it or save it for the last. Explain each criterion and give reasons why it applies if it isn't obvious. Provide specific examples of how well your subject meets or does not meet each criterion.

Anticipate and address opposing viewpoints

Acknowledge why others may have a different opinion than you do. Demonstrate why your evaluation is better by pointing out either why your criteria are better or why you have better evidence and reasons.

Conclude with strength

State your summary evaluation if you have not done so already. Offer a compelling example or analogy to end your essay. State explicitly what is at stake in your evaluation, especially if you are evaluating a policy or issue that affects many people.

Choose a title that will interest your readers

A bland, generic title like "An Evaluation of X" gives little incentive to want to read the essay.

Writer at work

Based on her lists of criteria, her conclusions about her audience, and her research, Jenna Picchi sketched out a rough outline for her essay.

1. Opening personal anecdote about trying to shop organic near campus. End with claim.

2. Specific example about issues related to industrial organic farming: the image of natural, healthy foods produced with traditional methods vs. reality of factory farms

3. Look at industrial organic food industry
   a. What is it
   b. Why is it growing
   c. What are its origins (the move from small organic to Big Organic)

4. First criterion: good organic food policy should produce healthy foods that are sustainably produced
   a. Better for the environment
   b. Better for individuals and for public health
   c. Better for taxpayers

5. Second criterion: good policy should protect consumers and guarantee valid organic certifications
   a. Organic standards hard to police
   b. Federal investigations into major organic milk producers breaking rules
   c. If organic label isn't protected consumers won't trust it

6. Third criterion: good policy avoids negative impacts on small farms
   a. Industrial organic companies help define organic standards
   b. Industrial organic companies involved in setting prices
   c. Local farms can be held accountable about standards and sustainability, earn consumer trust

7. Conclusion and perspective

4: Revise, Revise, Revise

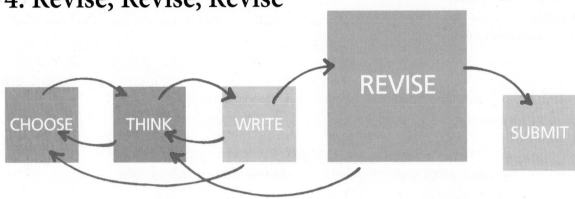

Skilled writers know that the secret to writing well is rewriting. Leave correcting errors for last.

Does your paper or project meet the assignment?	• Look again at your assignment. Does your paper or project do what the assignment asks?
	• Look again at the assignment for specific guidelines, including length, format, and amount of research. Does your work meet these guidelines?
Is your evaluative claim arguable?	• Do enough people disagree with you to make the evaluation worthwhile?
	• Does anyone but you care about this topic?
Are your criteria reasonable, and will your audience accept them?	• Do you provide compelling reasons for readers to accept your criteria for evaluation, if they weren't predisposed to do so?
	• Do you weight criteria appropriately, balancing aesthetic, ethical, and practical considerations?
Is your evidence convincing and sufficient?	• Will readers believe what you say about the thing you are evaluating? What proof do you offer that it does or doesn't meet your criteria?
Do you address opposing views?	• Have you acknowledged the opinions of people who disagree with you?
	• Where do you show why your evaluation is better?
Is the writing project visually effective?	• Is the font attractive and readable?
	• Are the headings and visuals effective?
	• If you use images or tables as part of your evaluation, are they legible and appropriately placed?
Save the editing for last.	• See guidelines for editing and proofreading on page 59.

A peer review guide is on page 58.

Writer at work

Working with a group of her fellow students, Jenna Picchi noted their suggestions on her rough draft, and she used them to help produce a final draft.

This starts to sound like conspiracy or rumors—find some quotes or anecdotes to illustrate it so people believe it really happens, and that it really affects consumers.

Organic foods that are industrially produced may mislead consumers into thinking they are more natural and wholesome than they really are. For the most part, government agencies carefully regulate and define the meanings of the words on food labels. Consumers should be able to expect that foods with the organic label are healthy food choices that are sustainably produced. Organic foods are marketed as more wholesome or more humanely raised and harvested than other foods in the store. Packaging suggests organic foods are pure, natural, and simply better. But in reality, many of these organic products are grown by big, industrial companies that produce foods in a way that are not consistent with organic principles. The reality of the organic foods we find at Walmart, Target, and other major retail chains is that they are produced on a mass scale—the same industrial-sized operations that bring us cheap, "regular" products. These industrial "Big Organic" producers are stretching organic standards to become more vaguely worded and harder to enforce. Organic standards are not being met.

The "us" versus "them" tone will alienate people who feel differently about convenience foods. Many people are busy and want food that is convenient and also healthy and sustainably produced.

If the goal is to offer healthy choices to consumers who are trained to expect cheap, convenient options, industrial producers of organic foods have made significant contributions. They have put organic foods within reach for average consumers, not just affluent ones. But the growth of the organic food industry has come at a great price. Early on, the organic movement encouraged people to choose more whole foods rather than processed ones. Now all kinds of processed convenience foods containing synthetic additives carry the organic label. Although industrially produced organic foods are convenient, they present a natural, earth-friendly image that is often not the reality. The organic ideal has been polluted when it is applied to processed foods that include corn syrup along with other confusing additives. The marketing message and the reality of what is in many processed foods with the organic label do not match. Small, local organic farmers are well positioned to deliver on the organic movement's original ideals and give consumers foods grown using meaningful organic standards. It is worth questioning whether organic standards mean what they seem and worth it to seek out the local, organic farmers who are able to show their commitment to sustainably produced organic foods. Labeling foods organic cannot be just a marketing ploy, and the organic industry will continue to grow if it can ensure this label has real meaning.

Giving too much weight to ethics, not enough to practicality. What option would be better than supporting and buying only a watered-down definition of organic food, but still practical?

5: Submitted Version (MLA Style)

MyWritingLab™

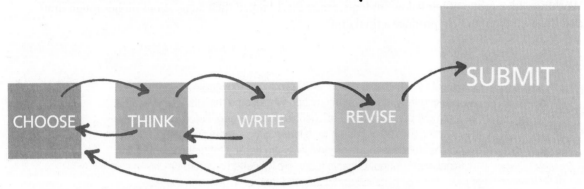

Picchi 1

Jenna Picchi

Professor Alameno

English 101

2 December 2014

Organic Foods Should Come Clean

   As a kid growing up not far from rural communities, I took for granted the access to local produce and the farm stands that my family frequented. When I moved to a college town, I assumed I would have access to an even wider variety of foods and better choices. I wanted to continue eating organic as I had at home, even though it would be more work than a campus-dining plan. I learned quickly that even in a large college town, it takes determined searching in most supermarkets to find the organic produce, bread, meat, and dairy products that are scattered in less-trafficked corners of the store. Instead of shopping at the farmers market (which keeps hours I cannot attend), I choose these supermarket fruits and vegetables from the lackluster and small display of things shipped in from California and Central America. Taking a recent look at these organic departments, I noticed that almost all the products are store or national brands. It never occurred to me that living in the middle of an agricultural state my choices would be so limited. After spending much time and energy seeking out organic products in stores all around town, I wondered whether the effort is worth it. How healthy are these foods in the local supermarket? And are these national brands as good for the environment as they seem?

Many people shop for organic foods in the belief that they are free of pesticides, additives, and other chemicals that can harm people and the environment over time. Visit an average supermarket's organic department and you will see signs and labels confirming this idea. Organic foods are marketed as more wholesome or more humanely raised and harvested than other foods in the store. Packaging suggests organic foods are pure, natural, and simply better. But the big businesses that bring these products to consumers are anything but simple. The reality of the organic foods we find at Walmart, Target, and other major retail chains is that they are produced on a mass scale—the same industrial-sized operations that bring us cheap, "regular" products. And it may be that the policy of producing and selling organic foods on a massive, industrial scale is not as good for the environment or consumers as producing and selling organic foods on a smaller scale. Although industrially produced organic foods are convenient, they present a natural, earth-friendly image that is often not the reality. The industrial organic food industry makes many claims that deserve a closer look.

Consumers willing to pay more for organic foods might be surprised to learn that mass-produced organic foods come from farms that barely resemble the old-fashioned images on their milk carton. The majority of organic food sales come via a very large industry, not an idealistic or environmentalist movement. In fact, organic foods are the fastest-growing category in the food industry, now worth about $11 billion (Pollan 136). The way food is produced has been changing more over the past fifty years than in the previous 10,000 years *(Food Inc.)*. Many organic foods are grown by big, industrial producers. These companies—often owned by large corporations—use many of the same practices as mainstream factory farms to keep costs low. They can distribute and market their products nationally, and while organic foods cost more overall, these corporations succeed because they have made organic food available to average customers (not just affluent ones). If the goal is to offer healthy choices to consumers who are trained to expect cheap, convenient options, industrial producers of organic foods have made significant contributions. The organic label works wonders in marketing—and the big corporations who produce and deliver the foods in our supermarkets are taking advantage of it.

The history of the organic food movement was originally small, locally based, and in response to the industrialization of food. The evolution away from an organic movement toward an organic food industry is fairly recent. The organic pioneers of the 1970s had "a vision of small farms, whole food, and local distribution" (Fromartz 194). They hoped to help people eat fewer processed foods, produced organically and distributed from local sources. But for some farmers the allure of reaching more consumers and national sales led to compromises. In *Omnivore's Dilemma*, Michael Pollan traces the pressure some farmers felt in the early 1990s to "sell out" and work with agribusiness (153). Farmers like Gene Kahn, the founder of Cascadian Farm (now owned by food giant General Mills), saw that he could change and redefine the way food is grown and still reach a mass market. Even though this meant giving up on two ideals of the organic movement—local distribution and eating more whole foods—organic foods were becoming a large-scale business, bringing more naturally produced choices to more and more consumers.

One concern for Pollan and others is that the organic label is being used by companies who are not invested in organic principles. In fact, chemical farming and big agribusiness had once been the enemy of the organic movement. But then agribusiness got into the organic market (Fromartz 194). The worry is, as industrial organic operations grow and adopt more and more big agribusiness methods, whether the term organic is becoming just another marketing gimmick.

As organic foods become increasingly industrial, it important for consumers to be able to verify whether the products they buy are defined and produced using truly organic standards. Organic standards have evolved

Picchi 4

in recent years and now regulate not just small farms but also large-scale industrial operations. But even as the standards are changing, they must at a minimum guarantee healthy foods that are sustainably produced. Organic agriculture is valuable for the way it protects the environment. Marion Nestle, a scholar on food and public health, describes research that organic farming uses less energy and leaves soils in better condition than traditional farms (213). In addition to protecting lands from excessive chemical use, another possible benefit of organic, local farming is that it can require less use of fossil fuels. Fossil fuels are spent whenever farm supplies must be shipped or when foods are sent for processing. Foods travel long distances across the country and foods are shipped from across the world, draining fossil fuels. But Pollan states that organic food can be produced with about one-third less fossil fuel than conventional food (183). Using fewer fossil fuels and chemicals should be a goal for any organic farmer or consumer concerned with pollution and creating a more sustainable food industry.

Less research is available to prove that organic foods are better nutritionally. Officially, Pollan says, the government takes the position that "organic food is no better than conventional food" (178). But he believes current research reveals organic foods grown in more naturally fertile soil to be more nutritious. And Nestle believes organic foods may be safer than conventional foods because people who eat them will have fewer synthetic pesticides and chemicals in their bodies (213). If consumers can rely on organic foods for their health benefits, a larger good would be granted in overall public health. As a society we all benefit when people eat whole foods and organic foods as part of diets that maintain a health and fight weight-related disease. Foods with an organic label should be able to guarantee these benefits to individuals and to public health.

Another benefit to taxpayers is that organic farms are far less subsidized and in particular do not receive direct government payments (Pollan 182). Many organic farms do not participate in the complicated system of paying farmers directly that mainstream farmers participate in, though Pollan points out that many industrial organic farms do benefit from less direct subsidies. For example, many states subsidize access to cheaper water and electricity to power farms. However, supporting the less subsidized farmers may bring savings taxpayers in the end.

Organic labels and standards are difficult but crucial to police and enforce. Consumers who are willing to pay extra for natural food choices will lose faith if it turns out the organic labels are not honest. Organic farmers traditionally set themselves up as an alternative to big agribusiness. But as Pollan explains, as giant manufacturers and chains sell more and more of the organic foods in supermarkets, organic agriculture has become more and more like the industrial food system it was supposed to challenge (151). As a result, it is more likely that without scrutiny organic standards are not being met.

Organic milk offers one example of a product where organic standards have recently been an issue. A handful of very large companies produce most of the organic milk we buy. Many chain stores have begun successfully competing, selling their own private label organic milk. These huge private label organic brands allow consumers to get organic goods at even lower prices. But one recent case of possible organic fraud involves Aurora Dairy, the supplier for many in-house brands of organic milk for stores such as Walmart and Costco. Aurora was discovered to have broken fourteen of the organic standards in 2007. The USDA cited them because their herds included cows that were fed inappropriate feed and because some cows had no access to pastures. It took a federal investigation to bring information about these violations to light and yet even then they continued to operate without penalty (Gunther). But when organic standards are vaguely worded and unenforceable or go unmonitored at factory dairy farms, violations of organic principles are bound to happen.

The overwhelming pressure for access to foods that are cheap and convenient is something all consumers feel. But most people interested in buying organic foods do so because they believe they're doing something positive for their health, for the health of their community, and in the best interests of the environment. Often these consumers have a strong sense of the ethical importance of sustainable produced food. Because of this interest in doing what is right, these consumers are likely to be especially upset by news that the goods they're paying extra for are being misrepresented. These consumers expect and welcome organic standards that are meaningfully set and policed. Good organic agriculture policy would help ensure strong standards; without them consumers will become jaded and not trust the organic label.

Consumers interested in the monitoring of these standards might be concerned to see how standards in the past decade have changed. In crafting these rules, the government consults with some of the biggest businesses involved in organic food production. Many long-time organic farmers believe that the role of these corporations has watered down organic standards. The farmers themselves are voicing concerns that regulations should be tougher. Elizabeth Henderson, an organic farmer and member of the large organic co-op, Organic Valley, spoke out in 2004 about the huge growth of organic food as coming "at an awful price, compromising standards, undercutting small farms, diluting healthy food, ignoring social justice—polluting the very ideals embodied in the word *organic*" (qtd. in Fromartz 190).

In one recent example, Horizon Organic, the giant milk producer, fought for the development of USDA rules that ensure its factory farms in Idaho would not be required to give all cows a specific amount of time to graze on pasture (Pollan 157). The watered down USDA standard Horizon helped to craft instead is very vague. The image most consumers have of organic milk coming from cows grazing in pasture is an ideal that many mainstream organic milk producers don't even approach. Many small dairy farmers follow older organic practices on their own, but current "organic" labels do not guarantee this.

Another challenge for consumers looking for sustainably produced organic products is that the industrial-sized producers are more efficient, making it hard for smaller farmers to compete. Local small farms, like personal gardens, are both "more expensive but also less efficient than larger operations in terms of transportation, labor, and materials required" (Dubner). Big organic companies can set lower prices, ship foods long distances quickly, and make distribution simpler for the supermarkets (Pollan 168). The growth of industrially produced organic foods has helped bring prices down overall. The competition is good in theory, allowing more people access to organic choices. But faced with these competing choices, perhaps only very informed consumers of organic foods may sympathize with and support their local organic farmers.

Good organic agriculture policy would ideally avoid having a negative impact on small, local producers. I would acknowledge that locally produced food is not necessarily more sustainable or by definition produced with less energy or better for the environment (McWilliams 22). The smaller-scale farm also has to be committed to sustainable practices. Local farms can be held accountable for whether they are meeting organic standards and following sustainable farming practices. A dairy farmer you can talk to at a local farmers market can, in theory, earn trust and be held accountable to customers.

Small, local organic farmers are well positioned to deliver on the organic movement's original ideals of sustainably produced foods. Consumers should have a right to know where their food comes from and how organic standards are defined. In fact, as organic foods become more widely available to most consumers—even college students—it is worth questioning whether organic standards mean what they seem. Labeling foods organic cannot be just a marketing ploy, and the organic industry will continue to reach and inform more consumers if it can ensure this label has real meaning.

Works Cited

Dubner, Stephen J. "Do We Really Need a Few Billion Locavores?" *Freakonomics*, 9 June 2008, freakonomics.com/2008/06/09/do-we-really-need-a-few-billion-locavores/.

Food Inc. Directed by Robert Kenner, Magnolia Pictures, 2009.

Fromartz, Samuel. *Organic, Inc.: Natural Foods and How They Grew*. Houghton Mifflin Harcourt, 2006.

Gunther, Marc. "An Organic Milk War Turns Sour." *The Cornucopia Institute*, 3 Oct. 2007, www.cornucopia.org/2007/10/an-organic-milk-war-turns-sour/.

McWilliams, James E. *Just Food: Where Locavores Get It Wrong and How We Can Truly Eat Responsibly*. Little, Brown, 2009.

Nestle, Marion. "Eating Made Simple." *Food Inc.: How Industrial Food Is Making Us Sicker, Fatter, and Poorer—and What You Can Do About It,* edited by Karl Weber, PublicAffairs Books, 2009, pp. 209-18.

Pollan, Michael. *The Omnivore's Dilemma: A Natural History of Four Meals*. Penguin Books, 2006.

Projects

Effective evaluation arguments depend on finding the right criteria and convincing your readers that these criteria are the best ones to use.

Film review

Select a film to review. Choose a specific magazine, newspaper, or online publication as the place where you would publish the review.

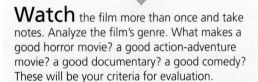

Watch the film more than once and take notes. Analyze the film's genre. What makes a good horror movie? a good action-adventure movie? a good documentary? a good comedy? These will be your criteria for evaluation.

Find information on the film. The Internet Movie Database (IMDB) is a good place to start.

Write a thesis that makes an evaluative claim: the film is a successful or unsuccessful example of its genre. Use evidence from the film to support your claim.

Evaluate a controversial subject

Think of controversial subjects on your campus or in your community for which you can find recent articles in your campus or local newspaper. For example, is your mayor or city manager an effective leader? Is your campus recreational sports facility adequate? Is a new condominium complex built on city land that was used as a park good or bad?

Identify what is at stake in the evaluation. Who thinks it is good or effective? Who thinks it is bad or ineffective? Why does it matter?

List the criteria that make something or someone good or bad. Which criteria are the most important? Which will you have to argue for?

Analyze your potential readers. How familiar will they be with what you are evaluating? Which criteria will they likely accept and which might they disagree with?

Write a draft. Introduce your subject, and give the necessary background. Make your evaluative claim either at the beginning or as your conclusion. Describe each criterion and evaluate your subject on each criterion. Be sure to address opposing viewpoints by acknowledging how their evaluations might be different.

Evaluate a campus policy

Identify a policy on your campus that affects you. Examples include the way your school schedules classes and has students register, the way parking spaces are allotted on campus, the library's late fee and returns policy, housing or admissions policies, or rules regulating student organizations.

Consider your target audience as the readers of your campus newspaper. Who else besides you does this issue affect? What office or division of the school is responsible for the program? Who implemented it in the first place? Keep in mind that your school's administration is part of your audience.

Determine the criteria for your evaluation. Which criteria will be most important for other students? for the faculty and staff? for the administration?

Take a clear position about the policy. If you think the policy is unfair or ineffective, acknowledge why it was put into place. Sometimes good intentions lead to bad results. If you think the policy is fair or effective, explain why according to the criteria you set out. In either case, give reasons and examples to support your judgment.

COMPOSE IN MULTIMEDIA

Video evaluation

Find a subject to evaluate by making a video. You might evaluate something you own, such as your phone, your television, or your bicycle. Or you might evaluate something on your campus, such as the student union, a campus gym, or a campus event.

Plan your content. In much the same way you write an evaluation essay, you will need to identify criteria and gather evidence. Think about whether you will need to interview anyone. Draft a storyboard, which is a shot-by-shot representation of your project, which will help you arrange your schedule.

Arrange for your equipment and compose your video. If you don't own a video camera, find out if you can get one from a campus lab. Quality video takes many hours to shoot and edit. Visit all locations in advance to take into account issues such as lighting and noise.

Edit your video. Editing software allows you to combine video clips and edit audio. Your multimedia lab may have instructions or consultants for using video editing software. Allow ample time for editing.

MyWritingLab™ Visit Ch. 11 in MyWritingLab to complete the chapter exercises, explore an interactive version of the Writer at Work paper, and test your understanding of the chapter objectives.

12 Position Arguments

Position arguments aim to change readers' attitudes and beliefs. This statue commemorates César Chávez, who spent his adult life arguing for civil rights for farm workers.

In this chapter, you will learn to

1 Recognize the different forms of position arguments *(see p. 371)*

2 Understand how to make a visual position argument *(see p. 372)*

3 Read and analyze a position argument *(see pp. 373–403)*

4 Describe the steps involved in the process of writing a position argument *(see pp. 404–405)*

5 Apply flexible strategies to write and revise a position argument *(see pp. 406–421)*

Writing a Position Argument

In a position argument you make a claim about a controversial issue. Position arguments often take two forms—definition arguments and rebuttal arguments.

Definition arguments set out criteria and then argue that whatever is being defined meets or does not meet those criteria.

Something is (or is not) _____ because it has (or does not have) Criteria A, Criteria B, and Criteria C (or more).

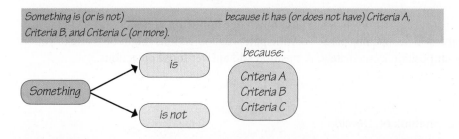

Graffiti is art because it is a means of self-expression. it shows an understanding of design principles, and it simulates both the senses and the mind.

Rebuttal arguments take the opposite position. They challenge either the criteria a writer uses to define something or the evidence that supports the claim.

The opposing argument has serious shortcomings that undermine the claim because
flawed reason 1
flawed reason 2

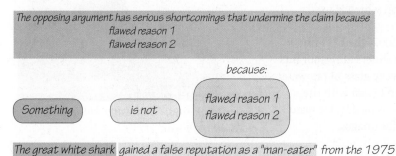

The great white shark gained a false reputation as a "man-eater" from the 1975 movie Jaws, but in fact attacks on humans are rare and most bites have been "test bites," which is a common shark behavior with unfamiliar objects.

What Makes a Good Position Argument?

1

Define the issue

Your subject should be clear to your readers. If readers are unfamiliar with the issue, you should give enough examples so they understand the issue in concrete terms.

2

Identify the stakeholders

Who is immediately affected by this issue? Who is affected indirectly?

3

Read about the issue

Before you formulate a claim about an issue, become familiar with the conversation about that issue by reading.

4

State your position

You may want to state your thesis in the opening paragraph to let readers know your position immediately.

5

Find reasons

List as many reasons as you can think of. Develop the ones that are most convincing.

6

Provide evidence

In support of your reasons, provide evidence—in the form of examples, statistics, and testimony of experts—that the reasons are valid.

7

Acknowledge opposing views

Anticipate what objections might be made to your position and answer those objections.

Visual Position Arguments

Images don't speak for themselves but they can combine with words to make powerful arguments. One type of visual argument is visual metaphor, which is used frequently in advertising.

On World Water Day, March 22, 2007, the US Fund launched their Tap project, in which diners at restaurants in select cities could donate $1 for every glass of tap water they order. The advertising campaign began with the striking visual metaphor of a boy pointing a water pistol at his head followed by other powerful images.

The caption says, "Bad water kills more children than war."

WRITE NOW   MyWritingLab™

Identify reasons that support conflicting claims

Select a controversial issue for which there are multiple points of view.
You can find a list of issues at **www.dir.yahoo.com/Society_and_Culture/Issues_and_Causes/**.

Explore the links for one of the issues to get a sense of the range of opinion.
Analyze two Web sites. Write down the following for each site.

- What is the main claim of the Web site?
- What reason or reasons are given?
- What evidence (facts, examples, statistics, and the testimony of authorities) is offered?

Write a one-page analysis that addresses these questions. How do the reasons differ for opposing claims? What assumptions underlie the reasons? How does the evidence differ?

Take My Privacy, Please!
Ted Koppel

Ted Koppel joined ABC News in 1963 and served from 1980 until 2005 as the anchor and managing editor of *Nightline,* the first late-night network news program. He has had a major reporting role in every presidential campaign since 1964. "Take My Privacy, Please!", which appeared in June 2005 in the *New York Times,* is an example of a position argument that doesn't begin with a thesis but first gives a series of examples.

HOW IS THIS READING ORGANIZED?

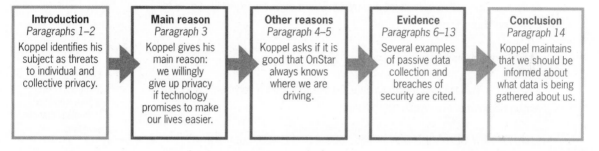

| **Introduction** *Paragraphs 1–2* Koppel identifies his subject as threats to individual and collective privacy. | **Main reason** *Paragraph 3* Koppel gives his main reason: we willingly give up privacy if technology promises to make our lives easier. | **Other reasons** *Paragraph 4–5* Koppel asks if it is good that OnStar always knows where we are driving. | **Evidence** *Paragraphs 6–13* Several examples of passive data collection and breaches of security are cited. | **Conclusion** *Paragraph 14* Koppel maintains that we should be informed about what data is being gathered about us. |

Take My Privacy, Please!

1 THE PATRIOT ACT—brilliant! Its critics would have preferred a less stirring title, perhaps something along the lines of the Enhanced Snooping, Library and Hospital Database Seizure Act. But then who, even right after 9/11, would have voted for that?

2 Precisely. He who names it and frames it, claims it. The Patriot Act, however, may turn out to be among the lesser threats to our individual and collective privacy.

3 There is no end to what we will endure, support, pay for and promote if only it makes our lives easier, promises to save us money, appears to enhance our security and comes to us in a warm, cuddly and altogether nonthreatening package. To wit: OnStar, the subscription vehicle tracking and assistance system. Part of its mission statement, as found on the OnStar Web site, is the creation of "safety, security and peace of mind for drivers and passengers with thoughtful wireless services that are always there, always ready." You've surely seen or heard their commercials, one of which goes like this:

ANNOUNCER -- The following is an OnStar conversation. (Ring)

ONSTAR -- OnStar emergency, this is Dwight.

Introduction:
Koppel announces his stance and his subject in the first two paragraphs. He questions the Patriot Act and then suggests that there may be bigger threats to privacy.

Evidence:
The OnStar commercial is described in detail as the first example.

DRIVER -- (crying) Yes, yes??!

ONSTAR -- Are there any injuries, ma'am?

DRIVER -- My leg hurts, my arm hurts.

ONSTAR -- O.K. I do understand. I will be contacting emergency services.

ANNOUNCER -- If your airbags deploy, OnStar receives a signal and calls to check on you. (Ring)

EMERGENCY SERVICES -- Police.

ONSTAR -- This is Dwight with OnStar. I'd like to report a vehicle crash with airbag deployment on West 106th Street.

EMERGENCY SERVICES -- We'll send police and E.M.S. out there.

DRIVER -- (crying) I'm so scared!

ONSTAR -- O.K., I'm here with you, ma'am; you needn't be scared.

4 Well, maybe just a little scared. Tell us again how Dwight knows just where the accident took place. Oh, right! It's those thoughtful wireless services that are always there. Always, as in any time a driver gets into an OnStar-equipped vehicle. OnStar insists that it would disclose the whereabouts of a subscriber's vehicle only after being presented with a criminal court order or after the vehicle has been reported stolen. That's certainly a relief. I wouldn't want to think that anyone but Dwight knows where I am whenever I'm traveling in my car.

5 Of course, E-ZPass and most other toll-collecting systems already know whenever a customer passes through one of their scanners. That's because of radio frequency identification technology. In return for the convenience of zipping through toll booths, you need to have in your car a wireless device. This tag contains information about your account, permitting E-ZPass to deduct the necessary toll—and to note when your car whisked through that particular toll booth. They wouldn't share that information with anyone, either; that is, unless they had to.

Evidence:
In the ad, OnStar is portrayed as a technology that can save lives.

Style:
The language is conversational and often satirical.

Reasons:
Koppel uses critical thinking to question the main assumption of the ad: Is it necessarily good that OnStar always knows where you are while driving?

Reasons:
Convenient technologies also keep track of our movements. Koppel gets his readers to think about what happens to personal information that is passively collected.

6 Radio frequency identification technology has been used for about 15 years now to reunite lost pets with their owners. Applied Digital Solutions, for example, manufactures the VeriChip, a tiny, implantable device that holds a small amount of data. Animal shelters can scan the chip for the name and phone number of the lost pet's owner. The product is now referred to as the HomeAgain Microchip Identification System.

7 Useful? Sure. Indeed, it's not much of a leap to suggest that one day, the VeriChip might be routinely implanted under the skin of, let's say, an Alzheimer's patient. The Food and Drug Administration approved the VeriChip for use in people last October. An Applied Digital Solutions spokesman estimates that about 1,000 people have already had a VeriChip implanted, usually in the right triceps. At the moment, it doesn't carry much information, just an identification number that health care providers can use to tap into a patient's medical history. A Barcelona nightclub also uses it to admit customers with a qualifying code to enter a V.I.P. room where drinks are automatically put on their bill. Possible variations on the theme are staggering.

Evidence: Technologies used to track pets can also track people.

8 And how about all the information collected by popular devices like TiVo, the digital video recorder that enables you to watch and store an entire season's worth of favorite programs at your own convenience? It also lets you electronically mark the programs you favor, allowing TiVo to suggest similar programs for your viewing pleasure. In February, TiVo announced the most frequently played and replayed commercial moment during the Super Bowl (it involves a wardrobe malfunction, but believe me, you don't want to know), drawing on aggregated data from a sample of 10,000 anonymous TiVo households. No one is suggesting that TiVo tracks what each subscriber records and replays. But could they, if they needed to? That's unclear, although TiVo does have a privacy policy. "Your privacy," it says in part, "is very important to us. Due to factors beyond our control, however, we cannot fully ensure that your user information will not be disclosed to third parties."

Evidence: The popular TiVo service admits that it does not fully protect the privacy of its subscribers.

9 Unexpected and unfortunate things happen, of course, even to the most reputable and best-run organizations. Only last February, the Bank of America Corporation notified federal investigators that it had lost computer backup tapes containing personal information about 1.2 million federal government employees, including some senators. In April, LexisNexis

unintentionally gave outsiders access to the personal files (addresses, Social Security numbers, drivers license information) of as many as 310,000 people. In May, Time Warner revealed that an outside storage company had misplaced data stored on computer backup tapes on 600,000 current and former employees. That same month, United Parcel Service picked up a box of computer tapes in New Jersey from CitiFinancial, the consumer finance subsidiary of Citigroup, that contained the names, addresses, Social Security numbers, account numbers, payment histories and other details on small personal loans made to an estimated 3.9 million customers. The box is still missing.

Evidence:
Numerous accidents and data thefts have given private information to unauthorized people.

10 Whoops!

11 CitiFinancial correctly informed its own customers and, inevitably, the rest of the world about the security breach. Would they have done so entirely on their own? That is less clear. In July 2003, California started requiring companies to inform customers living in the state of any breach in security that compromises personally identifiable information. Six other states have passed similar legislation.

12 No such legislation exists on the federal stage, however—only discretionary guidelines for financial institutions about whether and how they should inform their customers with respect to breaches in the security of their personal information.

Conclusion:
Koppel hopes by this point he has raised concerns about privacy for his readers. He now gives his thesis: The public has the right to know what is being done with private information they give to companies and services.

13 Both the House and Senate are now considering federal legislation similar to the California law. It's a start but not nearly enough. We need mandatory clarity and transparency; not just with regard to the services that these miracles of microchip and satellite technology offer but also the degree to which companies share and exchange their harvest of private data.

14 We cannot even begin to control the growing army of businesses and industries that monitor what we buy, what we watch on television, where we drive, the debts we pay or fail to pay, our marriages and divorces, our litigations, our health and tax records and all else that may or may not yet exist on some computer tape, if we don't fully understand everything we're signing up for when we avail ourselves of one of these services.

What to the Slave Is the Fourth of July?

Frederick Douglass

MyWritingLab™

On the fifth of July in 1852, former slave Frederick Douglass spoke at a meeting of the Ladies' Anti-Slavery Society in Rochester, New York. In this series of excerpts from his lengthy oration (published shortly thereafter as a pamphlet), Douglass reminds his audience of the irony of celebrating freedom and liberty in a land where much of the population was enslaved.

Return to these questions after you have finished reading.

Analyzing the Reading

1. Douglass spends considerable time telling his audience what points do not need to be argued: that a slave is human, that man is entitled to liberty, and so on. If in fact these points are agreed upon by all, why do you think Douglass spends so much time talking about them?

2. Douglass was speaking in the last few years before the American Civil War (1861–1865). How is the vivid imagery in this speech likely to have affected listeners? Read carefully through Douglass's descriptions of the slave trade and its impact on individuals and families. What values is he appealing to?

3. What impact does Douglass's personal history have on his credibility? Would the argument in this speech have been as compelling if it had been made by someone who had never experienced slavery firsthand?

4. What words would you use to describe the overall tone of Douglass's speech? Is it angry? threatening? hopeful? pessimistic? Why do you think Douglass chose the tone he used in this argument?

Exploring Ideas and Issues

Douglass was renowned as both an orator and a writer. His first autobiography, *Narrative of the Life of Frederick Douglass, an American Slave*, remains a major historical American document. In addition to working for the abolition of slavery, Douglass was also a passionate advocate for women's suffrage.

1. Douglass appeals to both reason and emotion in the speech he gives. What additional kinds of evidence might he have used? What kinds of evidence do you think an audience can absorb more easily through reading than through listening, and vice versa? Write a short essay in which you identify two additional kinds of evidence and explain why you believe they would be more suitable in a written than in a spoken argument.

2. Does society have an obligation to redress the injustices of the past? For example, is affirmative action in favor of minorities and women in college applications and hiring necessary or fair? Is the payment of slave reparations appropriate? What about prohibiting same-sex schools? Write an essay in which you argue for or against such measures. Include appeals to logic and emotion. If possible, do some research on the subject and include evidence from your research.

3. Some groups have advocated extending certain rights to nonhumans. Using Douglass's basic train of logic—that a slave is a man and therefore entitled to the same rights as nonslaves—construct an argument in favor of or against recognizing animals' rights. Write an essay in which you support your argument with appeals to emotion and examples of expert testimony, as well.

What to the Slave is the Fourth of July?

Fellow-citizens, pardon me, allow me to ask, why am I called upon to speak here to-day? What have I, or those I represent, to do with your national independence? Are the great principles of political freedom and of natural justice, embodied in that Declaration of Independence, extended to us? And am I, therefore, called upon to bring our humble offering to the national altar, and to confess the benefits and express devout gratitude for the blessings resulting from your independence to us?

But, such is not the state of the case. I say it with a sad sense of the disparity between us. I am not included within the pale of this glorious anniversary! Your high independence only reveals the immeasurable distance between us. The blessings in which you, this day, rejoice, are not enjoyed in common. The rich inheritance of justice, liberty, prosperity, and independence, bequeathed by your fathers, is shared by you, not by me. The sunlight that brought life and healing to you has brought stripes and death to me. This Fourth [of] July is yours, not mine. You may rejoice, I must mourn. To drag a man in fetters into the grand illuminated temple of liberty, and call upon him to join you in joyous anthems is inhuman mockery and sacrilegious irony. Do you mean, citizens, to mock me, by asking me to speak to-day?

Fellow-citizens, above your national, tumultuous joy, I hear the mournful wail of millions whose chains, heavy and grievous yesterday, are, to-day, rendered more intolerable by the jubilee shouts that reach them. To forget them, to pass lightly over their wrongs, and to chime in with the popular theme, would be treason most scandalous and shocking, and would make me a reproach before God and the world. My subject, then fellow citizens, is AMERICAN

SLAVERY. I shall see, this day, and its popular characteristics, from the slave's point of view. Standing, there, identified with the American bondman, making his wrongs mine, I do not hesitate to declare, with all my soul, that the character and conduct of this nation never looked blacker to me than on this 4th of July! Whether we turn to the declarations of the past, or to the professions of the present, the conduct of the nation seems equally hideous and revolting. America is false to the past, false to the present, and solemnly binds herself to be false to the future. Standing with God and the crushed and bleeding slave on this occasion, I will, in the name of humanity which is outraged, in the name of liberty which is fettered, in the name of the constitution and the Bible, which are disregarded and trampled upon, dare to call in question and to denounce, with all the emphasis I can command, everything that serves to perpetuate slavery—the great sin and shame of America! "I will not equivocate; I will not excuse"; I will use the severest language I can command; and yet not one word shall escape me that any man, whose judgment is not blinded by prejudice, or who is not at heart a slaveholder, shall not confess to be right and just.

But I fancy I hear some one of my audience say, it is just in this circumstance that you and your brother abolitionists fail to make a favorable impression on the public mind. Would you argue more, and denounce less, would you persuade more, and rebuke less, your cause would be much more likely to succeed. But, I submit, where all is plain there is nothing to be argued. What point in the anti-slavery creed would you have me argue? On what branch of the subject do the people of this country need light? Must I undertake to prove that the slave is a man? That point is conceded already. Nobody doubts it. The slaveholders themselves acknowledge it in the enactment of laws for their government. They acknowledge it when they punish disobedience on the part of the slave. There are seventy-two crimes in the State of Virginia, which, if committed by a black man, (no matter how ignorant he be), subject him to the punishment of death; while only two of the same crimes will subject a white man to the like punishment. What is this but the acknowledgement that the slave is a moral, intellectual and responsible being? The manhood of the slave is conceded. It is admitted in the fact that Southern statute books are covered with enactments forbidding, under severe fines and penalties, the teaching of the slave to read or to write. When you can point to any such laws, in reference to the beasts of the field, then I may consent to argue the manhood of the slave. When the dogs in your streets, when the fowls of the air, when the cattle on your hills, when the fish of the sea, and the reptiles that crawl, shall be unable to distinguish the slave from a brute, there will I argue with you that the slave is a man!

For the present, it is enough to affirm the equal manhood of the negro race. Is it not astonishing that, while we are ploughing, planting and reaping, using all kinds of mechanical tools, erecting houses, constructing bridges, building ships, working in metals of brass, iron, copper, silver and gold; that, while we are reading, writing and ciphering, acting as clerks, merchants and secretaries, having among us lawyers, doctors, ministers, poets, authors, editors, orators and teachers; that, while we are engaged in all manner of enterprises common to other men, digging gold in California, capturing the whale in the Pacific, feeding sheep and cattle on the hillside, living, moving, acting, thinking, planning, living in families as husbands, wives and children, and, above all, confessing and worshipping the Christian's God, and looking hopefully for life and immortality beyond the grave, we are called upon to prove that we are men!

Would you have me argue that man is entitled to liberty? That he is the rightful owner of his own body? You have already declared it. Must I argue the wrongfulness of slavery? Is it to be settled by the rules of logic and argumentation, as a matter beset with great difficulty, involving a doubtful application of the principle of justice, hard to be understood? How should I look to-day, in the presence of Americans, dividing, and subdividing a discourse, to show that men have a natural right to freedom? speaking of it relatively, and positively, negatively, and affirmatively. To do so would be to make myself ridiculous and offer an insult to your understanding. There is not a man beneath the canopy of heaven that does not know that slavery is wrong for him.

What, am I to argue that it is wrong to make men brutes, to rob them of their liberty, to work them without wages, to keep them ignorant of their relations to their fellow men, to beat them with sticks, to flay their flesh with the lash, to load their limbs with irons, to hunt them with dogs, to sell them at auction, to sunder their families, to knock out their teeth, to burn their flesh, to starve them into obedience and submission to their masters? Must I argue that a system thus marked with blood, and stained with pollution, is wrong? No! I will not. I have better employments for my time and strength, than such arguments would imply.

What, then, remains to be argued? Is it that slavery is not divine; that God did not establish it; that our doctors of divinity are mistaken? There is blasphemy in the thought. That which is inhuman, cannot be divine! Who can reason on such a proposition? They that can, may; I cannot. The time for such argument is past.

What, to the American slave, is your 4th of July? I answer: a day that reveals to him, more than all other days in the year, the gross injustice and cruelty to which he is the constant victim. To him, your celebration is a sham; your boasted liberty, an unholy license; your national greatness, swelling vanity; your sounds of rejoicing are empty and heartless; your denunciations of tyrants, brass fronted impudence; your shouts of liberty and equality, hollow mockery; your prayers and hymns, your sermons and thanksgivings, with all your religious parade, and solemnity, are, to him, mere bombast, fraud, deception, impiety, and hypocrisy—a thin veil to cover up crimes which would disgrace a nation of savages. There is not a nation on the earth guilty of practices, more shocking and bloody, than are the people of these United States, at this very hour.

Go where you may, search where you will, roam through all the monarchies and despotisms of the old world, travel through South America, search out every abuse, and when you have found the last, lay your facts by the side of the everyday practices of this nation, and you will say with me, that, for revolting barbarity and shameless hypocrisy, America reigns without a rival. Take the American slave-trade, which we are told by the papers, is especially prosperous just now. Ex-Senator Benton tells us that the price of men was never higher than now. He mentions the fact to show that slavery is in no danger. This trade is one of the peculiarities of American institutions. It is carried on in all the large towns and cities in one-half of this confederacy; and millions are pocketed every year, by dealers in this horrid traffic. In several states, this trade is a chief source of wealth. It is called (in contradistinction to the foreign slave-trade) "the internal slave trade." It is, probably, called so, too, in order to divert from it the horror with which the foreign slave-trade is contemplated. That trade has long since been denounced by this government, as piracy. It has been denounced with burning words, from the high places of the nation, as an execrable traffic. To arrest it, to put an end to it, this nation keeps a squadron, at immense cost, on the coast of Africa. Everywhere, in this country, it is safe to speak of this foreign slave-trade, as a most inhuman traffic, opposed alike to the laws of God and of man. The duty to extirpate and destroy it is admitted even by our DOCTORS OF DIVINITY. In order to put an end to it, some of these last have consented that their colored brethren (nominally free) should leave this country, and establish themselves on the western coast of Africa! It is, however, a notable fact that, while so much execration is poured out by Americans upon those engaged in the foreign slave-trade, the men engaged in the slave-trade between the states pass without condemnation, and their business is deemed honorable.

Behold the practical operation of this internal slave-trade, the American slave-trade, sustained by American politics and American religion. Here you will see men and women reared like swine for the market. You know what is a swine-drover? I will show you a man-drover. They inhabit all our Southern States. They perambulate the country and crowd the highways of the nation, with droves of human stock. You will see one of these human flesh-jobbers, armed with pistol, whip and Bowie-knife, driving a company of a hundred men, women, and children from the Potomac to the slave market at New Orleans.

These wretched people are to be sold singly, or in lots, to suit purchasers. They are food for the cotton-field, and the deadly sugar-mill. Mark the sad procession, as it moves wearily along, and the inhuman wretch who drives them. Hear his savage yells and his blood-chilling oaths, as he hurries on his affrighted captives! There, see the old man, with locks thinned and gray. Cast one glance, if you please, upon that young mother, whose shoulders are bare to the scorching sun, her briny tears falling on the brow of the babe in her arms. See, too, that girl of thirteen, weeping, yes! weeping, as she thinks of the mother from whom she has been torn! The drove moves tardily. Heat and sorrow have nearly consumed their strength; suddenly you hear a quick snap, like the discharge of a rifle; the fetters clank, and the chain rattles simultaneously; your ears are saluted with a scream, that seems to have torn its way to the centre of your soul! The crack you heard, was the sound of the slave-whip; the scream you heard, was from the woman you saw with the babe. Her speed had faltered under the weight of her child and her chains! that gash on her shoulder tells her to move on. Follow this drove to New Orleans. Attend the auction; see men examined like horses; see the forms of women rudely and brutally exposed to the shocking gaze of American slave-buyers. See this drove sold and separated forever; and never forget the deep, sad sobs that arose from that scattered multitude. Tell me citizens, WHERE, under the sun, you can witness a spectacle more fiendish and shocking. Yet this is but a glance at the American slave-trade, as it exists, at this moment, in the ruling part of the United States.

I was born amid such sights and scenes. To me the American slave-trade is a terrible reality. When a child, my soul was often pierced with a sense of its horrors. I lived on Philpot Street, Fell's Point, Baltimore, and have watched from the wharves, the slave ships in the Basin, anchored from the shore, with their cargoes of human flesh, waiting for favorable winds to waft them down the Chesapeake. There was, at that time, a grand slave mart kept at the head of Pratt Street, by Austin Woldfolk. His agents were sent into every town and county in Maryland, announcing their arrival, through the papers, and on flaming "hand-bills," headed CASH FOR NEGROES. These men were generally well dressed men, and very captivating in their manners. Ever ready to drink, to treat, and to gamble. The fate of many a slave has depended upon the turn of a single card; and many a child has been snatched from the arms of its mother by bargains arranged in a state of brutal drunkenness.

Allow me to say, in conclusion, notwithstanding the dark picture I have this day presented of the state of the nation, I do not despair of this country. There are forces in operation, which must inevitably work the downfall of slavery. "The arm of the Lord is not shortened," and the doom of slavery is certain. I, therefore, leave off where I began, with hope. While drawing encouragement from the Declaration of Independence, the great principles it contains, and the genius of American Institutions, my spirit is also cheered by the obvious tendencies of the age. Nations do not now stand in the same relation to each other that they did ages ago. No nation can now shut itself up from the surrounding world, and trot round in the same old path of its fathers without interference. The time was when such could be done. Long established customs of hurtful character could formerly fence themselves in, and do their evil work with social impunity. Knowledge was then confined and enjoyed by the privileged few, and the multitude walked on in mental darkness. But a change has now come over the affairs of mankind. Walled cities and empires have become unfashionable. The arm of commerce has borne away the gates of the strong city. Intelligence is penetrating the darkest corners of the globe. It makes its pathway over and under the sea, as well as on the earth. Wind, steam, and lightning are its chartered agents. Oceans no longer divide, but link nations together. From Boston to London is now a holiday excursion. Space is comparatively annihilated. Thoughts expressed on one side of the Atlantic are distinctly heard on the other. The far off and almost fabulous Pacific rolls in grandeur at our feet. The Celestial Empire, the mystery of ages, is being solved. The fiat of the Almighty, "Let there be Light," has not yet spent its force. No abuse, no outrage whether in taste, sport or avarice, can now hide itself from the all-pervading light.

Eat Food: Food Defined

MyWritingLab™

Michael Pollan

Author Michael Pollan is a "foodie intellectual" who achieved notable fame through two of his best-selling books, *The Omnivore's Dilemma* (2005) and *In Defense of Food* (2008). The first book follows the four basic ways human societies obtain food (industrial systems, organic operations, self-sufficient farming, and hunting/gathering). *In Defense of Food* explores how Western diets, which have been "intellectualized" by deconstructing foods into individual nutrients, are in fact very unhealthy. The following essay in an excerpt from this latter book, in which he urges readers to follow three simple dietary rules: "Eat food. Not too much. Mostly plants."

Return to these questions after you have finished reading.

Analyzing the Reading

1. According to Pollan, what is "real food"? What has replaced real food on our supermarket shelves?

2. Pollan makes a distinction between "ordinary food" and "foodlike substitutes." Based on what you have read, what "food" do you usually eat? How would he categorize your breakfast, lunch, dinner, and snack choices? Explain.

3. According to Pollan, what problems arise when we deconstruct whole foods into individual nutrients? Why isn't it enough to add nutrients to processed foods? Explain.

4. Pollan makes five suggestions for a better diet. Summarize each one and note how difficult or easy it would be to follow his recommendations.

Exploring Ideas and Issues

In his book, *In Defense of Food*, Pollan recommends that consumers "shop the parameter" of supermarkets where foods your great-grandmother would have recognized are most likely to be found—fresh, whole, and unprocessed foods. In 2007, University of Washington researchers Adam Drewnowski and Pablo Monsivais checked the prices of fresh fruits and vegetables, whole grains, fish, and lean meats at numerous stores in the Seattle area. They discovered that prices for healthy foods had risen nearly 20% compared to an overall 5% inflation rate in food prices. Moreover, prices for processed foods remained about the same, and in some cases had dropped.

1. Pollan advocates that people eat "real food." In a down-economy, can people afford to eat in the way he suggests? Why or why not?

2. Check the prices for food in your local supermarket. Compare the prices of unprocessed foods to those of processed ones offering a similar level of nutrition. Write a short essay on the economic challenges for a healthy diet.

3. According to the U.S. Department of Agriculture, Americans spend just under 6% of their income on food. As a comparison, people in Denmark spend almost 11%, and in Indonesia and Azerbaijan people spend around 50%. Write an editorial in which you explain why Americans should spend more, rather than less, of their income on food.

4. What steps would you need to take in order to eat healthier? Would you have to give up something in order to afford it? Would you have to travel far out of your daily sphere to have access to "real food"? What other challenges, if any, would you face?

Eat Food: Food Defined

The first time I heard the advice to "just eat food" it was in a speech by Joan Gussow, and it completely baffled me. Of course you should eat food—what else is there to eat? But Gussow, who grows much of her own food on a flood-prone finger of land jutting into the Hudson River, refuses to dignify most of the products for sale in the supermarket with that title. "In the thirty-four years I've been in the field of nutrition," she said in the same speech, "I have watched real food disappear from large areas of the supermarket and from much of the rest of the eating world." Taking food's place on the shelves has been an unending stream of foodlike substitutes, some seventeen thousand new ones every year—"products constructed largely around commerce and hope, supported by frighteningly little actual knowledge." Ordinary food is still out there, however, still being grown and even occasionally sold in the supermarket, and this ordinary food is what we should eat.

But given our current state of confusion and given the thousands of products calling themselves food, this is more easily said than done. So consider these related rules of thumb. Each proposes a different sort of map to the contemporary food landscape, but all should take you to more or less the same place.

DON'T EAT ANYTHING YOUR GREAT GRANDMOTHER WOULDN'T RECOGNIZE AS FOOD. Why your great grandmother? Because at this point your mother and possibly even your grandmother are as confused as the rest of us; to be safe we need to go back at least a couple generations, to a time before the advent of most modern foods. So depending on your age (and your grandmother), you may need to go back to your great- or even great-great grandmother. Some nutritionists recommend going back even further. John Yudkin, a British nutritionist whose early alarms about the dangers of refined carbohydrates were overlooked in the 1960s and 1970s, once advised, "Just don't eat anything your Neolithic ancestors wouldn't have recognized and you'll be ok."

What would shopping this way mean in the supermarket? Well imagine your great grandmother at your side as you roll down the aisles. You're standing together in front of the dairy case. She picks up a package of Go-Gurt Portable Yogurt tubes—and has no idea what this could possibly be. Is it a food or a toothpaste? And how, exactly, do you introduce it into your body? You could tell her it's just yogurt in a squirtable form, yet if she read the ingredients label she would have every reason to doubt that that was in fact the case. Sure, there's some yoghurt in there, but there are also a dozen other things that aren't remotely yoghurtlike, ingredients she would probably fail to recognize as foods of any kind, including high-fructose corn syrup, modified corn starch, kosher gelatin, carrageenan, tricalcium phosphate, natural and artificial flavours, vitamins, and so forth. (And there's a whole other list of ingredients for the "berry bubblegum bash" flavoring, containing everything but berries or bubblegum.) How did yoghurt, which in your great grandmother's day consisted of simply milk inoculated with a bacterial culture, ever get to be so complicated? Is a product like Go-Gurt Portable Yogurt still a whole food? A food of any kind? Or is it just a food product?

There are in fact hundreds of foodish products in the supermarket that your ancestors simply wouldn't recognize as food: breakfast cereal bars transacted by bright white veins representing, but in reality having nothing to do with, milk; "protein waters" and "non-dairy creamer"; cheeselike foodstuffs equally innocent of any bovine contribution; cakelike cylinders (with creamlike fillings) called Twinkies that never grow stale, *Don't eat anything incapable of rotting* is another personal policy you might consider adopting.

There are many reasons to avoid eating such complicated food products beyond the various chemical additives and corn and soy derivatives they contain. One of the problems with products of food science is that, as Joan Gussow has pointed out, they lie to your body; their artificial colors and flavours and synthetic sweeteners and novel fats confound the senses we rely on to assess new foods and prepare our bodies to deal with them. Foods that lie leave us with little choice but eat by numbers, consulting labels rather than our senses.

It's true that foods have long been processed in order to preserve them, as when we pickle or ferment or smoke, but industrial processing aims to do much more than extend shelf life. Today foods are processed in ways specifically designed to sell us more food by pushing our evolutionary buttons—our inborn preferences for sweetness and fat and salt. These qualities are difficult to find in nature but cheap and easy for the food scientist to deploy, with the result that processing induces us to consume much more of these ecological rarities than is good for us. "Tastes great, less filling!" could be the motto for most processed foods, which are far more energy dense than most whole foods: They contain much less water, fiber, and micronutrients, and generally much more sugar and fat, making them at the same time, to coin a marketing slogan, "More fattening, less nutritious!"

The great grandma rule will help keep many of these products out of your cart. But not all of them. Because thanks to the FDA's willingness, post-1973, to let food makers freely alter the identity of "traditional foods that everyone knows" without having to call them imitations, your great grandmother could easily be fooled into thinking that that loaf of bread or wedge of cheese is in fact a loaf of bread or a wedge of cheese. This is why we need slightly more detailed personal policy to capture these imitation foods; to wit:

AVOID FOOD PRODUCTS CONTAINING INGREDIENTS THAT ARE A) UNFAMILIAR, B) UNPRONOUNCEABLE, C) MORE THAN FIVE IN NUMBER, OR THAT INCLUDE D) HIGH-FRUCTOSE CORN SYRUP. None of these characteristics, not even the last one, is necessarily harmful in and of itself, but all of them are reliable markers for foods that have been highly processed to the points where they may no longer be what they purport to be. They have crossed over from foods to food products.

Consider a loaf of bread, one of the "traditional foods that everyone knows" specifically singled out for protection in the 1938 imitation rule. As your grandmother could tell you, bread is traditionally made using a remarkably small number of familiar ingredients: flour, yeast, water, and a pinch of salt will do it. But industrial bread—even industrial whole-grain bread—has become a far more complicated product of modern food science (not to mention commerce and hope). Here's the complete ingredients list for Sara Lee's Soft & Smooth Whole Grain White Bread. (Wait a minute—isn't "Whole Grain White Bread" a contradiction in terms? Evidently not any more.)

> Enriched bleached flour [wheat flour, malted barley flour, niacin, iron, thiamine mononitrate (vitamin B_1), riboflavin (vitamin B_2), folic acid], water, whole grains [whole wheat flour, brown rice flour (rice flour, rice bran)], high fructose corn syrup [hello], whey, wheat gluten, yeast, cellulose. Contains 2% or less of each of the following: honey, calcium sulfate, vegetable oil (soybean and/or cottonseed oils), salt, butter (cream, salt), dough conditioners (may contain one or more of the following; mono- and diglycerides, ethoxylated mono- and diglycerides, ascorbic acid, enzymes, azodicarbonamide), guar gum, calcium propionate (preservative), distilled vinegar, yeast nutrients (monocalcium phosphate, calcium sulfate, ammonium sulfate), corn starch, natural flavor, betacarotene (color), vitamin D_3, soy lecithin, soy flour.

There are many things you could say about this intricate loaf of "bread," but note first that even if it managed to slip by your great grandmother (because it is a loaf of bread, or at least is called one and strongly resembles one), the product fails every test proposed under rule number two: It's got unfamiliar ingredients (monoglycerides I've heard of before, but ethoxylated monoglycerides?); unpronounceable ingredients (try "azodicarbonamide"); it exceeds the maximum of five ingredients (by roughly thirty-six); and it contains high-fructose corn syrup. Sorry, Sara Lee, but your Soft & Smooth Whole Grain White Bread is not food and if not for the indulgence of the FDA could not even be labelled "bread."

Sara Lee's Soft & Smooth Whole Grain White Bread could serve as a monument to the age of nutritionism. It embodies the latest nutritional wisdom from science and government (which in its most recent food pyramid recommends that at least half our consumption of grain come from whole grains) but leavens that wisdom with the commercial recognition that American eaters (and American children in particular) have come to prefer their wheat highly refined—which is to say, cottonly soft, snowy white, and exceptionally sweet on the tongue. In its marketing materials, Sara Lee treats this clash of interests as some sort of Gordian knot—it speaks in terms of an ambitious quest to build a "no compromise" loaf—which only the most sophisticated food science could possibly cut.

And so it has, with the invention of whole-grain white bread. Because the small percentage of whole grains in the bread would render it that much less sweet than, say, all-white Wonder Bread—which scarcely waits to be chewed before transforming itself into glucose—the food scientists have added high-fructose corn syrup and honey to make up the difference; to overcome the problematic heft and toothsomeness of a real whole grain bread, they've deployed "dough conditioner," including guar gum and the aforementioned azodicarbonamide, to simulate the texture of supermarket white bread. By incorporating certain varieties of albino wheat, they've managed to maintain that deathly appealing Wonder Bread pallor.

Who would have thought Wonder Bread would ever become an ideal of aesthetic and gustatory perfection to which bakers would actually aspire—Sara Lee's Mona Lisa?

Very often food science's efforts to make traditional foods more nutritious make them much more complicated, but not necessarily any better for you. To make dairy products low fat, it's not enough to remove the fat. You then have to go to great lengths to preserve the body or creamy texture by working in all kinds of food additives. In the case of low-fat or skim milk, that usually means adding powdered milk. But powdered milk contains oxidized cholesterol, which scientists believe is much worse for your arteries than ordinary cholestrol, so food makers sometimes compensate by adding antioxidants, further complicating what had been a simple one-ingredient whole food. Also, removing the fat makes it that much harder for your body to absorb the fat-soluble vitamins that are one of the reasons to drink milk in the first place.

All this heroic and occasionally counterproductive food science has been undertaken in the name of our health—so that Sara Lee can add to its plastic wrapper the magic words "good source of whole grain" or a food company can ballyhoo the even more magic words "low fat." Which brings us to a related food policy that may at first sound counterproductive to a health-conscious eater:

AVOID FOOD PRODUCTS THAT MAKE HEALTH CLAIMS. For a food product to make health claims on its package it must first have a package, so right off the bat it's more likely to be a processed than a whole food. Generally speaking, it is only the big food companies that have the wherewithal to secure FDA-approved health claims for their products and then trumpet them to the world. Recently, however, some of the tonier fruits and nuts have begun boasting about their health-enhancing properties, and there will surely be more as each crop council scrounges together the money to commission its own scientific study. Because all plants contain antioxidants, all these studies are guaranteed to find something on which to base a health oriented marketing campaign.

But for the most part it is the products of food science that make the boldest health claims, and these are often founded on incomplete and often erroneous science—the dubious fruits of nutritionism. Don't forget that trans-fat-rich margarine, one of the first industrial foods to claim it was healthier than the traditional food it replaced, turned out to give people heart attacks. Since that debacle, the FDA, under tremendous pressure from industry, has made it only easier for food companies to make increasingly doubtful health claims, such as the one Frito-Lay now puts on some of its chips—that eating them is somehow good for your heart. If you bother to read the health claims closely (as food marketers make sure consumers seldom do), you will find that there is often considerably less to them than meets the eye.

Consider a recent "qualified" health claim approved by the FDA for (don't laugh) corn oil. ("Qualified" is a whole new category of health claim, introduced in 2002 at the behest of industry.) Corn oil, you may recall, is particularly high in the omega-6 fatty acids we're already consuming far too many of.

Very limited and preliminary scientific evidence suggests that eating about one tablespoon (16 grams) of corn oil daily may reduce the risk of heart disease due to the unsaturated fat content in corn oil.

The tablespoon is a particularly rich touch, conjuring images of moms administering medicine, or perhaps cod-liver oil, to their children. But what the FDA gives with one hand, it takes away with the other. Here's the small-print "qualification" of this already notably diffident health claim:

[The] FDA concludes that there is little scientific evidence supporting this claim.

And then to make matters still more perplexing:

To achieve this possible health benefit, corn oil is to replace a similar amount of saturated fat and not increase the total number of calories you eat in a day.

This little masterpiece of pseudoscientific bureaucratese was extracted from the FDA by the manufacturer of Mazola corn oil. It would appear that "qualified" is an official FDA euphemism for "all but meaningless." Though someone might have let the consumer in on this game: The FDA's own research indicates that consumers have no idea what to make of qualified health claims (how would they?), and its rules allow companies to promote the claims pretty much any way they want—they can use really big type for the claim, for example, and then print the disclaimers in teeny-tiny type. No doubt we can look forward to a qualified health claim for high-fructose corn syrup, a tablespoon of which probably does contribute to your health—as long as it replaces a comparable amount of, say, poison in your diet and doesn't increase the total number of calories you eat in a day.

When corn oil and chips and sugary breakfast cereals can all boast being good for your heart, health claims have become hopelessly corrupt. The American Heart Association currently bestows (for a fee) its heart-healthy seal of approval on Lucky Charms, Cocoa Puffs, and Trix cereals, Yoo-hoo lite chocolate drink, and Healthy Choice's Premium Caramel Swirl Ice Cream Sandwich—this at a time when scientists are coming to recognize that dietary sugar probably plays a more important role in heart disease than dietary fat. Meanwhile, the genuinely heart-healthy whole foods in the produce section, lacking the financial and political clout of the packaged goods a few sales aisles over, are mute. But don't take the silence of the yams as a sign that they have nothing valuable to say about health.

The Walkability Dividend

Jeff Speck

MyWritingLab™

Jeff Speck, a Harvard educated architect, is an acclaimed author, consultant, and urban planner. A frequent radio guest, TED Talks presenter, and guest speaker, Speck has authored or coauthored numerous books and articles on urban design and New Urbanism. "The Walkability Dividend" is excerpted from his 2012 book *Walkable City: How Downtown Can Save America, One Step at a Time.*

Return to these questions after you have finished reading.

Analyzing the Reading

1. Is Speck's a definition or rebuttal argument? Use the diagrams at the beginning of this chapter to map his argument and to support your assessment (see page 371).

2. Evaluate the evidence Speck employs to support his position. Point out passages in which he uses examples, statistics, and expert testimony and discuss the effectiveness and balance of his evidence.

3. Who is Speck's audience? Infer his social class based on his background. Examine the reasons for his position, its beneficiaries, his examples, and the experts he quotes, and draw an inference as to whom he's writing.

4. In the third paragraph, Speck writes, "While most American cities were amassing a spare tire of undifferentiated sprawl, . . ." Brainstorm the different connotations of "spare tire" and discuss possible interpretations. In the seventh paragraph he writes, "Almost 85 percent of money expended on cars [is] bound for the pockets of Middle Eastern princes." Examine Speck's language and metaphors and draw inferences about his position, audience, and persuasive appeals.

Exploring Ideas and Issues

In 2002, Richard Florida, an urban theorist and University of Toronto management professor, identified a demographic classification he called the "Creative Class." This group, up to 40% of American workers in 2014, includes engineers, artists, educators, computer scientists, and other "knowledge economy" professionals whose work involves the creation of innovative ideas, solutions, and products. Florida points out this highly educated and mostly affluent demographic impacts urban planning as its members seek out many of the benefits of Speck's "walkable cities." Creative Class members break from the restrictions of traditional corporate life to pursue individual lifestyle preferences. They seek out cities with vibrant street life comprised of cafés, boutiques, and other creative social spaces and which support active, participatory lifestyles such as hiking, bicycle riding, and travelling.

1. New Urbanism, of which Speck is a proponent, is gaining traction nationwide as cities large and small seek solutions to the negative effects of suburban sprawl and urban decline. Is New Urbanism a panacea? Can New Urbanism go too far? Is it the best or only solution to the problems? Write a rebuttal argument to Speck's position.

2. According to the 2010 US Census, in America's 51 largest metropolitan areas, 44 million live in the urban cores whereas 122 million reside in their suburbs. Write a position argument on the topic "In Defense of Suburbs" in which you examine the history, lure, and benefits of suburban living.

3. Suburbanization, urbanization, and gentrification often lead to displacement. As suburbs sprawl, farms and forests disappear. Inner cities become gentrified as long-term residents surrender to escalating taxes, rents, and housing costs driven by the creative class returning to the urban core. Interview people you know who have been displaced from farms, villages, or cities. Write an essay analyzing the effects of suburbanization, urbanization, and gentrification.

THE WALKABILITY DIVIDEND

In 2007, Joe Cortright published a report called "Portland's Green Dividend," in which he asked the question: What does Portland get for being walkable? Quite a lot, it turns out.

To set the stage, we should describe what makes Portland different. Clearly, it is not Manhattan. It is not particularly big or particularly small and its residential density, by American standards, is pretty normal. It has attracted a good amount of industry lately, but has shown no great historical predisposition to do so, nor is it gifted with mineral wealth. It rains a lot in Portland and, interestingly, locals pride themselves on not using umbrellas. Perhaps most fascinating is the way that Portlanders refuse to disobey DON'T WALK signs, even if it's 1:00 a.m. on a tiny two-lane street swathed in utter silence . . . and even if a blithe east-coaster is striding happily into the intersection (I'm not naming names here).

But what really makes Portland unusual is how it has chosen to grow. While most American cities were building more highways, Portland invested in transit and biking. While most cities were reaming out their roadways to speed traffic, Portland implemented a Skinny Streets program. While most American cities were amassing a spare tire of undifferentiated sprawl, Portland instituted an urban growth boundary. These efforts and others like them, over several decades—a blink of the eye in planner time—have changed the way that Portlanders live.

This change is not dramatic—were it not for the roving hordes of bicyclists, it might be invisible—but it is significant. While almost every other American city has seen its residents drive farther and farther every year and spend more and more of their time stuck in traffic, Portland's vehicle miles traveled per person peaked in 1996. Now, compared to other major metropolitan areas, Portlanders on average drive 20 percent less (Cortright 1).

Small change? Not really: according to Cortright, this 20 percent (four miles per citizen per day) adds up to $1.1 billion of savings each year, which equals fully 1.5 percent of all personal income earned in the region. And that number ignores time not wasted in traffic: peak travel times have actually fallen from 54 minutes per day to 43 minutes per day (1-2). Cortright calculates this improvement at another $1.5 billion. Add those two dollar amounts together and you're talking real money.

What happens to these savings? Portland is reputed to have the most independent bookstores per capita and the most roof racks per capita. The city is also said to have the most strip clubs per capita. These claims are all exaggerations, but they reflect a documented above-average consumption of recreation of all kinds. Portland has more restaurants per capita than all other large cities except Seattle and San Francisco. Oregonians also spend considerably more than most Americans on alcohol, which could be a good thing or a bad thing, but in any case makes you glad they are driving less (Cortright 2).

More significantly, whatever they are used for, these savings are more likely to stay local than if spent on driving. Almost 85 percent of money expended on cars and gas leaves the local economy—much of it, of course, bound for the pockets of Middle Eastern princes (Intelligent). A significant amount of the money saved probably goes into housing, since that is a national tendency: families that spend less on transportation spend more on their homes, which is, of course, about as local as it gets (Leinberger, *Option* 20).

The housing and driving connection is an important one, and has been the subject of much recent study, especially since transportation costs have skyrocketed. While transportation used to absorb only one-tenth of a typical family's budget (1960), it now consumes more than one in five dollars spent (Lutz and Fernandez 80). All told, the average American family now spends about $14,000 per year driving multiple cars (Lipman iv). By this measure, this family works from January 1 until April 13 just to pay for its cars. Remarkably, the typical "working" family, with an income of $20,000 to $50,000, pays more for transportation than for housing (Lipman 5).

This circumstance exists because the typical American working family now lives in suburbia, where the practice of drive-'til-you-qualify reigns supreme. Families of limited means move farther and farther away from city centers in order to find housing that is cheap enough to meet bank lending requirements. Unfortunately, in doing so, they often find that driving costs outweigh any housing savings (Doherty and Leinberger). This phenomenon was documented in 2006, when gasoline averaged $2.86 per gallon. At that time, households in the auto zone were devoting roughly a quarter of their income to transportation, while those in walkable neighborhoods spent well under half that amount (Doherty and Leinberger).

No surprise, then, that as gasoline broke $4.00 per gallon and the housing bubble burst, the epicenter of foreclosures occurred at the urban periphery, "places that required families to have a fleet of cars in order to participate in society, draining their mortgage carrying capacity," as Chris Leinberger notes. "Housing prices on the fringe tended to drop at twice the metropolitan average while walkable urban housing tended to maintain [its] value and [is] coming back nicely in selected markets today" (Leinberger, "Federal"). Not only have city centers fared better than suburbs, but walkable cities have fared better than drivable ones. Catherine Lutz and Anne Lutz Fernandez note that "the cities with the largest drops in housing value (such as Las Vegas, down 37 percent) have been the most car-dependent, and the few cities with housing prices gains . . . have good transit alternatives" (207).

This is bad news for Orlando and Reno, but it's good news for Portland . . . and also for Washington, D.C., which continues to benefit from earlier investments in transit. From 2005 to 2009, as the District's population grew by 15,862 people, car registrations fell by almost 15,000 vehicles. The National Building Museum, in its Intelligent Cities Initiative, notes that this reduction in auto use results in as much as $127,275,000 being retained in the local economy each year.

Those are the economic benefits of not driving. Are there additional economic benefits of walking, biking, and taking transit instead? The evidence here is a little more scarce, but the indications are positive. Ignoring the health benefits, there is a clear distinction to be made in the category of job creation. Road and highway work, with its big machines and small crews, is notoriously bad at increasing employment. In contrast, the construction of transit, bikeways, and sidewalks performs 60 percent to 100 percent better. A study of President Obama's American Recovery and Reinvestment Act documented a 70 percent employment premium for transit over highways. By this measure, that job-creation program would have created fifty-eight thousand more jobs if its road-building funds had gone to transit instead (Garrett-Peltier 1-2).

How does this translate at the local level? Portland has spent roughly $65 million on bicycle facilities over the past several decades. That is not a lot of money by infrastructure standards—it cost more than $140 million to rebuild just one of the city's freeway interchanges (Leinberger, *Option* 77–78; Mapes 143). Yet, in addition to helping to boost the number of bicyclists from near normal to fifteen times the national average, this investment can be expected to have created close to nine hundred jobs, about four hundred more than would have come from spending it on road building.

But the real Portland story is neither its transportation savings nor its bikeway employment, but something else: young, smart people are moving to Portland in droves. According to Cortright and coauthor Carol Coletta, "Over the decade of the 1990s, the number of college-educated 25 to 34 year-olds increased 50 percent in the Portland metropolitan area—five times faster than in the nation as a whole, with the fastest increase in this age group being recorded in the city's close-in neighborhoods." There is another kind of walkability dividend, aside from resources saved and resources reinvested: resources attracted by being a place where people want to live. This has certainly been the case in San Francisco, where headhunters for companies like Yelp and Zynga (the social-gaming developers who created FarmVille) actively use urbanism as a recruiting tool. "We're able to attract creative and tech talent because we are in the city," acknowledges Colleen McCreary, Zynga's head of human resources (Swartz).

Ultimately, though, it would seem that urban productivity has even deeper causes. There is mounting evidence that dense, walkable cities generate wealth by sheer virtue of the propinquity that they offer. This is a concept that is both stunningly obvious—cities exist, after all, because people benefit from coming together—and tantalizingly challenging to prove. This hasn't kept it from the lips of some of our leading thinkers, including Stewart Brand, Edward Glaeser, David Brooks, and Malcolm Gladwell.

Speaking at the Aspen Institute, David Brooks pointed out how most U.S. patent applications, when they list similar patents that influenced them, point to other innovators located less than twenty-five miles away. In a recent article, he also mentioned an experiment at the University of Michigan, where "researchers brought groups of people together face to face and asked them to play a difficult cooperation game. Then they organized other groups and had them communicate electronically. The face-to-face groups thrived. The electronic groups fractured and struggled."

Face-to-face collaboration is, of course, possible in any setting. But it is easier in a walkable city. Susan Zeilinski, managing director of the University of Michigan's SMART Center, puts it this way: "In Europe you can get five good meetings done in a day. In Australia, maybe three, and in Atlanta, maybe two, because you've gone way, way farther and way, way faster but you haven't been in an accessible place that allows a lot to happen. You've spent a lot of time sitting in traffic" (Mapes 268). This discussion raises a larger theoretical question that scientists have just begun to take on: are there underlying universal rules that govern the success of a place?

The theoretical physicists Geoffrey West and Luis Bettencourt believe so. They do not believe in urban theory—"a field without principles"—they are interested only in math. "What the data clearly shows," West notes, "is that when people come together they become much more productive" (qtd. in Lehrer 3). Do the same physical laws work in reverse? Writing about West's research in *The New York Times Magazine*, Jonah Lehrer notes:

> In recent decades, though, many of the fastest-growing cities in America, like Phoenix and Riverside, Calif., have given us a very different urban model. These places have traded away public spaces for affordable single-family homes, attracting working-class families who want their own white picket fences. West and Bettencourt point out, however, that cheap suburban comforts are associated with poor performance on a variety of urban metrics. Phoenix, for instance, has been characterized by below-average levels of income and innovation (as measured by the production of patents) for the last 40 years. (4)

These findings align with a recent Environmental Protection Agency study that found, state by state, an inverse relationship between vehicle travel and productivity: the more miles that people in a given state drive, the weaker it performs economically. Apparently, the data are beginning to support the city planners' bold contention that time wasted in traffic is unproductive.

In contrast, the Portland metro area is now home to more than twelve hundred technology companies. Like Seattle and San Francisco, it is one of the places where educated millennials are heading in disproportionate numbers. This phenomenon is what the demographer William Frey has in mind when he says: "A new image of urban America is in the making. What used to be white flight to the suburbs is turning into 'bright flight' to cities that have become magnets for aspiring young adults who see access to knowledge-based jobs, public transportation and a new city ambiance as an attraction" (qtd. in Leinberger, *Option* 170).

The conventional wisdom used to be that creating a strong economy came first, and that increased population and a higher quality of life would follow. The converse now seems more likely: creating a higher quality of life is the first step to attracting new residents and jobs. This is why Chris Leinberger believes that "all the fancy economic development strategies, such as developing a biomedical cluster, an aerospace cluster, or whatever the current economic development 'flavor of the month' might be, do not hold a candle to the power of a great walkable urban place" (*Option* 170).

Works Cited

Brooks, David. "The Splendor of Cities." *The New York Times*, 7 Feb. 2011, nyti.ms/1OAdjlg.

Cortright, Joe. *Portland's Green Dividend*. CEOs for Cities, July 2007, blog.oregonlive.com/commuting/2009/09/pdxgreendividend.pdf. White paper.

Cortright, Joe, and Carol Coletta. *The Young and the Restless: How Portland Competes for Talent*. Impresa Inc. / Coletta & Company, 2004, www.globalurban.org/Portland.pdf.

Doherty, Patrick C., and Christopher B. Leinberger. "The Next Real Estate Boom." *Washington Monthly*, Nov.-Dec. 2010, www.washingtonmonthly.com/features/2010/1011.doherty-leinberger.html.

Garrett-Peltier, Heidi. *Estimating the Employment Impacts of Pedestrian, Bicycle, and Road Infrastructure: Case Study: Baltimore.* Political Economy Research Institute, U of Massachusetts, Amherst, Dec. 2010, www.downtowndevelopment.com/pdf/baltimore_Dec20.pdf.

Intelligent Cities Initiative. Poster. 2009, National Building Museum, Washington, D.C.

Lehrer, Jonah. "A Physicist Solves the City." *The New York Times Magazine,* 17 Dec. 2010, pp. 1-7.

Leinberger, Christopher B. "Federal Restructuring of Fannie and Freddie Ignores the Underlying Cause of Crisis." *Urban Land,* 10 Feb. 2011, urbanland.uli.org/economy-markets-trends/federal-restructuring-of-fannie-and-freddie-ignores-underlying-cause-of-crisis/.

- - -. *The Option of Urbanism: Investing in a New American Dream.* Island Press, 2009.

Lipman, Barbara J. *A Heavy Load: The Combined Housing and Transportation Costs of Working Families.* Center for Housing Policy, 2006.

Lutz, Catherine, and Anne Lutz Fernandez. *Carjacked: The Culture of the Automobile and Its Effect on Our Lives.* St. Martin's Press, 2010.

Mapes, Jeff. *Pedaling Revolution: How Cyclists Are Changing American Cities.* Oregon State UP, 2009.

Swartz, Jon. "San Francisco's Charm Lures High-Tech Workers." *USA Today,* 6 Dec. 2010, p. A7.

Bethesda, Maryland, a suburb of Washington, DC, is an example of transit-oriented development, where stores and apartments are clustered around a Metro stop, eliminating the need to drive and park a car.

Games, Not Schools, Are Teaching Kids to Think   MyWritingLab™

James Paul Gee

As Mary Lou Fulton Presidential Professor of Literacy Studies at Arizona State University, James Paul Gee has published widely in the fields of linguistics and education. His book *Sociolinguistics and Literacies* (1990) helped establish the area of New Literacy Studies, an interdisciplinary field that combines language, learning, and literacy studies. Gee's most recent books deal with video games, language, and learning. He has published widely in academic journals as well as consumer publications. The following article appeared in the May 2003 issue of *Wired* magazine.

Return to these questions after you have finished reading.

Analyzing the Reading

1. The article opens with the question: "Why aren't kids learning?" What does the author say that schools are actually teaching kids? What is the author's definition of real learning?

2. In paragraph 3, the author praises five specific video games. What are they? What kinds of skills does he say the games teach?

3. What two characteristics of a successful video game's "underlying architecture" make it a "teaching machine"? How do schools exemplify, or not exemplify those characteristics, according to Gee?

4. What evidence does the article give that successful video games are the result of "free-market economics"?

Exploring Ideas and Issues

What's your experience with video games? Is playing video games an "educational" experience, purely an entertaining activity, or a waste of time?

1. One widespread understanding of games is that they are all learning experiences—helping to prepare children for adult activities. For example, when children play "house," they experiment with being parents and running a household. Think of other positive purposes that games might have for children. Write a short essay in which you explore three such purposes. Draw on examples from your own experience and the experiences of people you know to show how specific games fulfill these purposes.

2. Gee says, "Learning isn't about memorizing isolated facts." But is there a role for memorization in education? For example, do children gain anything by memorizing the capitals of states, the multiplication tables, or the words to a poem? Write a short essay in which you agree or disagree with Gee's statement. Be sure to include examples to support your ideas.

3. Gee says that schools are responding, ineffectually, "with more tests, more drills, and more rigidity" to the crisis in education demonstrated by studies that compare students in the United States with students in other countries. Do some research on suggested causes for this crisis—for example, lack of money, poor teacher training, and low parental involvement. What proposals are being put forth to address these issues? Do these proposals make sense to you? Write an essay in which you identify one possible cause of the education crisis and evaluate the recommendations advanced for remedying this problem.

Games, Not Schools,
Are Teaching Kids to Think

The US spends almost $50 billion each year on education, so why aren't kids learning? Forty percent of students lack basic reading skills, and their academic performance is dismal compared with that of their foreign counterparts. In response to this crisis, schools are skilling-and-drilling their way "back to basics," moving toward mechanical instruction methods that rely on line-by-line scripting for teachers and endless multiple-choice testing. Consequently, kids aren't learning how to think anymore—they're learning how to memorize. This might be an ideal recipe for the future Babbitts of the world, but it won't produce the kind of agile, analytical minds that will lead the high tech global age. Fortunately, we've got *Grand Theft Auto: Vice City* and *Deus X* for that.

After school, kids are devouring new information, concepts, and skills every day, and, like it or not, they're doing it controller in hand, plastered to the TV. The fact is, when kids play videogames they can experience a much more powerful form of learning than when they're in the classroom. Learning isn't about memorizing isolated facts. It's about connecting and manipulating them. Doubt it? Just ask anyone who's beaten *Legend of Zelda* or solved *Morrowind*.

The phenomenon of the videogame as an agent of mental training is largely unstudied; more often, games are denigrated for being violent or they're just plain ignored. They shouldn't be. Young gamers today aren't training to be gun-toting carjackers. They're learning how to learn. In *Pikmin*, children manage an army of plantlike aliens and strategize to solve problems. In *Metal Gear Solid 2*, players move stealthily through virtual environments and carry out intricate missions. Even in the notorious *Vice City*, players craft a persona, build a history, and shape a virtual world. In strategy games like *WarCraft III* and *Age of Mythology*, they learn to micromanage an array of elements while simultaneously balancing short- and long-term goals. That sounds like something for their resumes.

The secret of a videogame as a teaching machine isn't its immersive 3-D graphics but its underlying architecture. Each level dances around the outer limits of the player's abilities, seeking at every point to be hard enough to be just doable. In cognitive science, this is referred to as the "regime of competence principle," which results in a feeling of simultaneous pleasure and frustration—a sensation as familiar to gamers as sore thumbs. Cognitive scientist Andy diSessa has argued that the best instruction hovers at the boundary of a student's competence. Most schools, however, seek to avoid invoking feelings of both pleasure and frustration, blind to the fact that these emotions can be extremely useful when it comes to teaching kids.

Also, good videogames incorporate the principle of expertise. They tend to encourage players to achieve total mastery of one level, only to challenge and undo that mastery in the next, forcing kids to adapt and evolve. This carefully choreographed dialectic has been identified by learning theorists as the best way to achieve expertise in any field. This doesn't happen much in our routine-driven schools, where "good" students are often just good at "doing school."

How did videogames become such successful models of effective learning? Game coders aren't trained as cognitive scientists. It's a simple case of free-market economics: If a title doesn't teach players how to play it well, it won't sell well. Game companies don't rake in $6.9 billion a year by dumbing down the material—aficionados condemn short and easy games like *Half Life: Blue Shift* and *Devil May Cry 2*. Designers respond by making harder and more complex games that require mastery of sophisticated worlds and as many as 50 to 100 hours to complete. Schools, meanwhile, respond with more tests, more drills, and more rigidity. They're in the cognitive-science dark ages.

We don't often think about videogames as relevant to education reform, but maybe we should. Game designers don't often think of themselves as learning theorists. Maybe they should. Kids often say it doesn't feel like learning when they're gaming—they're much too focused on playing. If kids were to say that about a science lesson, our country's education problems would be solved.

"Are You Pouring on the Pounds?"
"Food Cops Bust Cookie Monster"

MyWritingLab™

"Are You Pouring on the Pounds?" was created by New York City's Health Department in 2009 as part of its public service campaign to fight obesity. The then mayor of New York City, Michael Bloomberg, pushed for a limit on soft drink sizes, and the Board of Health approved a limit of 16 ounces for sugary drinks sold in restaurants, movie theaters, and stadiums. The soft-drink industry vigorously opposed the ban on oversize sodas and succeeded in having the ban struck down in state's highest court in June 2014.

The Center for Consumer Freedom, an organization sponsored by restaurants and food companies, produced a series of ads taking a different position on obesity, including "Food Cops Bust Cookie Monster." These ads defend what the organization describes as "the right of adults and parents to choose what they eat, drink, and how to enjoy themselves."

Return to these questions after you have finished reading.

Analyzing the Reading

1. Both of these ads make visual arguments. Why do you think the producers of each ad chose the image they did? How effective is each visual in communicating the ad's central message?

2. The ConsumerFreedom.com ad refers to "food cops" and "nutrition nags." Why did the creators of this ad choose these terms? What type of audience are they trying to appeal to with these kinds of labels? And since the Center for Consumer Freedom is itself merely an advocacy group, like the health advocates it is lampooning, how responsibly is it arguing its case by using such terms to describe its opponents?

3. The New York City ad invites viewers to make a direct connection between drinking sugary sodas and resulting physical effect with the soda turning into blubber. How would this argument sound if they were stated as a simple claim plus reasons? Would the ad be as effective in non-visual form?

Exploring Ideas and Issues

Americans are among the fattest people on the planet. According to health experts two out of three adults and one out of three children are overweight or obese. Rising consumption of sugary drinks has been a major contributor to the obesity epidemic. A 64-ounce fountain soda drink can have 700 calories. Excess weight is not just a matter of looks. Obesity magnifies the risk of heart disease, diabetes, high blood pressure, and other ailments—already overtaking tobacco as the leading cause of chronic illness.

1. The 2014 documentary *Fed Up* presents evidence that the large quantities of sugar in drinks and processed foods are a major cause of obesity and that government should intervene to reduce sugar consumption. Food and soft-drink industries argue that moderation and physical activity are the long-term solutions to obesity, and they point out that the majority of Americans polled in surveys are not in favor of governmental controls on food. Write a position argument for or against government intervention in our diet, using a specific issue. For example, should a soda tax be imposed to raise funds for educating children and adults about the risks of obesity and how to follow healthy eating habits?

2. One cause of the skyrocketing rate of obesity in children is the increased marketing of food and sugary drinks to children. When the American public realized how effective Joe Camel ads were in reaching children, their outrage led to a ban on many forms of cigarette advertising. The food industry has no such restrictions and uses popular cartoon characters to pitch their products, a practice banned in most European countries. Write a position argument for or against limiting food and soft-drink advertising directed toward children.

ConsumerFreedom.com Editorial Infographic

Food Cops Bust Cookie Monster

Farce again became reality as the children's TV show *Sesame Street* has bowed to obesity hysteria from nutrition nags. In a nod to calorie killjoys, Cookie Monster will tout health foods, and his famous song, "C is For Cookie, That's Good Enough For Me," will be replaced with "A Cookie Is a Sometimes Food." This U-Turn may not be the last. Predictions:

C is for Cookie

Big Bird becomes Svelte Bird

Miss Piggy becomes Miss Moderation

Mayor McCheese voted out of office and replaced with Mayor McSoy-Slice

Keebler elves to make only unflavored rice cakes

Cap'n Crunch forced to sail in only skim milk

Count Chocula stabbed through heart with a carrot stick

Fat Albert becomes "Weight Watchers patient #00873-Albert"

How to Write a Position Argument

These steps for the process of writing a position argument may not progress as neatly as this chart might suggest. Writing is not an assembly-line process.

As you write and revise you may think of additional reasons to support your position. Your instructor and fellow students may give you comments that help you to rethink your argument. Use their comments to work through your paper or project again, strengthening your content and making your writing better organized and more readable.

1 FIND AN ISSUE

- Read your assignment slowly and carefully. Note key words like *argue for* and *take a stand* that indicate the assignment requires a position argument.

- Make a list of possible issues.

- Select a possible issue.

- Read about your issue.

- Analyze your potential readers. What do your readers likely know about the issue? Where are they most likely to disagree with you?

2 DEVELOP REASONS AND A THESIS

- Take a definite position.

- Develop reasons by considering whether you can argue from a definition, compare or contrast, consider good and bad effects, or refute objections.

- Support your reasons by making observations and finding facts, statistics, and statements from authorities.

- Write a working thesis.

3
WRITE A DRAFT

- Introduce the issue and give the necessary background. Explain why the issue is important.

- Think about how readers will view you, the writer.

- If you argue from a definition, set out the criteria.

- Avoid fallacies.

- Provide evidence to support your main points.

- Address opposing views. Summarize opposing positions and explain why your position is preferable.

- Make counterarguments if necessary. Examine the facts and assumptions on which competing claims are based.

- Conclude with strength. Avoid merely summarizing. Emphasize the importance of your argument and possibly make an additional point or draw implications.

- Choose a title that will interest readers.

4
REVISE, REVISE, REVISE

- Check that your position argument fulfills the assignment.

- Make sure that your claim is arguable and focused.

- Check your reasons and add more if you can.

- Add additional evidence where reasons need more support.

- Examine the organization.

- Review the visual presentation.

- Proofread carefully.

5
SUBMITTED VERSION

- Make sure your finished writing meets all formatting requirements.

1: Find an Issue

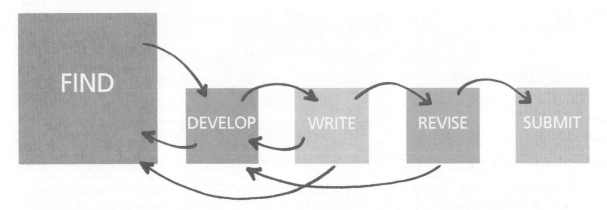

Analyze the assignment

Read your assignment slowly and carefully. Look for words like *argue for, take a stand,* or *write on a controversial issue,* which signal that you are writing a position argument. Highlight any information about the length specified, date due, formatting, and other requirements. You can attend to this information later. At this point you want to give your attention to finding an issue if one is not specified.

Make a list of possible campus issues

Think about issues that are debated on your campus such as these.

- Should smoking be banned on campus?
- Should varsity athletes get paid for playing sports that bring in revenue?
- Should admissions decisions be based exclusively on academic achievement?
- Should colleges offer financial incentives for students to graduate in three years rather than four?

Make a list of possible community issues

Think about issues that are debated in your community such as these.

- Should more tax dollars be shifted from building highways to public transportation?
- Should sex education be increased in schools to reduce teenage pregnancy?
- Should talking on phones and texting while driving be banned?
- Should bike lanes be designated on streets to encourage more people to ride bicycles?

Make a list of possible national and international issues

Think about national and international issues such as these.

- Should advertising be banned on television shows aimed at preschool children?
- Should people who are terminally ill be allowed to end their lives?
- Should animals be used for scientific research?
- Should any citizen who does not have a criminal record be permitted to carry a concealed handgun?

Select an issue and take stock of what you know

Freewrite or make a list of everything you know about the issue. Why are you interested in this issue? What is your stance on the issue? What do you need to know more about?

Read about your issue

Read broadly about your issue. You'll find that writers respond to the opinions and ideas of other writers. Major issues are the sites of ongoing conversations. By mapping the conversation, you may see an opportunity to enter the larger conversation (see page 30).

Analyze the stakeholders

For whom does this issue matter? Whose interests are at stake? Who stands to win and lose?

Analyze your potential readers

How familiar are your potential readers with your issue? What background will you need to supply? What attitudes and beliefs will your readers likely have about this issue? Where will you likely find common ground with your readers? Where will your readers most likely disagree with you?

WRITE NOW   MyWritingLab™

Choose an issue that you care about

1. Make a list of issues that fulfill your assignment.

2. Put a checkmark beside the issues that look most interesting to write about or the ones that mean the most to you.

3. Put a question mark beside the issues that you don't know very much about. If you choose one of these issues, you will probably have to do in-depth research—by talking to people, by using the Internet, or by going to the library.

4. Select a possible issue. What is your stand on this issue? Write nonstop for five minutes about why this issue is important and how it affects you.

Writer at work

Patrice Conley received an assignment to write a position argument. She made notes on and highlighted important parts of her assignment sheet.

English 101
Position Argument Assignment

Choose a current controversial issue that interests you. If no issue comes to mind immediately, visit these library databases: *Opposing Views in Context, Issue Tracker* (on *CQ Researcher*), and *Times Topics* (from *The New York Times*).

Gain an overview of the issue by reading several articles and possibly books. You will need to cite at least five sources in your paper.

Take a position on the issue. You will need to provide reasons and evidence in support of your position, and you will need to acknowledge and discuss opposing viewpoints. Also, most controversial issues have long histories, which you should summarize briefly.

HEART OF THE PAPER Give reasons and evidence for position and acknowledge opposing views.

Submitting a draft on April 14
For the workshop draft, submit two copies
- A paper copy for your in-class editor (print in advance of class)
- A digital copy to the Discussion Board

Paper and digital copies required

So that everyone in class will have easy access to your drafts, you will post them on the Discussion Board. Simply locate the appropriate forum, type in a brief introduction to the paper, and then upload the paper as an attachment to your message. In your introduction, discuss your writing process and what you hoped to achieve by the draft.

Format
Use MLA format in both the draft and final versions. The format is explained in Chapter 23 of the *Brief Penguin Handbook*, 5th ed. Pay particular attention to pages 267 and 281, which give checklists of formatting features. Note that MLA does not require a title page but does have a standard format for headings. Note too that MLA double-spaces everything.

Get the little things right

Length: 1200–1500 words (approximately 4-5 double-spaced pages)
Due dates:
April 14: Draft due
April 28: Final version due

Read the assignment closely
Patrice Conley began by marking information about the due dates and requirements.

Choose a topic
Patrice enjoys playing and watching sports, so she started by making a list of current controversial issues in college sports.

Explore the issue
Patrice made her initial search on *Google*, using the search terms "student athlete salaries," which turned up many articles She also searched library databases and the library catalog. In addition, she watched "Money & March Madness" on the PBS series *Frontline*. People interviewed on the program gave arguments against the NCAA's policy of not paying players. The President of the NCAA, Mark Emmert, defended the NCAA's definition of amateurism.

College sports controversies

1. *Equal opportunities for women athletes*

2. *Big-time sports overshadow education*

3. *Financing college sports*

4. *Paying student-athletes in big-time college sports*

5. *Ethics: win-at-all-costs philosophy*

6. *The BCS championship system in big-time college football*

NOTES

College sports is big business. NYT estimates NCAA's licensing deals at $4 billion in 2010.

Coaches receive outlandish salaries while players are paid nothing. John Calipari at Kentucky gets $4 million a year.

Univ. of North Carolina College Sports Research Inst. 2010 study: 54.8% of major college football players at 117 schools graduated within six years, compared to 73.7% of other full-time students. Gap greater in basketball, with 44.6 percent of athletes graduating compared to 75.7% of the general student body.

Tim Tebow–autographed Florida jerseys sell for $349.99 but Tebow gets nothing.

Student musicians can get paid; school even helps them find jobs. What's the difference between student musicians and student athletes?

Olympic Games dropped the professional-amateur distinction in 1988.

History: professional-amateur distinction arose in Britain in the 1800s when middle-class and upper-class students didn't want to play against working-class sportsmen, who had to be paid for time taken off work.

2: Develop Reasons and a Thesis

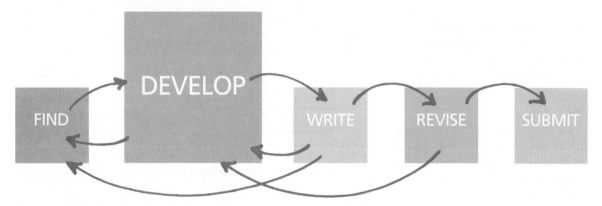

Take an arguable position

A position argument requires that you make a claim that a reasonable person could disagree with and support that claim with one or more reasons. Statements of facts that can be verified by doing research are not arguable. Likewise, claims of personal taste (e.g., your favorite food) and of faith are not arguable.

Write a working thesis

Is your thesis arguable? Statements of fact are not arguable unless the facts are disputed.

NOT ARGUABLE: The population of the United States grew faster in the 1990s than in any previous decade because Congress increased the level of legal immigration and the government stopped enforcing most laws against illegal immigration in the interior of the country.

ARGUABLE: Allowing a high rate of immigration helps the United States deal with the problems of an increasingly aging society and helps provide funding for millions of Social Security recipients.

ARGUABLE: The increase in the number of visas to foreign workers in technology industries is the major cause of unemployment in those industries.

Develop reasons

- Can you argue from a definition? Is _____ a _____? What criteria are necessary for _____ to be a _____? If you want to argue, for example, that zoos are guilty of cruelty to animals, you will have to argue for a definition of cruelty based on criteria, then assert that those criteria apply to zoos.

- Can you write a rebuttal to another position argument? There are two basic strategies for writing a rebuttal. In a **refutation**, you can demonstrate the shortcoming of an argument you wish to discredit. In a **counterargument**, you emphasize the strengths of the position you support in contrast to the argument you are opposing.

- Can you compare and contrast? Is _____ like or unlike _____? For example, should health care in the United States be more like the health care in Canada?

Support your reasons

Search for facts, statistics, statements from authorities, and textual evidence to support your reasons. If you are writing about a campus or community issue, you may also need to visit the site and make observations.

Writer at work

Patrice Conley decided to make a map in order to find a center for her broad topic of whether student athletes in big-time college sports should be paid.

She started with her general topic, stating it in a few words and drawing a box around it.

Next Patrice asked additional questions:

- What is the current situation?
- Who is involved?
- How long has it been going on?
- What else is like it?
- What exactly is the problem?
- What possible solutions are there for the problem?

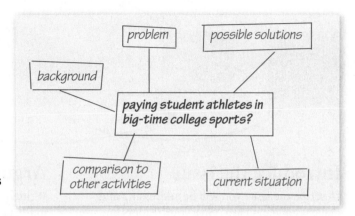

She thought of some general categories for her topic in response to those questions and drew boxes for each.

She then looked at her notes from what she had read. She began to generate ideas for each of the subcategories and put them on her map.

When she finished she took stock of her map. She picked up a marker and drew a box around a possible central idea for her project.

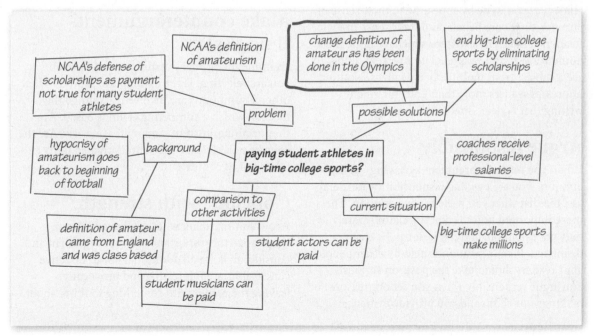

She succeeded in narrowing her general topic to the more specific topic of changing the definition of amateur as it applies to student athletes.

3: Write a Draft

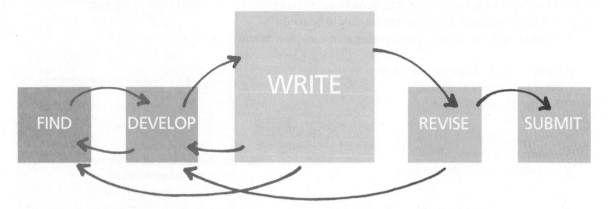

Introduce the issue

Describe the issue you will be addressing and make your claim early. Give your readers any background information they will need.

Think about your credibility

Think about how you can connect with your readers as you write by appealing to their sense of fairness, their core beliefs, and their sense of logic. Readers tend to trust writers who have done their homework, and they appreciate a writer's ability to see a subject from multiple perspectives. Nothing impresses readers more than graceful, fluent writing that is clear, direct, and forceful.

Argue responsibly

When you begin an argument by saying "In my opinion," you are evading responsibility. Readers assume that what you write is your opinion. The more important point is that the claim is rarely only your opinion, and if it is, it can be easily dismissed. If your position is held by other people, your readers should take the position seriously. You argue responsibly when you set out reasons for making your claim and you provide evidence.

Argue respectfully

Written arguments almost never end by getting in the last word. Think of arguments as ongoing conversations. Your goal is to create a dialogue. Show that you understand and respect opposing positions, even if you think the position is ultimately wrong.

Make counterarguments if necessary

Examine the primary assumption of the claim you are rejecting. Is the assumption flawed? What other assumptions are involved? Examine the facts on which a competing claim is based. Are they accurate, current, and representative? Are the sources reliable? Are the sources treated fairly or taken out of context?

Conclude with strength

Avoid summarizing what you have just said. Emphasize the importance of your argument and consider making an additional point. Effective conclusions are interesting and provocative, leaving the reader with something to think about.

Writer at work

Patrice Conley prefers to write a "zero draft" to generate ideas before she plans her organization. She knows that nearly all of what she writes will not make it into the final draft, but she finds that writing as fast as she can frees up her thinking. (You can read Patrice's zero draft on page 44.)

When Patrice finished her zero draft, she let it sit for a day and then took stock of the key points that she had underlined. She rearranged these key points into a working outline.

PATRICE CREATES A WORKING OUTLINE FROM HER ZERO DRAFT

WORKING TITLE: Should Student Athletes in Big-Time College Sports Be Paid?

SECTION 1:   Student athletes in college sign away their rights for payment.

SECTION 2:   College athletics are big business, and top coaches receive multimillion-dollar salaries.

SECTION 3:   NCAA defends classifying student athletes as amateurs to protect them from exploitation.

SECTION 4:   The history of amateurism arose in 19th c. Britain when middle- and upper-class sportsmen didn't want to play against working-class teams. The Olympics abandoned the distinction in 1988.

SECTION 5:   Student musicians and student actors get paid when they perform professionally.

SECTION 6:   Student athletes cannot be paid for use of their names and images even after they graduate.

SECTION 7:   Defenders of the current system claim that student athletes are paid with scholarships, but in big-time sports many do not graduate.

SECTION 8:   NCAA should adopt a different definition of amateur that allows athletes to be paid for what they earn for their schools.

4: Revise, Revise, Revise

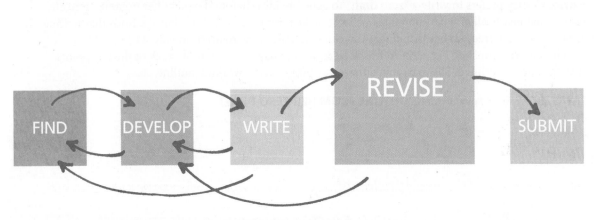

Skilled writers know that the secret to writing well is rewriting.

Does your position argument fulfill the assignment?	• Look again at your assignment. Does your paper or project do what the assignment asks? • Look again at the assignment for specific guidelines, including length, format, and amount of research. Does your work meet these guidelines?
Is your claim arguable and focused?	• Is your position arguable? Statements of fact and statements of religious belief are not arguable. • Can you make your claim more specific to avoid ambiguous language and situations where your claim may not apply?
Are your reasons adequate?	• Are your reasons clear to your readers? • Can you add additional reasons to strengthen your argument? • Have you acknowledged the views of people who disagree with your position?
Are your reasons supported with evidence?	• Have you found the most accurate information available about your issue? • Can you find additional evidence in the form of examples, quotations from experts, statistics, and observations?
Save the editing for last	• When you have finished revising, edit and proofread carefully.

A peer review guide is on page 58.

Writer at work

Patrice Conley received both global and local comments from her instructor. Patrice first dealt with her instructor's global comments.

RETURNED DRAFT WITH COMMENTS

> College athletics are big business. The most visible college sports—big-time men's football and basketball—generate staggering sums of money. Even more money comes in from video games, clothing, and similar licenses.

Your major claims need to be supported with evidence. Give specific examples.

Patrice did additional research to find examples to support her claim.

PATRICE'S REVISION

Make no mistake: college athletics are big business. The most visible college sports—big-time men's football and basketball—generate staggering sums of money. For example, the twelve universities in the Southeastern Conference receive $205 million each year from CBS and ESPN for the right to broadcast its football games (Smith and Ourand). Even more money comes in from video games, clothing, and similar licenses. In 2010, *The New York Times* reported, "the NCAA's licensing deals are estimated at more than $4 billion" per year (Thamel). While the staggering executive pay at big corporations has brought public outrage, coaches' salaries are even more outlandish. Kentucky basketball coach, John Calipari, is paid over $4 million a year for a basketball program that makes about $35-40 million a year, more than 10% of the entire revenue.

Then she moved on to her instructor's local comments. Her instructor noted a transition is needed between two paragraphs, and Patrice added a sentence, highlighted in yellow below.

PATRICE'S REVISION

The college sports empire in the United States run by the NCAA is the last bastion of amateurism for sports that draw audiences large enough to be televised. Colleges might be able to defend the policy of amateurism if they extended this definition to all students. A fair policy is one that treats all students the same. A fair policy doesn't result in some students getting paid for professional work, while other students do not.

5: Submitted Version (MLA Style)

MyWritingLab™

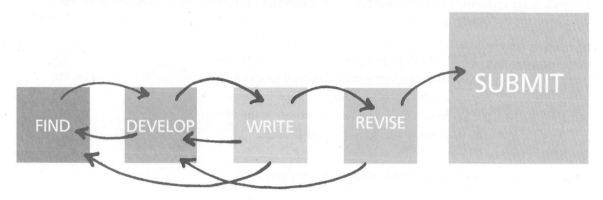

Conley 1

Patrice Conley

Professor Douglas

English 101

28 April 2014

Flagrant Foul: The NCAA's Definition of Student Athletes as Amateurs

Every year, thousands of student athletes across America sign the National Collegiate Athletic Association's Form 08-3a, the "Student-Athlete" form, waiving their right to receive payment for the use of their name and image (McCann). The form defines student athletes as amateurs, who cannot receive payment for playing their sports. While their schools and coaches may make millions of dollars in salaries and endorsement deals and are the highest-paid public employees in many states, student athletes can never earn a single penny from their college athletic careers. Former Nike executive Sonny Vacarro sums it up: "Everybody has a right except for the player. The player has no rights" ("Money").

Make no mistake: college athletics are big business. The most visible college sports—big-time men's football and basketball—generate staggering sums of money. For example, the fourteen universities in the Southeastern Conference receive $205 million each year from CBS and ESPN for the right to broadcast its football games (Smith and Ourand). Even more money comes in from video games, clothing, and similar licenses. In 2010, *The New York Times* reported, "the NCAA's licensing deals are estimated at more than $4 billion" per year (Thamel). While the staggering executive pay at big corporations has brought public outrage, coaches' salaries are even more outlandish. Kentucky basketball coach, John Calipari, is paid over $4 million a year for a basketball program that makes about $35-40 million a year, more than 10% of the entire revenue. Tom Van Riper observes that no corporate CEO commands this large a share of the profits. He observes that if Steve Ballmer, the CEO at Microsoft, had Calipari's deal, Ballmer would make over $6 billion a year.

How can colleges allow advertisers, arena operators, concession owners, athletic gear manufacturers, retailers, game companies, and media moguls, along with coaches and university officials, to make millions and pay the stars of the show nothing? The answer is that colleges define athletes as amateurs. Not only are student athletes not paid for playing their sport, they cannot receive gifts and are not allowed to endorse products, which may be a violation of their right to free speech. The NCAA, an organization of colleges and schools, forces student athletes to sign away their rights because, it says, it is protecting the students. If student athletes could accept money from anyone, the NCAA argues, they might be exploited, cheated, or even bribed. Taking money out of the equation is supposed to let students focus on academics and preserve the amateur status of college sports.

The definition of amateur arose in the nineteenth century in Britain, when team sports became popular. Middle-class and upper-class students in college had ample time to play their sports while working-class athletes had only a half-day off (no sports were played on Sundays in that era). Teams began to pay top working-class sportsmen for the time they had to take off from work. Middle-class and upper-class sportsmen didn't want to play against the working-class teams, so they made the distinction between amateurs and professionals. The definition of amateur crossed the Atlantic to the United States, where college sports became popular in the 1880s. But it was not long until the hypocrisy of amateurism undermined the ideal. Top football programs like Yale had slush funds to pay athletes, and others used ringers—players who weren't students—and even players from other schools (Zimbalist 7).

The Olympic Games maintained the amateur-professional distinction until 1988, but it was long evident that Communist bloc nations were paying athletes to train full-time and Western nations were paying athletes through endorsement contracts. The only Olympic sport that now requires amateur status is boxing. The college sports empire in the United States run by the NCAA is the last bastion of amateurism for sports that draw audiences large enough to be televised.

Colleges might be able to defend the policy of amateurism if they extended this definition to all students. A fair policy is one that treats all students the same. A fair policy doesn't result in some students getting paid for professional work, while other students do not. Consider the students in the Butler School of Music at the University of Texas at Austin, for example. Many student musicians perform at the professional level. Does the school prevent them from earning money for their musical performances? No. In fact, the school runs a referral service that connects its students with people and businesses who want to hire professional musicians. The university even advises its students on how to negotiate a contract and get paid for their performance ("Welcome").

Likewise, why are student actors and actresses allowed to earn money from their work and images, while student athletes are not? Think about actress Emma Watson, who enrolled at Brown University in Rhode Island. Can you imagine the university officials at Brown telling Watson that she would have to make the next two Harry Potter films for free, instead of for the $5 million she was offered? Can you imagine Brown University telling Watson that all the revenue from Harry Potter merchandise bearing her likeness would have to be paid directly to the university, for the rest of her life? They would if Watson were an athlete instead of an actress.

In fact, compared to musicians and actors, student athletes have an even greater need to earn money while they are still in college. Athletes' professional careers are likely to be much shorter than musicians' or actors'. College may be the only time some athletes have the opportunity to capitalize on their success.

(Indeed, rather than focusing student athletes on their academic careers, the NCAA policy sometimes forces students to leave college early, so they can earn a living before their peak playing years are over.) Student athletes often leave school with permanent injuries and no medical insurance or job prospects, whereas student musicians and actors rarely suffer career-ending injuries on the job.

Defenders of the current system argue that student athletes on scholarships are paid with free tuition, free room and board, free books, and tutoring help. The total package can be the equivalent of $120,000 over four years. For those student athletes who are motivated to take advantage of the opportunity, the lifetime benefits can be enormous. Unfortunately, too few student athletes do take advantage of the opportunity. Seldom does a major college football and men's basketball program have a graduation rate at or close to that of the overall student body. A study by the University of North Carolina's College Sports Research Institute released in 2010 accuses the NCAA of playing fast and loose with graduation rates by counting part-time students in statistics for the general student body, which makes graduation rates for athletes look better in a comparison. Student athletes must be full-time students; thus they should be compared to other full-time students. The North Carolina Institute reports that 54.8% of major college (Football Bowl Subdivision) football players at 117 schools graduated within six years, compared to 73.7% of other full-time students. The gap between basketball players was even greater, with 44.6% of athletes graduating compared to 75.7% of the general student body (Zaiger). For the handful of talented athletes who can play in the National Football League or the National Basketball Association, college sports provide training for their future lucrative, although short-lived, profession. But as the NCAA itself points out in its ads, the great majority of student athletes "go pro in something other than sports" ("NCAA"). For the 55% of college basketball players who fail to graduate, the supposed $120,000 package is an air ball.

The NCAA would be wise to return to the older definition of amateur, which comes from Latin through old French, meaning "lover of." It doesn't necessarily have to have anything to do with money. Whether it's a jazz performer or dancer or an athlete, an amateur ought to be considered someone in love with an activity—someone who cares deeply about the activity, studies the activity in depth, and practices in order to be highly proficient. NBA players, Olympians, college athletes, high school players, and even bird watchers, star gazers, and open-source programmers: they're all amateurs. If they are lucky enough to be paid, so be it.

Conley 6

Works Cited

McCann, Michael. "NCAA Faces Unspecified Damages, Changes in Latest Anti-Trust Case." *Sports Illustrated*, 21 July 2009, www.si.com/more-sports/2009/07/21/ncaa.

"Money and March Madness." *Frontline*, WGBH/Boston, 29 Mar. 2011, www.pbs.org/wgbh/pages/frontline/money-and-march-madness/.

"NCAA Launches Latest Public Service Announcements, Introduces New Student-Focused Website." *NCAA.org*, 13 Mar. 2007, fs.ncaa.org/Docs/Press Archive/2007/Announcements/NCAA%2BLaunches%2BLatest%2BPublic%2B Service%2BAnnouncements%2BIntroduces%2BNew%2BStudent-Focused%2 BWebsite.html.

Smith, Michael, and John Ourand. "ESPN Pays $2.25B for SEC Rights." *Street & Smith's SportsBusiness Journal*, 25 Aug. 2008, www.sportsbusinessdaily.com/Journal/Issues/2008/08/20080825/This-Weeks-News/ESPN-Pays-$225B-For-SEC-Rights.aspx.

Thamel, Pete. "N.C.A.A. Fails to Stop Licensing Lawsuit." *The New York Times,* 8 Feb. 2010, nyti.ms/1Ho5aOR.

Van Riper, Tom. "The Highest-Paid College Basketball Coaches." *Forbes*, 8 Mar. 2010, www.forbes.com/2010/03/05/calipari-donovan-pitino-business-sports-college-basketball-coaches.html.

"Welcome to the Music Referral Service." *Sarah and Ernest Butler School of Music*, U of Texas at Austin, ww4.austin.utexas.edu/bsomBridgeApp/gigReferral/. Accessed 3 Apr. 2014.

Zaiger, Alan Scher. "Study: NCAA Graduation Rate Comparisons Flawed." *ABC News*, 20 Apr. 2010, abcnews.go.com/topics/sports/ncaa-football.htm.

Zimbalist, Andrew. *Unpaid Professionals: Commercialism and Conflict in Big-Time College Sports*. Princeton UP, 2001.

Projects

Position arguments are not merely statements of opinion but are reasoned arguments backed by evidence that are intended to advance the discussion of an issue.

Position argument

Make a position claim on a controversial issue. See pages 406–407 for help on identifying an issue.

Identify the key term. Often position arguments depend on the definition of the key term. What criteria are necessary for something to meet this definition? How would others benefit from a different definition?

Analyze your potential readers. How does the claim you are making affect them? How familiar are they with the issue? How likely will they be to accept your claim or the definition that underlies your claim?

Write an essay on a controversial issue that takes a stand supported by developed reasons.

Rebuttal argument

Identify a position argument to argue against. What is its main claim or claims? A fair summary of your opponent's position should be included in your finished rebuttal.

Examine the facts on which the claim is based. Are the facts accurate? Are the facts current? Can the statistics be interpreted differently? How reliable are the author's sources?

Analyze the assumptions on which the claim is based. What is the primary assumption of the claim you are rejecting? What are the secondary assumptions? How are these assumptions flawed? What fallacies does the author commit (see pages 24–25)?

Consider your readers. To what extent do your potential readers support the claim you are rejecting? If they strongly support that claim, then how do you get them to change their minds? What beliefs and assumptions do you share with them?

Write a rebuttal. Make your aim clear in your thesis statement. Identify the issue you are writing about and give background information if the issue is likely to be unfamiliar to your readers. Question the evidence and show the flaws in the argument you are rejecting. Conclude on a strong note with your counterargument or counterproposal.

Narrative position argument

Think about an experience you have had that makes an implicit causal argument. Have you ever experienced being stereotyped? Have you ever had to jump through many unnecessary bureaucratic hoops? Have you ever been treated differently because of your perceived level of income? Have you ever experienced unfair application of laws and law enforcement?

How common is your experience? If other people have similar experiences, probably what happened to you will ring true.

Describe the experience in detail. When did it happen? How old were you? Why were you there? Who else was there? Where did it happen? If the place is important, describe what it looked like.

Reflect on the significance of the event. How did you feel about the experience when it happened? How do you feel about the experience now? What long-term effects has it had on your life?

Write an essay. You might need to give some background, but if the story is compelling, often it is best to jump right in. Let the story do most of the work. Avoid drawing a simple moral lesson. Your readers should feel the same way you do if you tell your story well.

COMPOSE IN MULTIMEDIA

Position argument brochure

Brochures are used by many organizations to make position arguments. They are easy to make with software and inexpensive to print and distribute.

Select an issue for your brochure (see pages 406–407). Identify your target audience. Think about what background they may need about your issue, and what you want them to take away from your brochure.

Develop a layout. A typical brochure has six panels—three on the front and three on the back. Take two pieces of standard paper, place them together, and fold them in three sections. Then sketch what will go on each panel.

Open your software program, create two new pages, and change the page layout to horizontal. Create text boxes for each panel, three boxes on each page. Add your content and images inside the boxes.

Check the formatting. Print your draft pages, put them together, and fold them in the correct order. Inspect the alignment and the readability of your text. You may need to enlarge the type size or insert blank space to set apart key points. Edit and proofread carefully when you finish.

MyWritingLab™ Visit Ch. 12 in MyWritingLab to complete the chapter exercises, explore an interactive version of the Writer at Work paper, and test your understanding of the chapter objectives.

13 Proposal Arguments

Proposal arguments aim to convince others to take action for change (or not to take action).

In this chapter, you will learn to

1. Recognize how proposal arguments work *(see p. 425)*

2. Understand how to use visuals in support of proposal arguments *(see p. 426)*

3. Read and analyze a proposal argument *(see pp. 427–463)*

4. Describe the steps involved in the process of writing a proposal argument *(see pp. 464–465)*

5. Apply flexible strategies to write and revise a proposal argument *(see pp. 466–485)*

Writing a Proposal Argument

Successful proposals use good reasons to convince readers that if they act, something positive will happen (or something negative will be avoided). If your readers believe that taking action will benefit them, they are more likely to help bring about what you propose.

The challenge for writers of proposal arguments is to convince readers to take action. It's easy for readers to agree that something should be done, as long as they don't have to do it. It's much harder to get readers involved with the situation or convince them to spend their time or money trying to carry out the proposal.

Proposal arguments take this form.

Genres of proposal arguments

- **Proposal essays** make general readers aware of a specific problem and present a solution.

- **Grant proposals** often aim to gain support for nonprofit organizations.

- **Internal proposals** try to persuade those in charge to get something done within an organization such as initiating a new project.

- **Business proposals** seek funding from bankers and investors for a new business or a business expansion.

Someone should → do something / not do something ───── because _____

We should *convert existing train tracks in the downtown area to a light-rail system and build a new freight track around the city* because we need to relieve traffic and parking congestion downtown.

What Makes a Good Proposal Argument?

1
Identify and define the problem
Sometimes, your audience is already fully aware of the problem you want to solve. The clearer you are about what must be done, and by whom, the stronger your argument will be.

2
State a proposed solution
A strong proposal offers a clear, definite statement of exactly what you are proposing. Vague statements that "Something must be done!" may get readers stirred up about the issue but are unlikely to lead to constructive action.

3
Convince readers that the proposed solution is fair and will work
Once your readers agree that a problem exists and a solution should be found, you have to convince them that your solution is the best one.

4
Consider other possible solutions
You may also have to show how your proposal is better than other possible actions that could be taken.

5
Demonstrate that the solution is feasible
Your solution not only has to work; it must be feasible, or practical, to implement.

Visual Proposals

Many proposal arguments depend on presenting information visually, in multimedia, or in images, in addition to using written language.

NASA global climate computer model (GCM) calculates many factors, such as the temperature of air and water, how much sunlight is reflected and absorbed, and the distribution of clouds, rain, and snow. NASA has released an educational version that runs on a PC so teachers and students can conduct the same kinds of experiments that scientists are running to predict climate change.

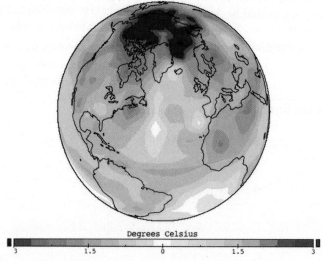

Surface air temperature increase by 2040. Source: NASA.

WRITE NOW   MyWritingLab™

Make a list of campus and community problems to solve

First, make a list of all the problems you can think of on your campus: the library closes too early, shuttle buses run late, long waits at the heath center, food options too limited, and so on. Next make a list of problems in your community: too few bike lanes, traffic, downtown in decline, off-campus housing too expensive, and so on.

Share your lists in a group of three or four students or with the entire class. Record any problems that turn up on more than one list. Discuss the following.

- Which problems are the most important?
- Which are possible to solve?
- Which are the most interesting? Which are the least interesting?

The Declaration of Independence
Thomas Jefferson and others

The American Revolution had already begun with the battles of Lexington, Concord, and Bunker Hill, and George Washington had been named to head the colonial army by June 7, 1776, when the Continental Congress moved to draft a Declaration of Independence. Thomas Jefferson was given eighteen days to complete the task with the help of Benjamin Franklin and John Adams.

HOW IS THIS READING ORGANIZED?

Introduction	**Reasons**	**Problem**	**Ethos**	**Conclusion**
Paragraph 1	*Paragraph 2*	*Paragraphs 3–30*	*Paragraph 31*	*Paragraph 32*
The *Declaration of Independence* announces the separation from Britain based on natural law.	The lengthy second paragraph argues that people have certain natural rights.	Paragraph 3 begins a long list of accusations against King George III.	The document claims that colonists attempted peaceful solutions to problems.	The proposal is asserted again.

IN CONGRESS, JULY 4, 1776.

The unanimous Declaration of the thirteen united States of America.

1   When, in the Course of human events, it becomes necessary for one people to dissolve the political bands which have connected them with another, and to assume among the powers of the earth, the separate and equal station to which the laws of nature and of nature's God entitle them, a decent respect to the opinions of mankind requires that they should declare the causes which impel them to the separation.

2   We hold these truths to be self-evident: That all men are created equal; that they are endowed by their Creator with certain unalienable rights; that among these are life, liberty and the pursuit of happiness. That, to secure these rights, governments are instituted among men, deriving their just powers from the consent of the governed; that, whenever any

Proposal:
Jefferson maintains that the drastic solution of declaring independence is justified if the problem is of great magnitude.

Reasons:
The rationale for the proposal is a definition argument. According to Jefferson, the purpose of a government is to ensure the rights of the governed. The British used similar arguments to justify the revolution against King James II in 1688.

form of government becomes destructive of these ends, it is the right of the people to alter or to abolish it, and to institute new Government, laying its foundation on such principles, and organizing its powers in such form, as to them shall seem most likely to effect their safety and happiness. Prudence, indeed, will dictate that governments long established should not be changed for light and transient causes; and accordingly all experience hath shown, that mankind are more disposed to suffer, while evils are sufferable, than to right themselves by abolishing the forms to which they are accustomed. But when a long train of abuses and usurpations, pursuing invariably the same object evinces a design to reduce them under absolute despotism, it is their right, it is their duty, to throw off such government and to provide new guards for their future security. Such has been the patient sufferance of these colonies, and such is now the necessity which constrains them to alter their former systems of government. The history of the present king of Great Britain is a history of repeated injuries and usurpations, all having in direct object the establishment of an absolute tyranny over these States. To prove this, let facts be submitted to a candid world.

3   He has refused his assent to laws, the most wholesome and necessary for the public good.

4   He has forbidden his governors to pass laws of immediate and pressing importance, unless suspended in their operation till his Assent should be obtained, and, when so suspended, he has utterly neglected to attend to them.

5   He has refused to pass other laws for the accommodation of large districts of people, unless those people would relinquish the right of representation in the legislature—a right inestimable to them and formidable to tyrants only.

6   He has called together legislative bodies at places unusual, uncomfortable, and distant from the depository of their public Records, for the sole purpose of fatiguing them into compliance with his measures.

Problem:
The burden for Jefferson is to convince others of the severity of the problem—that life is intolerable under the King. He goes on to detail a long list of complaints. His goal is to prove the need for change rather than to outline how the solution will work.

7   He has dissolved representative houses repeatedly, for opposing with manly firmness his invasions on the rights of the people.

8   He has refused for a long time, after such dissolutions, to cause others to be elected; whereby the legislative powers, incapable of annihilation, have returned to the people at large for their exercise; the State remaining in the mean time exposed to all the dangers of invasion from without, and convulsions within.

9   He has endeavored to prevent the population of these states; for that purpose obstructing the laws for naturalization of foreigners; refusing to pass others to encourage their migrations hither, and raising the conditions of new appropriations of lands.

10   He has obstructed the administration of justice by refusing his assent to laws for establishing judiciary powers.

11   He has made judges dependent on his will alone, for the tenure of their offices, and the amount and payment of their salaries.

12   He has erected a multitude of new offices, and sent hither swarms of officers to harass our people, and eat out their substance.

13   He has kept among us, in times of peace, standing armies without the consent of our legislatures.

14   He has affected to render the military independent of and superior to the civil power.

15   He has combined with others to subject us to a jurisdiction foreign to our constitution, and unacknowledged by our laws; giving his assent to their acts of pretended legislation:

16   For quartering large bodies of armed troops among us;

17   For protecting them, by a mock trial, from punishment for any murders which they should commit on the inhabitants of these States;

18   For cutting off our trade with all parts of the world;

19   For imposing taxes on us without our consent;

20   For depriving us in many cases, of the benefits of trial by jury;

Style:
The legalistic list of charges is made more vivid by the use of metaphors such as "swarms of officers," which likens the British to a plague of insects.

21   For transporting us beyond seas to be tried for pretended offences;

22   For abolishing the free system of English laws in a neighboring province, establishing therein an arbitrary government, and enlarging its boundaries so as to render it at once an example and fit instrument for introducing the same absolute rule into these colonies;

23   For taking away our charters, abolishing our most valuable laws, and altering fundamentally the forms of our governments;

24   For suspending our own legislatures, and declaring themselves invested with power to legislate for us in all cases whatsoever.

25   He has abdicated government here, by declaring us out of his protection and waging war against us.

26   He has plundered our seas, ravaged our coasts, burnt our towns, and destroyed the lives of our people.

27   He is at this time transporting large armies of foreign mercenaries to complete the works of death, desolation and tyranny, already begun with circumstances of cruelty and perfidy scarcely paralleled in the most barbarous ages, and totally unworthy the head of a civilized nation.

28   He has constrained our fellow citizens taken captive on the high seas to bear arms against their country, to become the executioners of their friends and brethren, or to fall themselves by their hands.

29   He has excited domestic insurrections amongst us, and has endeavored to bring on the inhabitants of our frontiers, the merciless Indian savages, whose known rule of warfare is an undistinguished destruction of all ages, sexes and conditions.

30   In every stage of these oppressions we have petitioned for redress in the most humble terms; our repeated petitions have been answered only by repeated injury. A prince, whose character is thus marked by every act which may define a tyrant, is unfit to be the ruler of a free people.

Style:
The strongest charges against the king are placed at the end of the list.

Ethos:
To build credibility Jefferson makes a case that the colonists' frustration with the British government is justified. He argues that the colonists have tried the peaceful approach only to be rebuffed.

31   Nor have we been wanting in attentions to our British brethren. We have warned them from time to time of attempts by their legislature to extend an unwarrantable jurisdiction over us. We have reminded them of the circumstances of our emigration and settlement here. We have appealed to their native justice and magnanimity, and we have conjured them by the ties of our common kindred to disavow these usurpations, which would inevitably interrupt our connections and correspondence. They too have been deaf to the voice of justice and of consanguinity. We must, therefore, acquiesce in the necessity, which denounces our separation, and hold them, as we hold the rest of mankind, enemies in war, in peace, friends.

32   We, therefore, the representatives of the United States of America, in general congress, assembled, appealing to the Supreme Judge of the world for the rectitude of our intentions, do, in the name, and by authority of the good people of these colonies, solemnly publish and declare, that these united colonies are, and of right ought to be free and independent states; that they are absolved from all allegiance to the British crown, and that all political connection between them and the state of Great Britain, is and ought to be totally dissolved; and that as free and independent states, they have full power to levy war, conclude peace, contract alliances, establish commerce, and to do all other acts and things which independent states may of right do. And for the support of this declaration, with a firm reliance on the protection of Divine Providence, we mutually pledge to each other our lives, our fortunes and our sacred honor.

Conclusion:
The proposal is that the colonies no longer have any political connection to Great Britain and possess all the rights of an independent country.

The Doodle Revolutionary's Manifesto

Sunni Brown

Brown is an author, consultant, and international speaker on doodling and visual literacy. "The Doodle Revolutionary's Manifesto" is from her book *The Doodle Revolution: Unlock the Power to Think Differently* (2014). *Fast Company* named her one of the "10 Most Creative People on Twitter" and "100 Most Creative People in Business 2011," and her 2011 TED Talk has received more than one million hits.

Return to these questions after you have finished reading.

Analyzing the Reading

1. Summarize Brown's proposal argument using the diagram on page 425 as a model. What are the main reasons supporting her claim that more of us should doodle?

2. Undoubtedly, Brown's position argument is serious, but some may find humor in the piece. Do you? If so, point out passages that create a humorous tone and examine how Brown creates the tone. Does humor contribute to or detract from Brown's seriousness?

3. Compare Brown's manifesto structure to the *Declaration of Independence*. Identify shared elements. How does she deviate from the structure? What would Brown need to add or revise to transform her manifesto into a more formal proposal argument? What might be gained or lost in doing so? Why?

4. Discuss the audience for this piece. Whom is Brown trying to convince to rise to action? What might you infer about their age group, education, employment, professional status? Whom is the revolution against?

Exploring Ideas and Issues

The word *doodle* first appeared in the seventeenth century, derived from the German word for simpleton or noodle. In fact, "simpleton" was the intended meaning when British troops, prior to the American Revolution, sang "Yankee Doodle Dandy." Nonetheless, doodling has a long distinguished history. Famous doodlers include Thomas Jefferson, John F. Kennedy, Ronald Reagan, both Bill and Hillary Clinton, and Barack Obama. Mathematician Stanislaw Ulam and astronomer Sir Martin Rees doodled explanations of complex concepts. Artist and author doodlers include Michelangelo, daVinci, Emerson, Twain, and Vonnegut. In recent times, doodling's reputation has risen from the random scribbles of simpletons and daydreamers to an effective technique to improve memory, create art, and spark innovative thinking. In a 2010 study at the University of Plymouth, psychologist Jackie Andrade found doodlers recalled more information than did nondoodlers.

1. Create an Infodoodle on a topic of your choice. Search "infodoodle" on the Internet to learn more about the form, the tools, and the process. Then, create an Infodoodle to capture a class or public discussion or lecture.

2. Like the *Declaration of Independence*, Brown's manifesto is grounded in the assertion of a series of "self-evident truths." Choose one of Brown's "self-evident truths," and make it the topic of an analytical research report. What kind of supporting evidence might be used to support the "truth"?

3. Are you a doodler? Write a personal narrative titled "My Life as a Doodler" in which you describe your doodling history and occasions. Reflect on why you might doodle and with what effect. As part of your narrative, share your doodles and analyze them to use as supporting evidence of your reflection. Do your personal experiences align with Brown's self-evident truths?

THE DOODLE REVOLUTIONARY'S MANIFESTO

TO DOODLE

: ~~to dillydally~~
: ~~to monkey around~~
: ~~to make meaningless marks~~
: ~~to do something of little value, substance, or import~~
: ~~to do nothing~~

FALSE.

TO DOODLE

: to make spontaneous marks with your mind and body to help yourself think

TRUE.

We, the Doodlers of every nation, in order to form a more perfect world, establish semantic truth, promote whole-minded learning, provide for the struggling knowledge worker and student, enhance educational well-being, and secure the benefits of the Doodle for ourselves and our posterity, do ordain and establish this Manifesto for Doodlers everywhere.

Contrary to popular belief, **THERE IS NO SUCH THING AS A MINDLESS DOODLE.**

   The very act of creating a Doodle necessarily engages the mind. Doodling IS thinking; it's just thinking in disguise. This Manifesto, therefore, intends to disrupt society's myths that—intentionally or otherwise—conspire to keep the Doodle down. We as Revolutionaries will illuminate the truth about Doodling and set the record straight after decades of misinformation. Because we, the millions of Doodlers around the world and the billions of Doodlers throughout history, know the impressive power of this universal act. And on this day and each day forth shall the rest of the world know, too. No longer will the Doodle live in a house of ill repute. No longer will simple visual language be underestimated, underused, and misunderstood. Forevermore, we acknowledge the

Doodle, in all its varied forms, as a tool for immersive learning. We wield its power deliberately and without restriction, in any learning environment we see fit.

We hold these truths to be self-evident:

✓ That doodling is as native to human beings as walking and talking;

✓ That human beings have been doodling in the sand, in the snow, and on cave walls for more than thirty thousand years;

✓ That we are neurologically wired with an overwhelmingly visual sensory ability;

✓ That doodling ignites four learning modalities—auditory, kinesthetic, reading/ writing, and visual—and dramatically enhances the experience of learning;

✓ That doodling promotes concentration and increases information retention;

✓ That doodling supports deep, creative problem solving, insight, and innovation;

✓ That doodling has been an ever-present tool, a precursor and a catalyst for the emergence of intellectual breakthroughs in science, technology, medicine, architecture, literature, and art;

✓ That doodling is and has been deployed by some of the best and brightest minds in history;

✓ That doodling lives outside of elite realms of high art and design and is a form of expression free and accessible to all.

Because of these truths of the Doodle, we hereby **DECLARE A DOODLE REVOLUTION**. We defy the modern definition of doodling and take the definition into our own hands. What we believe to be a fair and just definition of the Doodle is as follows:

> **to Doodle:** to make spontaneous marks with our minds and bodies in order to support thinking; to use simple visual language to activate the mind's eye, engage multiple learning modalities, and support creativity, problem solving, and innovation.

We believe that education around the power of Doodling is essential for a brighter future, and awareness will necessarily lead to its enhanced use. As Revolutionaries, we have designed an advanced method of applying and deploying the Doodle: Infodoodling.

> **to Infodoodle:** to intentionally track auditory or text-based content and translate it into words and pictures; to use both text- and picture-based language to clarify and communicate concepts; to explore and display complex information using a union of words and pictures, as a solo effort or with a group.

The practice of Infodoodling is for a complex and unpredictable future—one that will warrant knowledge of and proficiency in the building of visual displays. We believe that the opportunity to learn and practice Doodling and Infodoodling should be available to all people, so we will no longer tolerate the crippling of our native Doodling abilities in order to adhere to antiquated perceptions. We insist that the People be shown the value and real-world applications of both techniques.

To reach this lofty goal, we demand that teachers, bosses, and authority figures cease and desist any suspicion and disapproval that stigmatizes Doodling. We assert our belief that Doodling is most appropriate where society perceives it as least appropriate: in situations with high information density and high accountability for learning. Today, we liberate the Doodle and elevate it to its proper place in our world. We take up our pens, pencils, and markers and deploy Doodling—sophisticated and simple—wherever we deem it necessary. We will wield the power of the Doodle, and for this, we will not apologize. We will take the Doodle back and then put it to work.

Viva la Revolución!

I made you a promise at the beginning of this book. I promised that the Doodle Revolution would bring the possibility of higher-order thinking, the prospect of greater insight, the chance for deeper creativity, and the path to better problem solving. When this promise is fulfilled it will be because of you. You chose to explore a space where both hemispheres of your mind—left and right—are awakened. You chose to activate the fuller potential of what's possible. That choice will lift all of us from our myths and misinformation and result in a better future. One day, we'll all look back and marvel at a time when we used to rely almost exclusively on text, numbers, and verbal language at work and at school. Until that day comes, you as a Revolutionary will light the way. You, your tools, and your talent will be the agents of change. The path to visual literacy—a path that contributes to the creative and intellectual advancement of humankind—will be built by brave and noble people, just like you.

Sign the Manifesto: http://sunnibrown.com/doodlerevolution/manifesto/.

Love! Sunni

A Nation of Jailers
Glenn Loury

MyWritingLab™

Glenn C. Loury, a prominent African American intellectual, holds the posts of Merton P. Stoltz Professor of the Social Sciences and Professor of Economics at Brown University. His areas of study include game theory, industrial organization, welfare economics, natural resource economics, and the economics of income distribution. He has also written and spoken extensively on racial issues, with his most recent book being *Ethnicity, Social Mobility, and Public Policy: Comparing the US and the UK* (2005). The following essay appeared in the March 11, 2009, issue of *Cato Unbound*, an online forum of The Cato Institute, which is a public policy think tank "dedicated to the principles of individual liberty, limited government, free markets and peace."

Return to these questions after you have finished reading.

Analyzing the Reading

1. Loury states his thesis at the beginning of the essay, calling it "a preeminent moral challenge for our time." Restate his thesis in your own words.

2. The essay offers statistical evidence for the "truly historic expansion" of the penal system in the United States. What is that evidence? How effectively does it support Loury's thesis?

3. What does Loury say is the current purpose of the penal system? What role does rehabilitation play?

4. Loury talks about a "them" versus "us" mentality. How, in his view, is this responsible for the state of the penal system? What does he say about individual responsibility and societal responsibility? What does he claim are the causes for what he calls the "racially disparate incidence of punishment" in our society?

Exploring Ideas and Issues

One argument against capital punishment is that blacks convicted of essentially the same crime as whites are disproportionately likely to receive the death penalty. Moreover, recently DNA evidence has actually exonerated individuals on death row. Consequently, some observers believe that in the past innocent people, including perhaps a disproportionate number of African Americans, are likely to have been convicted and executed in our legal system.

1. In your view, what should the purposes of incarceration be? List at least three purposes and rank them in order of their value to society, prisoners, prisoners' families, and victims and their families. Write a short essay in which you give reasons for how you prioritized these goals. Remember to include examples to support your choices.

2. According to the author, society has collectively created the conditions that keep African Americans isolated and marginalized. He argues that society bears some responsibility for the actions of African Americans who suffer from those conditions. Do you agree with Loury's assessment of societal versus individual responsibility? Why or why not? Write an essay arguing your view. Give at least two reasons for your thesis and support each reason with personal or researched examples.

3. Stressing statistics about high school dropouts, the article implies a strong connection between lack of education and incarceration: "Inmates in state institutions average fewer than eleven years of schooling." Do some research on the relationship between education and incarceration for a range of races and ethnicities (African Americans, Hispanics, Asians, Native Americans, and whites). How do the rates compare for high school, two-year college, four-year college, and graduate school? Write an essay about your findings. What conclusions can you draw?

A Nation of Jailers

The most challenging problems of social policy in the modern world are never merely technical. In order properly to decide how we should govern ourselves, we must take up questions of social ethics and human values. What manner of people are we Americans? What vision would we affirm, and what example would we set, before the rest of the world? What kind of society would we bequeath to our children? How shall we live? Inevitably, queries such as these lurk just beneath the surface of the great policy debates of the day. So, those who would enter into public argument about what ails our common life need make no apology for speaking in such terms.

It is precisely in these terms that I wish to discuss a preeminent moral challenge for our time—that imprisonment on a massive scale has become one of the central aspects of our nation's social policy toward the poor, powerfully impairing the lives of some of the most marginal of our fellow citizens, especially the poorly educated black and Hispanic men who reside in large numbers in our great urban centers.

The bare facts of this matter—concerning both the scale of incarceration and its racial disparity—have been much remarked upon of late. Simply put, we have become a nation of jailers and, arguably, racist jailers at that. The past four decades have witnessed a truly historic expansion, and transformation, of penal institutions in the United States—at every level of government, and in all regions of the country. We have, by any measure, become a vastly more punitive society. Measured in constant dollars and taking account of all levels of government, spending on corrections and law enforcement in the United States has more than quadrupled over the last quarter century. As a result, the American prison system has grown into a leviathan unmatched in human history. This development should be deeply troubling to anyone who professes to love liberty.

Here, as in other areas of social policy, the United States is a stark international outlier, sitting at the most rightward end of the political spectrum: We imprison at a far higher rate than the other industrial democracies—higher, indeed, than either Russia or China, and vastly higher than any of the countries of Western Europe. According to the International Centre for Prison Studies in London, there were in 2005 some 9 million prisoners in the world; more than 2 million were being held in the United States. With approximately one twentieth of the world's population, America had nearly one fourth of the world's inmates. At more than 700 per 100,000 residents, the U.S. incarceration rate was far greater than our nearest competitors (the Bahamas, Belarus, and Russia, which each have a rate of about 500 per 100,000). Other industrial societies, some of them with big crime problems of their own, were less punitive than we by an order of magnitude: the United States incarcerated at 6.2 times the rate of Canada, 7.8 times the rate of France, and 12.3 times the rate of Japan.

The demographic profile of the inmate population has also been much discussed. In this, too, the U.S. is an international outlier. African Americans and Hispanics, who taken together are about one fourth of the population, account for about two thirds of state prison inmates. Roughly one third of state prisoners were locked up for committing violent offenses, with the remainder being property and drug offenders. Nine in ten are male, and most are impoverished. Inmates in state institutions average fewer than eleven years of schooling.

The extent of racial disparity in imprisonment rates exceeds that to be found in any other arena of American social life: at eight to one, the black to white ratio of male incarceration rates dwarfs the two to one ratio of unemployment rates, the three to one non-marital child bearing ratio, the two to one ratio of infant mortality rates and the one to five ratio of net worth. More black male high school dropouts are in prison than belong to unions or are enrolled in any state or federal social welfare programs. The brute fact of the matter is that the primary contact between black American young adult men and their government is via the police and the penal apparatus. Coercion is the most salient feature of their encounters with the state. According to estimates compiled by sociologist Bruce Western, nearly 60% of black male dropouts born between 1965 and 1969 had spent at least one year in prison before reaching the age of 35.

> **DISPROPORTIONATE INCREASE**
>
> **6.9 million**
> US population under corrective control in 2012
>
> **1.8 million**
> US population under corrective control in 1980
>
> **277%**
> Change in population under corrective control, 1980–2012
>
> **38%**
> Change in US population, 1980–2012

For these men, and the families and communities with which they are associated, the adverse effects of incarceration will extend beyond their stays behind bars. My point is that this is not merely law enforcement policy. It is social policy writ large. And no other country in the world does it quite like we do.

This is far more than a technical issue—entailing more, that is, than the task of finding the most efficient crime control policies. Consider, for instance, that it is not possible to conduct a cost-benefit analysis of our nation's world-historic prison buildup over the past

35 years without implicitly specifying how the costs imposed on the persons imprisoned, and their families, are to be reckoned. Of course, this has not stopped analysts from pronouncing on the purported net benefits to "society" of greater incarceration without addressing that question! Still, how—or, indeed, whether—to weigh the costs born by law-breakers—that is, how (or whether) to acknowledge their humanity—remains a fundamental and difficult question of social ethics. Political discourses in the United States have given insufficient weight to the collateral damage imposed by punishment policies on the offenders themselves, and on those who are knitted together with offenders in networks of social and psychic affiliation.

Whether or not one agrees, two things should be clear: social scientists can have no answers for the question of what weight to put on a "thug's," or his family's, well-being; and a morally defensible public policy to deal with criminal offenders cannot be promulgated without addressing that question. To know whether or not our criminal justice policies comport with our deepest values, we must ask how much additional cost borne by the offending class is justifiable per marginal unit of security, or of peace of mind, for the rest of us. This question is barely being asked, let alone answered, in the contemporary debate.

Nor is it merely the scope of the mass imprisonment state that has expanded so impressively in the United States. The ideas underlying the doing of criminal justice—the superstructure of justifications and rationalizations—have also undergone a sea change. Rehabilitation is a dead letter; retribution is the thing. The function of imprisonment is not to reform or redirect offenders. Rather, it is to keep them away from us. "The prison," writes sociologist David Garland, "is used today as a kind of reservation, a quarantine zone in which purportedly dangerous individuals are segregated in the name of public safety." We have elaborated what are, in effect, a "string of work camps and prisons strung across a vast country housing millions of people drawn mainly from classes and racial groups that are seen as politically and economically problematic." We have, in other words, marched quite a long way down the punitive road, in the name of securing public safety and meting out to criminals their just deserts.

And we should be ashamed of ourselves for having done so. Consider a striking feature of this policy development, one that is crucial to this moral assessment: the ways in which we now deal with criminal offenders in the United States have evolved in recent decades in order to serve expressive and not only instrumental ends. We have wanted to "send a message," and have done so with a vengeance. Yet in the process we have also, in effect, provided an answer for the question: who is to blame for the maladies that beset our troubled civilization? That is, we have constructed a narrative, created scapegoats, assuaged our fears, and indulged our need to feel virtuous about ourselves. We have met the enemy and the enemy, in the now familiar caricature, is them—a bunch of anomic, menacing, morally deviant "thugs." In the midst of this dramaturgy—unavoidably so in America—lurks a potent racial subplot.

This issue is personal for me. As a black American male, a baby-boomer born and raised on Chicago's South Side, I can identify with the plight of the urban poor because I have lived among them. I am related to them by the bonds of social and psychic affiliation. As it happens, I have myself passed through the courtroom, and the jailhouse, on my way along life's journey. I have sat in the visitor's room at a state prison; I have known, personally and intimately, men and women who lived their entire lives with one foot to either side of the law. Whenever I step to a lectern to speak about the growth of imprisonment in our society, I envision voiceless and despairing people who would have me speak on their behalf. Of course, personal biography can carry no authority to compel agreement about public policy. Still, I prefer candor to the false pretense of clinical detachment and scientific objectivity. I am not running for high office; I need not pretend to a cool neutrality that I do not possess. While I recognize that these revelations will discredit me in some quarters, this is a fate I can live with.

So, my racial identity is not irrelevant to my discussion of the subject at hand. But, then, neither is it irrelevant that among the millions now in custody and under state supervision are to be found a vastly disproportionate number of the black and the brown. There is no need to justify injecting race into this discourse, for prisons are the most race-conscious public institutions that we have. No big city police officer is "colorblind" nor, arguably, can any afford to be. Crime and punishment in America have a color—just turn on a television, or open a magazine, or listen carefully to the rhetoric of a political campaign—and you will see what I mean. The fact is that, in this society as in any other, order is maintained by the threat and the use of force. We enjoy our good lives because we are shielded by the forces of law and order upon which we rely to keep the unruly at bay. Yet, in this society to an extent unlike virtually any other, those bearing the heavy burden of order-enforcement belong, in numbers far exceeding their presence in the population at large, to racially defined and historically marginalized groups. Why should this be so? And how can those charged with the supervision of our penal apparatus sleep well at night knowing that it is so?

This punitive turn in the nation's social policy is intimately connected, I would maintain, with public rhetoric about responsibility, dependency, social hygiene, and the reclamation of public order. And such rhetoric, in turn, can be fully grasped only when viewed against the backdrop of America's often ugly and violent racial history: There is a reason why our inclination toward forgiveness and the extension of a second chance to those who have violated our behavioral strictures is so stunted, and why our mainstream political discourses are so bereft of self-examination and searching social criticism. An historical resonance between the stigma of race and the stigma of prison has served to keep alive in our public culture the subordinating social meanings that have always been associated with blackness. Many historians and political scientists—though, of course, not all—agree that the shifting character of race relations over the course of the nineteenth and twentieth centuries helps to explain why the United States is exceptional among democratic industrial societies in the severity of its punitive policy and the paucity of its social-welfare institutions. Put directly and without benefit of euphemism, the racially disparate incidence of punishment in the United States is a morally troubling residual effect of the nation's history of enslavement, disenfranchisement, segregation, and discrimination. It is not merely the accidental accretion of neutral state action, applied to a racially divergent social flux. It is an abhorrent expression of who we Americans are as a people, even now, at the dawn of the twenty-first century.

My recitation of the brutal facts about punishment in today's America may sound to some like a primal scream at this monstrous social machine that is grinding poor black communities to dust. And I confess that these facts do at times leave me inclined to cry out in despair. But my argument is intended to be moral, not existential, and its principal thesis is this: we law-abiding, middle-class Americans have made collective decisions on social and incarceration policy questions, and we benefit from those decisions. That is, we benefit from a system of suffering, rooted in state violence, meted out at our behest. Put differently our society—the society we together have made—first tolerates crime-promoting conditions in our sprawling urban ghettos, and then goes on to act out rituals of punishment against them as some awful form of human sacrifice.

It is a central reality of our time that a wide racial gap has opened up in cognitive skills, the extent of law-abidingness, stability of family relations, and attachment to the work force. This is the basis, many would hold, for the racial gap in imprisonment. Yet I maintain that this gap in human development is, as a historical matter, rooted in political, economic, social, and cultural factors peculiar to this society and reflective of its unlovely racial history. That is to say, it is a societal, not communal or personal, achievement. At the level of the individual case we must, of course, act as if this were not so. There could be no law, and so no civilization, absent the imputation to persons of responsibility for their wrongful acts. But the sum of a million cases, each one rightly judged fairly on its individual merits, may nevertheless constitute a great historic wrong. This is, in my view, now the case in regards to the race and social class disparities that characterize the very punitive policy that we have directed at lawbreakers. And yet, the state does not only deal with individual cases. It also makes policies in the aggregate, and the consequences of these policies are more or less knowable. It is in the making of such aggregate policy judgments that questions of social responsibility arise.

This situation raises a moral problem that we cannot avoid. We cannot pretend that there are more important problems in our society, or that this circumstance is the necessary solution to other, more pressing problems—unless we are also prepared to say that we have turned our backs on the ideal of equality for all citizens and abandoned the principles of justice. We ought to be asking ourselves two questions: Just what manner of people are we Americans? And in light of this, what are our obligations to our fellow citizens—even those who break our laws?

Without trying to make a full-fledged philosophical argument here, I nevertheless wish to gesture—in the spirit of the philosopher John Rawls—toward some answers to these questions. I will not set forth a policy manifesto at this time. What I aim to do is suggest, in a general way, how we ought to be thinking differently about this problem. Specifically, given our nation's history and political culture, I think that there are severe limits to the applicability in this circumstance of a pure ethic of personal responsibility, as the basis for distributing the negative good of punishment in contemporary America. I urge that we shift the boundary toward greater acknowledgment of social responsibility in our punishment policy discourse—even for wrongful acts freely chosen by individual persons. In suggesting this, I am not so much making a "root causes" argument—he did the crime, but only because he had no choice—as I am arguing that the society at large is implicated in his choices because we have acquiesced in structural arrangements which work to our benefit and his detriment, and yet which shape his consciousness and sense of identity in such a way that the choices he makes. We condemn those choices, but they are nevertheless compelling to him. I am interested in the moral implications of what the sociologist Loïc Wacquant has called the "double-sided production of urban marginality." I approach this problem of moral judgment by emphasizing that closed and bounded social structures—like racially homogeneous urban ghettos—create contexts where "pathological" and "dysfunctional" cultural forms emerge, but these forms are not intrinsic to the people caught in these structures. Neither are they independent of the behavior of the people who stand outside of them.

Several years ago, I took time to read some of the nonfiction writings of the great nineteenth century Russian novelist Leo Tolstoy. Toward the end of his life he had become an eccentric pacifist and radical Christian social critic. I was stunned at the force of his arguments. What struck me most was Tolstoy's provocative claim that the core of Christianity lies in Jesus' Sermon on the Mount: You see that fellow over there committing some terrible sin? Well, if you have ever lusted, or allowed jealousy, or envy or hatred to enter your own heart, then you are to be equally condemned! This, Tolstoy claims, is the central teaching of the Christian faith: we're all in the same fix.

Now, without invoking any religious authority, I nevertheless want to suggest that there is a grain of truth in this religious sentiment that is relevant to the problem at hand: That is, while the behavioral pathologies and cultural threats that we see in society—the moral erosions "out there"—the crime, drug addiction, sexually transmitted disease, idleness, violence and all manner of deviance—while these are worrisome, nevertheless, our moral crusade against these evils can take on a pathological dimension of its own. We can become self-righteous, legalistic, ungenerous, stiff-necked, and hypocritical. We can fail to see the beam in our own eye. We can neglect to raise questions of social justice. We can blind ourselves to the close relationship that actually exists between, on the one hand, behavioral pathology in the so-called urban underclass of our country and, on the other hand, society-wide factors—like our greed-driven economy, our worship of the self, our endemic culture of materialism, our vacuous political discourses, our declining civic engagement, and our aversion to sacrificing private gain on behalf of much needed social investments. We can fail to see, in other words, that the problems of the so-called underclass—to which we have reacted with a massive, coercive mobilization—are but an expression, at the bottom of the social hierarchy, of a more profound and widespread moral deviance—one involving all of us.

Taking this position does not make me a moral relativist. I merely hold that, when thinking about the lives of the disadvantaged in our society, the fundamental premise that should guide us is that we are all in this together. Those people languishing in the corners of our society are our people—they are us—whatever may be their race, creed, or country of origin, whether they be the crack-addicted, the HIV-infected, the mentally ill homeless, the juvenile drug sellers, or worse. Whatever the malady, and whatever the offense, we're all in the same fix. We're all in this thing together.

Just look at what we have wrought. We Americans have established what, to many an outside observer, looks like a system of racial caste in the center of our great cities. I refer here to millions of stigmatized, feared, and invisible people. The extent of disparity in the opportunity to achieve their full human potential, as between the children of the middle class and the children of the disadvantaged—a disparity that one takes for granted in America—is virtually unrivaled elsewhere in the industrial, advanced, civilized, free world.

Yet too many Americans have concluded, in effect, that those languishing at the margins of our society are simply reaping what they have sown. Their suffering is seen as having nothing to do with us—as not being evidence of systemic failures that can be corrected through collective action. Thus, as I noted, we have given up on the ideal of rehabilitating criminals, and have settled for simply warehousing them. Thus we accept—despite much rhetoric to the contrary—that it is virtually impossible effectively to educate the children of the poor. Despite the best efforts of good people and progressive institutions—despite the encouraging signs of moral engagement with these issues that I have seen in my students over the years, and that give me hope—despite these things, it remains the case that, speaking of the country as a whole, there is no broadly based demand for reform, no sense of moral outrage, no anguished self-criticism, no public reflection in the face of this massive, collective failure.

The core of the problem is that the socially marginal are not seen as belonging to the same general public body as the rest of us. It therefore becomes impossible to do just about anything with them. At least implicitly, our political community acts as though some are different from the rest and, because of their culture—because of their bad values, their self-destructive behavior, their malfeasance, their criminality, their lack of responsibility, their unwillingness to engage in hard work—they deserve their fate.

But this is quite wrongheaded. What we Americans fail to recognize—not merely as individuals, I stress, but as a political community—is that these ghetto enclaves and marginal spaces of our cities, which are the source of most prison inmates, are products of our own making: Precisely because we do not want those people near us, we have structured the space in our urban environment so as to keep them away from us. Then, when they fester in their isolation and their marginality, we hypocritically point a finger, saying in effect: "Look at those people. They threaten the civilized body. They must therefore be expelled, imprisoned, controlled." It is not we who must take social responsibility to reform our institutions but, rather, it is they who need to take personal responsibility for their wrongful acts. It is not we who must set our collective affairs aright, but they who must get their individual acts together. This posture, I suggest, is inconsistent with the attainment of a just distribution of benefits and burdens in society.

Civic inclusion has been the historical imperative in Western political life for 150 years. And yet—despite our self-declared status as a light unto the nations, as a beacon of hope to freedom-loving peoples everywhere—despite these lofty proclamations, which were belied by images from the rooftops in flooded New Orleans in September 2005, and are contradicted by our overcrowded prisons—the fact is that this historical project of civic inclusion is woefully incomplete in these United States.

At every step of the way, reactionary political forces have declared the futility of pursuing civic inclusion. Yet, in every instance, these forces have been proven wrong. At one time or another, they have derided the inclusion of women, landless peasants, former serfs and slaves, or immigrants more fully in the civic body. Extending to them the franchise, educating their children, providing health and social welfare to them has always been controversial. But this has been the direction in which the self-declared "civilized" and wealthy nations have been steadily moving since Bismarck, since the revolutions of 1848 and 1870, since the American Civil War with its Reconstruction Amendments, since the Progressive Era and through the New Deal on to the Great Society. This is why we have a progressive federal income tax and an estate tax in this country, why we feed, clothe and house the needy, why we (used to) worry about investing in our cities' infrastructure, and in the human capital of our people. What the brutal facts about punishment in today's America show is that this American project of civic inclusion remains incomplete. Nowhere is that incompleteness more evident than in the prisons and jails of America. And this as yet unfulfilled promise of American democracy reveals a yawning chasm between an ugly and uniquely American reality, and our nation's exalted image of herself.

Bound to Burn

Peter Huber

Peter Huber is a lawyer, an author, and senior fellow at the Manhattan Institute, a conservative "think tank." He is the author of many books, including *Hard Green: Saving the Environment from the Environmentalists* (2000), and *The Bottomless Well* (2010), coauthored with Mark Mills. Huber has also published articles in scholarly journals and magazines such as the *Harvard Law Review, Science, The Wall Street Journal, Reason*, and *National Review*. "Bound to Burn" appeared in 2009 in *City Journal*, published by the Manhattan Institute.

Return to these questions after you have finished reading.

Analyzing the Reading

1. What is an "indulgence" (paragraph 1)? How does it connect to our need for forgiveness of "carbon sins"?

2. According to Huber, why is it impossible for the "rich" West to stop the carbon emissions coming from the world's five billion poor? Does he seem to think there is nothing we can do to stop global warming from carbon emissions?

3. Why are carbon-based fuels so much cheaper and easier to use than greener alternatives? What does the expense of green energy mean in our global effort to reduce carbon emissions?

4. What is Huber's view of "green" advocates and of the people who control most of the world's carbon-based fuels? Identify passages and words he uses that reveal his viewpoint.

Exploring Ideas and Issues

Huber makes several references to the Kyoto Protocol. The Kyoto Protocol, initially adopted in December 1997, is an international agreement linked to the United Nations Framework Convention on Climate Change. The major feature of the Kyoto Protocol is that it sets binding targets for industrialized countries and the European community for reducing greenhouse gas emissions. By 2010, 191 countries signed and ratified the protocol. Read more about the Kyoto Protocol at http://unfccc.int/kyoto_protocol/items/2830.php.

1. The United States is one of the few Western countries that did not ratify the treaty. After reading more about the Kyoto Protocol, write a short essay expressing your own view on why the United States should or should not ratify it. You may wish to reference points Huber makes in his essay in your response.

2. In this essay, Huber notes that the Kyoto protocol has "hurt the anti-carbon mission far more than carbon zealots seem to grasp." How effective has the protocol been on reducing carbon emissions? Explain.

3. Huber observes that the United States was right to "steer clear" of unenforceable treaties like the Kyoto Protocol. Why is it unenforceable? Based on Huber's essay and what you research about the treaty, write an essay about the future of this treaty.

Bound to Burn

Humanity will keep spewing carbon into the atmosphere, but good policy can help sink it back into the earth.

Like medieval priests, today's carbon brokers will sell you an indulgence that forgives your carbon sins. It will run you about $500 for 5 tons of forgiveness—about how much the typical American needs every year. Or about $2,000 a year for a typical four-person household. Your broker will spend the money on such things as reducing methane emissions from hog farms in Brazil.

But if you really want to make a difference, you must send a check large enough to forgive the carbon emitted by four poor Brazilian households, too—because they're not going to do it themselves. To cover all five households, then, send $4,000. And you probably forgot to send in a check last year, and you might forget again in the future, so you'd best make it an even $40,000, to take care of a decade right now. If you decline to write your own check while insisting that to save the world we must ditch the carbon, you are just burdening your already sooty soul with another ton of self-righteous hypocrisy. And you can't possibly afford what it will cost to forgive that.

If making carbon this personal seems rude, then think globally instead. During the presidential race, Barack Obama was heard to remark that he would bankrupt the coal industry. No one can doubt Washington's power to bankrupt almost anything—in the United States. But China is adding 100 gigawatts of coal-fired electrical capacity a year. That's another whole United States' worth of coal consumption added every three years, with no stopping point in sight. Much of the rest of the developing world is on a similar path.

Cut to the chase. We rich people can't stop the world's 5 billion poor people from burning the couple of trillion tons of cheap carbon that they have within easy reach. We can't even make any durable dent in global emissions—because emissions from the developing world are growing too fast, because the other 80 percent of humanity desperately needs cheap energy, and because we and they are now part of the same global economy. What we can do, if we're foolish enough, is let carbon worries send our jobs and industries to their shores, making them grow even faster, and their carbon emissions faster still.

We don't control the global supply of carbon.

Ten countries ruled by nasty people control 80 percent of the planet's oil reserves—about 1 trillion barrels, currently worth about $40 trillion. If $40 trillion worth of gold were located where most of the oil is, one could only scoff at any suggestion that we might somehow persuade the nasty people to leave the wealth buried. They can lift most of their oil at a cost well under $10 a barrel. They will drill. They will pump. And they will find buyers. Oil is all they've got.

Poor countries all around the planet are sitting on a second, even bigger source of carbon—almost a trillion tons of cheap, easily accessible coal. They also control most of the planet's third great carbon reservoir—the rain forests and soil. They will keep squeezing the carbon out of cheap coal, and cheap forest, and cheap soil, because that's all they've got. Unless they can find something even cheaper. But they won't—not any time in the foreseeable future.

We no longer control the demand for carbon, either. The 5 billion poor—the other 80 percent—are already the main problem, not us. Collectively, they emit 20 percent more greenhouse gas than we do. We burn a lot more carbon individually, but they have a lot more children. Their fecundity has eclipsed our gluttony, and the gap is now widening fast. China, not the United States, is now the planet's largest emitter. Brazil, India, Indonesia, South Africa, and others are in hot pursuit. And these countries have all made it clear that they aren't interested in spending what money they have on low-carb diets. It is idle to argue, as some have done, that global warming can be solved—decades hence—at a cost of 1 to 2 percent of the global economy. Eighty percent of the global population hasn't signed on to pay more than 0 percent.

Accepting this last, self-evident fact, the Kyoto Protocol divides the world into two groups. The roughly 1.2 billion citizens of industrialized countries are expected to reduce their emissions. The other 5 billion—including both China and India, each of which is about as populous as the entire Organisation for Economic Co-operation and Development—aren't. These numbers alone guarantee that humanity isn't going to reduce global emissions at any point in the foreseeable future—unless it does it the old-fashioned way, by getting poorer. But the current recession won't last forever, and the long-term trend is clear. Their populations and per-capita emissions are rising far faster than ours could fall under any remotely plausible carbon-reduction scheme.

Might we simply buy their cooperation? Various plans have circulated for having the rich pay the poor to stop burning down rain forests and to lower greenhouse-gas emissions from primitive agricultural practices. But taking control of what belongs to someone else ultimately means buying it. Over the long term, we would in effect have to buy up a large fraction of all the world's forests, soil, coal, and oil—and then post guards to make sure that poor people didn't sneak in and grab all the carbon anyway. Buying off people just doesn't fly when they outnumber you four to one.

Might we instead manage to give the world something cheaper than carbon? The moon-shot law of economics says yes, of course we can. If we just put our minds to it, it will happen. Atom bomb, moon landing, ultracheap energy—all it takes is a triumph of political will.

Really? For the very poorest, this would mean beating the price of the free rain forest that they burn down to clear land to plant a subsistence crop. For the slightly less poor, it would mean beating the price of coal used to generate electricity at under 3 cents per kilowatt-hour.

And with one important exception, which we will return to shortly, no carbon-free fuel or technology comes remotely close to being able to do that. Fossil fuels are extremely cheap because geological forces happen to have created large deposits of these dense forms of energy in accessible places. Find a mountain of coal, and you can just shovel gargantuan amounts of energy into the boxcars.

Shoveling wind and sun is much, much harder. Windmills are now 50-story skyscrapers. Yet one windmill generates a piddling 2 to 3 megawatts. A jumbo jet needs 100 megawatts to get off the ground; Google is building 100-megawatt server farms. Meeting New York City's total energy demand would require 13,000 of those skyscrapers spinning at top speed, which would require scattering about 50,000 of them across the state, to make sure that you always hit enough windy spots. To answer the howls of green protest that inevitably greet realistic engineering estimates like these, note that real-world systems must be able to meet peak, not average, demand; that reserve margins are essential; and that converting electric power into liquid or gaseous fuels to power the existing transportation and heating systems would entail substantial losses. What was Mayor Bloomberg thinking when he suggested that he might just tuck windmills into Manhattan? Such thoughts betray a deep ignorance about how difficult it is to get a lot of energy out of sources as thin and dilute as wind and sun.

It's often suggested that technology improvements and mass production will sharply lower the cost of wind and solar. But engineers have pursued these technologies for decades, and while costs of some components have fallen, there is no serious prospect of costs plummeting and performance soaring as they have in our laptops and cell phones. When you replace conventional with renewable energy, everything gets bigger, not smaller—and bigger costs more, not less. Even if solar cells themselves were free, solar power would remain very expensive because of the huge structures and support systems required to extract large amounts of electricity from a source so weak that it takes hours to deliver a tan.

This is why the (few) greens ready to accept engineering and economic reality have suddenly emerged as avid proponents of nuclear power. In the aftermath of the Three Mile Island accident—which didn't harm anyone, and wouldn't even have damaged the reactor core if the operators had simply kept their hands off the switches and let the automatic safety systems do their job—ostensibly green antinuclear activists unwittingly boosted U.S. coal consumption by about 400 million tons per year. The United States would be in compliance with the Kyoto Protocol today if we could simply undo their handiwork and conjure back into existence the nuclear plants that were in the pipeline in nuclear power's heyday. Nuclear power is fantastically compact, and—as America's nuclear navy, several commercial U.S. operators, France, Japan, and a handful of other countries have convincingly established—it's both safe and cheap wherever engineers are allowed to get on with it.

But getting on with it briskly is essential, because costs hinge on the huge, up-front capital investment in the power plant. Years of delay between the capital investment and when it starts earning a return are ruinous. Most of the developed world has made nuclear power unaffordable by surrounding it with a regulatory process so sluggish and unpredictable that no one will pour a couple of billion dollars into a new plant, for the good reason that no one knows when (or even if) the investment will be allowed to start making money.

And countries that don't trust nuclear power on their own soil must hesitate to share the technology with countries where you never know who will be in charge next year, or what he might decide to do with his nuclear toys. So much for the possibility that cheap nuclear power might replace carbon-spewing sources of energy in the developing world. Moreover, even India and China, which have mastered nuclear technologies, are deploying far more new coal capacity.

Remember, finally, that most of the cost of carbon-based energy resides not in the fuels but in the gigantic infrastructure of furnaces, turbines, and engines. Those costs are sunk, which means that carbon-free alternatives—with their own huge, attendant, front-end capital costs—must be cheap enough to beat carbon fuels that already have their infrastructure in place. That won't happen in our lifetimes.

Another argument commonly advanced is that getting over carbon will, nevertheless, be comparatively cheap, because it will get us over oil, too—which will impoverish our enemies and save us a bundle at the Pentagon and the Department of Homeland Security. But uranium aside, the most economical substitute for oil is, in fact, electricity generated with coal. Cheap coal-fired electricity has been, is, and will continue to be a substitute for oil, or a substitute for natural gas, which can in turn substitute for oil. By sharply boosting the cost of coal electricity, the war on carbon will make us more dependent on oil, not less.

The first place where coal displaces oil is in the electric power plant itself. When oil prices spiked in the early 1980s, U.S. utilities quickly switched to other fuels, with coal leading the pack; the coal-fired plants now being built in China, India, and other developing countries are displacing diesel generators. More power plants burning coal to produce cheap electricity can also mean less natural gas used to generate electricity. And less used for industrial, commercial, and residential heating, welding, and chemical processing, as these users switch to electrically powered alternatives. The gas that's freed up this way can then substitute for diesel fuel in heavy trucks, delivery vehicles, and buses. And coal-fired electricity will eventually begin displacing gasoline, too, as soon as plug-in hybrid cars start recharging their batteries directly from the grid.

To top it all, using electricity generated in large part by coal to power our passenger cars would lower carbon emissions—even in Indiana, which generates 75 percent of its electricity with coal. Big power plants are so much more efficient than the gasoline engines in our cars that a plug-in hybrid car running on electricity supplied by Indiana's current grid still ends up more carbon-frugal than comparable cars burning gasoline in a conventional engine under the hood. Old-guard energy types have been saying this for decades. In a major report released last March, the World Wildlife Fund finally concluded that they were right all along.

But true carbon zealots won't settle for modest reductions in carbon emissions when fat targets beckon. They see coal-fired electricity as the dragon to slay first. Huge, stationary sources can't run or hide, and the cost of doing without them doesn't get rung up in plain view at the gas pump. California, Pennsylvania, and other greener-than-thou states have made flatlining electricity consumption the linchpin of their war on carbon. That is the one certain way to halt the displacement of foreign oil by cheap, domestic electricity.

The oil-coal economics come down to this. Per unit of energy delivered, coal costs about one-fifth as much as oil—but contains one-third more carbon. High carbon taxes (or tradable permits, or any other economic equivalent) sharply narrow the price gap between oil and the one fuel that can displace it worldwide, here and now.

The oil nasties will celebrate the green war on carbon as enthusiastically as the coal industry celebrated the green war on uranium 30 years ago.

The other 5 billion are too poor to deny these economic realities. For them, the price to beat is 3-cent coal-fired electricity. China and India won't trade 3-cent coal for 15-cent wind or 30-cent solar. As for us, if we embrace those economically frivolous alternatives on our own, we will certainly end up doing more harm than good.

By pouring money into anything-but-carbon fuels, we will lower demand for carbon, making it even cheaper for the rest of the world to buy and burn. The rest will use cheaper energy to accelerate their own economic growth. Jobs will go where energy is cheap, just as they go where labor is cheap. Manufacturing and heavy industry require a great deal of energy, and in a global economy, no competitor can survive while paying substantially more for an essential input. The carbon police acknowledge the problem and talk vaguely of using tariffs and such to address it. But carbon is far too deeply embedded in the global economy, and materials, goods, and services move and intermingle far too freely, for the customs agents to track.

Consider your next Google search. As noted in a recent article in *Harper's*, "Google . . . and its rivals now head abroad for cheaper, often dirtier power." Google itself (the "don't be evil" company) is looking to set up one of its electrically voracious server farms at a site in Lithuania, "disingenuously described as being near a hydroelectric dam." But Lithuania's grid is 0.5 percent hydroelectric and 78 percent nuclear. Perhaps the company's next huge farm will be "near" the Three Gorges Dam in China, built to generate over three times as much power as our own Grand Coulee Dam in Washington State. China will be happy to play along, while it quietly plugs another coal plant into its grid a few pylons down the line. All the while, of course, Google will maintain its low-energy headquarters in California, a state that often boasts of the wise regulatory policies—centered, one is told, on efficiency and conservation—that have made it such a frugal energy user. But in fact, sky-high prices have played the key role, curbing internal demand and propelling the flight from California of power plants, heavy industries, chip fabs, server farms, and much else.

So the suggestion that we can lift ourselves out of the economic doldrums by spending lavishly on exceptionally expensive new sources of energy is absurd. "Green jobs" means Americans paying other Americans to chase carbon while the rest of the world builds new power plants and factories. And the environmental consequences of outsourcing jobs, industries, and carbon to developing countries are beyond dispute. They use energy far less efficiently than we do, and they remain almost completely oblivious to environmental impacts, just as we were in our own first century of industrialization. A massive transfer of carbon, industry, and jobs from us to them will raise carbon emissions, not lower them.

The grand theory for how the developed world can unilaterally save the planet seems to run like this. We buy time for the planet by rapidly slashing our own emissions. We do so by developing carbon-free alternatives even cheaper than carbon. The rest of the world will then quickly adopt these alternatives, leaving most of its trillion barrels of oil and trillion tons of coal safely buried, most of the rain forests standing, and most of the planet's carbon-rich soil undisturbed. From end to end, however, this vision strains credulity.

Perhaps it's the recognition of that inconvenient truth that has made the anti-carbon rhetoric increasingly apocalyptic. Coal trains have been analogized to boxcars headed for Auschwitz. There is talk of the extinction of all humanity. But then, we have heard such things before. It is indeed quite routine, in environmental discourse, to frame choices as involving potentially infinite costs on the green side of the ledger. If they really are infinite, no reasonable person can quibble about spending mere billions, or even trillions, on the dollar side, to dodge the apocalyptic bullet.

Thirty years ago, the case against nuclear power was framed as the "Zero-Infinity Dilemma." The risks of a meltdown might be vanishingly small, but if it happened, the costs would be infinitely large, so we should forget about uranium. Computer models demonstrated that meltdowns were highly unlikely and that the costs of a meltdown, should one occur, would be manageable—but greens scoffed: huge computer models couldn't be trusted. So we ended up burning much more coal. The software shoe is on the other foot now; the machines that said nukes wouldn't melt now say that the ice caps will. Warming skeptics scoff in turn, and can quite plausibly argue that a planet is harder to model than a nuclear reactor. But that's a detail. From a rhetorical perspective, any claim that the infinite, the apocalypse, or the Almighty supports your side of the argument shuts down all further discussion.

To judge by actions rather than words, however, few people and almost no national governments actually believe in the infinite rewards of exorcising carbon from economic life. Kyoto has hurt the anti-carbon mission far more than carbon zealots seem to grasp. It has proved only that with carbon, governments will say and sign anything—and then do less than nothing. The United States should steer well clear of such treaties because they are unenforceable, routinely ignored, and therefore worthless.

If we're truly worried about carbon, we must instead approach it as if the emissions originated in an annual eruption of Mount Krakatoa. Don't try to persuade the volcano to sign a treaty promising to stop. Focus instead on what might be done to protect and promote the planet's carbon sinks—the systems that suck carbon back out of the air and bury it. Green plants currently pump 15 to 20 times as much carbon out of the atmosphere as humanity releases into it—that's the pump that put all that carbon underground in the first place, millions of years ago. At present, almost all of that plant-captured carbon is released back into the atmosphere within a year or so by animal consumers. North America, however, is currently sinking almost two-thirds of its carbon emissions back into prairies and forests that were originally leveled in the 1800s but are now recovering. For the next 50 years or so, we should focus on promoting better land use and reforestation worldwide. Beyond that, weather and the oceans naturally sink about one-fifth of total fossil-fuel emissions. We should also investigate large-scale options for accelerating the process of ocean sequestration.

Carbon zealots despise carbon-sinking schemes because, they insist, nobody can be sure that the sunk carbon will stay sunk. Yet everything they propose hinges on the assumption that carbon already sunk by nature in what are now hugely valuable deposits of oil and coal can be kept sunk by treaty and imaginary cheaper-than-carbon alternatives. This, yet again, gets things backward. We certainly know how to improve agriculture to protect soil, and how to grow new trees, and how to maintain existing forests, and we can almost certainly learn how to mummify carbon and bury it back in the earth or the depths of the oceans, in ways that neither man nor nature will disturb. It's keeping nature's black gold sequestered from humanity that's impossible.

If we do need to do something serious about carbon, the sequestration of carbon after it's burned is the one approach that accepts the growth of carbon emissions as an inescapable fact of the twenty-first century. And it's the one approach that the rest of the world can embrace, too, here and now, because it begins with improving land use, which can lead directly and quickly to greater prosperity. If, on the other hand, we persist in building green bridges to nowhere, we will make things worse, not better. Good intentions aren't enough. Turned into ineffectual action, they can cost the earth and accelerate its ruin at the same time.

Should Pandas Be Left to Face Extinction?

Chris Packham and Mark Wright

In September 2009, the well-known British naturalist, photographer, and writer Chris Packham created an international furor when during a radio interview he proposed that giant pandas ought to be allowed to go extinct. A fierce advocate for nature and wildlife, he nevertheless contends that "T-shirt animals" like pandas get far too much attention and draw resources from far more critical environmental concerns. On September 23, 2009, the British newspaper The *Guardian* carried a debate between Packham and Mark Wright, a leading scientist for the World Wide Fund for Nature.

Return to these questions after you have finished reading.

Analyzing the Reading

1. Packham argues that we should simply allow pandas to become extinct. List at least three reasons he gives for his point of view.

2. Wright argues that we should do our best not to allow pandas to become extinct. List at least three reasons he gives for his point of view.

3. Both debaters acknowledge points made by the other person. What effect does this strategy have on the reader?

4. To what extent do each person's arguments rely on *logos, ethos*, and *pathos*? Explain.

Exploring Ideas and Issues

Conservation of wildlife and wild habitats is a major concern of our time. It has drawn together ecologists and other scientists, as well as hunters, sport fishermen, organic farmers, and recreational users of the natural world, in what can be seen as an unlikely alliance. Yet the issues remain complex and not easily resolved.

1. Whose arguments—Packham's or Wright's—do you find more convincing? Why? Write a short essay explaining your view. Include examples from both debaters.

2. Both debaters concede that the panda attracts attention and sympathy while other animals, such as the river dolphin, do not. How is using attractive animals like pandas and tigers to gain support similar, or not similar, to using celebrities to sell a product? Write a short essay in which you defend or criticize the practice of using animals in this way.

3. Packham says, "I'm not trying to play God; I'm playing God's accountant." Do we have an obligation to save the giant panda and other endangered wildlife at all costs? What is the nature of that obligation? Write a short essay in which you argue yes or no, giving at least three reasons for your point of view.

4. Do some research on conservation issues in the United States. Choose one issue—for example, the forestry and logging practice of clearcutting. Write an essay in which you compare viewpoints of at least two competing interests—commercial, environmentalist, agricultural, and so on. If possible, include a current proposal aimed at reconciling these viewpoints.

SHOULD PANDAS BE LEFT TO FACE EXTINCTION?

Yes, says Chris Packham

I don't want the panda to die out. I want species to stay alive—that's why I get up in the morning. I don't even kill mosquitoes or flies. So if pandas can survive, that would be great. But let's face it: conservation, both nationally and globally, has a limited amount of resources, and I think we're going to have to make some hard, pragmatic choices.

A giant panda, an example of what Chris Packham calls "T-shirt animals"

The truth is, pandas are extraordinarily expensive to keep going. We spend millions and millions of pounds on pretty much this one species, and a few others, when we know that the best thing we could do would be to look after the world's biodiversity hotspots with greater care. Without habitat, you've got nothing. So maybe if we took all the cash we spend on pandas and just bought rainforest with it, we might be doing a better job.

Of course, it's easier to raise money for something fluffy. Charismatic megafauna like the panda do appeal to people's emotional side, and attract a lot of public attention. They are emblematic of what I would call single-species conservation: i.e., a focus on one animal. This approach began in the 1970s with Save the Tiger, Save the Panda, Save the Whale, and so on, and it is now out of date. I think pandas have had a valuable role in raising the profile of conservation, but perhaps "had" is the right word.

Panda conservationists may stand up and say, "It's a flagship species. We're also conserving Chinese forest, where there is a whole plethora of other things." And when that works, I'm not against it. But we have to accept that some species are stronger than others. The panda is a species of bear that has gone herbivorous, and that eats a type of food that isn't all that nutritious, and that dies out sporadically. It is susceptible to various diseases, and, up until recently, it has been almost impossible to breed in captivity. They've also got a very restricted range, which is ever decreasing, due to encroachment on their habitat by the Chinese population. Perhaps the panda was already destined to run out of time. Extinction is very much a part of life on earth. And we are going to have to get used to it in the next few years because climate change is going to result in all sorts of disappearances. The last large mammal extinction was another animal in China—the Yangtze river dolphin, which looked like a worn-out piece of pink soap with piggy eyes and was never going to make it on to anyone's T-shirt. If that had appeared beautiful to us, then I doubt very much that it would be extinct. But it vanished, because it was pig-ugly and swam around in a river where no one saw it. And now, sadly, it has gone for ever.

I'm not trying to play God; I'm playing God's accountant. I'm saying we won't be able to save it all, so let's do the best we can. And at the moment I don't think our strategies are best placed to do that. We should be focusing our conservation endeavours on biodiversity hotspots, spreading our net more widely and looking at good-quality habitat maintenance in order to preserve as much of the life as we possibly can, using hard science to make educated decisions as to which species are essential to a community's maintenance. It may well be that we can lose the cherries from the cake. But you don't want to lose the substance. Save the Rainforest, or Save the Kalahari: that would be better.

No, says Mark Wright

You are reading this because it is about giant pandas. We could have this argument about the frogs of the rainforest and the issues would be identical, but the ability to get people's attention would be far lower. So in that sense, yes, you could argue that conservationists capitalize on the panda's appeal.

And, to be fair, I can understand where Chris Packham is coming from. Everywhere you look on this planet there are issues to be addressed, and we have finite resources. So we do make really horrible choices. But nowadays, almost exclusively, when people work in conservation they focus on saving habitats.

Chris has talked about pandas being an evolutionary cul-de-sac, and it's certainly unusual for a carnivore to take up herbivory. But there are many, many other species that live in a narrowly defined habitat. When he says that if you leave them be, they will die out, that's simply not true. If we don't destroy their habitat they will just chunter along in the same way that they have for the thousands of years.

And besides, in terms of its biodiversity and the threats it faces, I think that the part of China where pandas live should be on the preservation list anyway. The giant panda shares its habitat with the red panda, golden monkeys, and various birds that are found nowhere else in the world. The giant panda's numbers are increasing in the wild, so I don't see them dying out, and I haven't heard anything to suggest that other biodiversity isn't thriving equally.

It is true, though, that there some cases where preserving an animal is not the best use of resources. If you asked 100 conservationists—even at the World Wide Fund—you would probably get 90 different answers, but look at what happened with the northern white rhino in Africa, which we're pretty sure has died out. We lament its loss. But at the same time it had gotten to the stage where the likelihood of success was at a critically low level. If you were doing a battlefield triage system, the rhino would probably have had to be a casualty.

Otherwise, charismatic megafauna can be extremely useful. Smaller creatures often don't need a big habitat to live in, so in conservation terms it's better to go for something further up the food chain, because then by definition you are protecting a much larger area, which in turn encompasses the smaller animals.

And of course they are an extraordinarily good vehicle for the messages we want to put out on habitat conservation. Look at Borneo, where you instantly think of the orangutans. In the southern oceans, you think of the blue whale. Then there are polar bears in the north. There are things you pull out from the picture because people can relate to them. And it does make a difference.

Connecting the City
San Francisco Bicycle Coalition

MyWritingLab™

The San Francisco Bicycle Coalition (SFBC) is a nonprofit public organization that aims to "transform San Francisco's streets and neighborhoods into more livable and safe places by promoting the bicycle for everyday transportation." Currently, the SFBC's primary goal is creating a citywide network of bike lanes that connect every neighborhood in San Francisco. Many citizens of San Francisco have embraced the project, and the coalition claims over 12,000 dues-paying members.

Return to these questions after you have finished reading.

Analyzing the Reading

1. What reasons are given for creating more bikeways in San Francisco?

2. What action does the information sheet ask the viewer to do? Is it clear to the reader?

3. If you received this information sheet in your mailbox or saw it in a newspaper or magazine, how likely would you be to stop and read it? Where would you expect to see it? Explain.

4. Examine the way this information sheet is designed. Where does your eye look first? Second? Why do you think the sheet was designed this way?

Exploring and Writing

The Netherlands is one of the most bike-friendly countries in the world, with a majority of the population regularly using bicycles as their primary mode of transportation. The country is well equipped with a network of cycle paths that reaches all parts of the nation. These "cycleways" have their own sets of rules including traffic signals/lights, tunnels, and lanes. Children begin cycling to school around the age of 8 and grow up with an appreciation and understanding of the traffic rules that govern cycling. The sheer number of cyclists has created a social structure in which the needs of cyclists come before the needs of motorists. In fact, auto insurers consider the driver to always be at fault in a collision with a bicyclist, making drivers extra careful driving where cyclists are also present.

1. If you were given the option of cycling on safe bike paths in your city or town, would you use a bicycle as your primary means of transportation?

2. The Netherlands is a very old country, but it redesigned the streets of most of its towns and many of its highways to accommodate bicycles. Do you think your city or town could adopt a similar model? Why or why not?

3. Write an essay exploring the multiple benefits of incorporating cycling path networks in urban planning. Include the social, ecological, financial, and personal benefits in your evaluation. Conversely, you could write an essay exploring why incorporating a cycling path network would not benefit your city or town.

CONNECTING THE CITY

Crosstown Bikeways
for Everyone!

What is Connecting the City?

Connecting the City addresses the question of how to make San Francisco a city that is easy to shop, live, work and play in while also preserving our unique neighborhoods and commercial districts. By designing our city's bike network for everyone, from an eight-year-old child to an eighty-year-old grandmother, we can provide inviting and safe door-to-door access to shop, commute and play by bicycle. Already, seven in 10 San Franciscans rode a bike last year thanks to improvements like the Market Street separated bike lanes and events like Sunday Streets — it's clear that more San Franciscans want to get around by bike.

Connecting the City builds on this demand and envisions the year 2020 when 100 miles of crosstown bikeways will help a growing population of San Francisco residents and visitors bike more often, relieving our crowded roadways and strained transit system. Elegantly designed bikeways that are physically separated from vehicles will help everyone from your boss, your neighbor's child or your mother-in-law to feel comfortable and safe biking on San Francisco streets. We are already working towards our first ambitious goal, to complete the Bay to Beach bikeway route by 2012 to showcase the comfort, safety and freedom of *Connecting the City*'s bikeways. Learn more about the bikeway routes.

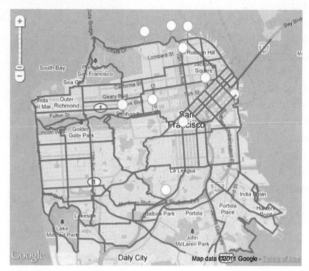

More Stories

Ask Mayor Lee for crosstown bikeways to connect the city

BAY TO BEACH   CONNECTING THE CITY

Goals

2011: Three continuous miles of bikeway

We will achieve this by getting 1.5 miles of separated bikeway on the Bay to Beach route on JFK Drive by May 2011, and connecting it with a bikeway on Fell and Oak streets and the traffic-calmed streets of the Wiggle route in the lower Haight by December 2011.

2011: Improvements to Market Street

We are already working to enhance our city's busiest bicycling street by: filling in the gaps in the bikeway between Octavia Boulevard and Eighth Street; enhancing the required right turn at Sixth Street by including right-turn arrows for drivers and a colored channel for people bicycling just south of the transit boarding island; trialing a "bike boardwalk" in the mid-Market area using Parklet technology to leverage the unused sidewalk edge and adding a new, flush surface to create a fully separated, continuous, raised green bikeway.

2012: First continuous, crosstown bikeway

A completed Bay to Beach route will give more people of all ages the confidence to bicycle more often and will be a great demonstration of a comfortable, safe and inviting bikeway.

2015: 25 miles of bikeway

The Bay to Beach, Bay Trail and North-South bikeways are complete making San Francisco an easier place to shop, work, live and play.

How to Write a Proposal Argument

These steps for the process of writing an argument for change may not progress as neatly as this chart might suggest. Writing is not an assembly-line process.

As you write and revise, imagine that you are in a conversation with an audience that contains people who both agree and disagree with you. Think about what you would say to both and speak to these diverse readers.

1 IDENTIFY THE PROBLEM

- Read your assignment carefully and note exactly what you are being asked to do.

- Identify the problem, what causes it, and whom it affects.

- Do background research on what has been written about the problem and what solutions have been attempted.

- Describe what has been done or not done to address the problem.

- Make a claim advocating a specific change or course of action. Put the claim in this form: "We should (or should not) do ___."

2 PROPOSE YOUR SOLUTION

- State your solution as specifically as you can.

- Consider other solutions and describe why your solution is better.

- Examine if the solution will have enough money and support to be implemented.

- Analyze your potential readers. How interested will your readers be in this problem? How would your solution benefit them directly and indirectly?

3
WRITE A DRAFT

- Define the problem. Give the background your readers will need.

- Discuss other possible solutions.

- Present your solution. Explain exactly how it will work, how it will be accomplished, and if anything like it has been tried elsewhere.

- Argue that your proposal will work. Address any possible arguments that your solution will not work.

- Describe the positive consequences of your solution and the negative consequences that can be avoided.

- Conclude with a call for action. Be specific about exactly what readers need to do.

- Write a title that will interest readers.

- Include any neccessary images, tables, or graphics.

4
REVISE, REVISE, REVISE

- Recheck that your proposal fulfills the assignment.

- Make sure that your proposal claim is clear and focused.

- Add detail or further explanation about the problem.

- Add detail or further explanation about how your solution addresses the problem.

- Make sure you have considered other solutions and explain why yours is better.

- Examine your organization and think of possible better ways to organize.

- Review the visual presentation of your report for readability and maximum impact.

- Proofread carefully.

5
SUBMITTED VERSION

- Make sure your finished writing meets all formatting requirements.

1: Identify the Problem

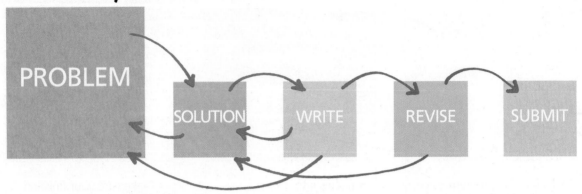

Analyze the assignment

Read your assignment slowly and carefully. Look for words like *propose, problem,* or *solution,* which signal that you are writing a proposal argument. Highlight any information about the length specified, date due, formatting, and other requirements. You can attend to this information later. At this point you want to zero in on your subject and your proposal claim.

Identify the problem

- What exactly is the problem?
- Who is most affected by the problem?
- What causes the problem?
- Has anyone tried to do anything about it? If so, why haven't they succeeded?
- What is likely to happen in the future if the problem isn't solved?

Do background research in online and print library sources and on the Web

- What has been written about the problem?
- What other solutions have been proposed?
- Where have other solutions been effective?
- Where have other solutions failed?
- Is there anyone involved with the problem whom you might interview?

Make a proposal claim

Proposal claims advocate a specific change or course of action. Put the claim in this form: "We should (or should not) do _____."

WRITE NOW   MyWritingLab™

Make an Idea Map

When you have a number of ideas and facts about a topic, write them on sticky notes. Then post the sticky notes and move them around, so you can begin to see how they might fit together. When you find an organization that suits your subject, make a working outline from your sticky notes.

PROBLEM:
Citizens of the United States born in another country cannot run for president

EXCEPTION:
Foreign-born citizens whose parents are American citizens

REQUIRED:
2/3s majority of Congress and 2/3s of state legislatures must approve

SOLUTION:
Amend the U.S. Constitution to allow foreign-born American citizens to run for and serve as the president of the United States

HOW WOULD IT WORK?
Grassroots campaign

WHO WOULD SUPPORT?
Probably Asian Americans, Mexican Americans, and other recent immigrant groups

WHO WOULD OPPOSE?
(1) politicians afraid of angering voters
(2) Americans who are afraid of foreigners

HOW LONG WOULD IT TAKE?
Probably years because of the approval process

PRO ARGUMENTS
(1) Fairness
(2) America's image of itself as a land of opportunity

COUNTERARGUMENT
Point out that foreign born doesn't mean untrustworthy

467

Writer at work

Kim Lee was asked to write a proposal argument for her Rhetoric and Writing course. Upon receiving the assignment, she made the following notes and observations.

RHE 306 Rhetoric and Writing
Policy Proposal

Change an old policy or make a new one.

For this assignment, you will write a policy proposal argument. Propose a change to an existing policy or law, or propose a new law, that will correct a problem. This problem might be a revenue shortfall, an existing inequality, poor living or working conditions, a safety or law-enforcement threat, or something similar. Your paper should be about 5–7 pages long.

Remember, a policy proposal typically deals with a problem that affects a large number of people, and is often concerned with bettering society in some way. It will require practical steps to implement of course, and you will need to describe these steps in your essay. What would it take to change a particular law? Who would have to approve your new policy? How would it be funded? Your audience will need to know these things to decide if they agree with your proposal.

have to show practical steps. U.S. laws don't change unless people protest, write to Congress, etc.

Must inspire them to do something.

Also think about moving your audience to action. No matter how easy or hard your proposal would be to implement, you must persuade people to act upon it.

Time line

We will review first drafts of your proposals in class one week from today. After this initial review, we will schedule one-on-one conferences during my office hours. Final versions will be due on May 10.

Ten days from review to final draft. Try to schedule conference early.

Evaluation

Grades for the final essay will break down as follows:

20% —description of problem
25% —description of solution (specifics, feasibility)
25% —persuasiveness/call to action
20% —overall support/citation of sources
10% —grammar and mechanics

Read the assignment closely

Kim Lee began by highlighting key words in the assignment and noting specifics about the length and due date.

Choose a topic

Kim listed possible topics and then considered the strengths and weaknesses of each. She chose one that could be developed adequately and could motivate her audience.

Plan research strategies

Kim made a list of possible sources of information to begin her research.

POSSIBLE TOPICS

— Create a standardized form of testing for steroid use in all American sports (professional, educational, recreational).

> Might be too broad. Also, the science involved might be hard to explain in 5–7 pages

— Move the U.S. capital to St. Louis.

> Too regional?

— Amend the Constitution to allow foreign-born American citizens (or naturalized citizens) to serve as president of the United States.

An issue of fair treatment.
Good for motivating audience.

— Revitalize Youngstown, Ohio, by building a tourist trade around its previous Mafioso reputation as "Little Chicago."

> Could give lots of specific steps (funding, building plans, tourist info).

— Reformulate the means by which the Corporation for Public Broadcasting receives federal funds.

> Would be very dry, though T.V. shows like Sesame Street could be used to provoke interest/make people want to act.

To Do:

— Search Web and library databases for current discussion on this topic. What kinds of sites are discussing the "natural-born" clause?

— Search periodicals for discussions of this topic.

— Search academic and law journals for more sophisticated discussions.

— Any books???

— What groups (political, ideological) are discussing this right now?

2: Propose Your Solution

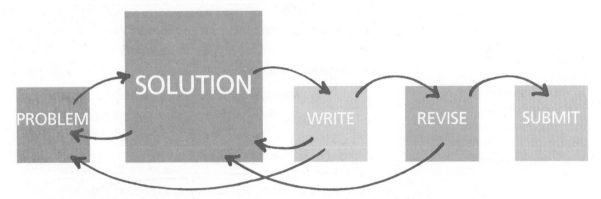

State your solution

Be as specific as possible.

- What exactly do you want to achieve?
- How exactly will your solution work?
- Can it be accomplished quickly, or will it have to be phased in over a few years?
- Has anything like it been tried elsewhere?
- Who will be involved?
- Is it possible that your solution might not work? Think of arguments against your solution and try to answer them.

Consider other solutions

What other solutions have been proposed for this problem, including doing nothing? What are the advantages and disadvantages of those solutions? You will need to acknowledge other solutions and argue for why your solution is better.

Examine the feasibility of your solution

- How easy is your solution to implement?
- Will people who are most affected go along with it? (For example, many people who support green energy still don't want wind farms in sight of their houses.)
- If it costs money, how do you propose paying for it?
- How can you best convince readers that your proposal can be achieved?

Analyze your potential readers

How interested will your readers be in this problem? Are they affected in any way by the problem? If they do not have an immediate stake in solving the problem, how can you gain their attention?

Acknowledging other points of view

Write for readers who may disagree with you

Proposal arguments that ignore other points of view and other possible solutions tend to convince only those who agree with you before you start writing. Your goal is to convince those who haven't thought about the problem and those who might disagree at the outset but can be persuaded. Think about why readers might disagree.

- Are they misinformed about the problem? If so, you will need to provide accurate information.
- Do they have different assumptions about the problem? If so, can you show them that your assumptions are better?
- Do they share your goals but think your solution is not the right one? If so, you will need to explain why your solution is better.

You might have to do some research to find out the views of others. If you are writing about a local problem, you may need to talk to people.

Deal fairly with other solutions and other points of view

OFF TRACK

Free tuition for all state high school graduates who attend state colleges is an idea too ridiculous to consider.
(No reason is given for rejecting an alternative solution, and those who propose it are insulted.)

ON TRACK

Free tuition for all state high school graduates is a desirable solution to get more students to attend college, but it is not likely to be implemented because of the cost. A merit-based solution similar to the HOPE scholarship program in Georgia, which is funded by state lottery money, could be implemented in our state.
(The author offers a reason for rejecting an alternative solution and proposes a solution that has some common ground with the alternative.)

Writer at work

Kim Lee began laying out her proposal by first stating her solution as specifically as possible. She used the following list of questions to guide her proposal argument.

PROPOSAL: Amend the U.S. Constitution to allow foreign-born American citizens to run for and serve as the president of the United States.

- *How exactly will my solution work?*

Through a nonpartisan grassroots campaign, we will work to pressure members of the U.S. Congress to propose the amendment. Ultimately, this proposal is both for the people of the United States and the governmental body.

- *Can it be accomplished quickly, or will it have to be phased in over a few years?*

This is a tricky area. An amendment such as lowering the voting age to 18 during the Vietnam War did pass within four months. It often takes at least a couple years to work a proposed amendment through Congress.

- *Who will be involved?*

This will have to be a two-front battle. (1) the American people (specifically underrepresented voting blocks such as Asian Americans, Mexican Americans, and others, who are most directly affected by the limitations put forth by the current regulation). (2) the members of the United States Congress.

- *Are any reasons why my solution might not work?*

This has been brought up a number of times and never really gotten very far. It is a hot-button topic, especially as related to national security. Congressmen/women may not want to ruffle their constituents who may see this as a national threat and direct decrease in their own personal rights.

- *How will I address those arguments?*

Through pointing out the faulty logic that states foreign born=shifty and natural-born=patriotic.

- *Can I think of any ways of strengthening my proposed solution in light of those possible criticisms?*

I believe the strength in this is pointing to the contradictions that exist between the rule and the governing notion of the United States as "melting pot," "land of freedom," and "a land where everyone can grow up to be president." The heart of this argument is to drive home its illogical nature, highlight contradictions in its logic, and include stipulations that ensure that the individual who is running for president is not merely a drop-in from another country.

OTHER SOLUTIONS

- *Solutions that have been discussed recently seem to differ in the length of required residence.*

Not necessarily disadvantages, but have been ineffective in achieving the goal. It comes from the people and not in support of one candidate, but an idea.

FEASIBILITY

- *How easy is my solution to implement?*

It all depends on the people's ability to move Congress to action.

- *Will the people who will be most affected be willing to go along with it?*

I believe the answer is yes.

- *How will we pay for it?*

Again, grassroots political fundraising. A major source may be ethnic/immigrant groups, etc.

- *Who is most likely to reject my proposal because it is not practical enough?*

Most likely (a) politicians who see support of the change as a threat to their positions (due to voter dissent) and (b) citizens who live in a state of fear.

- *How can I convince my readers that my proposal can be achieved?*

It must be proposed as being about the people and their ability to enact change.
It is about empowerment.

POTENTIAL READERS

- *Whom am I writing for?*

American people (specifically the immigrant population).

- *How interested will my readers be in this problem?*

It is currently a hot topic, and hopefully making it more personally relevant will peak interest (not just about where President Obama was born).

- *How much does this problem affect them?*

Withholds a basic right for them and their children.

- *How would my solution benefit them directly and indirectly?*

Directly, it allows for naturalized citizens to run for president (or vice president). Indirectly, it fosters a sense of pride in one's ethnic identity and helps (through visibility and legislative legitimacy) to create an image of diversity and success.

3: Write a Draft

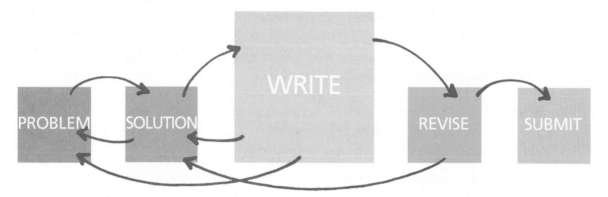

Define the problem

Set out the issue or problem. If the problem is local, you might begin by telling about your experience or the experience of someone you know.

Present your solution

- Describe other solutions that have been attempted and others that are possible. Explain why other solutions either don't solve the problem or are unrealistic.

- Make clear the goals of your solution. Many solutions cannot solve problems completely, but they can make things better.

- Describe in detail the steps in implementing your solution and how they will solve the problem you have identified. You can impress your readers by the care with which you have thought through this problem.

- Explain the positive consequences that will follow from your proposal. What good things will happen and what bad things will be avoided if your proposal is implemented?

Argue that your solution can be accomplished

Your proposal for solving the problem is a truly good idea only if it can be put into practice. If people have to change the ways they are doing things now, explain why they would want to change. If your proposal costs money, you need to identify exactly where the money would come from.

Conclude with a call for action

Make a call for action. Be direct that if your readers agree with you, they should be willing to take action. Restate and emphasize exactly what they need to do.

Writer at work

Here is the working outline upon which Kim Lee built the first draft of her proposal essay.

I. SET UP PROBLEM
    A. Story about son not being able to run
    B. Statistics
    C. Why it goes beyond just the hype

II. BACKGROUND
    A. Historical
        1. How this came about
        2. What is the historical logic behind it
    B. Current — Controversy over where Barack Obama was born

III. PROPOSAL
    A. Why
        1. Nation built on the melting pot
        2. Why is this issue important now?
        3. What have foreign-born Americans achieved?
        4. Who has it barred?
        5. Haven't we learned anything from past biases?
            a. Gitmo and Japanese American internment
            b. Natural-born traitors
        6. Tie to raising of voting age during Vietnam War
        7. Not a threat
    B. What
        1. Remove the "natural-born" clause
        2. Replace that clause with a different stipulation for president
            a. Must have been living in residence of the United States for at least 25 years
            b. Preserves the spirit of the clause
    C. How to do so in the most efficient and secure fashion
        1. Grassroots campaign to effect change with men and women of Congress
            a. We elect them
            b. Make this a major issue
            c. Use the minority voices who are often marginalized
        2. Ultimately it must be driven to Congress while keeping voices heard
    D. The actual governmental process

IV. CONCLUSION
    A. This will provide hope for the disenfranchised
    B. This will right an illogical wrong
    C. This will not place the country at risk
    D. This will create role models
    E. This will be one more step toward making this country what it professes to be

4: Revise, Revise, Revise

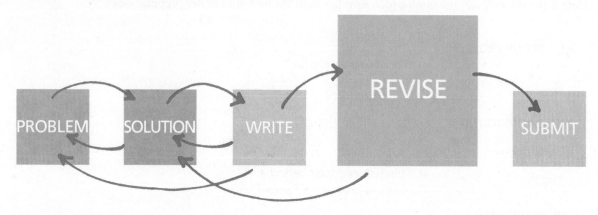

Take a break from your writing and come back to it with "fresh eyes." When you return, imagine you are someone who has never seen your proposal before. Read the proposal out loud. When you are done, ask yourself: Do I understand the problem? Does it really seem like a problem that must be dealt with? Is the solution clear? Does it seem like it is worth the trouble? Do I think it will really work? How much will it cost me, in money, effort, or inconvenience? The biggest trap you can fall into is starting off with the little stuff first. Leave the small stuff for last.

Does your paper or project meet the assignment?	• Look again at your assignment. Does your paper or project do what the assignment asks? • Look again at the assignment for specific guidelines, including length, format, and amount of research. Does your work meet these guidelines?
Is the proposal claim clear and focused?	• Does the proposal claim address the problem? • Does the proposal claim issue a clear call to action?
Do you identify the problem adequately?	• Do you need more evidence that the problem exists and is a serious concern? • Will your readers find credible any sources you include? Can you think of other sources that might be more persuasive?
Is it clear how your solution will address the problem?	• Can you find more evidence that your solution will resolve the problem? • Do you address potential objections to your solution? • Do you provide evidence that your solution is feasible? For example, if your solution requires money, where will the money come from?

Do you consider alternative solutions?	• Do you explain why your solution is better than the alternatives?
Is your organization effective?	• Is the order of your main points clear to your reader? • Are there any places where you find abrupt shifts or gaps? • Are there sections or paragraphs that could be rearranged to make your draft more effective?
Is your introduction effective?	• Can you get off to a faster start, perhaps with a striking example? • Can you think of a better way to engage your readers to be interested in the problem you identify? • Does your introduction give your readers a sense of why the problem is important?
Is your conclusion effective?	• Does your conclusion have a call for action? • Do you make it clear exactly what you want your readers to do?
Do you represent yourself effectively?	• To the extent you can, forget for a moment that you wrote what you are reading. What impression do you have of you, the writer? • Does "the writer" create an appropriate tone? • Has "the writer" done his or her homework?
Is the writing project visually effective?	• Is the font attractive and readable? • Is the overall layout attractive and readable? • If headings are used, do they make clear what comes under each of them? • Is each photograph, chart, graph, map, or table clearly labeled? Does each visual have a caption?
Save the editing for last	When you have finished revising, edit and proofread carefully.

A peer review guide is on page 58.

Writer at work

During peer review of her paper with fellow classmates, and in her meeting with her instructor, Kim Lee made notes on her rough draft. She used these comments to guide her revision of the essay.

The history of the United States of America is punctuated with rhetoric that positions the nation as one that embraces diversity and creates a land of equal opportunity for all of those who choose to live here. As the Statue of Liberty cries out "bring us your tired, your poor, your huddled masses yearning to breathe free," American politicians gleefully use such images to frame the United States a bastion for all things good, fair, and equal. As a proud American, however, I must nonetheless point out one of the cracks in this façade of equality ~~(and that is without even mentioning the repeated failed ratification of the women's Equal Rights Amendment). What flaw could this be?~~ Any foreign-born person with foreign parents is not eligible to be elected our president, even if that person became an American as a baby through adoption.

Think about the recent "birther" controversy about whether Barack Obama was born in Hawaii. The White House released the long-form birth certificate in April 2011. But does it really matter where Obama was born?

We as a nation must take this time to take a stand against this discriminatory and antiquated aspect of the Constitution.

Opening sentence is too clunky. Need something more engaging.

Stay focused. Don't ask unnecessary questions. Give an example.

Transition—the info does not lead naturally into the renewed call for change. Need a link to show the relationship between this info and my proposal.

Look for ways to focus	Kim Lee responded to suggestions from her teacher and her peers to make her opening paragraph less wordy and better focused on her main point. She removed material that did not obviously inform readers about the problem she was interested in.
Check transitions	She also worked on strengthening transitions between paragraphs.
Read your paper aloud	Finally, Kim Lee read her essay aloud to check for misspelled words, awkward phrasing, and other mechanical problems.

STAYING ON TRACK

Reviewing your draft

Give yourself plenty of time for reviewing your draft. For detailed information on how to participate in a peer review, how to review it yourself, and how to respond to comments from your classmates, your instructor, or a campus writing consultant, see pages 60–61.

Some good questions to ask yourself when reviewing an argument for change

- Do you connect the problem to your readers? Even if the problem doesn't affect them directly, at the very least you should appeal to their sense of fairness.

- Can you explain more specifically how your solution will work?

- If resources including people and money are required for your solution, can you elaborate where these resources will come from?

- Do you include other possible solutions and discuss the advantages and disadvantages of each? Can you add to this discussion?

- Does your conclusion connect with the attitudes and values of your readers in addition to making clear what you want them to do? Can you add an additional point? Can you sharpen your call to action?

5: Submitted Version (MLA Style)

MyWritingLab™

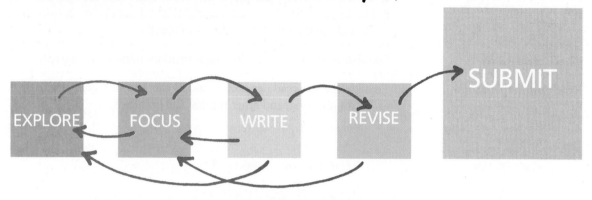

Lee 1

Kim Lee

Professor Patel

RHE 306

10 May 2014

Let's Make It a Real Melting Pot with Presidential Hopes for All

The image the United States likes to advertise is a country that embraces

diversity and creates a land of equal opportunity for all. As the Statue of Liberty

cries out, "give me your tired, your poor, your huddled masses yearning to

breathe free," American politicians gleefully evoke such images to frame the

United States as a bastion for all things good, fair, and equal. As a proud

American, however, I must nonetheless highlight one of the cracks in this

façade of equality. Imagine that a couple decides to adopt an orphaned child

from China. They follow all of the legal processes deemed necessary by both

countries. They fly abroad and bring home their (once parentless) six-month-old

baby boy. They raise and nurture him, and while teaching him to embrace

his ethnicity, they also teach him to love Captain Crunch, baseball, and

The Three Stooges. He grows and eventually attends an ethnically diverse American public school. One day his fifth-grade teacher tells the class that anyone can grow up to be president. To clarify her point, she turns to the boy, knowing his background, and states, "No, you could not be president, Stu, but you could still be a senator. That's something to aspire to!" How do Stu's parents explain this rule to this American-raised child? This scenario will become increasingly common, yet as the Constitution currently reads, only "natural-born" citizens may run for the offices of president and vice president. Neither these children nor the thousands of hardworking Americans who chose to make America their official homeland may aspire to the highest political position in the land. While the huddled masses may enter, it appears they must retain a second-class citizen ranking.

The issue arose most recently when bloggers, media personalities, and some elected officials alleged that Barack Obama was born in Kenya, not Hawaii, and that his birth certificate is a forgery. The release of a certified copy of Obama's Certificate of Live Birth (the "long form") and other evidence including birth announcements in two Hawaii newspapers in August 1961 answered Donald Trump and other prominent "birthers" (Shear). Lost in the controversy was the question: Should it matter where Obama or any other candidate was born? In a land where everyone but American Indians are immigrants or descendants of immigrants, why should being born in the United States be considered an essential qualification for election as President?

The provision arose from very different circumstances than those of today. The "natural-born" stipulation regarding the presidency stems from

the self-same meeting of minds that brought the American people the
Electoral College. During the Constitutional Convention of 1787, the Congress
formulated the regulatory measures associated with the office of the president.
A letter sent from John Jay to George Washington during this period reads
as follows:

> "Permit me to hint," Jay wrote, "whether it would not be wise and
> seasonable to provide a strong check to the admission of foreigners into
> the administration of our national government; and to declare expressly
> that the Commander in Chief of the American army shall not be given to,
> nor devolve on, any but a natural-born citizen." (Mathews A1)

> Shortly thereafter, Article II, Section I, Clause V, of the Constitution

declared that "No Person except a natural born Citizen, or a Citizen of the
United States at the time of the Adoption of this Constitution, shall be eligible
to the Office of President." Jill A. Pryor states in *The Yale Law Journal* that
"some writers have suggested that Jay was responding to rumors that
foreign princes might be asked to assume the presidency" (881). Many cite
disastrous examples of foreign rule in the eighteenth century as the impetus
for the "natural-born" clause. For example, in 1772—only 15 years prior to
the adoption of the statute—Poland had been divided up by Prussia, Russia,
and Austria (Kasindorf). Perhaps an element of self-preservation and not
ethnocentrism led to the questionable stipulation. Nonetheless, in the twenty-
first century this clause reeks of xenophobia.

The Fourteenth Amendment clarified the difference between "natural-born"
and "native-born" citizens by spelling out the citizenship status of children born

to American parents outside of the United States (Ginsberg 929). This clause qualifies individuals such as Senator John McCain—born in Panama—for presidency. This change, however, is not adequate. I propose that the United States abolish the natural-born clause and replace it with a stipulation that allows naturalized citizens to run for president. This amendment would state that a candidate must have been naturalized and must have lived in residence in the United States for a period of at least twenty-five years. The present time is ideal for this change. This amendment could simultaneously honor the spirit of the Constitution, protect and ensure the interests of the United States, promote an international image of inclusiveness, and grant heretofore-withheld rights to thousands of legal and loyal United States citizens.

In our push for change, we must make clear the importance of this amendment. It would not provide special rights for would-be terrorists. To the contrary, it would fulfill the longtime promises of the nation. Naturalized citizens have been contributing to the United States for centuries. Many nameless Mexican, Irish, and Asian Americans sweated and toiled to build the American railroads. The public has welcomed naturalized Americans such as Bob Hope, Albert Pujols, and Peter Jennings into their hearts and living rooms. Individuals such as German-born Henry Kissinger and Czechoslovakian-born Madeleine Albright have held high posts in the American government and have served as respected aides to its presidents. The amendment must make clear that it is not about one man's celebrity. Approximately seven hundred foreign-born Americans have won the Medal of Honor, and over sixty thousand proudly serve in the United States military today (Siskind 5). The "natural-born" clause must be removed to provide each of these people—over 700,000 naturalized in 2013 alone—with equal footing to those who were born into citizenship rather than working for it ("Naturalization").

Since the passing of the Bill of Rights, only 17 amendments have been ratified. This process takes time and overwhelming congressional and statewide support. To alter the Constitution, a proposed amendment must pass with a two-thirds "supermajority" in both the House of Representatives and the Senate. In addition, the proposal must find favor in two-thirds (38) of state legislatures. In short, this task will not be easy. In order for this change to occur, a grassroots campaign must work to dispel misinformation regarding naturalized citizens and to force the hands of senators and representatives wishing to retain their congressional seats. We must take this proposal to ethnicity-specific political groups from both sides of the aisle, business organizations, and community activist groups. We must convince representatives that this issue matters. Only through raising voices and casting votes can the people enact change. Only then can every American child see the possibility for limitless achievement and equality. Only then can everyone find the same sense of pride in the possibility for true American diversity in the highest office in the land.

Works Cited

Ginsberg, Gordon. "Citizenship: Expatriation: Distinction between Naturalized and Natural Born Citizens." *Michigan Law Review*, vol. 50, no. 6, Apr. 1952, pp. 926-29. *JSTOR*, www.jstor.org/stable/1284568.

Kasindorf, Martin. "Should the Constitution Be Amended for Arnold?" *USA Today*, 2 Dec. 2004, usatoday30.usatoday.com/news/politicselections/2004-12-02-schwarzenegger-amendment_x.htm.

Mathews, Joe. "Maybe Anyone Can Be President." *Los Angeles Times*, 2 Feb. 2005, articles.latimes.com/2005/feb/02/local/me-arnold2.

"Naturalization Fact Sheet." *United States Citizenship and Immigration Services*, 24 Oct. 2012, www.uscis.gov/archive/archive-news/naturalization-fact-sheet. Accessed 17 Apr. 2014.

Pryor, Jill A. "The Natural Born Citizen Clause and Presidential Eligibility: An Approach for Resolving Two Hundred Years of Uncertainty." *The Yale Law Journal*, vol. 97, no. 5, Apr. 1988, pp. 881-99. *JSTOR*, www.jstor.org/stable/796518.

Shear, Michael D. "With Document, Obama Seeks to End 'Birther' Issue." *The New York Times*, 27 Apr. 2011, nyti.ms/1I3u31R.

Siskind, Lawrence J. "Why Shouldn't Arnold Run?" *The Recorder*, 10 Dec. 2004. *Academic OneFile*, go.galegroup.com/ps/i.do?id=GALE%7CA126125737&v=2.1&u=nysl_me_wls&it=r&p=AONE&sw=w&asid=e872b81d47c6e794f28cd523533e16c3.

Projects

If you want to persuade your readers to do something, you must convince them that a problem exists and that something needs to be done about it.

Teamwork: counterproposals

Find a proposal argument that you and three or four classmates are interested in. This might be a proposal to widen a road in your town, to pass a law making English the official language of your state government, or something similar.

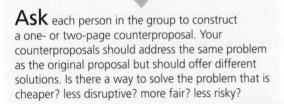

Ask each person in the group to construct a one- or two-page counterproposal. Your counterproposals should address the same problem as the original proposal but should offer different solutions. Is there a way to solve the problem that is cheaper? less disruptive? more fair? less risky?

Present your counterproposals to the rest of your group, and discuss which is the most appealing. You may find that a combination of elements of the different proposals ends up being the best.

Proposal essay

Write a proposal of 1000–1250 words (about three to four double-spaced pages) that would solve a problem that you identify.

Choose a problem with which you have personal experience, but you should also think about how many other people this problem affects. Your proposal should take them into account as part of your audience.

Find out who would be in a position to enact your proposal. How can you make your solution seem like a good idea to these people?

Propose your solution as specifically as you can. What exactly do you want to achieve? How exactly will your solution work? Has anything like it been tried elsewhere? Who will be involved?

Consider other solutions that have been or might be proposed for this problem, including doing nothing. What are the advantages and disadvantages of those solutions? Why is your solution better?

Examine how easy your solution is to implement. Will the people most affected be willing to go along with it? Lots of things can be accomplished if enough people volunteer, but groups often have difficulty getting enough volunteers to work without pay. If it costs money, how do you propose paying for it?

Reconstructing a proposal

You may not have a lot of experience writing proposals. Nevertheless, proposals have had a profound impact on your life. Almost every program, law, policy, or business that affects you had to be proposed before it became a reality.

Think of some things in your life that were proposed by people: the building where you attended high school, for example. At some point, that building was proposed as a way of solving a certain problem—perhaps your town had one old, overflowing high school, and your building was proposed to solve the overcrowding. Its location was probably chosen carefully, to avoid causing more problems with traffic, and to ensure that it was easy for students to reach.

Choose something you are familiar with that went through a proposal process. Try to reconstruct the four components of the original proposal. What problem do you think people were trying to solve? How did concerns about fairness and feasibility shape the program, building, or policy?

Outline your re-created proposal in a page or two.

Ask yourself if this policy, program, or business truly solved the problem it was intended to solve? Clearly, the proposal itself was successful, for the school was built, the law was passed, or the business was started. But how successful was the proposed solution in reality?

COMPOSE IN MULTIMEDIA

Nonprofit proposal on the web

Nonprofit organizations depend to a large extent on external funding. Many rely on help from volunteers, including students, to compose proposals, both on paper and on the Web. Find a nonprofit organization in your community that seeks funding. Select a project that the organization wishes to undertake. Compose a Web site that includes the following elements.

Problem statements describe the need and the target population. Individuals and funding agencies must be convinced that what you are proposing is important.

Goals and objectives should describe in detail what will be accomplished, how the community will benefit, and how success will be measured. Long-term strategies for maintaining the successes of the project should also be described.

Organizational information explains the broad mission of the organization and its history.

Conclude with how much money will be required and how to contact the nonprofit.

MyWritingLab™ Visit Ch. 13 in MyWritingLab to complete the chapter exercises, explore an interactive version of the Writer at Work paper, and test your understanding of the chapter objectives.

14 Composing in Multimedia

Readers today expect writers to communicate using photos, graphics, audio, and video in addition to words.

In this chapter, you will learn to

Communicate with Visuals and Words

The word *writing* makes us think of words, yet in our daily experience reading newspapers, magazines, advertisements, Web sites, and signs, along with watching television, we find words combined with images and graphics. Understanding the relationships of words and visuals will make you a better writer.

What do visuals do best?

Visuals work well when they

- Deliver spatial information, especially through maps, floor plans, and other graphic representations of space
- Represent statistical relationships
- Produce a strong immediate impact, even shock value
- Emphasize a point made in words

What do words do best?

Words can do many things that images cannot. Written words work best when they

- Communicate abstract ideas
- Report information
- Persuade using elaborated reasoning
- Communicate online using minimal bandwidth

When do you combine words and images?

- Most Web sites and brochures do use images and graphics because readers expect to see their subjects in addition to reading about them.
- Think about the purpose of an image or graphic. Does it illustrate a concept? highlight an important point? show something that is hard to explain in words alone?
- Think about the placement of an image or graphic in your text. It should be as close as possible to a relevant point in your text.
- Think about the focus of an image. Will readers see the part that matters? If not, you may need to crop the image.
- Provide informative captions for the images and graphics you use and refer to them in your text.

Uninformative caption:
Ghost town

Informative caption:
Following the discovery of quicksilver in the 1880s, Terlingua became a boom town, but the people left when the mines ceased production at the end of World War II.

Understand the Process of Composing in Multimedia

Composing in multimedia requires you to combine different objects—texts, pictures, audio clips, video clips, and graphics—to communicate with other people. Today's technology has made it easy to create these objects and to publish them on the Internet. You can do it all on a smart phone.

But as you have no doubt recognized, very few people can create effective multimedia beyond a video of their cat. The ease of the technology is part of the problem. Sure, you can get your cat video on *YouTube* almost instantly, and if it is funny enough, it may go viral. But what if you want to inform people about the problem of abandoned cats and you want cat owners to become more responsible for their pets? A funny cat video is not going to get your message conveyed.

Multimedia composing, like composing in writing, is all about your audience and purpose

What do you want your audience to take from your multimedia presentation? Can they Tweet it? If you cannot Tweet the main goal, your audience will not be able to either.

Another key difference between strictly verbal texts and multimedia is the simple fact that your audience will be using multiple channels to take in what you have to say and show. Multimedia texts have the advantage that people better remember multimedia than just words or pictures alone, but you have to give your audience some guidance on putting things together. Give them your agenda up front and announce the main points before you get into the details.

Plan before you start

The temptation in multimedia is to jump right in. Instead you should step back and take stock of what you want to present. Various planning software tools are available, but working first in analogue mode with pen and paper is always a good way to start.

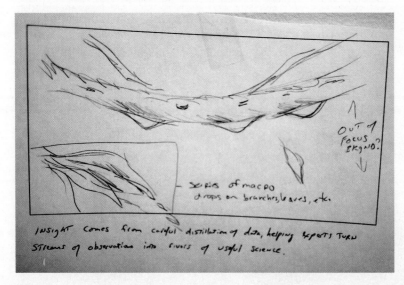

An example of a storyboard for the 2014 NASA film Water Falls. *Source: http://pmm.nasa.gov/node/830*

Take Pictures That Aren't Boring

No matter how easy it is now to take photographs, the great majority of pictures look the same. Why? It's because most people think pictures should look the same, taken at eye level with the subject in the center.

The result is boring, boring, boring.

This kind of picture has been taken many, many times. How else might you see this subject?

Change the angle

Find a new eye level

Kneel

Squat

Lie down

Climb a tree

Most people never stop to experience the visual richness of the world. Look for detail. Be open to what you see.

Compose Images

A common misperception is that a photograph is a direct representation of reality. Nothing could be further from the truth. A photograph shows not so much what the photographer sees but rather *how* the photographer sees. The key to becoming a good photographer is not to take pictures that show things exactly as they appear but to take pictures that convey meaning, organization, and an emotional response to the subject.

Eliminate nonessential elements Most people include too much in their photographs. Decide what is essential and concentrate on getting those elements in the frame.

The mud on a tired horse after a race shows his exhaustion.

Framing

If you are taking a portrait, usually the closer you can get to your subject, the better. If your camera has a zoom, use it.

Decide what you want in a frame. If your goal is to show the habitat of pelicans, you'll need a wide shot.

But if you want a portrait of a pelican, get in tight.

Create Graphics

Graphics can display information to support your text in an at-a-glance format. Select the type of visual that best suits your purpose.

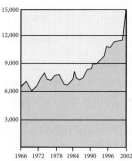

Table 25.1
Population Change for the Ten Largest U.S. Cities, 1990 to 200

| City and State | Population | | Change, 1990 to 2000 | |
	April 1, 2000	April 1, 1990	Number	Percentage
New York, NY	8,008,278	7,322,564	685,714	9.4
Los Angeles, CA	3,694,820	3,485,398	209,422	6.0
Chicago, IL	2,896,016	2,783,726	112,290	4.0
Houston, TX	1,953,631	1,630,553	323,078	19.8
Philadelphia, PA	1,517,550	1,585,577	-68,027	-4.3
Phoenix, AZ	1,321,045	983,403	337,642	34.3
San Diego, CA	1,223,400	1,110,549	112,851	10.2
Dallas, TX	1,188,580	1,006,877	181,703	18.0
San Antonio, TX	1,144,646	935,933	208,713	22.3
Detroit, MI	951,270	1,027,974	-76,704	-7.5

Source: U.S. Cencus Bureau, Census 2000; 1990 Census, Population and Housing Unit Counts, United States (1990 CPH-2-1).

Tables

A table is used to display numerical data and similar types of information.

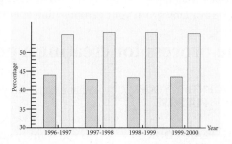

Bar Graphs

A bar graph compares the values of two or more items.

Line Graphs

A line graph shows change over time.

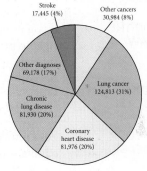

Pie Charts

A pie chart shows the parts making up a whole.

WRITE NOW   MyWritingLab™

Create a Google Map

Google Maps have become a new way of thinking about making connections between places and ideas in visually stimulating and interactive ways. Create a map about some aspect of your town or campus that not everyone knows about. Select your sites either by a specific area or a specific theme (e.g., best graffiti art, best food trailers, best places to watch sunset).

Your map should contain a minimum of five placemarks. Each placemark should have at least a paragraph of original text and a photograph taken at the site. You can make hyperlinks, but do not depend on links to do your work for you. Tell the story yourself. When you finish, submit the URL of your map to your instructor.

Create Audio

Podcasts are easy to create using your own audio editor and your Web site or you can create them in a multimedia lab and post them on a third-party site. For a podcast with high audio quality, you'll need a headset with a noise-canceling microphone, a portable voice recorder, and podcasting software. All these may be available from your campus multimedia lab.

The process for creating a podcast

IDENTIFY YOUR PURPOSE	What exactly do you want to accomplish?
PLAN YOUR CONTENT	Do you want to conduct interviews about a subject or an issue? Do a documentary of an event? Give practical advice or instructions? Give a history or an analysis? Make a persuasive argument?
COMPOSE YOUR AUDIO	Arrange and record interviews. Write a script.
KNOW THE LAW	If you use music created by someone else, you likely will have to pay for the right to broadcast that music. If someone agrees to be your guest, you have the right to broadcast that person's voice.
RECORD YOUR PODCAST	Reserve a campus audio production lab or record on your computer. Create an audio file by combining the interviews with your narration.
EDIT YOUR PODCAST	Your multimedia lab may have instructions or consultants for using audio editing software. Allow ample time for editing.
PUBLISH YOUR PODCAST	Export the audio into a format such as WAV or MP3 that you can put on the Web or share as a downloadable file.

Create Video

The cost and technical barriers for creating video have been significantly reduced. Phones and PDAs can now record video along with simple-to-use camcorders. Most new computers come with video editors installed including Apple's *iMovie* or Windows' *MovieMaker*. *YouTube* and other videosharing Web sites make it easy to publish your video.

Nonetheless, making a high-quality video requires a great deal of effort. In addition to the technical demands, producing quality videos requires the hard work of planning and revising that extended writing tasks demand.

The process for creating a video

IDENTIFY YOUR SUBJECT AND PURPOSE	What exactly do you want to accomplish?
DECIDE ON YOUR APPROACH	Do you want to conduct interviews? Do a documentary of an event? Make an announcement? Re-enact a past event?
PLAN YOUR CONTENT	Will all the video be original? Will you incorporate other video such as *YouTube* clips? Will you include still images? Maps or graphs? Music? Voiceover?
DRAFT A SCRIPT AND A STORYBOARD	A storyboard is a shot-by-shot representation of your project that will help you organize your shooting schedule.
MAKE A SCHEDULE AND PLAN YOUR LOCATIONS	Quality videos take many hours to shoot and edit. Visit all locations in advance to take into account issues such as lighting and noise.
ARRANGE FOR YOUR EQUIPMENT	At minimum you will need video and sound recording equipment and an editing suite. Find out what is available from your campus multimedia lab.
COMPOSE YOUR VIDEO	You can create more dynamic video by using techniques of still photographers. You can add movement by using the zoom feature on your camera.
CAPTURE AUDIO	The microphone installed in your camera is usually not the best option. Your multimedia lab may have external microphones that will give you better quality. Microphones record ambient noises—such as the wind noise, traffic, and computer fans—which you need to minimize.
EDIT YOUR VIDEO	Editing software allows you to combine video clips and edit audio. Your multimedia lab may have instructions or consultants for using video-editing software. Allow ample time for editing.
PUBLISH YOUR VIDEO	Export the video into a format such as *QuickTime* that you can put on the Web or share as a downloadable file.

Create a Photo Essay

A combination of words and images often work best to help your readers understand an unfamiliar subject. Christine Vasquez received the following assignment in her environmental studies class.

Photo essay about an environmentally threatened place

Compose a short photo essay (no more than 6 photos) on a place that has a significant environmental issue. Many places locally are possible—polluted creeks, illegal dumping of hazardous chemicals, factories, sewage leaks, and noise from jets taking off at our airport, just to name a few. Or you can choose a place outside our area if you have original photographs. Describe the place visually and explain how it is threatened using photographs.

A native of Ecuador, Christine knew she wanted to submit a photo essay on the Cotacachi Cayapas Ecological Reserve in central Ecuador, a tropical cloud forest where she had volunteered in past summers and had taken numerous photos. She realized, however, that most of her classmates had never been to a cloud forest and had no idea where they existed. Thus she had to inform her audience what a cloud forest is and why cloud forests are an important ecosystem before she stated the threat they face.

Protecting the Cloud Forest: Cotacachi Cayapas Ecological Reserve
Christine Vasquez

The first slide should have a descriptive title. It should give a strong visual introduction to the content of the photo essay. Christine chose a photo that shows both the mountain environment and the cloud forest.

Maps are critical when a place is unfamiliar.

The Cotacachi Reserve is located in the mountains of northern Ecuador, near the border with Columbia.
Source: Google Maps

An explanation of the subject should come early in a photo essay.

Cloud forests have persistent, low-level cloud cover with an abundance of ferns and mosses.

499

Details should follow after the subject is introduced.

Over 500 species of birds live in the reserve including this Toucan Barbet.

People who are environmentally concerned understand threats to wildlife, but few are aware of the enormous loss of plant life, or that many of those plants can provide benefits to people such as medicine. Photographs allow people to see rare plants.

Over 2,000 types of flora have been identified in the reserve.

Only 5% of Ecuador's cloud forest remains. Much land has been cleared for growing crops, and illegal mining within the Cotacachi Reserve causes great environmental destruction because of erosion.

Christine waited until the end to present the current threat to the Cotacachi Reserve because she had to establish first why the reserve is a valuable environmental asset.

WRITE NOW

MyWritingLab™

Campus architectural and visual details

Your task in this photo essay assignment is to show your instructor and classmates something they walk past often and never really see. If your photo essay succeeds, your instructor and classmates will look more closely at what surrounds them on or near campus. Take 5 photographs of the details of one building or one statue or one sculpture (or something else) on or near campus.

For example, look closely at the architectural details on older buildings or details on statues on campus. Or even graffiti. Your photos should tell a visual story about your subject. You can submit your photos as a photo essay.

MyWritingLab™ Visit Ch. 14 in MyWritingLab to complete the chapter exercises and to test your understanding of the chapter objectives.

15 Designing for Print and Digital Readers

Successful design should be both functional and handsome.

In this chapter, you will learn to

① Start with your readers *(see p. 503)*

② Use headings and subheadings effectively *(see p. 504)*

③ Design pages *(see p. 505)*

④ Understand typography *(see p. 506)*

⑤ Evaluate your design *(see p. 507)*

You know at a glance who is telling the truth.

Start with Your Readers

Will your readers be seeing your text on a screen or on paper? Your strategies will differ according to what medium you use. Print texts usually assume that readers will turn pages in linear order. Online readers expect to move easily between different parts of a text.

Tell your reader what you are writing about

Whether in print or on paper, an accurate and informative title is critical for readers to decide if they want to read what you have written. If you are creating a Web site, the opening page should orient your readers to what they can find by clicking on your links.

Some genres require **abstracts**, which are short summaries of a document. Abstracts are required for scholarly articles in the sciences and social sciences as well as dissertations. Business reports and other reports often have executive summaries, which are similar to abstracts but often briefer.

Make your organization visible to readers

Most longer texts and many shorter ones include headings, which give readers an at-a-glance overview and make the text easier to follow and remember. Headings visually indicate the major and subordinate sections of a text.

Help your reader to navigate your text

Do the little things that help readers. Always include page numbers on a print document. Make links on a Web page to other pages when a subject is covered elsewhere. If you are citing sources, make sure they are all in your list of works cited.

Help your reader to understand the purposes of different parts of your text

Writers have traditionally relied on footnotes to add information that they did not want to interrupt the running text. Today writers often use boxes or sidebars to supply extra information. The key is to make what is different look different.

You do research every day. If you compare prices online before you buy an airline ticket, or if you look up a detailed course description before registering for a class, you are doing research. If you want to settle an argument about the first African American to win an Olympic gold medal, you need to do research. In college, research means both investigating existing knowledge that is stored on computers and in libraries, and creating new knowledge through original analysis, surveys, experiments, and theorizing. When you start a research task in a college course, you need to understand the different kinds of possible research and to plan your strategy in advance.

If you have an assignment that requires research, look closely at what you are being asked to do.

The assignment may ask you to review, compare, survey, analyze, evaluate, or prove that something is true or untrue. You may be writing for experts, for students like yourself, or for the general public. The purpose of your research and your potential audience will help guide your strategies for research.

Pull quotes are often set off from the body text with a larger font and a different color.

503

Use Headings and Subheadings Effectively

Readers of print and digital texts increasingly expect you to divide what you write into sections and label those sections with headings. A system of consistent headings should map the overall organization.

Determine levels of headings

Determine the level of importance of each heading by making an outline to see what fits under what. Then make the headings conform to the different levels by choosing a size and an effect such as boldfacing for each level. The type, the size, and the effect should signal the level of importance.

Phrase headings consistently

Headings should be similar in how they are worded. For example, if you are writing headings for an informative brochure about a service, you might use the most frequently asked questions as your headings.

TITLE

Saepe et multum hoc mecum cogitavi, bonine an mali plus attulerit hominibus et civitatibus copia dicendi ac summum eloquentiae studium.

Major Heading

Ac me quidem diu cogitantem ratio ipsa in hanc potissimum sententiam ducit, ut existimem sapientiam sine eloquentia parum prodesse civitatibus, eloquentiam vero sine sapientia nimium obesse plerumque, prodesse numquam.

Level 2 heading Ac si volumus huius rei, quae vocatur eloquentia, sive artis sive studii sive exercitationis cuiusdam sive facultatis ab natura profectae considerare principium, reperiemus id ex honestissimis causis natum atque optimis rationibus profectum.

Be a Quitter! Join Quitters

Why quit smoking?

- You'll lower your risk for heart attack, stroke, and cancer.
- You'll look, feel, and smell a whole lot better.
- You'll have extra money to spend on things other than cigarettes.

How will the Quitters class help me?

- You'll find out your individual level of nicotine-dependence.
- You'll utilize a brand-switching technique.
- You'll explore the use of nicotine replacement therapies.

Headings function like gateways from one section to another.

Design Pages

Computers, laptops, and other digital devices design pages for you with their default settings for margins, paragraph indentations, and justification. Even if you use the default settings, you still have a range of options. Thinking about design will lead to better decisions.

Choose the orientation, size of your page, and columns

You can normally use the default settings for academic essays (remember to select double-spacing for line spacing if the default is single-spaced).

Divide your text into units

The paragraph is the basic unit of extended writing, but think also about when to use lists. This list is a bulleted list. You can also use a numbered list.

Use left aligned text with a ragged right margin

Fully and justified text aligns the right margin, which gives a more formal look but can also leave unsightly rivers of extra white space running through the middle of your text.

Be conscious of white space

White space can make your text more readable and set off more important elements. Headings stand out more with white space surrounding them. Leave room around graphics. You don't want words to crowd too close to graphics because both the words and the visuals will become hard to read.

Be aware of MLA and APA design specifications

MLA and APA styles have specifications for margins, indentations, reference lists, and other things. See the sample papers in Chapters 24 and 25 if you are using MLA or APA style.

3

stay in the military after their commitment ends. Congress first gave the military the authority to retain soldiers after the Vietnam War when new volunteers were too few to replace departing soldiers. In November 2002 the Pentagon gave stop-loss orders for Reserve and National Guard units activated to fight terrorism (Robertson).

- This policy is neither forthcoming, safe, nor compassionate toward those most directly impacted—the soldiers and their families.
- As the United States became more and more entrenched in the conflict in Iraq, the military was stretched thinner and thinner.
- By 2004, approximately 40% of those serving in Iraq and Afghanistan came from the ranks of the part-time soldiers: the Reserves and the National Guard (Gerard).

While these individuals did know that their countries could call if they enlisted, they continue to bear an inordinate burden of actual combat time, and this new policy continues to create situations further removed from the job for which they had enlisted. Recruiters often pitch the military—including the Reserves and the Guard–to young, impressionable, and often underprivileged kids.

The Pitch

I have experienced this pitch firsthand and seen the eyes of my classmates as the recruiter promised them a better and richer tomorrow. Seeing a golden opportunity for self-respect and achievement, young men and women sign on the dotted line. Today, other young men and women

Understand Typography

Just as people communicate with body language, texts have a look and feel created by the layout, typefaces, type size, color, density, and other elements.

Typography is the designer's term for letters and symbols that make up the print on the page. You are already using important aspects of typography when you use capital letters, italics, boldface, or different sizes of type to signal a new sentence, identify the title of a book, or distinguish a heading from the body text.

You can use dozens of different typefaces (fonts), bold and italic versions of these fonts, and a range of font sizes. Fortunately, you can rely on some simple design principles to make good typographic choices for your documents.

Choosing a font

A font family consists of the font in different sizes as well as in its boldface and italic forms. Although computers now make hundreds of font styles and sizes available to writers, you should avoid confusing readers with too many typographical features. Limit the fonts in a document to one or two font families. A common practice is to choose one font family for all titles and headings and another for the body text.

A Font Family
Futura Light Condensed
Futura Light Condensed Italic
Futura Book
Futura Book Italic
Futura Heavy
Futura Heavy Italic
Futura Bold

The font family Futura, shown above in 14 point, is composed of style variations on the Futura design that include a variety of weights.

Serif and sans serif typefaces

Typefaces are normally divided into two groups— serif and sans serif. Serif typefaces include horizontal lines—or serifs—added to the major strokes of a letter or character such as a number. Sans serif typefaces, by contrast, do not have serifs. Notice the difference opposite.

The typical use and stylistic impact of the typefaces vary considerably. Serif typefaces are more traditional, conservative, and formal in appearance. By contrast, sans serif typefaces offer a more contemporary, progressive, and informal look. Serif is often used for longer pieces of writing, such as novels and textbooks. It is also the best bet for college papers.

The difference between serif and sans serif fonts

The horizontal lines make serif easier to read because they guide the eye from left to right across the page.

This **SERIF** font is called Garamond

This **SANS SERIF** font is called Helvetica

Evaluate Your Design

1. Goals	What are you trying to accomplish? Inform your readers? Analyze a text, object, or event? Offer a fresh point of view? Persuade your readers to take action?
2. Audience	Who is the intended audience? Will the design be appealing to them? How does the design serve their needs?
3. Genre	What is the genre? Does the design meet the requirements of the genre? For example, a brochure should fit in your pocket.
4. Medium	What medium will readers use to read what you compose? If you are writing for readers who will be using digital devices, you have to be compact. There's a reason why Tweets are limited to 140 characters.
5. Organization	Is the organization clear to readers? If headings are used, are they in the right places? If headings are used for more than one level, are these levels indicated consistently?
6. Readability	Is the typeface attractive and readable? Are the margins sufficient? Is any contrasting text, such as boldface, italics, or all caps, brief enough to be legible? If color is used, does it direct emphasis to the right places?
7. Layout	Can the basic layout be made more effective? Is there adequate white space around headings, images, and graphics?

WRITE NOW MyWritingLab™

Design a menu

Collect menus from a few restaurants, either in print or on the Web. Study the design of each menu.

Design a menu of your own. First, you have to decide what kind of food you will serve: burgers, Italian, Thai, seafood, and so on. Second, think about the clientele you want to attract: college students, families, office lunch crowd, or another demographic. Third, list a few food items for your menu. Fourth, name your restaurant and give it a theme.

Make a sketch of your menu. Decide what graphics, photographs, and backgrounds you want to use. Then create your menu.

MyWritingLab™ Visit Ch. 15 in MyWritingLab to complete the chapter exercises and to test your understanding of the chapter objectives.

16 Delivering Presentations and Portfolios

Effective presentations require putting the interests of the audience first.

In this chapter, you will learn to

1. Plan a presentation
   (see p. 509)
2. Design effective visuals
   (see p. 510)
3. Deliver a successful presentation *(see p. 511)*
4. Create a portfolio *(see p. 512)*

Plan a Presentation

A successful presentation, like a successful writing project, requires careful planning. Read your assignment carefully for guidance on how to plan your presentation.

FIND A TOPIC	Choosing and researching a topic for a presentation is similar to choosing and researching a topic for a writing assignment. Ask these questions. • Does the topic fit the assignment? • Will you enjoy speaking on this topic? • Do you know enough to speak on this topic? ➔ **See page 12**
IDENTIFY YOUR AUDIENCE	Who is your audience? How interested will they be in your topic? What will they likely know and believe about your topic? ➔ **See page 14**
IDENTIFY YOUR PURPOSE	Your assignment often specifies your purpose. ➔ **See page 9**
IDENTIFY YOUR CENTRAL IDEA	The central idea of a presentation is similar to a working thesis. It includes your purpose, your audience, and your objective. **Purpose:** To persuade **Audience:** my fellow students **Objective:** that they should volunteer at no-kill animal shelters. ➔ **See page 38**
DO THE NECESSARY RESEARCH	Find supporting material from sources. ➔ **See Chapters 20 and 21**
CREATE A WORKING OUTLINE	Make a list of key points and think about how best to order them. ➔ **See page 46**
PLAN YOUR INTRODUCTION	You must gain the attention of your audience, introduce your subject, indicate why it is important, and give a sense of where you are headed. ➔ **See page 48**
PLAN YOUR CONCLUSION	Give your audience something to take away—a compelling example or an idea that captures the gist of your presentation. ➔ **See page 50**

Design Effective Visuals

Less is more with slides. One text-filled slide after another is mind-numbingly dull. Create a presentation that engages your audience.

Keep it simple

Imagine you are making an argument that fewer animals would be euthanized at animal shelters if more people in your city knew that they could save a pet's life by adopting it. You could fill your slides with statistics alone. Or you could tell your audience the facts while showing them slides that give emotional impact to your numbers.

Keep in mind these principles.

- One point per slide
- Very few fonts
- Quality photos, not clip art
- Less text, more images
- Easy on the special effects

But what if you have a lot of data to show? Make a handout that the audience can study later. They can take notes on your handout during your presentation. Keep your slides simple and emphasize the main points in the presentation.

Compare the following examples.

Pet Overpopulation in the United States

- Estimated number of animals that enter shelters each year: 6-8 million
- Estimated number of animals euthanized at shelters each year: 3-4 million
- Estimated number of animals adopted at shelters each year: 3-4 million

Source: "HSUS Pet Overpopulation Estimates." *Humane Society of the U.S.* Humane Society of the U.S., 9 Nov. 2009. 18 Oct. 2010.

Save a life. Adopt a pet.

Which slide makes the point most effectively?

Deliver a Successful Presentation

If you are not passionate about your subject, you will never get your audience involved, no matter how good your slides are. Believe in what you say; enthusiasm is contagious.

It's all about you

The audience didn't come to see the back of your head in front of slides. Move away from the podium and connect with them. Make strong eye contact with individuals. You will make everyone feel like you were having a conversation instead of giving a speech.

Prepare in advance

Practice your presentation, even if you have to speak to a mirror. Check out the room and equipment in advance. If you are using your laptop with a projector installed in the room, make sure it connects. If the room has a computer connected to the projector, bring your presentation on a flash drive and download it to the computer.

Be professional

Pay attention to the little things.

- **Dress appropriately.** Think in advance about what your audience expects.

- **Invite response during your presentation.** Leave time for questions at the end.

- **Add a bit of humor.** Humor can be tricky, especially if you don't know your audience well. But if you can get your audience to laugh, they will be on your side. Remember to smile.

- **Slow down.** When you are nervous, you tend to go too fast. Stop and breathe. Let your audience take in what's on your slides.

- **Proofread carefully.** A glaring spelling error can destroy your credibility.

- **Be consistent.** If you randomly capitalize words or insert punctuation, your audience will be distracted.

- **Pay attention to the timing of your slides.** Stay in sync with your slides. Don't leave a slide up when you are talking about something else.

- **Finish on time or earlier.** Your audience will be grateful.

WRITE NOW　　　　　　　　　　　　　　MyWritingLab™

Moving across media

Convert a paper you have written into a presentation using visuals. Presentation software can help you create the visuals.

Think about your main points and how to support each point with facts, statistics, or other evidence. Think too about how to engage your audience at the beginning. Perhaps you will need to find a vivid example or anecdote to get your audience interested.

Avoid making the common mistake of putting too much text on your slides. Cutting and pasting from your written text often produces a dull, wordy presentation.

Create a Portfolio

Your instructor may ask you to submit a portfolio of written work as part of your grade. Some schools also require a writing portfolio in the junior or senior year. A portfolio includes a range of documents, giving readers a broader, more detailed picture of your writing than a single document could. Portfolios have different purposes and different requirements. For some portfolios, you might assemble a notebook of printed writing, while for others you might submit documents online into an electronic portfolio system. For any kind of portfolio, your goal is to provide tangible evidence of your learning. Your instructor should give you instructions about the purpose of your portfolio, what it should contain, and how you should arrange and submit it.

Types of portfolios

What you choose to include will depend on your portfolio guidelines. Here are some common portfolio types, their purposes, and documents they might contain.

Developmental	A developmental writing portfolio demonstrates a writer's developing skills over a given period of time—perhaps a semester, a year, or several years. Developmental portfolios may focus on skills like critical thinking, research, argument, style, collaboration, and mechanical competence. A developmental portfolio will usually include examples of revised work, providing evidence to readers that you have learned to evaluate and improve your own work.
Disciplinary	A disciplinary or professional writing portfolio demonstrates the writer's mastery of important writing forms in a field or discipline. For example an engineering writing portfolio might include examples of a survey, an accident report, an e-mail to clients, a competitive bid, and similar documents.
	Like a developmental portfolio, a disciplinary portfolio may also reflect how your knowledge about a subject progressed over a period of time. To show how you learned, you might provide examples of informal writing where you wrestle with new concepts; short papers where you research, expand, or connect your growing knowledge; and drafts or sections of longer analytical papers that demonstrate how you have learned to manipulate complex ideas.
Stylistic	Some portfolios are used to give readers a sense of the various styles and genres a writer can employ. Such a portfolio might include humorous writing, formal oratory, descriptive writing, and other types of writing that aim to produce different effects for the reader.

Sample portfolio

Here is a sample portfolio assignment for a rhetoric class.

End of Semester Portfolio Requirements
Rhetoric 309: 19th-Century Rhetoric—Professor Morrison

Your grade for the semester will be based upon a portfolio of your writing, chosen by you, and submitted the final week of class. I will meet individually with each of you at least twice during the semester to talk about your portfolios and answer any questions you have about them. I will also make periodic suggestions about work that you should include in your portfolio.

I will evaluate your portfolio for evidence of the following.

- Awareness of rhetorical terms and techniques.
- Comprehension of the ways rhetoric was used in the nineteenth century, and ability to discuss individual examples.
- A growing ability to use and to discuss the use of rhetorical techniques in your own writing and in that of your peers.
- Steady improvement in the power and readability of your own prose, including mechanical facility and vocabulary.

Of course, I do not expect you to know all the course material the minute you walk through the door. Nor do I expect you to be a perfect writer on the first day of class. That is what this class is for: to teach you about rhetoric and to help you improve your writing. Therefore, your portfolio should demonstrate to me how you have approached each element of the class—the readings, the class discussions, the writing process, and the research—and what you have learned from it. You should begin your portfolio with a reflective letter that sums up your experience in the class. In particular, I am interested in how the class experience might be useful to you in the future.

Please follow the letter with a list of your portfolio contents. Arrange your materials in whatever order you like, and place them in a three-ring binder with your name on the outside. The portfolio is due at the beginning of class on May 2.

Here is a Table of Contents for a completed sample portfolio.

Portfolio Contents

1. First informal writing assignment: What do I know about rhetoric?

2. Last informal writing assignment: What would you do with your final research project if you had another semester to work on it?

3. First draft (with instructor comments): "Investigating 'Independence': An Analysis of Frederick Douglass's Speech, 'What to the Slave Is the Fourth of July?'"

4. Peer review of "Investigating 'Independence': An Analysis of Frederick Douglass's Speech, 'What to the Slave Is the Fourth of July?'"

5. Final draft: "Investigating 'Independence': An Analysis of Frederick Douglass's Speech, 'What to the Slave Is the Fourth of July?'"

6. Peer review for Kevin Gi

7. Discussion forum transcript: "Special Elements of Oratory"

8. Proposal and annotated bibliography for final research paper

9. Final draft of research paper: "Discrepancies in Newspaper Transcriptions of Abolitionist Orations"

The reflective letter or summary

Usually, a portfolio includes a reflective letter, a summary statement, or some other written document in which you provide an overview of the material and your experience in the course. You may be asked to explain why you chose the pieces you did, or to discuss what you feel you have accomplished. The reflective letter is your opportunity to frame the different documents in the portfolio and explain how they add up to a single, comprehensive picture of your performance as a writer.

The letter does not simply make a claim that you performed well; it tracks your experience in the course, using the writing samples as a step-by-step guide to your learning. You will get the most out of your reflective letter if you perform an honest, impartial examination of your challenges, setbacks, and successes in the course.

Here is the reflective letter in Grace Bernhardt's portfolio.

Dear Professor Morrison,

I learned a great deal about writing, speaking, and thinking this semester. When I first started this class I had only done freewriting in a creative writing workshop. The exercises we did almost every day showed me how writing can get me started thinking and can help get me out of feeling stuck when I am not sure where to go next. I have included two examples of my freewriting from the beginning and the end of semester so you can see how much more useful they became to me.

I also learned how to take criticism. I was proud of my first draft of the paper on Frederick Douglass and was shocked to get it back with many comments and suggestions from you. But when I sat down and read your comments, I realized how much better the paper could be. Your advice, along with our peer review and a session with a consultant in the writing center, helped me improve the paper. The experience taught me that I can improve any paper and that I should always try to do so. My final research paper is probably the best writing I've done so far in my life, but I hope to get even better.

I discovered how helpful my peers could be to my learning. Writing peer reviews taught me how to look closely at someone else's words and consider how they could be stronger. The discussions were the best part of class, and it was on the online class discussion forum that I worked out the focus for my final research project. I have included a transcript of this forum discussion.

The research we did for our final project was difficult and time consuming, but I learned much about the resources in our library. You can see from my annotated bibliography that I finally figured out the difference between primary and secondary sources!

Finally, this class taught me so much about history and the power of words. I feel like I know more about why America is the way it is. I am considering majoring in Radio, Television, and Film, and this class helped me understand the impact of words on audiences.

Thanks for a great class!
Sincerely,
Grace Bernhardt

 **MyWritingLab**™ Visit Ch. 16 in MyWritingLab to complete the chapter exercises and to test your understanding of the chapter objectives.

17 Writing for Online Courses

When you enroll in a course with an online component, your participation and engagement are the keys to your success.

In this chapter, you will learn to

1 Keep track of online coursework *(see p. 517)*

2 Participate in online discussions *(see p. 518)*

3 Manage online writing *(see p. 519)*

Keep Track of Online Coursework

You will excel in online courses if you communicate well, stay motivated, and produce outstanding work. If you miss assignments, you can fall behind in a hurry.

Use courseware

Many courses—not just those that meet only online—now offer online tools and content that are located within a course management system (such as Blackboard, Moodle, Canvas, or Coursera). Whatever course management system your school uses, take advantage early in the semester of tutorials and help documents that guide you in how to e-mail, post to a discussion, or submit an assignment for your course.

Plan your time

Even more than in traditional face-to-face-classes, online courses require self-discipline and strong organization to keep your work on track. At the beginning of the term, use the course syllabus or online course schedule to create your own detailed schedule to be sure you keep up with reading and assignments.

Then stick to the schedule you have outlined. Know the course policy for late assignments, for written work, and other participation. The sooner you start the work for the course the better. As in any other class, keeping up with reading and due dates is essential.

WRITE NOW   MyWritingLab™

Create a blog

Blogs assigned for courses sometimes allow students a great deal of freedom to select their subject matter and sometimes course blogs are on an assigned topic, such as responses to the readings. Your school may have a Web site where you can publish a blog, or you can use one of the many free sites such as these:

- Blogger
- edublogs
- WordPress

Great bloggers who attract many readers share four qualities. They write with a lively, personal voice. They are well informed. They are honest about what they know and don't know. And they write their blog entries to initiate conversations, not to have the last word on a subject. Keep these points in mind:

- Develop a personal voice that conveys your personality.
- Offer something new. If you don't have anything new, then point readers to the interesting writing of others.
- Do your homework. Let your readers know the sources of your information.
- Keep it short. If you have a lot to say about different subjects, write more than one entry.
- Provide relevant links.
- Remember that informal writing is not sloppy, error-filled writing.

Participate in Online Discussions

Discussion board posts are frequent assignments in writing classes. Usually they are short essays, no more than 300 words. Sources of any information still need to be cited.

When you are posting the first entry in a discussion thread, give your post a clear, specific subject line that lets readers know what you are writing before they open it. For new or response posts, offer the context (the assignment or reading name) and other background.

Discussion board posts are often similar to blogs, but they are typically written as a response to a question or posting by the instructor. The assignment for the post below was to find and analyze an example of a visual metaphor.

Thread: "Use Only What You Need": The Denver Water Conservation Campaign
Author: Chrissy Yao
Posted Date: March 1, 2014 1:12 PM

In 2006, Denver Water, the city's oldest utility, launched a ten-year conservation plan based on using water efficiently ("Denver"). Denver Water teamed up with the Sukle Advertising firm and produced the "Use Only What You Need Campaign" to help alleviate the water crisis that the city was enduring (Samuel). The campaign uses billboard advertising, magazine ads, and even stripped-down cars to impart messages of water conservation and efficiency. ◀

> Yao describes the ad campaign that uses the partial bus bench.

Clever visual metaphors are at the heart of the campaign. One example is a park bench with available seating only for one individual. The words, "USE ONLY WHAT YOU NEED," are stenciled in on the back of the bench. The bench, which can actually be used for sitting, conveys the idea that if only one person were using the bench, that person would only need a small area to sit on, not the whole thing. The bench makes concrete the concept of water conservation. ◀

> Yao analyzes the visual metaphor.

The innovative ad campaign that uses objects in addition to traditional advertising has proven successful. The simplicity and minimalist style of the ads made a convincing argument about using resources sparingly. The average water consumption of Denver dropped between 18% and 21% annually from 2006 to 2009.

Works Cited
"Denver Water's Conservation Plan." *Denver Water*, www.denverwater.org/
    Conservation/ConservationPlan/. Accessed 23 Feb. 2014.
Samuel, Frederick. "Denver Water." *Ad Goodness*, 16 Nov. 2006,
    www.frederiksamuel.com/blog/2006/11/denver-water.html.

Manage Online Writing

As in any course, be sure you back up files as a regular part of your routine to avoid losing your work.

Stay organized

In most online courses that you will be saving and then exchanging drafts with classmates. To avoid problems with lost drafts or confusing file names, develop a system for organizing drafts for each course. Set up a system of folders with one for your drafts, one for those from classmates and save files in these separate folders.

Give each of your drafts a name that includes specifics of the assignment and, if you plan to share it with others, your name (Sheri Harrison Reflection Draft 1). Your instructor may require or suggest a system for you. Including your name in the draft's file name helps your instructor and classmates keep track; also, put dates in the file names if you are writing multiple drafts.

Observe netiquette

In online courses your discussion posts, wiki entries, and other written work speak for and create an impression of you. Follow commonsense rules of netiquette.

- **Remember your classmates are people like you.** Address them by name if possible, and sign your post with your name. Don't say things online that you would not say to a classmate face-to-face.

- **Be aware of tone.** Often sarcasm and attempts at humor come off poorly when you are having a discussion online.

- **Be a forgiving reader.** You don't need to point out every minor error. If you feel strongly about a mistake, send the writer a private e-mail rather than addressing the entire class.

- **Keep the discussion civil.** Often a reply like "what a stupid idea" leads to a flame war with name calling, and the possibility of exploring an issue ends.

- **Don't spam your classmates.** Refrain from sending off-topic messages to everyone. Your classmates have enough to sort through without having to deal with frivolous messages.

- **Make yourself credible.** Check for punctuation, grammar, and spelling errors before you post.

WRITE NOW   MyWritingLab™

Review drafts online

When you are reviewing drafts online, be sure you know what formats your instructor recommends and your classmates can read and open. After you comment on another student's draft, remember to change the file name.

See page 58 for a guide for responding to others' work.

MyWritingLab™ Visit Ch. 17 in MyWritingLab to complete the chapter exercises and to test your understanding of the chapter objectives.

18 Working as a Team

The better you understand how to write effectively with others, the more enjoyable and the more productive the process will be for you.

In this chapter, you will learn to

1 Organize a team *(see p. 521)*

2 Brainstorm as a team *(see p. 522)*

3 Work as a team *(see p. 523)*

Organize a Team

Unlike sports teams where a coach is in charge, writing team members often have to organize themselves.

Analyze the assignment	• Identify what exactly you are being asked to do. • Write down the goals as specifically as you can and discuss them as a team. • Determine which tasks are required to meet those goals. Be as detailed as you can. Write down the tasks and arrange them in the order they need to be completed.
Make a work plan	• Make a time line. List the dates when specific tasks need to be completed and distribute it to all team members. Charts are useful tools for keeping track of progress. • Assign tasks to all team members. Find out if anyone possesses additional skills that could be helpful to the team.
Keep goals in mind	• Revisit the team's goals often. To succeed, each team member must keep in mind what the team aims to accomplish. • Communicate often. Most writing teams will not have an assigned leader. Each team member shares responsibility.

What makes a good team?

In sports, in the workplace, and in everyday life, successful teams have well-defined goals and work together to achieve these goals. Successful teams communicate well, make good decisions together, act quickly on their decisions, and continuously evaluate their progress. Successful teams achieve the right balance so that each team member can contribute.

WRITE NOW   MyWritingLab™

Plan an oral presentation as a team

Much of the work in organizations, companies, and laboratories is done by teams of people. Frequently these teams give in-progress and summary oral presentations to report what they have accomplished.

• Determine the goals of the presentation and how long the presentation should last.
• Decide if visuals would be useful, especially if you are presenting statistical data.
• Assign each team member a role in the presentation.
• Find time to rehearse as a team to make sure the presentation meets the goals and time limit.

Brainstorm as a Team

Teams have the potential to generate many more ideas than individuals can, and teams bring the full experience of everyone to the issue or problem.

Online tools: Chat sessions, discussion boards, wikis, and collaborative documents all can be used for brainstorming. Online tools have the advantage of bringing together people who may not be able to meet in person.

Face-to-face tools: Team brainstorming sessions draw energy from the immediacy of the group. Simple tools like whiteboards, flipcharts, and sticky notes help team members to visualize problems and ideas.

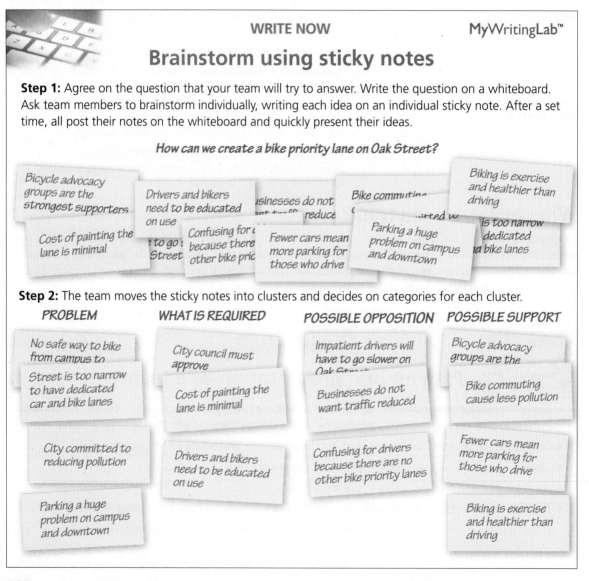

WRITE NOW

MyWritingLab™

Brainstorm using sticky notes

Step 1: Agree on the question that your team will try to answer. Write the question on a whiteboard. Ask team members to brainstorm individually, writing each idea on an individual sticky note. After a set time, all post their notes on the whiteboard and quickly present their ideas.

How can we create a bike priority lane on Oak Street?

Bicycle advocacy groups are the strongest supporters

Drivers and bikers need to be educated on use

...sinesses do not ...reduce...

Bike commuting...

Biking is exercise and healthier than driving

Cost of painting the lane is minimal

...to go... Street...

Confusing for... because there... other bike pric...

Fewer cars mean more parking for those who drive

Parking a huge problem on campus and downtown

...itted w... ...dedicated ...a bike lanes

is too narrow

Step 2: The team moves the sticky notes into clusters and decides on categories for each cluster.

PROBLEM	WHAT IS REQUIRED	POSSIBLE OPPOSITION	POSSIBLE SUPPORT
No safe way to bike from campus to	City council must approve	Impatient drivers will have to go slower on Oak Str...	Bicycle advocacy groups are the
Street is too narrow to have dedicated car and bike lanes	Cost of painting the lane is minimal	Businesses do not want traffic reduced	Bike commuting cause less pollution
City committed to reducing pollution	Drivers and bikers need to be educated on use	Confusing for drivers because there are no other bike priority lanes	Fewer cars mean more parking for those who drive
Parking a huge problem on campus and downtown			Biking is exercise and healthier than driving

Work as a Team

Work closely together in creating and revising content. You'll enjoy writing more and you'll have the benefit of more ideas.

Carry out the plan

- Decide on a process for monitoring progress. Set up specific dates for review and assign team members to be responsible for reviewing work that has been done.
- When you have a complete draft, each team member should evaluate it by providing written comments.
- Meet to compare evaluations and decide on a plan for revising and adding content.
- After revising, arrange for one or more persons to review the project. Meet again to determine if additional changes are needed.

Be aware of team dynamics

Teamwork requires some flexibility. Different people have different styles and contribute in different ways. Keep talking to each other along the way.

- Deal with problems when they come up.
- If a team member is not participating, find out why.
- If team members have different ideas about what needs to be done, find time to meet so that the team can reach an agreement.
- Get the team together if you are not meeting the deadlines you established in the work plan and, if necessary, devise a new plan.

WRITE NOW   MyWritingLab™

What to do when problems arise

Working together in a team is most often a rewarding experience, but you need to know how to deal with problems when they arise. Generally it is better to make an effort to resolve problems within the team before asking your instructor to intervene. In a group of four or five students, discuss how you might respond as a group to a team member who

1. is "missing in action,"
2. doesn't come prepared,
3. doesn't answer e-mail,
4. is disrespectful to others,
5. refuses to allow anyone to critique or revise his or her work.

MyWritingLab™ Visit Ch. 18 in MyWritingLab to complete the chapter exercises and to test your understanding of the chapter objectives.

Part 4

The Writer as Researcher

Guide to Research

Research is a creative process, which is another way of saying that it is a messy process. Even though the process is complex, your results will improve if you understand what the process involves and what you need to do. This research map will help you keep the big picture in mind while you are immersed in research.

1 PLAN A RESEARCH PROJECT

- **Analyze your assigment**
  (see p. 529)

- **Ask a question about a topic that interest you and narrow that topic**
  (see p. 530)

- **Determine what kinds of research you will need**
  (see p. 531)

- **Decide if you need to do field research**
  (see Chapter 22)

- **Draft a working thesis**
  (see p. 533)

2 FIND SOURCES

- **Identify the kinds of sources that you will need**
  (see p. 535)

- **Search using keywords**
  (see p. 536)

- **Find sources in databases**
  (see p. 538)

- **Find sources on the Web**
  (see p. 540)

- **Find multimedia sources**
  (see p. 543)

- **Find print sources**
  (see p. 544)

- **Start a working bibliography**
  (see p. 545)

3 EVALUATE SOURCES

- **Determine if a source is relevant for your research**
  (see p. 547)

- **Determine the kind of source**
  (see p. 548)

- **Determine if a source is trustworthy**
  (see p. 549)

- **Recognize the special challenges of Web sources**
  (see p. 550)

4 WRITE A DRAFT

- **Review your working thesis and revise if necessary**
  (see p. 533)

- **Take stock of your research to identify which sources are critical for your project and what further research you may need to do**
  (see p. 533)

- **Plan your organization by making a working outline**
  (see p. 40)

- **Avoid plagiarism when quoting, summarizing, and paraphrasing sources**
  (see p. 561)

- **Integrate quotations**
  (see p. 565)

5 DOCUMENT SOURCES AND REVISE

- **Decide which documentation style to use**
  (for MLA-style documentation, go to Chapter 24)
  (for APA-style documentation, go to Chapter 25)

- **Review and revise your research project, beginning with high-level issues of content and organization**
  (see p. 569)

19 Planning Research

Understand the different kinds of possible research and plan your strategy in advance.

In this chapter, you will learn to

1. Analyze the research task
   (see p. 529)

2. Ask a research question
   (see p. 530)

3. Determine what information you need
   (see p. 531)

4. Draft a working thesis
   (see p. 533)

Analyze the Research Task

If you have an assignment that requires research, look closely at what you are being asked to do.

ANALYZE YOUR ASSIGNMENT	Often your assignment will tell you what is expected.
	An assignment that asks you to *inform* or *explain* signals an informative essay or project.
	→ See Chapter 8
	An *analysis of causes* requires you to write a causal argument.
	→ See Chapter 10
	An *evaluation* requires you to make critical judgments based on criteria.
	→ See Chapter 11
	An *argument* requires you to assemble evidence in support of a claim that you make.
	→ See Chapter 12
	A *proposal* requires you to offer a solution to a problem or a call for the audience to do something.
	→ See Chapter 13
ASSESS THE PROJECT'S LENGTH, SCOPE, AND REQUIREMENTS	• What kind of research are you being asked to do?
	• What is the length of the project?
	• What kinds and number of sources are required?
	• Which documentation style is required, such as MLA or APA?
	→ See Chapter 24 for MLA and Chapter 25 for APA
FIND A TOPIC	• Visit "Research by Subject" on your library's Web site. Clicking on a subject such as "African and African American Studies" will take you to a list of resources.
	• Look for topics in your courses. Browse your course notes and readings.
	• Browse a Web subject directory. Web subject directories, including Yahoo Directory, are useful when you want to narrow a topic or learn what subcategories a topic might contain.
	• Look for topics as you read. When you read actively, you ask questions and respond to ideas in the text.
IDENTIFY YOUR POTENTIAL READERS	• How familiar are your readers with your subject?
	• What background information will you need to supply?
	• If your subject is controversial, what opinions or beliefs are your readers likely to hold?
	• If some readers are likely to disagree with you, how can you convince them?

529

Ask a Question

Often you'll be surprised by the amount of information your initial browsing uncovers. Your next task will be to identify in that mass of information a question for your research project. This researchable question will be the focus of the remainder of your research and ultimately of your research project or paper. Browsing on the topic of solid waste recycling might lead you to these broad researchable questions.

Broad questions

- Do cities save or lose money on recycling programs?
- Why can't all plastics be recycled?
- Are Americans being persuaded to recycle more paper, aluminum, and plastic?

Focused questions

Think about how to make your research question specific enough so that you can treat it thoroughly in a paper. Reading about your subject will help you to focus your research question.

- Why did the number of tons of recycled plastic and glass in our city peak in 2012 and decline slightly ever since?
- Should our state mandate the use of degradable plastics that decay along with kitchen and yard waste in compost heaps?
- Besides paper bags that deplete forests, what are the alternatives to plastic bags that contaminate soil in landfills and sabotage the recycling system by jamming the machinery that sorts bottles and cans?

Determine what kinds of research you need to do

Once you have formulated a research question, begin thinking about what kind of research you will need to do to address the question.

Secondary research

Most researchers rely partly or exclusively on the work of others as sources of information. Research based on the work of others is called **secondary research**.

Primary research

Much of the research done in college creates new information through **primary research**: experiments, data-gathering surveys and interviews, detailed observations, and the examination of historical documents. Although some undergraduates do not do primary research, sometimes you may be researching a question that requires you to gather firsthand information (see Chapter 22).

Determine What You Need

Is the scope of your issue . . .	Then research might include . . .
local? (Inadequate bike lanes, local noise ordinances, school policies)	• interviews and observations • local newspapers • other local media: television, radio, blogs, social media
regional? (County taxes, toll road construction, watershed protection)	• some of the sources above • state government offices • regional organizations, clubs, or associations—e.g., the Newark Better Business Bureau, Brazos Valley Mothers Against Drunk Driving
national? (Federal agricultural subsidies, immigration, major league sports)	• some of the sources above • federal government offices • national organizations, clubs, or associations—e.g., the American Automobile Association • national network news on television and radio • national newspapers or magazines—e.g., the *New York Times* or *Rolling Stone*
international? (Trade imbalances, military conflicts, global climate change)	• some of the sources above • international agencies such as UNICEF • international news outlets such as Reuters • foreign newspapers or magazines like *Le Monde* and *der Spiegel*

You can also find sources you need by thinking about people affected by your issue and noting where it is being discussed.

Who is interested in this issue?	**Where would they read, write, talk, or hear about it?**	**In what media might the information appear?**
scientists teachers voters minors senior citizens policy makers stock brokers	scientific journals political journals scholarly journals newspapers books Web forums government documents	Web sites social media television radio print film/DVD

Set a schedule

To schedule your research, use your assignment, your personal schedule, and your knowledge of the sources you'll need. Allow yourself some large blocks of uninterrupted time, especially during the browsing stage.

Project: Research paper for a government course, analyzing a recent financial fraud

Days until first draft is due: 17

Days 1-3: PRELIMINARY research, one hour each evening
Days 4-6: IN-DEPTH library research— Schedule appointment with reference librarian for periodicals search tutorial
Days 7-9: Go over collected material, think about research question/hypothesis
Days 10-12: Begin drafting
Days 13-14: Revise rough draft for clarity, organization, and ideas
Days 15-16: Follow-up research or verify questionable sources as needed
Day 17: Fine-tune draft

Project: Paper utilizing field research for an introduction to social research course

Weeks until project due: 7

Week 1: Research and brainstorm topics; discuss short list of possible topics/methods with professor; make final decision
Week 2: Research survey/interview methods; design appropriate method
Week 3: Conduct field research
Week 4: Analyze data and do follow-up if necessary
Week 5: Draft paper—go back to library if necessary
Week 6: Take draft to writing center; revise
Week 7: Proofread, fine-tune, and make sure all charts and images print correctly

Draft a Working Thesis

Once you have done some preliminary research into your question, you need to craft a working thesis. Perhaps you have found a lot of interesting material on the home economics movement of the 1950s and 1960s. You have discovered that food companies—particularly makers of packaged foods—were deeply involved in shaping and funding the movement. As you research the question of why food companies fostered the home economics movement, a working thesis begins to emerge.

Write your topic, research question, and working thesis on a notecard or in a file that you keep handy. You may need to revise it several times until the wording is precise. As you research, ask yourself, does this information tend to support my thesis? Information that does not support your thesis is still important! It may lead you to adjust your thesis, or even abandon it altogether. You may need to find another source or reason that shows your thesis is still valid.

TOPIC:

The Home Economics Movement of the 1950s and 1960s.

RESEARCH QUESTION:

Why did the major American food corporations fund the Home Economics movement of the '50s and '60s?

WORKING THESIS:

Major American food corporations invested in the development and spread of Home Economics in order to create a ready market for their products by teaching women to rely on prepared foods instead of cooking "from scratch." They used Home Economics programs to change the way Americans thought about food and cooking.

WRITE NOW MyWritingLab™

Determine what information you need

Select one of the possible topics below or identify a topic that will work for your assignment. Write a brief list or paragraph describing the types of research that might be used to investigate the question. What kinds of information would you need? Where would you look for it?

1. How much does an average American couple spend to adopt a child from overseas?

2. What determines the price of gasoline that you pay at the pump?

3. How effective was drafting soldiers in the North and South during the Civil War?

4. What percentage of U.S. power generation comes from renewable energy?

MyWritingLab™ Visit Ch. 19 in MyWritingLab to complete the chapter exercises and to test your understanding of the chapter objectives.

533

20 Finding Sources

In this chapter, you will learn to

1. Identify the kinds of sources that you need *(see p. 535)*
2. Search using keywords *(see p. 536)*
3. Find sources in databases *(see p. 538)*
4. Find sources on the Web *(see p. 540)*
5. Find multimedia sources *(see p. 543)*
6. Find print sources *(see p. 544)*

Identify the Kinds of Sources That You Need

Searches using *Google*, *Yahoo!*, or *Bing* turn up thousands of items, many of which are often not useful for research. Knowing where to start is the first step.

Start with your research question and working thesis

Look at your research question and working thesis.

- If your topic is more than a year or two old, scholarly books and articles in scholarly journals often are the highest-quality sources because they have undergone peer review by experts in the field before publication.

- If your topic concerns events and issues in the past few weeks or months, you likely will not find current coverage in scholarly books and journals because of the lag time required for peer review. You may have to use Web and newspaper sources, which demand extra care in evaluating for quality (see Chapter 21).

- If your topic requires current statistics, government Web sites and publications are often the best for finding them and are also valuable for researching science and medicine.

Research librarians in your library can help you locate sources quickly.

Type of source	Types of information	How to find them
Scholarly books	Extensive and in-depth coverage of nearly any subject	Library catalog
Scholarly journals	Reports of new knowledge and research findings by experts	Online library databases
Trade journals	Reports of information pertaining to specific industries, professions, and products	Online library databases
Popular magazines	Reports or summaries of current news, sports, fashion, entertainment subjects	Online library databases
Newspapers	Recent and current information; foreign newspapers are useful for international perspectives	Online library databases
Government publications	Government-collected statistics, studies, and reports; especially good for science and medicine	Library catalog and city, state, and federal government Web sites
Videos, audios, documentaries, maps	Information varies widely	Library catalog, Web, and online library databases

Search Using Keywords

In most cases, you will begin your research with a keyword search or a subject search.

Identify keywords in your working thesis

Underline possible keywords in your working thesis.

> **EXAMPLE:**
> The <u>NCAA</u> should adopt a different definition of <u>amateur</u> that allows <u>student athletes</u> to be <u>paid</u> a <u>stipend</u> to cover <u>living expenses</u> in light of what they <u>earn</u> for their <u>colleges</u>.

Think of synonyms (words similar in meaning) to the words you underline. For example, you might list synonyms for the word paid such as earnings, money, payment, income, or salary.

Find keywords in your library's online catalog

Entries for subjects in your library's online catalog and in databases will help you find keywords. If you find a book or article that is exactly on your topic, use the subject terms to locate additional items.

> **EXAMPLE:**
> TITLE:
> The digital person : technology and privacy in the information age / Daniel J. Solove.
> SUBJECTS:
> Data protection–Law and legislation–United States.
> Electronic records–Access control–United States.
> Public records–Law and legislation–United States.
> Government information–United States.
> Privacy, Right of–United States.

Search using AND or OR

The operator AND combines different keywords in a search. The search engine limits the results to documents that contain all the terms. Use AND when you want to narrow search results.
as search terms (*college athlete* AND *salary*).

The operator OR finds synonyms of search terms. The search engine limits the results to documents that contain all the terms. Use OR when you want to broaden search results.

Limit searches

Another strategy to limit your search is to specify what you don't want, by using NOT.

> **EXAMPLE:**
> If you are interested in air pollution control policies, but not those used in the state of California.
>
> Type **air pollution control policies** NOT **California**

Use a thesaurus to find synonyms for keywords

A thesaurus is a reference work that lists words similar in meaning (synonyms) and words opposite in meaning (antonyms). You can find several general thesauri on Web sites and apps that yield results like the example below.

Main Entry:	**earn**
Part of Speech:	*verb*
Definition:	make money
Synonyms:	be gainfully employed, collect, draw, gain, gross, make, net, profit, receive

Many databases have thesauri, and there are also specialized thesauri for particular subjects including law, business, medicine, science, anthropology, education, psychology, sociology, and others. You can find them on your library's online catalog.

WRITE NOW　　　　　　　　　　　MyWritingLab™

Freewrite to find keywords

If you have difficulty coming up with keywords, another method of finding keywords is to freewrite. For a set time (fifteen to twenty minutes is typical), write anything that comes to mind about your topic, ignoring grammatical mistakes.

When you finish, use a spelling checker to clean up any spelling mistakes. (Keyword searches require accurate spelling.) Grammar and punctuation mistakes don't matter during a freewrite.

Then create a Wordle, which is a tool for generating "word clouds" that give greater prominence to the words that appear most frequently in a text. Go to Wordle and paste your text in the box provided under the Create tab. Click the Go button, and then click the Randomize button until you find a visually appealing result. This Wordle was created from Patrice Conley's freewrite on p. 44.

Look at the largest words, and enter them into an online thesaurus to generate synonyms.

Find Sources in Databases

Sources found through library databases have already been filtered for you by professional librarians. They will include some common sources like popular magazines and newspapers, but the greatest value of database sources are the many journals, abstracts, studies, e-books, and other writing produced by specialists whose work has been scrutinized and commented on by other experts. When you read a source from a library database, chances are you are hearing an informed voice in an important debate.

Locate databases

You can find databases on your library's Web site. Sometimes you will find a list of databases. Sometimes you select a subject, and then you are directed to databases. Sometimes you select the name of a database vendor such as EBSCO or ProQuest. The vendor is the company that provides databases to the library.

Common databases

Academic OneFile	Indexes periodicals from the arts, humanities, sciences, social sciences, and general news, with full-text articles and images. (Formerly *Expanded Academic ASAP*)
Academic Search Premier and Complete	Provide full-text articles for thousands of scholarly publications, including social sciences, humanities, education, computer sciences, engineering, language and linguistics, literature, medical sciences, and ethnic-studies journals.
ArticleFirst	Indexes journals in business, the humanities, medicine, science, and social sciences.
EBSCOhost Research Databases	Gateway to a large collection of EBSCO databases, including *Academic Search Premier* and *Complete*, *Business Source Premier* and *Complete*, *ERIC*, and *Medline*.
Factiva	Provides full-text articles on business topics, including articles from *The Wall Street Journal*.
Google Books	Allows you to search within books and gives you snippets surrounding search terms for copyrighted books. Many books out of copyright include the full text. Available for everyone.
Google Scholar	Searches scholarly literature according to criteria of relevance. Available for everyone.
General OneFile	Contains millions of full-text articles about a wide range of academic and general-interest topics.
LexisNexis Academic	Provides full text of a wide range of newspapers, magazines, government and legal documents, and company profiles from around the world.
JSTOR	Provides scanned copies of scholarly journals.
ProQuest Databases	Like EBSCOhost, ProQuest is a gateway to a large collection of databases with over 100 billion pages, including the best archives of doctoral dissertations and historical newspapers.

Use databases

Your library has a list of databases and indexes by subject. If you can't find this list on your library's Web site, ask a reference librarian for help. Follow these steps to find articles.

1. Select a database appropriate to your subject or a comprehensive database.

2. Search the database using your list of keywords.

3. Once you have chosen an article, print or e-mail to yourself the complete citation to the article. Look for the e-mail link after you click on the item you want.

4. Print or e-mail to yourself the full text if it is available.

5. If the full text is not available, check the online library catalog to see if your library has the journal.

Sometimes the images are not reproduced in the HTML versions, but the PDF versions show the actual printed copy. Get the PDF version if it is available. Articles in HTML format usually do not contain the page numbers.

Locate elements of a citation

To cite a source from a database, you will need the

- Author if listed
- Title of article
- Name of periodical
- Volume and issue number (for journals)

- Date of publication (and edition for newspapers)
- Section (for newspapers) and page numbers
- Name of database
- URL for the article, or a DOI (digital object identifier) if one is assigned to the article.

A sample article from the Academic Search Complete search for "steroids" and "high school." The confusing part of citing this example is distinguishing between the database and the vendor. The vendor's name often appears at the top of the screen, making the vendor's name look like the name of the database. In this case, EBSCO is the vendor—the company that sells your library access to Academic Search Complete and many other databases. Often you have to look carefully to find the name of the database.

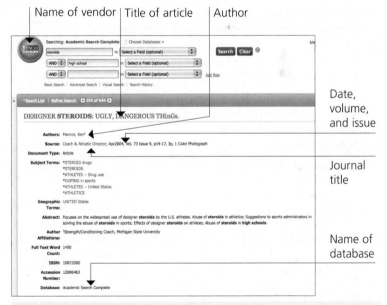

Mannie, Ken. "Designer Steroids: Ugly, Dangerous Things." *Scholastic Coach and Athletic Director,* vol. 73, no. 9, Apr. 2004, pp. 14-17. *Academic Search Complete,* web.a.ebscohost.com/ehost/detail/detail?vid=3&sid=a0137e71-62ef-4ed8-9d58-feeec994758a%40sessionmgr4003&hid=4104&bdata=JnNpdGU9ZWhvc3QtbGl2ZQ%3d%3d#AN=12696463&db=a9h.

A citation for an article that you find on a database looks like this in MLA style:

Find Sources on the Web

Because anyone can publish on the Web, there is no overall quality control and there is no system of organization—two strengths we take for granted in libraries. Nevertheless, the Web offers you some valuable resources for current topics.

Use search engines wisely

Search engines designed for the Web work in ways similar to library databases and your library's online catalog but with one major difference. Databases typically do some screening of the items they list, but search engines potentially take you to everything on the Web—millions of pages in all. Consequently, you have to work harder to limit searches on the Web or you can be deluged with tens of thousands of items.

Kinds of search engines

A search engine is a set of programs that sort through millions of items at incredible speed. There are three major kinds of search engines.

1. **Keyword search engines** (e.g., *Bing, Google, Yahoo!*). Keyword search engines give different results because they assign different weights to the information they find.

2. **Web directories** (e.g., *Britannica.com, Yahoo! Directory*). Web directories classify Web sites into categories and are the closest equivalent to the cataloging system used by libraries. On most directories professional editors decide how to index a particular Web site. Web directories also allow keyword searches.

3. **Specialized search engines** are designed for specific purposes:

   - regional search engines (e.g., *Baidu* for China)
   - medical search engines (e.g., *WebMD*)
   - legal search engines (e.g., *Lexis*)
   - job search engines (e.g., *Monster.com*)
   - property search engines (e.g., *Zillow*)

Advanced searches

The advanced searches on *Google* and *Yahoo!* give you the options of using a string of words to search for sites that contain (1) all the words, (2) the exact phrase, (3) any of the words, or (4) that do not contain certain words. They also allow you to specify the site, the date range, the file format, and the domain. For example, if you want to limit a search for *identity theft statistics* to reliable government Web sites, you can specify the domain as **.gov**, either by using the advanced search window or by adding *site:.gov* to your search terms.

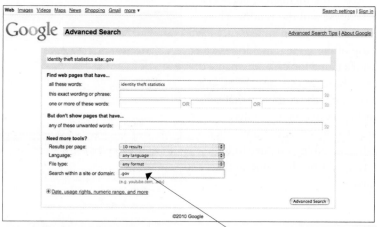

An advanced search on Google for government (.gov) sites only.

Limiting the domain to .gov eliminates commercial sites from the search.

The **OR** operator is useful if you don't know exactly which term will get the results you want, especially if you are searching within a specific site. For example, you could try this search: *face-to-face OR f2f site: webworkerdaily.com*.

You can also exclude terms by putting a minus sign before the term. If you want to search for social network privacy, but not *Facebook*, try *social network privacy –Facebook*.

Find online government sources

The federal government has made many of its publications available on the Web. Also, many state governments now publish important documents on the Web. Often the most current and most reliable statistics are government statistics. Among the more important government resources are the following.

- **Bureau of Labor Statistics** (www.bls.gov/). Source for official U.S. government statistics on employment, wages, and consumer prices

- **Census Bureau** (www.census.gov/). Contains a wealth of links to sites for population, social, economic, and political statistics, including the *Statistical Abstract of the United States* (www.census.gov/compendia/statab/)

- **Centers for Disease Control and Prevention** (www.cdc.gov/). Authoritative and trustworthy source for health statistics

- **CIA World Factbook** (www.cia.gov/library/publications/the-world-factbook/). Resource for geographic, economic, demographic and political information on the nations of the world

- **Library of Congress** (www.loc.gov/). Many of the resources of the largest library in the world are available on the Web

- **National Institutes of Health** (www.nih.gov/). Extensive health information including MedlinePlus searches

- **NASA** (www.nasa.gov/). A rich site with much information and images concerning space exploration and scientific discovery

- **THOMAS** (thomas.loc.gov/). The major source of legislative information, including bills, committee reports, and voting records of individual members of Congress

- **USA.gov** (www.usa.gov/). The place to start when you are not sure where to look for government information

Find online reference sources

Your library's Web site has a link to reference sites, either on the main page or under another heading like research tools.

Reference sites are usually organized by subject, and you can find resources under the subject heading.

- **Business information** (links to business databases and sites like *Hoover's* that profile companies)

- **Dictionaries** (including the *Oxford English Dictionary* and various subject dictionaries and language dictionaries)

- **Education** (including *The College Blue Book* and others)

- **Encyclopedias** (including *Britannica Online* and others)

- **Government information** (links to federal, state, and local Web sites)

- **Reference books** (commonly used books like atlases, almanacs, biographies, handbooks, and histories)

- **Statistics and demographics** (links to federal, state, and local government sites; *FedStats* [www.fedstats.gov/] is a good place to start)

Search interactive media

The Internet allows you to access other people's opinions on thousands of topics. Millions of people post messages on discussion lists and groups, *Facebook* groups, blogs, RSS feeds, *Twitter*, and so on. Much of what you read on interactive media sites is undocumented and highly opinionated, but you can still gather important information about people's attitudes and get tips about other sources, which you can verify later.

Several search engines have been developed for interactive media. *Facebook* and *Twitter* also have search engines for their sites.

Discussion list search engines

- **Big Boards** Tracks over two thousand of the most active discussion forums

- **Google Groups** Archives discussion forums dating back to 1981

- **Yahoo Groups** A directory of groups by subject

Blog search engines

- **Bloglines** Web-based aggregator that delivers RSS feeds

- **Google Blog Search** Searches blogs in several languages besides English

- **IceRocket** Searches blogs, *MySpace*, and *Twitter*

- **Technorati** Searches blogs and other user-generated content

STAYING ON TRACK
Know the limitations of *Wikipedia*

Wikipedia is a valuable resource for current information and for popular culture topics that are not covered in traditional encyclopedias. You can find out, for example, that SpongeBob SquarePants's original name was "SpongeBoy," but it had already been copyrighted.

Nevertheless, many instructors and the scholarly community in general do not consider *Wikipedia* a reliable source of information for a research paper. The fundamental problem with *Wikipedia* is stability, not whether the information is correct or incorrect. *Wikipedia* and other wikis constantly change. The underlying idea of documenting sources is that readers can consult the same sources that you consulted. Consult other sources to confirm what you find on *Wikipedia* and cite those sources.

Find Multimedia Sources

Text sources in print and on the Web are not your only option for research. Massive collections of images; audio files including music, speeches, and podcasts; videos; maps, charts, and graphs; and other resources are now available on the Web.

Find images

The major search engines for images include the following.

- **Bing Images**
- **Google Image Search**
- **Picsearch**
- **Yahoo! Image Search**

Libraries and museums also offer large collections. For example, the American Memory collection in the Library of Congress offers an important visual record of the history of the United States (memory. loc.gov/ammem/).

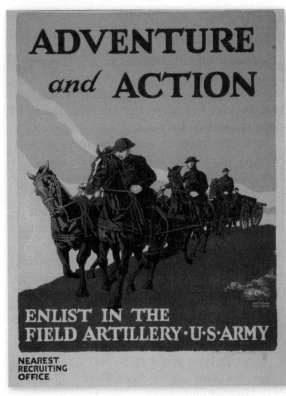

A search for World War I army recruiting posters turns up this poster in the Library of Congress.

Find videos

- **Bing Videos**
- **blinkx**
- **Google Videos**
- **Yahoo! Video Search**
- **YouTube**

Find podcasts

- **iTunes Podcast Resources**
- **PodcastDirectory.com**

Find charts, graphs, and maps

You can find statistical data represented in charts and graphs on many government Web sites.

- **Statistical Abstract of the United States** (www.census.gov/compendia/statab/)
- **Google Earth**
- **National Geographic Map Machine**
- **Perry Casteñada Map Collection, University of Texas** (www.lib.utexas.edu/maps/map_sites/ map_sites.html)

Respect copyright

Just because images, videos, and other multimedia files are easy to download from the Web does not mean that everything is available for you to use. Look for the creator's copyright notice and suggested credit line. This notice will tell you if you can reproduce the multimedia file.

Find Print Sources

Print sources may seem "old fashioned" in the Internet era, but they are the starting point for much of the research done by experts. In college and beyond, they are indispensable. No matter how current the topic you are researching, you will likely find information in print sources that is simply not available online.

Print sources have other advantages as well.

- Books are shelved according to subject, allowing easy browsing.
- Books often have bibliographies, directing you to other research on the subject.
- You can search for books in multiple ways: author, title, subject, or call letter.
- The majority of print sources have been evaluated by scholars, editors, and publishers, who decided whether they merited publication.

Find books

Nearly all college libraries now shelve books according to the Library of Congress Classification System, which uses a combination of letters and numbers to give you the book's unique location in the library. The Library of Congress call number begins with a letter or letters that represent the broad subject area into which the book is classified.

Locating books in your library

The floors of your library where books are shelved are referred to as the stacks. The call number will enable you to find the item in the stacks. You will

need to consult the locations guide for your library, which gives the level and section where an item is shelved.

The signs in the stacks guide you to the books you are looking for.

Locating e-books

Use your library's online catalog to find e-books the same way you find printed books. You'll see on the record "e-book" or "electronic resource." Click on the link and you can read the book and often download a few pages.

Find journal articles

Like books, scholarly journals provide in-depth examinations of subjects. The articles in scholarly journals are written by experts, and they usually contain lists of references that can guide you to other research on a subject.

Popular journals are useful for gaining general information. Articles in popular magazines are usually short with few, if any, source references and are typically written by journalists. Some instructors frown on using popular magazines, but these journals can be valuable for researching current opinion on a particular topic.

Many scholarly journals and popular magazines are available on your library's Web site. Find them the same way you look for books, using your library's online catalog. Databases increasingly contain the full text of articles, allowing you to read and copy the contents onto your computer. If the article you are looking for isn't available online, the paper copy will be shelved with the books in your library.

Create a Working Bibliography

As you begin to collect your sources, make sure you get full bibliographic information for everything you might want to use in your project: articles, books, Web sites, and other materials. This will save you a great deal of time and trouble later. Determine which documentation style you will use. If your instructor does not tell you which style is appropriate, ask. (Two major documentation styles—MLA and APA—are explained in detail in Chapters 24 and 25.) You can compile this information in a computer file, a notebook, or on notecards.

For books in print

You will need, at minimum, the following information. This information can typically be found on the front and back of the title page.

- Author's name
- Title of the book
- Name of publisher
- Date of publication

You will also need

- page numbers if you are quoting directly or referring to a specific passage.
- title and author of the individual chapter if your source is an edited book with contributions by several people.
- call numbers for the book or journal so you can find it easily in the future.

> HQ
> 799.7
> K36
> 2006
>
> Kamenetz, Anya. *Generation Debt: Why Now Is a Terrible Time to Be Young*. Riverhead Books, 2006.

For journals

- Author's name
- Title of the article
- Title of the journal
- Volume and issue of the journal
- Date of the issue
- Page numbers of the article
- URL (for online articles)

If you find the article in a database, you will also need the following information:

- Name of the database
- URL or DOI (digital object identifier), if one has been assigned to the article.

> Jurecic, Ann. "Neurodiversity." *College English*, vol. 69, no. 5, May 2007, pp. 421-42. *JSTOR*, www.jstor.org/stable/25472229.

 Visit Ch. 20 in MyWritingLab to complete the chapter exercises and to test your understanding of the chapter objectives.

21 Evaluating Sources

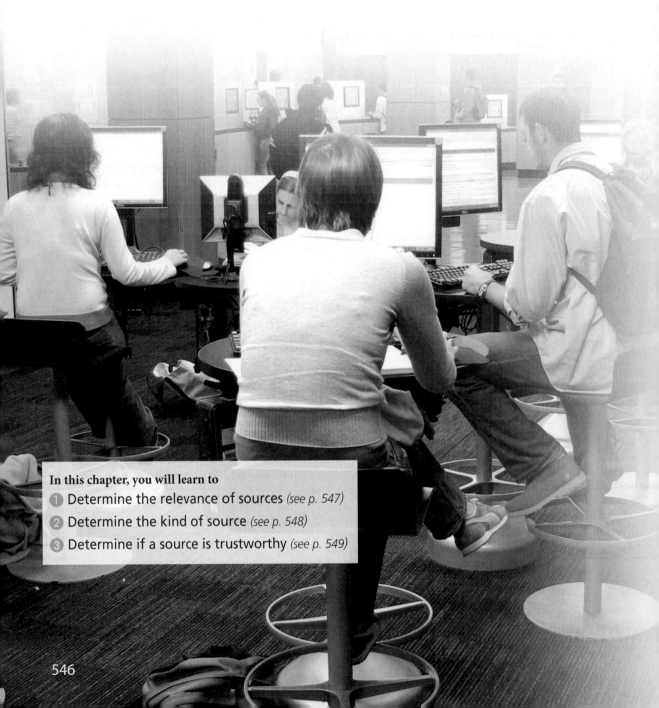

In this chapter, you will learn to

1. Determine the relevance of sources (see p. 547)
2. Determine the kind of source (see p. 548)
3. Determine if a source is trustworthy (see p. 549)

Determine the Relevance and Quality of Sources

Whether you use print or online sources, a successful search will turn up many more items than you can expect to use in your final product. You have to make a series of decisions as you evaluate your material. Use your research question and working thesis to create guidelines for yourself about importance and relevance.

If you ask a research question about contemporary events such as the NCAA's policy that college athletes should not be paid (see pages 416–521), you will need to find both background information and current information. You will need to know, for example, the most recent statistics on how many scholarship athletes actually graduate because the NCAA's main defense of not paying scholarship athletes is that they get a free education.

For each source, you must decide if the source is relevant and trustworthy.

Relevant?

Look at your assignment and research question.

- Does your research question require you to consult primary or secondary sources?
- Does a source you have found address your question?
- Does a source support or disagree with your working thesis? (You should not throw out work that challenges your views. Representing opposing views accurately enhances your credibility.)
- Does a source add significant information?
- Is the source current? (For most topics try to find the most up-to-date information.)

Trustworthy?

First determine what kind of source you have.

- Self-published or edited?
- Scholarly or popular?
- Primary or secondary?
→ **See page 548**

Then ask these questions.

- Who published it?
- Who is the author? What are the author's qualifications?
- Is the author associated with a reputable organization or college?
- Does the author state goals or exhibit a particular bias?
- How valid is the information and evidence?
- How current is the source?
- Is advertising a prominent part of the content?
→ **See page 549**

Determine the Kind of Source

Your assignment may have suggestions about the kinds of sources you need to use. Even if there are no instructions about sources, you still need to evaluate each source to ensure quality.

Distinguish individual and anonymous sources from edited sources

Anyone with a computer and access to the Internet can put up a Web site. Furthermore, they can put up sites anonymously or under an assumed name. It's no wonder that there are so many sites that contain misinformation.

In general, sources that have been edited and published in scholarly journals, scholarly books, major newspapers, major online and print magazines, and government Web sites are considered of higher quality than what an individual might put on a personal Web site, a *Facebook* page, a user review, or in a blog.

Distinguish popular sources from scholarly sources

Scholarly books and **scholarly journals** are published by and for experts. Scholarly books and articles published in scholarly journals undergo a **peer review** process in which a group of experts in a field reviews them for their scholarly soundness and academic value. Scholarly books and articles in scholarly journals include

- Author's name and academic credentials
- A list of works cited

Newspapers, popular books, and **popular magazines** vary widely in quality. Popular sources are not peer reviewed and require more work on your part to determine their quality. EBSCOhost databases allow you to limit searches to scholarly journals.

Popular vs. Scholarly Sources

	Popular books and magazines	Newspapers	Scholarly books and journals
Author	staff writers, journalists	journalists	scholars, researchers
Audience	general public	general public	scholars, college students
Reviewed by	professional editor	professional editor	editorial boards of other scholars and researchers
Purpose	entertain, express an opinion	entertain, express an opinion, inform	share information with the scholarly community
Documentation	usually none	usually none	extensive, with lists of works cited
Advertisements	frequent in magazines	frequent	a few ads for scholarly products
Evidence of bias	usually some bias	usually some bias	little bias
Examples	**Magazines:** *Cosmopolitan, GQ, Rolling Stone, Sports Illustrated, Time*	*The New York Times, The Globe and Mail, The Washington Times*	**Journals:** *American Journal of Mathematics, College English, JAMA: Journal of the American Medical Association*

Distinguish primary sources from secondary sources

Another key distinction for researchers is primary versus secondary sources. In the humanities and fine arts, **primary sources** are original, creative works and original accounts of events written close to the time they occurred. **Secondary** sources interpret creative works and primary sources of events.

In the sciences, **primary sources** are the factual results of experiments, observations, and other data. **Secondary sources** interpret those results.

Determine if a Source Is Trustworthy

In the Internet era, we don't lack for information but we do lack filters for finding quality information. You have to evaluate each source using your critical reading skills. Think about each of these questions, and come to an overall evaluation of the trustworthiness of the source.

Ask critical questions	Find answers
Who published it?	For books and articles, search the Web for the publisher's Web site. Scholarly books and scholarly journals are generally more reliable than popular magazines and popular books, which tend to emphasize what is sensational and entertaining.
Who is the author? What are the author's qualifications?	Can you identify the author? What can you find out about the author? Enter the author's name on *Google* or another search engine. Does the author represent an organization?
Is the author associated with a reputable organization or college?	Search the Web for the Web site of the organization or college. Look in directories in your library such as the *Encyclopedia of Associations and Research Centers Directory*.
Does the author state goals or exhibit a particular bias?	Read the introduction or abstract. Look closely at the author's arguments and supporting facts. What conclusions does the author draw? If the author uses sources, where are they from? Authors with particular biases often use only sources that support their point of view.
How valid is the information and evidence?	Where does the information and evidence come from? Is the evidence adequate to support the author's claims?
How current is the source?	Find the date of publication. If you are researching a fast-breaking topic such as treating ADHD, then currency is very important. Even historical topics are subject to controversy and revision.
Is advertising a prominent part of the content?	If advertising is prominent, how might advertising influence the content?

Compare the quality of Web sources

A Web search on the research question "Should all schoolchildren be required to get a vaccination for influenza (flu) every year?" might turn up an article titled "Annual Flu Deaths: The Big Lie." The article concludes that more people will die who receive the flu vaccine than those who do not get the flu shot. If you look at the home page, you'll find that the site's sponsor, ThinkTwice Global Vaccine Institute, opposes all vaccinations of children.

Source: Miller, Neil Z. "Annual Flu Deaths: The Big Lie." *ThinkTwice Global Vaccine Institute*, 2005, www.thinktwice.com/flu_lie.htm.

Publisher	The ThinkTwice Global Vaccine Institute opposes mandatory vaccinations and accuses researchers of falsifying the results of vaccine studies.
Author	A search for Neil Z. Miller turns up sites that list him as the director of the ThinkTwice Global Vaccine Institute. He has a degree in psychology but is not a medical doctor.
Bias	This article along with other articles on the site express a strong bias against vaccinations.
Evidence	The primary evidence is from the Centers for Disease Control's statistics on flu deaths. Miller disputes the CDC's assertion that many pneumonia deaths, which number in the tens of thousands, are the result of the flu virus.
Currency	The article was written in 2005.
Advertising	Links on the site go to advertisements for books published by ThinkTwice that oppose vaccinations.

Conclusion:

The article takes a controversial position opposing the flu vaccine. The author's argument is based exclusively on the claim that flu does not lead to pneumonia. The only source listed is a review by a graduate student, not a report of research. The author's bias, the lack of currency, and the lack of supporting evidence makes this source less trustworthy.

Source:

United States, Department of Health and Human Services. "Seasonal Influenza (Flu) Vaccination." *Centers for Disease Control and Prevention*, 16 May 2014, www.cdc.gov/vaccines/vpd-vac/flu/default.htm.

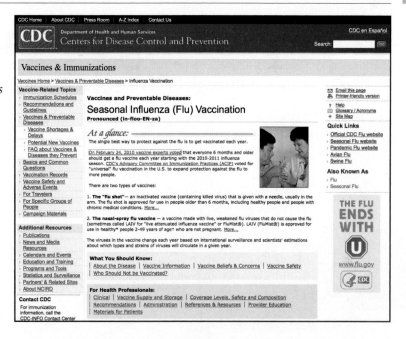

Publisher	The Centers for Disease Control and Prevention (CDC) is a United States federal agency charged with protecting and improving public health.
Author	The author is the agency, which has a staff of over 15,000 including more than half who have earned advanced degrees. The recommendations are from fifteen experts who have been selected to provide advice to the CDC along with representatives of other federal agencies and organizations that bring immunization expertise.
Bias	The language is neutral. The larger site covers many medical topics and is considered an authoritative source of medical information.
Evidence	Many links to research studies and other sites are on this long page (only the top is shown here).
Currency	The site is current. It was updated on the day of access.

Conclusion:

This site is published by the United States government and reflects the judgment of experts in the field, various organizations concerned with immunization, and the input of individuals. The page includes links to a great deal of evidence. The quality is high.

MyWritingLab™   Visit Ch. 21 in MyWritingLab to complete the chapter exercises and to test your understanding of the chapter objectives.

22 Exploring in the Field

Gather information through interviews, surveys, and observation.

In this chapter, you will learn to

① Conduct interviews *(see p. 553)*

② Administer surveys *(see p. 554)*

③ Make observations *(see p. 556)*

Conduct Interviews

College campuses are a rich source of experts in many areas, including people on the faculty and in the surrounding community. Interviewing experts on your research topic can help build your knowledge base. You can use interviews to discover what the people most affected by a particular issue are thinking, such as why students object to some fees and not others.

Arrange interviews

Before you contact anyone, think carefully about your goals; knowing what you want to find out through your interviews will help you determine whom you need to interview and what questions you need to ask.

- Decide what you want or need to know and who best can provide that for you.
- Ask the person to grant an interview in advance, and let the person know why you are conducting the interview. Estimate how long your interview will take, and tell your subject how much time you will need.
- Choose a location that is convenient for your subject, but not too chaotic or loud. An office or study room is better than a noisy cafeteria.
- If you want to record the interview, ask for permission in advance.

Plan questions

- Start writing questions in advance.
- Ask some specific questions such as "What exactly are your responsibilities in your position?"
- Ask some open-ended questions such as "How have the administration's new policies changed your relationship with the people you serve?"

Conduct interviews

- Come prepared with your questions and a computer, mobile device, or pen and paper.
- If you plan to record the interview (with your subject's permission), make sure whatever recording device you use has an adequate power supply and memory.
- Ask your specific questions first, then move to the open-ended questions that allow your subject to express opinions.
- Listen carefully so you can follow up on key points. Make notes when important questions are raised or answered, but don't attempt to transcribe every word the person is saying.
- When you are finished, thank your subject, and ask his or her permission to get in touch again if you have additional questions.

Analyze interviews

- Schedule at least 30 minutes after the interview to flesh out the notes you took while the interview is still fresh in your mind.
- Think about your own reactions including what you found unusual or suprising.
- When you are ready to incorporate the interview into a paper or project, think about what you want to highlight about the interview and which direct quotations to include.

Administer Surveys

Extensive surveys that can be projected to large populations, like the ones used in political polls, require the effort of many people. Small surveys, however, often can provide insight on local issues, such as what percentage of students might be affected if library hours were reduced.

Plan surveys

Decide what exactly you want to know: What information do you need for your research question? Then design a survey that will provide that information. Likely you will want both close-ended questions (multiple choice, yes or no, rating scale) and open-ended questions that allow detailed responses. Create a list of no more than ten questions.

- Write a few specific, unambiguous questions. People will fill out your survey quickly, and if the questions are confusing, the results will be meaningless.
- Include one or two open-ended questions, such as "What do you like about X?" "What don't you like about X?" Open-ended questions can be difficult to interpret, but sometimes they turn up information you had not anticipated.

Test surveys in advance

- Make sure your questions are clear by testing them on a few people before you conduct the survey.
- Think about how you will interpret your survey. Multiple-choice formats make data easy to tabulate, but often they miss key information. Open-ended questions will require you to figure out a way to sort responses into categories.

Administer surveys

- Decide on the people you will need to survey and how many your survey will require.
- Decide how you will contact participants in your survey. If you are conducting your survey on private property, you will need permission from the property owner.
- If you mail or e-mail your survey, include a statement about what the survey is for.

Analyze surveys

- Tally the results of the specific questions.
- Analyze the open-ended questions by determining categories for the responses to each question and assigning each answer to a category.
- When writing about the results, be sure to include information about who participated in the survey, how the participants were selected, and when and how the survey was administered.

Make surveys appealing

So many people want information from us—marketers, politicians, pollsters, corporations—that we often feel bombarded by surveys and polls. To keep people from tuning out your survey, you need to appeal to them without annoying them.

Technique	Less Effective	More Effective
Get attention with a title or subject heading that interests people and makes clear that they have something to contribute. However, don't resort to exclamations and capitalized words; these will remind people of spam e-mail and advertising pitches.	• Survey for part-time students • Please take our survey • Important: student survey • Take this survey and WIN A FREE CAR!!!!!	• Share your opinion of cafeteria food. • Help the Biology Department improve lab classes. • Sound off about bus service.
Ask people for their help, and tell them why you need it.	• We appreciate your taking the time to answer this survey.	• Your answers to this survey will provide insight into the strengths and weaknesses of our school's current admissions policy.
Briefly describe the project and its audience.	• I'm taking this survey for a class I'm in.	• This survey is part of a group research project for Business Administration 118. We hope to present our final report to the University Student Services Committee.
Most people prefer to take surveys anonymously. Ensure confidentiality if necessary.	• Please note your name and phone number below for follow-up.	• Your answers will be kept confidential and your identity will not be associated with your answers in any way.
State up front how long the survey will take the respondent to complete.		• We estimate this survey will take you 5 to 10 minutes to complete.
Provide your contact information so respondents can learn more about your project or results.		• Please feel free to contact us at 555-4567 or bizkids@mail.edu if you have any questions about this survey.
Thank your respondents by reminding them what they are helping you accomplish.		• Thank you once again for taking the time to share your opinions. Your contribution will help to improve student services at our school.

Make Observations

Observing can be a valuable source of data. For example, if you are researching why a particular office on your campus does not operate efficiently, observe what happens when students enter and how the staff responds to their presence.

Choose a place

- Choose a place where you can observe with the least intrusion. The less people wonder about what you are doing, the better.

Collect observations

- Carry a notebook and write extensive field notes. Record as much information as you can, and worry about analyzing it later.

- Record the date, exactly where you were, exactly when you arrived and left, and important details like the number of people present.

- Write on one side of your notebook so you can use the facing page to note key observations and analyze your data later.

Analyze observations

You must interpret your observations so they make sense to your audience. Ask yourself the following questions.

- What patterns of behavior did you observe?

- How was the situation you observed unique? How might it be similar to other locations? What constituted "normal" activity during the time when you were observing? Did anything out of the ordinary happen?

- Why were the people there? What can you determine about the purposes of the activities you observed?

Children in Egypt are taught in school to be friendly to tourists, and they are outgoing with visitors.

November 8, 2014

After visiting the Great Pyramids at dawn, I walked back to Cairo on the Sharia-al-Ahram. The number of foreign tourists was dwarfed by groups of visiting Egyptian schoolchildren, all well dressed in contrast to the homeless children on the streets of Cairo. The children greeted me as we passed. I photographed one group whose teacher was giving them a mock stern lecture (that's his arm in the picture), and the children responded with mock stern expressions that broke into smiles. Unlike most of the other groups, these children were not wearing their school uniforms.

WRITE NOW MyWritingLab™

Compose interview questions

Think of a specific person who fits one of the categories below and a specific purpose. For example, write a series of interview questions for your U.S. Senator on immigration policy. Write five to ten interview questions.

- A celebrity you admire
- A potential employee
- A potential employer
- The author of a book you have read recently
- A Fortune 500 CEO
- A professional athlete
- A well-known scientist in a field you don't know much about
- An "invisible person"—a custodian, gardener, security guard, or other person who has an impact on your life but with whom you never or rarely interact

MyWritingLab™ Visit Ch. 22 in MyWritingLab to complete the chapter exercises and to test your understanding of the chapter objectives.

23 Writing the Research Project

Thorough research gives you a wealth of ideas and information to communicate.

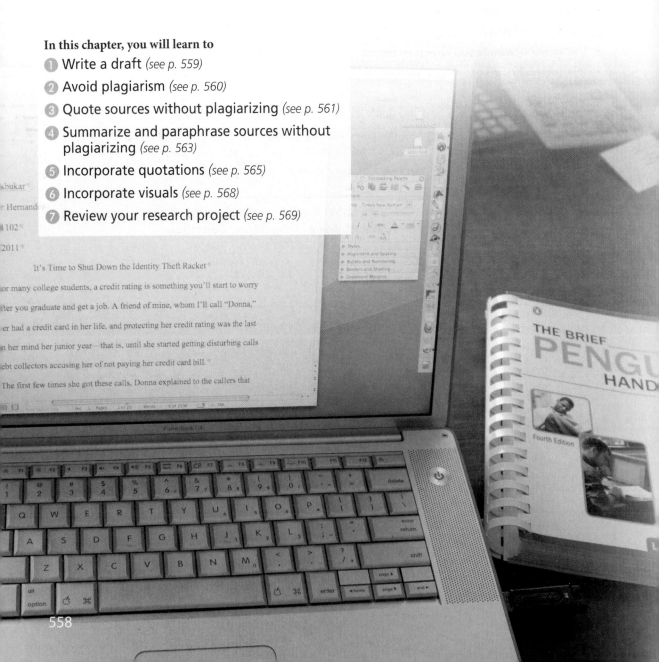

It's Time to Shut Down the Identity Theft Racket

For many college students, a credit rating is something you'll start to worry

after you graduate and get a job. A friend of mine, whom I'll call "Donna,"

ever had a credit card in her life, and protecting her credit rating was the last

in her mind her junior year—that is, until she started getting disturbing calls

debt collectors accusing her of not paying her credit card bill.

The first few times she got these calls, Donna explained to the callers that

Write a Draft

Before you begin writing your project, review the assignment and your goals (see Chapter 19). Your review of the assignment will remind you of your purpose, your potential readers, your stance on your subject, and the length and scope you should aim for.

REVIEW YOUR WORKING THESIS	Often you will find that one aspect of your topic turned out to be more interesting and produced more information. At this stage your working thesis may be rough and may change as you write your draft, but having a working thesis will help you stay focused.
TAKE STOCK OF YOUR RESEARCH	A convincing research project includes the ideas of others and responds to those ideas. It also presents your original thinking on the subject. • Who do you agree with? • Who do you disagree with? • What can you add to points you agree with? • What original analysis or theorizing do you have to offer?
PLAN YOUR ORGANIZATION	Look over your notes and decide how to group the ideas you have researched. • Determine what your main points will be and how they support your thesis. • Create a working outline. → **See page 41**
AVOID PLAGIARISM WHEN QUOTING, SUMMARIZING, AND PARAPHRASING SOURCES	The best way to avoid unintentional plagiarism is to take care to distinguish source words from your words. → **See pages 560–564**
INTEGRATE QUOTATIONS	Decide when to quote directly and when to paraphrase. Introduce quotations with signal phrases (X argues that . . . , X claims that . . . , X theorizes that . . .). → **See pages 565–567**
DOCUMENT YOUR SOURCES	→ **See Chapter 24** for how to document sources in MLA style. → **See Chapter 25** for how to document sources in APA style.
REVIEW AND REVISE YOUR RESEARCH PROJECT	A systematic review of your project is critical to identifying your goals in revising. → **See page 569**

Avoid Plagiarism

You know that copying someone else's paper word for word or taking an article off the Internet and turning it in as yours is plagiarism. That's plain stealing, and people who take that risk should know that the punishment can be severe. But plagiarism also means using the ideas, melodies, or images of someone else without acknowledging them, and it is important to understand exactly what defines plagiarism.

What you don't have to document

Fortunately, common sense governs issues of academic plagiarism. The standards of documentation are not so strict that the source of every fact you cite must be acknowledged. Suppose you are writing about the causes of maritime disasters and you want to know how many people drowned when the *Titanic* sank on the early morning of April 15, 1912. You check the *Britannica Online* Web site and find that the death toll was around 1,500. Since this fact is available in many other reference works, you would not need to cite Britannica Online as the source.

But let's say you want to challenge the version of the sinking offered in the 1998 movie *Titanic*, which repeats the usual explanation that the *Titanic* sideswiped an iceberg, ripping a long gash along the hull that caused the ship to go down. Suppose that, in your reading, you discover that a September 1985 exploration of the wreck by an unmanned submersible did not find the long gash previously thought to have sunk the ship. The evidence instead suggested that the force of the collision with the iceberg broke the seams in the hull, allowing water to flood the ship's watertight compartments. You would need to cite the source of your information for this alternative version of the *Titanic*'s demise.

What you do have to document

For facts that are not easily found in general reference works, statements of opinion, and arguable claims, you should cite the source. You should also cite the sources of statistics, research findings, examples, graphs, charts, and illustrations. For example, if you state that the percentage of obese children aged 6 to 11 in the United States rose from 4% in 1974 to 18% in 2012, you need to cite the source.

As a reader you should be skeptical about statistics and research findings when the source is not mentioned. When a writer does not cite the sources of statistics and research findings, there is no way of knowing how reliable the sources are or whether the writer is making them up.

Careful citing of sources gives you credibility as a writer. When in doubt, always document the source.

Be careful when taking notes and copying material online

The best way to avoid unintentional plagiarism is to take care to distinguish source words from your own words.

- Don't mix words from the source with your own words. If you copy anything from a source when taking notes, place those words in quotation marks and note the page number(s) where those words appear.

- Write down all the information you need for each source for a list of works cited or a list of references (see Chapters 24 and 25).

- If you copy words from an online source, take special care to note the source. You could easily copy online material and later not be able to find where it came from.

- Photocopy printed sources and print out online sources. Having printed copies of sources allows you to double-check later that you haven't used words from the source by mistake and that any words you quote are accurate.

Quote Sources Without Plagiarizing

Effective research writing builds on the work of others. You can summarize or paraphrase the work of others, but often it is best to let the authors speak in your text by quoting their exact words. Indicate the words of others by placing them inside quotation marks.

Most people who get into plagiarism trouble lift words from a source and use them without quotation marks. Where the line is drawn is easiest to illustrate with an example. In the following passage, Steven Johnson takes sharp issue with the metaphor of surfing applied to the Web.

> The concept of "surfing" does a terrible injustice to what it means to navigate around the Web. . . . What makes the idea of cybersurfing so infuriating is the implicit connection drawn to television. Web surfing, after all, is a derivation of channel surfing—the term thrust upon the world by the rise of remote controls and cable panoply in the mid-eighties. . . . Applied to the boob tube, of course, the term was not altogether inappropriate. Surfing at least implied that channel-hopping was more dynamic, more involved, than the old routine of passive consumption. Just as a real-world surfer's enjoyment depended on the waves delivered up by the ocean, the channel surfer was at the mercy of the programmers and network executives. The analogy took off because it worked well in the one-to-many system of cable TV, where your navigational options were limited to the available channels.
>
> But when the term crossed over to the bustling new world of the Web, it lost a great deal of precision. . . . Web surfing and channel surfing are genuinely different pursuits; to imagine them as equivalents is to ignore the defining characteristics of each medium. Or at least that's what happens in theory. In practice, the Web takes on the greater burden. The television imagery casts the online surfer in the random, anesthetic shadow of TV programming, roaming from site to site like a CD player set on shuffle play. But what makes the online world so revolutionary is the fact that there are connections between each stop on a Web itinerant's journey. The links that join those various destinations are links of association, not randomness. A channel surfer hops back and forth between different channels because she's bored. A Web surfer clicks on a link because she's interested.
>
> Steven Johnson. *Interface Culture: How New Technology Transforms the Way We Create and Communicate.* HarperCollins Publishers, 1997, pp. 107–09.

If you were writing a paper or putting up a Web site that concerned Web surfing, you might want to mention the distinction that Johnson makes between channel surfing and surfing on the Web. You could then expand on the distinction. The next pages show you how to do it without plagiarizing.

Use quotation marks for direct quotations

If you quote directly, you must place quotation marks around all words you take from the original.

> One observer marks this contrast: "A channel surfer hops back and forth between different channels because she's bored. A Web surfer clicks on a link because she's interested" (Johnson 109).

Notice that the quotation is introduced and not just dropped in. This example follows Modern Language Association (MLA) style, where the citation—(Johnson 109)—goes outside the quotation marks but before the final period. In MLA style, source references are made according to the author's last name, which refers you to the full citation in the list of works cited at the end of the paper. Following the author's name is the page number where the quotation can be located. (Notice also that there is no comma after the name.)

Attribute every quotation

If the author's name appears in the sentence, cite only the page number, in parentheses.

> According to Steven Johnson, "A channel surfer hops back and forth between different channels because she's bored. A Web surfer clicks on a link because she's interested" (109).

Quoting words that are quoted in your source

If you want to quote material that is already quoted in your source, use single quotes for that material.

> Steven Johnson uses the metaphor of a Gothic cathedral to describe a computer interface: " 'The principle of the Gothic architecture,' Coleridge once said, 'is infinity made imaginable.' The same could be said for the modern interface" (42).

Summarize and Paraphrase Sources Without Plagiarizing

Summarizing

When you summarize, you state the major ideas of an entire source or part of a source in a paragraph or perhaps even a sentence. The key is to put the summary in your own words. If you use words from the source, you have to put those words within quotation marks.

PLAGIARIZED

Steven Johnson argues in *Interface Culture* that the concept of "surfing" is misapplied to the Internet because channel surfers hop back and forth between different channels because they're bored, but Web surfers click on links because they're interested.

[Most of the words are lifted directly from the original; see page 561.]

ACCEPTABLE SUMMARY

Steven Johnson argues in *Interface Culture* that the concept of "surfing" is misapplied to the Internet because users of the Web consciously choose to link to other sites while television viewers mindlessly flip through the channels until something catches their attention.

Paraphrasing

When you paraphrase, you represent the idea of the source in your own words at about the same length as the original. You still need to include the reference to the source of the idea. The following example illustrates what is not an acceptable paraphrase.

PLAGIARIZED

Steven Johnson argues that the concept of "surfing" does a terrible injustice to what it means to navigate around the Web. What makes the idea of Web surfing infuriating is the association with television. Web surfing and channel surfing are truly different activities; to imagine them as the same is to ignore their defining characteristics. A channel surfer skips around because she's bored while a Web surfer clicks on a link because she's interested (107-09).

Even though the source is listed, this paraphrase is unacceptable. Too many of the words in the original are used directly here, including most words of entire sentences.

When a string of words is lift ed from a source and inserted without quotation marks, the passage is plagiarized. Changing a few words in a sentence is not a paraphrase. Compare these two sentences.

SOURCE

Web surfing and channel surfing are genuinely different pursuits; to imagine them as equivalents is to ignore the defining characteristics of each medium.

UNACCEPTABLE PARAPHRASE

Web surfing and channel surfing are truly different activities; to imagine them as the same is to ignore their defining characteristics.

The paraphrase takes the structure of the original sentence and substitutes a few words. It is much too similar to the original.

A true paraphrase represents an entire rewriting of the idea from the source

ACCEPTABLE PARAPHRASE

Steven Johnson argues that *surfing* is a misleading term for describing how people navigate on the Web. He allows that *surfing* is appropriate for clicking across television channels because the viewer has to interact with what the networks and cable companies provide, just as the surfer has to interact with what the ocean provides. Web surfing, according to Johnson, operates at much greater depth and with much more consciousness of purpose. Web surfers actively follow links to make connections (107-09).

Even though there are a few words from the original in this paraphrase, such as *navigate* and *connections*, these sentences are original in structure and wording while accurately conveying the meaning of the source.

Frame each paraphrase

Each paraphrase should begin by introducing the author and conclude with a page reference to the material that is paraphrased.

Incorporate Quotations

Quotations are a frequent problem area in research papers. Review every quotation to ensure that each is used effectively and correctly.

- Limit the use of long quotations. If you have more than one blocked quotation on a page, look closely to see if one or more can be paraphrased or summarized.

- Check that each quotation supports your major points rather than making major points for you. If the ideas rather than the original wording are what's important, paraphrase the quotation and cite the source.

- Check that each quotation is introduced and attributed. Each quotation should be introduced and the author or title named. Check for verbs with a signal phrase: Smith *claims*, Jones *argues*, Brown *states*.

- Check that you cite the source for each quotation. You are required to cite the sources of all direct quotations, paraphrases, and summaries.

- Check the accuracy of each quotation. It's easy to leave out words or mistype a quotation. Compare what is in your paper to the original source. If you need to add words to make the quotation grammatical, make sure the added words are in brackets.

- Read your paper aloud to a classmate or a friend. Each quotation should flow smoothly when you read your paper aloud. Put a check beside rough spots as you read aloud so you can revise later.

When to quote directly and when to paraphrase

Use direct quotations when the original wording is important.

DIRECT QUOTATION

Smith notes that

> Although the public grew to accept film as a teaching tool, it was not always aware of all it was being taught. That was because a second type of film was also being produced during these years, the "attitude-building" film, whose primary purpose was to motivate, not instruct. Carefully chosen visuals were combined with dramatic story lines, music, editing, and sharply drawn characters to create powerful instruments of mass manipulation. (21)

Prose quotations longer than four lines (MLA) or forty words (APA) should be indented one-half inch from the left margin in both MLA and APA style. Note that in this MLA example of a block quotation the page number within parentheses goes after the period at the end.

PARAPHRASE

Smith points out that a second kind of mental hygiene film, the attitude-building film, was introduced during the 1940s. It attempted to motivate viewers, whereas earlier films explicitly tried to teach something. The attitude-building films were intended to manipulate their audiences to feel a certain way (21).

PARAPHRASE COMBINED WITH QUOTATION

In his analysis of the rise of fascism in twentieth-century Europe, George Mosse notes that the fascist movement was built on pre-existing ideas like individualism and sacrifice. It "scavenged" other ideologies and made use of them. "Fascism was a new political movement but not a movement which invented anything new," Mosse explains (xvii).

In the second example, the original wording provides stronger description of the attitude-building films. The direct quotation is a better choice.

Often, you can paraphrase the main idea of a lengthy passage and quote only the most striking phrase or sentence.

Verbs that introduce quotations and paraphrases

acknowledge	comment	express	reject
add	compare	find	remark
admit	complain	grant	reply
advise	concede	illustrate	report
agree	conclude	imply	respond
allow	contend	insist	show
analyze	criticize	interpret	state
answer	declare	maintain	suggest
argue	describe	note	think
ask	disagree	object	write
assert	discuss	observe	
believe	dispute	offer	
charge	emphasize	point out	
claim	explain	refute	

Quotations don't speak for themselves

OFF TRACK

Don't rely on long quotations to do the work of writing for you.

These quotations are picked up out of context and dropped into the paper. Readers have no clue about why they are relevant to the writer's text.

> Richard Lanham writes:
>> Economics . . . studies the allocation of scarce resources. Normally we would think that the phrase "information economy," which we hear everywhere nowadays, makes some sense. It is no longer physical stuff that is in short supply, we are told, but information about it. So, we live in an "information economy," but information is not in short supply in the new information economy. We're drowning in it. What we lack is the human attention needed to make sense of it all. (xi)
>
> Lanham goes on to say:
>> "Rhetoric" has not always been a synonym for humbug. For most of Western history, it has meant the body of doctrine that teaches people how to speak and write and, thus, act effectively in public life. Usually defined as "the art of persuasion," it might as well have been called "the economics of attention." It tells us how to allocate our central scarce resource, to invite people to attend to what we would like them to attend to. (xii-xiii)

ON TRACK

When sources are used effectively, they are woven into the fabric of a research project but still maintain their identity.

Most of the source is paraphrased, allowing the discussion to be integrated into the writer's text. The writer centers on how two key concepts, the "information economy" and "rhetoric," are reinterpreted by Richard Lanham. Only those words critical to representing Lanham's position are quoted directly.

> In *The Economics of Attention*, Richard Lanham begins by pointing out that the "information economy" stands traditional economics on its head because there is no shortage of information today. Instead Lanham argues that attention is what is in short supply and that the discipline of rhetoric can help us to understand how attention is allocated. Rhetoric historically has meant the art and study of speaking and writing well, especially for participating in public life. Lanham maintains that what rhetoric has really been about is what he calls "the economics of attention" (xii). The central goal of rhetoric, according to Lanham, is "to invite people to attend to what we would like them to attend to" (xii-xiii).

Incorporate Visuals

Here are a few guidelines to keep in mind for incorporating visual sources into your research paper.

- Use visuals for examples and supporting evidence, not for decoration. For example, if the subject of your research is Internet crime in San Francisco, including a picture of the Golden Gate Bridge is irrelevant and will detract from your paper.

- Refer to images and other graphics in the body of your research paper. Explain the significance of any images or graphics in the body of your paper.

- Respect the copyright of visual sources. You may need to request permission to use a visual from the Web.

- Get complete citation information. You are required to cite visual sources in your list of works cited just as you are for other sources.

- Describe the content of the image or graphic in the caption.

Façade of the Last Judgment, Orvieto, Italy, c. 1310–1330. Medieval churches frequently depicted Christ as a judge, damning sinners to hell.

WRITE NOW MyWritingLab™

Summarize, paraphrase, and quote directly

Read this quotation and then
- write a summary of it;
- write a paraphrase of it;
- incorporate a direct quotation from it into a sentence.

There is no strife, no prejudice, no national conflict in outer space as yet. Its hazards are hostile to us all. Its conquest deserves the best of all mankind, and its opportunity for peaceful cooperation may never come again. But why, some say, the moon? Why choose this as our goal? And they may well ask why climb the highest mountain? Why, 35 years ago, fly the Atlantic? Why does Rice play Texas?

We choose to go to the moon. We choose to go to the moon in this decade and do the other things, not because they are easy, but because they are hard, because that goal will serve to organize and measure the best of our energies and skills, because that challenge is one that we are willing to accept, one we are unwilling to postpone, and one which we intend to win, and the others, too (President John F. Kennedy, September 12, 1962).

Review Your Research Project

Read your project aloud and put checks in the margin in places where you think it sounds rough or might need more development. When you finish, try to imagine yourself as a reader who doesn't know much about your subject or has a different viewpoint. What could you add to benefit that reader?

Reviewing another student's research project

Read through a paper twice. The first time you read through a paper, concentrate on comprehension and overall impressions. On your second reading show the writer where you got confused or highlight parts that were especially good by adding comments in the margins.

Questions for reviewing a research project

- Does the title describe the subject of the paper? Does it create interest in the subject?

- Are the introductory paragraphs effective and relevant to the paper that follows?

- Is the thesis clearly stated in the beginning paragraphs of the paper?

- Does the writer offer support for the thesis from a variety of valid and reliable sources?

- Does the paper go into enough detail to support the thesis, and are the details relevant to the thesis?

- Do the arguments presented in the paper flow logically? Is the paper well organized?

- Is the tone of the paper consistent throughout? Is the word choice varied and appropriate throughout?

- Did you have to read some parts more than once to fully understand them?

- Are quotations properly introduced and integrated into the text?

- Are all facts and quotations that are not common knowledge documented?

- Is the documentation in the correct form?

- Is the paper free of errors of grammar and punctuation?

Revise your research project

From your review and possibly reviews of other students, make a list of changes you might make. Start with the large concerns—reorganizing paragraphs, cutting unnecessary parts, and adding new sections. When you have finished revising, edit and proofread carefully.

MyWritingLab™ Visit Ch. 23 in MyWritingLab to complete this chapter's exercises and to test your understanding of the chapter objectives.

24 MLA Documentation

MLA is the preferred style in the humanities and fine arts.

In this chapter, you will learn to

MLA
HANDBOOK
EIGHTH
EDITION

official
MLA
Style

SIN
and
SYNTA

HOW TO C
wickedly EF
PRO

Cons
Edito

KAREN E

BRYAN

Elements of MLA Documentation

In MLA style, quotations, summaries, and paraphrases from outside sources are indicated by in-text citations in parentheses. When readers find a parenthetical reference in the body of a paper, they can turn to the list of works cited at the end of the paper to find complete publication information for the cited source.

If you have questions that the examples in this chapter do not address, consult the *MLA Handbook,* 8th ed. (2016) or *The MLA Style Center* site at https://style.mla.org.

Walker 3

. . . But how important is face-to-face interaction to maintaining good, "social" behavior in a group?

Describing humans as "innate mind readers," one observer argues that "our skill at imagining other people's mental states ranks up there with our knack for language and our opposable thumbs" (Johnson 196). The frequency of "flame wars" on Internet message boards and list serves, however, 1§

The writer quotes a passage from page 196 of Johnson's book.

Walker 5

Works Cited

Darlin, Damon. "'Wall-E': An Homage to Mr. Jobs." *The New York Times,* 29 June 2008, nyti.ms/1fx6bEc.

Johnson, Steven. *Emergence: The Connected Lives of Ants, Brains, Cities, and Software.* Scribner, 2001.

"Listen to the Brain Drain." *The Irish Times,* final ed., 24 June 2008, p.17.

The reader can find the source by looking up Johnson's name in the list of works cited. The information there can be used to locate the book, to check whether the writer accurately represents Johnson, and to see how the point quoted fits into Johnson's larger argument.

Entries in the Works-cited List

The list of works cited is organized alphabetically by authors or, if no author is listed, the first word in the title other than *a*, *an*, or *the* (see page 599).

1. Works-cited entries for books

Entries for books have three main elements:

1. Author's name.

2. *Title of book.*

3. Publication information.

Sterling, Bruce. *Shaping Things.* MIT P, 2005.

1. Author's name.
- List the author's name with the last name first, followed by a period.

2. Title of book.
- Find the exact title on the title page, not the cover.
- Separate the title and subtitle with a colon.
- Italicize the title and put a period at the end.

3. Publication information.
- The name of the publisher,
- The date of publication.

Use complete publisher names, except for university presses (like MIT P) which are abbreviated. The publisher name is followed by a comma.

2. Works-cited entries for periodicals

Entries for periodicals have three main elements:

1. Author's name.

2. "Title of article."

3. Publication information.

Danielewicz, Jane. "Personal Genres, Public Voices."
    College Composition and Communication,
    vol. 59, no. 3, Feb. 2008, pp. 420-50.

1. Author's name.
- List the author's name with the last name first, followed by a period.

2. "Title of article."
- Place the title of the article inside quotation marks.
- Insert a period before the closing quotation mark.

3. Publication information
- Italicize the title of the journal.
- For scholarly journals include the volume number (preceded by *vol.*) and issue number (preceded by *no.*) of the journal.
- List the date of publication.
- List the page number(s), using *p.* for a single page article, *pp.* for multi-page articles.

3. Works-cited entries for Web sources

Publications on the Web vary widely. For works other than newspapers, magazines, and other journals published on the Web, include the following components if you can locate them.

1. **Author's name.**

2. **"Title of work."**

3. *Title of overall Web site,*

4. **Version or edition used,**

5. **Publisher or sponsor of the site,**

6. **Date of publication,**

7. **URL or DOI.**

Dickler, Jennifer. "Economy Makes People Sick."
 CNNMoney, Cable News Network, 7 June
 2011, money.cnn.com/2011/06/07/pf/
 financial_stress_health/.

---

4. Works-cited entries for database sources

Basic entries for database sources have four main elements:

1. **Author's name.**

2. **Complete print publication information.**

3. *Name of database,*

4. **URL or DOI.**

Jurecic, Ann. "Neurodiversity." *College English,*
 vol. 69, no. 5, May 2007, pp. 421-42.
 JSTOR, www.jstor.org/stable/25472229.

---

1. **Author's name.**
 - List the author's name if you can find it; otherwise begin with the title of the work.

2. **"Title of work."**
 - Place the title of the work inside quotation marks if it is part of a larger Web site.

3. **Title of overall Web site,**
 - Italicize the name of the overall site if it is different from 2.

4. **Version or edition used,**
 - Some Web sites are updated, so list the version if you find it (e.g., 2006 edition).

5. **Publisher or sponsor of the site,**
 - Include the publisher's or sponsor's name if it is different than the title of the overall Web site.

6. **Date of publication,**
 - Use day, month, and year if available.

7. **URL or DOI.**
 - Do not include *http://* or *https://* as part of the URL in your citation. Precede DOI with *doi:.*

8. **Date of access.**
 - If your Web source has no publication date of any kind or is likely to be updated often, then include a date of access at the end of your citation. List the day, month, and year you accessed the source.

1. **Author's name.**
 - List the author's name with the last name first, followed by a period.

2. **Print publication information.**
 - Give the print publication information in standard format, in this case for a periodical (see page 572).

3. **Name of database,**
 - Italicize the name of the database, followed by a comma.

4. **URL or DOI.**
 - Include the URL or DOI (digital object identifier). Use a DOI or stable URL if available, since these are more permanent than a standard URL.

For each source you want to document, use this index to find a model in-text citation and a model entry for the list of works cited.

In-text Citations in MLA Style

1. Author named in your text

Put the author's name in a signal phrase in your sentence.

> Sociologist Daniel Bell called this emerging U.S. economy the "postindustrial society" (3).

2. Author not named in your text

> In 1997, the Gallup poll reported that 55% of adults in the United States think secondhand smoke is "very harmful," compared to only 36% in 1994 (Saad 4).

3. Work by one author

The author's last name comes first, followed by the page number. There is no comma.

> (Bell 3)

4. Work by two authors

The authors' last names follow the order of the title page. If there are two authors, join the names with *and*.

> (Francisco and Lynn 7)

5. Work by three or more authors

Write the first author's last name, followed by the phrase *et al.* (meaning "and others"). Do not italicize the phrase or insert a comma after it.

> (Abrams et al. 1653)

6. Work by no named author

Use a shortened version of the title that includes at least the first important word. Your reader will use the shortened title to find the full title in the works-cited list.

> A review in *The New Yorker* of Ryan Adams's new album focuses on the artist's age ("Pure" 25).

Notice that "Pure" is in quotation marks because it refers to the title of an article. If it were a book, the short title would be italicized.

7. Work by a group or organization	Treat the group or organization as the author. Try to identify the group author in the text and place only the page number in the parentheses.

> According to the *Irish Free State Handbook*, published by the Ministry for Industry and Finance, the population of Ireland in 1929 was approximately 4,192,000 (23).

8. Quotations longer than four lines	NOTE: Indent quotations that are longer than four lines ("block quotations") 1/2 inch (5 spaces) from left margin. Place period before (not after) the parenthetical citation.

> In her article "Art for Everybody," Susan Orlean attempts to explain the popularity of painter Thomas Kinkade:
>> People like to own things they think are valuable. . . .The high price of limited editions is part of their appeal: it implies that they are choice and exclusive, and that only a certain class of people will be able to afford them—a limited edition of people with taste and discernment. (128)
>
> This same statement could possibly also explain the popularity of phenomena like PBS's *Antiques Road Show*.

9. Web sources including Web pages, blogs, podcasts, wikis, videos, and other multimedia sources	MLA prefers that you mention the author in the text instead of putting the author's name in parentheses.

> Andrew Keen ironically used his own blog to claim that "blogs are boring to write (yawn), boring to read (yawn) and boring to discuss (yawn)."

If you cannot identify the author, mention the title in your text.

10. Work in an anthology	Cite the name of the author of the work within an anthology, not the name of the editor of the collection. Alphabetize the entry in the list of works cited by the author, not the editor. For example, Melissa Jane Hardie published the chapter "Beard" in *Rhetorical Bodies*, a book edited by Jack Selzer and Sharon Crowley.

> In "Beard," Melissa Jane Hardie explores the role assumed by Elizabeth Taylor as the celebrity companion of gay actors including Rock Hudson and Montgomery Cliff (278-79).

Note that Hardie, not Selzer and Crowley, is named in parenthetical citations.

> (Hardie 278-79)

11. Two or more works by the same author

Use the author's last name, followed by a comma, and then a shortened version of the title of each source.

> The majority of books written about coauthorship focus on partners of the same sex (Laird, *Women* 351).

Note that *Women* is italicized because it is the name of a book.

---

12. Different authors with the same last name

If your list of works cited contains items by two or more different authors with the same last name, include the initial of the first name in the parenthetical reference. Note that a period follows the initial.

> Web surfing requires more mental involvement than channel surfing (S. Johnson 107).

---

13. Two or more sources within the same sentence

Place each citation directly after the statement it supports.

> Many sweeping pronouncements were made in the 1990s that the Internet is the best opportunity to improve education since the printing press (Ellsworth xxii) or even in the history of the world (Dyrli and Kinnaman 79).

---

14. Two or more sources within the same citation

If two sources support a single point, separate them with a semicolon.

> (McKibbin 39; Gore 92)

---

15. Work quoted in another source

When you do not have access to the original source of the material you wish to use, put the abbreviation *qtd. in* (quoted in) before the information about the indirect source.

> National governments have become increasingly what Ulrich Beck, in a 1999 interview, calls "zombie institutions"—institutions that are "dead and still alive" (qtd. in Bauman 6).

---

16. Literary works

To supply a reference to literary works, you sometimes need more than a page number from a specific edition. Readers should be able to locate a quotation in any edition of the book. Give the page number from the edition that you are using, then a semicolon and other identifying information.

> "Marriage is a house" is one of the most memorable lines in *Don Quixote* (546; pt. 2, bk. 3, ch. 19).

Books in MLA-style Works Cited

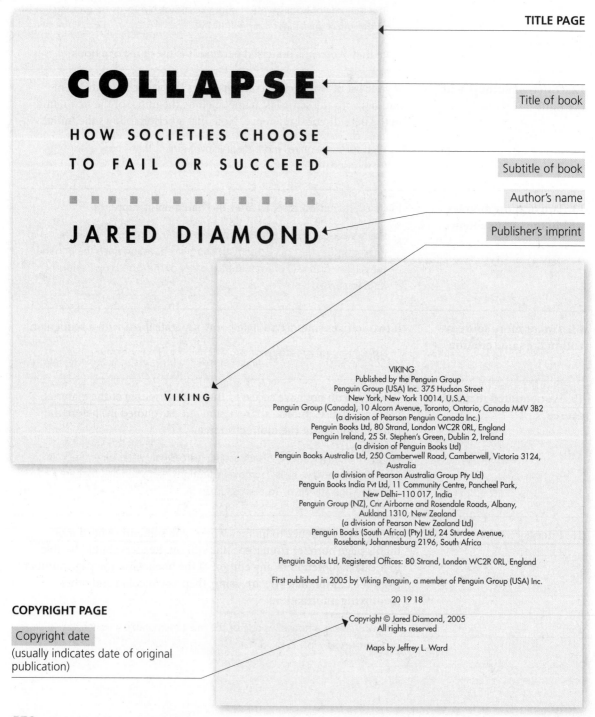

TITLE PAGE

COLLAPSE

Title of book

HOW SOCIETIES CHOOSE
TO FAIL OR SUCCEED

Subtitle of book

Author's name

JARED DIAMOND

Publisher's imprint

VIKING
Published by the Penguin Group
Penguin Group (USA) Inc. 375 Hudson Street
New York, New York 10014, U.S.A.
Penguin Group (Canada), 10 Alcorn Avenue, Toronto, Ontario, Canada M4V 3B2
(a division of Pearson Penguin Canada Inc.)
Penguin Books Ltd, 80 Strand, London WC2R 0RL, England
Penguin Ireland, 25 St. Stephen's Green, Dublin 2, Ireland
(a division of Penguin Books Ltd)
Penguin Books Australia Ltd, 250 Camberwell Road, Camberwell, Victoria 3124,
Australia
(a division of Pearson Australia Group Pty Ltd)
Penguin Books India Pvt Ltd, 11 Community Centre, Pancheel Park,
New Delhi–110 017, India
Penguin Group (NZ), Cnr Airborne and Rosendale Roads, Albany,
Aukland 1310, New Zealand
(a division of Pearson New Zealand Ltd)
Penguin Books (South Africa) (Pty) Ltd, 24 Sturdee Avenue,
Rosebank, Johannesburg 2196, South Africa

Penguin Books Ltd, Registered Offices: 80 Strand, London WC2R 0RL, England

First published in 2005 by Viking Penguin, a member of Penguin Group (USA) Inc.

20 19 18

Copyright © Jared Diamond, 2005
All rights reserved

Maps by Jeffrey L. Ward

VIKING

COPYRIGHT PAGE

Copyright date
(usually indicates date of original
publication)

Diamond, Jared. *Collapse: How Societies Choose to Fail or Succeed*. Viking, 2005.

1. Author's or editor's name

- The author's last name comes first, followed by a comma and the first name.
- For edited books, put the label *editor* after the name, preceded by a comma: Kavanaugh, Peter, editor.

2. Book title

- Use the exact title, as it appears on the title page (not the cover).
- Italicize the title.
- All nouns, verbs, pronouns, adjectives, and subordinating conjunctions, and the first word of the title are capitalized. Do not capitalize articles, prepositions, or coordinating conjunctions, unless they are the first word of the title.

3. Publication information

Publisher

- Use complete publisher names.
- However, omit business words and abbreviations such as Inc., Company (Co.), and Corporation (Corp.) from publisher names. So, shorten W. W. Norton & Co. to W. W. Norton.
- For university presses, use the abbreviation *UP*: New York UP, or U of Chicago P.

Date of publication

- Give the year as it appears on the copyright page.
- If no year is given, but can be approximated, put a c. ("circa") and the approximate date in brackets: [c. 1999].

Other information

- For online books, additional information (such as a URL) must be added to the citation. See p. 589.

Sample Works-cited Entries for Books

One author

17. Book by one author

The author's last name comes first, followed by a comma and the rest of the name, as presented in the work. End the name with a single period.

> Doctorow, E. L. *The March*. Random House, 2005.

18. Two or more books by the same author

In the entry for the first book, include the author's name. In the second entry, substitute three hyphens and a period for the author's name. List the titles of books by the same author in alphabetical order.

> Gladwell, Malcolm. *Outliers: The Story of Success*. Little, Brown, 2008.
> ---. *What the Dog Saw: And Other Adventures*. Little, Brown, 2009.

Multiple authors

19. Book by two authors

Second and subsequent author's name appear in standard order (not reversed). A comma separates the authors' names. If all are editors, use *editors* after the names.

> Cruz, Arnaldo, and Martin Manalansan, editors. *Queer Globalizations: Citizenship and the Afterlife of Colonialism*. New York UP, 2002.

20. Book by three or more authors

List the first author's name (last name first) followed by a comma and then the phrase *et al.* (meaning "and others"). You need to use the same method in the in-text citation as you do in the works-cited list.

> Britton, Jane, et al. *The Broadview Anthology of Expository Prose*. Broadview Press, 2001.

Anonymous and group authors

21. Book by an unknown author

Begin the entry with the title.

> *Pocket World in Figures*. Profile Books, 2011.

22. Book by a group or organization

Treat the group as the author of the work.

> United Nations. *The Charter of the United Nations: A Commentary*. Oxford UP, 2000.

23. Religious texts

The Talmud: A Selection. Edited by Norman Solomon, Penguin Classics, 2009.

Editions, reprints, and illustrated books

24. Book with an editor

List an edited book under the editor's name if your focus is on the editor. Otherwise, cite an edited book under the author's name.

Maxwell, Richard, editor. *A Tale of Two Cities*. By Charles Dickens, Penguin Classics, 2011.

25. Reprinted works

For works of fiction that have been printed in many different editions or reprints, give the original publication date after the title.

Wilde, Oscar. *The Picture of Dorian Gray*. 1890. W. W. Norton, 2001.

26. Illustrated book or graphic narrative

After the title of the book, give the illustrator's name, preceded by the description *Illustrated by*. If the emphasis is on the illustrator's work, place the illustrator's name first, followed by the description *illustrator*, and list the author after the title, preceded by the word *By*.

Strunk, William, Jr., and E. B. White. *The Elements of Style Illustrated*. Illustrated by Maira Kalman, Penguin Books, 2005.

Parts of books

27. Introduction, Foreword, Preface, or Afterword

Give the author and then the name of the specific part being cited. If the author for the whole work is different, put that author's name after the word *by*. Place inclusive page numbers after the date of publication.

Benstock, Sheri. Introduction. *The House of Mirth*, by Edith Wharton, Bedford St. Martin's, 2002, pp. 3-24.

28. Single chapter written by same author as the book

Ardis, Ann. "Mapping the Middlebrow in Edwardian England." *Modernism and Cultural Conflict: 1880–1922*, Cambridge UP, 2002, pp. 114-42.

29. Selection from an anthology or edited collection

McEwan, Ian. "On John Updike." *The Best American Essays 2010*, edited by Christopher Hitchens and Robert Atwan, Houghton Mifflin Harcourt, 2010.

Periodicals in MLA-style Works Cited

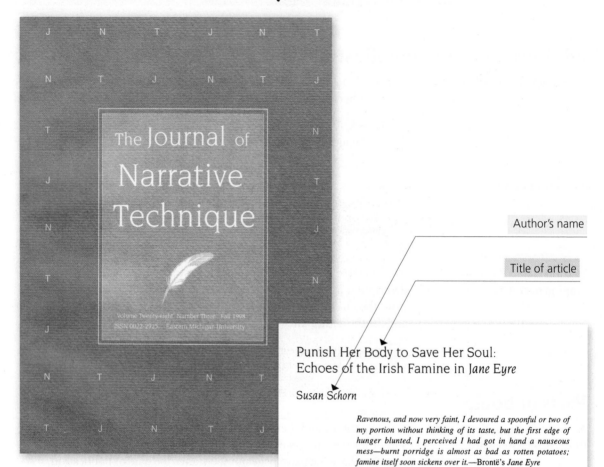

Author's name

Title of article

Punish Her Body to Save Her Soul:
Echoes of the Irish Famine in *Jane Eyre*

Susan Schorn

> *Ravenous, and now very faint, I devoured a spoonful or two of my portion without thinking of its taste, but the first edge of hunger blunted, I perceived I had got in hand a nauseous mess—burnt porridge is almost as bad as rotten potatoes; famine itself soon sickens over it.*—Brontë's *Jane Eyre*

In 1846, the second year of the Irish Potato Famine, Charles Trevelyan, Assistant Secretary in charge of the relief of Ireland, stated "The great evil with which we are to contend is not the physical evil of famine, but the moral evil of the selfish, perverse and turbulent character of the people" (Clarity). That same year, Charlotte Brontë penned the following speech for the character of Mr. Brocklehurst in her novel *Jane Eyre*: "Oh, madam, when you put bread and cheese, instead of burnt porridge, into these children's mouths, you may indeed feed their vile bodies, but you little think how you starve their immortal souls!" The similarity between the sentiment and policy of these two men, one fictional, one very real indeed, is no coincidence. Both express ideas that were then common currency with regard to "the Irish Problem." The connections between starvation, moral improvement, discipline, and nationality were familiar ones in Victorian England, and Brontë's use of this public, political sentiment in her novel—and of numerous other images borrowed from accounts of the

Name of journal, volume number, issue number, date of publication, page number

The Journal of Narrative Technique 28.3 (Fall 1998): 350–365. Copyright © 1998 by *The Journal of Narrative Technique.*

Schorn, Susan. "'Punish Her Body to Save Her Soul': Echoes of the Irish Famine in *Jane Eyre*." *The Journal of Narrative Technique,* vol. 28, no. 3, Fall 1998, pp. 350-65.

1. Author's or editor's name
- The author's last name comes first, followed by a comma and the first name.

2. Title of Article
- Use the exact title, which appears at the top of the article.
- Put the title in quotation marks. If a book title is part of the article's title, italicize the book title. If a title requiring quotation marks is part of the article's title, use single quotation marks around it.
- All nouns, verbs, pronouns, adjectives, and subordinating conjunctions, and the first word of the title are capitalized. Do not capitalize articles, prepositions coordinating conjunctions, unless they are the first word of the title.

3. Publication information

Name of journal
- Italicize the title of the journal or periodical.

Volume, issue, and page numbers
- For scholarly journals give the volume number (preceded by the abbreviation *vol.*) and issue number (if there is one, preceded by the abbreviation *no.*), separated by a comma.
- Some scholarly journals use issue numbers only.
- Give the page numbers for the entire article, preceded by *p.* for a single page article and by *pp.* for multi-page articles.

Date of publication
- Abbreviate the names of all months except May, June, and July.
- For magazines and journals identified by the month or season of publication, use the month (or season) and year.
- For weekly or biweekly magazines, give the day, month, and year of publication. Note that the day precedes the month and no comma is used: 6 Apr. 2016.

Other information
- For online periodicals, the citation needs additional information. See pp.587-89.

Sample Works-cited Entries for Periodicals

Journal articles

30. Article by one author

> O'Rourke, Frank. "Joyce's Early Aesthetic." *Journal of Modern Literature*, vol. 34, no. 2, Winter 2011, pp. 97-120.

31. Article by two authors

> Higgins, Lorraine D., and Lisa D. Brush. "Personal Experience Narrative and Public Debate: Writing the Wrongs of Welfare." *College Composition and Communication*, vol. 57, no. 4, June 2006, pp. 694-729.

32. Article by three or more authors

List the first author's name (last name first) followed by a comma and then the phrase *et al.* (meaning "and others").

> Mahli, Ripan S., et al. "Patterns of mtDNA Diversity in Northwestern North America." *Human Biology*, vol. 76, no. 1, Feb. 2004, pp. 33-54.

Pagination in journals

33. Article in a scholarly journal

After the title of the article, give the journal name in italics, the volume and issue number, the publication date, and the inclusive page numbers.

> Duncan, Mike. "Whatever Happened to the Paragraph?" *College English*, vol. 69, no. 5, May 2007, pp. 470-95.

34. Article in a scholarly journal paginated by issue that uses only issue numbers

Some scholarly journals use issue numbers only. List the issue number after the name of the journal.

> McCall, Sophie. "Double Vision Reading." *Canadian Literature*, no. 194, Autumn 2007, pp. 95-97.

Magazines

35. Monthly or seasonal magazines

Use the month (or season) and year. Remember to abbreviate the names of all months except May, June, and July.

> Anderson, Chris. "A History of Collaborative Circles." *Wired*, Jan. 2011, p. 117.

36. Weekly or biweekly magazines

Give both the day and month of publication, as listed on the issue.

> Toobin, Jeffrey. "Crackdown." *The New Yorker*, 5 Nov. 2001, pp. 56-61.

Newspapers

37. Newspaper article by one author

The author's last name comes first, followed by a comma and the first name.

> Marriott, Michel. "Arts and Crafts for the Digital Age." *The New York Times*, late ed., 8 June 2006, p. C13.

38. Newspaper article by two authors

The second author's name is shown in regular order, first name first.

> Davis, Howard, and June Allstead. "Rice's Testimony to 9/11 Commission Leaves Unanswered Questions." *The Dallas Morning News*, final ed., 9 Apr. 2004, p. C5.

39. Newspaper article by an unknown author

Begin the entry with the title of the article.

> "The Dotted Line." *The Washington Post*, final ed., 8 June 2006, p. E2.

Reviews, editorials, letters to the editor

40. Review

If the review has no title, name the author of the review, then include the description (*Review of*) and the name of the work being reviewed.

> Mendelsohn, Daniel. "The Two Oscar Wildes." Review of *The Importance of Being Earnest*, directed by Oliver Parker. *The New York Review of Books*, 10 Oct. 2002, pp. 23-24.

41. Editorial

> "Reading Turkey's Vote." Editorial. *The New York Times*, 14 June 2011, p. A24.

42. Letter to the editor

> Patai, Daphne. Letter to the editor. *Harper's Magazine*, Dec. 2001, p. 4.

Online Sources in MLA-style Works Cited

Publisher

Title of Web site

Title of work

Author's name

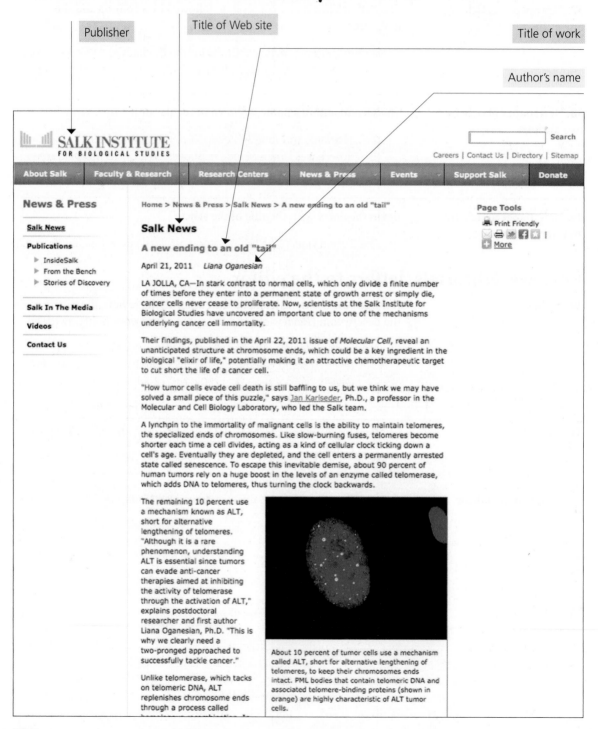

SALK INSTITUTE
FOR BIOLOGICAL STUDIES

Search

Careers | Contact Us | Directory | Sitemap

About Salk Faculty & Research Research Centers News & Press Events Support Salk Donate

News & Press

Salk News

Publications
▶ InsideSalk
▶ From the Bench
▶ Stories of Discovery

Salk In The Media

Videos

Contact Us

Home > News & Press > Salk News > A new ending to an old "tail"

Salk News

A new ending to an old "tail"

April 21, 2011   *Liana Oganesian*

LA JOLLA, CA—In stark contrast to normal cells, which only divide a finite number of times before they enter into a permanent state of growth arrest or simply die, cancer cells never cease to proliferate. Now, scientists at the Salk Institute for Biological Studies have uncovered an important clue to one of the mechanisms underlying cancer cell immortality.

Their findings, published in the April 22, 2011 issue of *Molecular Cell*, reveal an unanticipated structure at chromosome ends, which could be a key ingredient in the biological "elixir of life," potentially making it an attractive chemotherapeutic target to cut short the life of a cancer cell.

"How tumor cells evade cell death is still baffling to us, but we think we may have solved a small piece of this puzzle," says Jan Karlseder, Ph.D., a professor in the Molecular and Cell Biology Laboratory, who led the Salk team.

A lynchpin to the immortality of malignant cells is the ability to maintain telomeres, the specialized ends of chromosomes. Like slow-burning fuses, telomeres become shorter each time a cell divides, acting as a kind of cellular clock ticking down a cell's age. Eventually they are depleted, and the cell enters a permanently arrested state called senescence. To escape this inevitable demise, about 90 percent of human tumors rely on a huge boost in the levels of an enzyme called telomerase, which adds DNA to telomeres, thus turning the clock backwards.

The remaining 10 percent use a mechanism known as ALT, short for alternative lengthening of telomeres. "Although it is a rare phenomenon, understanding ALT is essential since tumors can evade anti-cancer therapies aimed at inhibiting the activity of telomerase through the activation of ALT," explains postdoctoral researcher and first author Liana Oganesian, Ph.D. "This is why we clearly need a two-pronged approached to successfully tackle cancer."

Unlike telomerase, which tacks on telomeric DNA, ALT replenishes chromosome ends through a process called

About 10 percent of tumor cells use a mechanism called ALT, short for alternative lengthening of telomeres, to keep their chromosomes ends intact. PML bodies that contain telomeric DNA and associated telomere-binding proteins (shown in orange) are highly characteristic of ALT tumor cells.

Page Tools

🖨 Print Friendly

More

Oganesian, Liana. "A New Ending to an Old 'Tail.'" *Salk News,* Salk Institute for Biological Studies, 21 Apr. 2011, www.salk.edu/news-release/a-new-ending-to-an-old-tail/.

1. Author's name
- Authorship is often difficult to determine for Web sources. If you know the author or creator, follow the rules for books and periodicals.
- If you cannot identify the author or creator, begin with the title.

2. Title of work and title of overall Web site
- Place the title of the work inside quotation marks if it is part of a larger Web site.
- Untitled works may be identified by a label (e.g., *Home page, Introduction*). List the label in the title slot without quotations marks or italics.
- Italicize the name of the overall site if it is different from the work.
- The name of the overall Web site will usually be found on its index or home page. If you can not find a link back to the home page, look at the URL for clues. You can work backward through the URL by deleting sections (separated by slashes) until you come to the home page.

3. Publication information
- For online periodicals (magazines, newspapers, journals) do not include a publisher name.
- For other online sources, list the publisher's or sponsor's name followed by a comma. You may omit the publisher's or sponsor's name from the citation if it is essentially the same as the title of the overall Web site.
- List the date of publication or the date of uploading by day, month, and year if available. If there is both an original publication date and a more recent "last modified date" listed on the site, then use the most recent date in your citation.
- List the URL or DOI and end with a period. Omit *http://* and *https://* from the URL in your citation.

4. Date of access
- If a site has no publication date of any kind or is likely to be updated often, then at the end of your citation, include the date you accessed the site. List the date in the format of day, month, and year: Accessed 7 April 2016.

About URLs

MLA style recommends including URLs for Web sources to help readers locate those sources. If a Web source has a stable URL or a permanent URL (sometimes called a permalink), it is preferable to include that URL in your citation instead of using the URL that appears in your browser. If a scholarly journal article has a DOI (digital object identifier) assigned to it, then include that DOI (preceded by *doi:*) in place of a URL in your citation. DOIs are permanent unique numbers assigned to some types of online documents, especially journal articles, and they are the most reliable way to locate those online sources.

Sample Works-cited Entries for Online Sources

Online publications

43. Publication by a known author

If you know the author or creator, follow the rules for periodicals and books.

> Hurley, Jack F. "Lee, Russell Werner." *The Handbook of Texas*, Texas State Historical Association, 15 June 2010, tshaonline.org/handbook/online/articles/fle71.

44. Publication by an anonymous author

If a work has no author's or editor's name listed, begin the entry with the title of the source.

> "Welcome to the Music Referral Service." *Sarah and Ernest Butler School of Music*, U of Texas at Austin, ww4.austin.utexas.edu/bsomBridgeApp/gigReferral/. Accessed 3 Apr. 2016.

45. Publication by a group or corporate author

If the group or organization that authored the publication is also the publisher or sponsor for the publication, then start the citation with the title of the work and list the organization as the publisher.

> North American Bird Conservation Initiative, U.S. Committee. *The State of the Birds 2014 Report*. United States Department of Interior, 2014, www.stateofthebirds.org/2014%20SotB_FINAL_low-res.pdf.

46. Government publication on the Web

If you cannot locate the author of the document, give the name of the government and agency that published it.

> United States, Department of Health and Human Services. "Seasonal Influenza (Flu) Vaccination." *Centers for Disease Control and Prevention*, 3 Feb. 2016, www.cdc.gov/vaccines/vpd-vac/flu/default.htm.

Online periodicals

47. Article in a scholarly journal

Some scholarly journals are published on the Web only. List articles by author, title, name of journal in italics, volume and issue number, and the date of publication (including month or season, if available, and the year). Conclude with the URL followed by a period.

> Fleckenstein, Kristie. "Who's Writing? Aristotelian Ethos and the Author Position in Digital Poetics." *Kairos*, vol. 11, no. 3, Summer 2007, kairos.technorhetoric.net/11.3/binder.html?topoi/fleckenstein/index.html.

48. Article in a newspaper

Be sure to include the title and publication date of the article as it appears online. Include a URL instead of page numbers.

> Brooks, David. "How Covenants Make Us." *The New York Times*, 5 Apr. 2016, nyti.ms/1S6CHfw.

49. Article in a popular magazine

Remember that publisher names do not need to be included in citations for periodicals such as magazines, newspapers, and journals.

> Petrusich, Amanda. "The Discovery of Roscoe Holcomb and the 'High Lonesome Sound.'" *The New Yorker*, 17 Dec. 2015, www. newyorker.com/culture/culture-desk/the-discovery-of-roscoe-holcomb-and-the-high-lonesome-sound.

Online books and scholarly projects

50. Online book

If the book was printed and then scanned, give the complete print publication information. Then give the name of the database or Web site in italics, and the URL.

> Stoker, Bram. *Dracula*. Grosset and Dunlap Publishers, 1897. *Project Gutenberg*, www.gutenberg.org/files/345/345-h/345-h.htm.

51. E-book on Kindle, iPad, or another device

For a book originally published in print but read on an electronic device, treat the work as you would a printed book. Include a description of the type of e-book reader device being used and treat it as you would an edition.

> Morrison, Toni. *Home*. Kindle ed., Vintage, 2013.

Library database

52. Work from a library database

Follow the standard guidelines for citing the print publication (usually a periodical or book). Give the name of the database in italics and then include the URL or DOI. Remember that a DOI is preferable to a URL, if one is available for your source.

> Duncan, Mike. "Whatever Happened to the Paragraph?" *College English*, vol. 69, no. 5, May 2007, pp. 470-95. *JSTOR*, www.jstor.org/stable/25472231.

Other Sources in MLA-style Works Cited

53. E-mail

Give the name of the writer, the subject line, the name of recipient of the message, and the date.

> Ballmer, Steve. "A New Era of Business Productivity and Innovation." Received by Steve Jobs, 30 Nov. 2006.

54. Blog

> Arrington, Michael. "Think Before You Voicemail." *TechCrunch,* 5 July 2008, techcrunch.com/2008/07/05/think-before-you-voicemail/.

55. Posting on social media

Give the author, the title of the post (or first sentence of the post if it is not titled), the name of the site (e.g., *Facebook*), the date and time, and the URL.

> The Metropolitan Museum of Art, New York. "Arbus was particularly sensitive to children." *Facebook,* 5 June 2016, 1:00 p.m., www.facebook.com/metmuseum/posts/10153744054572635.

56. Untitled online posting, such as a tweet

Include the entire tweet in your citation and treat it as the title of the source, set in quotation marks. Include the date and time of publication.

> @BarackObama (BO). "The economy added 215,000 jobs in March—a record-breaking 73 months of private-sector job growth." *Twitter,* 1 Apr. 2016, 12:16 p.m., twitter.com/BarackObama/status/715909089113432064.

57. Film

If you are discussing a film in a general way, then follow the first example below. If you are focusing on the work of a particular person connected with the film, then follow the second example below and include that person's name and their role in your citation. List the the company primarily responsible for distributing the film, and the year the film was released.

> *Star Wars: Episode VII - The Force Awakens.* Walt Disney Studios, 2015.
> *Star Wars: Episode VII - The Force Awakens.* Directed by J. J. Abrams, performance by Daisy Ridley, Walt Disney Studios, 2015.

58. Podcast

> Dubner, Stephen J. "The Economics of Sleep, Part 1." *Freakonomics Radio,* 23 Mar. 2016, freakonomics.com/podcast/economics-sleep-part-1-freakonomics-radio-rebroadcast/.

59. Television episode

If you are discussing an episode in a general way, then follow the first example below. If you are focusing on the work of a particular person, then follow the second example. Provide the title of the episode, title of the series, and the season and episode numbers. List the name of the company primarily responsible for distributing the episode and the original broadcast date.

"Garage Sale." *The Office,* season 7, episode 19, NBC, 24 Mar. 2011.

"Garage Sale." *The Office,* performance by Steve Carell, season 7, episode 19, NBC, 24 Mar. 2011.

Visual Sources in MLA-style Works Cited

60. Cartoon

Trudeau, Gary. "Doonesbury." *The Washington Post,* 21 Apr. 2008, p. C15.

61. Advertisement

"Nike – Better For It." Advertisement. ABC, 5 May 2015.

62. Map, graph, or chart

Treat a map, graph, or chart as an anonymous book, but add the descriptive label *Map* after the name of the map.

Greenland. Map. International Travel Maps, 2004.

63. Painting, sculpture, or photograph

Give the artist's name, the title of the work in italics, the date the work was created, the name of the institution that houses it and the city where that institution is located. In your research project, mentioning the work and the artist is preferable to using a parenthetical citation.

Manet, Édouard. *Olympia.* 1863, Musée d'Orsay, Paris.

Visual sources on the web

64. Video on the Web

Begin the entry with a title if you cannot find a creator or author of the video. Include the date that the video was uploaded or posted.

"Alex Honnold—El Sendero Luminoso." *YouTube,* uploaded by The North Face, 12 Feb. 2014, youtu.be/Phl82D57P58.

65. Photograph on the Web

Gardner, Alexander. *The Home of a Rebel Sharpshooter.* Library of Congress, [circa 1863], lccn.loc.gov/2012647605.

66. Map on the Web

"Lansing, Michigan." Map. *GoogleMaps,* 2016, www.google.com/maps/@42.7088481,-84.6994643,11z.

Sample MLA Paper

Abukar 1

George Abukar

Professor Hernandez

English 1102

19 May 2014

It's Time to Shut Down the Identity Theft Racket ◀

For many college students, a credit rating is something you'll start to worry about after you graduate and get a job. A friend of mine, whom I'll call "Donna," has never had a credit card in her life, and protecting her credit rating was the last thing on her mind her junior year—that is, until she started getting disturbing calls from debt collectors accusing her of not paying her credit card bill.

The first few times she got these calls, Donna explained to the callers that she didn't have a credit card and didn't know what account they were talking about. Then one debt collector threatened to take her to court. Donna got scared.

It took several days of phone calls to her parents, her bank, the police, and a credit-reporting agency before Donna found out what was going on. During spring break of her sophomore year, Donna had lost her wallet at a beach in South Carolina. She got a new driver's license from the Department of Motor Vehicles when she returned home, but she didn't report the lost wallet to the police because it didn't have any money or credit cards in it.

But whoever found Donna's wallet used her driver's license information to apply for a credit card, and got one, with Donna's name on it. He or she used the card to rack up several thousand dollars in bills, mostly for clothes and electronic equipment. When this criminal didn't pay the bill, the creditors came looking for Donna instead.

It's bad enough that someone stole Donna's identity. What was worse, to her, was that none of the people who should have helped stop the crime did. The credit card company that issued the card did not bother to check the applicant's identity. The credit reporting agencies did nothing to help her get the bad information off her files. In fact, even after she has filled out

Include your last name and page number as page header, beginning with the first page, 1/2" from the top

Center the title. Do not underline the title, put it inside quotation marks, or type it in all capital letters.

Indent each paragraph five spaces (1/2" on the ruler in your word processing program).

Specify 1" margins all around. Double-space everything.

MLA style does not require a title page. Check with your instructor to find out whether you need one.

Abukar 2

forms for all three national credit reporting agencies, asking to have the information about the unpaid credit card bills removed from her file, the bad debts are still showing up. Donna worries that she will never have a clean credit record, and that she'll have trouble buying a house or car after she graduates. "All this information about me has been falsified," Donna said in an interview, "and I don't even get to set the record straight." Only the credit reporting agencies have the ability to do that, and since they do not stand to make any money from helping Donna, they are in no hurry to do it.

As long as credit-reporting agencies are protected from the effects of identity theft, they will not take steps to protect consumers. Therefore, I propose that the United States Congress pass federal legislation making credit-reporting agencies liable for damages when their actions or negligence lead to loss from identity theft.

This legislation is necessary because identity theft is increasingly out of control. In 2007 there were 8.4 million adult victims of identity theft in the United States for a total loss of $49.3 billion (Kim). For example, in April 2011 when hackers who infiltrated Sony's Playstation Network obtained the personal data, possibly including credit card information, for about 77,000 subscribers worldwide, Sony simply warned its customers to "remain vigilant" for signs of identity theft and other fraud (Bilton and Stelter). Clearly, identity theft is a huge and expensive problem. What is being done to prevent it?

Mostly, consumers are being told to protect themselves. The United States Federal Trade Commission has an entire Web site devoted to telling consumers how to minimize their risk of identity theft. Some of their advice is obvious, like "Keep your purse or wallet in a safe place at work." Some tips are more obscure: "Treat your mail and trash carefully." Some assume that people have a lot more time, patience, and knowledge than they really do:

> Ask about information security procedures in your
> workplace or at businesses, doctor's offices or other
> institutions that collect your personally identifying
> information. Find out who has access to your personal
> information and verify that it is handled securely. Ask

Akubar states his thesis in this paragraph after he has described the problem using the example of Donna.

Quotations of more than four lines should be indented 1/2 inch or five spaces.

593

Abukar 3

about the disposal procedures for those records as well. Find out if your information will be shared with anyone else. If so, ask how your information can be kept confidential. (*Identity Theft: Minimizing*)

Not many people are prepared to spend twenty minutes grilling the checkout person at Old Navy when she asks for their phone number. But even if someone takes all these steps and avoids even a simple mistake like Donna made by losing her wallet, is that enough.

Daniel J. Solove, in his book *The Digital Person: Technology and Privacy in the Information Age*, argues that it is not. "The underlying cause of identity theft," he says, "is an architecture that makes us vulnerable to such crimes and unable to adequately repair the damage" (115). He notes that

> We are increasingly living with digital dossiers about our lives, and these dossiers are not controlled by us but by various entities, such as private-sector companies and the government. These dossiers play a profound role in our existence in modern society. The identity thief taps into these dossiers and uses them, manipulates them, and pollutes them. The identity thief's ability to so easily access and use our personal data stems from an architecture that does not provide adequate security to our personal information and that does not afford us with a sufficient degree of participation in its collection, dissemination, and use. (115)

Solove's proposal for reducing identity theft is to change the structure, or "architecture," of the systems we use to collect and store personal information. He recommends giving individuals more control over their personal information and requiring the companies that use that information to inform people whenever something unusual happens to their files. This sounds like a good plan, but I think the second half of it is far more important. Solove says that any new system should be "premised on the notion that the collection and use of personal information is an activity that carries duties and responsibilities" (121). This statement is an indirect way of saying, "Companies that handle personal information ought to be held liable for damages caused by identity theft." I would argue that if you make companies

---

Do not include a page number for items without pagination, such as Web sites.

Introduce blocked quotations rather than just dropping them into the text.

Do not place blocked quotations within quotation marks.

Abukar 4

responsible to consumers by making them liable (the second half of Solove's plan), then they will automatically give consumers more control over their own information (the first half).

As Solove himself points out, "Credit reporting agencies don't work for the individuals they report on; rather they are paid by creditors" (117). Individuals already have the motivation to take care of their credit rating. But companies that make huge profits by collecting and selling our personal information have absolutely zero motivation to take even minimal steps to protect us.

How big are the profits? There are only three major American credit reporting agencies: Equifax, Experian, and TransUnion. Equifax reported an annual profit of $246.5 million in 2005 ("Companies"). TransUnion, the smallest of the three, is privately held and does not report its annual revenue, but it employs 3,600 people. Experian, the largest of the three companies, had an annual revenue of $2.5 billion dollars in 2007 (Moyer). These companies are raking in money while they do next to nothing about identity theft. Why would they want to change things? It is much easier, and more profitable, for them to place the burden on consumers and blame them whenever identity theft occurs. If these companies actually lost money every time identity theft occurred, would they change their attitude?

> Cite publications by the name of the author (or authors).

To answer that question, let's look at the banking industry. In an article in *American Banker*, Don A. Childears, the president and chief executive officer of the Colorado Bankers Association, reports that Colorado banks "lose up to $150 million each year to fraud" (qtd. in Kuehner-Herbert 3).

> For a source quoted in another source, use the abbreviation *qtd. in*: ("quoted in").

The article also points out that "Along with consumers, financial institutions are hit hardest by fraud from identity theft because they have to assume most of the losses." Credit reporting agencies, by contrast, see little or no loss from identity theft. At most, they may spend some extra time processing paperwork when fraud has occurred. But Donna's experience shows they don't even take this responsibility very seriously. Indeed, credit-reporting agencies may take the time to resolve a claim only if they deem the consumer a VIP. A recent *New York Times* article said the agencies have a "two-tiered system" for investigating complaints—"one for the rich, the well-connected, the well-known and the powerful, and the other for everyone else." Apparently, celebrities get "special help" from agency personnel. But an average consumer's complaint is processed in an "automated system," with workers spending "about two minutes" on what amounts to a "perfunctory check" of the agency's records. No wonder agencies can seem so unresponsive: "Consumers who have trouble fixing errors through the dispute process can quickly find themselves trapped in a Kafkaesque no man's land, where the only escape is through the court system" (Bernard).

It gets worse. The credit reporting agencies are not content with letting consumers and banks foot the bill for their sloppy handling of our digital identities. They want to make more money off the insecurity they have created. Kevin Drum reports in *Washington Monthly,*

> For their part, the major credit-reporting bureaus—Experian, Equifax, and TransUnion—don't seem to care much about the accuracy of their credit reports. In fact, they actually have a positive incentive to let ID theft flourish. Like mobsters offering "protection" to frightened store owners, credit-reporting agencies have recently begun taking advantage of the identity-theft boom to offer information age protection to frightened consumers. For $9.95 a month, Equifax offers "Credit Watch Gold," a service that alerts you whenever changes are made to your credit report. Experian and TransUnion offer similar services. In effect, customers are being asked to pay credit agencies to protect them from the negligence of those same agencies.

Unlike consumers, who usually at least try to act responsibly to protect their credit rating, credit-reporting agencies avoid responsibility for, and profit from, identity theft. Therefore, the most important step to take in reducing identity theft is to implement legislation that holds credit reporting agencies responsible for the damage their actions or inactions cause consumers.

Legislation, of course, must be passed by the government. And because of the Fair and Accurate Credit Transactions Act (FACTA) passed by the U.S. Congress in 2003, states cannot pass

Abukar 6

any laws that are stricter than the federal laws on identity theft (Solove 113). Therefore, a new federal law is needed. To determine whether U.S. Representatives and Senators could be convinced to pass such a law, I conducted a sample survey asking people about this issue. I asked fifty people who were sitting or walking on the University Commons the following questions:

1. Have you, or has someone you know, ever been the victim of identity theft?
2. Do you feel identity theft is an important problem?
3. If a credit-reporting company reports false information about you, and you suffer as a result, should the company be held responsible?
4. Are you registered to vote?

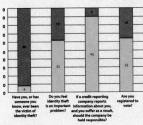

Fig. 1. Identity theft survey results

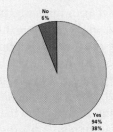

Fig. 2. Is ID theft an important problem? (Overall response)

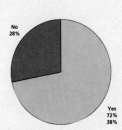

Fig. 3. Is ID theft an important problem? (Registered voters only)

Fig. 4. Should credit-reporting companies be held responsible for harm? (Overall results)

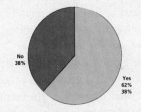

Fig. 5. Should credit-reporting companies be held responsible for harm? (Registered voters only)

The results of this survey indicate that most people, and the vast majority of registered voters, believe credit-reporting agencies should be held responsible for the damage they cause (see fig. 1). Furthermore, registered voters felt even more strongly about the issue than non voters (see figs. 2–5).

Although this survey was very limited, I believe its results could be replicated on a much larger scale. Almost 13% of Americans surveyed by the FTC had gone through the same ordeal as Donna (*Identity Theft Survey* 4), and the frequency of identity theft is increasing.

Drum points out that the type of law I am proposing is very similar to the Truth in Lending Act passed in 1968, which regulated banks and lending institutions. He explains,

> One notably simple provision was that consumers could be held liable for no more than $50 if their credit cards were stolen and used without their authorization. For anything above that, it was the credit-card issuer who had to pay. The result was predictable: Credit-card companies have since taken it upon themselves to develop a wide range of effective anti-fraud programs.

So it would be hard for anyone to claim (as the credit-reporting agencies probably will) that a law like this would bankrupt the credit-reporting companies. The credit-card business has flourished since 1968, and is now a multi billion dollar industry. The lesson here is that responsible behavior is even better for business than irresponsible behavior.

The person who took Donna's driver's license still hasn't been caught. The credit-reporting agencies still haven't repaired her credit rating. The thief made money by stealing Donna's identity. The credit-reporting agencies are still making money by selling Donna's name and the false information associated with it. Donna's financial history is a wreck, and she worries about it constantly. Why is one person who profited from her misery labeled a criminal, while the others are considered good corporate citizens? It's time to shut down the identity theft racket, and make corporate responsibility the law of the land.

Abukar 8

Works Cited

Bernard, Tara Siegel. "Credit Error? It Pays to Be on V.I.P. List." *The New York Times*, 14 May 2011, nyti.ms/1UJCm4h.

Bilton, Nick, and Brian Stelter. "Sony Says PlayStation Hacker Got Personal Data." *The New York Times*, 2 Apr. 2011, nyti.ms/1LGQM4d.

"Companies with annual revenue of $1 billion or more." *Atlanta Business Chronicle*, 20 Mar. 2006, www.bizjournals.com/atlanta/stories/2006/03/20/focus2.html.

Donna. Personal interview. 30 Mar. 2014.

Drum, Kevin. "You Own You." *Washington Monthly*, Dec. 2005, www.washingtonmonthly.com/features/2005/0512.drum.html.

Kim, Rachel. 2007 *Identity Fraud Survey Report - Consumer Version*. Javelin Strategy and Research, Feb. 2007, graphics8.nytimes.com/images/blogs/freakonomics/pdf/Javelin%20Report%202007.pdf.

Kuehner-Hebert, Katie. "Colorado Banks Would Fund ID Theft Task Force." *American Banker*, 21 Mar. 2006, pp. 1-4. *Academic OneFile,* go.galegroup.com/ps/i.do?id=GALE%7CA143466405&v=2.1&u=nysl_me_wls&it=r&p=AONE&sw=w&asid=af17c4ba5785f3bef81324a6646267fb.

Moyer, Liz. "Credit Agencies in the Clover." *Forbes*, 7 June 2005, www.forbes.com/pushfiles/omnisky/cx_lm_0608equifax.html.

Solove, Daniel J. *The Digital Person: Technology and Privacy in the Information Age*. New York UP, 2004.

United States, Federal Trade Commission. *Identity Theft Survey Report*. Synovate, Sept. 2003, www.ftc.gov/sites/default/files/documents/reports/federal-trade-commission-identity-theft-program/synovatereport.pdf.

---, ---. *Identity Theft: Minimizing Your Risk*. July 2005, www.consumer.ftc.gov/topics/identity-theft.

Center "Works Cited" on a new page.

Double-space all entries. Indent all but the first line in each entry one-half inch.

Alphabetize entries by the last names of the authors or by the first important word in the title if no author is listed.

Italicize the titles of books and periodicals.

If an author has more than one entry, list the entries in alphabetical order by title. Use three hyphens in place of the author's name (for government names, include three hyphens for any name repeated) in the second and subsequent entries.

Go through your text and make sure all the sources you have used are in the list of works cited.

MyWritingLab™ Visit Ch. 24 in MyWritingLab to test your understanding of the chapter objectives.

25 APA Documentation

APA style is followed in the social sciences and education.

References

Clayton, M. (2006, September 24). He tallies hidden costs of free parking—one sp

Christian Science Monitor. Retrieved from http://www.csmonitor.com

County of Ventura (California) Planning Department. (n.d.). Build it smart! `

http://www.builditsmartvc.org/how/team.php

Kloeppel, J. E. (2006, October 24). Weight gain of U.S. drivers has inc

consumption. Retrieved from University of Illinois at Urban

Bureau Web site: http://www.news.uiuc.edu/

Main, D. (2007, September 11). Parking spaces outnumber dr

warming. Retrieved from Purdue University News `

Miller, P. (2005, April). Design for active living theme f

[Electronic version.] *Recreation Management*

APA Citations

APA style emphasizes the date of publication. When you cite an author's name in the body of your paper, always include the date of publication. Notice too that APA style includes the abbreviation for page (p.) in front of the page number. For a detailed treatment of APA style, consult the *Publication Manual of the American Psychological Association*, sixth edition (2010).

Zukin (2004) observes that teens today begin to shop for themselves at age 13 or 14, "the same age when lower-class children, in the past, became apprentices or went to work in factories" (p. 50).

When you cite an author's name in the body of your paper, always include the date of publication.

One sociologist notes that teens today begin to shop for themselves at age 13 or 14, "the same age when lower-class children, in the past, became apprentices or went to work in factories" (Zukin, 2004, p. 50).

APA style includes the abbreviation for page *(p.)* in front of the page number.

If the author's name is not mentioned in the sentence, the reference looks like this.

References

Zukin, S. (2004). *Point of purchase: How shopping changed American culture.* New York: Routledge.

The corresponding entry in the references list would be

Where do you put the date?

You have two choices. You can put the date in your text in parentheses

Zhang, Liu, and Cao (2006) specify . . .

or between the author's name and the page number in the citation note.

. . . visual languages (Zhang, Liu, & Cao, 2006, p. 192).

When do you need to give a page number?

- Give the page number for all direct quotations.
- For electronic sources that do not provide page numbers, give the paragraph number when available. Use the abbreviation *para.*
- If the source does not include page numbers, it is preferable to reference the work and the author in the text.

In Wes Anderson's 1998 film *Rushmore*, . . .

In-text Citations in APA Style

1. Author named in your text

Influential physicist Stephen Hawking (2005) asserts that "today, we are closer than ever before to understanding the nature of the universe" (p. 2).

2. Author not named in your text

In 1997, the Gallup poll reported that 55% of adults in the United States think secondhand smoke is "very harmful," compared to only 36% in 1994 (Saad, 1997, p. 4).

3. Work by a single author

(Hawking, 2005, p. 2)

4. Work by two authors

Notice that APA uses an ampersand (&) with multiple authors' names rather than *and*.

(Suzuki & Irabu, 2014, p. 404)

5. Work by three to five authors

The authors' last names follow the order of the title page.

(Francisco, Vaughn, & Romano, 2014, p. 7)

Subsequent references can use the first name and *et al.*

(Francisco et al., 2014, p. 17)

6. Work by six or more authors

Use the first author's last name and *et al.* for all in-text references.

(Swallit et al., 2013, p. 49)

7. Work by a group or organization

Identify the group author in the text and place only the page number in the parentheses.

The National Organization for Women (2001) observed that this "generational shift in attitudes towards marriage and childrearing" will have profound consequences (p. 325).

8. Work by an unknown author

Use a shortened version of the title (or the full title if it is short) in place of the author's name. Capitalize all key words in the title. If it is an article title, place it in quotation marks.

("Derailing the Peace Process," 2014, p. 44)

9. Quotations 40 words or longer	Indent long quotations one-half inch and omit quotation marks. Note that the period appears before the parentheses in an indented "block" quote.

> Orlean (2001) has attempted to explain the popularity of the painter Thomas Kinkade:
>> People like to own things they think are valuable. . . . The high price of limited editions is part of their appeal; it implies that they are choice and exclusive, and that only a certain class of people will be able to afford them. (p. 128)

10. Two works by one author with the same copyright date	Assign the dates letters (*a*, *b*, etc.) according to their alphabetical arrangement in the references list.

> The majority of books written about coauthorship focus on partners of the same sex (Laird, 2001a, p. 351).

11. Two or more sources within the same sentence	Place each citation directly after the statement it supports.

> Some surveys report an increase in homelessness rates (Alford, 2004) while others chart a slight decrease (Rice, 2003a) . . .

If you need to cite two or more works within the same parentheses, list them in the order they appear in the references list and separate them with a semicolon.

> (Alford, 2004; Rice, 2003a)

12. Work cited in another source	Name the work and give a citation for the secondary source.

> Saunders and Kellman's study (as cited in McAtee, Luhan, Stiles, & Buell, 2014) . . .

Books in APA-style References List

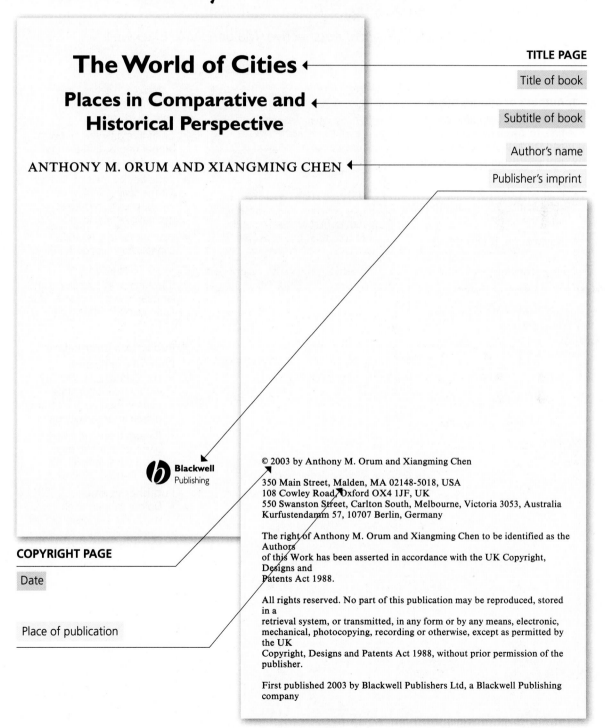

TITLE PAGE

The World of Cities ← Title of book

Places in Comparative and Historical Perspective ← Subtitle of book

ANTHONY M. ORUM AND XIANGMING CHEN ← Author's name

Publisher's imprint

Blackwell
Publishing

© 2003 by Anthony M. Orum and Xiangming Chen

350 Main Street, Malden, MA 02148-5018, USA
108 Cowley Road, Oxford OX4 1JF, UK
550 Swanston Street, Carlton South, Melbourne, Victoria 3053, Australia
Kurfustendamm 57, 10707 Berlin, Germany

The right of Anthony M. Orum and Xiangming Chen to be identified as the Authors
of this Work has been asserted in accordance with the UK Copyright, Designs and
Patents Act 1988.

All rights reserved. No part of this publication may be reproduced, stored in a
retrieval system, or transmitted, in any form or by any means, electronic,
mechanical, photocopying, recording or otherwise, except as permitted by the UK
Copyright, Designs and Patents Act 1988, without prior permission of the
publisher.

First published 2003 by Blackwell Publishers Ltd, a Blackwell Publishing
company

COPYRIGHT PAGE

Date

Place of publication

605

Orum, A. M., & Chen, X. (2003). *The world of cities: Places in comparative and historical perspective.* Malden, MA: Blackwell.

1. Author's or editor's name
- The author's last name comes first, followed by a comma and the author's initials.
- Join two authors' names with an ampersand.
- If an editor, put the abbreviation *Ed.* in parentheses after the name:

Kavanaugh, P. (Ed.).

2. Year of publication
- Give the year the work was copyrighted in parentheses. If no year of publication is given, write *n.d.* ("no date") in parentheses:

Smith, S. (n.d.).

- If it is a multivolume edited work published over a period of more than one year, put the span in parentheses:

Smith, S. (1999–2001).

3. Book title
- Italicize the title.
- Capitalize only the first word, proper nouns, and the first word after a colon.
- If the book is part of a series, list the series name immediately after the title. Do not italicize or underline it.
- Use the same rules for capitalization as for the title.
- Close with a period.
- If the title is in a foreign language, copy it exactly as it appears on the title page.

4. Publication information
Place of publication
- For all books, list the city with a two-letter state abbreviation (or full country name) after the city name.
- If more than one city is given on the title page (as in this example), list only the first.

Publisher's name
- Do not shorten or abbreviate words like *University* or *Press.*
- Omit words such as *Co., Inc.,* and *Publishers.*

Sample references for books

13. Book by one author

The author's last name comes first, followed by a comma and the author's initials.

> Hagedorn, J. M. (2008). *A world of gangs: Armed young men and gangsta culture*. Minneapolis, MN: University of Minnesota Press.

If an editor, put the abbreviation *Ed.* in parentheses after the name.

> Conrad, C. (Ed.). (2011). *The handbook of stress: Neuropsychological effects on the brain*. New York, NY: Wiley.

14. Book by two authors

Join two authors' names with a comma and ampersand.

> Hardt, M., & Negri, A. (2000). *Empire*. Cambridge, MA: Harvard University Press.

15. Book by three or more authors

List last names and initials for up to seven authors, with an ampersand between the last two names. For works with eight or more authors, list the first six names, then an ellipsis, then the last author's name.

> Anders, K., Child, H., Davis, K., Logan, O., Orr, J., Ray, B., . . . Wood, G.

16. Chapter in an edited collection

Add the word *In* after the selection title and before the names of the editor(s).

> Ferguson-Patrick, K. (2009). Writers develop skills through collaboration: An action research approach. In R. Schmuck (Ed.), *Practical action research* (pp. 3–24). Thousand Oaks, CA: Corwin.

17. Published dissertation or thesis

If the dissertation you are citing is available online, give the name of the database and the order number.

> Tzilos, G. K. (2010). *A brief computer-based intervention for alcohol use during pregnancy* (Doctoral dissertation). Available from ProQuest Dissertations and Theses database. (UMI No. 3373111)

18. Government document

When the author and publisher are identical, use the word *Author* as the name of the publisher.

> U.S. Environmental Protection Agency. (2002). *Respiratory health effects of passive smoking: Lung cancer and other disorders*. (EPA Publication No. 600/6-90/006 F). Washington, DC: Author.

Periodicals in APA-style References

JOURNAL COVER

Publication information

Authors' names

Date

Title of article

JRRD

Volume 48, Number 2, 2011
Pages 89–102

Journal of Rehabilitation Research & Development

Department of Veterans Affairs

Measurement of community reintegration in sample of severely wounded servicemembers

Linda Resnik, PT, PhD;[1-2]* Melissa Gray, MOT, OTR/L;[3] Matthew Borgia, BS[2]
[1]Providence Department of Veterans Affairs Medical Center, Providence, RI; [2]Department of Community Health, Brown University, Providence, RI; [3]Brooke Army Medical Center, San Antonio, TX

Abstract—The Community Reintegration of Servicemembers (CRIS) is a new measure of community reintegration. The purpose of this study was to test the CRIS with seriously injured combat veterans. Subjects were 68 patients at the Center for the Intrepid. Each patient completed three CRIS subscales, the 36-Item Short Form Health Survey for Veterans (SF-36V), the Quality of Life Scale (QOLS), and two Craig Handicap Assessment and Reporting Technique subscales at visit 1 and the 3-month follow-up. Of the patients, 11 also completed the measures within 2 weeks of visit 1. We abstracted diagnoses and activities of daily living from the medical record. We evaluated test-retest reliability using intraclass correlation coefficients (ICCs). We evaluated concurrent validity with Pearson product moment correlations. We used multivariate analyses of variance to compare scores for subjects with and without posttraumatic stress disorder (PTSD), traumatic brain injury (TBI), and depression. Responsiveness analyses evaluated floor and ceiling effects, percent achieving minimal detectable change (MDC), effect size (ES), and the standardized response mean (SRM). CRIS subscale ICCs were 0.90 to 0.91. All subscales were moderately or strongly correlated with QOLS and SF-36V subscales. CRIS subscale scores were lower in PTSD and TBI groups ($p < 0.05$). CRIS Extent of Participation and Satisfaction with Participation subscales were lower for subjects with depression ($p < 0.05$). Of the sample, 17.4% to 23.2% had change greater than MDC. The ES ranged from 0.227 to 0.273 (SRM = 0.277–0.370), showing a small effect between visit 1 and the 3-month follow-up. Results suggest that the CRIS is a psychometrically sound choice for community reintegration measurement in severely wounded servicemembers.

Key words: community reintegration, disability, measurement, military healthcare, outcomes assessment, participation, psychometric testing, reliability, traumatic brain injury, veterans.

INTRODUCTION

Evidence to date suggests that demobilization and return home after combat can be challenging for military servicemembers. Numerous reintegration problems have been reported among veterans from the gulf war and more recent conflicts in Iraq and Afghanistan, including marital difficulties, financial difficulties, problems with alcohol or substance abuse, medical problems, behavioral problems such as depression or anxiety [1], homelessness [2], and motor vehicle accidents [3]. Readjustment to

Abbreviations: ADL = activity of daily living, ANOVA = analysis of variance, BAMC = Brooke Army Medical Center, CFI = Center for the Intrepid, CHART = Craig Handicap Assessment and Reporting Technique, CRIS = Community Reintegration of Servicemembers, ES = effect size, ICC = intraclass correlation coefficient, ICF = International Classification of Function, IED = improvised explosive device, MANOVA = multivariate analysis of variance, MDC = minimal detectable change, OEF = Operation Enduring Freedom, OIF = Operation Iraqi Freedom, PF-10 = 10-Item Physical Functioning Subscale, PTSD = posttraumatic stress disorder, QOLS = Quality of Life Scale, SD = standard deviation, SF-36V = 36-Item Short Form Health Survey for Veterans, SRM = standardized response mean, TBI = traumatic brain injury, VA = Department of Veterans Affairs.
*Address all correspondence to Linda Resnik, PT, PhD; Providence VA Medical Center, 830 Chalkstone Ave, Providence, RI 02908; 401-273-7100, ext 2368; fax: 401-863-3489. Email: Linda_Resnik@brown.edu
DOI:10.1682/JRRD.2010.04.0070

89

DOI

Resnik, L., Gray, M., & Borgia, M. (2011). Measurement of community reintegration in sample of severely wounded servicemembers. *Journal of Rehabilitation Research and Development, 48*(2), 89–102. doi:10.1682/JRRD.2010.04.0070

1. Author's name
- The author's last name comes first, followed by the author's initials.
- Join two authors' names with a comma and an ampersand.

2. Date of publication
- Give the year the work was published in parentheses.
- Most popular magazines are paginated per issue. These periodicals might have a volume number, but are more often referenced by the season or date of publication.

3. Title of article
- Do not use quotation marks.
- If there is a book title in the article title, italicize it.
- The first word of the title, the first word of the subtitle, and any proper nouns in the title are capitalized.

4. Publication information
Name of journal
- Italicize the journal name.
- All nouns, verbs, pronouns, adjectives, and adverbs, as well as the first word of the title, are capitalized.
- Do not capitalize any article or coordinating conjunction unless it is the first word of the title or subtitle. Capitalize prepositions of four or more letters only.
- Put a comma after the journal name.

Volume, issue, and page numbers
- Italicize the volume number and follow it with a comma.
- If each issue of the journal begins on page 1, give the issue number in parentheses, followed by a comma.
- Give inclusive page numbers for the article.
- See sample references 22 and 23 for more on different types of pagination.

DOI
- Scholarly articles are often assigned a unique registration code, called a digital object identifier (DOI).
- If the article has a DOI, list it after the page numbers but without a period at the end.

Sample references for periodical sources

A digital object identifier (DOI) is a unique, permanent alphanumeric string that many scholarly publishers now attach to their articles. Include a DOI if available.

19. Article by one author

Sitzmann, T. (2011) A meta-analytic examination of the instructional effectiveness of computer-based simulation games. *Personnel Psychology, 64*(2), 489-529. doi:10.1111/j.1744-6570.2011.01190.x

20. Article by multiple authors

List last names and initials for up to seven authors, with an ampersand between the last two names. For works with eight or more authors, list the first six names, then an ellipsis, then the last author's name.

Blades, J., & Rowe-Finkbeiner, K. (2006). The motherhood manifesto. *The Nation, 282*(20), 11–16.

21. Article by a group or organization

National Organization for Women (2002). Where to find feminists in Austin. *The NOW guide for Austin women.* Austin, TX: Chapter Press.

22. Article in a journal with continuous pagination

Include only the volume number and the year.

Engen, R., & Steen, S. (2000). The power to punish: Discretion and sentencing reform in the war on drugs. *American Journal of Sociology, 105*, 1357–1395. doi:10.1086/210433

23. Article in a journal paginated by issue

List the issue number in parentheses (not italicized) after the volume number. For a popular magazine that does not commonly use volume numbers, use the season or date of publication.

McGinn, D. (2006, June 5). Marriage by the numbers. *Newsweek*, 40–48.

24. Monthly publications

Fallows, J. (2008, June). China's silver lining. *Atlantic Monthly*, 36–50.

25. Newspaper article

de Vise, D. (2008, July 3). Italian American groups speak up to save AP language test. *The Washington Post*, p. A1.

Web Sources in APA-style References List

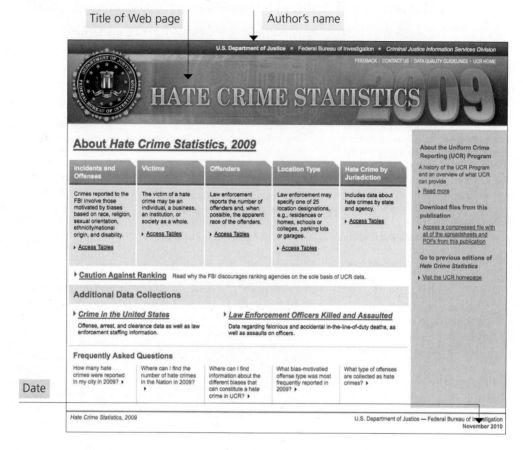

Title of Web page

Author's name

Date

Titles and URLs in APA-style references

Web sites are often made up of many separate pages or articles. Each page or article on a Web site may or may not have a title. If you are citing a page or article that has a title, treat the title like an article in a periodical. No retrieval date is necessary if the content is not likely to be changed or updated.

Heiney, A. (2004). A gathering of space heroes. Retrieved from the National Aeronautics and Space Administration Web site: http://www.nasa.gov/missions/

If you need to cite the Web site itself, treat it as you would a book.

U.S. Department of Justice. Federal Bureau of Investigation. (2010, November). *Hate crime statistics, 2009*. Retrieved from http://www2.fbi.gov/ucr/hc2009/

1. Author's name, associated institution, or organization
- Authorship is sometimes hard to determine for online sources. If you do have an author or creator to cite, follow the rules for periodicals and books.
- If the only authority you find is a group or organization (as in this example), list its name as the author.
- If the author or organization is not identified, begin the reference with the title of the document.

2. Dates
Two dates are possible for a Web site.
- The date the site was produced or last revised is required. Sometimes this date is the copyright date, sometimes listed at the bottom of a page. This date might be just a year.
- Give the date you retrieved the Web source if the Web site is likely to change or be updated. Place this second date (month, day, and year) just before the URL, preceded by the word *Retrieved* and followed by a comma and the word *from*. No retrieval date is necessary for journal articles, books, and other material unlikely to be revised.

3. Name of site and title of page or article
- Web sites are often made up of many separate pages or articles. Each page or article on a Web site may or may not have a title. If you are citing a page or article that has a title, treat the title like an article in a periodical. Otherwise, treat the name of the Web site itself as you would a book.
- The name of a Web site will usually be found on its index or home page. If you cannot find a link back to the home page, look at the address for clues. You can work your way backward through the URL, deleting sections (separated by slashes) until you come to a home or index page.

4. URL
- Copy the address exactly as it appears in your browser window. You can copy and paste the address into your text for greater accuracy.
- Note that there are no angle brackets around the URL and no period after it.
- If a URL does not fit on one line, break before most punctuation, except after a double slash (//).

Sample references for Web sources

26. Web publication by a known author

Authorship is sometimes hard to discern for online sources. If you do have an author or creator to cite, follow the rules for periodicals and books.

> Carr, A. (2003, May 22). *AAUW applauds senate support of Title IX resolution*. Retrieved from http://www.aauw.org

27. Scholarly article on the Web with DOI assigned

Because URLs frequently change, many scholarly publishers have begun to use a digital object identifier (DOI), a unique alphanumeric string that is permanent. If a DOI is available, use the DOI instead of the URL. The article was retrieved from the PsychARTICLES database, but there is no need to list the database, the retrieval date, or the URL if the DOI is listed.

> Erdfelder, E. (2008). Experimental psychology: Good news. *Experimental Psychology, 55*(1), 1-2. doi:0.1027/1618-3169.55.1.1

28. Scholarly article on the Web with no DOI assigned

If no DOI is assigned, give the exact URL.

> Brown, B. (2004). The order of service: The practical management of customer interaction. *Sociological Research Online, 9*(4). Retrieved from http://www.socresonline.org.uk/9/4/brown.html

29. E-book with DOI

> Chaffe-Stengel, P., & Stengel, D. (2012). *Working with sample data: Exploration and inference*. doi:10.4128/9781606492147

30. E-book with no DOI assigned

> Burton, R. (1832). *The anatomy of melancholy*. Retrieved from http://etext.library.adelaide.edu.au/b/burton/robert/melancholy

31. Document from a database

APA no longer requires listing the names of well-known databases. Include the name of the database only for hard-to-find books and other items. Include the DOI when available.

> Jones, J. (2008). Patterns of revision in online writing: A study of Wikipedia's featured articles. *Written Communication, 25*(2), 262–289. doi:10.1177/0741088307312940

Other Sources in APA-style References List

32. Television program

Weiner, M. (Writer). (2011). Public relations. [Television series episode]. In M. Weiner (Producer), *Mad men*. Bethpage, NY: AMC.

33. Film, Video, or DVD

Guggenheim, D. (Director). (2010). *Waiting for superman* [DVD]. United States: Paramount Vantage.

Unedited online sources

34. Blog entry

Spinuzzi, C. (2010, January 7). In the pipeline [Web log post]. Retrieved from http://spinuzzi.blogspot.com/search?updated-max=2010-01-25T12%3A35%3A00-06%3A00

35. Social media (e.g., *Facebook*) update

The Daily Show. (2013, March 18). Political speeches contain much more than empty promises. http://on.cc.com/114V1xk [*Facebook* update]. Retrieved July 29, 2014, from https://www.facebook.com/thedailyshow

36. *Twitter* post

Collins, F.S. (2013, April 30). Check out my NPR interview this afternoon with Marketplace's @kairyssdal about #NIH research [Tweet]. Retrived from https://twitter.com/NIH

37. Wiki

Machu Picchu [*Wikipedia* entry]. (n.d.) Retrieved June 7, 2014 from http://en.wikipedia.org/wiki/Machu_Picchu

38. E-mail

E-mail sent from one individual to another should be cited as a personal communication. Personal communication is cited in text but not included in the reference list.

(M. Rodriguez, personal communication, March 28, 2014)

Sample APA Paper

APA style uses a title page.

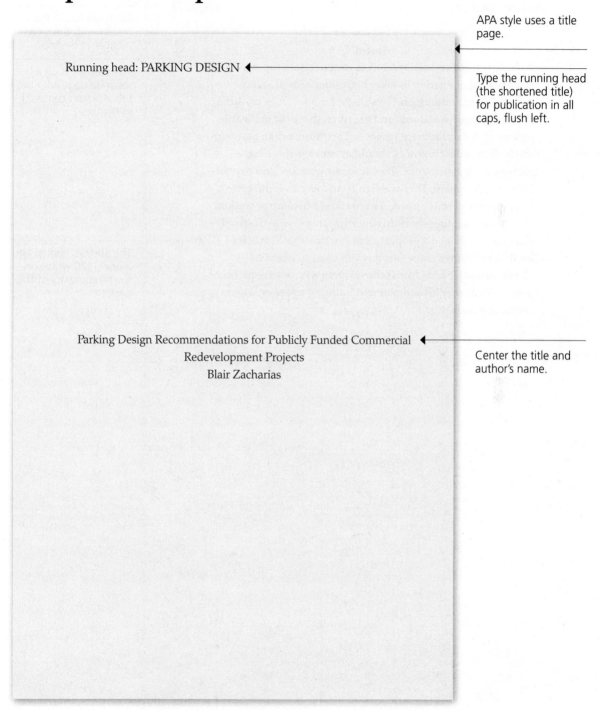

Running head: PARKING DESIGN

Type the running head (the shortened title) for publication in all caps, flush left.

Parking Design Recommendations for Publicly Funded Commercial
Redevelopment Projects
Blair Zacharias

Center the title and author's name.

Continue to use the header with the page number at the top.

Abstract

Publicly funded redevelopment of commercial property has a special obligation to meet high standards of safety, environmental impact, and health. Parking facilities contribute directly to these standards and are often the most malleable portion of redevelopment projects. Therefore, urban planners involved in redevelopment should encourage three basic parking design elements: sharing, centralization, and rear-of-building placement. These design elements can reduce the total amount of space needed for parking, encourage walking, reduce fuel-wasting short driving trips, improve pedestrian safety, and enhance a property's aesthetic value. Costs for implementation of these designs will vary, so planners should prioritize bids from redevelopers who use them. Local governments may also implement building codes or laws to encourage their use.

The abstract is on a separate page with the title *Abstract* centered at the top.

The abstract should be a brief (120 words or fewer) summary of the paper.

Parking Design Recommendations for Publicly Funded
Commercial Redevelopment Projects

Redevelopment of underused commercial space
presents a unique opportunity for communities. As cities
fight to counteract the outward pull of suburban sprawl,
redevelopment offers a counterweight that can draw people
and revenue into city centers. The National Association of
Local Housing Finance Agencies (2005) reports that the United
States Department of Housing and Urban Development spent
$4.7 billion in 2005 just on Community Development Grants.
According to the Web site of the U.S. Department of Housing
and Urban Development (2008), Community Development
Grants are used in part for "provision of assistance to profit-
motivated businesses to carry out economic development and
job creation/retention activities." State, and local governments
spend billions more dollars annually to transform outdated
commercial real estate, through tax breaks, direct investment,
and bond packages.

Often private investors partner with government to
redevelop properties, expecting to profit from their investment.
But the use of taxpayer dollars to fund redevelopment projects
places an extra burden of accountability on project planners.
Publicly funded redevelopment should benefit all members
of the public, not just the investors hoping to profit from it. A
profitable commercial real estate holding should not be the
only goal of redevelopment. Rather, city planners have an
obligation to produce urban spaces that are safe, aesthetically
pleasing, environmentally responsible, and health-promoting.
To accomplish these goals, planners must incorporate design
features that reduce traffic congestion, encourage walking
and biking, protect pedestrians and cyclists, reduce energy
consumption, and minimize impervious ground cover.

Compared with regular commercial development,
redevelopment presents different challenges and possibilities.
Redeveloped commercial properties are already sited;
they cannot be moved to better locations. The streets and
infrastructure supporting them are already in place (though

Give the full title at the
beginning of the body
of the paper.

Specify 1-inch margins
on all sides.

they may be modified). Therefore, parking is often the easiest feature of redeveloped properties to improve in terms of aesthetics, environmental impact, and health promotion. Three basic parking designs—centralized, shared, and rear-of-building—contribute directly to a development's aesthetic, environmental, and public health profile. Responsible city planners should rely heavily on these designs for publicly financed redevelopment projects.

Shared Parking

Many redevelopment projects involve mixed-use space, including offices, retail stores, and residences. In such developments, the total amount of parking capacity for all types of use is normally calculated by simply summing the expected number of users, and providing spaces for a certain percentage of the total. The result is often an excess of space dedicated to parking. When designing the project and choosing tenants, planners should consider when each service will be most in use, and adjust parking capacity to account for overlap. For example, retail space will be most heavily used from 9 a.m. until 5 p.m. Entertainment venues such as bars, restaurants, and theaters, will have their heaviest traffic after 5 p.m. If a mixed-use development contains both kinds of space, customers of the entertainment venues can park in spaces that have been vacated by customers of the retail stores.

Using shared parking to reduce the amount of total parking cuts costs and leaves more space available for other uses. It also lessens the problem of runoff pollution contaminating a community's water supply. Researchers at Purdue University recently estimated that parking lots in a single Midwestern county produced almost 1,000 pounds of heavy metal runoff annually. One of the researchers, professor Bernard Engel, explains that parking lots "accumulate a lot of pollutants—oil, grease, heavy metals and sediment—that cannot be absorbed by the impervious surface. Rain then flushes these contaminants into rivers and lakes" (Main, 2007, para. 5). Reducing parking area by using shared parking,

Center the headings if you use only one level of heads.

then, makes a significant difference in a development's environmental imprint.

Centralized Parking

In the short term, people may prefer the convenience of parking immediately in front of the business they are patronizing. In fact, Americans have grown accustomed to this convenience, and it is supported by the design of many of our retail spaces. Few of us consider what this convenience costs us in terms of health, expense, and environmental impact.

The average American now walks less than a quarter of a mile per day (Miller, 2005), but American drivers drive over 13,000 miles per year—a 40% increase over the last 25 years (Veno, Brady, Burjhard, & Yergin, 2007, para. 5). We are the most well-traveled sedentary society in history. In fact, researchers at the University of Illinois have determined that, with the average American weighing 24 pounds more than he or she did in 1960, we as a nation now burn an extra 938 million gallons of gasoline each year just to drive around the weight we've gained (Kloeppel, 2006, para. 7, 11).

As a result of the "convenience" of curbside parking, we are more overweight and in poorer health, spend more of our household income on gasoline, breathe worse air, and drink dirtier water than ever before. The design of retail space with "as-close-as-you-can-get" parking contributes to these problems. It habituates people to driving as far as necessary in order to walk as little as possible. A redesign of our environment is called for to get us to change our habits.

Centralized parking is the redesign called for. It addresses all of the problems engendered by de-centralized parking. Concentrating parking spaces in a central area of a shopping district encourages people to park once and walk from location to location within the development. This increases their activity level and reduces their total amount of driving—especially the number of very short drives from one parking spot to another. The U.S. Department of Energy (2008) advises that several short driving trips can use up to twice as

Include authors and date in parentheses when you do not mention authors in the text.

Indent each paragraph five to seven spaces (1/2").

much gas as a longer, combined-purpose trip. Knowing that they will be walking to several locations, people are also more likely to combine trips, rather than driving to the shopping center each time they need something. Combined trips thus increase physical activity, save energy and reduce air pollution.

Centralized parking also makes it far easier to control runoff pollution from parked cars. Drainage and filtration for a single parking garage is much simpler to design, easier to monitor, and more cost effective than run-off control for acres of paved parking.

Rear-of-Building Parking

Finally, commercial buildings should be located toward the front of the redeveloped center, near the sidewalk and street, with parking placed behind. This immediately makes a development more aesthetically pleasing. It makes merchandise and services more visible, instead of foregrounding parked cars. It also encourages walking in much the same way that centralized parking does.

Moreover, rear-of-building parking makes streets safer for pedestrians. Advocates of "complete streets" note that with rear-of-building parking, "pedestrians are more likely to walk from one building to the next rather than drive because they do not have to compete with cars to get through the parking lots that normally separate buildings from the street" (County of Ventura, n.d., para. 15).

Use *n.d,* when no date is provided for a source.

Consider the driving and walking patterns encouraged around the intersection by the design in Figure 1.

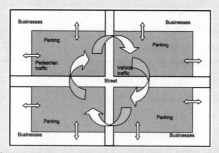

Number figures and tables. Give each figure a descriptive title.

Figure 1. Traffic flow with front-of-building parking design.

Because shops are widely separated by large, busy parking lots, shoppers will use their cars to navigate safely through the lots, across the streets (crowded with more cars also trying to hop from lot to lot), and into another parking spot. This arrangement greatly increases the vehicular traffic pedestrians must confront if they try to walk from place to place within the development. Bicycles must navigate many more cars at the intersection when they enter or leave the center. Overall, this design encourages driving and discourages walking and bicycling.

Compare this to the behavior likely to result from the design in Figure 2.

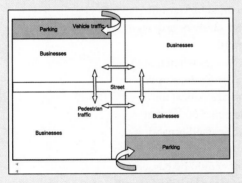

Figure 2. Traffic flow with rear-of-building parking design.

Here, cars are parked in centralized garages located behind two building clusters. Shoppers can walk easily from one area to another. Drivers are encouraged to leave their cars parked and travel from store to store on foot. The distances between destinations are shorter and vehicular traffic is lighter, which encourages walking and bicycling. The parking garages can be placed with an eye toward which building clusters are most likely to involve bulky purchases—for example, a grocery store or office supply store.

Encouraging walking improves health in another important way: by improving pedestrian and cyclist safety.

Research shows that increased pedestrian traffic actually improves pedestrian safety, possibly by heightening driver awareness. Researcher Noah Raford at the University of California-Berkeley's Traffic Safety Center states: "From a public policy standpoint, from a safety standpoint, the message is, if you want safer streets, have more people on them" (Traffic Safety Center, 2004, para. 9).

Conclusion

The design elements described here are not necessarily cheap to implement, which is why private developers might not use them unless they are required. But responsible urban planning, even if it cuts into profit margins, is responsible, and should be mandatory for projects that receive even partial funding from taxpayers. Governments must hold profit-seeking investors accountable for the health and safety of taxpayers who are helping to pay for redevelopment.

Considering proposed parking changes when taking bids for redevelopment projects and favoring developers who propose the most responsible plan are critical for implementing a pedestrian-friendly design. Should that approach prove inadequate, cities might consider passing zoning and development ordinances that encourage the use of these features. Such ordinances and laws could be passed to affect even projects that are entirely financed by private funds, and new commercial construction as well. The end result will be healthier, safer, more sustainable communities for all who use them.

Start a new page for references.

References

Clayton, M. (2007, September 24). He tallies hidden costs of free parking—one space at a time. *Christian Science Monitor*. Retrieved from http://www.csmonitor.com

County of Ventura (California) Planning Department. (n.d.). *Build it smart!* Retrieved from http://www.builditsmartvc.org/how/team.php

Kloeppel, J. E. (2006, October 24). *Weight gain of U.S. drivers has increased nation's fuel consumption.* Retrieved from University of Illinois at Urbana-Champaign News Bureau Web site: http://www.news.uiuc.edu/NEWS/06/1024auto.html

Main, D. (2007, September 11). *Parking spaces outnumber drivers 3-to-1, drive pollution and warming.* Retrieved from Purdue University News Web site: http://www.purdue.edu

Miller, P. (2005, April). *Design for active living theme focuses on recreational resources* [Electronic version]. *Recreation Management*. Retrieved from http://www.recmanagement.com

National Association of Local Housing Finance Agencies. (2005). 2006 *HUD Appropriations*. Retrieved from http:// www.nalhfa.org

Traffic Safety Center, University of California-Berkeley. (2004). Safety in numbers. *SafeTREC Newsletter, 2*(1). Retrieved from http://www.tsc.berkeley.edu

U.S. Department of Energy. (2008). *Tips: Planning and combining trips.* Retrieved from http://www.fueleconomy.gov

U.S. Department of Housing and Urban Development. (2008). *Community development block grants: Entitlement communities grants.* Retrieved from http://www.hud.gov

Veno, W., Brady, A., Burkhard, J., & Yergin, D. (2007) *Gasoline and the American people.* Retrieved from Cambridge Energy Research Associates Web site: http://www2.cera.com/gasoline/summary

Alphabetize entries by last name of the author.

Double-space all entries.

Indent all but the first line of each entry 1/2".

MyWritingLab™ Visit Ch. 25 in MyWritingLab to test your understanding of the chapter objectives.

ETOSHA NATION

60

DEAR GUE

Please adhere to the follow

DO NOT FEED THE ANIMALS

NO MOTORBIKES OR QUADBIKES ALLOWED

NO PETS ALLOWED

STAY IN YOUR VEHICLE EXCEPT AT DESIGNATED AREAS

NO PERSONS ALLOWED ON THE BACK OF OPEN VEHICLE

REPORT TO THE NEAREST OFFICE BEFORE PROCE

PLEASE ENSURE THAT BOTH E

AND ACCOMMODATION FEES HAVE

PLEASE KEEP THE PARK CLEAN - DO NOT LIT

**BEWARE OF
DANGEROUS ANIMALS**

AL PARK

ST

ng regulations

NOT SIT
EN WINDOW
RAVE YOUR
OR OPEN

NO DRIVING
AFTER SUNSET
OR BEFORE
SUNRISE

DO NOT DRIVE
OFF THE ROADS

ING THROUGH THE PARK

TRANCE FEES

BEEN FULLY PAID

Part 5

The Writer as Editor

26 Writing Effective Sentences

Effective sentences bring energy, clarity, and shape to a writer's ideas.

In this chapter, you will learn to

Pay Attention to Verbs

The importance of verbs

A teacher may have once told you that verbs are "action words." Where are the action words in the following paragraph?

Reading much prose like this would put you to sleep quickly. →

LeBron James was the leader in the Miami Heat's win over the San Antonio Spurs in Game 6. James was the star in the victory with 16 points in the fourth quarter even without his trademark headband. His totals were 32 points, 10 rebounds, and 11 assists for a triple-double.

James played a dynamic game, but the above description deflates his achievement. Changing *was* and *were* to verbs that express action brings to life his outstanding performance.

LeBron James **denied** the San Antonio Spurs a win in Game 6 that would have **clinched** the 2013 NBA championship. He **powered** the Miami Heat to victory, **exploding** for 16 points in the fourth quarter, even though he **lost** his trademark headband. James **scored** 32 points, **grabbed** 10 rebounds, and **dished out** 11 assists for a triple-double.

Strengthen your verbs when you revise

Circle every *is*, *are*, *was*, and *were*. Think about the action. Does the verb express the action? Can you think of a better verb?

WEAK VERBS

Jack Black **is** considerably skilled in physical comedy, and his overblown mannerisms **are** wisely downplayed.

STRONG VERBS

Jack Black **excels** in physical comedy, and he wisely **downplays** his overblown mannerisms.

627

Stay Active

Active versus passive

The passive voice reverses the order of a sentence, allowing whoever or whatever did the action expressed in the verb to be deleted.

Who misplaced the laptop? It's a mystery.	The laptop containing personal data on 38,000 employees was misplaced. [passive]

Revise passive sentences

Most of the time your goal is not to conceal but to communicate.

Watch for passive sentences and convert them to active voice whenever possible. Listen to the difference:	The pear tree in the front yard **was demolished** by the storm. [passive]
	The storm **demolished** the pear tree in the front yard. [active]
Ask who or what is doing the action. If the doer is not the subject, consider rewriting so the doer is the subject.	A request on your part **will be reviewed** by the admissions committee. [passive]
	The graduate admissions committee **will review** your request. [active]

Uses of the passive

In some situations, passive voice can be used in academic and workplace writing. Passive sentences are useful when you want to keep the focus on the person or thing being acted on.

The focus is on *increased January sales*, not *deep discounts*.	Our January sales **were increased** substantially by our deep discounts.
The process of simulation is the focus, not the unknown people who perform the simulations.	Analog and digital data **are simulated** together before the company commits to the expense of manufacturing.

Focus on People and Actors
Ask "What is going on?"

Reading much of what's written today is like digging for clams in a mud flat. Read this sentence adapted from a university admissions Web site. You can figure out what it says if you read it two or three times. But it doesn't have to be this bad.

The secret to writing clearly is to begin by asking "What is going on?" Make the doer the subject and what is being done the verb. In this case—an admissions Web site—the doer is you, the visitor to the site who wants to apply.

ORIGINAL

Eligibility for transfer admission as defined by Big State U is restricted to persons who have begun coursework at another college or university and now wish to study at Big State U, which includes persons who have obtained an undergraduate degree at another institution and now wish to pursue a different degree plan at Big State U.

REVISED

If you want to attend Big State U but you've already started your studies at another college or university, you should apply as a transfer student. Even if you earned an undergraduate degree at another college or university and want to work toward a different degree, you should apply for transfer admission.

Focus on people

If people are involved, make them the grammatical subjects. Keeping the focus on people makes your writing more emphatic because people do things that you can express in active verbs.

ORIGINAL

When the process of freeing a vehicle that has been stuck results in ruts or holes, the operator is required to fill the rut or hole created by such activity before removing the vehicle from the immediate area.

REVISED

If you make a hole while freeing a stuck vehicle, you must fill the hole before you drive away.

Find actors

When people are not present, identify the institutions and concepts involved and make them the subjects.

ORIGINAL

The celebration of Martin Luther King Day had to be postponed because of inclement weather.

REVISED

The severe ice storm forced the city to postpone the Martin Luther King Day celebration.

Write Concise Sentences

Revise wordy sentences

Unnecessary words creep into writing in the form of clutter and wordy phrases. Writers who are unsure of themselves overuse phrases like "in my opinion" or "I think" to qualify their points. Stock phrases plague writing in the media and workplace, where some writers may think that "at this point in time" sounds more impressive than "now." If you find wordy phrases in your own prose, cut them.

The words in **bold** are unnecessary. You can say the same thing with half the words and gain more impact as a result.

In regards to the Web site, the content is **pretty** successful **in consideration of** the topic. The site is **fairly** good **writing-wise** and is **very** unique in telling you how to adjust the rear derailleur one step at a time.

Writers who impress us most are those who use words efficiently.

The well-written Web site on bicycle repair provides step-by-step instructions on adjusting your rear derailleur.

Eliminate redundancy

Some words act as modifiers, but when you look closely at them, they repeat the meaning of the word they pretend to modify. Have you heard expressions such as *red in color*, *small in size*, *round in shape*, or *honest truth*? Imagine *red* not referring to color or *round* not referring to shape.

Intensifiers modify verbs, adjectives, and other adverbs, and they often are overused. *Very* and *totally* are but two of a list of empty intensifiers that usually can be eliminated with no loss of meaning. Other empty intensifiers include *absolutely, awfully, definitely, incredibly, particularly,* and *really*.

Replace wordy phrases

Wordy	Concise
at this point in time	now
due to the fact that	because
have the ability to	can
in the modern world of today	today
in spite of the fact that	although
the great writer by the name of William Shakespeare	William Shakespeare

Write Ethical Sentences

Avoid stereotypes

A stereotype makes an assumption about a group of people by applying a characteristic to all of them based on knowledge of only a few of them. Of course you want to avoid harmful and inaccurate stereotypes, such as *People on welfare are lazy*, or *NASCAR fans are rednecks*.

More subtle stereotypes, however, may be harder to identify and eliminate. If you want to offer an engineer as an example, will you make theengineer a man? Try to choose examples that go against stereotypes.

Avoid bias

Pay attention to the way your language characterizes individuals and groups of people on the basis of their gender, race, ethnicity, sexual orientation, or age. While the conventions of language change continually, three guidelines for inclusive language toward all groups remain constant:

- Do not point out people's differences unless those differences are relevant to your argument.
- Call people whatever they prefer to be called.
- When given a choice of terms, choose the more precise one. (*Vietnamese*, for example, is preferable to *Asian*.)

Eliminate gender bias by using the following tips.

- Use *men and women* or *people* instead of *man*.
- Use *humanity* or *humankind* in place of *mankind*.

Make your writing user friendly

Too much writing is excessively complicated and wordy. Think about what your readers need to know. Medicare Beneficiary Services receives thousands of fraud complaints each year. The agency revised its reply letter to get to the point.

ORIGINAL

Investigators at the contractor will review the facts in your case and decide the most appropriate course of action. The first step taken with most Medicare health care providers is to reeducate them about Medicare regulations and policies. If the practice continues, the contractor may conduct special audits of the providers' medical records. Often, the contractor recovers overpayments to health care providers this way. If there is sufficient evidence to show that the provider is consistently violating Medicare policies, the contractor will document the violations and ask the Office of the Inspector General to prosecute the case. This can lead to expulsion from the Medicare program, civil monetary penalties, and imprisonment.

REVISED

We will look into this matter: We will find out if it was an error or fraud.
We will let you know the result.

Match Structure with Ideas

Use parallel structure with parallel ideas

When writers neglect to use parallel structure, the result can be jarring. Reading your writing aloud will help you catch problems in parallelism. Read this sentence aloud.

> At our club meeting we identified problems in **finding** new members, **publicizing** our activities, and **maintenance** of our Web site.

The end of the sentence does not sound right because the parallel structure is broken. We expect to find another verb + *ing* following *finding* and *publicizing*. Instead, we run into *maintenance*, a noun. The problem is easy to fix: Change the noun to the *-ing* verb form.

> At our club meeting we identified problems in finding new members, publicizing our activities, and **maintaining** our Web site.

Use parallel structure with lists

Lists are an effective way of presenting a series of items at the same level of importance. The effectiveness of a list is lost, however, if the items are not in parallel form. For example, in a bulleted list of action items, such as a list of goals, beginning each item with a verb emphasizes the action.

> **Sailing Club goals**
> - **Increase** membership by 50% this year
> - **Offer** beginning and advanced classes
> - **Organize** spring banquet
> - **Publicize** all major events

Pair grammatical elements

Match grammatical elements to provide strong parallelism in sentences with parallel ideas or lists.

> Purchasing the undeveloped land **not only gives us a new park but also is something that our children will benefit from in the future**. [awkward]

> Purchasing the undeveloped land **not only will give our city a new park but also will leave our children a lasting inheritance**. [parallel]

Summary for Editing Sentences

Pay attention to verbs
Circle every *is*, *are*, *was*, and *were*. Think about the action. Does the verb express the action? Can you think of a better verb?

Amanda **was** a teacher of new skills to our unit.
BETTER
Amanda **taught** new skills to our unit.

Stay active
Ask who or what is doing the action. If the doer is not the subject, consider rewriting so the doer is the subject.

Making a video rather than writing a paper **was chosen** by one-third of our class.
BETTER
One-third of our class **chose** to make a video rather than write a paper.

Find characters
Use characters as the subjects of sentences.

Strong disagreements arose over the decision to close Hill Elementary School.
BETTER
Neighborhood residents expressed their outrage when the **school board** voted to close Hill Elementary School.

Write concise sentences
Eliminate wordy phrases, redundant modifiers, and empty intensifiers from your sentences.

In ~~one of his more famous nature writings entitled~~ *Walden*, ~~the great American writer~~ Henry David Thoreau writes of one of nature's smaller entities: ants.

Write ethical sentences
Avoid stereotypes and biased language by using inclusive and accurate language instead. Be specific rather than using broad labels.

The **very old seniors** living in nursing homes are often **senile**.
BETTER
Many nursing home **residents over ninety** suffer from **symptoms of Alzheimer's disease**.

Match structure with ideas
Match grammatical elements to provide strong parallelism in sentences with parallel ideas or lists.

If you run on hot, sunny days, **drink** water before you run, **drink** water while you run, **avoiding** coffee and alcohol, **wearing** sunscreen while **looking** for some shade.
BETTER
If you run on hot, sunny days, **drink** water before you run, **drink** water while you run, **avoid** coffee and alcohol, **wear** sunscreen, and **choose** routes with some shade.

MyWritingLab™ Visit Ch. 26 in MyWritingLab to test your understanding of the chapter objectives.

27 Avoiding Errors

Most common errors can easily be corrected once they are spotted.

In this chapter, you will learn to

1 Fix sentence fragments *(see p. 635)*

2 Fix run-on sentences *(see p. 636)*

3 Fix comma splices *(see p. 637)*

4 Make verbs and pronouns agree with subjects *(see pp. 638–639)*

5 Fix shifts *(see p. 640)*

6 Use modifiers correctly *(see p. 641)*

7 Place modifiers carefully *(see p. 642)*

Department of Conservation
Te Papa Atawbai

Fix Fragments

Fragments are incomplete sentences. They are punctuated to look like sentences, but they lack a key element—often a subject or a verb—or else are a subordinate clause or phrase. Remember that every sentence must have a subject and a complete verb, and that a subordinate clause cannot stand alone as a sentence. Ask these questions when you are checking for sentence fragments.

Does the sentence have a subject? Except for commands, sentences need subjects.

Jane spent every cent of credit she had available. **And then applied for more cards.**

Does the sentence have a complete verb? Sentences require complete verbs. Verbs that end in *-ing* must have an auxiliary verb to be complete.

Ralph keeps changing majors. **He trying to figure out what he really wants to do after college.**

If the sentence begins with a subordinate clause, is there a main clause in the same sentence?

Even though Seattle is cloudy much of the year, no American city is more beautiful when the sun shines. **Which is one reason people continue to move there.**

Use these strategies for turning fragments into sentences

Incorporate the fragment into an adjoining sentence.

INCORRECT

I was hooked on the game. Playing it constantly day and night.

CORRECT

I was hooked on the **game, playing** it constantly day and night.

Add the missing element. If you cannot incorporate a fragment into another sentence, add the missing element.

INCORRECT

When aiming for the highest returns, and also thinking about the possible losses.

CORRECT

When aiming for the highest returns, **investors** also **should think** about possible losses.

Fix Run-on Sentences

Run-ons jam together two or more sentences, failing to separate them with appropriate punctuation.

The problem is that the two main clauses are not separated by punctuation.

A period should be placed after *was*, and the next sentence should begin with a capital letter.

I do not recall what kind of printer it was all I remember is that it could sort, staple, and print a packet at the same time.

I do not recall what kind of printer it was **|** all I remember is that it could sort, staple, and print a packet at the same time.

I do not recall what kind of printer it was. All I remember is that it could sort, staple, and print a packet at the same time.

Use a three-step strategy to correct run-on sentences

1. Identify the problem. If you find two main clauses with no punctuation separating them, you have a run-on sentence.

(**bold black** = subject green type = verb)
Internet businesses are not bound to specific locations or old ways of running a business **they are** more flexible in allowing employees to telecommute and to determine their working hours.

2. Determine where the run-on sentence needs to be divided.

Internet businesses are not bound to specific locations or old ways of running a business **|** they are more flexible in allowing employees to telecommute and to determine their working hours.

3. Choose the punctuation that indicates the relationship between the main clauses.

Insert a period.
Internet businesses are not bound to specific locations or old ways of running a business. They are more flexible in allowing employees to telecommute and to determine their working hours.

Insert a semicolon (and possibly a transitional word).
Internet businesses are not bound to specific locations or old ways of running a business; therefore, they are more flexible in allowing employees to telecommute and to determine their working hours.

Insert a comma and a coordinating conjunction (*and, but, or, nor, for, so, yet*).
Internet businesses are not bound to specific locations or old ways of running a business, so they are more flexible in allowing employees to telecommute and to determine their working hours.

Fix Comma Splices

Comma splices occur when two or more sentences are incorrectly joined by a comma; a comma should not link two clauses that could stand on their own.

Most of us were taking the same classes, if someone had a question, we would all help out.

Use one of these strategies to fix a comma splice

- **Change the comma to a period.**

  It didn't matter that I worked in a windowless room for 40 hours a ~~week, on~~ the Web I was exploring and learning more about distant people and places than I ever had before.
  [CORRECTION: **week. On**]

- **Change the comma to a semicolon.**
  A semicolon indicates the close connection between the two main clauses.

  It didn't matter that I worked in a windowless room for 40 hours a ~~week,~~ on the Web I was exploring and learning more about distant people and places than I ever had before.
  [CORRECTION: **week;**]

- **Insert a coordinating conjunction.**
  Some comma splices can be repaired by inserting a coordinating conjunction (*and, but, or, nor, so, yet, for*) to indicate the relationship of the two main clauses.

  Digital technologies have intensified a global culture that affects us daily in large and small ways**, yet** their impact remains poorly understood.

- **Make one of the main clauses a subordinate clause.**

  ~~Community~~ is the vision of a great society trimmed down to the size of a small town, it is a powerful metaphor for real estate developers who sell a mini-utopia along with a house or condo.
  [CORRECTION: **Because community**]

- **Make one of the main clauses a phrase.**

  Community—**the vision of a great society trimmed down to the size of a small town**—is a powerful metaphor for real estate developers who sell a mini-utopia along with a house or condo.

637

Make Verbs Agree with Subjects

A verb must match its subject. If the subject is singular (*I, you, he, she,* or *it*), the verb must take a singular form. If the subject is plural (*we, you, they*), the verb must take a plural form. Therefore, verbs are said to *agree in number* with their subjects. This single rule determines subject-verb agreement.

When two subjects are joined by *and*, treat them as a compound (plural) subject.

The teacher and the lawyer are headed west to start a commune.

When two nouns linked by *and* are modified by *every* or *each*, these two nouns are likewise treated as one singular subject.

Each night and day brings no new news of you.

If a subject is joined by *or*, *either . . . or*, or *neither . . . nor*, make sure the verb agrees with the subject closest to the verb.

Is it **the sky or the mountains** that **are** blue?

Is it **the mountains or the sky** that **surrounds** us?

Check for agreement when words come between the subject and verb

When you check for subject-verb agreement, identify the subject and the verb. Ignore any words that come between them.

Students is plural and *read* is plural; subject and verb agree.

INCORRECT   Ignore this phrase

Students at inner-city Washington High **reads** more than suburban students.

CORRECT

Students at inner-city Washington High **read** more than suburban students.

The plural noun *sharks* that appears between the subject *the whale shark* and the verb *feeds* does not change the number of the subject. The subject is singular and the verb is singular. Subject and verb agree.

INCORRECT   Ignore this phrase

The whale shark, the largest of all sharks, **feed** on plankton.

CORRECT

The whale shark, the largest of all sharks, **feeds** on plankton.

Make Pronouns Agree

Because pronouns usually replace or refer to other nouns, they must match those nouns in number and gender. The noun that the pronoun replaces is called its **antecedent**. If pronoun and antecedent match, they are in **agreement**. When a pronoun is close to the antecedent, usually there is no problem.

> **Maria** forgot **her** coat.
>
> The band **members** collected **their** uniforms.

Pronoun agreement errors often happen when pronouns and the nouns they replace are separated by several words.

INCORRECT

> **The players**, exhausted from the double-overtime game, picked up **his** sweats and walked toward the locker rooms.

Careful writers make sure that pronouns match their antecedents.

CORRECT

> The **players,** exhausted from the double-overtime game, picked up **their** sweats and walked toward the locker rooms.

Agreement with *every, each, or,* and *nor*

Words that begin with *any, some,* and *every* are usually singular.

INCORRECT

> **Everybody** can choose **their** roommates.

CORRECT

> **Everybody** can choose **his or her** roommate.

Use singular pronouns for antecedents preceded by *each* or *every*.

CORRECT

> **Every male cardinal and warbler** arrives before the female to define **its** territory.

Use a pronoun that agrees with the nearest antecedent when compound antecedents are joined by *or* or *nor*.

INCORRECT

> **Either the Ross twins or Sue** should bring **their** iPods.

When you put the plural *twins* last, the correct choice becomes the plural pronoun *their*.

CORRECT

> **Either Sue or the Ross twins** should bring **their** iPods.

639

Fix Shifts

Unintentional shifts in tense, voice, person, or number often distract readers.

Shifts in tense

The shift from present tense (*looks*) to past tense (*relied*) is confusing. Correct the mistake by putting both verbs in the present tense.

INCORRECT

While Brazil **looks** to ecotourism to fund rain forest preservation, other South American nations relied on foreign aid.

CORRECT

While Brazil **looks** to ecotourism to fund rain forest preservation, other South American nations **rely** on foreign aid.

Shifts in voice

Watch for unintended shifts from active (*I ate the cookies*) to passive voice (*the cookies were eaten*).

The unexpected shift from active voice (*toppled*) to passive (*were broken*) forces readers to wonder whether it was the sudden storm, or something else, that broke the windows.

AWKWARD

The sudden storm **toppled** several trees and numerous windows were shattered.

CORRECT

The sudden storm **toppled** several trees and **shattered** numerous windows.

Shifts in person and number

Sudden shifts from third person (*he, she, it, one*) to first (*I, we*) or second (*you*) are confusing to readers and often indicate a writer's uncertainty about how to address a reader.

INCORRECT

When one is reading a magazine, you often see several different type fonts used on a single page.

CORRECT

When reading a magazine, **you** often see several different type fonts used on a single page.

Use Modifiers Correctly

Modifiers come in two varieties: adjectives and adverbs. Adjectives answer the questions *Which one? How many?* and *What kind?* Adverbs answer the questions *How often? To what extent? When? Where? How?* and *Why?*

Comparative modifiers weigh one thing against another. They either end in *-er* or are preceded by *more*.	Road bikes are **faster** on pavement than mountain bikes. The **more courageous** juggler tossed flaming torches.
Superlative modifiers compare three or more items. They either end in *-est* or are preceded by *most*.	April is the **hottest** month in New Delhi. Wounded animals are the **most ferocious**.

Absolute modifiers are words that represent an unvarying condition and thus aren't subject to the degrees that comparative and superlative constructions convey. Common absolute modifiers include *complete, ultimate*, and *unique*. Absolute modifiers should not be modified by comparatives (*more* + modifier or modifier + *-er*) or superlatives (*most* + modifier or modifier + *-est*).

Avoid errors in comparisons

Do not use both a suffix (*-er* or *-est*) and *more* or *most*.	*INCORRECT* The service at Jane's Restaurant is more slower than the service at Alphonso's. *CORRECT* The service at Jane's Restaurant is **slower** than the service at Alphonso's.
Be sure to name the elements being compared if they are not clear from the context.	*UNCLEAR COMPARATIVE* Mice are cuter. *CLEAR* Mice are **cuter than rats**. *UNCLEAR COMPARATIVE* Nutria are the creepiest. *CLEAR* Nutria are the **creepiest rodents**.

641

Place Modifiers Carefully

Words such as *almost, even, hardly, just, merely, nearly, not, only,* and *simply* are called **limiting modifiers**. Although people often play fast and loose with their placement in everyday speech, limiting modifiers should always go immediately before the word or words they modify in your writing.

Place limiting modifiers immediately before the words they modify

Many writers have difficulty with the placement of *only*. Like other limiting modifiers, *only* should be placed immediately before the word it modifies.

The word *only* modifies one in this sentence, not *Gross Domestic Product*.

INCORRECT

The Gross Domestic Product **only** gives one indicator of economic growth.

CORRECT

The Gross Domestic Product gives **only** one indicator of economic growth.

Connect modifiers clearly to the words they modify

A **dangling modifier** does not seem to modify anything in a sentence; it dangles, unconnected to the word or words it presumably is intended to modify.

When still a girl, my father joined the army.

It sounds like *father* was once a girl. The problem is that the subject, *I*, is missing.

When I was still a girl, my father joined the army.

Dangling modifiers usually occur at the head of a sentence when a subject is implied but never stated.

INCORRECT

After lifting the heavy piano up the stairs, the apartment door was too small to get it through.

CORRECT

After lifting the heavy piano up the stairs, **we discovered** the apartment door was too small to get it through.

Summary for Editing for Errors

Fix fragments	• Incorporate the fragment into an adjoining sentence. • Add the missing element.
Fix run-on sentences	1. Identify the problem. If you find two main clauses with no punctuation separating them, you have a run-on sentence. 2. Determine where the run-on sentence needs to be divided. 3. Choose the punctuation that indicates the relationship between the main clauses.
Fix comma splices	• Change the comma to a period. • Change the comma to a semicolon. • Insert a coordinating conjunction. • Make one of the main clauses a subordinate clause. • Make one of the main clauses a phrase.
Make verbs agree with subjects	When you check for subject-verb agreement, identify the subject and the verb. Ignore any words that come between them.
Make pronouns agree	• Words that begin with *any*, *some*, and *every* are usually singular. • Use plural pronouns for antecedents joined by *and*. • Use singular pronouns for antecedents preceded by *each* or *every*. • Use a pronoun that agrees with the nearest antecedent when compound antecedents are joined by *or* or *nor*.
Fix shifts	Watch for sudden shifts in tense, voice, person, or number and edit them out of your writing unless you are certain that their purpose is clear and evident to your readers.
Use modifiers correctly	• Do not use both a suffix (*-er* or *-est*) and *more* or *most*. • Be sure to name the elements being compared if they are not clear from the context.
Place modifiers carefully	• Place limiting modifiers immediately before the word(s) they modify. • Modifiers should be clearly connected to the words they modify, especially at the beginning of sentences.

MyWritingLab™ Visit Ch. 27 in MyWritingLab to test your understanding of the chapter objectives.

28 Understanding Punctuation and Conventions

Punctuation and other conventions give readers vital clues about how to read.

In this chapter, you will learn to

1. Identify where commas are needed *(see p. 645)*
2. Place commas correctly with modifiers *(see p. 646)*
3. Place commas correctly with clauses and phrases *(see p. 647)*
4. Use colons and semicolons correctly *(see p. 648)*
5. Use hyphens, dashes, and parentheses correctly *(see p. 649)*
6. Use quotation marks correctly *(see p. 650)*
7. Understand print conventions *(see p. 652)*

Identify Where Commas Are Needed

Use commas with introductory words and phrases

Introductory words like *also*, *however*, *instead*, *likewise*, *therefore*, and *thus* are conjunctive adverbs. Conjunctive adverbs and introductory phrases that signal a shift in ideas usually need to be set off by commas.

Commas allow the reader to pause and take notice of these pivotal elements.	Therefore, Graceland will remain open despite rumors of Lisa putting it up for sale. Above all, remember to order your Pearl Jam tickets as soon as they go on sale.
When a conjunctive adverb comes in the middle of a sentence, set it off with commas before and after. Occasionally fthe conjunctive adverb or phrase blends into a sentence so smoothly that a pause would sound awkward.	If you really want great seats, however, plan to get in line with your sleeping bag a day early. *AWKWARD* Even though Pearl Jam began a grueling concert tour of twenty-three cities in ten countries in June 2014, they play each show as if it were their last, nevertheless. *BETTER* Even though Pearl Jam began a grueling concert tour of twenty-three cities in ten countries in June 2014, they play each show as if it were their last nevertheless.

Use commas with compound sentences

Compound sentences have two or more main clauses. Each main clause can stand by itself as a sentence.

Punctuate compound sentences by putting a comma after the first main clause.	Sandy borrowed my iPod on Tuesday, and she returned it on Friday.
Do not use a comma to separate two verbs with the same subject. This sentence has only one main clause. *Sandy* is the subject of *borrowed* and *returned*.	Sandy borrowed my iPod on Tuesday and returned it on Friday.

Place Commas Correctly with Modifiers

Use commas with free modifiers

Free or nonrestrictive modifiers add information without changing the meaning of the base sentence. You can identify free modifiers by deleting the modifier and then deciding if the essential meaning of the sentence has changed.

For example, delete *which host Jon Stewart claims is nothing other than satire and comedy* in this sentence.

The Daily Show, which host Jon Stewart claims is nothing other than satire and comedy, has won major awards for news and journalism.

The result leaves the meaning of the base sentence unchanged. Thus, the modifier should be set off with commas.

The Daily Show has won major awards for news and journalism.

Use commas with coordinate adjectives

Coordinate adjectives modify the same noun independently and require a comma.

Coldplay is an introspective, alternative band from London.

Use commas with items in a series

In a series of three or more items, place a comma after each item except the last one.

Ellen DeGeneres has succeeded as a stand-up comedian, a television and film actor, a producer, a television host, and an author.

Use commas to introduce quotations

Commas set off phrases that attribute quotations such as *he argues*, *they said*, and *she writes*.

Liz Winstead wrote, "I think, therefore I'm single."

Place Commas Correctly with Clauses and Phrases

Use commas after introductory clauses and long introductory phrases

Introductory clauses and long introductory modifiers should be followed by a comma.

Because Ang Lee's first Hollywood films were not as successful at the box office as his earlier Chinese-language films, he went to China to direct *Crouching Tiger, Hidden Dragon*.

After directing the award-winning and commercially successful *Crouching Tiger, Hidden Dragon*, Ang Lee won the Academy Award for Best Director for *Brokeback Mountain*.

Avoid unnecessary commas

Do not use a comma to separate two verbs with the same subject.

Ang Lee completed his mandatory military service in Taiwan and came to the United States to study theater at the University of Illinois at Urbana-Champaign.

Do not use a comma before a list.

Ang Lee's films have some common themes such as the interaction of tradition and modernity, deep secrets that come to the surface, and internal torment.

Do not use a comma before *because* and similar subordinate conjunctions (*although, if, since, unless, until, when, where, while*) that follow the main clause.

Many viewers in China objected to *Crouching Tiger, Hidden Dragon* because some actors spoke Mandarin with unfamiliar accents.

Do not use a comma before *than*.

Ang Lee's 2012 film *Life of Pi* received more Academy Award nominations than all other films but Steven Spielberg's *Lincoln*.

Use Semicolons and Colons Correctly

Use semicolons with closely related ideas

Director Spike Lee has never shied away from controversy; he has criticized the African American community for wrongfully associating "intelligence with acting white and ignorance with acting black."

Use semicolons with conjunctive adverbs that join main clauses

This sentence pattern is frequently used; therefore, it pays to learn how to punctuate it correctly.

Spike Lee's films are perceptive in depicting race relations in the United States; however, he rejects Martin Luther King Jr. as a role model for African Americans.

Use colons to link a main clause that expands another main clause

Colons, like semicolons, join closely related ideas. A colon signals that the second idea expands the first one.

Spike Lee let everyone know who made the Nike commercials featuring Michael Jordan: Lee appears in several of the ads.

Use colons correctly with lists

Colons are used correctly to introduce lists only when a complete sentence is before the colon.

INCORRECT

The actors that Spike Lee helped launch include: Wesley Snipes, Laurence Fishburne, Samuel L. Jackson, Halle Berry, and Denzel Washington.

CORRECT

Spike Lee helped launch the careers of some of today's best actors: Wesley Snipes, Laurence Fishburne, Samuel L. Jackson, Halle Berry, and Denzel Washington.

Use colons correctly with quotations

Colons are used correctly to introduce quotations only when a complete sentence is before the colon.

Spike Lee directly blamed the US government for the Hurricane Katrina disaster: "I don't find it too far-fetched that they tried to displace all the black people out of New Orleans."

Use Hyphens, Dashes, and Parentheses Correctly
When to hyphenate

Hyphenate a compound modifier that precedes a noun.	middle-class values	self-fulfilling prophecy
Hyphenate a phrase when it is used as a modifier that precedes a noun.	out-of-body experience	step-by-step instructions
Hyphenate the prefixes *pro-*, *anti-*, *post-*, *pre-*, *neo-*, and *mid-* before capitalized nouns.	mid-Atlantic states	pre-Columbian art
Hyphenate a compound modifier with a number when it precedes a noun.	eighteenth-century drama	tenth-grade class

Use dashes and parentheses to set off additional information

Stephen Colbert left *The Daily Show* in 2005 to host a spin-off series, *The Colbert Report*—a parody of *The O'Reilly Factor* and other personality-driven political opinion shows.

Don't use dashes as periods

INCORRECT

Unlike Jon Stewart, Stephen Colbert played the role of a political pundit on *The Colbert Report*—he made frequent use of humorous fallacies in logic to argue his points.

CORRECT

Unlike Jon Stewart, Stephen Colbert on *The Colbert Report* played the role of a political pundit—a character that allowed him to make frequent use of humorous fallacies in logic to argue his points.

Use Quotation Marks Correctly

Use quotation marks with direct quotations

Put other people's verbatim words inside quotation marks and cite the source.

Julius Henry Marx, known to the world as Groucho, never used profanity in a performance but got his laughs instead from one-liners like "I was married by a judge; I should have asked for a jury" (Kanfer 45).

Use single quotation marks for quotations within quotations

Groucho recalled his early years in comedy: "Because we were a kid act, we traveled at half-fare, despite the fact that we were all around twenty. Minnie insisted we were thirteen. 'That kid of yours is in the dining car smoking a cigar,' the conductor told her. 'And another one is in the washroom shaving.'"

"Minnie shook her head sadly. 'They grow so fast.'"

Use quotation marks with periods, commas, and question marks inside them

Place periods and commas inside closing quotation marks. Place question marks inside unless the entire sentence is a question.

"Those are my principles," Groucho announced. "If you don't like them, I have others."

"Why should I care about posterity? What's posterity ever done for me?" is a typical Groucho quip.

Place the titles of essays, short stories, short poems, articles, and other short works inside quotation marks

"Self-Reliance," by Ralph Waldo Emerson (essay)
"Light Is Like Water," by Gabriel García Márquez (short story)
"We Real Cool," by Gwendolyn Brooks (poem)
"Sudan Leader Is Accused of Genocide," by Marlise Simons and Jeffrey Gettleman (newspaper article)
"Purple Haze," by Jimi Hendrix (song)

Use Other Punctuation Correctly

Use periods with abbreviations

Many abbreviations require periods; however, there are few set rules. Use the dictionary to check how to punctuate abbreviations on a case-by-case basis. The rules for punctuating two types of abbreviations do remain consistent: postal abbreviations for states and most abbreviations for organizations do not require periods. When an abbreviation with a period falls at the end of a sentence, do not add a second period to conclude the sentence.

Use question marks with direct questions

A direct question is one that the questioner puts to someone outright. In contrast, an indirect question merely reports the asking of a question.

INDIRECT QUESTION

Desirée asked whether Dan rides his motorcycle without a helmet.

DIRECT QUESTION

Desirée asked, "Does Dan ride his motorcycle without a helmet?"

Use exclamation points to convey strong emotion

Exclamation points conclude sentences and, like question marks, tell the reader how a sentence should sound.

When asked in 1975 if he had seen any recent movies, Groucho replied, "*Jaws* . . . would have been funnier if a guppy had swallowed the boat instead of the shark!"

Use exclamation points correctly with quotation marks

In quotations, exclamation points follow the same rules as question marks. If a quotation falls at the end of an exclamatory statement, place the exclamation point outside the closing quotation mark.

The singer forgot the words to "America the Beautiful"!

Use ellipses to indicate an omission from a quotation

When you quote only a phrase or short clause from a sentence, you usually do not need to use ellipses. When you omit words from the middle of a passage from a source, use ellipses.

"The female praying mantis . . . tears off her male partner's head during mating."

651

Understand Print Conventions

Capitalize the initial letters of proper nouns (nouns that name particular people, places, and things)

Do not capitalize the names of seasons, academic disciplines (unless they are languages), or job titles used without a proper noun.

African **A**merican bookstore

Avogadro's number

Irish music

Italicize the titles of entire works (books, magazines, newspapers, films)

Also italicize the names of ships and aircraft.

I am fond of reading ***USA Today*** in the morning.

Italicize unfamiliar foreign words

Italicize foreign words that are not part of common English usage. How do you decide which words are common? If a word appears in a standard English dictionary, it can be considered as adopted into English.

Use conventions for using abbreviations with years and times

BCE (before the common era) and CE (common era) are now preferred for indicating years, replacing BC (before Christ) and AD (*anno Domini* ["the year of our Lord"]). Note that all are now used without periods.

The preferred written conventions for times are a.m. (*ante meridiem*) and p.m. (*post meridiem*).

479 **BCE** (or **BC**)

9:03 **a.m.**   3:30 **p.m.**

Use conventions for using abbreviations in college writing

Most abbreviations are inappropriate in formal writing except when the reader would be more familiar with the abbreviation than with the words it represents. When your reader is unlikely to be familiar with an abbreviation, spell out the term the first time you use it in a paper, followed by the abbreviation in parentheses.

The Office of Civil Rights (OCR) is the agency that enforces Title IX regulations.

Spell out any number that can be expressed in one or two words

Hyphenate two-word numbers from twenty-one to ninety-nine. In scientific reports and some business writing that requires the frequent use of numbers, using numerals more often is appropriate. Most styles do not write out in words a year, a date, an address, a page number, the time of day, decimals, sums of money, a percentage, phone numbers, rates of speed, or the scene and act of a play. Use numerals instead.

> In 2014 only 33% of respondents said they were satisfied with the City Council's proposals to help the homeless.

Summary for Punctuation and Conventions

Commas	• Place commas after introductory elements and between main clauses joined by *and*, *but*, *or*, *nor*, *yet*, and *so*. • Use commas with nonrestrictive modifiers, coordinate adjectives, and items in a series. • Use a comma after an introductory clause or a long introductory phrase but not to set off a because clause at the end.
Semicolons and colons	• Pay close attention to semicolons and colons that join main clauses.
Hyphens, dashes, and parentheses	• Know the difference in how hyphens and dashes are used, and don't use dashes as periods.
Quotation marks	• Check that all direct quotations are within quotation marks and that periods and commas are inside the closing quotation mark.
Other punctuation	• Check all periods, question marks, exclamation points, and ellipses.
Print conventions	• Check all capitalization, italics, abbreviations, and numbers.

29 Writing in a Second Language

You can overcome the challenges of writing in a second language.

In this chapter, you will learn to

1. Understand the demands of writing in a second language *(see p. 655)*

2. Understand nouns in English *(see p. 656)*

3. Understand articles in English *(see p. 657)*

4. Understand verbs and modifiers in English *(see pp. 658–659)*

5. Understand English sentence structure *(see p. 660)*

Understand the Demands of Writing in a Second Language

Talk with other writers

When you write in an unfamiliar situation, you might find it helpful to locate a few examples of the type of writing you are trying to produce. If you are writing a letter of application to accompany a résumé, for example, ask your friends to share similar letters of application with you and look for the various ways they present themselves in writing in that situation. Ask them to read their letters and to explain the decisions they made as they wrote and revised their letters.

Use your native language as a resource

You can also use your native language to develop your texts. Many people, when they cannot find an appropriate word in English, write down a word, a phrase, or even a sentence in their native language and consult a dictionary later. Incorporating key terms from your native language is also a possible strategy.

A Japanese term adds perspective to this sentence.

> "Some political leaders need to have *wakimae*—a realistic idea of one's own place in the world."

Use dictionaries

Bilingual dictionaries are especially useful when you want to check your understanding of an English word or when you want to find equivalent words for culture-specific concepts and technical terms. Some bilingual dictionaries also provide sample sentences.

Learner's dictionaries, such as the *Longman Dictionary of American English*, include information about count/noncount nouns and transitive/intransitive verbs. Many of them also provide sample sentences to help you understand how the word is used.

Understand English idioms

Some English idioms function like proverbs. In the United States, for example, if people have to "eat crow," they have been forced to admit they were wrong about something. But simpler examples of idiomatic usage—word order, word choice, and combinations that don't follow any obvious set or rules—are common in even the plainest English.

If you are unsure about idioms, use *Google* or another Web search engine to find out how they are used.

"INCORRECT" IDIOM

Here is the answer **of** your question.

ACCEPTED IDIOM

Here is the answer **to** your question.

"INCORRECT" IDIOM

I had jet **legs** after flying across the Pacific.

ACCEPTED IDIOM

I had jet **lag** after flying across the Pacific.

Understand Nouns in English

Perhaps the most troublesome conventions for nonnative speakers are those that guide usage of the common articles *the*, *a*, and *an*. To understand how articles work in English, you must first understand how the language uses **nouns**.

Proper nouns and common nouns

There are two basic kinds of nouns. A **proper noun** begins with a capital letter and names a unique person, place, or thing: *Elvis Presley*, *Russia*, *Eiffel Tower*.

The other basic kind of noun is called a **common noun**. Common nouns do not name a unique person, place, or thing: *man*, *holiday*, *tower*. Common nouns are not names and are not capitalized unless they are the first word in a sentence.

PROPER NOUNS

Beethoven	Michael Jordan	Africa
Honda	South Korea	Empire State Building

COMMON NOUNS

composer	athlete	continent
vehicle	country	building

Count and noncount nouns

Common nouns can be classified as either *count* or *noncount*. **Count nouns** can be made plural, usually by adding *-s* (*finger*, *fingers*). Some common nouns have distinctive plural forms (*person*, *people*; *datum*, *data*).

Noncount nouns cannot be counted directly and cannot take the plural form (*information*, but not *informations*; *garbage*, but not *garbages*).

CORRECT USE OF HAIR AS A COUNT NOUN

Three blonde hairs were in the sink.

CORRECT USE OF HAIR AS A NONCOUNT NOUN

My roommate spent an hour combing his hair.

Singular and plural forms

Count nouns usually take both singular and plural forms, while noncount nouns usually do not take plural forms and are not counted directly. A count noun can have a number before it (as in *two books*, *three oranges*) and can be qualified with adjectives such as *many* (as in *many books*), *some* (as in *some schools*), and *few* (meaning almost none, as in *few people volunteered*).

Noncount nouns can be counted or quantified in only two ways: either by using general adjectives that treat the noun as a mass (*much* information, *some* news) or by placing another noun between the quantifying word and the noncount noun (two *kinds* of information, a *piece* of news).

INCORRECT

five horse	many accident

CORRECT

five horses	many accidents

INCORRECT

three breads	I would like a mustard on my hot dog.

CORRECT

three loaves of bread
I would like some mustard on my hot dog.

Understand Articles in English

Articles indicate that a noun is about to appear, and they clarify what the noun refers to. There are only two kinds of articles in English: definite and indefinite.

1. **the:** *The* is a **definite article**, meaning that it refers to (1) a specific object already known to the reader, (2) one about to be made known to the reader, or (3) a unique object.

2. **a, an:** The **indefinite articles** *a* and *an* refer to an object whose specific identity is not known to the reader. The only difference between *a* and *an* is that *a* is used before a consonant sound (*man, friend, yellow*), while *an* is used before a vowel sound.

Look at these sentences, identical except for their articles, and imagine that each is taken from a different newspaper story.

> Rescue workers lifted **the** man to safety.
>
> Rescue workers lifted **a** man to safety.

By use of the definite article *the*, the first sentence indicates that the reader already knows something about the identity of this man and his needing to be rescued. The news story has already referred to him.

The indefinite article *a* in the second sentence indicates that the reader does not know anything about this man. Either this is the first time the news story has referred to him, or there are other men in need of rescue.

Rules for using articles

1. *A* or *an* is not used with noncount nouns.

INCORRECT

> The crowd hummed with **an** excitement.

CORRECT

> The crowd hummed with excitement.

2. *A* or *an* is used with singular count nouns whose particular identity is unknown to the reader or writer.

INCORRECT

> Detective Johnson was reading book.

CORRECT

> Detective Johnson was reading **a** book.

3. *The* is used with most count and noncount nouns whose particular identity is known to readers.

CORRECT

> I bought a book yesterday. **The** book is about kayaking.

4. *The* is used when the noun is accompanied by a superlative: for example, *best, worst, highest, lowest, most expensive, least interesting.*

CORRECT

> **The** most interesting book about mountaineering is Jon Krakauer's *Into Thin Air.*

Understand Verbs and Modifiers in English

Verbs in English can be divided between simple verbs like *run*, *speak*, and *look*, and verb phrases like *may have run*, *have spoken*, and *will be looking*. The words that appear before the main verbs—*may*, *have*, *will*, and *be*—are called auxiliary (or helping) verbs. Helping verbs help express something about the action of main verbs: for example, when the action occurs (tense), whether the subject acted or was acted upon (voice), or whether or not an action occurred.

Indicating tense with *be* verbs

Like the other auxiliary verbs *have* and *do*, *be* changes form to signal tense. In addition to *be* itself, the *be* verbs are *is*, *am*, *are*, *was*, *were*, and *been*.

To show ongoing action, *be* verbs are followed by the present participle, which is a verb ending in *-ing*.

INCORRECT

I **am think** of all the things I'd rather **be do**.

CORRECT

I **am thinking** of all the things I'd rather **be doing**.

To show that an action is being done to, rather than by, the subject, follow *be* verbs with the past participle (a verb usually ending in *-ed*, *-en*, or *-t*).

INCORRECT

The movie **was direct** by John Woo.

CORRECT

The movie **was directed** by John Woo.

Modal auxiliary verbs

Modal auxiliary verbs *will*, *would*, *can*, *could*, *may*, *might*, *shall*, *must*, and *should* express conditions like possibility, permission, speculation, expectation, obligation, and necessity. Unlike the auxiliary verbs *be*, *have*, and *do*, modal verbs do not change form according to the grammatical subject of the sentence (*I*, *you*, *she*, *he*, *it*, *we*, *they*).

Two basic rules apply to all uses of modal verbs. First, modal verbs are always followed by the simple form of the verb.

INCORRECT

She should **studies** harder to pass the exam.

CORRECT

She should **study** harder to pass the exam.

The second rule is that you should not use modals consecutively.

INCORRECT

If you work harder at writing, you **might could** improve.

CORRECT

If you work harder at writing, you **might** improve.

Ten conditions that modals express

- **Speculation**: If you had flown, you **would** have arrived yesterday.
- **Ability**: She **can** run faster than Jennifer.
- **Necessity**: You **must** know what you want to do.
- **Intention**: I **shall** wash my own clothes.
- **Permission**: You **may** leave now.
- **Advice**: You **should** wash behind your ears.
- **Possibility**: It **might** be possible to go home early.
- **Assumption**: You **must** have stayed up late last night.
- **Expectation**: You **should** enjoy the movie.
- **Order**: You **must** leave the building.

Placement of modifiers

Modifiers will be unclear if your reader can't connect them to their associated words. The proximity of a modifier to the noun or verb it modifies provides an important clue to their relationship.

Clarity should be your first goal when you use a modifier.

UNCLEAR

Many pedestrians are killed each year by motorists **not using sidewalks**.

CLEAR

Many pedestrians **not using sidewalks** are killed each year by motorists.

An **adverb**—a word or group of words that modifies a verb, adjective, or another adverb—should not come between a verb and its direct object.

AWKWARD

The hurricane destroyed **completely** the city's tallest building.

BETTER

The hurricane **completely** destroyed the city's tallest building.

Try to avoid placing an adverb between to and its verb. This construction is called a **split infinitive**.

AWKWARD

The water level was predicted **to not rise**.

BETTER

The water level was predicted **not to rise**.

Understand English Sentence Structure

Words derive much of their meaning from how they function in a sentence.

With the exception of **imperatives** (commands such as *Watch out!*), sentences in English usually contain a subject and a predicate. A **subject** names who or what the sentence is about; the predicate contains information about the subject.

(SUBJECT)	(PREDICATE)
The lion	is asleep.

A predicate consists of at least one main verb. If the verb is **intransitive**, like *exist*, it does not take a direct object. Some verbs are **transitive**, which means they require a **direct object** to complete their meaning.

INCORRECT

James beat.

CORRECT

James beat Eli at chess.

Some verbs (*write, learn, read,* and others) can be either transitive or intransitive, depending on how they are used.

INTRANSITIVE

Pilots fly.

TRANSITIVE

Pilots fly airplanes.

Formal written English requires that each sentence include a subject and a verb, even when the meaning of the sentence would be clear without it. In some cases you must supply an expletive such as *it* or *there*.

INCORRECT

Is snowing in Alaska.

CORRECT

It is snowing in Alaska.

Summary for Second-language Writers

Understand the demands of writing in a second language	• Ask a peer to respond to your first draft by focusing on your main ideas and purpose. • If your reader can summarize your main ideas, then move on to consider the organization and content of your draft. • Address grammar, vocabulary, and mechanics in editing after you are comfortable that your main ideas are clear.
Understand nouns in English	• Use plural forms of count nouns even if a plural number is otherwise indicated. • Correct form in English is to indicate the singular or plural nature of a count noun explicitly, in every instance.
Understand articles in English	• Noncount nouns are never used with the indefinite articles *a* or *an*.
Understand verbs and modifiers in English	• To show ongoing action, *be* verbs are followed by the present participle, which is a verb with an *-ing* ending. • Check that modals are followed by the simple form of the verb and that only one modal is used before the verb. • Readers usually link modifiers with their nearest word. Whenever you use a modifier, ask yourself whether its relationship to the word it modifies will be clear to your reader.
Understand English sentence structure	• Altering the basic subject + verb + object word order in English often changes the meaning of a sentence. As a general rule, try to keep the verb close to its subject, and the direct object close to its verb.

MyWritingLab™ Visit Ch. 29 in MyWritingLab to test your understanding of the chapter objectives.

Text Credits

Index